EXPERIENCES IN LANGUAGE

TOOLS AND TECHNIQUES FOR LANGUAGE ARTS METHODS

Sixth Edition

Walter T. Petty   **Dorothy C. Petty**

Richard T. Salzer   *State University of New York at Buffalo*

Marjorie F. Becking   *(contributed to previous editions)*

ALLYN AND BACON

Boston   London   Toronto   Sydney   Tokyo   Singapore

This edition is dedicated to the thousands of teachers with whom the authors—during their combined 100 years in education—have had contact. We have known them as colleagues, students, consultants, and friends (and spouses for two of us) and have found them to be the most admirable group of persons anyone is likely to meet. Much of the content of this book derives directly from our experiences with outstanding teachers, whether in our classrooms or theirs. We wish to thank them for all that they and the children in their charge have taught us.

Series Editor: Virginia Lanigan
Editorial Assistant: Nicole DePalma
Editorial-Production Service: Spectrum Publisher Services
Composition Buyer: Linda Cox
Manufacturing Buyer: Louise Richardson
Cover Administrator: Linda K. Dickinson
Cover Designer: Susan Paradise

Library of Congress Cataloging-in-Publication Data

Petty, Walter Thomas
    Experiences in language : tools and techniques for language arts methods / Walter T. Petty, Dorothy C. Petty, Richard T. Salzer. — 6th ed.
        p. cm.
    Includes bibliographic references and index.
    ISBN 0-205-16078-6
    1. Language arts (Elementary) I. Petty, Dorothy C. II. Salzer, Richard T. III. Title.
LB1576.P552 1991
372.6′044—dc20   93-39672
                                                                              CIP

Printed in the United States of America
10 9 8 7 6 5 4 3 2 1   99 98 97 96 95 94

Photos on pages 15, 18, 23, 28, 32, 38, 47, 64, 70, 91, 98, 110, 119, 121, 149, 153, 156, 173, 183, 195, 199, 221, 226, 228, 245, 251, 279, 299, 304, 318, 329, 337, 348, 364, 382, 387, 389, 391, 402, 406, 410, 417, 426, and 428 by Christina J. Bogan.

Contents

Chapter 3   Language Learning and the Young Child   55

Chapter 4 **Beginning Language Arts Programs** **77**

Chapter 5 **Using Oral Language** **119**

Chapter 6   Listening, Thinking, and Learning   **149**

Chapter 7   Grammar and Language Usage   173

Chapter 8   Learning About Words: Vocabulary, Spelling, and Dictionary Use   195

Chapter 9   Writing by Hand and Machine   221

Chapter 10   The Writing Process   241

Chapter 11   Writing in the Classroom Program   273

Chapter 12   Children and Reading   299

Chapter 13   Reading and Studying   **329**

Chapter 16   Serving Children with Special Needs   417

Preface

*W*e believe that, over the years, the strength of *Experiences in Language* has been that the content of each edition reflects the latest research findings and the best of evolving teaching practices. Our intent in preparing this edition was to follow that precedent, and we think that we have. In this version we have given particular attention to the importance of viewing language arts instruction as based on a comprehensive instructional plan composed of many different teaching strategies and types of materials. We have also continued our emphasis on such areas as early education and the use of electronic teaching aids as an integral aspect of the classroom program.

Newer trends have been recognized where they appear likely to be beneficial. Promising developments in elementary education include a greater emphasis on writing as a way of learning in all curriculum areas, the increased use of nonfiction trade books in science and social studies, the integration of skill learning in unit and thematic teaching of topics, and the inclusion of special-needs students in the regular classroom. We have given attention to all of these because they relate in significant ways to the teaching of the language arts and offer means of helping all students become better educated.

Though we support greater integration of the language areas in the overall school curriculum we continue to present separate chapters and sections on each area of the language arts. We believe that readers, particularly those new to the profession, can profit from both systematic treatment of all topics and suggestions for teaching about them in relation to one another and in connection with other school subjects.

Acknowledgments

We would like to extend our thanks to the following professors for their valuable comments and insights: Howard Blake, Temple University; Pose Lamb, Purdue University; Anna Nardelli, SUNY–Plattsburgh; Beverly Shields, Joliet Junior College; and Roger Wess, Chadron State College.

W.T.P.
D.C.P.
R.T.S.

Chapter 1

Language and the Language Arts

*T*he successful exchange of knowledge through language is crucial to every person's well-being. Those who lack facility in communication will find it increasingly difficult to participate fully in our complex society, whether as students, family members, employees, or simply individual citizens. The importance of raising the level of communicative competence in the general society must be recognized, and institutions must cooperate with one another to improve the literacy of the population. Nothing is more important than promoting children's language abilities. The home and family are instrumental in the early acquisition of language and in stimulation of its development, but the role of the school system is central.

Books such as *Ways with Words*, by Shirley Brice Heath, and *Family Literacy*, by Denny Taylor, describe many interesting language-learning episodes children experience at home.

LANGUAGE

Language may be defined in a number of ways, but human speech is usually thought of first. Communication occurs in additional ways, however. Animals communicate with one another or even with humans by wagging their tails as dogs do and screeching in different ways to convey messages as some monkeys have been observed doing. Computer languages enable humans to control the workings of complex machines and even permit the machines to "talk" with one another. There are communicative sounds other than speech, including drums, fog horns, and sirens. There are various types of graphic symbols, from marks cut into trees to the international codes commonly used on highway signs or restroom doors. There are gestures, with or without speech; sign language; and body language (well known to teachers, especially as exhibited by students who are restless or bored).

All of these means of communication constitute language in the broader sense because they are used to communicate—and both teachers and children should be aware of this. The principal focus in the classroom, however, is on language as defined in the narrower sense, that is, as the symbols, either vocal or graphic, that are produced in systematic patterns by one person in order to convey meaning to one or more others. The primary concern of this book is with teaching and learning the use of language defined in this way.

Language and Culture

Language grows out of people's need to communicate. The shared collection of understandings that accumulate from interactions in daily life is called culture. That is, culture is the set of beliefs and ways of doing things that characterize a group of people and differentiate it from other such groups, or societies. Language is a means of storing knowledge, but it is also the means by which people see the world and process information.

Language, culture, and thinking are interrelated in complex ways. For example, the English statement "The path runs around the lake" seems rather foolish when taken in a literal sense. In another language the same observation might be stated as "With respect to the path and the lake, they are concentric," which appears to come closer to describing reality. In English one of the preferred sentence patterns implies that something does something to something else, even though that way of perceiving events does not always make literal sense. This is a cultural characteristic: English speakers expect events to have causes and therefore look for explanations. People from other cultures may be more likely to take things as they come, without thinking and talking so much about causes and reasons. Clearly, culture, thought, and language are interrelated in important ways.

The Alaskan natives of the North Slope are said to identify many different kinds of snow—and to have words for all of them.

Word meanings provide much evidence of connections between language and culture. For instance, names for objects and events are created by a language group as communication needs arise. Seventeenth-century English did not include the word *electricity,* but this does not mean that the language was deficient or its users primitive; there was simply no need for such a word. Today, visitors unfamiliar with American English may express confusion about what menu to expect and how to dress when invited to attend a *lunch, brunch, supper, dinner,* or *cook-out.* And we are amazed when it is reported that some languages have no word for lying, or "saying that which is not." We might wonder what such a society would be like! Such language differences convey much about a culture, and this is why language experts and other scholars insist that a people cannot be fully understood unless their language is fully understood.

One of the most important ways in which language and culture are interrelated is that those with a way to communicate can share one another's experiences. Talking, singing, writing, and reading all combine to promote the development of common understandings. Through language we know about the lives of our ancestors, and we can speculate as to the fate of generations that are to come. We can know every detail of an imagined event that could never have taken place, and we can even become emotionally involved in a made-up character's adventures or problems.

Personal use of language is also related to culture. Conversations among individuals are always governed by certain rules that have been learned. For example, when meeting a prospective mother-in-law for the first time, the average person would not use the same vocabulary as he or she would when relaxing with friends. Every society has its own standards; there may be expectations about when eye contact is permitted or how close faces should be during conversation. Language permits us to think and communicate, but culture structures the methods and content of communication and thought.

Characteristics of Language

Language is symbolic.
Language symbols are arbitrary.
Language is systematic.
Language is a form of human behavior.
Language is a social instrument.
Language continually changes.

Characteristics of Language

The systematic arrangement of symbols is a key characteristic of language. The systematic nature of any language is shown by intertwined and interrelated principles that cause the language to operate in regular ways. Each language has its own system—a system peculiar in at least some respects to no other language—but every language is systematic and every language has vocal (and generally graphic) symbols that have been arbitrarily attached to the ideas and objects that are a part of the culture it serves.

Thus, arbitrariness of a language relates to its systematic nature. The people who use a language have come to designate a sound or set of sounds to represent something they need to talk about. The French *le chien* and the English *dog* are arbitrarily designated symbols (both in sound and graphic forms) that represent the same object, and they do so regularly and systematically. Those who use a language also make it as complete as necessary for their culture. Modern English has the term *nuclear physics;* a Native American language of the year 1600 had no need for such a term. This difference makes neither language any less "advanced," complete, or systematic than the other. Each is a social instrument facilitating communication between people about objects and events significant in their lives.

Still another characteristic of language is that it changes. Evidence of the change in English is apparent, for example, if one compares pages from the King James version of the Bible, a Shakespeare play, a Hemingway novel, and an issue of *Time*. These changes in language occur in many ways. We readily think of new meanings being attached to words and of new words or combinations of words being used for new or changed objects or ideas. Perhaps we can think of pronunciation changes or spelling changes, though the latter tend to take longer to occur, and we may not be aware of them unless we read something written a hundred or so years ago. And if we look back far enough we can even find changes in word order.

The 1993 edition of *Merriam-Webster's Collegiate Dictionary* has a total of 10,000 new words and meanings.

New Words

BYTE
COWABUNGA
DISINFORMATION
GREENMAIL
NIMBY
WANNABE

Some children speak one language at home and another at school.

Language in Use

The many ways language is used are thoroughly discussed in *Language Learning Through Communication,* by Allen, Brown, and Yatvin.

Most of the time we are not aware of the scientific aspects of language; we are simply using it in all aspects of life. Through face-to-face and telephone conversations, electronic media, newspapers, magazines, books, and advertising, we are constantly exposed to language in one form or another. The effectiveness of the communication that occurs in these encounters depends on the degree to which both the speaker and the listener know the language and have, relatively speaking, the same abilities in using it. Knowing the language in this sense means having attained a level of development of those elements discussed above that make possible language use, including being aware (though perhaps not at a conscious level) of any social or cultural forces that may bear on the communication.

Language also often serves as a means of releasing tensions or reacting to a specific personal incident. Many of us talk to ourselves—sometimes using expletives—or sing or talk to a pet or even an inanimate object. We may mutter imprecations after a poor golf shot or while working on an income tax form, exclaim aloud at the sight of the Grand Canyon, or shout "Bravo!" in appreciation of an outstanding musical performance. Language used in such instances as these is personal; no communication to someone else is generally intended.

The role of language in thinking is possibly its most important use. Although not all of the symbols used in the mental manipulation necessary for thinking are language symbols, the majority are. Primitive people could think in terms of mental images as they sought food and shelter, but as the need for communication developed and as rules, laws, customs, and social mores were established, representational symbols became necessary. Thus, language evolved, and now language symbols representing the many abstractions of our culture are crucial to thinking.

Language Variety

To get water do you turn on the *faucet, hydrant, spigot,* or *tap?*

The language each of us uses is largely a reflection of early environment and education and the social situation of the moment. The variation in language that is most obvious is in **dialect.** Dialects, like the language of which they are a part, are systematic, adequate for communication among their users, and, to a large extent, predictable in structure and use. In general, dialects differ in matters of pronunciation and vocabulary more than they do in sentence arrangement. Some dialects are also characterized by rate of speech and variation in pitch. The slow drawl associated with the South and Southwest and the nasality of the southern hills are familiar examples. *Mary, marry,* and *merry* are pronounced identically by most natives of the northern Midwestern states, whereas native speakers in New England pronounce these words differently. Groceries are placed in a *bag* in some sections of the country but in a *sack* or perhaps a *poke* in others. There are many other instances of differences in pronunciation and vocabulary, but in the United States dialectal differences ordinarily do not extend to such basic features as the order of words in sentences.

How do you say these words?

creek
greasy
roof
wash
stomach
hog

Even though everyone (not just people in the South or Brooklyn or Boston) speaks a dialect of English, each person's language within a dialect is, to some extent at least, unique. This is an individual's **idiolect.** Also, each of us varies his or her language from one expressional situation to another, particularly after becoming an adult. Such variation is known as **register switching,** or, more commonly in written expression, changing styles. Each of us uses a colloquial or homely language in speaking with close friends and family. This language is certainly less formal than that used in giving a speech or writing a term paper. A person may also use particular words and expressions—localisms—in his or her own town or neighborhood that would probably be avoided or even unknown in another geographical location. Thus, although we may say that a person speaks a certain dialect, that dialect has variations, just as there are variations among dialects.

Any dialect is an adequate means of communication for its users, but if it deviates too much from what the community at large considers to be standard or acceptable English (see Chapter 7), a problem is created for the speaker, one that the school must recognize and attempt to solve.

Language Change

English is a particularly adaptable and flexible language, partly because it is a polyglot one, rich in words taken from languages with origins in other parts of the world; examples are:

Europe
> Dutch: *buoy, yacht, sleigh, waffle, skate*
> French: *rouge, bayou, toboggan, vignette, coup*
> Italian: *violin, replica, ghetto, broccoli*
> German: *bagel, delicatessen, kindergarten*
> Spanish: *rodeo, corral, mosquito, guitar*

North America (Native American): *caribou, hominy, squash*
West Africa: *gumbo, voodoo, okra*
Middle East: *camel, bazaar, sabbath, muslin*

Finding examples of how other languages have enriched our own provides opportunities to point out to students that we live in a multicultural society to which all have contributed.

And, of course, other languages have adopted English words; speakers of French or German use such Americanisms as *weekend* and *drugstore*.

Besides adopting words from other languages, we create words to describe new commercial products, processes, or discoveries or new ways of thinking about things: *motorcade, jetliner, stereo, amplifier, missile, sneakers, Freon*. Other words actually are abbreviations, compounds, or acronyms: *OPEC, TV, pro, hype, motel, houseplant, scuba, offbeat, paperback, software*. Still others move into the language from slang, although much slang gives new meaning to words already in the language. However, very little slang gains permanent acceptance (one period's *square* is another's *nerd*), although such words as *crank, fad, pluck,* and *slump* were once considered slang.

Early settlers created these:

underbrush
bluff
gap
warpath

Examining the Language

We use language as a complete experience of communication, but all communicative acts can be broken down into component parts and examined. Those who do this systematically are referred to as **linguists,** scientists who study language. Linguistics as a field of knowledge focuses on such areas as sounds of a language, combinations of sounds used as words or word parts, arrangements of words in sentences or parts of sentences, and the processes by which meanings are assigned to language experiences.

Phonemes are represented in written form by using virgules in order to distinguish between letters and the sounds they represent. For example, to show the sounds in *mat,* the linguist writes /m/ /a/ /t/.

Sounds. The basic sounds of a language are called **phonemes.** A phoneme is the smallest unit of sound that produces a change in meaning. It is often not precisely a single sound; there are slight differences in the sounds indicated by *p* in *pin, spin,* and *lip.* Native speakers of English learn to hear these sounds as identical, however, and make no distinctions among them. On the other hand, the sound difference represented by *b* in *bit* and *p* in *pit,* although also slight, is one that native speakers know carries meaning and therefore acknowledge.

Phonemes are not the same as letters of the alphabet in English. One sound may be represented by different letters or even combinations of letters. The phoneme /s/ is represented by *s* in *send, c* in *cent,* and *sc* in *scent.* Conversely, one letter of the alphabet may represent different phonemes. For instance, *g* is the graphic form of the initial sound in *gun* and *gene* and the medial sound in *regime.* These complexities are one of the important outcomes of the historical growth of the English language.

Phonemes identifiable in the flow of speech as a speaker uses voice, teeth, and mouth parts are called **segmental phonemes.** They can be segmented, or isolated, from other phonemes and are recognizable as meaningful units. Differences in analysis procedures and classification systems lead some authorities to state that there are only thirty-three phonemes in English and others to conclude that there are more than forty.

In addition to segmental phonemes, there are **suprasegmental features** that also describe speech. These include four degrees of stress in the flow of language, three levels of **pitch** in the voice, and four **junctures,** or interruptions in the stream of speech. Stress is most readily apparent when it shifts, as in the pronunciations of *expert* and *expertise.* Changing the pitch of the voice is done almost automatically when asking questions and even when the sentence is not in the form of a question (try saying, "His name was Billy," giving the last word a higher pitch than the others). Juncture is exemplified by comparing "light housekeeping" with "lighthouse keeping."

Words. In ordinary speech we do not pay much attention to phonemes; words are thought of as the meaningful elements. Even quite young children learn that words have power to secure assistance and even to cause hurt. Linguists study morphemes rather than words. A **morpheme** is defined as the smallest unit of language that cannot be divided without eliminating meaning or changing it drastically. A morpheme is, in fact, often a word, such as *cat, walk,* or *laugh.* These are called **free,** or **lexical, morphemes** because they can stand alone in terms of meaning. A **bound,** or **grammatical, morpheme** is one that must be combined with another morpheme; examples are *-s, -ed,* and *anti-.* Thus, *cat* is one morpheme (three phonemes), and *cats* is two morphemes (four phonemes). The *s* in *cats* conveys meaning ("more than one"); this is an example of why morphemes may be thought of as the building blocks of language.

Words may be classified into four large **form classes,** or parts of speech (nouns, verbs, adjectives, and adverbs). Placement in these classes in most contemporary descriptions of language is determined by four basic considerations, none of which gives particular emphasis to meaning or function in the traditional sense (for example, that a noun is the name of a person, place, or thing). The considerations that are used include affixes, word order, particular structures or function, and the sound stress given. Thus, a noun is a word that will take the inflectional endings *-s* or *-es, -'s,* and *-s';* that will take derivational suffixes such as *-er, -or, -ment, -ness,* and *-ism;* that may be signaled or marked by such words as *the, a, each, some, many,* and *my;* or that receives major stress on the beginning syllable (for example, *sus'pect* is a noun, whereas *suspect'* is a verb). A word can be classified as a noun if it meets one of these criteria, and there are a few instances in which all can be applied. For the other form classes—verbs, adjectives, and adverbs—word order, signal words, and affixes are used to determine the classification.

In addition to the form classes, English has **structure,** or **function, words.** These include the signal words already mentioned and qualifiers (*very, rather, quite,* etc.), prepositions (*on, in, after,* etc.), and conjunctions (*but, and,* etc.). The structure words relate words of the different form classes to one another and provide the framework that gives the language fluidity and cohesion.

Functions, or Signal Words

Noun markers—*my, some, two, the, an*
Verb markers—*am, is, were, had, will*
Phrase markers—*into, above, down, up, out*
Clause markers—*because, that, if, why, how*
Question markers—*who, when, where, why*

Sentences. The arrangement or order of words in sentences or parts of sentences is **syntax,** which may also be defined as the grammar or description of a language. There are several approaches to describing word order in English sentences (see Chapter 7). Syntax is particularly important in English because it is the major way of showing relationships among words and is essential in making meaningful sentences. For example, each of the words in the string "selected book the quickly girl the" expresses grammatical meaning via structure signals and endings, but taken as a group their meaning is not clear until they are arranged into the syntactically correct "the girl quickly selected the book."

Meaning. Language conveys meaning, and making yourself understood and comprehending what others say and write are important areas of knowledge about language. Some linguists conduct studies of **semantics,** the meanings associated with words. They are concerned with the literal or objective meanings (a *plum* is a fruit) and also feelings and emotions that become attached to words (a *plum* is anything highly desired). The study of word meanings also involves examination of dialects and cultural influences (*calling* in British English refers to a personal visit, not a telephone conversation).

British English

flat
lift
vest
biscuit
cooker
lorry
nappy

American English

apartment
elevator
undershirt
cookie
stove
truck
diaper

Other areas of meaning touch on psychology and intellectual development, aspects of **psycholinguistics.** A person cannot understand language if the ideas expressed are totally unfamiliar or if they are complex beyond that individual's ability to comprehend. **Sociolinguistics** recognizes that social factors are also relevant in determining meaning. Class background, dialect, and sophistication with respect to context are all of significance. No teenager who has just demolished the family car would take the statement at face value when the parent says, "Well, we're certainly proud of you today."

LEARNING LANGUAGE

Nearly all children learn to talk without much difficulty. This learning begins at birth; the first sounds a child hears seem to trigger communication attempts. The fact that language is systematic facilitates this learning, as does the desire of persons around the child to communicate with her or him. As the child experi-

Language learning results from experiences and from talking about them.

ments and others respond, discovery and reinforcement proceed, and the language system begins to come under the child's control. Of course, not everything is grasped at the outset. For many years, including those spent in elementary school, children continue to learn about their language.

Children learn the language of the adults with whom they are in contact, but just how this learning occurs is not a matter of consensus. Several different theories to explain the learning of language have been advanced by linguists; these are discussed in the following section.

Theories of Language Acquisition

Theories of language acquisition and the work of Piaget are discussed in Chapter 1 of Pflaum's *The Development of Language and Literacy.*

The theories concerning how language is acquired are complex and controversial. Advancing our understanding of the language acquisition process brings a better grasp of the nature of language. The theories are discussed here in terms of initial language learning, but the principles set forth in each theory also apply to how older children learn in all of the language arts areas.

See Chapter 6 in *Inquiries into Child Language,* by Diane Nelson Bryen.

Behaviorist Theory. The behaviorist point of view is that each newborn infant has a potential for learning in general but no specific capacity for language learning. The development of language is a result of the environment: Japanese children learn Japanese, and American children learn English. More specifically, each child first learns a dialect, the language spoken in his or her immediate environment.

Under this theory, all learning, including language, results from positive reinforcement of desirable behavior and nonreinforcement of what is not wanted.

Thus, the babbling infant is reinforced or rewarded for making certain sounds rather than others. Furthermore, according to behaviorists, the environment controls a baby's language efforts in that those around the child respond positively when he or she produces an utterance close to something recognizable in the language. Sounds such as *buh-buh-buh* may be repeated by others, with accompanying laughter, smiling, and cuddling. Then, at some time near the first birthday, the child says "dada" or "mama," and much excitement results. More words are learned in the same way, and the child gains the ability to try to say what others say. Repeating known words becomes enjoyable and reinforcing in itself, and the child goes on to say them over and over without urging.

The behaviorist theory, unlike other points of view, treats language learning (and all other learning) as essentially imitation and repetition guided by external events. In learning the language to which they are exposed, infants are not always able to repeat everything they hear, but, according to this theory, the stimuli and reinforcement provided encourage them to make the effort, to experiment, until they master the system to the extent necessary to function successfully in the environment where they find themselves.

Young children differ greatly in their tendency to imitate as well as their ability to do so.

Nativist Theory. The nativist point of view is not as well defined as behaviorism and differs principally from that theory in the assumption that humans are endowed with a specific capacity for learning language. According to the nativist theory, this innate ability or mechanism gives the learner a start in "knowing" the system of a language in its basic design. This inborn ability, called the **language acquisition device (LAD),** needs only to be triggered by the language environment of the infant for the expression of language to occur rapidly.

Advocates of this theory hold that the imitation and reinforcement conditions of the behaviorists cannot account for the rapidity with which a child in any culture learns the essentials of language structure. Nativists also point out that a young child speaks sentences or parts of sentences that are not imitations of adult speech, which seems to indicate that exposure to adult models is needed only to give the learner examples from which to deduce the underlying rules that govern how the language system works. Although the LAD remains basic to the nativist theory, many nativists currently emphasize the interaction between the child and adults. The nature of this interaction, which is not entirely verbal since facial expressions and touching are included, is that adults use language differently when speaking with children than they do when talking to other adults. Adults do everything possible to help the learner see how the sounds relate to meanings and what the underlying language organization is.

In further support of their theory, nativists cite studies of language acquisition in different cultures; these have shown that children of differing intellectual abilities or even ones with physical or environmental handicaps will learn whatever language they have access to, and the acquisition sequence will always be substantially the same. On the other hand, experiments in teaching language to chimpanzees have seemed to challenge the nativist position that acquisition of language is restricted to humans. Some researchers have shown that chimps can be taught to utilize such language symbols as electronic sign boards and American Sign Language. The nativists counter this evidence by stressing the difference between acquiring a language from nothing more than exposure to it and being carefully taught to use it. They also point out that the chimpanzees do not go on to develop language use beyond the linking of a few symbols or signs.

Cognitivist Theory. A third point of view relates language to cognitive processes, or thinking. Although cognitivists accept the uniqueness of humans in language learning, they emphasize the development of basic thought structures prior to the development of corresponding linguistic structures, implying that thought is at least initially independent of language. Before being able to use language, the infant does solve some problems that appear to call for thought (for example, finding a toy by removing the cover placed over it). The LAD is not discounted in this theory but is considered to be related more to relationships of meanings than to the underlying organization of sentences and other word combinations. Semantic concepts are viewed as the generating force in the learning process, as the child constructs the meanings of the words he or she hears. Such construction is facilitated by language users in the child's environment, of course; thus, interaction with adults is considered important, as it is in the other theories.

Language Development

A child begins at birth to experiment with his or her vocal organs and to make sounds. This experimenting progresses through cries and cooing, sounds that are identified as expressing pain, fear, anger, or joy. These early vocalizations show little system or little relationship to the language spoken by those caring for the child. At about four months of age the infant shows signs of responding to human sounds—turning the head and eyes to look for the speaker. Shortly thereafter the cooing will change to babbling, which with increasing practice shows considerable mastery of the basic elements of the vocal mechanism. The child does more "practicing," gaining a great deal of control of volume, pitch, and articulation, as shown by the ability to repeat sounds that are heard. By the time the normal child has reached the first birthday, he or she is producing sounds to which adult listeners can genuinely attach meaning. Usually these first "words" are consonant-vowel in form—*ma-ma, da-da, bye-bye*—and the child may not be attaching the same meaning to them as the adoring father and mother do, although experimenting will soon enable the child to relate the sounds to the adult meanings. The majority of first words are usually nouns—*ball, man, bird,* and so on—but such action words as *want, give,* and *more* also appear before the child begins to put two or more words together.

Children's first words often seem to be attempts to express complex ideas, suggesting a words-as-sentences hypothesis. The term **holophrastic speech** is often used to convey this idea. Of course, there is no way for us to know if a child has the idea of the content of a sentence in mind. The child who says "milk" is likely to get more milk, but the adult who hears the word doesn't know whether the child had "I want more milk" in mind but was limited by memory, attention, or linguistic skill or simply recognized that the one word was sufficient to accomplish communication.

Children normally, however, begin to put words together at around eighteen to twenty months of age. The experimenting in doing this is similar to that done

Most children acquire at least fifty words before beginning to put two or more of them together.

with words. The first combinations of words tend to follow the pattern of a few words in a particular utterance position joined with a variety of other words ("bye-bye, daddy," "bye-bye, mommy," "bye-bye, doggie"). The experimenting continues, with more of these singled-out words being tried out with other words and combinations of words. Gradually, then, the child perceives the notion of word order—that some words belong first and some words second. Sometimes this early perception is faulty with respect to the language system. More often, though, word order is satisfactory, but frequently some words are omitted. The child says "I see car" for "I can see the car." This is **telegraphic speech** (as in telegrams) and is simply further experimenting. All such experimenting is a normal stage in development, a stage in learning how the language works.

By the time most children are two years old they have a fund of words that represent objects and actions and are able to use them in ways that are understood. They test hypotheses about noun and verb endings, frequently overgeneralizing from the rules by saying "foots," "goed," or "mines." This "sorting out" continues for some time (for some aspects of syntax to about age nine and even beyond), but by the time the average child reaches kindergarten age he or she speaks in sentences, the complexity of which depends on mental maturity, language aptitude, and experiences.

From the very beginning, the child's use of language is purposeful, not perfunctory. The child who has learned to talk enough to use language for satisfying immediate physical needs soon becomes absorbed in making the acquaintance of a great variety of things. Children ask, "What's that?" over and over. Asking questions is the characteristic type of language activity at this stage of preschool language development. Two- to five-year-olds struggle to identify the many objects in the environment; they seek to bring order into a wide world of sight, sound, smell, and feeling. The responses to this exploring are very important to language development. Thus, narrow experiences and limited responses result in language development that is less advanced than that of the child who has had broad experiences and has secured responses to expressions of curiosity.

The family environment is the most important factor other than the child's maturity pattern in determining the language facility that develops and the speed with which it develops. For instance, an only child may have closer association with adults than does a child who has brothers and sisters. This closeness may result in the development of a larger vocabulary and more maturity in expression. Similarly, the child who is talked with a great deal develops language facility earlier than does one who grows up being ignored or told to be quiet. In addition to providing the child with language experiences, the family provides the language model—the kind of language to imitate.

In *The Meaning Makers,* Wells describes how a group of British children developed language from early speech through the intermediate grades.

Children's mental development and progress in using language move along together, thoroughly interwoven with the experiences of life. Once children have a basic command of language the relationship between thinking and communication becomes significant. According to Piaget's theory of intellectual or cognitive development, the age of about six or seven is the beginning of the *Concrete-Operational Period* and marks an important change in a child's thinking. One important consequence regarding language is that children past this age are much more likely to understand that a word may have more than one meaning. This is why kindergartners do not understand puns and riddles, whereas

Ask children to draw
a "head" of lettuce
a "toe" truck
a "flower" bed
a "school" of fish

first and second graders love them. A child has to know that two meanings of a word can exist simultaneously in order to see the joke in the mayonnaise asking for the refrigerator door to be closed because "I'm dressing." Third graders are bored by all this because they are well aware of multiple meanings for words.

As children approach the age of ten or eleven, most are moving into what Piaget calls the *Stage of Formal Thinking.* At this time they are ready for greater abstractions, so vocabulary involving amounts, comparisons, qualities, and characteristics takes a substantial leap. The reasoning ability of children advances, and they have more need for connectives such as *since, because, whenever,* and *although.* They are able to suspend judgment and do propositional thinking, and this ability has some effect on their interest in such activities as reading science fiction and writing stories of their own.

Although there are different degrees of maturity in children of the same chronological age, the general relationships between levels of maturity and thought processes are of special concern in teaching, significantly influencing, as they do, the grade placement of curriculum content. Also, teachers who know how children think and how that thought is reflected in their language will be better able to plan appropriate classroom programs and carry out effective learning activities.

THE LANGUAGE ARTS

The instructional program of the elementary school is commonly thought of as being composed of several curriculum areas, often referred to as "subjects." Those usually included are reading, mathematics, science, social studies, music, art, physical education, and language arts. Though other terms such as "English" or "language" may be used instead of "language arts," the school program areas referred to are the same—handwriting, spelling, grammar, and the other topics included in this book. (We also emphasize that reading should be considered one of the language arts.)

Studying the components of language arts leads to development of skills, knowledge, and attitudes required for the individual to become competent in communication. The **skills** of language performance include the ability to form letters correctly in handwriting, use dictionaries, speak loudly and clearly, and successfully perform many other specific acts. Important **knowledge** in the field of language arts consists of understandings as to why some forms of expression are more acceptable than others in particular situations, what types of poetry there are, when to use a semicolon, and how the English language developed through history. **Attitudes** are also important in the language arts. Individuals should be helped to see themselves as effective users of language and to develop their desire to read widely, spell correctly, listen actively, and enjoy discussion and conversation.

Objectives of Language Arts Teaching

No one doubts the importance of the language arts as a part of the school program. The many reasons for assigning this area of the curriculum a central place may be summarized under three major goals: learning English, learning about the English language, and using that language to learn in all areas of the school program.

Learning English. Although some children may enter elementary school with little ability to use English and others may speak a form considered non-standard, teachers must assist all pupils in becoming proficient in the language. Such a goal must go well beyond skill development to the establishment of good language habits and the creation of a desire to achieve competence in speaking, listening, writing, and reading.

This discussion is adapted from similar content in Learning How to Mean *by M. A. K. Halliday.*

Learning about English. Children in elementary school are expected to make a start in learning about the English language, its words, forms, authors, and literature. (Of course, how students of this age are taught is important; the emphasis must be on direct, concrete methods rather than abstractions unrelated to their experiences.) Such study is a significant part of the pupils' shared cultural heritage and general education and is thought of as complementary to understandings many youngsters gain from their families and other sources. We also expect that learning more about English will lead children to become interested in other languages and language in general.

Learning through English. Good command of English has an extremely strong influence on how well a learner does in any subject, and this is as true in the elementary classroom as in any other school setting. Whether the topic is fractions or frogs, the learner needs to be able to comprehend and process relevant information. While some of the language encountered will be particular to the content studied (*quotient*), most will be relevant to a large number of topics (*symmetry*).

Elements of the Language Arts

The language areas are often thought of as listening, speaking, reading, and writing. Of course, all of these are based on the ability to think, so thinking is sometimes considered one of the language arts. Also, given the impact of television and other modern technology allowing electronic storage of words, sounds, and images, use of such media should be included as a component of the language arts program.

Chapter 6 of this book contains material on listening and thinking.

Thinking. As a teacher you need to focus on the intimate connection between thinking and language. In order to think effectively children need to know how to manipulate various symbols—words, numbers, signs, and concepts—with respect to their possible meanings and their relationships to one another and to ideas. Experience shows that students will improve in their ability to think if they have a school program that is rich in challenging and authentic language experiences.

Speaking. Speaking involves saying what has been thought. Talking and thinking are so closely connected that it sometimes seems that we don't really know what we think about a topic until we talk about it. This appears to be particularly true of children. Of course, speaking well also depends on vocabulary, use of the voice, and facility in producing a variety of types of sentences, along with knowledge of several alternative ways of organizing what we want to say.

Writing. Writing resembles speaking in that what is expressed is written or typed rather than spoken. Some of what we write is only for our own use or for communicating informally with others, but much other writing involves thinking about and expressing complicated and significant ideas. In such writing, as with speaking, students need to learn to use appropriate words and language forms. Writing with care involves a rather complex process whereby we revise our written product several times until it communicates as we want it to, and then we thoroughly examine it for appropriate word usage, spelling, punctuation, and so forth.

Reading. Reading plays an important role in daily life. We read such materials as newspapers, magazines, and books for the information we can get from them, and we also read for enjoyment, looking for stories, poems, articles, and other texts that appeal to us. Learning to read is a developing process that begins with being read to as a young child and continues as the individual learns how to deal with different kinds of content, recognize thousands of words in print, and think effectively about what she or he is reading.

Listening encourages us to supply our own "pictures"—whether the content is poetry, stories being read or told, an audiotape, or a play heard on radio.

Listening. Listening and speaking are closely related in conversation and in more formal exchanges such as interviews. In listening, as in speaking, such

Reading sometimes involves listening and laughing.

matters as general familiarity with language structures, possession of an adequate vocabulary, and the ability to think about a topic are all important. The same kinds of similarities exist between listening and reading as we learn to listen for different purposes and integrate newer with existing content. Efficient listening is often difficult and, as a result, memories of what has been heard often need to be supported by note-taking or the electronic recording of what was heard.

Electronic Viewing. Although some viewing may be done in silence, we usually find that images are presented in combination with sound. In contrast to television or other sound-picture media, however, use of the radio or recordings requires those of us who ordinarily can see to imagine visual material, an experience considered much more stimulating by some authorities. With most television programming almost nothing is left to the imagination, and the viewer appears to make very little contribution to the total communicative experience. On the other hand, the content of films, videotapes, and compact discs, with sound or without, can profoundly stimulate thinking; carefully prepared and properly used they can be powerful educational tools.

Interrelationships Among the Language Arts

In addition to the general sorts of connections among listening, speaking, reading, writing and viewing, relationships exist among specific areas of the language arts such as vocabulary development, writing, and spelling. This is true in both the communication activities of daily life and the teaching-learning situations found in classrooms.

Everyday Life. Appropriate attitudes, relevant knowledge, and effective skills come together with thinking ability to produce successful language performance in daily life.

When you send a letter you might include photos, news clippings, a child's drawing—or even a five-dollar bill!

For example, in writing a letter to a family member or friend, you consider what you want to include, using your thinking ability to recall events that might be mentioned, to organize content so that it makes sense, and to devise especially effective or entertaining ways to express yourself. You also read as you write, going over what you've written, perhaps doing this aloud. You may even talk to yourself ("She'll go ballistic over this!") or to someone else or listen to that person ("Don't forget to tell about the cat").

More thought is involved as you project events into the future, perhaps creating an image of what the recipient will look like or be doing while reading the letter or what the response to a particularly humorous (you hope) part will be. You may write with a pen or type, in either case doing so with some care: you want to be courteous and provide a legible text. The words you write are ones you have learned through all kinds of experiences. Most are those that appear in anyone's English, but a few may not be appropriate for "polite" conversation, and you might even use a word or expression that has meaning only for your family or circle of friends. The sentences you compose are likely to be of different types: simple statements ("I have my vacation in June"), questions ("How was your trip?"), exclamations ("They were impossible!"), and more complex constructions ("With the baby coming, a bigger place is something we have to think about"). Thus, even though producing a letter is basically a writing activity, there is significant involvement in the other principal language arts areas, all related to one another.

You write a letter, however, without giving attention to each separate aspect of language. You are not likely to be greatly concerned about the location of a comma or the size of a loop on a letter, even though you do realize that such matters may interfere with personal communication, which is your principal goal. You are also unlikely to pay much attention to issues of spelling, word choice, and sentence patterns unless your thought processes cause you to be aware of detractions from the effectiveness of your message. Concern about how the letter looks or whether there are errors depends on circumstances, especially the nature of the audience. When writing to a newspaper, for instance, or to someone you don't know very well, you would probably watch the organization of the letter, the structure of sentences, and the spelling more closely than when writing to a close friend or relative. And, of course, when writing a letter of application for a job, you would likely be very concerned with good form and correctness.

Whether writing something or engaging in other everyday communicative acts—watching television, talking on the telephone, listening to a sermon, typing on a word processor, reading the newspaper—the individual is thinking at least to some extent and utilizing several areas of the language arts.

School Situations. In the classroom, teachers need to give attention to all facets of the language arts curriculum. Though they will do this in different ways, it should be kept in mind that, because of the interrelationships among the language arts, growth in one area usually strengthens development in others. Classroom activities should be rich and varied so that students will be motivated to make use of what they know about language and continue to learn more.

In a teaching-learning activity there are opportunities to see many possible connections among the language arts themselves (just as in the letter-writing experience described in the preceding section, Everyday Life) and between the language arts and other curriculum areas. Connections with other subjects are particularly apparent when the activities of the class are focused on a large-scale project, unit, or theme.

Names teachers may give to teaching that includes all subjects:

Activity Approach
Project Teaching
Theme Cycle
Unit Teaching
Inquiry Teaching

Books about space:

Mysteries of Outer Space by F. M. Branley (Lodestar, 1985)
Beyond the Milky Way by C. Schoberle (Crown, 1986)
Commander Toad in Space by J. Yolen (Coward McCann, 1980)

When a topic such as "The Space Station" is studied, for example, all aspects of the classroom program can be involved. Several areas of science can be included—astronomy, space travel, rockets, and needs of humans in space, at a minimum. Social studies content might involve studying the roles of government agencies in planning and financing the space program, mapping the trajectory of rockets, and becoming familiar with a world globe as a representation of what Earth looks like from space. Mathematics-related learning activities in areas such as weight, pay loads, rocket thrust, costs, and time schedules could be important. The arts can also contribute: for example, music from the sound tracks of space-related films, drawings and paintings of space stations, and body movements that interpret what humans experience in a weightless environment.

All these activities imply much use of the language arts as teacher and pupils talk about aspects of the topic and carry out their plans. In addition to speaking and listening in a general way, children will be reading a variety of materials (encyclopedias, informational library books, stories and novels about space

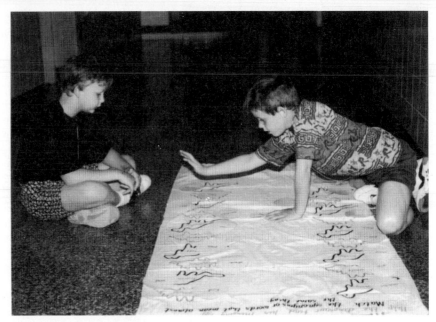

Language is involved in all learning activities.

travel, newspapers, magazines, and poetry related to space), doing several types of writing (reports, made-up diaries of space-station occupants, reviews of related television programs and movies, responses to fictionalized accounts of life in space, and scripts to be dramatized), listening (interviewing an expert, reviewing recordings of conversations between astronauts and control personnel on the earth's surface, and listening to related film or television dialogues), or speaking (presenting oral reports, dramatizing space-station events, and making audio- and videotapes). There will also be numerous specific learning experiences: spelling of scientific terms, practice in reading technical materials, opportunities to use several types of indexes in reference works, and using such electronic communication aids as camcorders, audiocassettes, word processors, and laser disk information systems.

In an effective classroom program, students are, as we said, developing skills, knowledge, and attitudes. These aspects of learning belong not only to language arts but also to other areas of the curriculum, and, indeed, promote important interrelationships among school subjects.

Teaching the Language Arts

Approaches to teaching the language arts vary from keeping subjects almost entirely separate from one another to including nearly all of what is thought of as the content of the language arts in studies in other areas of the curriculum. The major types of program organization are Separate Subjects, Integrated Language Arts, and Whole Language.

Separate Subjects. In the Separate Subjects approach time periods are scheduled during the school day or week for the different areas of the curriculum. The list of subjects includes handwriting, spelling, English, and reading, as well as mathematics, social studies, science, art, physical education, music and, perhaps, foreign language, library, and computers. Most subjects are taught from a textbook and without much connection to the others. Each language arts lesson is ordinarily taken directly from a spelling, handwriting, or English book, or a dictionary. Reading is almost always considered a subject in itself rather than a component of the language arts. The Separate Subjects organization is based on the assumption that pupils will study the text materials in a sequential fashion and then be able to use the skills and content they have learned when these are needed.

If the Separate Subjects type of organization were in use in a classroom where "The Space Station" was being studied, most of what was being learned would be thought of as science. During other periods of the day, the class would study spelling, writing, and the rest of the language arts, but the content covered would not necessarily have anything to do with the space station activities. It would be expected that what was taught in the language arts subjects could be used more or less automatically as needed in any other subject.

Integrated Language Arts. The approach known as Integrated Language Arts treats the language arts as a field that includes handwriting, spelling, composition, grammar, punctuation, listening, speaking, and, to some extent, reading. Teaching emphasizes the relationships among these components, encouraging pupils to see, for instance, that good handwriting and knowledge of spelling are both involved in producing words that can be read easily. Also, the language content of other subjects receives attention. A science report may involve consideration of reading, writing, and speaking content, for example.

In an Integrated Language Arts approach, attention is given both to systematic teaching of necessary skills and to actual use of what has been learned when there are opportunities to do so. Accordingly, in a classroom studying "The Space Station," there would be many attempts by the teacher to use what students had learned in their language arts classes as they engaged in the various project activities. However, he or she would also spend a substantial amount of time teaching language separately in developmental sequences (handwriting, spelling, etc.), with this content coming from textbooks and completely unrelated to the space theme.

Much useful information is available in *The Whole Language Catalog.*

Whole Language. The Whole Language approach to teaching does not stress classroom activities neatly separated into subjects. Usually larger blocks of time are scheduled for projects such as publishing a classroom newspaper or carrying out a survey of local traffic problems. A project would involve much learning in writing, interviewing, editing, and the other language arts, as well as art, mathematics, social studies, and science. Little use is made of textbooks in a Whole Language approach; instead, learning activities focus on children's own, often self-selected, experiences. Also, library books—both fiction and non-fiction—replace most conventional reading materials. In Whole Language teaching, it is expected that pupils will improve their performance through actual use of growing abilities in meaningful situations.

A Whole Language teacher ordinarily expects to include nearly all language arts teaching within the framework of major program features, including extensive reading of library books, televising of the school news, or building models of space stations. Conventional school textbooks are used as resource materials, if at all. There is very little attention to scheduling classes in each area of the language arts, although students might do independent study in some aspect of language of particular interest—a comparison of English and French words for the same objects and activities, perhaps.

A FINAL WORD

In recent times the English language has become a virtually worldwide medium for commerce, science, technology, and transportation. Not surprisingly, then, English is widely studied, with people in many nations seeking to master it. All languages are worthy of study, of course, but, considering the international prominence of English, it is all the more necessary that children learn to use English well. To ensure this proficiency, teachers must have a thorough knowledge of the English language—the way it works, how it grows and changes, how children learn it, and the ways it affects the lives of all of us. In addition, teachers need to know what to teach, when to teach it, and the best procedures to use in teaching. The chapters that follow were developed to help you acquire such knowledge.

References

Allen, R. R.; Brown, Kenneth L.; and Yatvin, Joanne. *Learning Language Through Communication: A Functional Perspective*. Wadsworth, 1985.

Baron, Naomi S. *Growing Up with Language: How Children Learn to Talk*. Addison-Wesley, 1992.

Bryen, Diane Nelson. *Inquiries into Child Language*. Allyn and Bacon, 1982.

Burgoon, Judee K.; Buller, David B.; and Woodall, W. Gill. *Nonverbal Communication: The Unspoken Dialogue*. Harper and Row, 1986.

Chapman, Robert L., ed. *New Dictionary of American Slang*. Harper and Row, 1986.

Claiborne, Robert. *Our Marvelous Native Tongue: The Life and Times of the English Language*. Times Books, 1983.

De Vito, Joseph A., and Hecht, Michael L. *The Nonverbal Communication Reader*. Waveland Press, 1990.

Goodman, Kenneth. *What's Whole in Whole Language?* Heinemann, 1986.

Goodman, Kenneth S.; Bird, Lois Bridges; and Goodman, Yetta M. *The Whole Language Catalog*. American School Publishers, 1991.

Halliday, M. A. K. *Learning How to Mean*. Elsevier North Holland, 1975.

Heath, Shirley Brice. *Ways with Words*. Cambridge University Press, 1983.

Henderson, Edmund. "History of English Spelling," in *Teaching Spelling*. Houghton Mifflin, 1985, pp. 5–36.

Hiebert, Elfrieda H., ed. *Literacy for a Diverse Society: Perspectives, Practices, and Policies*. Teachers College Press, 1991.

Holzman, Mathilda. *The Language of Children*. Prentice-Hall, 1983.

Ingram, David. *First Language Acquisition: Method, Description and Explanation*. Cambridge University Press, 1989.

Klopf, Donald W. *Intercultural Encounters: The Fundamentals of Intercultural Communication*. Morton, 1987.

Linn, Michael D., and Zuber, Maarit-Hannele. *The Sound of English: A Bibliography of Language Recordings*. National Council of Teachers of English, 1984.

McCrum, Robert; Cran, William; and MacNeil, Robert. *The Story of English* (companion to the Public Broadcasting System's series). Viking, 1986.

Myers, Doris T. *Understanding Language*. Boynton/Cook, 1984.

Newman, Judith M., ed. *Whole Language: Theory in Use*. Heinemann, 1985.

Olson, David R.; Torrance, Nancy; and Hildyard, Angela. *Literacy, Language, and Learning: The Nature and Consequences of Reading and Writing.* Cambridge University Press, 1985.

Pflaum, Susanna W. *The Development of Language and Literacy in Young Children.* Charles E. Merrill, 1986.

Powell, Rebecca Eller. "Goals for the Language Arts Program: Toward a Democratic Vision." *Language Arts* 69 (September 1992), pp. 342–349.

Seiler, William J.; Schuelke, L. David; and Lieb-Brilhart, Barbara. *Communication for the Contemporary Classroom.* Holt, Rinehart and Winston, 1984.

Taylor, Denny. *Family Literacy.* Heinemann, 1983.

Tompkins, Gail E., and Yaden, David B., Jr. *Answering Students' Questions about Words.* National Council of Teachers of English, 1986.

Walmsley, Sean A., and Walp, Trudy P. "Integrating Literature and Composing into the Language Arts Curriculum." *The Elementary School Journal* 90 (January 1990), pp. 251–274.

Wells, Gordon. *The Meaning Makers: Children Learning Language and Using Language to Learn.* Heinemann, 1986.

Teaching Resources

Adelson, Leone. *Dandelions Don't Bite: The Story of Words.* Pantheon, 1972 (grades 3–5).

Ashton, Christina. *Words Can Tell: A Book About Our Language.* Silver Burdett Press, 1989.

The Birth, Life—and Death?—of the Printed Word. Knowledge Unlimited (filmstrip).

A Common Tongue. Encyclopaedia Britannica (videotape).

Greene, Carol. *Language.* Children's Press, 1983 (grades 1–4).

Language—The Social Arbiter. Stuart Finley (film series).

Nevins, Ann. *From the Horse's Mouth.* Prentice-Hall, 1981 (grades 4–6).

News Words. Knowledge Unlimited (filmstrip).

Our Changing Language. National Council of Teachers of English (record).

Schwartz, Alvin, ed. *Tall Talk and Other Talk Collected from American Folklore.* Harper and Row, 1981 (grades 4–8).

Steckler, Arthur. *101 More Words and How They Began.* Doubleday, 1981 (grades 4–6).

The Story of English. Public Broadcasting System (videotapes).

Terban, Marvin. *Superdupers!: Really Funny Real Words.* Clarion, 1989.

Weiss, Ann E. *What's That You Said? How Words Change.* Harcourt Brace Jovanovich, 1980 (K–grade 3).

Activities for Preservice Teachers

1. Make a list of slang expressions currently used by high-school and college students. Ask people of various ages and backgrounds what these expressions mean. Report your findings to the class.

2. Analyze your own language history. What variety of English (or other language) is spoken by your relatives, friends, and neighbors? What influence has this had on you? What steps might you take to "improve" your English?

3. Watch several television situation comedies and quiz shows, paying particular attention to speech. What differences do you hear in sounds, vocabulary, and sentence structures?

4. Visit with some elderly people and ask what words they used in their youth to refer to games, candy, toys, and relations between boys and girls.

5. Videotape a two-year-old engaged in play or book reading with an adult. Note the child's range of vocabulary, speech patterns, and responses to what the adult says.

6. Look up the pronunciations of *aunt, berserk, data, heinous, orange,* and *route* in several dictionaries and then listen to how your classmates say them. What do you find?

7. Visit an elementary classroom for about two hours and closely observe one child. How much language does he or she use? What kinds of language? With whom does he or she talk? For what purposes? What proportion of class time is spent in listening, speaking, reading, or writing?

8. Begin a file of readings and language activities related to animal communication. Start with material from encyclopedias about bees, whales, and primates.

9. Examine the language arts textbooks for a particular grade level, and for spelling, handwriting, reading, and English. Note the extent to which attempts are made to

relate one area to another. Is spelling discussed in the English book? Handwriting in spelling? Storytelling in the reading book? Then look for writing activities suggested in the science, social studies, and math books.

10. See if you can identify the region of the country associated with each of the words or phrases in these pairs: string beans and snap beans, pail and bucket, sweet corn and roasting ears, porch and stoop, cherry pit and cherry seed, pavement and sidewalk. Perhaps friends and family members can help.

11. Visit a classroom and talk with children who did not begin their education in the school they are now attending. Find out the reasons for their having moved. As the children talk, listen for variety in language patterns and usage. Identify three or four language features that you believe might be significant for language arts teaching.

Activities for Inservice Teachers

1. Watch two or three of the programs from the Public Broadcasting System's series *The Story of English*. Identify content that might be adapted for teaching to elementary students.

2. Videotape yourself as you make a presentation in your classroom or work with a group of students. What do you notice about your speech and general style of communication that might be improved?

3. Ask children to write about the meanings of well-known expressions such as those listed below. Tailor the selection to the maturity and sophistication of your group. Let the students take their lists home for discussion with others. If you ask about the expressions' derivations, be sure to make homework discussion a part of the activity.

neat as a pin	look a gift horse in the mouth
picture of health	on cloud nine
once in a blue moon	get up on the wrong side of the bed
raining cats and dogs	
	barking up the wrong tree

4. Identify a problem concerning language arts teaching in your school. Find out the names of state or federal resource people, and write to them for advice.

5. Discuss with pupils what constitutes appropriate talk for various settings: the dinner table at home, the living room when their parents have guests, the school bus, and so forth. Take note of the particulars they mention, the factors they consider important, and any language-related generalizations they make.

6. Talk with a highly experienced or retired teacher about how emphases in language arts teaching have changed over the years with regard to interrelatedness among the language arts.

7. Find some books about words for children (*The First Book of Words* by Epstein and Epstein or *More About Words* by Ernst, for example). Use these as a departure point for a unit on vocabulary, dictionary study, or spelling.

8. Read the 1989 statement on recommended teaching procedures by the National Council of Teachers of Mathematics. Note that they emphasize that reading and writing activities be used extensively in math teaching.

9. Consider joining the National Council of Teachers of English so that you will receive their journal, *Language Arts*. See if there is a local affiliate of the Whole Language Umbrella and attend one of its meetings if possible.

Chapter 2

Teaching the Language Arts

A hundred years ago, the list of language areas studied by students was long, including oral and silent reading, spelling, etymology, penmanship, elocution, composition, grammar, and literature. What do you remember about the language arts you studied when you were in elementary school? Possibly you engaged in many learning activities similar to those of a century earlier—participating in spelling contests, identifying parts of speech, diagramming sentences, filling in blanks, giving reports, drilling on handwriting forms, and taking your turn reading aloud.

Increasingly, today's teachers are dropping or modifying these time-honored activities or adopting new ones in recognition of evidence from research. Also, newer techniques such as videotaping or using a word processor have been introduced in many classrooms. Even though what to include in a program is determined to some extent by state and district requirements, the need to make fundamental decisions concerning the requirements and the organization of a class of children and the physical aspects of the classroom itself presents difficult problems a teacher must deal with every year and to some extent every day.

The purpose of this chapter is to give you an overview of effective language arts teaching and the planning and organizing that are so important in maximizing children's learning. The content of this chapter has application in each of the chapters that follow; you may find yourself referring back to it as you study them.

PREPARATION FOR TEACHING

Who are the children?
How are they alike?
How are they different?
What are their needs?
How will you find answers to these questions?

As a teacher, you need to know whom you are teaching, what it is that they should learn, and how you plan to go about helping them do that. You may know quite a bit about children in general, but every class is somewhat different, and individual students can be extremely difficult to understand. You need to know what *abilities, knowledge, skills,* and *attitudes* your students have and what their interests, problems, and needs are. Determining all this for more than a few children is a huge task—one that has to be worked at all year long. Getting to know children is a rewarding experience, however, and one that will enrich your life as well as make you a more effective teacher. You can refer to test scores and other school records, of course, and consult previous teachers, but keep in mind that these records and opinions may be accurate or may be biased against a child because of personality conflicts, cultural differences, or judgments made hastily. Use records and others' judgments carefully, depending primarily on your own methods for learning about children (see the section Recognizing Pupil Differences later in this chapter).

Other important matters to consider when preparing to teach include the content of the program and the learning principles on which to base teaching activities as well as the decision-making process by which you integrate what you know about children, subject matter, and effective teaching strategies.

Content—What to Teach

What should be taught is important in organizing a language arts program, but how content is selected—on what premises and by what principles—is of utmost concern if teaching effort is to accomplish anything worthwhile. The findings of research, the contents of curriculum guides and textbooks, and the policies and standards of the school provide guides, but the responsibility for determining what is taught is primarily the teacher's. Teachers often contend that this is not true—that school administrators tell them what to teach or that the textbooks and other materials structure the program for them. In some situations there may be justification for such concern, but for the most part teachers have substantial control over what they present to their students.

Guiding principles for exercising this responsibility include the following:

Gradually we are learning how parents, teachers, and school administrators can collaborate to assess programs and decide on changes and new directions.

- The nature of the classroom program should be decided in conjunction with consideration of the expectations of the school district involved. Statements of objectives may have been formulated by the school system, but these may require reformulation in more specific or meaningful terms. Or the recommended program might be somewhat out-of-date, in which case the staff should initiate systematic examination of content and teaching approaches.

- The emphasis in teaching should be on developing communication abilities rather than on drilling on skills in isolation. It is more important for a child to have the strategies necessary for effective expression and reception of ideas and information than to know rules about language structure, punctuation, and similar sorts of content.

Don't forget that published materials were planned for children in general—not necessarily for *your* students.

- The selection of content should take into account the communication needs of the children in the classroom—their experiences and development, the types of communication they need experience with, what they require as they progress further in the school system, and the opportunities provided by the ongoing activities that develop from day to day in the classroom.

Carefully examine some elementary-level textbooks. To what extent is it apparent that the books have been compiled with these content guides in mind?

To help you decide what skills, attitudes, and knowledge the children in your class need immediately and as they progress through their school years, you should ask yourself the questions listed as follows. Answering them may not be easy, but you should rely on your own honest, sensible judgment in seeking the answers rather than first turning to the teacher next door or to textbooks and their teachers' manuals. Both of these resources—and others—may help you to find answers, but essentially the answers must be yours.

When considering a skill, understanding, or other specific item for inclusion in your classroom program ask these questions:

- *How frequently is this needed and used in the life activities of children and adults?* For example, writers use colons much less frequently than they use commas; people do more storytelling than choral speaking; and seldom does one need to identify the adverbs in a sentence.

- *How important is this when the need for it arises?* For instance, many people do not write business letters frequently, but when the time arrives, it is usually important that the letter be well written.
- *How universally is this encountered in people's experiences?* For example, the presentation of a book report is only a school activity for most people, but a conversation is something everyone does at one time or another.
- *What evidence is there that this will meet a permanent need?* For example, some of the first words a child should learn to spell are the same words adults use frequently in their writing.
- *Which children, if any, in my classroom are ready to learn this?* In other words, attention must be given to the needs of the children, the experiences they have had, and what they have already learned. Dictionary instruction will have little value for the child who has not learned alphabetical order.

Using Principles of Learning—How to Teach

In planning your program—*how* you will teach as well as *what* you will teach—you must recognize that learning is a complex act, and descriptions of the process are sometimes superficial or misleading. Research based on observations of learning, however, provides evidence as to how learning may be expedited. This evidence can be stated in several principles that every teacher must heed.

Can you think of a college class in which these principles were successfully applied?

Learning Is Different for Each Individual. Children differ from one another in many ways, and most certainly in their ability to learn. This difference is apparent in learning capacities and rates and in responsiveness to various instructional techniques. Furthermore, in addition to differences in inherited intellectual and physical endowments, children vary in their emotions, previous experiences, and motivation as well as in age, gender, maturation, and health status. You may expect that children's participation in a classroom activity will reflect these characteristics and conditions. A teacher can do something about some of them but not others, yet all have to receive consideration in teaching.

Learning Is an Active Process. Although some kinds of learning do not require much effort on the part of the learner, the type of learning involved in most school work is an active, seeking process. Pupils almost constantly interact with the classroom environment, constructing interpretations of what is experienced and thus developing their ideas. Taking into account children's backgrounds and needs will facilitate the types of transactions likely to produce meaningful learning for everyone. That is, teachers must match learning tasks appropriately to the students so that the seeking process will be productive. This is a key factor in enhancing children's positive attitudes toward school and learning.

Learning Is Cooperative. The active process of learning often occurs more effectively when small groups of learners are working together toward a common objective. In such situations information is pooled, there is shared ownership of responsibility for task completion, individuals with varied competencies may make significant contributions, and those with particular understandings and skills help other members of the group; students teach one another.

Learning Is Developmental. Anything learned is built on and adds to previous learning. Learning will not occur without readiness; therefore, it is important to be aware of children's prior knowledge, their maturation levels, and their learning rates and capacities as well as to plan for appropriate sequencing of their experiences.

Learning Is Motivated. In the classroom, the best source of motivation is the pupils' inherent interest in the activities presented. Extrinsic motivation is readily apparent in schools, of course, as learners seek the approval of the teacher or compete for grades and other symbols of success. The teachers who provide the best learning environments, however, will be the ones whose students are motivated by a need to understand and a desire to do their best and produce something worthwhile.

Learning Requires Reinforcement. Anything learned but not used moves rather quickly out of the conscious mind and may be entirely forgotten. ("Use it or lose it" is more than just an expression.) Also, practice needs to be meaningful, so it should take place in realistic situations. Constant drill and practice without actual use is empty.

Learning May Transfer. Ordinarily, transfer of learning takes place from one situation to another to the extent that identical elements are shared by both. Learning will transfer if proper attention is given to what is taught, when it is taught, and whether children are helped to see the similarity in situations and the applicability of what they know.

Thinking about Teaching—Making Decisions

Determining the content you plan to teach and acknowledging relevant principles of learning will contribute significantly to your preparation for teaching, but other important decisions remain to be made. You must be sure that the content given priority receives adequate attention and occurs in situations that provide students with the best opportunities for learning. This requires that you constantly reflect on what you and the students are doing and whether or not the activities planned appear to be worth the time and effort expended.

As a teacher you should also be ready to capitalize on events and situations that occur in unexpected ways and have the potential for becoming excellent teaching opportunities (*embedded lessons* are discussed in the section A Basic Instructional Approach). The chances are very good that these unplanned activities will be memorable for the children and will contribute to the achievement of important instructional goals. They may also lead to the planning of additional valuable learning experiences.

All decision making does not have to be done by the teacher alone. Teachers who plan cooperatively with their students find that this approach leads to improved performance and good attitudes toward learning and school. Effective sharing of decision-making responsibility does not just happen, though; it must be learned through gradual expansion of the children's role. Children and teacher need to learn how to plan together. The following suggestions should help that process along.

Don't overpraise students. "Good job," constantly repeated may teach children to always look to adults for approval rather than to take satisfaction in their own knowledge that they have done well.

Every day a teacher makes dozens of decisions. Good teaching is largely a matter of the ratio of better decisions to poorer ones.

The best teachers take big risks occasionally.

In nursery classes three-
year-olds make choices.
Can't third graders be given
such opportunities?

- Keep your responsibility as a teacher in mind. Know what the children's abilities are at any given point, and share decision making appropriately.

- Make sure that genuine choices are available. This is the only way for students to develop a feeling of ownership over their learning experiences.

- Attempt to implement the plans that have been made. It is worthwhile for even the results of poor planning to be experienced.

- Make certain that planning is not being done by only a few members of the class. True sharing means that everyone is included.

INSTRUCTIONAL PLANNING

An instructional plan is not something that can be made once and then shelved; a plan needs to be modified slightly or revised substantially as circumstances change and as children progress. Although a long-term plan (what should be

Effective planning requires wide participation.

In multigrade classrooms children will stay with a teacher for two years or even more. This provides a superb basis for planning students' experiences.

accomplished this year, this term, this month) is crucial, plans must be made also for intermediate periods of time and for daily activities.

This section describes the elements of an instructional plan—for any period of time—and suggests a model of a basic plan for teaching in the various language arts areas and for integrating this teaching with some aspect of a content subject that is a part of the classroom's total curriculum. Finally, an illustration of such a plan is given.

A Basic Instructional Approach

The Language Arts Instructional Plan outlined in the figure illustrates a framework for thinking about planning. The diagram depicts the relationships among the major factors at work as classroom planning is done and as instruction occurs.

Language Arts Instructional Plan

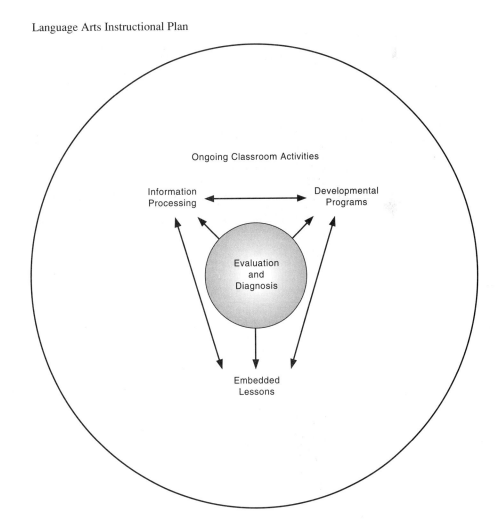

The larger circle represents the ongoing **classroom program,** instruction as it moves along from day to day, each day building on learning that has been gained and taking into consideration children's interests and their needs as determined by evaluation and diagnosis. The setting for classroom activities includes not only the curriculum requirements and the children but also external influences such as state-required and local testing, community preferences, and district policies. These and many other factors influence planning and, in turn, instruction.

Evaluation is an ongoing process, not something done only periodically.

The smaller circle represents the **evaluation and diagnosis**—both formal and informal—that should be integral parts of all classroom activities. As a teacher, you assess the progress of students and evaluate the success of learning activities and the appropriateness of particular instructional materials. Most important, you evaluate the effectiveness of your own planning and teaching. It is important to remember, though, that children have a responsibility for evaluating their own daily work and academic progress. Diagnosis seeks to determine each student's specific learning needs. Responsibility for diagnosis falls primarily on the teacher, but students can learn to identify their own weaknesses. They can also participate in discussions of problems they are having and how these might be handled. With practice and guidance children can, as they become more mature, learn to honestly diagnose their own learning efforts.

Diagnosis also means finding out what is going well.

The diagram focuses on three principal types of teaching activities: those based on instructional materials of a sequential, developmental nature; information-processing activities involving use of language to accomplish something specific; and embedded lessons, which occur on an unscheduled basis when students encounter a learning situation and the teacher capitalizes on it to further understanding or skill growth.

Developmental Programs. As discussed in Chapter 1, the Separate Subjects approach to teaching is strongly influenced by instructional materials designed to be presented in a developmental, sequential way. These materials primarily consist of textbooks but also include curriculum guides and, to some extent, kits, duplicated worksheets, computer-aided instruction, and games. The developmental materials most widely used in language arts teaching are the basal readers, series of books that take children through a sequential set of experiences designed to lead to competency in reading. In addition, it is common for schools to have children study spelling and handwriting by completing programs that provide a definite sequence of learning activities.

If a teacher proceeds through textbooks page by page, little planning will be required, but this is not a justifiable way to teach. Certainly, as you plan learning activities with your students, you will very likely see ways to use textbooks as resources to be drawn on as needed rather than as a curriculum to be covered. Using texts as resources is characteristic of an Integrated Language Arts program. After some experience you may even create your own developmental sequence, which will be different from that used by anyone else. Teachers using a Whole Language approach attempt to do without most ordinary developmental materials entirely and rely on their ability to include specific teaching episodes within comprehensive learning activities such as storybook reading.

Students process information as they:

clarify
identify
compare
inquire
survey
judge
create
solve
analyze
evaluate

Information Processing. Information-processing activities in the language arts area are those in which students use writing, reading, listening, and speaking to express themselves and gain knowledge. Information-processing strategies involving all school subjects and various thinking and language abilities will become increasingly significant as you create a classroom program that involves thoughtful responses to subject matter. Such strategies as identifying important ideas, making comparisons, and considering cause-effect relationships are important if thinking is to develop. (See Chapter 6 for further discussion of thinking.)

Reading, though often thought of as a subject taught mostly for its own sake, should be considered an important means of processing information. As a teacher, you will want to plan reading experiences that are based in other areas of the curriculum. In science, for example, students will read about the process of photosynthesis and begin to understand the role of the sun, water, air, and nutrients in producing chlorophyll in plants. Reading of this type (a good example of information processing) is demanding with respect to comprehension but much more meaningful than the reading-for-sequence exercises ("How to Build a Birdhouse") often presented in reading workbooks.

Children will use listening as they are introduced to poetry and other types of literature and (in social studies, for example) they are asked to listen to recorded speeches and perhaps to reports made by their classmates. They must try to follow each presentation and grasp meaning at several different levels. When giving oral reports themselves, children will require assistance in learning how to prepare their material and make an effective delivery. Writing presents a great number of possibilities for information-processing experiences.

These learning opportunities will have to be carefully planned if children are to derive maximum benefit from them. Some activities will be described in the teachers' manuals of textbook series in social studies and other subject fields, but the best ideas are likely to be your own because only you know the students and what activities will be most appropriate for them.

Of course, connections exist between developmental programs and information-processing activities. It seems logical from the Separate Subjects perspective that students should learn something in a developmental program (how to make an inference from a text) and then be able to apply this directly to their content experiences, but studies of human learning seem to indicate that this sort of transfer takes place for only a small proportion of learners. Most of us need to learn something in a context highly similar to the one in which it will be used.

Teachers using the Integrated Language Arts approach will be more effective if they have their students review the relevant language arts content when they are about to do something involving use of that material. In Integrated Language Arts teaching, textbooks and other guides in spelling and handwriting may frequently be used as resources to support information-processing activities. This is also true in Whole Language teaching, since helping children see how they might employ a variety of resources is of concern to a teacher using that method. However, as a Whole Language teacher, you would expect that in a highly meaningful information-processing situation the pupils would learn much language arts content in the process of actually using it, whether or not it had been previously "taught."

Embedded Lessons. Embedded lessons can involve information processing, but usually only a single student or small group will have your attention for a brief time, during which the focus is on a specific understanding. Embedded lessons cannot be planned because of the impossibility of predicting when a productive situation will occur. Experience will reveal what to expect in a general way, though, so you need to be alert for good teaching opportunities. When children write stories, for example, they may be vaguely aware of the need for quotation marks in dialogue but will have to be assisted in seeing how this kind of punctuation is used. This, then, is the best time to provide a few minutes of instruction—just when the child is ready.

Developmental program materials can be used to support embedded lessons. For example, the pupil who is interested in writing dialogue may be referred to relevant pages in the language textbook. Also, both language and spelling books

A minute or even less with students can result in a successful embedded lesson.

are likely to include lists of commonly misspelled words, and children should be taught how and when to use these resources. Writers' guides covering many matters related to word choice, punctuation, and other questions are found in some language textbooks; this is a good type of aid to have in mind at a time when students are writing. Also, when a child's handwriting seems to need attention, you can refer him or her to a handwriting book for help and practice in correcting the problem.

Embedded lessons are closely related to information-processing activities because such specific teaching is most likely to succeed when children are studying content in a subject area or preparing to organize and present what they have learned. Within the context of these comprehensive experiences there will be numerous opportunities to help children learn the specifics of spelling, handwriting, reading, using the dictionary, punctuating, learning vocabulary, listening, and improving speech. You can improve your teaching by learning to use a few seconds to good advantage, knowing when a student is likely to be ready for a particular learning experience, and regularly refreshing your memory concerning the abilities and skills you want to emphasize.

Although embedded lessons are not a necessary part of the Separate Subjects approach to organization, an individual teacher might well take the opportunity to teach something even when it was not the "time" for that particular skill or understanding. In the Integrated Language Arts approach, opportunities for embedded lessons are something to look for, and in the Whole Language approach they constitute much of the teaching program.

Planning in Action

As indicated in the preceding section, daily language arts activities have many sources. A few may come from textbook series and other materials that include detailed plans telling teachers what to do. As a teacher, you should use or modify these materials as needed, making decisions about what to leave out and which aspects to emphasize and extend. Even if you tried to do it, you could not possibly find enough class time to carry out all of the activities recommended in each set of published materials; so it is advisable to rely heavily on your own judgment.

Decisions often involve choosing what to omit.

Another major consideration when developing lesson plans is to provide for language experiences within the framework of other classroom events. In science or social studies, for example, you will be planning lessons about magnets or elections that should involve children in writing, speaking, listening, and reading. Thus, language abilities are important in all subjects and will occasionally require specific attention—a few minutes on the use of capital letters for place names or how to find topics in an index, for instance. This kind of embedded lesson advances language performance without diverting pupils from the subject matter being studied. In such situations learning opportunities for the language arts, just as those for mathematics or some other area of the curriculum, are often included for purposes of reinforcement and transfer (discussed in the earlier section Using Principles of Learning).

In addition to lessons already planned for you and lessons embedded in various activities, you can use fully developed lesson plans that are truly your own. These you devise because of needs in the class, subject matter that is expected to be taught, something that has come up in an activity, your desire to provide an experience you consider important for the children to have, and so on. Detailed planning is often required in one situation or another, and even the most experienced teachers will at least make a few notes about what is needed and what will be done. Those with less experience will usually want to be more thorough and complete a fully developed lesson plan.

Planning a Lesson

You probably have read about how to plan a lesson, or you may have done such planning yourself. A lesson plan may be for a single day or, in the case of a social studies or science unit, for several days. Lesson plans also vary in amount of detail specified and in format; the extent of the detail included often depends on the teacher's level of experience. Every lesson, however, involves tasks and learning opportunities that require planning, and careful thought must be given to *what* is to be included, *why* it is being taught, *how* the teaching will be done, and *ways* to measure the effectiveness of the teaching.

As an example of lesson planning, suppose that the social studies curriculum for your school includes a unit on colonial America. Understanding about national history is a **broad goal,** so delineation is required for a specific class situation. First, you and the children might discuss what they expect to learn from this unit. Perhaps the discussion would lead to the following questions:

What famous people lived during that period? Why are they famous?
What events occurred during the period that are important to us today?
How did the people of that time live?

Because all of these questions cannot be answered in a single lesson, one or two **specific objectives** should be identified for the plan being developed. Suppose, then, that you and the children decide to concentrate on the third question about people's lives.

With the objective determined, the next step is to consider what you will need to do, what materials and other **resources** will be needed, and what learning activities the children will engage in. With these considerations in mind, attention should be given first to resources. The children, knowing and understanding the objective, can provide some input. For example, they might suggest that they use the encyclopedia and other books in the classroom and school libraries. Someone might also suggest that a nearby museum could be visited. You might propose drawing on such resources as a film, a local collector of antiques, or a speaker knowledgeable about the topic.

Certainly, then, you need to list the long-range goals, broad objectives, the specific objective, and the resources, and it is also a good idea to list these on the board or a chart for the benefit of the children. Be realistic about resources, however. For example, if transportation to a museum is not likely to be available, a museum visit is not a viable resource for the activity.

The next step in development of the plan is deciding what procedures will be used to help the children attain the specific objective. You may want to have the children work in small groups or as individuals to gather information on such aspects of colonial life as food, clothing, housing, jobs, transportation, religion, and recreation. Of course, a museum visit, a speaker, or a film would provide information to the class and perhaps give an overall picture of colonial life; specific and more complete information about the various narrower aspects requires that the groups or individuals read and do research on their own. You, throughout all of this, should be guiding children as they find resources, take notes, and consider how they might report their information to the class (for example, by means of oral presentations, written summaries, demonstrations, displays, or dramatizations).

Beginners often find it helpful to include a time schedule in lesson plans. This provides a target for pacing—moving neither too quickly nor too slowly.

You need to plan how much time will be given to gathering information and how much to reporting, thereby putting a time frame around the lesson. The broad objective of the planning example discussed here dictates that it will not be a one-day activity but will likely extend over a week or more following the introductory experience. A given day's learning activities are usually most productive when they grow out of what was done the previous day.

As noted in the section A Basic Instructional Approach, a significant component of teaching—and one that should be included in all planning—is **evaluation** of the learning and of the effectiveness of the procedures followed. Maybe having the children summarize orally is adequate; perhaps testing is appropriate. Certainly, evaluation must also include deciding what to do if the objective has not been reached. The children should be included in the latter aspect of evaluation and in looking ahead to the next lesson. Of course, your evaluation often needs to be more than that done by or with the children, if such evaluation consists only of oral discussion and summarizing, important as these may be. You may need to consider what experiences were provided and note which particular skills or processes need more practice or attention. It is to be hoped, of course, that the children will eventually learn to evaluate themselves in terms of skills and appropriate behavior.

Although the example presented here is a social studies lesson, the same kind of planning is appropriate whether the focus is science, health, literature, or any other subject area. The significant point is that effective communication must also be a center of attention, along with the content involved. This includes *authentic* use of listening, speaking, viewing, reading, writing and thinking, and it is through real-life, hands-on activities (letters are really sent and received, not just written as a textbook exercise) that language is most effectively taught.

Thus, planning a lesson involves certain necessary steps or stages. Also necessary is the children's participation in the planning and in execution of the plan. A plan for a single lesson, for example, might be recorded in a form like the one presented on the following page.

PLANNING FOR INDIVIDUAL LEARNERS

Refer to Chapter 16 for discussion of "special needs" children and services for them.

Because it is the individual child who learns effectively or doesn't, planning must be based in part on the progress of each pupil. Though learning activities are often group experiences, all teachers realize that there are important differences among the individuals who participate in them. We know that each person is unique. Yet, aside from observing obvious physical differences, a teacher may not fully recognize the degree of variation among the children in his or her class. In terms of pupil achievement, only about one-third of a typical class achieve at or near the *norm,* the average for that grade level on a standardized achievement test. The

OBJECTIVES:

Broad—Learning about life in colonial America
Specific—Gaining information about how life necessities were acquired by
          colonists
          Improving skills in researching, studying, and reporting

MATERIALS:

Chapter 2 of the social studies textbook
Encyclopedias in the classroom and in the library
Books on colonial America that have been set aside in the school library
Large pictures of Plymouth Plantation

PROCEDURES:

1. Initiate discussion of camping (a topic familiar to many of the children), relating this to situations faced by colonists. Involve children in listing life necessities and discussing how these are met when camping.
2. Use pictures of Plymouth Plantation to show what a colony was like and to suggest how the colonists lived.
3. Encourage discussion about life necessities: which are truly basic and which are merely important? Have the class formulate a list.
4. Form groups consisting of four or five pupils, and have each group select a life necessity to investigate and report on.
5. Discuss available resources, at the same time providing lessons that review using a table of contents, skimming, and note taking.
6. Suggest that groups begin to plan how they will make their reports.
7. Conclude by reviewing what has been done and what will be done during the next class.

EVALUATION:

1. Do children have a clear idea of what the necessities of life are? Does each group understand what kind of information they are looking for?
2. Are pupils skimming resources to see whether they contain needed information? Is further practice in this skill needed by some or all of the children?
3. Are the notes that have been taken so far accurate and likely to be useful?
4. Are group members working well together, with each child making a contribution?

SUMMARY AND FOLLOW-UP:

1. Plan for a review of skimming and/or note taking for those who need it.
2. Decide, with the children, what other aspects of colonial life and times should be examined (plantation residents' relationships with their Native American neighbors, perhaps).
3. Plan for variety in resources, grouping, and methods of reporting.
4. Determine what kinds of experiences can be included in the total unit, both those provided by you (trips, films, etc.) and those provided by the pupils (skits, demonstrations, oral and written reports, displays, etc.).

other two-thirds are usually about equally divided above and below the norm, with the *range* (distance from lowest to highest score) increasing as the grade level advances. For example, a classroom of sixth graders may show 40 percent at grade level, 20 percent at seventh-grade level, 10 percent at eighth-grade level or above, 20 percent at fifth-grade level, and 10 percent at fourth-grade level or below. And because the achievement test does not measure many of the specific language skills, the range among all pupils for all skills, abilities, and attitudes important to language communication is likely to be even more startling.

Teacher Assessment of Pupils

To identify important differences among pupils in order to determine their instructional needs, it is necessary to carry on a continuing program of pupil assessment. Relying on your memory for information regarding each child's strengths and needs is likely to result in instruction that is less effective than it could be. Techniques such as quietly speaking your observations into a small audiotape recorder as you work with the children or making videotapes of their performance for later analysis provide opportunities to augment your observational notes. Also, keeping a portfolio of school work, tests, and other related materials for each child will enable you to observe how the pupils assess their own progress. The recommendations that follow are discussed throughout the text in chapters devoted to particular aspects of the language arts program.

1. Observe and record the listening and speech performance of each child, including his or her speaking skills, mannerisms, and behavior in various settings.
2. Analyze a pupil's patterns of English usage in oral and written language by taking samples at regular intervals.
3. Use checklists or inventory forms to note achievements and areas of concern in specific language activities such as conversations, discussions, letter writing, or reporting.
4. Construct tests to determine each pupil's knowledge and abilities in choosing correct spellings, punctuating and capitalizing properly, and identifying types of sentences.
5. Tabulate the types of spelling errors a pupil makes.
6. Use standardized measures (see the discussion of reading tests in Chapter 12) in a planned program to assess growth and achievement in specific areas, including achievement tests and reading inventories.
7. Keep anecdotal records (brief reports of behavior or incidents having to do with children) of significant events and share these with special teachers, parents, or others who may find such information of use in helping the child.
8. Interview pupils regularly concerning their perceptions of how they are succeeding, what they see as their problems, what they enjoy doing, and what goals they want to set for themselves.

We are all well aware that record keeping is a chore, but the procedures suggested above are relatively easy to implement. The task can be simplified by varying procedures throughout the year, by using checklists whenever possible, and particularly by keeping records up to date. Much of the material mentioned may be added to the child's language arts portfolio.

The range of achievement found among a group of students usually gets wider as they grow older.

A student's portfolio may include work from all subjects or could be restricted to language arts.

Involving Pupils in Self-Assessment

Portfolios need to be reviewed regularly, with items examined, deleted, and added.

Helping a child to identify his or her own language strengths and needs is a procedure that will pay rich dividends. If each pupil has a language arts portfolio, a variety of inventories, tapes, work samples, and other assessments may be systematically collected. These will furnish evidence that the child is making progress, an important source of motivation in itself, and will also provide a most valuable base for individual and group planning. Several activities will yield useful results.

1. Checklists may be kept for oral language, preferably ones that the child has helped to devise and that he or she has had an opportunity to use in reviewing a personal videotape.

2. Proofreading checklists should be used by students to edit their own written work. Copies of edited work may be included in the portfolio.

Students should learn to keep records of their own progress.

3. Handwriting may be analyzed for difficulties caused by improperly formed letters or other characteristics.

4. Audiotapes may be made of the child reading particular selections and notes kept regarding her or his thoughts regarding progress in such areas as expression or ability to deal with unknown words.

5. Videotapes of oral reports may be made and progress noted by the child in her or his ability to use notes, maintain eye contact, vary voice and summarize presentations.

6. Lists should be kept of what the pupil has read (biographies, science fiction, myths, adventures) and what she or he has written in response.

7. Copies (or photocopies) of standardized tests a pupil has been administered may be kept, along with teacher's written comments on test results.

8. A pupil might keep lists of what needs attention—new vocabulary to consider using, spelling words or aspects of handwriting that have been a problem, books that sound interesting, etc.

A portfolio provides a very good basis for pupil self-assessment and for conferences with parents. Of special importance are periodic reviews of the portfolio by the pupil and the teacher as they jointly assess what the pupil has done and plan what might be the next set of goals for her or him.

ORGANIZING FOR TEACHING AND LEARNING

There are many ways of organizing the programs of an entire school or those of classrooms. The intent of each plan is to facilitate teaching and learning by influencing how the interaction of teachers and learners takes place. Apparently, however, no one plan of organization of a school or of a class of youngsters is the ideal, the one that research or practice has shown to be the most effective. Each plan is affected by many factors, including the number of children involved, the characteristics of the children as a group, the community and its traditions, legal regulations, fiscal and space requirements and limitations, curriculum decisions that have been made, and the specific approaches favored by school board members, administrators, and teachers.

This section will not review all possible organizational plans or discuss any in great depth. There are published resources that do both. However, every language arts teacher needs to know something about school organizational plans and how he or she may best organize a classroom of children for the maximum learning of each individual to occur.

Classroom Grouping

Group only when doing so will facilitate learning. Don't group for your convenience or for administrative expediency.

In the elementary school there are many appropriate groupings for language arts experiences. Several classes may come together in an auditorium to hear a storyteller or view a dramatic performance, for example. Within classrooms the entire group will do choral reading, listen to poetry, interview a guest speaker, receive instruction on types of science fiction, or watch a television program.

Small-group activities also have an important place in the language arts program. Groups of pupils may be formed for a variety of reasons, including similarity of learning requirements, shared interests, and involvement in a particular project. Reading groups based on ability are common, especially in the primary-grades classrooms. (See criticism of this practice in Chapter 4, Reading Activities.)

Other types of grouping for instruction include those for short-range needs such as learning more about how sentences are formed or how certain types of punctuation should be used. Often intended to be of help to pupils who are accelerated in their learning or encountering problems, instructional groups are formed or abandoned, depending on circumstances.

Interest groups in language arts may include those related to particular kinds of literature. Children interested in the same book, or books by a certain author, or books on a topic may come together for a period of time. Other interests may be in a different type of literature or in a form of writing—limericks, plays, or fables, perhaps. Project groups may choose to become involved in videotaping a scene from a book, participating in a "pen pal" program with students in another state, or starting a class magazine. Once the project is in operation or completed, the group may be disbanded or reorganized. In interest and project groups, and even in skill-learning groups, children of different levels of ability may participate together, since studies of "cooperative learning" indicate that all members benefit from well-organized small-group experiences.

In considering how and when to use groups, you should recognize that such organization must grow naturally from the setting of goals and planning. If interested in promoting student participation in planning and giving children many opportunities to accept responsibilities, you should emphasize small-group activities. Of course, you need to know your students and apply that knowledge in helping them to make best use of the group experience. And group activities need to be planned carefully, especially when first introduced. You should ensure that objectives are clear, guidelines are understood, and materials are available. Just as with many other experiences, pupils must be helped to learn how to be a participant in a small-group setting.

Group activities present many good opportunities for listening and speaking experiences, as described in Chapters 5 and 6.

Read the book by Johnson and Johnson (listed at the end of this chapter) for information on *cooperative learning.*

Individualizing Learning

There are many ways to provide instruction directed at meeting the individual needs of children. Some school and classroom organizational features seem particularly beneficial in accomplishing individualization. The suggestions given below are ones related to practices found in schools and classrooms where good results have been observed.

- **Flexible Scheduling** involves setting up a classroom program that provides large time blocks that can be used in various ways. This permits pupils some opportunity to make choices about activities such as reading library books, typing on a word processor, or practicing spelling. Most of the suggestions for individualized learning can only be implemented in settings where there is substantial flexibility in the use of time.

- **Learning Centers** are classroom areas that children are free to use when they have available time. Centers may be tables or partly screened-off areas or a grouping of materials on shelves. There are usually centers for writing, listening, science, or mathematics activities. Some centers may be used according to the interests of the student, whereas others are designed to be used only in certain ways.

- **Media Resources** include recorders, projectors, computers, and copiers that pupils have been taught to use. Individualization might be in the form of computer-assisted instruction as the pupil interacts with a particular program. Other activities could involve viewing a videotape, taking a recorded spelling test, listening to a taped story, or making a book or a filmstrip.

- **Unit Studies,** projects, or themes on topics such as transportation or dinosaurs present many opportunities for children to do individual study. They may enrich their learning by going well beyond what was originally planned, investigating matters that would ordinarily be the work of much older students. Or they may be able to capitalize on artistic or other talents and make a unique and valued contribution to the project.

Chapter 14 describes some important contributions of library media centers.

- **Library media centers** in schools are particularly important for individualization. In a well-supplied center, pupils can find not only books and magazines but also reference materials, films, tapes, recordings, and even computerized information-retrieval services. Of great importance for individualization is the availability of a staff member who knows how to assist a child in doing research.

Regularly occurring teacher–student conferences related to writing (Chapter 10) and reading (Chapter 12) should be a basic aspect of classroom organization.

- **Pupil–Teacher Conferences** provide opportunities for consultation about the child's progress and interests. When pupils meet regularly with their teacher, they can receive guidance in identifying what they need to do and how their goals might be reached. The teacher can make assessments of progress and plan jointly with each pupil, perhaps making contracts specifying what the child will do in areas of special interest.

Much individualization of learning is possible when a classroom has learning centers, ongoing major projects or units of various kinds, large blocks of time flexibly organized, regular availability of computers and other types of electronic equipment, access to superior library services, and provision for conferences between youngsters and the teacher. Teaching methods of a general nature are also significant, of course. If entire areas of the program such as spelling and handwriting are individualized, this sets the tone for the program. Then all resources support a particular thrust and pupils begin to learn how they might apply certain strategies to other areas. On the other hand, if whole-class, teacher-centered instruction predominates, there will not be much time or support for individualized learning.

Be wary of commercially published individualized learning packets. They may impose a rigidity that you want to avoid.

Many suggestions for making individualization a reality are given in the chapters that follow, and at the end of each chapter specific examples of independent learning activities are listed. Like all the other activities presented in this book, these are only suggestions. If experiences are to meet the specific needs of particular children, they must be designed with those needs and those children in mind.

MAXIMIZING CONDITIONS FOR LEARNING

Children are constantly learning, and your program should capitalize on their abilities, backgrounds, and interests to ensure that what they learn is valuable and appropriate rather than trivial and of questionable validity. Planning and organization are important, but the specifics of daily experiences and how the pupils respond to them are matters that require your careful and constant attention.

Experience and Learning

An effective language arts program recognizes the importance of pupils' learning experiences in three important ways.

> *First,* the program is based on an awareness that every child entering school, from whatever family or cultural situation, has a varied background. Although students' experiences—including those involving language—may not be the ones that school programs have usually been built upon, they are important and deserve serious consideration.
>
> *Second,* the program provides experiences that build vocabulary and concepts and familiarize children with the kinds of language patterns and modes of expression they will encounter in school.
>
> *Third,* the program provides these experiences in settings that focus on genuine, lifelike communication activities that have meaning for the children involved and promote in them a love of language and learning.

Awareness that every child has a language background developed prior to entering school—one that continues to develop outside of the classroom—means more than overcoming any bias with respect to a "disadvantaged" or "deprived" child's having had little language experience or being "nonverbal." Children's life experiences vary and nothing should be assumed because of family economic condition, race, or ethnicity. It is important to recognize that cultural differences are a valuable resource in teaching, for they provide many learning opportunities in human relations as well as all areas of the curriculum. Of course, the school situation is itself a culture, so children need to learn how to get along in that particular environment, too.

Chapter 15 discusses literature in relation to the cultural background of children.

As we said in the first chapter, language and culture are closely intertwined, so you need to explore what communication differences may be characteristic of particular groups in a community. A common example is that children from certain backgrounds are often taught to keep their eyes averted when being addressed by a person in authority, and this may be taken as an indication of evasion or nonattention by the teacher who wants to be "looked in the eye" during conversations. (The chart below, about school expectations and cultural differences, may cause you to think of some important possibilities for students with whom you come in contact.)

Possible Cultural Differences Relating to School Practices

THE SCHOOL MAY URGE THE STUDENT TO:	BUT THE CULTURE MAY HAVE TAUGHT:
Do your own work.	Help your friends.
Be proud of your success.	Don't praise yourself.
Compete with others.	Cooperate with others.
Always tell the truth.	Always protect family honor.
Speak up in a group.	Talk only in private.
Work now for future rewards.	The future cannot be known.
Convince others that your ideas are best.	Collaborative decisions are best.
Bring problems to teachers.	Don't reveal inadequacies.

Other types of home-related problems also occur. For instance, when a teacher assumes that all families celebrate a particular holiday or that each child has both a mother and a father at home, those for whom such expectations are inappropriate may conclude that they are somehow so different as to be unwanted in the school.

Although it is advisable to take students' cultural differences into account when planning learning activities, you should also be sure that all have the sorts of language experiences needed for school success. Of course, depending on your school situation, many members of your class have had these experiences at home and in English. Others may have had valuable language interactions with family and friends—stories, discussions, reading, and conversations—but in a language other than English. Still others have had few good opportunities to learn any language well.

Whatever the language background of a child, the kinds of activities needed are the ones with the greatest potential to bring about desired types of learning. Above all, your teaching program, for any student, must not be restricted to drill and practice exercises unrelated to opportunities for genuine expression of needs and concerns. The activities planned should be authentic, as closely related to real life as you can make them.

Building on Experiences

Prepare children for experiences. For example, before a field trip, encourage them to help plan it, raise questions, anticipate what will be seen and heard.

Because of differences among students, provision should be made for diversity in their school experiences. At the same time, since successful teaching depends in part on children's shared experiences, you should plan a common core of class activities that will be meaningful to all. Each activity, whether it is reading about "early morning on the farm" or discussing the shape of snowflakes, must be examined in terms of whether or not class members have background knowledge or direct experience related to what you plan to do. If you have serious questions about this, you must reconsider your planned activities.

Helping children be more aware of their senses is particularly important in providing experiences and encouraging language growth. Children, like most adults, are seldom good observers, although too often time for observing is simply not provided for in a crowded school day, and this is sometimes the case on a field trip or some other experience-building activity. Although various observation games are available or can be created—such as displaying a number of objects, removing one, and asking what is missing—the observation of natural phenomena is more meaningful. Taking time to observe cloud formations, sand drifted by the wind, a flock of geese overhead, or the spread of the roots of a sprouting bean seed will interest children, cause them to use language, and facilitate their learning of new ideas and words. Children themselves can provide much input. With very little encouragement they will bring butterflies, leaves, worms, rocks, and innumerable other objects to the classroom.

Activities such as the following are all useful in adding to children's knowledge and creating communication opportunities.

- keeping an aquarium or terrarium
- noting temperature differences in sunshine and shade
- watching flying formations of birds

Talking about things that are real and important is beneficial.

- collecting leaves of different kinds or colors
- collecting rocks of different types and shapes
- tasting particular substances, such as pickles, berries, fruits, spices, or nuts
- feeling various materials, such as velvet, fur, aluminum foil, sand, wool, and silk
- caring for classroom animals
- observing the growth of different kinds of seeds
- keeping a weather chart
- bringing in pictures of things of interest, such as a new baby at the zoo
- feeding birds or squirrels
- observing soil erosion
- listening to stories and recordings
- participating in singing games

The Learning Climate

Children's lives and learning will benefit if the classroom atmosphere is warm, accepting, and friendly.

Children's growth in language depends on many factors, not the least of which is the atmosphere or climate of a classroom. The climate desired is one that fosters goodwill, respect, and friendliness on the part of all concerned. It is one in which an effort is made to ensure that each child will feel relaxed, at ease, and accepted as an important member of the group. Such a climate respects each child's personality, his or her heritage, and the social and emotional effects of his or her out-of-school environment. Creating a climate that will enhance each child's development is largely the teacher's responsibility and will evolve chiefly from the children's feelings of acceptance, freedom, and shared responsibility.

Although there are differences among teachers (and who would want it otherwise?), every teacher ought to be a vital, interesting person, one who is sensitive and supportive. These qualities are reflections of attitude, which can be shown in many ways. These include the following:

- Show each child that he or she is an important and valued member of the classroom group.
- Encourage an attitude of friendliness and mutual respect among the children—including respect for differences in gender, race, social background, and culture.
- Talk with and listen to the children individually and in groups, and encourage them to exchange ideas and experiences.
- Be receptive to ideas and interests expressed by the children.
- Show appreciation of each child's efforts at expression.
- Be enthusiastic—and encourage the children to be—about classroom activities.
- Show sensitivity to and awareness of the world about you. Help children to notice the way things look, sound, smell, and feel.
- Let children see your own enjoyment of the stories you read, the way words sound, and the images they create.

Classroom climate is also affected by the general learning environment or atmosphere of the school. The principal, office workers, lunchroom helpers, custodians, bus drivers, and teacher aides are all involved in influencing the learning conditions in classrooms. The principal, especially, plays a key role. He or she must understand children, know the curriculum and materials, and see the importance of a busy and interesting classroom, one in which the children are active participants. If a teacher has an aide, this person certainly should share the teacher's feelings about children and seek to develop the same attitudes that the teacher has or is developing. A custodian needs to be interested in what children are doing and be willing to accept possible personal inconveniences such as a disarranged classroom. Other school personnel should also appreciate children's curiosity and enthusiasm. You cannot control the actions and reactions of these people, but you can do much to influence their attitudes by talking with them about what the children are doing and why they are doing it. Try inviting each of them to be a special guest of the class for a particular activity or program. Also, involve them in a class activity, perhaps getting them to tell about an experience they had or to help the pupils make something.

Physical materials in the classroom are also important. Little language growth or creativity will come from drabness. Wall and bulletin-board decorations, displays, pictures, and objects to handle and talk about all provide effective stimulation. Of course, there must be language: signs, titles, and name plates to show the use of words; records, tapes, and tables and shelves of books as evidence of the delight and knowledge they can bring. Further, a classroom where language growth is taking place is one that shows evidence that the children themselves have taken part in planning, preparing, and arranging the decorations and displays and that many activities are in progress there. This does not necessarily mean neatness, though children must learn that materials left strewn around the room are not easily found when needed or may not be in condition to be used again. Nor does it mean that absolute peace and quiet must reign; children learn as they share their experiences, discuss their activities, and help one another with problems.

RESOURCES FOR TEACHING THE LANGUAGE ARTS

Anything in the children's world—in the classroom and outside of it—may be a teaching resource. Certainly the chief teaching resources have been textbooks and materials intended to supplement them. Though these continue to be important, other resources are finding a significant place in the school setting, including other print materials and electronic equipment, such as computers. Children need and can profit from exposure to many types of instructional aids.

Textbooks

Textbooks are the most commonly available classroom resource, but they ought to be considered aids to teaching, not directors or regulators. To begin a year's teaching by starting a group of children on the first page of a textbook and then proceeding through it page by page, day after day, fails to take into account the language abilities and needs of the pupils. On the other hand, textbooks do provide a general overview of the content that some authors believe to be suitable for certain grade levels. They can, then, serve as a general guide and as a standard to which the instructional program may be compared.

The NCTE has a publication that is helpful: *Guidelines for Judging and Selecting Elementary Language Arts Textbooks* by Shanahan and Knight (listed at the end of this chapter).

Textbooks are usually associated with the often-criticized Separate Subjects method of teaching. Certainly, when there is a textbook for each subject and what is taught depends mostly on the books' contents, such a program is likely to be much too formal, with little involvement of the children in planning and too few direct-experience learning experiences. A major difficulty is that many language-learning experiences must be oral in nature, and books simply cannot provide these. In addition, the emphasis in language textbooks is often on aspects of study that children either know already or have no valid reason for learning.

In the Integrated Language Arts and Whole Language approaches to teaching, textbooks are likely to be used mostly as resources or guides to instruction. Particularly in the Integrated Language Arts method, pupils may study something in the textbook for the specific purpose of using the knowledge (how words have changed in their spelling over the years or how a type of poetry known as the *cinquain* is constructed) in a class project. In the Whole Language approach, teaching texts may not be used at all, other source materials being emphasized.

Computers

Although computers have become widely available as instructional resources in the elementary schools, not all staff members have learned to use them effectively. One of the difficulties is that computer-based learning and teaching tools

Use of the computer can begin at a young age.

Riedesel and Clements, in *Coping with Computers in the Elementary and Middle Schools,* review the possibilities and problems associated with these important teaching aids.

proliferate at a faster rate than they can be incorporated into classroom organization and procedures. At the same time, computers are increasingly affecting other aspects of the school program, such as information storage in the library.

Computers have made their most dramatic impact in the language arts field as word processors (see Chapters 9 and 10). Besides writing, computers can serve to enhance several other areas of language learning:

- *Spelling.* The computer can flash a word on the screen, accompanied by an illustration or even the correct pronunciation. The word then disappears, and the student has a few seconds to type the word correctly.

- *Vocabulary building.* Simulation experiences involving such activities as operating a small business provide opportunities to use new terms—in this case, *asset, liability, inventory,* and *profit,* for example.

- *Beginning literacy.* A child types letters and the computer names them. After a group of letters has been typed (such as *CAT* or *MNXEOFU*), the child signals the computer to pronounce what has been written.

- *Reference skills.* Students can learn about information retrieval by supplying information to create a classroom data base. The computer can then call up phone numbers, for instance, or the names of all students having a dog as a pet.

The use of computers requires careful selection of software. Some programs are a waste of time; either they do not make much of a contribution to learning or what they provide is better done in some other way. Often programs are simply not appealing to children; material presented in a boring manner by means of a computer will not improve children's learning.

When selecting computer programs for classroom use, you should be guided by several general questions:

1. Does the program contribute to the achievement of appropriate long-term educational objectives?
2. Does the program make a contribution because it does something faster, better, or for more students than other approaches do?
3. Is the program attractive to students in terms of usability, color, movement, graphics, and sound?
4. Does the program teach rather than simply test?
5. Are there procedures for varying the difficulty level of the program through adjustments in speed and provision of more or less material?
6. Is it easy for the teacher to intervene at various points in the program in order to assist the student?
7. Is a record automatically kept of the student's successful and unsuccessful responses so that this information may be used for follow-up?
8. Is information on how well the student is doing in the program immediately available?

Professional magazines such as *The Reading Teacher* and *Language Arts,* as well as many others entirely devoted to computer materials, provide reviews of educational software.

In addition to these general concerns, there are many specific points to consider when selecting and using software. When you need such information, the best advice will probably come from an experienced teacher who uses computers extensively. There are also libraries and resource centers where programs may be tried as well as numerous periodicals that contain relevant information for teachers.

Other Resources

An effective language arts program uses virtually everything and anything as a teaching resource. Children are interested in the world and want to communicate about it. They learn outside the classroom as well as inside; in fact, they may learn more outside. Thus, teachers lose touch with much of the child's world if they limit teaching resources to just those found within the school walls. Additional resources include trade and reference books, magazines, newspapers, displays, artwork, maps, puppets, bulletin boards, television and radio, film, audio- and videocassettes, filmstrips, transparencies, photographs, and slides. Because such resources play an important role in maintaining an effective language arts program, some are listed at the end of each chapter so that you can incorporate them into your planning and instruction.

Instructional aids are sometimes inappropriately used, and this applies particularly to television. Too often in the classroom, television is watched with little follow-up and even less preparation. With the increased variety of content available on videotape, television can become an effective classroom resource in all subject areas. It is a way of communicating that deserves an important place in the language arts curriculum. Reading and writing activities readily grow out of television programs viewed both in the classroom and at home.

The greater availability of equipment necessary for videotape recording, photography, and audio recording means that students can often make use of such resources to produce their own work, a development that has important implications for language arts activities as well as learning in other subject areas. Children might write their own version of a historical event, for example, and

Audio and video recorders make a significant contribution to the language arts program.

then produce and videotape it with accompanying narration, recordings of music, costumes, and sound effects.

EVALUATION

The Instructional Plan presented in this chapter includes evaluation as an important part of the planning process. As a teacher you are responsible for determining the extent to which the major goals of your program are being achieved, how well the learning activities are being carried out, and the degree of success individual children are having. Information gathered to answer these needs should be used in appropriate ways to improve program planning and student learning. Too often evaluation is thought of as something done to the students so that marks and grades may be assigned. Even when such procedures are a requirement, you should be sure to maintain a broader view.

The Role of Evaluation

Evaluation is a process whereby teachers, learners, and other interested parties determine the degree to which program goals are being achieved in general and by each learner. Chapter 1 presented three major language arts goals: learning English, learning about English, and using English to learn about other school subjects. For all aspects of your classroom program you need to have specific objectives that correspond to these goals. In spelling, for example, the following questions would be relevant:

Finding out what a child knows or can do is the first step in good teaching. Too much emphasis is sometimes given to what the student *cannot* do. Not many of us would want to spend hours trying to do something we found extremely difficult.

1. To what extent are words being spelled correctly when pupils are using words unfamiliar to them?
2. When pupils of a given age try to spell unfamiliar words, do their attempts indicate that they have appropriate knowledge concerning features of English spelling?
3. Are pupils learning to spell important words in science, social studies, mathematics and other fields?

Of course, whether or not pupils are accomplishing such objectives is an indication of how well the program and the teacher are succeeding. If there are concerns, then examination of the other elements of your instructional plan would be necessary: what types of Developmental Programs you have adopted or devised, how you use information-processing activities in the subjects areas, and what success you are having with embedded lessons.

As far as the learners themselves are concerned, they should be significantly involved in establishing objectives and assessing how well they are doing in accomplishing these. Self-evaluation is very important and can be a significant part of the language arts program. Parents, school officials, and interested members of the community also have contributions to make in the area of evaluation, and means of gathering their views should be found.

Techniques and Instruments

In the preceding sections, Teacher Assessment of Pupils and Involving Pupils in Self-assessment, several different sorts of evaluation techniques were mentioned, as was the use of a portfolio for each student.

Certainly instruments and procedures for evaluation vary widely in type, structure, and function. The usual procedures involve the use of tests, questionnaires, inventories, checklists, and observation forms, as well as conferences with students and careful examination of their work. Tests vary, too; they may be oral or written, standardized or teacher-made, essay or short-answer. Additional techniques include models of good handwriting, statements of standards, spelling progress charts, and learning logs and literature response journals.

In the following chapters, many instruments and procedures are discussed where they have special applications. At this point our emphasis is on the significance of evaluation and the fact that there are many evaluative instruments and procedures available. It is also important to acknowledge the many serious weaknesses of the usual sorts of tests. We encourage you to recognize that you are the person who knows your program, your students, and what you expect. This is an excellent basis for making assessments of each child's progress and of the success of your teaching program. Various techniques may assist you in gathering relevant information, but findings from particular measurement instruments should not be allowed to overrule your own judgment.

Reporting Results

Conferences with parents can be very helpful, especially if the teacher is prepared to listen and if there is a portfolio of the child's materials to discuss. (Some teachers also provide videotapes of the child reading.)

A teacher must observe the reporting policies of the school and district, of course, and in many cases this means putting letter grades or other codes on a report card. You can go further than this, though, by communicating more useful information to parents. For example, you can include letters with report cards and in these provide comments on particular accomplishments of the youngsters as well as areas of their learning that require attention. You can also discuss what the class will be doing and send home samples of children's work. Sharing evaluative statements with parents and providing explanations of test results are good ideas, too. Although this is time-consuming, it will be well worth the effort in promoting effective communication with the home. In addition to providing better and more detailed written reports, you should arrange to confer with parents about their children's progress.

Children should also be reported to, but again this does not mean that every paper or activity has to be marked with a grade. Pupils will appreciate talking with you about their progress, seeing your marks on checklists and observation forms, and participating in interpreting data obtained by means of instruments such as tests and scales. This kind of active participation, along with helping to establish criteria before activities are begun, will help children to learn habits of self-evaluation and to understand how they can participate in the management of their own educational activities.

A FINAL WORD

This chapter has given an overview of the organizing and planning needed to teach language arts effectively; suggestions will be expanded on in the chapters that follow. Principles for selecting content and guidelines for planning become operational only when the teacher applies them in light of the particular children in a classroom—how well they speak and write, how well they listen and read, and what problems they seem to have. In the same way, the instructional plan and the means for implementing it can become truly meaningful only when considered in connection with specific content and procedures for teaching speaking, listening, reading, and writing.

References

Barchers, Suzanne I. *Creating and Managing the Literate Classroom.* Teacher Ideas Press, 1989.

Busching, Beverly A., and Schwartz, Judith I., eds. *Integrating the Language Arts in the Elementary School.* National Council of Teachers of English, 1983.

Carkhuff, Robert R. *The Productive Teacher II: An Introduction to Instruction.* Human Resources Development Press, 1984.

Chew, Charles R. *Whole Language in Urban Classrooms: Encounters with Literacy.* Berrent Publications, 1991.

Cushenbery, Donald C. *Directing an Effective Language Arts Program for Your Students.* Charles C Thomas, 1986.

Glazer, Susan M., and Brown, Carol. *Portfolios and Beyond: Collaborative Assessment in Reading and Writing.* Christopher-Gordon, 1993.

Goodman, Kenneth S.; Goodman, Yetta M.; and Hood, Wendy J. *The Whole Language Evaluation Book.* Heinemann Educational Books, 1989.

Goodman, Kenneth S.; Smith, E. Brooks; Meredith, Robert; and Goodman, Yetta. *Language and Thinking in School.* Richard C. Owen, 1987.

Graves, Donald. *The Reading/Writing Teacher's Companion: Building a Literate Classroom.* Heinemann, 1991.

Harp, Bill. *Assessment and Evaluation in Whole Language Programs.* Christopher-Gordon, 1991.

Hydrick, Janie, ed. *Whole Language: Empowerment at the Chalk Face.* Scholastic, 1991.

Johnson, D., and Johnson, R. *Learning Together and Alone: Cooperative, Competitive, and Individualistic Learning.* Prentice-Hall, 1987.

Johnston, Peter H. *Constructive Evaluation of Literate Activity.* Longman, 1992.

Last, Ellen. *A Guide to Curriculum Planning in English Language Arts.* Wisconsin Department of Public Instruction, 1990.

Pappas, Christine C.; Kiefer, Barbara; and Levstik, Linda S. *An Integrated Language Perspective in the Elementary School.* Longman, 1990.

Perrone, Vito. *Expanding Student Assessment.* Association for Supervision and Curriculum Development, 1991.

Pollard, Rita, ed. *Reading, Writing, Thinking, Learning.* National Council of Teachers of English, 1986.

Riedesel, C. Alan, and Clements, Douglas H. *Coping with Computers in the Elementary and Middle Schools.* Prentice-Hall, 1985.

Selfe, Cynthia L.; Rodrigues, Dawn; and Oates, William R., eds. *Computers in English and the Language Arts.* National Council of Teachers of English, 1989.

Shanahan, Timothy, and Knight, Lester. *Guidelines for Judging and Selecting Language Arts Textbooks.* National Council of Teachers of English, 1991.

Shepherd, Gene D., and Ragan, William B. *Modern Elementary Curriculum.* Harcourt Brace Jovanovich, 1991.

Thaiss, Christopher. *Language Across the Curriculum in the Elementary Grades.* National Council of Teachers of English, 1987.

Tierney, Robert J.; Carter, Mark A.; and Desai, Laura E. *Portfolio Assessment in the Reading-Writing Classroom.* Christopher-Gordon Publishers, 1991.

Teaching Resources

MAGAZINES FOR ELEMENTARY-SCHOOL TEACHERS

Childhood Education. The Association for Childhood Education International, 3615 Wisconsin Avenue, N.W., Washington, DC 20016.

Early Years. Allen Raymond, Inc., P.O. Box 1266, Darien, CT 06820.

The Horn Book. Park Square Building, 31 St. James Avenue, Boston, MA 02116.

Instructor. The Instructor Publications, Inc., 757 Third Avenue, New York, NY 10017.

Language Arts. National Council of Teachers of English, 1111 Kenyon Road, Urbana, IL 61801.

Pre-K Today. Scholastic, Inc., P.O. Box 644, Lyndhurst, NJ 07071-0644.

The Reading Teacher. International Reading Association, 800 Barksdale Road, P.O. Box 8139, Newark, DE 19711.

School Library Journal. P.O. Box 1978, Marion, OH 43305-1978.

Teacher. Macmillan Professional Magazines, Inc., 77 Bedford Street, Stamford, CT 06901.

OTHER RESOURCES

Computer Teaching Tips. Sunburst Communications.

Making Meaning: Integrated Language Arts Series. Association for Supervision and Curriculum Development (videotapes with ancillary materials).

Selfe, Cynthia. *ComputerAssisted Instruction: Create Your Own.* National Council of Teachers of English, 1986.

Shillingburg, Patricia M.; Bareford, Kenneth C.; Pacita, Joyce A.; and Townsond, Janice Lubinsky. *The Teacher's Computer Activities Book.* Teachers College Press, 1986.

Tiedt, Sidney W., and Tiedt, Iris M. *Language Arts Activities for the Classroom.* Allyn and Bacon, 1987.

Watson, Dorothy J., ed. *Ideas and Insights: Language Arts in the Elementary School.* National Council of Teachers of English, 1987.

Activities for Preservice Teachers

1. Develop a lesson plan that shows how you would try to teach average third graders social studies or science material to give them experience in thinking and writing about a sequence of events.

2. Interview a college professor or school administrator who is particularly concerned with evaluation in the language arts. Find out what practices are common in evaluation and how problems are being addressed.

3. Discuss with an elementary teacher the children in her or his class. Ask about the ranges of their intellectual abilities and academic achievement and how he or she deals with these.

4. Describe the mandated language and reading proficiency tests for classroom teachers, college students preparing for teaching, and elementary and secondary pupils in your state. Compare these with the requirements of other states.

5. Make an appointment with a school administrator, and ask to be shown the different types of records kept in children's cumulative folders. Consider what relevance these might have for language arts teaching.

6. Go to your college's curriculum library or your school district's facility and examine a basal language series for elementary schools. Identify elements that appear to be developmental or related to information processing as discussed in this chapter. Is there any mention of what might be thought of as embedded lessons?

7. Interview several elementary-school teachers from different school systems and ask how they group for instruction in various subjects. List as many different grouping designs as you can as well as what the teachers believe to be the strengths and weaknesses of each.

8. Obtain copies of your state and district syllabi for language arts. Study these to determine what children are expected to learn at each grade level.

9. List the advantages and disadvantages of subject matter departmentalization in elementary schools. Indicate the sources you used for determining these.

10. Contact a school where portfolios and portfolio assessment are being tried, either generally for all subjects or for language arts. Ask to see a child's portfolio.

Activities for Inservice Teachers

1. Interview other teachers at your grade level in your school system, asking them to identify language arts topics not receiving sufficient attention in the program. Can they (and you) agree on how time might be taken from other topics to make reallocation possible?

2. Find textbooks from language arts series that are at least eight years old. Note the similarities and differences between them and the materials currently in use.

3. Try language arts portfolios with your students. Decide on three or four sorts of things to collect first (photocopies of journal pages, lists of books read and the student's reaction, samples of spelling, etc.). Continue for several weeks and then decide if the results indicate that you ought to continue.

4. Plan a presentation for parents designed to explain your language arts program. Be sure that you cover your teaching goals, the program's importance, evaluation procedures used, and how parents might help at home or as volunteer aides in your classroom. Discuss what you've planned with your administrator before making the presentation.

5. Examine several pieces of language arts software with which you are unfamiliar. Use the criteria presented in this chapter to evaluate them.

6. Talk with people who are on curriculum development committees in your building or school system and find out if there is any interest in making a concerted effort to teach language arts "across the curriculum,"—perhaps in conjunction with increased attention to information processing or children's thinking.

7. Over a period of two weeks note the number of embedded lessons you teach to individuals and small groups. Can you increase the number by consciously looking for opportunities?

8. Examine some standardized achievement tests in language arts. Do the items match the content of your program? What do you think of the questions and format? Are the results reported in a way that makes them useful to you?

9. Review the electronic equipment and media available in your school. Draw up a list of needs, justifying each item on the grounds of its contribution to language arts teaching.

Chapter 3

Language Learning and the Young Child

In 1965 (the first year of Head Start) 500,000 children attended nursery schools. Twenty-five years later the total was more than 2,500,000.

*T*eachers rightly believe that the home has a powerful effect on a child's educational progress. In addition, most adults would agree that much of that influence is a result of the amount and kind of language experience provided by the parents. A high proportion of today's young children learn language, and much more, not only at home but also in group programs they attend regularly. Not only parents but all other adults who interact with this age group need to be particularly well informed about language development and literacy learning.

This chapter deals with the preschool years, although that may no longer be an entirely accurate term, because prekindergarten classes have been introduced into the elementary schools of a growing number of communities. Teachers of four-year-olds in these schools usually have degrees in elementary education. You may be considering such a career yourself or already involved in prekindergarten, nursery school, or day care programs. Of course, mothers and fathers don't automatically know what to do for their youngsters; teachers and others concerned with helping parents will find in this chapter much content explaining what can be done at home to promote learning. And, of course, if you are a parent of a young child or likely to be one, you will find this chapter especially interesting. In many ways it is the foundation for what will be presented in the rest of the book.

EARLY CHILDHOOD EDUCATION

For information on day care write to:
Day Care Council of America
Capital Publications, Inc.
1300 North Seventeenth St.
Arlington, VA 22209

A good general text on early childhood education is Morrison's *Early Childhood Education Today*.

Until children go to kindergarten they may spend all their time at home or they may be enrolled in an organized group program or cared for in a babysitter's home. Whatever the setting, the learning principles operating are the same and are usually thought of as making up a point of view referred to as "early childhood education." Because of the age of the participants, so-called traditional teaching practices involving scheduled lessons directed by teachers are not appropriate. Such practices usually indicate that the adult involved—whether a teacher or someone in the teacher's role—does not understand what is required for young children to learn effectively. The following list provides a review of the basic principles of early childhood education.

1. *Young children require opportunities to move around and interact with others.* "Sit down and be quiet" is a nearly useless request when directed at young children. They cannot do either unless especially fascinated by something they see and hear. They learn by engaging in physical activity and interaction with other children and adults.

2. *Interaction with concrete materials—blocks, puzzles, balls, paint brushes and all kinds of objects—is essential.* In manipulating objects, young children find out

how materials feel, what can be done with them, and how they respond when treated in certain ways. Important concepts and understandings grow out of such activities.

3. *Both large- and small-muscle activities are needed by young children.* Such small-muscle experiences as solving puzzles, cutting with scissors, and stringing beads should be made possible, as should activities involving large muscles—running, climbing, sliding, and riding wheeled toys.

4. *Pretending and other expressive and creative experiences are necessary.* Young children need opportunities to draw, paint, sing, dance, dramatize stories, pretend to be someone or something else, and otherwise express their ideas and feelings.

5. *There should be balance and alteration in young children's activities.* The experiences of the young child should be balanced between active and quiet times, large- and small-muscle movement, and individual and group involvement.

6. *Adults should follow the lead of the child.* Parents and teachers should watch children for clues to their responses to experiences and be prepared to switch to other activities if reactions seem to be unfavorable. Adults should not use bribes and threats to enforce their wishes.

7. *Young children must have opportunities to make choices.* Children should have much latitude in selecting activities and deciding how long to remain with them. Among the choices available to them, children should be able to decline to participate.

8. *The way something is done is more important than the result.* As the expression goes, "Process, not Product." How children feel about themselves and an experience is of significance; the tunefulness of their singing or the beauty of their picture is not.

The NAEYC publication, *Developmentally Appropriate Practice in Early Childhood Programs Serving Children from Birth Through Age 8,* makes clear distinctions between good and poor teaching at this level.

These principles apply to all types of experiences in a young child's life—playing at home, participating in a group, going shopping, visiting a relative, and so on. In this chapter we explore what the principles mean for language learning, recognizing, of course, that this is only one area of growth and development.

YOUNG CHILDREN'S USE OF LANGUAGE

As discussed in Chapter 1, an infant may be observed listening to human voices, often moving the body in rhythm with the language heard. An infant will recognize some speech, especially the mother's, and will react to familiar voices by stopping its crying or by waving and kicking in anticipation of being picked up or played with.

Babies do a great deal of vocalizing and, as the end of the first year of life approaches, may begin to produce sounds that are more and more like words. These utterances lack meaning in the beginning, but gradually some are associated with people and objects. The vocalizations lengthen, often lasting several seconds ("ooh-wa-duh-da-da-muh"), and babies will engage in a conversation-like game of taking turns making speech sounds. Hearing others talk and participating in vocal exchanges stimulate very young children's language development, and so does having adults recite nursery rhymes and sing to them, activities often accompanied by holding, rocking, and bouncing. Words in the child's vocabulary accumulate slowly at first but then increase to several dozen rather quickly, particularly if others respond to her or his speech attempts, try to encourage language production, and show enjoyment of these activities.

Toddlers (children aged from about eighteen to thirty months) have learned to walk and talk and so are able to engage in much interaction with family members and, very likely, other people as well. By age two or soon afterward children often know a hundred words or more, including the names of objects and of people and pets and some action words. They use this stock of words in many different ways: to make their needs known ("More milk"), to describe actions ("Throw ball"), and to relate to others ("Mommy kiss"). They can ask questions ("Daddy come?"), use modifiers ("red truck"), show possession ("Grandma car"), describe a situation ("Juice all gone"), and, of course, characteristic negativism ("No! No bed!"). These two- and three-word utterances are gradually replaced by standard sentences or close approximations ("Me want that") as the child adds the classes of speech required to hold the language together. At this age articulation is not perfect (for example, "wif" for "with" and "tar" for "car"), but improvement will come gradually and does not require direct teaching and correction.

By the time they are just over three years old, children have generally mastered the basics of speech. They have good vocabularies—over a thousand words in many cases, although meanings may not always be well established.

Children learn language best when in close contact with adults.

Some pronunciation difficulties persist, and there may be occasional stammering as the desire to talk outstrips the physical ability to speak rapidly.

Most three-year-olds (threes) successfully employ several different kinds of sentences, including those starting with dependent clauses ("When it rains . . . ") and prepositional phrases ("In the morning . . . "). Although they continue to use language in the same ways as toddlers, threes add such abilities as reporting events ("And then we rode the ponies and then we . . . ") and making observations ("The smoke means it's hot"). They also ask numerous questions, often as a way to maintain a conversation with an adult. Most importantly, however, threes begin to use language to talk about language: ("What's *adopted* mean?" or "What rhymes with *bunny*?")

Four-year-olds (fours) have language under rather good control. They may even hold fairly complex conversations with adults and moderately interesting ones among themselves. Vocabulary is increasing rapidly and is likely to reach two thousand words. Additional language uses for some fours will include recalling past events ("Remember when we . . . ?"), discussing projected ones ("Next summer on our vacation . . . "), and describing imaginary situations ("The rockets will blast the dinosaurs").

LANGUAGE EXPERIENCES FOR INFANTS AND TODDLERS

See Cataldo's book (listed in the references) for descriptions of programs at this level.

Children younger than three may be in day care but most are found at home with their families. Home environments vary substantially, so it is not easy to generalize about the daily language experiences of infants and toddlers. In some cases English is not spoken much in the family. Although the child may be learning to use the home language rather well, he or she will need to develop English later, often in school. Also, some children grow up speaking a dialect that is significantly different from the English used at school. Another source of concern about language experience is that in a few homes very little speaking of any kind is directed at children; instead, communication is restricted to a few commands and gestures.

Most young children, however, have good opportunities to learn a usable form of English. They may not enunciate perfectly or always choose the right word, and they sometimes put words in a peculiar order, but they know what someone is saying to them and can make themselves understood. They learn through talking and participating in the many forms of communication used around them.

Talking with Infants and Toddlers

Nothing is more important for language development than speaking to a young child regularly and with loving attention. Babies smile and show delight when spoken to and, as they grow a bit older, they join in singing, recitations, and conversations as best they can.

Parents and other adults who spend a great deal of time with infants and toddlers need to find an appropriate balance between encouraging development and allowing natural processes to occur. The following guidelines are suggested for those who interact with very young children:

1. *Be a good listener.* Take the time to hear what the child wants to talk about and show interest in what he or she says.
2. *Be a good talker.* Speak with the child often about daily events and planned activities.
3. *Be a good speech model.* Without exaggerating, speak distinctly and at an appropriate speed.
4. *Be a model of courteous conversation.* Children who are given a good opportunity to talk without being interrupted will learn to treat others respectfully.
5. *Be careful in offering corrections.* Avoid criticism of the child's language and only occasionally discuss the pronunciation of a word or a different way to say something.
6. *Be sure the child has chances to express her or his needs through speech.* Create opportunities for the child to ask questions and make requests by deliberately not doing everything for her or him.
7. *Be sensitive to the child's need for assistance.* A child who wants to say something may require special attention, such as touching, vocal encouragement, or extra time without interruption.
8. *Be a good provider of experiences.* Read to the child, go on walks together, look at picture books, tell stories, play with toys, sing, and enjoy language.

The Influence of Television

Some young children are exposed to TV for thirty hours a week—and even more.

Television sets are turned on for many hours each day in the average home, and infants and toddlers are exposed to what is being transmitted. For the most part they go about their usual activities without paying much attention to what is on the screen. Gradually, however, they begin to watch—commercials at first and then cartoons and other shows, particularly those directed at children when they are available. Color, motion, repeating images, and music are all quite attractive to young children, and they easily learn to recognize musical selections and advertising announcements. Very often they stop what they are doing to watch favorite commercials and then resume the previous activity. That this is a meaningful experience for youngsters is demonstrated by their ability to identify many products in supermarkets and other stores.

By age two or even younger, some children are watching certain programs regularly—everything from *Sesame Street* and other network and local programs, such as *Mr. Rogers' Neighborhood* and *Reading Rainbow,* to music videos. *Sesame Street* is popular for several reasons. The characters, including both real people and puppets (some confusion about which is which may exist for children), appear regularly and are distinctive, so the young viewers readily learn who they are and what they are likely to do. The same episodes appear frequently, and this familiarity also makes the program attractive. Academic and intellectual activities on the program include classifying objects that go together and noting attributes such as shape and color. A large proportion of the episodes are specifically related to academic skills, counting, for example, and learning the alphabet and how letters, sounds, and words are related. Most of this content is intended for nursery-school-age children, but toddlers very likely profit to some extent from being exposed to it.

Certainly children seem to learn a good deal from television viewing, *especially when adults watch with them and discuss what is on the screen.* Follow-up activities are important, too, and parents can make use of the *Sesame Street Magazine* and other books and learning aids produced in conjunction with *Sesame Street* and similar shows.

As children begin to give much attention to television, it is important to monitor what they see. When many viewing channels are accessible—and given the availability of video recordings of nursery rhymes and stories through public libraries—many possibilities exist for all homes, schools, and day care centers to expose young children to high-quality viewing experiences.

Reading to Infants and Toddlers

In many homes reading to the child begins quite early, often when he or she is no more than six months old. Infants and toddlers love to be read to, and there is every reason to believe that the activity is very important. Fortunately, there are many attractive books available, some of which are made of materials that can withstand the sort of treatment likely to be received from infants and toddlers.

Reading and Writing in the Home

In *Awakening to Literacy,* Anderson and Stokes report their findings that, in homes identified as economically disadvantaged, toddlers averaged eight literacy experiences a day— evidence that exposure to reading and writing is common in all households (Goelman et al., eds.).

In every household writing and reading activities take place in which the young child is either an observer or a participant. Mail is received and read, letters are written and greeting cards sent, and papers are brought from school by older siblings. In addition there are newspapers, advertising circulars, and pamphlets from churches and community organizations to be read, grocery lists to be made, and telephone messages to be taken. Even if there are few books or magazines around, the family has the opportunity to offer the child important literacy-related experiences.

Obtain the pamphlet *How Can I Prepare My Young Child for Reading?* from International Reading Association P.O. Box 8139 800 Barksdale Road Newark, DE 19714

When a family is strongly oriented toward reading and writing, the child will become aware of printed material of all kinds, not only in the home but also in libraries and bookstores. In some homes children will be exposed to typing and computerized word-processing as well as handwriting. Also, parents may make paper and markers available, supply plastic alphabet sets for the refrigerator door, encourage the scribbling of "letters to Grandma," take down the child's dictation of stories, play word games and supply related electronic toys, and generally support their child's exploration of written language.

Additional Literacy Experiences

Investigators showed the "golden arches" to hundreds of young children. All knew what the symbol meant.

Even the youngest children have many literacy-related experiences in their daily lives. They see advertising on signs as well as on television (not many fail to recognize the logos of their favorite fast-food restaurants). They may also be aware of words on street signs and buildings, **STOP** and **EXIT**, for instance. At the supermarket they recognize brand names and packages associated with breakfast cereals, toothpaste, and soap products. Children see some words so often that they begin to recognize what the letters *m-i-l-k* or *j-u-i-c-e* stand for.

Books about Signs

Children fascinated with alphabet letters will enjoy finding their "friends" in these books.

Black, Irma S. *The Little Old Man Who Could Not Read*. Whitman, 1968.
Crews, Donald. *School Bus*. Greenwillow, 1984.
Crews, Donald. *Truck*. Penguin, 1985.
Goor, R., and Goor, N. *Signs*. Harper and Row, 1983.
Hoban, Tana. *I Read Signs*. Morrow, 1987.
Hoban, Tana. *I Walk & Read*. Greenwillow, 1984.
Karlin, Bertie, and Karlin, Mati. *Night Ride*. Simon and Schuster, 1988.
Maestro, Betsy. *Harriet Reads Signs and More Signs*. Crown, 1981.

LANGUAGE EXPERIENCES FOR THREE- AND FOUR-YEAR-OLDS

In many homes children of ages three and four years benefit from the same sorts of language-related experiences as those described for infants and toddlers; they learn much from the everyday events in the household and from the special activities provided by their parents. In increasing numbers, however, children of this age group attend organized programs—nursery schools, Head Start classes, day care centers, and prekindergarten groups—where they speak, listen, look at books, engage in dramatic play, scribble and draw, and interact with others.

The various areas of language growth are discussed separately in this section, but this does not mean that such experiences ought to be conducted in isolation from one another. Rather, as a teacher in an organized program for three- and four-year-old children, you should emphasize "holistic" activities—songs, poems and finger plays—that offer possibilities for several different kinds and levels of learning. Also, threes and fours should have wide latitude in selection of their own activities; there must be no attempt to impose "language lessons" at this level of education. All experiences should, of course, be planned in accordance with the principles presented in the section Early Childhood Education.

Oral Language

Nearly everything that transpires in the early education environment promotes speaking and listening. You should have plans for encouraging children to acquire new words, use sentences of different kinds, and employ language in various ways as they explain their side of a dispute, ask questions when curiosity is aroused, and explore learning situations.

Of course, you can do much to stimulate a child's language. The following guidelines are important:

1. Talk one-to-one and face-to-face as much as possible.
2. Talk about what is meaningful to young children: pets, holidays, birthdays, and home and classroom events.
3. Talk about what the children are doing as they do it, supplying needed words.
4. Ask them to tell what they are doing or planning to do.

Young children will listen carefully if there are good reasons to do so.

5. With an unhappy child, show empathy by describing the emotions being experienced as well as you can.

6. Ask children to use language to express their feelings—to tell another child to stop taking toys rather than hitting or pushing the presumed guilty party, for example.

7. Show enjoyment of language by reciting poems, making up stories using the children's names, and bringing rhyming words into conversations.

8. Give children opportunities to memorize by using finger plays, poems, and stories over and over again and then providing extension activities that make use of the memorized material.

9. Expand children's statements. When a child says, "scissors," respond with "Betty wants scissors to do some cutting. What color, Betty?"

10. Relate language learning to classroom activities. Block building, picture painting, modeling with play dough, and many other experiences provide good learning opportunities.

11. Make possible specific sensory experiences in touching, smelling, tasting, listening, examining, and lifting. Use a variety of expressions to accompany the activities.

12. Recognize that concepts develop slowly. Provide many opportunities to use such words as *green, tall,* and *triangle,* and do this over several weeks or months.

13. Encourage careful listening by asking children to listen for sounds in the environment, playing recordings of sounds for them, and having them listen for particular parts of stories.

The Alphabet

Young children see letters of the alphabet all around them, with the result that some become so interested in reciting and naming the ABCs that they learn the complete alphabet by age three or even earlier. Parents and teachers can easily capitalize on such interest by providing alphabet-related experiences at home or in the daily program of the school. Singing the alphabet can be included in the child's repertoire of songs and ABC books of several types can be supplied. Reciting the alphabet may not mean much to some youngsters ("KLMNO" is often heard as one word), but others know it well, often from *Sesame Street,* and will associate names with specific letters.

In providing alphabet-related learning experiences you should particularly adhere to two principles of early childhood education: the instructional materials must be of a size and type that can be easily handled by the children and the decision to explore them must be made by each child. Several kinds of alphabet sets are appropriate. Large wooden ones, about four inches in height are popular, but somewhat smaller types made of rubber or plastic are also satisfactory. Magnetized plastic letters are good for moving around on metal surfaces. Alphabet sets may be either loose letters or in forms showing the A-to-Z sequence. Traditional cube-shaped wooden blocks with letters, pictures, and numbers on them should not be neglected.

A visitor to one home with young children in it counted fourteen alphabet sets distributed among all the rooms—including the bathroom.

Environmental Materials

Signs, advertising, and packaging materials readily attract children's attention, and you should be alert for opportunities to bring these into the classroom. Good

Alphabet letters should be available to young children in many forms.

possibilities are posters, fast-food packages, cereal boxes, milk and juice cartons, brand insignias from toy products, and advertising items from local stores and markets. Such materials may be included in the dramatic play of the group; playhouse areas and pretend stores are particularly effective settings for such use.

In addition to the use of commercial packages and signs, there are many other ways to introduce printed matter into the early childhood classroom. The playhouse corner, for instance, can contain telephone books, magazines, and newspapers, just as at home, as well as note pads for making lists and taking messages.

When you create pizza restaurants or doctors' offices as settings for dramatic play, there will be additional opportunities to make use of notices, menus, order blanks, prescriptions, and charts. The same is true of outside play involving traffic signs for wheeled toys or advertising for refreshment stands that dispense juice and crackers.

Classroom Centers

Permanent classroom centers may also be the focus of reading and writing experiences. Near the fish, gerbils, or plants, for instance, there might be charts that give their names and other information about them, pictures drawn by the children, and related library books. Writing supplies can be placed nearby to accommodate children who want to draw or make an attempt to write something about the plants or animals. Even in the block corner a child may wish to make signs for buildings or traffic control.

Reading Books

Discussed later in the chapter (in the section Young Children and Books) as a rich language-learning experience in and of itself, reading to very young children is also important in relationship to other language-learning experiences. The young child sitting with you as you read is not only listening to a story but is also being given an important opportunity to hear a particular kind of language—the vocabulary (*the old troll*), the cadence (*once upon a time*), and the structure (*three pigs, three wishes*) of literature. Reading to children provides them an introduction to the stories and poetry that comprise part of the world's storehouse of cultural heritage. When reading to a single child or perhaps a few at a time there will be many opportunities for oral activities, too, as they discuss characters and events and their own relevant experiences.

Group activities can also be productive. When you read to an audience of twelve or more young children, however, you should not expect that the experience will be exactly like what occurs with an individual youngster. The attention of many group members will be lost if much time is taken for discussion. More likely, you will need to read the book, show the pictures, acknowledge a few comments, and assure the children that the book will be available in the room to be read again. Such reading does provide the class with an opportunity to listen and experience what it means to be members of an audience, and this is worth discussing.

Reading, whether to individuals, small groups, or whole classes, supports much literacy-related development. You should occasionally point to the print, showing that this is what is being read and that it goes from left to right and from top to bottom of the text (in many books for young children the text does not

Learning about literature begins with nursery rhymes and traditional tales. Some adults wouldn't know what was meant if they were called a "Chicken Little."

See Schickedanz's *More Than the ABCs: The Early Stages of Reading and Writing* for many good ideas about how to include literacy experiences in an early childhood program.

begin at the top of the page). You may even indicate which words you are reading, pronouncing them as you point. Some children will begin to recognize common words or even make a connection between the first letter of a word and how it is pronounced, and you should acknowledge these insights.

Young children will want to have some books read repeatedly and this ought to be done, along with the introduction of new ones. And be sure to provide follow-up experiences after a book is read. There are audiotaped book sets which permit children to listen to the story while looking at the book as well as videocassettes of many popular titles. Favorites may be dramatized or recreated through the use of flannel-board figures or puppets. All of these activities, plus others you can think of or find described in various sources, should be provided.

Writing for Children

Children should regularly be given opportunities to see what they have said written down in some form. Individual experiences are possible; for example, you can transcribe what a child wishes to tell about a recently completed painting. Of course, there should be no requirement to name a painting or tell something about it: initiation of all writing should come from the child.

Opportunities for group experiences will also occur. The children can describe what they saw on a trip to the zoo, and you can record their descriptions in the form of an experience chart. This permits them to see their own ideas produced in print: letters are made, there is space between words, there are punctuation marks, and the lines of writing are placed under one another. Depending on the maturity of the group, you might mention some of these aspects of print.

Other kinds of personalized experiences can be made available, too. You may act as an interviewer and guide a child to make her or his own book. This can be done by talking with the youngster about preferred play activities, favorite foods or television programs, interest in animals, and home experiences. You then incorporate the child's responses into a booklet with one sentence on each page: "Billy lives with his mother and his brother," "Billy has a new sweatshirt," and so on. The child supplies drawings that illustrate the sentences, and a book results, one that can be taken home and read to the family. Class books can also be produced, with each youngster providing a drawing and a dictated sentence.

Writing by Children

In their early years most children will have seen family members writing at home (and if not, they will likely have such experiences in an organized program). Beginning as toddlers, most of them have also spent some time scribbling on paper or chalkboards (and walls, perhaps). Because of their limited coordination ability, threes and fours ordinarily cannot produce recognizable letters. A few can, however, and others want to write and draw, so you should be sure that they have access to the necessary materials.

The Beginnings of Writing, by Temple et al., presents many examples of children's first attempts.

A classroom writing center is easily established; it can be called the writing table or office, and children should use it as they would any other activity area. Such a center should have a variety of markers, pens and pencils of various kinds, and crayons, as well as a good supply of old stationery, envelopes, scrap paper, and blank forms. (Many love to fill in the forms with markings.) Add

A Three-Year-Old's Responses to Requests to "Write Something" (Left) and "Draw Something" (Right)

printing sets, stencils, and alphabet letters for tracing and copying when the children seem ready. Other possible accessories are staplers, safe scissors, old magazines, and paste or glue.

Near the writing center there should be a chalkboard for the children to use. If fastened to the wall (a good idea where possible), it should be placed close to the floor. An easel chalkboard will usually need to be lowered, too. Both drawing and writing with chalk should be encouraged. Magnetic letters and numerals and other similar items should be supplied when the chalkboard is made of the appropriate material.

Children's Names

Children's names are very important to them. At home and at school they become aware that their names can be written and they enjoy seeing this done. You should make sure that names appear on storage cubicles, paintings, and other projects, and also on charts, lists, and rosters. You might give the children the opportunity each day to find cards bearing their names and place them in an "I am here" pocket attached to the daily calendar.

Knowledge of their names helps children learn other aspects of literacy. A child may first recognize the initial letter of his or her name and will learn the others a bit later. Being familiar with the letters in their names encourages children to look for these letters on signs and in other printed materials. Of course, some will be interested in writing their own names in some form or another.

These efforts should be accepted without correction or any attempt to "teach them how"; progress will come gradually and naturally. Some children may begin to notice phonics relationships as they realize that their names sound like other words beginning with the same letter (Bobby says, "*Burger* has my letter in it!"). When young writers first begin to use real letters in their attempts to produce text, the writing often consists of the rearranged letters of their own names, since these are the ones they know best.

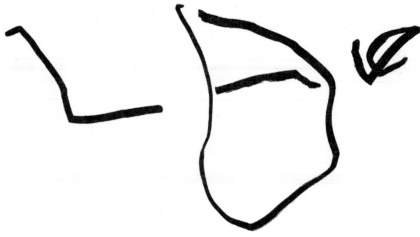

Letter-Like Figures by a Four-Year-Old

YOUNG CHILDREN AND BOOKS

Local libraries often have a story hour for preschoolers, and there are librarians whose special interest is books for very young children.

Stories and books are very important for young children. Those who are read to regularly, have their own collections of books, go to libraries, and participate in family reading activities not only make good progress in school but also develop a lifelong love of reading. Nearly everyone can learn to read reasonably well, but those read to throughout their childhood years have the greatest likelihood of developing into *real* readers.

In a literacy-rich home or school environment children are surrounded by books, even when quite young. By age two some have personal favorites that they carry around with them. At three, they are likely to be familiar with a large

An Early Attempt by Jerry to Write His Name

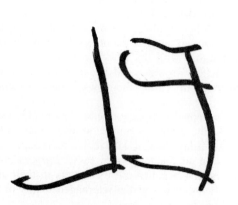

Four-Year-Old Phillip Writes His Name

number of titles and may even have bookshelves of their own. By the time they are four most will have developed a preference for certain kinds of books or those about particular characters.

Families should give much attention to book reading with young children, and many do so. However, there are homes where not much reading occurs, by adults or children. When you are responsible for teaching children from such backgrounds, it is imperative that you make book reading a regular activity. By giving systematic attention to reading, which means choosing the books with care—not just picking up whatever is handy— you will be providing a good start toward genuine literacy and a productive and enjoyable life.

Books and Babies

When reading to a baby you should sit with the child on your lap and hold the book upright so that it can be seen. You should talk about the book, point to the pictures, and read the text if there is one. Gradually the child will begin to become involved in the activity, hitting the pages, vocalizing, and grabbing at the book. All of this ought to be encouraged.

As the baby becomes a few months older, she or he behaves differently. Taking turns at talking occurs as the child vocalizes after you have said something. The baby may begin to point at illustrations and by his or her first birthday will likely enjoy turning pages and holding the book.

There are even "board books" made of heavy material and plastic books especially for bath time.

Infants ought to have their own books, but these must be durably made of cloth, plastic, or other water-resistant materials. It should be pointed out that the very young child will play with these books as with any available object but will also sometimes look at them as well. You may respond to a child's fascination with tearing of book pages by supplying old magazines and newspapers for that purpose, but naturally this activity must be supervised.

A thorough discussion of the benefits of reading to young children will be found in William Teale's chapter in *Awakening to Literacy* (Goelman et al., eds.).

Infants receive several benefits from being read to:

- The association of reading and books with the pleasurable sensations of sitting on someone's lap and being held

With experience babies learn how to handle books.

- The hearing of sentence patterns and voice intonations that are different from those of ordinary speech
- Seeing how books are handled—how they are held and manipulated

Toddlers and Reading

Reading should be a regular event in the toddler's daily routine at home, involving both parents as well as other family members. In an organized program outside the home there should be a place for regular book reading with individual children and very small groups.

As children approach their second birthday, they are likely to become more involved in reading experiences. They begin to pay close attention to illustrations, often pointing to small details as you ask them to find Big Bird or the pig's hat. They can point and vocalize alternately with you, too. Animal books are popular at this time, and a routine often becomes apparent.

ADULT: Look! A cow. Where's the cow?

CHILD: *(pointing)* Dah!

ADULT: Yes, a brown cow. The cow says "moo."

CHILD: Muh!

A sort of game soon develops in which the child learns to say the names of animals and to give their characteristic sounds. This is significant, because looking at books and talking about them represents one of the first kinds of conversation the child engages in.

In addition to animal books, toddlers enjoy Mother Goose and alphabet books and books with pictures of toys and common household objects. These books should have large, colorful illustrations that are relatively simple in design. Toddlers will learn how to handle books without damaging them and so should have some access to the family or classroom library. Whenever possible, you should store books with the front covers visible so that children can easily find their favorites.

Toddlers get several benefits from being read to, in addition to those identified in Books and Babies:

- The ability to identify entire pictures and small pictorial components on the pages
- Increased vocabulary acquired from the content and from discussion of the illustrations
- The pleasure derived from repetition of poems, stories, and picture captions

Threes and Books

As with younger children, threes and fours can benefit from watching videotapes of the stories listed at the end of this chapter rather than many of the programs on TV.

Enjoyment of simple storybooks begins at about age three. Rhymes and stories with predictable patterns are popular, along with ABC, counting, and shape books. Threes are interested in a variety of types of books, so this is an excellent time to begin making regular trips to the public library.

Threes can begin to understand some things about stories—that they have a beginning, middle, and end, for example. Easily understood predictable stories, such as *The Three Little Kittens* should be introduced, since children of this age enjoy knowing what is coming next and joining in. They are also likely to begin to say "the end" as you finish a book.

Since comprehension is a concern and youngsters are more likely to listen carefully, you should be sure to read stories from beginning to end without interruptions on your part. The child, of course, may want to comment or ask a question. Discussion is important, but the youngster's lead ought to be followed; it may be that a book has to be really familiar before the child wants to talk about it. And threes will insist that the same book be read over and over again—something that you may not enjoy but should do cheerfully, recognizing it as an important contribution to their development of literacy. Additional benefits three-year-olds derive from being read to:

- The successful memorization of stories, with the resultant enjoyment of paging through books and retelling what they have heard
- Growing familiarity with particular characters and types of stories and the pleasure found in repeated readings
- A rudimentary understanding of the characteristic features of stories and poems

Some of the material on children of kindergarten age presented in the following chapter applies to four-year-olds growing up in a highly literate home.

Reading and Fours

A high proportion of four-year-old children will spend time alone looking at books, and those who have been read to extensively will have solid knowledge of books and print. They will be able to discuss a book's title and will sometimes recognize the name of an author. They are very likely to have some understanding that, although pictures are attractive and interesting, it is the print that you read to them.

Some fours will be able to listen to rather long stories, perhaps parts of one over several days. They may very well develop preferences for certain kinds of books and stories—simple folk and fairy tales, perhaps, or books about trucks and machinery. Finally, other benefits fours may gain from being read to are:

- Greater understanding of what makes a story: characters, place, sequence of events, and so forth
- Participation in more involved discussions of books and stories, about matters such as cause and motivation
- Greater familiarity with print and the realization that print is read from left to right and down the page

Suggestions for Reading with Young Children

Although the act of reading to a child should not be reduced to a formula, useful guidelines have been analyzed that can be referred to from time to time.

1. Before reading, talk about the book.
2. Point to the words in the title as you read it.
3. Let children turn the pages.
4. Point to features of illustrations and name them or ask the child to do so.
5. Point to a line of print and follow it across the page.
6. Read with expression in your voice.
7. Change voices for different characters.
8. Encourage children to participate by pausing for them to supply the next word, reading repetitious parts slowly so that they can join in, and giving them adequate time to answer questions.
9. Read in a soft, pleasant voice.
10. Be sure children can see the pictures as you read.
11. After reading the book, talk about it together.
12. Ask story-related questions that have more than one answer.
13. When reading aloud, keep interruptions to a minimum.

A FINAL WORD

A good home and a high-quality early education program have much in common. In both settings the child is treated with respect and his or her special abilities are valued. This extends to language; the child is talked with and encouraged to use his or her capacity to discuss, recite, describe, pretend, imagine, and create. The best kinds of home and school environments stimulate interest in literacy.

When in them children have frequent direct contact with books, are read to regularly, and see adults read. They also have access to writing materials and may explore writing just as they do reading. Your responsibility as teacher or parent is to act as a good model and supportive collaborator in these crucially important activities.

References

Beaty, Janice J. *Skills for Preschool Teachers,* 2nd ed. Charles E. Merrill, 1984.

Bredekamp, Sue, ed. *Developmentally Appropriate Practice in Early Childhood Programs Serving Children From Birth Through Age 8*. National Association for the Education of Young Children, 1987.

Butler, Dorothy, and Clay, Marie. *Reading Begins at Home*. Heinemann, 1981.

Cataldo, Christine Z. *Infant and Toddler Programs: A Guide for Very Early Childhood Education*. Addison-Wesley, 1983.

Cawlfield, Mildred. "Velcro Time: The Language Connection." *Young Children* 47 (May 1992), pp. 26–30.

Clay, Marie. *Writing Begins at Home*. Heinemann, 1988.

Conlon, Alice. "Giving Mrs. Jones a Hand: Making Group Storytime More Pleasurable and Meaningful for Young Children." *Young Children* 47 (March 1992), pp. 14–18.

Fallen, Nancy H., and Umansky, Warren. *Young Children with Special Needs,* 2nd ed. Charles E. Merrill, 1985.

Goelman, Hillel; Oberg, Antoinette; and Smith, Frank, eds. *Awakening to Literacy*. Heinemann, 1984.

Grinnell, Paula C. *How Can I Prepare My Young Child for Reading?* International Reading Association, 1984.

Harste, Jerome C.; Woodward, Virginia A.; and Burke, Carolyn L. *Language Stories and Literacy Lessons*. Heinemann, 1984.

Hill, Mary. *Home: Where Reading and Writing Begin*. Heinemann, 1989.

Jalongo, M. R. *Young Children and Picture Books: Literature from Infancy to Six*. National Association for the Education of Young Children, 1992.

Lamme, Linda Leonard, ed. *Learning to Love Literature: Preschool Through Grade 3*. National Council of Teachers of English, 1981.

Lawton, Joseph T. *Introduction to Child Care and Early Childhood Education*. Scott, Foresman, 1988.

Machado, Jeanne M. *Early Childhood Experiences in Language Arts,* 2nd ed. Delmar Publishers, 1980.

Mahoney, Ellen, and Wilcox, Leah. *Ready, Set, Read: Best Books to Prepare Preschoolers*. Scarecrow Press, 1985.

Morrison, George M. *Early Childhood Education Today*. Charles E. Merrill, 1991.

Peck, J.; McCaig, G.; and Sapp, M. E. *Kindergarten Policies: What Is Best for Children?* National Association for the Education of Young Children, 1988.

Rogers, Cosby S., and Sawyers, Janet K. *Play in the Lives of Children*. National Association for the Education of Young Children, 1988.

Schickedanz, Judith A. *More Than the ABCs: The Early Stages of Reading and Writing*. National Association for the Education of Young Children, 1986.

Schickedanz, Judith A.; Chay, Soyoung; Gopin, Paula; Sheng, Lan Lan; Song, Soo-Mi; and Wild, Nancy. "Preschoolers and Academics: Some Thoughts." *Young Children* 48 (November 1990), pp. 4–13.

Seefeldt, Carol, ed. *The Early Childhood Curriculum: A Review of Current Research*. Teachers College Press, 1986.

Stone, Janet. "Caregiver and Teacher Language—Responsive or Restrictive?" *Young Children* 48 (May 1993), pp. 12–18.

Temple, Charles; Nathan, Ruth; Temple, Frances; and Burris, Nancy A. *The Beginnings of Writing,* 3rd ed. Allyn and Bacon, 1993.

Teaching Resources

Beginner Books Filmstrips. Random House (various sets with six filmstrips and cassettes in each set).

Cole, Joanna, and Calmenson, Stephanie. *The Eentsy, Weentsy Spider: Fingerplays and Action Rhymes*. Morrow, 1991.

Coletta, Anthony, and Coletta, Kathleen. *Year Round Activities for Four-Year-Old Children*. Center for Applied Research, 1986.

———. *Year Round Activities for Three-Year-Old Children*. Center for Applied Research, 1986.

Croft, Doreen J., and Hess, Robert D. *An Activities Handbook for Teachers of Young Children,* 4th ed. Houghton Mifflin, 1984.

Great Beginnings Activity Card Library. Thompson (box of cards with songs, games, finger plays, and language activities on them).

Hirsch, L., ed. *The Block Book.* National Association for the Education of Young Children, 1984.

Literacy Development in the Preschool. Heinemann, 1986 (filmstrip).

Mister Rogers' Plan and Play Book. Family Communications (records and audio cassettes).

Mother Goose Treasury. Greenleaf (videotape).

Taetzsch, Sandra Zeitlin, and Taetzsch, Lyn. *Preschool Games and Activities.* Fearon, n.d.

COMPUTER SOFTWARE

Easy as ABC. Springboard.

Rhymes and Riddles. Spinnaker (K–grade 3).

Stickybears ABC. Scholastic.

Suggested Stories and Books for Infants and Toddlers

TRADITIONAL STORIES FOR THE VERY YOUNG

The Three Bears
The Three Little Pigs
The Three Little Kittens
Jack and the Beanstalk
The Three Billy Goats Gruff
The Gingerbread Man

FOR THOSE WHO ARE A LITTLE OLDER

The Elves and the Shoemaker
Rumplestiltskin
The Ugly Duckling
Peter Rabbit
Cinderella
Hansel and Gretel
Snow White
Little Red Riding Hood

DURABLE BOOKS FOR INFANTS

Bruna, Dick. *My Toys.* Methuen, 1980.
———. *Out and About.* Methuen, 1980.
Ford, George. *Baby's First Picture Book.* Random House, 1979.
Hoban, Tana. *Red, Blue, Yellow Shoe.* Greenwillow, 1986.
Kunhardt, D. *Pat the Bunny.* Western, 1962.
Pfloog, Jan. *Kittens.* Random House, 1977.
Sesame Street. *Ernie and Bert Can . . . Can You?* Random House, 1982.
Smollin, Mike. *The Cow Says Moo.* Random House, 1979.

Sets: Playshapes Books (Dial Publishers)
Chunky Books (Random House)
My Teddy Books (Barron's)

OTHER BOOKS FOR INFANTS

Ahlberg, J., and Ahlberg, A. *Peek-a-Boo!* Viking, 1978.
Broomfield, Robert. *The Baby Animal ABC.* Penguin, 1968.
Bruna, Dick. *B Is for Bear.* Methuen, 1967.
Campbell, Rod. *Buster Gets Dressed.* Barron's, 1988.
Charao, Kay. *Baby's Lap Book.* Dutton, 1977.
Curry, Nancy. *An Animal Is Red.* Bowmar, 1977.
Fujikawa, Gyo. *Gyo Fujikawa's A to Z Picture Book.* Grosset and Dunlap, 1974.
Rojankovsky, Feodor. *Animals in the Zoo.* Alfred A. Knopf, 1962.
Scarry, Richard. *Early Words.* Random House, 1976.
Tudor, Tasha. *Mother Goose.* Henry Z. Walck, 1976.
Weisgard, Leonard. *My First Picture Book.* Grosset and Dunlap, 1964.

BOOKS FOR TODDLERS

Bonforte, Lisa. *Farm Animals.* Random House, 1981.
Brown, Margaret. *Goodnight Moon.* Harper and Row, 1947.
Campbell, Rod. *Buster Gets Dressed.* Barron's, 1988.
Carle, Eric. *Do You Want to Be My Friend?* Crowell, 1971.
Conover, Chris. *Six Little Ducks.* Crowell, 1976.
Freeman, Don. *Corduroy.* Viking, 1976.
Krauss, Ruth. *The Carrot Seed.* Harper and Row, 1976.
Rojankovsky, Feodor. *The Tall Book of Mother Goose.* Harper and Row, 1942.
Slobodkina, Esphyr. *Caps for Sale.* Addison-Wesley, 1947.
Van Fleet, Matthew. *One Yellow Lion.* Dial, 1992.

Sets: Talk-About-Books (Annick Press)
Little Poke & Look Books (Grosset & Dunlap)

Suggested Books for Threes and Fours

Ahlberg, A., and Ahlberg, J. *Each Peach, Pear, Plum.* Viking, 1978.

Anno, Mitsumasa. *Anno's Counting Book.* Crowell, 1977.

Barton, Bryon. *Wheels.* Crowell, 1977.

Carle, Eric. *Pancakes, Pancakes.* Pantheon, 1975.

Crews, Donald. *School Bus.* Greenwillow, 1984.

de Paolo, T. *Pancakes for Breakfast.* Harcourt Brace Jovanovich, 1978.

Dr. Seuss. *Green Eggs and Ham.* Random House, 1960.

———. *Hop On Pop.* Random House, 1963.

Eastman, P. D. *Go, Dog, Go!* Random House, 1961.

Gag, Wanda. *Millions of Cats.* Coward-McCann and Geoghegan, 1977.

Gramatsky, Hardie. *Little Toot.* Putnam, 1978.

Gretz, Susanna. *Teddy Bear's ABC.* Follett, 1975.

Hoban, Tana. *Count and See.* Macmillan, 1972.

———. *Is It Red? Is It Yellow? Is It Blue?* Greenwillow, 1978.

———. *Round and Round and Round.* Greenwillow, 1983.

Hopkins, Lee Bennett. *Go to Bed! A Book of Bedtime Poems.* Alfred A. Knopf, 1979.

Keats, Ezra Jack. *The Snowy Day.* Viking, 1962.

Kellogg, Steven. *Pinkerton, Behave.* Dial, 1979.

Kraus, R. *Leo the Late Bloomer.* Dutton, 1973.

Lear, Edward. *An Edward Lear Alphabet.* Lothrop, 1983.

———. *The Owl and the Pussy Cat and Other Nonsense.* Viking, 1978.

Lionni, Leo. *Swimmy.* Pantheon, 1963.

Lowery, Janette. *The Poky Little Puppy.* Golden, 1942.

Maestro, Betsy. *Harriet Goes to the Circus.* Crown, 1977.

McCloskey, Robert. *Make Way for Ducklings.* Viking, 1941.

Piper, Watty. *The Little Engine That Could.* Scholastic, 1979.

Prelutsky, Jack. *Read-Aloud Rhymes for the Very Young.* Knopf, 1986.

Rey, Hans. *Curious George.* Houghton Mifflin, 1941.

Sendak, Maurice. *Where the Wild Things Are.* Harper, 1963.

Stevenson, Robert Louis. *A Child's Garden of Verses.* Franklin Watts, 1966.

Viorst, Judith. *Alexander and the Terrible, Horrible, No Good Very Bad Day.* Atheneum, 1972.

———. *The Tenth Good Thing About Barney.* Atheneum, 1971.

Zion, Gene. *Harry the Dirty Dog.* Harper and Row, 1976.

Zolotow, Charlotte. *William's Doll.* Harper and Row, 1972.

Activities for Preservice Teachers

1. Interview the parent of a two-year-old. Find out how much the child is read to, which are the child's favorite books, and how much access the child has to writing materials.

2. Visit a nursery school or a day-care center that enrolls preschoolers. Note the room arrangement, equipment and materials, child/teacher interaction, and scheduled activities. Pay particular attention to how language development is encouraged and how much contact there is with books.

3. Visit a preschool or kindergarten class. Make a note of differences among the children in size, physical coordination, willingness and ability to express themselves orally, and extent of vocabulary.

4. Try some software intended for young children. Evaluate the content and mode of presentation. What would be likely to appeal to young children? What are some problems that you see in the use of such software?

5. From friends who teach prekindergarten classes or parents of children aged three to five, collect samples of children's "writing." Can you read it? Are some letters conventional in shape? Is there evidence of linear motion in putting them on paper? Are some figures (possibly letters) repeated frequently?

6. Go to a library or bookstore and examine books for preschoolers. Which do you judge to be the best? What are your criteria?

7. Tell a story such as "The Three Little Pigs" to a three-year-old and then to a four-year-old. Have each child tell it back to you. What do you notice about the children's ability to tell the story in sequence?

8. Watch several *Sesame Street* programs and pick out some episodes that are designed to teach language. To what extent are the principles of early childhood education followed?

9. Begin a collection of poems and stories to be used with young children. Keep these on file cards in a box.

10. Examine several college textbooks on early childhood education. Note what they contain on such topics as language development and beginning writing and reading experiences.

11. Assemble numerous objects—blocks of various sizes and colors, puzzles, beads, cartons, toy vehicles, puppets,

picture books, and so forth—and give them to a three-year-old. Observe what the child is interested in first, second, and so on, how long the interest lasts, and what the child does with the articles. Report your observations to the class.

Activities for Inservice Teachers

1. Interview some parents of preschoolers. Try to find out what they want the preschool to provide for their children. How informed are they about the intellectual development and learning abilities of their preschool children? Do they seem to favor an emphasis on academic learning or on social experiences?

2. Find out about your state's policy on providing early childhood education for all children. If a specific policy statement has been issued, obtain a copy and see whether it comments on the kind of program that ought to be provided for this age group.

3. Videotape a discussion with a three- or four-year-old child. Analyze the child's speech in terms of the number of different words used and the average length of utterances. Be prepared to report your analysis to your class as well as possibly to show the videotape.

4. Examine some recently published versions of such old favorites as "Little Red Riding Hood" or "The Three Bears." How do they compare with the ones you remember from your childhood in terms of content and illustrations?

5. Observe young children (aged two to four) in a public place such as a restaurant, supermarket, park, or department store. What do the children seem to notice, and how do they investigate what they notice? Take notes on what they are interested in and what they do.

6. Interview some prekindergarten teachers. Find out about their expectations for the children's progress, the stated goals of the program, and their confidence that the results will be what is expected.

7. Prepare a checklist of language-related characteristics that could be used in discussions with the parents of young children to help them see how language development proceeds and how a good preschool program makes a contribution.

8. Make a list of dramatic play activities that would provide especially good opportunities for young children to use writing materials.

Activities for Children

1. Following a discussion of a topic such as "Our Pets," "My House," or "What I Like to Eat," write the title on a chart or chalkboard. Then ask the children to tell something related to the topic and write this for the group to see. You can read it back to them, with some joining in after they have heard the sentences a few times. Analyze the learning experiences provided.

2. Make a "Rhyming Box," a box containing objects such as a shell, a cork, a spoon, a rubber mouse, and so on. Ask the children to find in the box an object whose name rhymes with, for example, *house, bell,* or *fork.*

3. Provide a box of old clothing, shoes, and hats for children to use in creative play. Videotape them as they try various activities.

4. Discuss news items with the children—both ones that you suggest and those you hear them talking about. Follow up by providing them with paper to make individual drawings about what interests them. See if any do a drawing related to the discussion.

5. Make a display of materials for children to handle and talk about. For example, a display of different cloth (silk, burlap, suede, velvet, nylon, wool, canvas, etc.) will lead to talk about differences, likenesses, feel, and so forth.

6. Give children pictures from magazines and ask them to talk about them. Mount the pictures on cardboard so that they will last, or even put flannel patches on the backs so that they may be placed on a flannel board. See if they begin to make up stories about the people, animals, or objects in the pictures.

7. Provide a box of odds and ends from which children may choose materials to create imaginary animals or other objects. Children may show these to the class, thus stimulating discussion, which, among other things, should lead to more use of the box.

8. Children may have innumerable learning experiences in a sandbox or with a tub of water. For example, they may build roads, houses, and lakes or check what will float and discuss what causes bubbles. Make sure these materials are provided.

Chapter 4

Beginning Language Arts Programs

*T*his chapter extends the discussion of the language development of children begun in Chapter 3, providing an overview of language arts programs for kindergarten and first and second grades. The language arts receive major attention at these levels because they are foundational for other learning and because young children naturally gain competence in using language and are eager to learn to read and write. Emphasizing continuity in children's language development, the chapter suggests learning experiences that will be meaningful to children and appropriate to their ability levels.

Some kindergarten and early-primary programs are too structured and ask more of children of this age group than they are prepared to do from a developmental perspective. On the other hand, activities should be sufficiently challenging to pupils who are more mature and eager for the opportunity to engage in a wide variety of learning experiences, including those related to beginning literacy. It is important that differences in the development of children be recognized and dealt with appropriately by teachers.

LANGUAGE ARTS IN KINDERGARTEN

About 95 percent of eligible children currently attend kindergarten.

The Nebraska State Education Department and many professional organizations have taken a position opposed to making the kindergarten program heavily academic.

There are several types of kindergarten programs. What many people still mean by "kindergarten" is a half-day session devoted mainly to free-choice activities in room centers, along with music, stories, art activities, and outside play. In recent years, however, there has been a tendency for the kindergarten program to move toward the direct teaching of material usually taught in first and second grades. The result is that in some kindergartens much less time is given to a playhouse corner, block building, easel painting, and other similar activities. Instead, teachers in these programs have total-class or even ability-group lessons on letters of the alphabet, writing, phonics, and numbers. The amount of time devoted to these lessons leaves little time in a half-day session for anything else. The response in some situations has been to change to an all-day schedule, meaning that five-year-olds attend for just as many (or almost as many) hours as older students. This arrangement has been justified on the basis that it satisfies all needs: there is time to conduct formal teaching, and there is time for free-choice and expressive activities. Concern has been expressed by many, particularly some authorities in early childhood education, that the full-day schedule may not be the best use of a young child's time, especially if play opportunities diminish and the direct teaching ignores children's levels of readiness for and interest in what is being taught.

Many types of experiences develop the language of young children.

Several rationales have been advanced for these changes in the kindergarten: that children know more today, that they have been attending group programs before kindergarten entrance, and that parents want the full-day schedule and more emphasis on academic study. These reasons do not seem sufficient to warrant substantial changes in the kindergarten. Five-year-olds need a program that balances in-school and out-of-school experiences and provides for much self-selection of activities in an interesting and varied environment. There is every reason to believe that such experiences will produce the kinds of individual development and academic progress that everyone wants.

Oral Expression in Kindergarten

Children's development in all areas of the language arts and, for that matter, their achievement in every school subject, is so dependent on their capacity for oral expression that such ability should be considered central to all kindergarten activities. This means that there must be free-choice time during which children may talk freely with one another about the bridge being built, a just-completed painting, the fish in the aquarium, or sprouting seeds. There must also be opportunities in the playhouse area or on the climbing frame for them to engage in dramatic play, talking in what they believe to be the language of parents or circus performers. And pairs of children or groups of three or four must be allowed time to quietly engage in personal conversations about pets, baby sisters, or plans to go to a birthday party.

If you make sure that opportunities for oral expression are plentiful, you will find it possible to identify a youngster who seems to be making only limited use of language or who has specific difficulties. Observations may lead you to realize, for example, that James seems to stammer hardly at all when playing with Bobby but has serious difficulty when anyone else is involved. Dialect patterns can be easily noted in these informal moments, so pronunciations, common expressions, and usage variations can be recorded. Although some of this is only useful for you to know as background, other factors may be significant for program planning.

In addition to encouraging oral language during free-choice times, you will want to plan specific speaking activities and give guidance. Total-class and group sessions should include discussions, sharing, storytelling, dramatizing, and creative play. In interaction with individuals and in small-group settings you can introduce matters based on observations made during informal periods.

Discussion. Discussion, or talking together as a fairly large group, often occurs in the kindergarten as children gather around a teacher who is preparing to play the piano or read a story or talk about future events while showing a calendar. The children should be seated on the floor and the atmosphere ought to be reasonably informal. At this age, considering how self-centered a five-year-old is, it is not appropriate to expect children to raise their hands and be recognized before speaking. With practice this may be learned, but rigid rules are not conducive to the spontaneous use of language.

Discussions, of course, don't always have to focus on something the teacher is doing; extending the informal activities of the classroom is appropriate. For example, a tub of water in the room, although sloppy, stimulates children's talking. It reduces shyness and leads to discussions about what will float, what won't, animals that live in water, and so forth. Children will have a great deal of fun, and the possibilities for discussion are innumerable.

A display of cloth materials that children are encouraged to handle will bring about new understanding of words, as well as awareness of everyday things in our world. Remember to encourage discussion of how the items look, feel, and smell, as well as of likenesses, differences among them, and their possible uses. The display might consist of pieces of burlap, cotton, suede, velvet, wool, and nylon. The amounts needed are small and can usually be easily obtained.

Things that can be smelled provide another way to bring about a good deal of talking. Children can be encouraged to describe the various odors (and the word *odor* can be introduced or even *aroma*) and to talk about smells they have encoun-

Sensations, concepts, and words are all related to one another.

tered and they like or dislike and why. This may lead to a discussion of what smells tell us and the recognition that not all liquids that look like water are indeed water. In fact, using water, rubbing alcohol, and white vinegar is a good way to begin a discussion of the differences between appearance and reality. Such a discussion can lead to further vocabulary development and concept building.

Another simple way to stimulate discussion is to ask everyone in the class to bring in the top from a jar or bottle (this is their "homework"). Each child may show his or her top to the others, who handle it and ask questions. For example, a discussion may begin with: "Is this from a ketchup bottle?" "What do you use ketchup for?" "Why are the tops for ketchup and mustard different?" "Could we put a ketchup cap on mustard?" Such a discussion might lead to the discovery that differences may be very slight or not immediately obvious. For example, though the consistency of both appears much the same, ketchup will pour, whereas mustard will not.

Other activities might include planting flowers, blowing soap bubbles, preparing fruit for eating, making and wearing paper masks, or looking at objects through a magnifying glass. Handling and attempting to describe unseen objects in a "mystery box" is an effective stimulator of discussion, too.

There are many occasions for discussion when direct leadership by the teacher is needed. For instance, you will need to talk with the children about the room and its management—such housekeeping matters as where to keep papers until taken home, who will care for the hamsters during vacation, or what will be done about costumes for the Halloween party. The calendar can be the focus for talking about the days of the week, what can be expected during a particular month, and whose birthday is approaching. Discussion of the weather brings up matters of clothing, outside play, and waiting for the bus.

Having a visitor in the room is an event that presents you with the chance to do some important direct teaching. Before a visit is the time to talk about such courtesies as raising hands for permission to speak, not interrupting others, and listening carefully to what is said. After a guest leaves is a good time to discuss what was said, who the visitor was, and what he or she does. The behavior of the class during the visit can also be talked about, giving you the opportunity to review the things discussed before the visit.

Some welcome guests in kindergarten:

police officers
fire fighters
musicians
dentists
doctors
parents

Children can "Show and Tell" about:

a colorful rock
a bird's nest
a photograph
a self-drawn picture
foreign stamps
books
seashells

Sharing. Sharing and the related activity "Show and Tell" are common language experiences in the kindergarten (and beyond). Children may bring toys or other objects to show and talk about, or they may share personal experiences, for example, a visit with relatives or something seen on the way to school. For some children sharing is easy; many are eager to participate. For others, holding an object while telling about it may relieve nervousness by shifting attention away from self. Either type of sharing may be conducted in a total-class setting or in small groups, perhaps at tables. Sometimes shy youngsters will participate only if the group is small and composed mainly of friends. To promote sharing activities, keep the following suggestions in mind:

1. Urge children to talk to the group rather than to you.
2. Encourage questions and comments.
3. Encourage attention and good listening.
4. Be a good listener yourself.
5. Be prepared to limit the number of children sharing each day, if necessary, to ensure that the others will be able to pay attention.

6. Do not overemphasize taking turns. Enthusiastic participants can stimulate others.

7. Invite and suggest, but do not require, participation.

8. Take special care to praise the efforts of shy children.

9. Do not fall into a pattern in which the children show while you do the telling.

Subjects for group pantomimes:

playing catch
a mouse is loose in the room
raising the flag
raking leaves
putting up a tent

Dramatic Play and Dramatization. Besides describing briefly activities based on dramatization and dramatic play (see Environmental Materials), Chapter 3 presented principles and guidelines to observe in fostering these activities (Early Childhood Education). Kindergartners should have many opportunities for creative role playing since so much of children's emotional and social growth, cognitive development, knowledge about their environment, and, certainly, language development depends on this form of experimentation and expression. Opportunities for creative play and dramatizing occur throughout the school day. As a part of both indoor and outdoor play, children in the kindergarten should be given the opportunity to pretend to do housekeeping, shop at the market, drive a car, be a bus driver, and so on.

Another activity to continue is that of listening to and reciting rhymes. More may be expected of kindergartners with respect to listening to and acting out in sequence the events in a finger play or nursery rhyme. It is usually helpful, though, to select the most extroverted children for the first efforts at "acting out." Though children know much about rhyming and may pick up the wording of rhymes, memorization should not be required.

Keep in mind that spontaneity of expression and ease with language are the goals. Some children, particularly those who are extremely self-conscious, may not readily respond to these activities, and doing so may take months, even with six-year-olds. Gently encouraging these children will help. Patience and knowledge of the particular child involved are essential in planning such activities.

Some possible Mother Goose rhymes to dramatize are the following:

The Old Lady Who Lived in a Shoe
Rock-a-Bye-Baby
Jack Be Nimble
One, Two, Buckle My Shoe
Jack and Jill
Humpty Dumpty
Little Miss Muffet
Three Little Kittens
Baa, Baa, Black Sheep
Simple Simon
Old King Cole
Polly, Put the Kettle On
Old Mother Hubbard
Wee Willie Winkie

Many others are as appropriate as those listed. Always be on the lookout for poems that are well suited to dramatization or that simply offer pure enjoyment.

Other Teaching Considerations

In every kindergarten class attention needs to be given to several factors related to language performance. Some of these supplement the oral language experi-

Much that was said about programs for three- and four-year-olds in Chapter 3 also applies to kindergarten classes.

The average kindergarten child has watched 5,000 hours of television.

ences just discussed; others are important to the writing and reading activities to follow. Kindergarten teachers must also be aware of certain potential problems and their effect on program planning.

Listening. Listening is not something new to kindergartners; they have been listening from early infancy. They have heard hundreds of people talking, perhaps speaking different dialects or even other languages. They have listened to mechanical and natural sounds and to music of all kinds. They have listened to radio, records, and television. Most of what they know in the way of concepts and understandings has been gained through listening.

Listening is crucial to language learning, and this learning continues in kindergarten in very important ways. Therefore, among many other considerations, you should attempt to provide a good speech model so that children will have an opportunity to hear, for example, that it is not "liberry" that's said but "library." You should also ask children of this age to listen and make distinctions between sounds of words, because hearing the difference between "pan" and "pen" is important in reading and spelling.

Many classroom activities provide listening experiences, and, with planning, all may be used to teach important skills. Children listen for their own names when you call them to get their coats in preparation for going home. They listen to find out about the sequence of the day's schedule and to follow directions for completing a classroom project. And the stories you read or tell furnish much to listen to—new words, accounts of interesting events, and character descriptions. (Chapter 6 discusses listening in detail and suggests various activities, many of which are appropriate for kindergarten.)

Speech. Speech is a major concern in kindergarten; as many as one-third of the youngsters are likely to use speech forms that may lead to problems. The speech difficulties of this age group range from the common "baby talk" to serious problems that may prevent the child from being understood even by you. It is important, though, to distinguish between genuine problems and speech characteristics that are likely to disappear with maturity. To assist teachers in this, school districts often check all kindergartners' speech and hearing (sometimes speaking difficulties are caused by hearing losses) at the time of entrance or early in the school year.

If a child has a serious speech problem, you should be aware of what the assigned clinician is doing and be prepared to support that plan. Even children with minor difficulties may be seen by a therapist, possibly for only a few sessions, and the therapist will have suggestions as to what you can do to help in these cases. You should not, however, decide that every child who does not pronounce words in standard adult ways has a speech problem. In many cases maturity will eliminate all difficulties. (See Chapters 5 and 16 for further discussion of speech.)

Vocabulary. The development of vocabulary occurs rapidly in the kindergarten without any specific program for teaching about words and their meanings. Children of this age know as many as two thousand words and are constantly learning new ones. You can make an important contribution to this aspect of language growth by continuing the activities begun during the preschool years. That is, you should provide a good model; introduce words associated with the learning activities; play word games of all kinds; and, especially, read to the children and engage in discussions with them. Every kindergarten room should have numerous objects that require naming. Some of these may be part of the furnishings, such as a *balance beam* to walk on or *triangles* for making music. Others might be a *turtle*, a *microscope*, or a *scale*. Especially valuable is anything that may provide an entirely new kind of experience, perhaps a *work bench* where children can *hammer* and *saw*.

Besides helping children learn new words, you are responsible for clarifying meanings for them. It is difficult for young children to grasp that a word may have more than one meaning, but once this occurs, new areas of thinking and enjoyment (such as riddles) open up to them.

You will find it revealing to administer a standardized instrument (such as the *Peabody Picture Vocabulary Test*) to children from different backgrounds.

Studies based on vocabulary testing indicate that some children have particular strengths and weaknesses. For example, a number of youngsters from disadvantaged backgrounds seem not to know very many verbs. They are just as likely as other children to climb, peek, and pull, but they appear not to have these words in their vocabularies. You need to be aware of this and look for the chance to link activities and vocabulary. The backgrounds of these children have influenced more than vocabulary, however. Such aspects of development as self-image and freedom of expression are likely to have been affected, and a teacher must keep this in mind.

On the other hand, even if children speak reasonably well and seem to use words correctly, that does not mean teaching is unnecessary. Children may distort what they hear to make a word or statement fit their own ideas about language, as is exemplified by reports concerning the words children actually say in pledging allegiance to the flag ("just dust for all"). Such an account points to the need for you to listen carefully and to attempt to clarify when necessary. One little girl, for instance, seemed to be confused about the words "neighbor" and "store," but her teacher finally realized that what she had been hearing was "next store neighbor."

Young children learn best when they have meaningful experiences. Direct observations of people, things, and processes made possible by trips away from the classroom are particularly supportive of vocabulary development. These may be full-fledged field trips to such sites as a museum, a farm, a factory, or city hall, or they may be short excursions to places close by, such as to the shrubbery at the edge of the school grounds to see the birds' nests or to the principal's office to learn what equipment is used there. Each trip should be a focus for discussion—on planning the trip; what will be, or was, seen and heard; and what to write on an experience chart. Each such experience can build vocabulary.

Studies indicate that the typical child entering kindergarten recognizes fourteen letters of the alphabet.

The Alphabet. Some children entering kindergarten may know the alphabet; that is, they may know the names of all or most of the letters and perhaps be able to recite or sing these in the correct order. Some of the children may be able to identify uppercase ("capital" or "big") and lowercase ("little") letters and write several of them, most likely ones in their names. Other children will know somewhat less, and a few will not be able to name or recognize more than a letter or two. Such a range of achievement levels makes it absolutely necessary to provide many different learning experiences, several alphabet sets to manipulate, and a writing table similar to the one described in Chapter 3.

Group and individual recitation of the alphabet should be part of the daily routine in a kindergarten class. Saying the alphabet will do no harm to those children who already know it, and the practice is necessary to those who are still learning. In general, children need to know the alphabet and to recognize uppercase letter forms before much emphasis is put on writing either uppercase or lowercase letters.

The article by Salzer listed in the references at the end of this chapter contains a statement on kindergarten adopted by the International Reading Association.

Learning the names of the letters and being able to recognize them is important, but you need to exercise judgment concerning what to introduce and how much to expect at any given time. Some school systems mandate the use of rather inflexible programs for teaching the alphabet. Often, though, the use of inappropriate activities within such programs can be minimized. Although learning if *R* comes before or after *P* will be important some day, it really isn't necessary for kindergarten children to do any more than pick up such knowledge from informal experiences.

Several alphabet books should be available in the classroom (and there should be others in the school library). Some good ones are

Anno, Mitsumasa. *Anno's Alphabet: An Adventure in Imagination.* Crowell, 1975.
Base, Graeme. *Animalia.* H. N. Abrams, 1986.
Duke, Kate. *The Guinea Pig ABC.* Dutton, 1983.
Elting, Mary, and Folsom, Michael. *Q Is for Duck.* Clarion Books, 1980.
Feelings, Muriel. *Jambo Means Hello: Swahili Alphabet Book.* Dial, 1974.
Fujikawa, Gyo. *A to Z Picture Book.* Grosset and Dunlap, 1974.
Gardner, Beau. *Have you ever seen . . . ?* Dodd, Mead, 1986.
Grant, Sandy. *Hey, look at me!* Bradbury Press, 1973.
Hague, Kathleen. *Alphabears: An ABC Book.* Holt, Rinehart and Winston, 1984.
Lobel, Anita, and Lobel, Arnold. *On Market Street.* Greenwillow, 1981.
MacDonald, Suse. *Alphabatics.* Bradbury Press, 1986.
Martin, Bill, Jr. *Chicka Chicka Boom Boom.* Simon and Schuster, 1989.
Palotta, Jerry. *The Bird Alphabet Book.* Charlesbridge, 1991.
Rankin, Laura. *The Handmade Alphabet.* Dial, 1991
Rey, H. A. *Curious George Learns the Alphabet.* Houghton Mifflin, 1963.
Tobias, Hosea, and Baskin, Liza. *Hosie's Alphabet.* Viking, 1972.
Wildsmith, Brian. *Brian Wildsmith's ABC.* Franklin Watts, 1963.

Writing in Kindergarten

Kindergarten writing experiences should include what you do and what the children get involved in. You should write regularly for them by using the chalkboard or chart paper to record daily news and what they want to say about experiences they have had. The whole group can be involved, since children of various maturity levels are learning different sorts of things. Those without much experience see lots of alphabet letters and note that writing proceeds from the left side and new lines of letters are placed underneath existing ones. More mature children will begin to see where capital letters are used and can try to supply some of the letters that are associated with particular sounds. Writing while the pupils watch is very important and should be done frequently.

Kindergartners should also try writing themselves. In Chapter 3, which discussed the writing interests and abilities of three- and four-year-old children, it was pointed out that many fours can make a few letters and some can print their

A proud beginning writer shows her work.

own names. Entering kindergartners can often print several letters other than those in their names, and a few will do more. Nearly all can make letterlike forms, although these may be upside down or backward.

With whatever writing ability they have, and because they know that pictures often accompany writing, kindergartners can begin to draw pictures and write texts to accompany them. Usually all that is required is for the teacher to say, "Draw a picture and write about it. Use any letters you know." Some will say that they do not know how to write, but when the teacher's response is, "Pretend you can," most will go ahead (some teachers try to relieve a reluctant child's anxiety by referring to what is done as "children's writing"). When the climate is an accepting one, this suggestion is enough in nearly every case. Those who won't take the risk (sometimes these are very able children who need to feel they are always correct) may have to see the others participating happily for a few days before they can join in. Your acceptance or, even better, encouragement of what they do, along with their pride in their work, will keep them writing, and the writing will keep on maturing.

As their writing develops, kindergartners will experiment in making letter forms. This experimentation will be very evident in the texts they include with their drawings, which will also exhibit various interpretations of what the children mean by "writing":

- *Writing the ABCs.* Writing to some kindergarten pupils means making the alphabet letters; they will draw a picture and write all twenty-six letters or some of them.

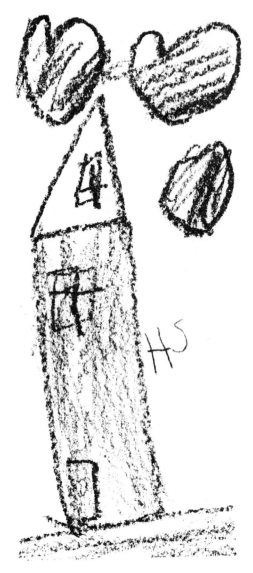

House is Spelled with Beginning and Ending
Sounds Only

Young children usually
learn capital letters first. If
presented with a word written in lower-case print some
will even copy it in uppercase form.

These are usually uppercase letters written in order from left to right, but less
conventional arrangements are found, too. When asked to "read" such a text,
children are likely to supply a story or description related to the picture.

- *Using letters of their names.* Again, using what is familiar, beginning writers may
  rearrange and repeat the letters of their own names when asked to write. For
  example, Margaret's text is a string of letters, *MTERG*, which, when "read" by her,
  tells a tale: "Me and my sister made a snowman."

- *Combining letters from several sources.* Some kindergarten students begin to use letters other than those in their names, often scattering them around the page. When they string letters together, they sometimes appear to be observing "rules," such as "Letters next to each other have to be different—no doubles." To increase their supply of letters they will look around the room and copy from signs and books. Nevertheless, they are usually willing to "read" what they have written as something about the drawing or why they drew it.

- *Clustering of letters.* Groups of letters appear as kindergartners begin to make wordlike forms. Sometimes they will place a cluster of letters near a component of the picture. There is a figure of a dog, for example, and the cluster *KTMO* nearby is identified as *dog*. Many of these clusters will be written left to right but some may not.

- *Single letters as sounds.* As young writers become more familiar with the letters, they may try to represent words or parts of them with single letters. First, letter names may be used (*U* stands for *you*) and then single letters that represent the initial sound of a word (*H* for *house*). This step signifies discovery of a very important idea, the **alphabetic principle,** which points out that alphabet letters are associated with sounds of speech.

- *Beginnings of invented spelling.* The alphabetic principle is soon extended to multisyllable words. *RB* is read as "rainbow," and *AP* as "airplane." Final sounds are then included; "house" is spelled *HS*, and "pond" is written *PD*. A few adventurous kindergartners will even try to spell long words such as *magnificent* and may come close to the actual spelling.

The active engagement of kindergartners in writing stories throughout the school year is accompanied by physical and intellectual maturing, so their handwriting will improve steadily. Those who have not already learned to do so will begin to form letters correctly, orient them on the page in conventional ways, and reduce them in size. Unlined paper should be used and the exclusive use of uppercase letters allowed, since these are the ones the children know best.

Progress related to the conventions of writing is important, but the most significant element in anyone's writing—a child's or an adult's—is the content, the message. Young children's first scribbles are done for the joy of movement and the satisfaction felt in making marks. With the knowledge that the letters signal meaning comes the desire to convey meaning: this is the real learning children achieve through kindergarten writing experiences.

Reading in Kindergarten

If the language arts program is a complete one—including regular reading to the group, much talk and oral expression, reciting of nursery rhymes, writing by you for the children, and attempts by them to write—some kindergartners will evolve into beginning readers rather easily. This is because they are learning the language of books and ways of responding to print. Also, as they write, they are making such important discoveries as how to associate speech sounds with the letters of the alphabet. Most important, they are having many opportunities to see that writing conveys meaning.

A comprehensive language arts program will enable you to respond to questions about what is being done to prepare pupils for reading. A complete response is important because many administrators and parents believe that only a highly structured program with ability groups, daily lessons, and textbooks can assure readiness. In pointing out the possible difficulties with such a formal approach, you will find it helpful to discuss the principles of reading readiness and the importance of offering a program that grows out of activities children find interesting and challenging.

Reading Readiness. The term reading readiness as used in discussions of kindergarten (and, very often, first-grade) programs has three possible meanings.

1. *Reading readiness is primarily a matter of maturity.* This perspective is based on the assumption that most kindergarten pupils require only time to mature before real progress in reading can be made. Youngsters who are not "ready" do not appear to have the physical, linguistic, and other abilities needed for reading but may be expected to develop these in a few weeks or months. While the children are getting a little older, a reasonably good general education program ought to be available to them but there needn't be much direct teaching of specific skills or understandings. Rather, children should interact socially, build with blocks, sing songs, and otherwise experience a varied early education program. Those who take this position on reading readiness often say, "Let them grow up; let them be children."

2. *Reading readiness is a curriculum to be taught.* This programmatic definition identifies reading readiness as an instructional sequence intended to teach children what they need to know and be able to do in order to read. Specific learning activities are often part of a published basal reading series, with the kindergarten component usually considered the readiness program. In this approach, daily lessons are provided in such areas as discussion of story sequences and names and sounds of alphabet letters. The point of view is: "If children are taught prereading skills, they will be prepared for reading."

3. *Reading readiness is an aspect of emergent literacy.* The "emergent literacy" view of readiness is that children's reading, like their writing and oral expression, may be expected to develop continuously in a classroom where there are varied opportunities for language arts experiences. The kindergarten program that provides appropriate speaking, listening, and writing activities, and then includes appropriate book and other reading-related experiences, will enable children to begin to read without a great deal of direct teaching of skills and understandings. Those who support this view of readiness say, "They will learn to read naturally, the way they learned to talk—through much exposure to ordinary activities and with the support of a teacher who understands the natural progression of literacy learning."

> Increased use of the term *emergent literacy* instead of *reading readiness* reflects growing acceptance of the concept that reading is a process that begins to develop in the first months of life.

Being Aware of Readiness. Although "reading readiness tests" are available and many schools require that entering kindergartners be interviewed and administered several tests, such procedures provide much less information than you can gain by interviewing parents and observing children. A few minutes spent with parents can tell you much about a child's general background of experience and specific reading-related home activities. Observation of a child as she or he engages in the activities provided in a well-planned kindergarten classroom is always the best means of finding out what you need to know.

The list of questions that follows highlights important aspects of a child's development. As you can see, some items refer to overall development and maturity, some suggest possible teaching considerations, and others indicate specifics to look for when you are observing. How you define readiness influences what emphasis you give to particular items in your classsroom program.

A. *Physical condition.* Is the child:
1. in general good health?
2. sufficiently rested and nourished?
3. able to see and hear adequately?
4. physically coordinated as well as others of the same age?
5. able to articulate sounds and pronounce words normally?
6. established as to eye, hand, and foot dominance?

B. *Intellectual and perceptual ability.* Does the child:
1. have the general intelligence and maturity of other children of the same age?
2. have the ability to discriminate visually among shapes, letters, and words?
3. identify words that rhyme or begin alike?

C. *Background experiences.* Has the child:
1. been on shopping trips to various kinds of stores?
2. visited places such as a zoo, farm, or office building?
3. gone on trips of some distance?
4. been to the library?
5. been read to and looked at many books?

D. *Language ability.* Does the child:
1. have the ability to describe experiences to others in a comprehensible way?
2. understand a variety of concepts and words, for example, that a peach is a fruit and a cow's baby is a calf?
3. know the meanings of common prepositions such as *over, under, between,* and *above?*
4. use and understand the language of the school, that is, what is meant by such expressions as "sit in a circle," "library corner," and "sharing time"?
5. have the ability to understand and restate oral directions?

E. *Social-emotional status.* Does the child:
1. adjust behavior when the situation changes?
2. work independently?
3. have the desire to learn and the ability to complete tasks?
4. relate well to other children?
5. listen to and react appropriately to others?
6. have a positive self-image?

F. *Letter knowledge.* Can the child:
1. identify uppercase letters?
2. identify lowercase letters?
3. identify some letters in his or her own name?
4. match some letters with speech sounds?

G. *Environmental reading.* Can the child:
1. identify common advertising signs?
2. recognize names on cereal boxes and other containers?
3. find common words such as milk on packages and containers?

H. *Book and print familiarity.* Does the child:
1. know how to find the front and back of a book and its title?
2. know that the print is read rather than the illustrations?
3. point from left to right with a finger to show how print is read?
4. recognize a few letters and words in printed material?

**Differences in Children
That Affect Learning:**

1. Intellectual abilities
2. Maturity levels
3. Experiential backgrounds
4. Verbal facility
5. Emotional adjustment
6. Attitude toward learning
7. Exposure to literacy
   events
8. Visual and auditory acuity

The list is long and indicates that a great deal is expected of a child beginning to learn to read. Observations should, of course, be comprehensive, but a few negative answers to the questions must not be taken as an indication that the child involved is likely to have serious difficulties. Also keep in mind that reading readiness is a concern related to first grade as much as to kindergarten.

Moving into Reading. Kindergarten children should have varied reading experiences. Some of these will be similar to activities provided in programs for three- and four-year-olds—the same sorts of experiences described in Chapter 3 made somewhat more involved and complex. Most kindergarten reading activities will be related to the other components of the classroom program, especially listening, speaking, and writing. Selection of unit or project topics for class study will have implications for reading, too.

While many types of experiences ought to be available, you will have to exercise judgment in deciding how much emphasis to give to certain aspects of

Access to many interesting books is important.

the program. Adjustments will be needed to provide appropriate opportunities for all the children. Also, kindergarten students change a great deal during the year: their needs in April will be different from what may have been appropriate in October. In terms of the room itself, furnishings should include, in addition to a writing center, shelves of books, an easel to hold large-format books, a rug to lie on when looking at books, and other places to read—a loft, a carpeted bath tub, or an appliance box with cushions and pillows. Nothing is more important at this level than that children should enjoy their reading experiences, so emphasis should be placed on creating a pleasant setting for looking at and reading books.

Functional Reading. Just as in environments for younger children, kindergarten classrooms should have signs, labels, notices, and charts that further the operation or functioning of the classroom. These will include signs telling how to use equipment and learning centers, information on classroom pets and plants, lists of contents of drawers and cabinets, and so forth. You should read these regularly with individual children and the class so they not only understand the information that is on the signs and charts but also so that they have opportunities to see reading used for real purposes.

Of particular importance are instances of the writing of the children's own names. They can try to find their names on attendance charts and on their paintings and other projects as well as on lists of classroom helpers. Environmental-print items such as cereal boxes and fast-food containers may also be included as learning materials.

Reading by the Teacher. As a kindergarten teacher you should read to the entire class daily and to individuals and small groups when there are opportunities to do so. If there are aides or volunteers who can help (including older students in the school), even more reading to children is possible. Both old favorites and new selections should be included. (And some story telling and poetry should be mixed in.) Guidelines on how to read are the same as those presented in conjunction with the discussion of reading to fours.

Books to be read may be of several types: traditional tales (*Peter Rabbit; The Little Red Hen*), modern stories (*The Cat in the Hat; Caps for Sale*), predictable books (*Greedy Cat; Brown Bear, Brown Bear*), or real-life concerns (*A Baby Sister for Frances; My Momma Says There Aren't Any Zombies, Ghosts, Vampires, Creatures, Demons, Monsters, Fiends, Goblins or Things*). Not only stories should be read, but also information books related to class concerns, such as topics being investigated (plants), a field trip (zoo animals), a holiday (Halloween), or a local event (how a building is constructed, when that is occurring nearby). If the group seems likely to be interested, you might try a longer book with them, too, perhaps reading a bit of *Peter Pan* each day. Books that have been read to the class ought to be placed on a table or in the library corner so that class members will have the opportunity to look at them. (Other titles are suggested in Chapter 15.)

"Big books" are available from:
  Holt, Rinehart and Winston
  Rigby Education
  Scholastic
  The Wright Group

Shared Reading. After children have heard a book a few times, they may know it very well and this makes it possible for them to have a shared book experience. When the entire class or a large group is involved it is best to have a large-format version, a "big book" that all can see easily. Benefits of the activity include having a satisfying group experience, enjoying a story, seeing how print is placed on a page, and noting that pronounced words correspond one-to-one with printed words.

Shared reading is also possible when several copies of the same book are available and someone, an older reader or one of the children, knows the book very well and can read it aloud while the others follow along or join in. And, of course, two or three can share the same story, perhaps lying on the floor with the large version or using multiple copies. Other valuable shared reading experiences include repeated readings of class books made when each child contributes a page on a topic—"Thanksgiving," maybe, or "The Class Trip to the Airport." Group reading of poems on charts is also a valuable form of sharing.

Independent Reading Activities. An extensive classroom library allows many possibilities for individual children to use books. Most kindergartners are quite interested in paging through picture books, naming the items depicted, talking about the text, or repeating it if it has been memorized. The large-format big books used in shared reading periods may also be looked at and the text repeated just as is done with the whole group. (And there may be regular-sized versions of stories that were first memorized as big books.) If a class has made its own books, these should be available in the classroom library. Also, it may be possible for kindergartners to go to the building library alone or in small groups to look at books there.

Writing–Reading Connections. Kindergartners begin to write because they see print in the environment and want to try to produce some themselves. They also see books and hear them read, which gives them an appreciation for the significance of writing. Of course, they want to read what you have written after listening to them tell about a classroom experience.

Kindergarten children have valuable experiences as they move back and forth between writing and reading. As mentioned in the section on writing, they may put down several alphabet letters on a sheet of paper and then proceed to attempt to read this to someone. A few letters (*MKRN*) may stand for a rather lengthy text: "Our family went to visit my cousins and I saw. . . ."). More letters may mean additional story material.

As you write and they watch there will be many important opportunities to demonstrate what happens when writing occurs, and much of this relates to reading. "We will leave some space between words because that helps us to read." "After each part we write we should put a mark to say that the sentence is finished." "What letter does *Terminator* begin with?"

Using Phonics. Kindergarten children, because of their interest in rhyming and other kinds of word play, are usually receptive to thinking about "phonics," the relationship between speech sounds and writing. As we pointed out in the discussion of writing, many kindergartners will at some point begin to use the alphabetic principle; they will spell a word by using letters they believe have some connection with the way the word is pronounced. Those who have advanced that far will also very likely already have begun to connect speech sounds with the letters they see and to "sound out" some words. Certainly, these attempts should be encouraged because such a strategy is being learned naturally during an enjoyable activity.

Having children learn the "phonics rules" and expecting them to apply these to words is not an appropriate teaching activity in beginning reading, however. (See the discussion of the *letter-sound system* in the section Reading in First and Second Grades.) Some youngsters of kindergarten age do not yet have all the "sounds" of the language in their own speech repertoires, much less the ability to give them in response to alphabet letters.

In her article *Testing in the Kindergarten,* Durkin points out that readiness programs often involve too much phonics.

Kindergarten Reading Outcomes. In a kindergarten classroom that provides a comprehensive language arts program, several children will likely be reading by the end of the year and others will have made a good start. Those who are operating at the very beginning levels will continue to make progress, but without developing any feelings of frustration or failure.

Literature in Kindergarten

At several points in this discussion we have mentioned contributions children's literature can make to the kindergarten classroom. When youngsters of this age are exposed to various kinds of stories and books over several months all aspects of their language development are enhanced. They gain practice in listening; they learn new vocabulary; they have opportunities to discuss new friends such as Curious George and Ramona Quimby; they begin to develop a sense of story and may try to retell familiar ones; and they find out that books are created by people called authors and illustrators. Equally important is the emotional gain from literature. Through hearing books and poems read, kindergartners begin to experience the joys and satisfactions of literature, how what is written by others can be funny or sad or exciting.

During the kindergarten year some pupils will visit the school library media center and this can be a very important experience. In the center they will be introduced to many books and to the librarian, someone who will help them find the books they want and tell them about new ones. If there is no school library or if kindergartners don't go there, a trip to the local public library may be possible. You should have a permanent classroom book collection, of course, one that you add to regularly as a book is introduced to the class and then made available to them. It may also be possible to borrow books from a school district or public library collection and keep these in the room for several months.

LANGUAGE ARTS IN FIRST AND SECOND GRADES

Children in the primary grades are still quite young, so the principles of early childhood education apply to how they learn. Pupils of this age do best when classroom experiences have maximum meaning for them; much of what is done in the class should grow out of their interests and events close to their lives. They need opportunities to experience language in varied contexts and to use what they know in realistic situations.

Of course, developmental programming needs to be provided, teaching content that must be learned. But learning objectives will be achieved more successfully when specific concerns are embedded in activities that contribute to the pupils' education in several areas. First- and second-graders should not spend much time completing worksheets and answering questions for which there is only one acceptable response; such activities result in, at most, limited learning.

Young children benefit most from experiences that utilize various forms of communication—movement, drawing, and music, as well as all of the language arts. Spelling, writing, reading, handwriting, and speech are certainly important, but concern with teaching of specific skills must be balanced by activities that include

Additional suggestions regarding literature and stories may be found in Chapter 15.

Make efforts to see that each child has a card for the local public library.

Many activities described in Chapters 5 and 6 can be adapted for use with children in the primary grades.

attention to daily human experiences of a much more comprehensive type. If a class takes up the topic Our Fire Department, for example, they should learn about local government, fire protection, water pressure, and many other areas of knowledge. They might interview fire fighters or speak to other classes about fire hazards. They should certainly read several kinds of printed materials, learn new words, and do much writing. They might also paint pictures of fire trucks and try movement activities in which they pretend to be pulling hoses and climbing ladders.

The elements of the instructional planning guide presented in Chapter 2 have relevance for the following discussion of separate program areas. That is, developmental sequences should receive attention, but there should also be many opportunities for information processing as topics in social studies and science are explored and as other learning experiences develop. And, of course, writing activities and those in other language arts areas need to be regarded as fertile ground for embedded lessons of all kinds, for individuals, small groups, and the total class.

Language Development

Much that was said about kindergarten programs regarding language growth also applies to the teaching of first and second grades, but there are important differences. Once children enter first grade, for example, there are nearly always more restrictions on their behavior than there were in kindergarten. There will likely be fewer and shorter periods during the day when they can move around the room and talk with classmates. In many classrooms they will find that they are expected to remain in their seats and to speak only under certain conditions. However, teachers of the primary grades tend to be tolerant of the problems children have with following rules exactly, so restrictions are often not imposed rigidly. Although spontaneous language does gradually become less frequent, oral expression continues to be a prominent part of programs in the primary grades.

The average first grader knows nearly all of the words most adults use most of the time.

Discussion Activities. In the first and second grades, discussion activities should, to a large extent, be similar to those provided in kindergarten but should also reflect growth in the children's abilities. Sharing at the beginning of the day leads to discussion of the weather, school activities, community events, and children's personal experiences. Other topics for discussion might include behavior on the bus, proper ways to treat one another, and management of the room. Discussions might also center around learning experiences—talking about what trees need in order to grow and how they are used by people, for example.

You and the children can plan both total-class and group discussion sessions. The group settings will work better if the children have had a fair amount of experience in total-class discussion and have received guidance in how to have good discussions. An agreement should be reached about what the discussion is to accomplish, deciding, for example, which of two television programs is better for children to watch. Specifying a goal will provide a focus for the discussion and thus make possible a decision. It's a good idea to work out with the children some guidelines or standards that should be observed:

Speak loudly enough to be heard, but don't shout.
Give everyone a chance to talk.
Listen to what each person says.
Be polite when disagreeing.

Of course, there should be many opportunities for small-group and total-class discussions in connection with activities in social studies and science and as an important aspect of the children's responses to books that they have heard or read themselves.

Speaking. Related to discussion is the area of speaking. First and second graders continue to have some of the speech problems of kindergartners. You need to be aware of the common ones and of the importance of competent treatment. Refer to Chapters 5 and 16 for further information on speech.

Speaking before a group, which begins with "Show and Tell" in nursery school and kindergarten, needs to be continued in the primary grades. While the show-and-tell format is applicable at this level, it can be altered in terms of focus. During "sharing time," for example, when the entire group may be seated on a rug with you, individual children can tell about something that happened to them or what they will be doing. These accounts may refer to classroom events or those that take place outside of school.

Guidance is called for so that the sharing may be used to benefit each youngster. If Jimmy has brought a toy and simply wants to hold it up for everyone to see, questions must be asked about its name, how he got it, how he plays with it, and so forth. These questions help Jimmy and also demonstrate to the others what is expected when you are telling about a toy. When Taquita says, "I went to Tammy's house," classmates may be encouraged to ask what else they would like to be told by the speaker. This procedure not only promotes careful listening but also transfers to writing when children reach the point where they are sharing their writing with classmates.

Dramatization. Drama activities are important to language development in first and second grades, in particular as they relate to speech. The opportunities for such activities may be similar to those suggested for kindergarten, but additional ones will be appropriate because of the expanded curriculum. Dramatizations may also be suggested by conversations or situations that occur on the playground or in the classroom. For example, suppose children playing a game get into an argument about the rules. Later, the situation could be dramatized, and the children themselves could work out a solution to the problem. Naturally, the focus should be on discovering a better way to resolve the disagreement, *not* on placing any child or children in an awkward or embarrassing position. This will not happen, of course, if the classroom is one in which every child feels that he or she is an accepted and valued member of the group.

Formal dramatization with elaborate sets and costumes and long parts to memorize is not desirable at this level. If you wish to plan a program for parents or another group of children, keep the procedures minimal. Rehearsal will be needed, of course, but have only enough to establish some kind of organization. A few lines of speech to connect songs and dances usually works best.

Drama in the classroom is valuable because children are likely to feel more secure there and be willing to take more risks in their pretending. They can begin by dramatizing traditional stories (*The Three Billy Goats Gruff*) and scenes from favorite books (*Where the Wild Things Are*). Again, productions do not need to be elaborate. Simple props are sufficient to stimulate the children's imaginations. Puppets can also be used (as described in Chapter 5).

Vocabulary Development and Word Study. Consideration of words should have a prominent place in the language arts program of the primary grades. As with any other type of learning experience for pupils at this level, progress in vocabulary development is best accomplished through direct experiences that require the use of new words or those not completely understood. You should stress children's involvement with concrete materials—making things, solving real problems, painting murals, and doing science demonstrations. Meaningful activities such as these provide the most advantageous settings for learning new words and new meanings through actual use. Of course, good results will depend on your ability to introduce relevant words and to continue to use them with the class.

New words will also be learned from stories as you read aloud to the group. (This is one reason for using books that are several levels of difficulty beyond what most class members would be able to read on their own.) Study of words encountered in such reading should be voluntary, though; students with genuine interest in words will pick up vocabulary readily from the context. Discussions of stories will provide opportunities to use new words and consider their meanings, and at such times all members of the class will add at least a few items to their vocabularies.

In science, mathematics, and social studies and in discussions of the day's news there are numerous opportunities to introduce the names of things (*missile, hurricane,* and *sympathy*), action words (*elected, divide,* and *fertilize*) and words that describe (*rapidly, huge,* and *impossible*). Mention of such word categories (without yet using the terms *noun, verb, adjective,* or *adverb,* however) will be of some interest to the more able learners and will begin to lay the groundwork for the use of grammar terminology in the writing program of the middle grades.

With students in first and second grades you can, of course, provide charts on which interested class members can record words that they identify, "quiet" words, "sad" words, or "winter" words, for example. Words connected with various topics such as football, musical instruments, trains, and cats can also be listed on charts and reviewed occasionally.

Children can be encouraged to keep personal lists of words they have learned and want to use in their writing. This is their own "dictionary," which may simply be composed of blank sheets fastened together, with each page devoted to words beginning with a letter of the alphabet. This is not only a vocabulary and word list for reading but also involves spelling, the learning of alphabetical order, and the beginning stages of dictionary use. (Vocabulary, spelling, and dictionary use are all treated in Chapter 8.)

Listening. Listening is an important skill area in the primary grades, as teachers often ask children to pay attention while directions are given, materials are distributed, questions are asked, and discussions occur. Children are also expected to listen to films, to audiotapes and videotapes, to visitors, and to each other. Because of these varied expectations, listening should receive particular attention in the classroom program.

Vocabulary development may occur from:

1. making a mural
2. planning and giving a puppet show
3. discussing pictures
4. talking about news events
5. listening to stories
6. preparing an exhibit
7. interviewing visitors

The discussion of vocabulary development presented in Chapter 8 makes the point that students learn many words through their reading.

Shared reading can lead to choral reading and speaking.

You can further careful listening in many ways. For example, a story might be introduced by saying that it has funny parts or a surprise ending that should be listened for. With predictable books the children can listen for parts they know, joining in when they are ready. Reading a poem about rain can provide an opportunity to listen for words that make "water sounds." (Chapter 6 gives many suggestions for teaching listening skills, and some are appropriate to use in the early primary grades.)

The Alphabet and Alphabetical Order. At the beginning of the first-grade year many pupils will need the kind of alphabet-related experiences described as appropriate for kindergarten. As they recite the alphabet, look at ABC books, and make progress in writing, first graders will become more familiar with the letters.

Picture Dictionaries

The American Heritage Picture Dictionary (Houghton Mifflin, 1986)
The Macmillan Picture Dictionary (Macmillan, 1983)
My First Picture Dictionary (Scott, Foresman, 1987)
My Second Picture Dictionary (Scott, Foresman, 1987)
The New Color Picture Dictionary for Children (Children's Press, 1981)

Other activities are also appropriate. Large sheets of paper can be used to make a class ABC book, either before the children make individual books or at the same time. You may use any available wall space to post individual pages before they are added, one by one, to the large book. As the children bring in pictures whose names begin with a particular alphabet letter, they will be pronouncing the words and relating sounds to the letters. An activity such as this increases the children's feeling that the classroom belongs to them (You can be certain that Sarah, who pasted on the picture of a walrus, will always be able to find the *W* page!) and also adds color and interest to the room's appearance.

Alphabet books should be available in primary classrooms just as in kindergartens. You should select ABC books with more in mind than simply teaching letter names, alphabetical order, vocabulary, and phonics, though. Many are quite worthwhile as picture books. For instance, *Brian Wildsmith's ABC* could be selected on the basis of its excellent illustrations alone, as could *Animalia.* And *Q Is for Duck* introduces the letters through riddles (*A* is for *ZOO* because animals live in the zoo; *Q* is for *DUCK*, of course, because they quack).

A variety of activities can be devised to supplement books in the teaching of alphabetical order. For example, 26 cards, each with a letter of the alphabet on it, can be distributed to members of the class and then the person with the *M* asked to sit in a chair facing the group while those with the letters before and after *M* identify themselves and find their appropriate places on either side of that chair. The number of letters on either side can be increased to two and then to three or more in order to involve additional children and make the task more complex.

The individual word lists described in the section Vocabulary Development and Word Study, organized so that all the words beginning with the same letter are on the same page or on several pages grouped together, provide opportunities to use alphabetical order frequently. Looking through their list for *thermometer,* a word they need to spell, pupils know that it begins with *T,* so they first look for that section of the list. (Does *T* come before or after *G*?). Then they go through the *T* words (also getting some practice on word recognition). If there are so many that these have been alphabetized, there will be a group beginning with *TH* that must be looked at, focusing attention on the third letter. In such an activity, spelling, reading, and alphabetical order are all involved.

In some classrooms, particularly those in buildings where there are good library services, students in the primary grades will become involved in using the card catalog or other methods for finding books by a particular author or those on a certain topic. At these times they will also need to be helped to see how what they know about the alphabet may be used. Practice in using the class list of names, the telephone book, classroom dictionaries, and encyclopedias should also be provided to those who seem to be ready.

Primary-grade pupils usually enjoy using computer programs that provide alphabet-learning activities.

Handwriting in the Primary Grades

When children have experienced the kind of kindergarten program described in this chapter, many will come to first grade able to write their own names and at least some other alphabet letters. Usually what they do will differ somewhat from the letter forms and the procedures for making them that you are going to teach. Although it is advisable to work toward consistency among class members, with all writing done in a similar manner—preferably using movements that are economical in terms of time and energy—this can be overemphasized. Too much attention to the "one right way" at the outset can even cause a child who already writes to lose confidence. (One girl, who had been writing her name in capitals for over a year and was trying other words, stopped writing entirely when her first-grade teacher said that she was not using lowercase letters as taught and was making some of the uppercase ones incorrectly.) It is usually best to build on what the child already knows and can do.

Beginning Instruction. Direct teaching of handwriting commonly begins in first grade or even earlier. Encouraging children to write in kindergarten may, in fact, lead to the adoption of a rigid program of handwriting at that level (staying

Paper Position for Manuscript Writing

For manuscript writing, the paper is usually perpendicular to the front edge of the desk. Some teachers prefer an angle of about 10 degrees, however, with the top of the paper tilted to the left for right-handed pupils and to the right for left-handers. (See Chapter 9 for further discussion of handedness.)

between lines; trying to duplicate a model exactly). Even in first grade no instruction should be given until a child possesses the necessary muscular coordination, the emotional and mental maturity required for learning the skills, and the desire to try. Many of the experiences recommended for kindergartners in this chapter help to develop the needed conditions. In addition, it may be helpful for children who are less mature to have some practice in the basic movements needed for making letters: drawing clocks, stick figures, circles, various geometrical shapes, and so on.

Children are first taught printscript—more often called *manuscript writing.* One of the reasons for teaching manuscript rather than the *cursive* form of writing is that it is easier to learn than cursive, since only simple curves and straight lines are required to form the letters, and the configuration of letters in manuscript is similar to the print encountered in reading. You can provide instruction in manuscript while children continue to write in less than perfect ways in their journals and on other papers. Their writing of stories makes important contributions to their progress in reading and spelling; such a productive activity should not be interrupted while handwriting is stressed.

The teachers in a school must make several decisions with respect to handwriting instruction. The most notable of these concerns whether or not to use a particular method, since a program may include detailed teaching procedures that are not considered to be worth the time and effort required. Commercial materials need not be used, of course, although even language and reading textbooks often include sections on handwriting.

Published handwriting programs introduce manuscript forms in particular ways and prescribe how letters ought to be made. Some teachers also give their own directions: "The *n* is one hill to slide down, and the *m* is two." Although individuality in giving directions may be appropriate and expected, it is best if a second-grade teacher (or a teacher of a later grade) does not teach letter forms and ways of making them that differ from those first taught.

The most commonly taught manuscript style is the *vertical form,* which consists primarily of straight lines, circles, and parts of circles. Straight lines are usually made from top to bottom and circles from left to right. The pencil is lifted from the paper as a new line in a letter is made. There is also the *D'Nealian* (or *slanted*) *form,* in which letters are oval rather than round, slanted rather than vertical, and often have additional curves for connections with other letters. Most of the lowercase letters for this form are made in one continuous movement, without lifting the pencil. Advocates of this approach claim that it facilitates the transfer to cursive writing. On the other hand, continuous movement is more difficult, and the letter forms look less like print than do the vertical ones. Both of these types of manuscript alphabets are illustrated in the pages that follow.

The chalkboard is a good place to begin handwriting instruction, and some handwriting programs advocate it. There is space on the board to make large letters, which may be easier for some children (of course, children who have done a lot of writing on paper will not need to make such large letters), and corrections can be made easily.

Paper with lines is often used from the beginning in first grade, and this may be all right for those who have been writing in kindergarten. Many beginners need to concentrate on making the letter forms rather than on keeping between

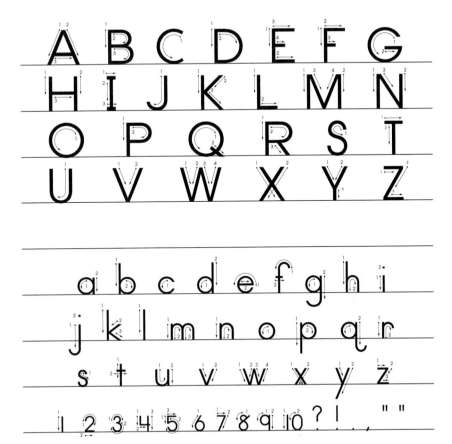

Zaner-Bloser Manuscript Alphabet

Used by permission of Zaner-Bloser, Inc., Columbus, Ohio. Copyright © 1984.

Follow the lead of the child. Don't ask her or him to use a particular type of paper unless it is clear that the necessary skills have developed.

lines, though, so writing on the chalkboard and on large pieces of unlined paper should precede writing on lined paper. As writing comes under the child's control, he or she will begin to align the letters and reduce their size; these are signals that paper with lines may be successfully introduced. Usually it is best to start with only a single line, something for the letters to "sit on." Just making the letters is enough challenge for some.

Pencils and markers of all kinds have generally been used by young children before they enter first grade. Therefore, large crayons or pencils may be needed by only a few first graders. Be as flexible about the writing instruments children want to use as about the paper they choose to write on.

Continuing Development. Handwriting must continue to be developed after the introduction of manuscript forms. You should enable your pupils to practice manuscript in meaningful writing experiences. In addition, you must teach it to those children who still require instruction; even some second graders

D'Nealian® Manuscript Alphabet

From *D'Nealian® Handwriting* by Donald Thurber. Copyright © 1987 by Scott, Foresman and Company. Reprinted by permission.

may not yet have learned all of the manuscript forms. Objectives for handwriting development in second grade should include the following:

- Refining manuscript ability: keeping the letters well rounded; making firm, straight lines; spacing letters closely and evenly within words; leaving a space between words; and orienting all letters to lines appropriately.
- Writing all the uppercase and lowercase letter forms correctly by the end of the year.
- Maintaining a consistently acceptable hand position: holding the pencil about an inch from the point, keeping the hand and elbow below the base line of writing, and keeping an air space under the wrist.

Of course, at the second-grade level, some teachers give instruction in cursive forms. See Chapter 9 for discussion of this.

First and Second Graders Doing Their Own Writing

Beginning in the first weeks or even days of the year, you may have your first graders draw pictures and write about them. If this activity was introduced in kindergarten, the children will easily continue to produce such writing. Those who have not had the opportunity before will do what kindergartners do: produce a few alphabet letters or perhaps their names or copy words visible in the room (*CRAYOLA*, for instance). Especially able pupils may make attempts to write

Writing is an excellent independent activity.

words and will carry out a suggestion that they put down sufficient letters to help them remember what they wrote. First graders who are practicing letter forms for manuscript writing, reading books with you, and listening to stories will make steady progress in their ability to write. Second graders who have had this background will produce very good results.

Collaborative writing by the class as done in kindergarten should continue in the early grades. The "Morning News" strategy is useful because children have something to say ("My aunt and uncle came to visit"), and you can record these items on chart paper for group reading aloud.

In first and second grades, writing matures if the purposes for writing and the process being used are given adequate attention. Certain types of writing are especially appropriate for children of this age—journals, stories, and their own books—although, as we will see, these do not always involve different types of writing but merely different formats. With proper guidance, regardless of the type of writing, the activity involves three stages, or aspects, of the writing process (discussed extensively in Chapter 10): **prewriting, writing,** and **postwriting.**

Journal Writing. In its simplest sense, journal writing means keeping some kind of record in a "journal," a place for writing that is the writer's own. For young children a journal may simply be a few blank pages stapled together, although spiral notebooks or other forms of bound paper are desirable. The objective is to encourage the children to draw and write in the journal regularly. Of course, children have to learn what a journal is for and how it should be used. Thus, you may need to set aside time to explain this kind of writing and to tell children that they may draw pictures and write about them in their journals.

Doing journal writing early in the morning works out well, since children usually come into school bursting to tell about the squirrel they saw, or their new sneakers, or a planned camping trip. You can respond by suggesting that such an event is something to be recorded in the journal—both sharing and writing should be encouraged.

After a few weeks some children will want to show their drawings and read their journals to others. You can easily make such reading a part of sharing time. There is no need to be concerned with handwriting and spelling because the children will be doing the reading themselves and will need only a few clues from their drawing and writing to recall the content.

Journal writing may involve all three stages of the writing process. In the *prewriting* stage the child thinks about what to write. For young children this is accomplished almost immediately, since the usual topics are themselves and their own activities. Their natural self-centeredness enables them to write unselfconsciously about friends, new toys, pets, and family events. In the beginning, much time and effort will be invested in the drawings, but by late in the first grade some

Correct spelling is of great concern to some parents. Be sure that you have explained your program and that parents know how to look for progress in their child's writing.

A Child Invents a Spelling for *snake*.

children may not want to draw before writing, and many second graders will be ready for prewriting activities other than drawing.

During the *writing* stage the child produces letters, words, and sentences with a proficiency that reflects her or his maturity level. Those children having difficulty spelling a word may attempt to spell it as best they can, ask a friend for help, or look for it on a word list or in a book. Every first- and second-grade classroom ought to have beginning dictionaries. If you spell words for children, you will be spending much time that could be devoted to other more helpful activities. However, if you do help with spelling, the words should be written on slips of paper and given to the children rather than spelled orally. (Such words then may be copied into their own word lists so that they can find them when needed again.)

Postwriting experiences for some children of this age may be similar to those described in Chapter 10. Most frequently, though, the postwriting stage for first and second graders consists of a child reading what she or he has written to a partner or to you or reading from their journals during sharing time.

Story Writing. A story often evolves out of the interests and experiences that children have written about in their journals. For example, Val's journal contains a great deal about her dog, Ollie, and she has also talked with you frequently about him. Thus, it is natural for her to decide to write a story about Ollie. The prewriting phase in this case has been fairly long and rich; Val has drawn pictures of Ollie and has written and talked about what he does. Additional prewriting activities may include bringing a photo of Ollie to school and talking with others about their dogs or other pets. Before Val begins to write, you might also suggest that she make a *topic web* to help her remember the things she wants to tell about Ollie. Children need help in learning to use this type of schematic diagram. You draw a circle and write *Ollie* in its center, adding several other circles around the

Common Invented Spellings

WEN
WR
GRIL
CLOS

Less Common Ones

FEEMAILS
STRUCKSHURE
OMOOSTE
VISTETER
SELAPERATE
PONIT
OWIS
FERSBYEE
UNICIL
DICIS
WOCHD
KCIINTS

In a small-group situation children read what they have written.

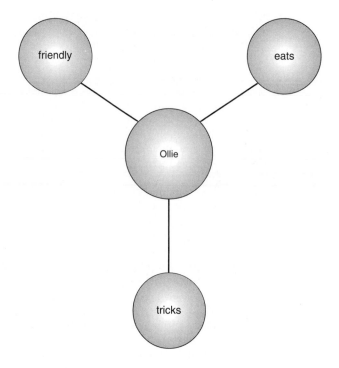

topic circle and connecting them to it with lines, while explaining to Val that she can write words in the surrounding circles to show what she wants to say about Ollie: what he eats, the tricks he does, how friendly he is, and so on. Later, when Val has developed the habit of making webs for herself, she will find them very useful in writing stories (see Chapter 10). Keep in mind, however, that a web (or *semantic map*, as it is also called) is not an end but only a means and should be used only to the extent that it supports the actual writing.

As Val's story evolves, the writing stage may require several days because there is so much to say. Again, the content is what is important. You should encourage her to get ideas and words down on paper without much concern for appearance. False starts are simply crossed out, and arrows used to show where something has been added to a sentence. Val should then be invited to read over what she has written, sharing it with you and classmates. Reading and discussion may cause her to think of more that she wants to write about Ollie.

In the postwriting stage, after Val has made some changes, she can read her story to others, including family members and even Ollie. She may also prepare it carefully, with attention to spelling and handwriting, so that it could be made available for someone else to read, perhaps in the form of a book.

Book Making. As an extension and refinement of story writing, making a book is a postwriting activity that can be very satisfying to children. Emphasis should be on the experience, so expectations should not be too high. On the other hand, if children are to become effective writers, they need to accept responsibility for doing their best. After a child's book is completed it may be read to the class, placed in the classroom library for others to read, or taken home. If it

Children enjoy reading the books they have written to adults, such as the principal.

becomes part of the library, a comment sheet may be placed in the back so that those who read it can give their reaction to the story.

Some children in kindergarten and the primary grades begin to use word processors to do their writing (see Chapter 9).

Additional Writing. Several other kinds of writing will be done by first- and second-grade students, including lists and charts having to do with classroom activities. Their work in other subjects will usually involve some writing, too. Some may want to do books on particular topics—dinosaurs, for example—and this ought to be encouraged. You should help them find and use informational books, as this is the beginning of study and research, important activities related to all facets of the curriculum. Other kinds of writing should be done, too, including poetry, responses to literature, and letters to be mailed.

Spelling. In the primary grades spelling is a part of the writing program and children learn much about finding the alphabet letters they need for writing a particular word. They may, for example, at some point think that *when* begins with *y,* and a little later that it is spelled *wn,* then *wen,* and, eventually, the accepted form is written. The sequence of development of children's ability to spell and ways of supporting such growth are discussed in Chapter 8.

In The Whole Language Catalog (p. 98), Kenneth Goodman discusses the cueing systems that operate in reading.

Reading in the First and Second Grades

Even at the beginning stages reading should not be thought of as a simple act but as a process involving three distinct systems that constantly interact: the **meaning system**, the **language system**, and the **letter-sound system**.

Dear dad,
I wold like
you to take
me Somwhere

Actsitcing

Love Kayce

A First Grader's Illustrated Note to Her Father

As when they listen to speech, young children expect reading to mean something, to make sense. Of course, the meaning derived from a nursery rhyme may not be the same as that understood by an adult ("Bad men pushed Humpty"). Children also derive their own meanings from environmental experiences—reading convenience-food logos as saying "hamburger," for instance. They also realize that the signs in their classroom provide important information about hamsters and the contents of cupboards. With regard to story reading they have begun to understand that stories have a beginning, middle, and end; that they have characters who get into difficulties or solve problems; and that by writing on paper meaningful content may be produced and read.

I have
to teach my brother how
to fish. How can I fish if I'm
teaching.

A Page From a Child's Book About Her Family's Fishing Activities

Altogether, such understanding indicates that reading activities for children, even at the beginning level, must necessarily stand the test of meaningfulness. When a program emphasizes phonics rules ("A medial vowel in a short word has its short sound"; "When *L* and *K* occur together, the *L* is silent") or the content is selected to use only a few words (*Oh! Oh! Look! Look!*) or words in a pattern (*The fat cat sat on the mat*), meaning is sacrificed. Children can learn to read in many ways, but an emphasis on meaningful materials offers a better possibility that they will grow up to enjoy reading fully.

It is English that is being read, so the child who has good familiarity with the language is at a great advantage. The child reading *The Three Little Pigs*, for example, is not surprised when there are references to *the first little pig, the second little pig,* and *the third little pig* rather than *pig number one, pig number two,* and so forth.

As discussed in Chapter 3, children who have grown up in an English-speaking environment have the language under reasonably good control by age three or four and understand how it operates. They expect what they hear and read to follow familiar patterns (this is part of making sense as described in the preceding paragraphs). Of course, they cannot discuss how plurals are formed, but they do know that car means one car and cars means two or more. When a well-informed person, even in first grade, reads about two cars being driven by small rodents the expectation is that, in the sentence *The red cars were being driven by two grey* _____ , the word will be *mice*. If "mices" or "mouses" is read the implication is clear: the reader's meaning system is operating well but there may be other difficulties.

Certainly, there are beginning readers whose dominant language system is not English, or not the school's kind of English. But no matter what kind of program these children participate in, they should have many opportunities to learn English. (See Chapter 16.)

The letter–sound system, usually referred to as "phonics," has been discussed in connection with kindergarten reading and primary writing and spelling. The alphabetic principle does operate in English but with many exceptions. Certainly there is enough consistency in the letter–sound system to provide help when the reader uses such knowledge in conjunction with the meaning and language systems. In the case of the sentence about the cars and mice, for example, the reader may be helped by seeing that the first letters of the word in question are *mi* and that there is no *s* at the end.

In a total language arts program such as that described in this chapter, the three reading-act systems have an opportunity to develop. An emphasis on meaning is reflected in a concern with literature and genuine discussions of real events. Children learn about English through extensive exposure to the language of books and the good example provided by teachers. As they write, children

Students enjoy reading the books that their friends have written.

begin to understand how sentences are put together and they also learn a great deal about the sounds of English and how these are represented by alphabet letters.

Components of Reading Programs

In the primary grades the reading program should contain the same elements as those identified as necessary for the kindergarten classroom. Pupils should hear much high-quality literature, including the usual stories, poetry, fables, and folk tales (see Chapter 15 for suggestions), and they should have access to the school and public libraries. There should be whole-class reading of big books, an enjoyable activity and one through which children learn to recognize words and gain practice in using the context of the material along with letter–sound relationships to read words they don't immediately recognize. They ought to have an opportunity each day to read books they have selected themselves, including class books compiled from writing done by the members of the class. And you should be sure that they have many experiences that involve talking and writing about what they have read.

Explain your classroom reading program in detail to parents. Send home a newsletter regularly, telling about class activities, children's favorite books, and other matters related to reading.

Program Organization

Just as there should be a writing time each day when pupils write in their journals, draft and revise the pieces they are working on, and make their books, there should be a reading period. It should be a large block of time and involve several activities. A possible schedule for a 55-minute period would be:

reading aloud by teacher	15 minutes
lesson	10 minutes
independent reading	15 minutes
varied activities	15 minutes

Reading Aloud.   As in kindergarten, literature selections to be read aloud to first and second graders ought to include favorites as well as newer titles. With these older pupils more complex books may be read (*chapter books,* with a portion read each day). You may read classics such as *Heidi* or *The Secret Garden* as well as modern stories like *Charlie and the Chocolate Factory.* The books should be more advanced in difficulty than those most of the children can read on their own, but there will likely be a few who will want to find their own copies and read along—or even go ahead. Occasionally you may want the group to discuss some event in the book or speculate about what may happen next, but care should be taken that analysis does not interfere with enjoyment.

Other material may be read aloud, too. Poems are a good idea, as are fairy stories, folk tales, fables, humor, adventures, and information books. Additional suggestions are presented in Chapter 15. These selections from literature can serve as departure points for drama activities as children portray favorite scenes. Also, hearing the language of literature will lead to growth in the flexibility of children's writing and to an increase in their desire to write.

Lessons.   Children will be learning from all aspects of the reading program, and much of this will come rather easily. There will be times, however, when you

Brief, specific lessons are best in reading—not more than a few minutes.

want to focus on something specific. For example, you may want to use shared reading of big books to show how an unknown word may be deciphered by using its first letters in conjunction with the context of the story and sentence. And you need to be aware of when learners could probably benefit from a presentation by you and discussion followed by practice. Some of this can be done with the entire class, because such matters as strategies for identifying an unknown word or seeing how an author develops a plot apply to reading at all levels. Occasionally, several students will have a particular need—seeing how some words are made up of root words with prefixes and suffixes, for example—and can profit from working on this together, so a small group is formed to meet for a few days. Much of what you cover in such lessons should be presented so that it easily transfers to the child's reading experience. What they can do with your guidance they can begin to do on their own.

Young children, often excluded from schoolwide activities, seem to particularly enjoy knowing that everyone is reading at the same time.

Independent Reading.   In many schools there are times during the day when everyone reads. These are often called SSR (Sustained Silent Reading) or DEAR (Drop Everything and Read) periods. Whatever the term, this emphasis on book reading is very important and should be thought of as part of the classroom reading program. At these times nothing occurs but reading. You should read as well, to demonstrate to pupils how important it is. You will find that some children need guidance in selecting books so that they do not become frustrated or remain fixed too long on one type of book, but most will use this time effectively to develop the fluency and love of reading that is so important. With a few classes the period of such independent reading will have to be brief at first (only a few minutes, maybe), and then it may be expanded as the students gain more experience.

Studies reviewed in *Becoming A Nation of Readers* found that children in reading groups often read only about six minutes a day. (Some watch TV six *hours* each day!)

Reading Activities.   All of this reading will generate the need for a number of other activities. Some of these will involve groups but these groups should not be permanent. (The existence of ability groups that meet daily for twenty minutes or so is common, but many teachers have reduced or eliminated use of them because of their negative effects on low-ability readers' self-concepts and the small amount of actual reading time they allow for pupils). Groups should be set up to accomplish specific purposes and then disbanded.

As individuals or as members of small groups, students should occasionally participate in a directed reading activity which you organize. Whether reading a story or informational content, students can identify and set purposes for reading, prepare for reading by drawing on what they already know about the topic or type of story, discuss what they expect to find, and then justify their positions by reading aloud from relevant text material. After demonstrating such strategies a few times, you can assist students by encouraging them to try these procedures in their independent reading.

Children can read to:

partners
small groups
classroom aides
senior volunteers
parents and others at home
older students from other
    classrooms
you
Some have even been known to read to the class's pet rabbit.

"Circles" of readers are groups created because of common interest in particular kinds of stories or a certain book. It may be, for instance, that several students have been reading "Clifford" books and would find it enjoyable and productive to come together to discuss this character and his exploits. It is their interest in dog stories that causes the group to form, even though the reading abilities of the group members vary. Such a discussion is a good way to provide the children with opportunities to do some oral reading, too. (See Chapter 5 for a related discussion of "readers' theater" activities that involve oral reading and drama.)

Group activity could also involve specific instruction in word recognition, summarizing what has been read, and other skill areas. (See Chapter 12 for further discussion of specific reading skills.) Practice materials may sometimes be needed for pupils who can benefit from systematic attention to specific strategies and skills, but you should expect to teach most such content as embedded lessons as children read material in which they are interested.

Individual pupils may also use the activity period as a time to record information in their reading logs, an aspect of their language arts portfolio described in Chapter 2. They should record titles of what they have read, their reactions, and descriptions of any projects they have carried out in response to reading. And, of course, you will want to hold reading conferences with individual students during this period, examining their logs, talking with them about what they have been reading, having them read for you, and making your notes and observations.

The schedule and content of reading periods will vary from day to day, and you should exercise judgment about what would be best for the class. If you are in a situation where you are expected to make use of a basal reading series, you can occasionally use basal activities as a developmental check to see how well your pupils are doing in a program intended for their grade level (a possible use of textbooks we discussed in Chapter 2).

EVALUATION IN THE EARLY YEARS

Use folders of children's writing as a departure point for parent conferences. They furnish much to talk about: interests, creativity, use of language, and improvement in handwriting and spelling.

The successful teacher of young children is constantly evaluating how well the program is functioning and also noting the children's progress in it. Development and learning in language and the language arts at the beginning levels in kindergarten and the primary grades lend themselves easily to certain types of assessment, much of which is very concrete. The quality of a program may be judged to some extent by simply examining the reading materials made available to pupils and the writing they are doing. If the only books are texts and the writing involves little more than completion of worksheets, this tells you a great deal about what goes on in the room. If the activities are more varied and the students are engaged in tasks that make use of content that has significant meaning for them, the message received is a much more positive one.

The progress of individual students becomes apparent from comparisons made of their performance over time. Especially useful in this respect are portfolios for each child containing samples of her or his products and indicators of performance. Examples of handwriting and story writing taken at monthly intervals reveal a great deal. A list of words successfully spelled during the year also provides useful information. A reading log of all books read and comments made about them is an excellent indicator in that area. Audio- and videotapes of story reading will help in assessment of growth in competence and fluency. Other tapes of oral presentations and dramatizations may also be available. Checklists demonstrating that speech and listening difficulties have been dealt with are helpful, too. Results of testing may be included as well.

A FINAL WORD

This chapter emphasizes interrelationships among the language arts, a holistic approach to teaching in the early years of the elementary school, and the central place of children's books in the classroom program. In the discussion of writing and reading we have stressed that both of these significant processes must be based on authentic classroom experiences growing out of activities that are meaningful to students.

Relationships among aspects of reading and writing are important for even the youngest students. When they write they draw on the language they have learned from listening, being read to, and having read themselves. When engaged in reading, children make full use of all the language experiences they have had, from their first experiences with environmental print and picture books to their own attempts at writing.

In the chapters that follow, we discuss each area of the language arts program separately, from speaking and listening to handwriting and spelling. We continue to emphasize the interrelationships among all of these, however, and the use of language abilities to learn in all areas of the curriculum.

References

Adams, Marilyn J. *Beginning to Read: Thinking and Learning about Print*. Massachusetts Institute of Technology Press, 1990.

Anderson, Richard C.; Hiebert, Elfrieda H.; Scott, Judith A.; and Wilkinson, Ian A. G. *Becoming a Nation of Readers*. National Institute of Education, 1985.

Barclay, Kathy D., and Walwer, Lynn. "Linking Lyrics and Literacy Through Song Picture Books." *Young Children* 47 (May 1992), pp. 76–85.

Clay, Marie M. "Introducing a New Storybook to Young Children." *The Reading Teacher* 45 (December 1991), pp. 264–273.

Cochran-Smith, Marilyn. *The Making of a Reader*. Ablex, 1984.

Cunningham, Patricia, and Cunningham, James. "Making Words: Enhancing the Invented Spelling-decoding Connection." *The Reading Teacher* 46 (October 1992), pp. 106–113.

Durkin, Dolores. "Testing in the Kindergarten." *The Reading Teacher* 40 (April 1987), pp. 766–770.

Dyson, Anne Haas. *Multiple Worlds of Child Writers: Friends Learning to Write*. Teachers College Press, 1989.

Fields, Marjorie V., and Lee, Dorris. *Let's Begin Reading Right*. Charles E. Merrill, 1986.

Fromberg, Doris Pronin. *The Full-Day Kindergarten*. Teachers College Press, 1987.

Goodman, Yetta M., ed. *How Children Construct Literacy: Piagetian Perspectives*. International Reading Association, 1990.

Hart-Hewins, Linda, and Wells, Jan. *Real Books for Reading: Learning to Read with Children's Literature*. Heinemann, 1990.

Hatch, J. Amos. "Improving Language Instruction in the Primary Grades." *Young Children* 47 (September 1992) pp. 54–59.

Hoot, J. L., and Silvern, S. B., eds. *Writing with Computers in the Early Grades*. Teachers College Press, 1988.

Jewell, Margaret Gree, and Zintz, Miles. *Learning to Read Naturally*. Kendall/Hunt, 1986.

Kagan, Sharon L. "Readiness Past, Present, and Future: Shaping the Agenda." *Young Children* 48 (November 1992), pp. 48–53.

Lamme, Linda L., and McKinley, Linda. "Creating a Caring Classroom with Children's Literature." *Young Children* 48 (November 1992), pp. 65–71.

Loughlin, Catherine E., and Martin, Mavis D. *Supporting Literacy: Developing Effective Learning Environments*. Teachers College Press, 1987.

Martinez, Miriam. "Motivating Dramatic Story Reenactments." *The Reading Teacher* 46 (May 1993), pp. 682–688.

Mayesky, Mary E. *Creative Activities for Children in the Early Primary Grades*. Delmar, 1986.

McGee, Lea M., and Richgels, Donald J. *Literacy's Beginnings*. Allyn and Bacon, 1990.

McVitty, Walter, ed. *Getting It Together: Organizing the Reading-Writing Classroom*. Heinemann, 1986.

Nebraska State Board of Education. *Position Statement on Kindergarten*, 1984.

O'Flahavan, John F., and Blassberg, Renee. "Toward an Embedded Model of Spelling Instruction for Emergent Literates." *Language Arts* 69 (October 1992), pp. 409–417.

Parker, Robert P., and Davis, Frances A., eds. *Developing Literacy: Young Children's Use of Language*. International Reading Association, 1983.

Raines, Shirley C., and Canady, Robert J. *The Whole Language Kindergarten*. Teachers College Press, 1990.

Routman, Regie. *Invitations*. Heinemann, 1991.

Salinger, Terry. *Language Arts and Literacy for Young Children*. Merrill, 1988.

Salzer, Richard. "Why Not Assume They're All Gifted Rather Than Handicapped?" *Educational Leadership* 44 (November 1986), pp. 74–77.

Schwartz, Judith I. *Encouraging Early Literacy: An Integrated Approach to Reading and Writing in N-3*. Heinemann, 1988.

Spodek, Bernard, ed. *Today's Kindergarten*. Teachers College Press, 1986.

Stahl, Steven A. "Saying the 'P' Word: Nine Guidelines for Examplary Phonics Instruction." *The Reading Teacher* 45 (April 1992), pp. 618–625.

Steffel, Nancy, and Swenson, Susan. *Inspiring Young Authors Year-Round: A Handbook for Teachers and Parents*. Treetop Publishing, 1989.

Teale, William H., and Sulzby, Elizabeth, eds. *Emergent Literacy: Reading and Writing*. Ablex, 1986.

Temple, Charles; Nathan, Ruth; Temple, Frances; and Burris, Nancy A. *The Beginnings of Writing*. 3rd ed. Allyn and Bacon, 1993.

Wolter, Deborah L. "Whole Group Story Reading?" *Young Children* 48 (November 1992), pp. 72–75.

Teaching Resources

COMPUTER SOFTWARE

Easy as ABC. Springboard Software, 1984 (five games to teach alphabet).

Kids on Keys. Spinnaker.

Kindercomp. Listening Library. (K–grade 3)

Letters and First Words. C and C Software, 1984 (identifying letters, letter sounds, simple spelling; preschool–grade 2).

Listen and Learn/Sound Ideas Series. Houghton Mifflin, 1986 (series of word-attack and comprehension disks; K–grade 2).

Picture Dictionary. D. C. Heath.

Talking Text Writer. Scholastic.

Tiger Tales. Sunburst Communications, 1986 (disks and guide; reading practice for individuals and groups; K–grade 2).

Write On! Humanities.

KITS

Alphabet Fun. Random House (four filmstrips and four audiocassettes; K–grade 3).

Basic Reading Skills: Reading Readiness. Society for Visual Education (six filmstrips, six audio cassettes, skill sheets, and guide).

Books Talk Back. Library Filmstrip Center, 1986 (filmstrip, cassette, and guide; K–grade 3).

Fable Plays for Oral Reading. Curriculum Associates.

Fairy Tale Plays for Oral Reading. Curriculum Associates.

New Goals in Listening. Listening Library (nine cassettes and guide; grades 1–3).

Ready to Read. Richard C. Owen.

VIDEOTAPES

Aesop's Fables. Society for Visual Education (with guide; preprimary and primary).

Animals in Verse. Society for Visual Education.

Fairy Tale Masterpieces. Society for Visual Education.

Four by Dr. Seuss. Society for Visual Education.

Readers of the Lost Alphabet. Greenleaf.

Sesame Street: Learning about Letters. Greenleaf.

The Story Book Series. Society for Visual Education.

Writing the Alphabet. Greenleaf.

OTHER RESOURCES

Chappel, Bernice M. *Listening and Learning*. Fearon Teacher Aids (games and activities).

Geller, Linda Gibson. *Wordplay and Language Learning for Children*. National Council of Teachers of English, 1985.

Live Oak Media produces videocassettes, books, and sound filmstrips related to the content of this chapter.

Activities for Preservice Teachers

1. Collect samples of the writing of children aged four to six. Compare these samples with the samples reproduced in *The Beginnings of Writing*.

2. Collect samples of the writing of children in grades two and three. Compare these with those you collected for the preceding activity and with examples in published handwriting books. Can you draw any conclusions from these comparisons?

3. Observe a reading group in a first- or second-grade classroom. What activities take place? What are the responses of the pupils? If a basal series is used, does the teacher follow the manual? What conclusions can you report to your class?

4. Visit a kindergarten or first- or second-grade class. Make notes on the differences you observe among the children in size, physical coordination, willingness and ability to express themselves orally, interest and ability in writing, and extent of vocabulary.

5. Do some manuscript writing yourself on chart paper, an overhead projector, the chalkboard, and paper on which you might write a note. Where do you need to improve? How fast can you write?

6. Collect pictures of objects that children can use in a variety of ways: to identify beginning sounds, to find words that rhyme, to practice vocabulary by making up descriptions, and to match images and the appropriate words.

7. Interview a speech therapist. Find out what the common articulation problems of young children are. Ask which of these are serious and what teachers might do about them.

8. Investigate commercial materials intended for use in grades one or two. The listing under Teaching Resources represents only a small sample of materials available for reading and language. Which materials do you believe to be good? Why do you prefer them? What criticisms of others do you have?

9. Investigate the use of computers in the elementary schools in your town or area. In particular, find out how often a child—any child in a class—can actually use a computer and for what purposes.

10. Observe a class doing the "Morning News," during which the teacher does chart writing. See how many opportunities there are for the inclusion of embedded lessons in speaking, listening, skills related to reading, and punctuation and capitalization.

11. Develop lists of words that will interest children in early primary grades. These may be words whose meanings they do not necessarily know (*jillions*) or ones they hear older students using (*dude*). Occasionally you will need to talk about the words that are not to be used in school. Most will know what you mean by the "S" word or the "F" word.

12. Start a file of ideas for dramatizing traditional tales such as *The Three Billy Goats Gruff* or *The Tortoise and the Hare*. Make flannel-board cutouts of the characters and try these with a child.

Activities for Inservice Teachers

1. Examine two or three reading readiness tests. What areas do they test? Using the list included in this chapter, note what they do not test.

2. Find a second grader who has not received much formal spelling instruction. Ask her or him to try some typical words from second-grade spelling lists and see what the results are.

3. Videotape a "Show and Tell" or "Morning News" session. Use it as a basis for talking about oral expression, listening, and other language arts areas.

4. Examine *Writing with Computers in the Early Grades* for some ideas about using word processing with this age group.

5. Plan a unit on a familiar topic, such as the zoo. See how many relevant children's books you can find, and use these as bases for various activities.

6. Describe steps that might be taken to help a shy child participate more in classroom activities.

7. Use poetry to stimulate children to think of good words to use for specific descriptions. Try such authors as Shel Silverstein and Lee Bennett Hopkins.

8. Regardless of the grade level you are teaching, have the children compose a group story with yourself as the scribe. What evidence do you find of the children's sequencing and organizing abilities? What else can you report about the experience?

9. Find out what is occurring in your school or a neighboring one with respect to writing and reading in the kindergarten.

10. Locate a basal reading series that uses selections from literature for most of its content. What has been used for the beginning levels? How well does it seem to work?

Activities for Children

1. A materials center, including such items as fabrics, crayons, clay, clothespins, and whatever else you have available, can encourage both creativity and language use. Children can make various kinds of objects that they then name or tell about, either orally or in writing.

2. Collect and make a variety of puppets and, with the children's help, make a puppet stage. The children can use these to do puppet shows whenever they have time.

3. Make available to the children several children's magazines and encourage individual children to engage in some of the activities suggested. Note the ones that most interest the children so that you may extend them.

4. Provide a writing center supplied with paper, pencils, crayons, and so forth, and encourage the children to use it. Each child should have his or her own place for storing whatever has been written or drawn. Visit the center frequently to assist children who want help.

5. Provide materials such as telephone books, encyclopedias, dictionaries, atlases, and other reference books for children to practice looking things up. Suggest topics the children can look for that are related to the ongoing activities of the classroom.

6. Individual children can look in magazines for words, phrases, and sentences to describe pictures that have been placed on a bulletin board. These can then be cut out and placed around the pictures.

7. Collect some of the alphabet books listed in this chapter—or others that you choose—and place them in a corner or on a table where they are readily available to the children. They will do their own exploring.

8. Individual children or small groups may make lists of words by categories. For example, a child might list all the food words he or she can think of. Or the category might be divided into lists of vegetables, fruits, and dairy products. Another child might list words identifying kinds of pets. Still another might list types of occupations. Lists can be exchanged, added to, talked about, and so on.

9. Find several versions of a well-known story such as *The Little Red Hen* or *The Gingerbread Boy* (see the lists in Chapter 3 for other titles), and make them available to the class. This should lead to group discussions about the different treatments.

10. Make it possible for children to create their own greeting cards to give to relatives and friends. This can be done by adding blank cards, half-sheets, envelopes, fabrics, or whatever is available to the materials in the writing center.

11. Some children who have become familiar with such patterned poems as *The House that Jack Built* may enjoy trying to create additional verses.

Chapter 5

Using Oral Language

Chapters 3 and 4 stressed the importance of oral language as the basis for the young child's learning of writing, reading, and the other language arts. Although early speech development is particularly significant, it is also important that children make steady progress in oral language competence as they move through the elementary school. To accomplish this goal, teachers should focus substantial attention on each pupil's production of speech and her or his ability to converse with others and communicate successfully in a group situation. This chapter addresses matters related to the effective use of oral language and relationships between speaking and the other language arts.

THE PLACE OF ORAL LANGUAGE

Most teachers provide opportunities for children to talk, knowing that this is the way language power develops and also recognizing that children have practical needs for speaking, both in and outside the classroom. However, evidence of wide support for the generalization "the good classroom is a quiet classroom" still may be found, and there are also classrooms where students talk a good deal but receive little guidance in learning appropriate behavior and attitudes.

A growing number of teachers recognize the contribution of oral language to children's success in attaining competence in the language arts and other areas of the school program. Of course, levels of language maturity are not *always* reflected in a child's (or adult's) speech, but the preponderance of research evidence indicates that they usually are. For example, Loban, in reporting his thirteen-year study, stated that children "superior in oral language in kindergarten and grade one before they learned to read and write are the very ones who excel in reading and writing by the time they are in grade six."

The relationship between a child's proficiency in oral expression and his or her personal and social development is significant, bearing on the child's potential for learning and affecting self-concept. Teachers have often noted that personality differences among children seem to be related to their oral language performance in group situations. An assertive child frequently assumes a leadership role in the classroom, possibly monopolizing speaking activities. Perhaps the child's assurance in speaking fosters this behavior, or possibly the aggressive personality provides speech confidence.

On the other hand, a shy, retiring personality could be associated with reluctance to speak out in some situations, or it may be that shyness has undermined his or her confidence in speaking. Cause and effect aren't easy to determine, but the fact that there apparently is a relationship between personality and oral language performance adds to the reasons for providing all students with much oral language experience. Surveys have shown that many adults fear speaking before a group; surely it is reasonable to assume that giving little—or haphazard and sporadic—attention to speaking situations during children's school years may well result in their becoming such adults.

As was pointed out in Chapter 2, the language arts program is best implemented in a classroom when *developmental, information-processing,* and *embedded-lesson* aspects of teaching and learning are all included. Oral language is, of course, already well developed when children first come to school (in many respects it has completed the most important phases of growth). But much remains to be done in such areas as speech improvement, social usage in conversations and discussions, self-expression, dialect, and so forth. Use your knowledge of the students to decide what is most important to emphasize. (Of course, you may teach several children for whom English is another language; this kind of situation is discussed in Chapter 16.)

Although it might not appear so at first, information processing is related in important ways to oral language. For elementary-school youngsters a strong relationship exists between understanding and talk. As children attempt to explain what they are seeing and thinking in mathematics, for example, they are clarifying their ideas and gaining insights into the subject matter. If you provide opportunities for them to talk and share with others, as in cooperative learning

The classroom that is rich in talk promotes learning in many ways.

activitities, you may be sure that students are learning more than if you were doing all the talking. Also, with a classroom program that emphasizes much oral language and presents many varied experiences you will have many opportunities to teach brief embedded lessons just at the appropriate time—when a group of students are preparing to do an interview or videotape a dramatic scene or when an individual is reviewing how well she or he did in presenting an oral report, for instance.

THE CHARACTERISTICS OF SPEECH

One fourth grade set the following standards for oral expression:

1. Don't talk too fast.
2. Speak clearly and loudly enough that everyone can hear.
3. Be sure that you know how to pronounce all the words.
4. Don't use too many *and*s.
5. Look at your audience.
6. Use good facial expressions and gestures.
7. Show your interest in what you are saying.
8. Try to look relaxed; don't fidget.

Skill in oral expression results from practice in the various situations in which an individual needs to speak. The instructional program, then, must provide many oral language experiences, and it must utilize these experiences to direct attention to speech skills, to behavioral attitudes and habits, and to content.

Naturally, *what* is said, the content, is of primary importance in any speaking situation. But effectiveness in communicating content is affected by its organization and development; by the vocabulary used; and by certain skills, including control and use of the vocal mechanism and use of facial and bodily expression.

Vocal Control

Effective speech is pleasing to the ear and is produced with ease and confidence. It is rhythmic and free from hesitations, repetitions, and interruptions. The tempo and volume are suitable to the content and the audience, and all sounds are clearly articulated and distinctly enunciated. To aid children in developing this kind of fluency the teacher must provide assistance intended to

- help each child to feel confident and secure in speaking situations
- help each child to identify his or her own areas of strengths and need
- help each child develop the desire to improve
- help each child learn to speak as clearly and distinctly as is physically possible

A child's emotional state is often indicated by voice **quality** (tense or strained), **tone** (angry or sad), **pitch** (normal or high), **volume** (unusually high or low), and **tempo** (speed). Youngsters who are upset, frustrated, angry, or worried often reveal their state in their voice. A self-reliant, alert child shows confidence by a pleasing voice. An eager, happy child is usually friendly and talkative. A diffident child who is emotionally and socially insecure is sometimes unable to achieve fluent, articulate speech. A child who is overly aggressive, perhaps because of emotional insecurity, is apt to speak in a strident voice and insist on monopolizing speaking situations.

You cannot, of course, be expected to solve all of your children's personal and social problems, but you can create a classroom atmosphere in which children feel secure and free to speak. You can provide many activities and experiences that encourage talk and, by your personal and verbal interactions with each child, build his or her self-concept.

One of the best ways to help children discover their individual needs with respect to pitch, volume, and rate of speaking is to record their voices and have them listen to the recordings. This can be done by means of audio recordings, but videotapings give better results. In a classroom where camcorders are used a great deal, there will be numerous opportunities for a child to view herself or himself in different situations. If a checklist is used (Am I speaking loudly enough to be heard? Am I louder than the other people? Do I seem to be speaking too rapidly or too slowly?) children can identify areas that require attention. (It is probably best to have individuals rate themselves or to let them do this cooperatively with a good friend. If others are involved the situation may become negative or appear threatening to the person being rated.) When a need has been identified, the youngster can use the camcorder frequently in practice sessions. An important advantage of videotape is that it may be edited to include several episodes over two or three months so that the student can look for evidence of progress. Such a tape may also be placed in the student's language arts portfolio.

Once made, a videotape can be used in several ways: as a basis for comparing later performance, a sample of behavior for self-evaluation, and a focus for conferences with parents.

Articulation

Children in the early grades sometimes do not articulate sounds clearly. This may be because of the retention of early speech habits, missing teeth, or eagerness in talking. Generally, such articulation difficulties are eliminated by the time children reach the middle grades, especially if teachers have been good speech models and the children have engaged in numerous speaking activities. However, some children may still have real problems in making particular sounds. The problems of these children should be brought to the attention of a speech therapist so that they may receive appropriate treatment.

Gestures and Bodily Expression

Children need to be aware that oral communication often includes more than speech. It is virtually impossible for a person to express herself or himself orally without using some body movements, which should be natural and in harmony with the speech activity and the content of the communication. Rhythmic activities, finger plays, and action verses used with younger children are both enjoyable and a means for developing harmony between speech and physical movements.

Lack of such harmony manifests itself in annoying mannerisms such as fidgeting, head jerking, hand twisting, and exaggerated facial expressions. The development of such mannerisms may be avoided if children have ample opportunity to engage in rhythmic activities and thus become more comfortable in a variety of oral language situations. In general, self-consciousness can be dealt with much more easily in the elementary school than at succeeding levels of the school system.

For a child in the primary grades the activity of showing an object while telling about it may relieve nervousness by taking the child's attention away from himself or herself. Similarly, the use of a map, chart, or some other object by a middle- or upper-grade child in giving a report may also encourage natural gestures and more purposeful body movements. Group and individual panto-

Showing aids telling in many different ways.

mimes, discussed in another section of the chapter, as well as creative dramatics, can also teach the value and proper use of gestures and movement. Of course, you are a constant source of modeling; just as you try to set an example in speech, so you should also be aware of your own use of facial expressions, gestures, and body movements throughout the school day.

ORAL EXPRESSION IN DAILY LIFE

Natural situations—the class discussing a trip, a small group working on a project, two or three children conversing—should be the basis for much of the instruction in oral expression. Genuine and meaningful activities that are truly concerned with communication provide the best opportunities for giving attention to specific speech skills, to behavior related to speech activities, and to the content of the speech. (It should also be kept in mind that, at such times, listening is receiving equal emphasis with speaking.)

Each school day will offer many such natural situations, since teaching and learning in every subject area require at least some oral expression. In virtually every chapter in this book you will find some reference to using language orally, with suggestions or implications for its teaching. As a result of such emphasis, we hope for some transfer of what is taught to life outside the classroom. Striving for conversational courtesy in school might even reduce the incidence of sibling quarrels at home!

Conversation

A responsible teacher shows interest in students by being available to talk with them when they first come to school in the morning and at other times during the day. Such "chatting time" should not be considered simply a courtesy, since these sorts of exchanges provide you with opportunities to establish relationships with children and get to know them in ways that are not possible through ordinary classroom activities. As an important principle you will find repeated throughout the text, we suggest that you have conferences with pupils about such mattters as their writing or the books they have read. These one-to-one sessions will be more valuable if based on a relationship that is well established through regular conversation.

> Children have a natural desire to move around and talk with friends. However, in schools both activities are usually discouraged.

Just as we enjoy talking with our colleagues throughout the day, children have a desire to communicate with their classmates. Rather than "shushing" constantly, teachers should recognize that conversations are natural, identify times when they are appropriate, and take steps to further their beneficial effects. Opportunities to watch for include the following:

- When a group of students is assembling to undertake a particular task, conversations that may or may not have something to do with that activity will be taking place, very likely.

> The most productive classrooms are neither very quiet nor very noisy—but somewhere in between.

- As the class changes from one activity to another or moves through the building, conversations will occur (this does not include shouting that disturbs other classes, of course).

- In specialized settings such as the library or art room, conversations should be permitted, as long as a teacher is not making a presentation and there is no other need to be especially quiet.
- The lunchroom is ordinarily a place where much conversing occurs. (In some schools there is too much emphasis on attempting to have quiet in the lunchroom.)
- Children visit with one another on the bus and the playground, while walking to and from school, and as they come into the room in the morning and prepare to leave at the end of the day.

Since conversations are to be expected and encouraged, you should find opportunities to discuss aspects of them with students. For greatest impact, use positive statements. Doing so will enable you to deal more effectively with quarrels among students, lack of courtesy, and even name calling.

For a conversational situation to be productive every participant ought to be friendly and responsive. A conversationalist needs to be attentive, too, so that he or she can react to what a speaker is saying, and those involved must be polite (even when angry) and tactful (especially when being forthright). A good conversationalist is also enthusiastic about what she or he has to say and about what others are saying.

It is important to remember that having a conversation is an activity involving some intimacy and that the necessary atmosphere is not easily created in a formal setting with a classroom group. A shy child who will not speak from his or her seat may find it easier to contribute in a conversational group of four or five children where it will be acceptable to talk at a reduced volume and where a feeling of security exists. However, even in a small-group setting it may be necessary to include one or more self-confident children to keep the conversation rolling and to foster the participation of the other children.

Some children absolutely will not speak up in a large-group setting. This is often related to cultural background.

Planning sessions can be times for genuine conversations.

How you operate your classroom, especially the emphasis given to small-group work and your conferences with students, will have a profound influence on the amount of genuine conversation that takes place and where this leads. For many pupils the progression is from conversations with you or a friendly class-mate, to participation in a small group, to more responsiveness in class, to making a brief oral report—the final result being much greater success in speaking situations.

Participation is a learning process.

Discussion

Classroom discussions are of several kinds, including cooperative learning groups, student and teacher consideration of problems in the operation of the room, book discussions, and panels talking about a topic with other members of the class as an audience. (Organization of book-discussion groups is described in Chapter 12.)

Discussion differs from conversation in that it ordinarily has a focus that was at least somewhat agreed upon in advance and an identifiable outcome as a goal (deciding if the class should publish a magazine or a newspaper, for example). Discussions are similar to conversations with regard to the need to take account of what others say, to be courteous, and to speak so that all can hear. A discussion does not always involve arguing, although disputes may occur. If you have given your students guidance in developing their conversational abilities, much of what you have done with them will transfer to discussion situations.

Discussions are an important educational tool. Through them children gain information, learn to stick to a topic, and gain practice in expressing themselves "on their feet." With your help, discussions can enable children to develop abilities in reasoning, critical thinking, problem solving, and expressing ideas orally in an organized manner—all significant goals for a language arts program. Also, as we point out in Chapters 10 and 11, thorough discussion in which an individual has many opportunities to formulate thoughts and express them is excellent preparation for writing.

The establishment of ground rules for a discussion is itself a useful activity for pupils. They can ponder the significance of questions about whether to have a discussion leader, how long the discussion will continue, how the time will be shared, and how interruptions and disputes will be handled. If the group is expected to report the results of its deliberations to the class, the question will arise about who will do that. It should be recognized that summarizing a discussion accurately and objectively are difficult and important tasks.

In assessing how well a discussion has gone, students might develop a checklist based on some of the points mentioned in this section:

How We Discuss a Topic

1. Everyone thinks before speaking.
2. Only one person talks at a time.
3. Everyone listens carefully.
4. Everyone gets a chance to talk.
5. We keep to the subject.
6. We are polite.

Did the discussion remain on the topic?
Was the time shared among the participants?
Could everyone be heard?
Were the participants polite to one another?
Were the results helpful?

If discussions are videotaped there will be opportunities to view the tape and point out instances where procedures went well and times when they didn't.

Individual participants can consider how they themselves were involved. (Some of what they see and hear will also apply to their assessment of their roles in conversations.)

Telephoning

Some teachers believe that, because so many children begin using the telephone prior to their coming to school, instruction and guidance in telephoning skills and courtesies are not necessary. To some extent this may be true; however, it is still likely that a moderate amount of teaching and reviewing will be worthwhile. Certainly telephoning is an activity that provides its own motivation and opens the way to numerous language arts activities. If possible, realistic situations involving the use of the telephone that arise either at school or at home should be the focus of teaching. Such authentic school activities might include telephoning the mother of a child who is ill to give information about assignments or class activities, phoning to make arrangements for an interview, using the telephone to ask someone to come and speak to the class, or calling to inquire about suitable dates for a trip to a museum or another place of interest.

Having a unit on using the telephone is sometimes a good idea since it stimulates interest and provides an excellent opportunity to address telephoning skills and courtesies. Ways of reporting emergencies and requesting assistance should be thoroughly rehearsed. (Refer to actual instances in which children have made life-saving telephone calls as examples of real-life situations.)

Telephone companies often have kits that may be borrowed for teaching. Such kits may include materials about using telephones as well as telephone hookups for the classroom. Because it is increasingly possible to buy telephones relatively inexpensively and because a good many children in the upper grades have strong science interests, some schools may be able to supply telephoning equipment themselves.

Announcements and Directions

Giving announcements has become a part of school life, and many schools broadcast regular opening announcements over a speaker system. In some buildings students make the schoolwide morning announcements, and there are many additional opportunities in classrooms for children to make announcements or give directions. Outside of school, children may make announcements at scout meetings, club meetings, and church events.

Announcements should be given in a clear, brief, and friendly manner. They usually have a "who, what, when, and where" format. Standards for announcements should be developed by the class, taking into consideration the recommended format and the manner of presentation. These standards can then be used as the basis for instruction and as a guide for the preparation and delivery of announcements by members of the class.

Children also have ample opportunity to give and follow directions during a school day. They may give directions for playing a game, participating in a scavenger hunt, performing a science experiment, or getting to their homes. Guidelines for giving directions should also be established by the class as a group; these should stress accuracy and sequence, as well as delivery.

The skills and abilities necessary for making announcements and for giving directions are similar to those needed in most oral language situations. The language used must be organized and presented in terms that will be understood by the audience. Acceptable language should be used, but the most important aspects are the conciseness and clarity of the message and its appropriateness for the particular audience. (Preparing the text of an announcement is a challenging writing task.)

Again, videotaping can be productive. A tape of "Morning Announcements" (an expanded version of the messages presented over the school public address system, perhaps) could be made by a group of students and then circulated through the building or to all the rooms interested in viewing it.

Debate

Debating is ordinarily considered a secondary-school or college speech activity. However, some children in the upper grades of the elementary school may be attracted to the idea of a "formalized" argument. If they are mature enough, doing the research that goes into preparing the arguments will be good practice in using reference skills and doing some careful thinking. (Local topics are usually best: where the new stadium should be located or whether the list of school clubs should be expanded.)

Debating calls for two children to present one side of the debate topic and two children to present the other. Each speaker makes a presentation and a rebuttal, with a time limit set for each turn at speaking. A debate is a good listening experience for the audience, too, as they judge whether points raised by one side are adequately responded to by the other.

Meetings

Intermediate-grade children are at the "let's form a club" age. When interest in such an organization is expressed, it may be time to teach parliamentary procedure. The name and type of a club should be chosen by the children. It is possible, for example, to have science, book, and hobby clubs all at the same time, with different members and officers. A fair amount of guidance will be needed, though, since children sometimes become quite cliquish within clubs and may become unnecessarily competitive or exclusive.

Interest in forming a club does not always mean interest in parliamentary procedure. At the time of starting a club, you may need to initiate discussion about the importance of operating it effectively and the contribution rules and regulations can make. Only a minimum of regulations should be used at first with, perhaps, the posting of a chart listing them. As the members become more experienced with clubs and meetings, they will likely become more interested in developing an understanding of parliamentary procedure.

Storytelling

Storytelling was mentioned in Chapter 4 and receives further attention in Chapter 15, but children should not only listen to stories being told, they should tell them, too. Storytelling is an activity they enjoy, both as tellers and as listeners, so it should be engaged in at all grade levels.

Children's first storytelling is usually the recounting of personal experiences, since storytelling is essentially an act of sharing. These first stories may be laced with both reality and fantasy, reflecting children's actual experiences as well as things they have heard about or seen on television. But even very young storytellers show a recognition that stories have a framework, although a teller's eagerness sometimes disguises this. Sketchy as such a framework may be, it does indicate that organization has begun to influence the child's thinking—an element vital to all communication, both oral and written.

These first experiences in sharing may be followed by your encouraging the children to tell stories they've heard and liked and, later, ones they've read. The telling of these will incorporate story beginnings and endings, characters and settings, and story lines—again, aspects of composition. As important as this foundational activity is, however, the major reason for encouraging children to tell stories should be the enjoyment they will gain from both listening to a good story and being able to tell one—a joy that may be experienced throughout life. And, of course, telling stories leads directly to writing them.

Storytelling is more informal than most other forms of expression, but the speech abilities needed are those required for all speaking activities. Listening to and watching an adult who is a good storyteller will help children to see the advantages of using voice tone, gestures, and facial expressions. But experience is still the best teacher: children must practice the skills for oral interpretation and the techniques for holding an audience.

Group reconstruction of a story that has been heard can be preparation for group writing of a story.

Riddles and Jokes

When children are about seven years old, they develop a real interest in telling jokes and riddles. This interest can be exploited in building oral language skills. Begin by having joke and riddle books in the classroom library and occasionally reading a joke or riddle to the class.

A bulletin board composed of riddles and jokes attracts lots of attention in the classroom. One paper star with a question on it can be superimposed on a second star on which the answer is written. The two stars can be taped together so that the answer is not revealed for a few days while people try to solve the riddle or come up with the punch line. The bulletin board title might be "The Answer Is in the Stars" or "The Stars Know—Do You?" Possible questions and answers include:

What did one wall say to the other? Meet you at the corner!
What is black and white and red (read) all over? Newspaper!
What can go up the chimney down but can't go down the chimney up? Umbrella!

Another display might be made of "knock-knock" jokes. The cutouts can be of doors, with the words *knock-knock* on the outside and the rest of the joke inside, perhaps on successive pages: *"Who's there?"* "Tank." *"Tank who?"* "You're welcome!"

After a bulletin-board display has been made and used, the children have listened as you read jokes and riddles, and they have looked at the joke and riddle books on the library table, they should be sufficiently motivated to want to tell jokes themselves. A class discussion must be held to establish rules for telling

Books Children Will Enjoy

Beastly Riddles: Fishy, Flighty and Buggy by Joseph Low (Macmillan, 1983)
Monica Beisner's Book of Riddles (Farrar, Straus and Giroux, 1983)
Too Hot to Hoot: Funny Palindrome Riddles by Marvin Terban (Clarion, 1985)
Unriddling: All Sorts of Riddles to Puzzle Your Guessery by Alvin Schwartz (Lippincott, 1983)
What's Gnu? Riddles from the Zoo by Thomas Mase (Lerner, 1991)
Wing It! Riddles about Birds by Scott Peterson (Lerner, 1991)

jokes and the types of jokes to tell. The discussion may be used to bring out the point that jokes should never hurt another person's feelings or make fun of someone in any way. Children may want to tell jokes about nationalities, races, or religions because they have heard their parents or friends tell them and know that people have laughed. A child may say, "My dad tells jokes about _____ all the time." There is no good answer to this; certainly jokes about nationality, race, and religion are told. Perhaps you might say that adults sometimes see things differently (children should certainly agree with that) and suggest that you might laugh at a joke about teachers when told by another teacher but be very hurt if it was told by one of the children in the class. In short, avoid even implied criticism of a child's family or friends, but reemphasize that a joke should not be harmful. If interest is present and the class sufficiently mature, you might even go into the changes that have taken place in comedy—the disappearance of the blackface comedian, the lazy servant, and the Irish cop, for example.

From the class discussion, lead the children to set up rules for telling jokes. Following are some examples:

1. Tell the joke or riddle to the teacher first to be certain that it is a good joke for the class. (Children do not always realize that a joke without offensive words may still not be appropriate.)
2. Look at the audience when telling a joke.
3. Know the order in which events happen in the joke so you don't have to say, "No, wait a minute; I forget; let's see—ah—then . . . "
4. Don't laugh at your own joke until you have told it.
5. Remember the punch line. Use your voice to lead up to the punch line, and then deliver it quickly.

One way to begin is to let the children take turns telling jokes or asking riddles as a part of the daily sharing time. Later, consider extending the class time for telling jokes and riddles to a program for parents or another class or several classes. Humorous songs might be included, too. For such a program each child in the class might dress as a clown or wear some other costume.

The telling of jokes and riddles is a good way to develop many oral language skills. It is especially useful with children who have negative attitudes toward school and learning, since it will develop interest and may persuade them that school can be fun. Telling jokes and riddles also encourages reading development, as children turn to books to find new ones. For a child to remember a joke it is essential that he or she comprehend and remember what was read and understand the sequence of events. Even children with poor attitudes toward reading will happily read a book of riddles or jokes.

Oral Language and Social Behavior

It is not enough to be able to speak at a functional level in order to get along in society; good manners and courtesy are needed to create and maintain an atmosphere of good will. Discussion of these matters with your students will go a long way toward establishing a productive climate for life in the classroom. Establishment of a minimum number of rules and ways of operating can easily grow out of such discussion. (The process might well begin with small-group sessions, with reports to the total class as described in the Discussion section of this chapter.) When students have a significant role in deciding what behavior guidelines will be adopted in the room, they are more likely to remember what these are and accept them.

Classroom courtesy ordinarily covers such matters as who can speak and when, how much latitude students have in moving around the room, what happens when one student interferes with the productive activity of another, and so forth. Determining what regulations relate to certain situations and whether or not a rule has been violated are all matters for discussion and resolution. It is important that students learn to negotiate in ways that do not involve loud and abusive language, and it is part of your responsibility to encourage courteous behavior, not only in the room but throughout the school, in the lunchroom, on the buses, on field trips and even at times when students are not under the supervision of the school.

Stress on mutual respect and nonabusive language will help to create a positive classroom atmosphere.

Certain forms of behavior—called *manners* or *social amenities*—involve common social interactions such as extending and responding to greetings, making requests of another, apologizing, expressing thanks, and making introductions. It is worthwhile to give these matters attention in school in order to support and reinforce whatever has been taught in the home. Polite behavior and manners are best taught as rehearsals for occasions when they will be needed.

Students may need to practice being pleasant and civil to one another.

In making introductions, for instance, children should learn to say "Mrs. Smith, this is Sue," or "Mary, I'd like you to meet Jimmy." The first name mentioned should be the person honored—an older person or a special guest. Children should also learn how to respond ("I'm very glad to meet you, Sue," or "How do you do"). Encourage them to shake hands firmly (but not too firmly) and to look at the person they are being introduced to.

Once students have been taught about the conventions of polite behavior, practice is best accomplished at the time of genuine occasions that arise in every classroom. For example, visitors who come into the classroom may be greeted by a room host or hostess, who introduces them to the teacher and the other children. Valuable practice for older children can also occur during an open house, parents' night, or similar occasion. Useful guidelines about introductions are to

- Speak each person's name clearly (if a name is not understood, see that it is repeated).
- Use an introduction to start a conversation, with the person making the introduction beginning the conversation.
- Be certain to give your name clearly and add some identifying remark when introducing yourself to someone else.
- Speak the name of a person to whom you are introduced and use it when speaking to him or her to help remember it.

Other social situations to discuss with children include the following:

- What can be said to make a new classmate feel welcome?
- What should be said in awkward situations, when, for example, a boy must thank his aunt who has given him a shirt he thinks is ugly? What can he say about the shirt without fibbing or hurting the aunt's feelings?

- What might be said and done if a group of children are playing ball and notice some strange children watching?
- Suppose you are having dinner at a friend's house. What do you do and say after dinner?
- What do you say if you want a person to sit in a particular place?
- A friend invites you to a movie but you know that you cannot go. What do you say?
- What are some situations in which you should offer assistance? For example, in removing a coat, what do you say?
- If you must interrupt someone who is talking, what do you say?
- Suppose the teacher asks, "Who discovered America?" and a child replies, "George Washington." Is it polite to laugh?
- How do you respond to courtesies shown you?
- Someone knocks at the door when your parents aren't at home, and they have told you not to let anyone in. What should you do?

Again, the videotape recorder will be useful as students rehearse such situations, view the results, make some changes, and then rerecord.

ORAL LANGUAGE: GROUP EXPERIENCES

Oral language is not only functional but it is also beautiful and expressive at times, and the classroom program should provide opportunities for children to enjoy various forms of speech production. As with any creative activity it is the process that is important—what the participants learn about life and themselves. It is also possible to learn from the process of making something so good that you want others to see only the finished product; having your students perform for an audience occasionally is worth considering, even though those invited might be limited to families and students from another class.

Choral Speech

Group singing, recitation, and reading possess qualities that make them highly important and enjoyable human activities. Group rendition of chants, songs, and prayers have been significant aspects of culture for thousands of years, supplying the kinds of experiences that bind people together, especially in nonliterate societies. With reading and writing came additional opportunities for reading poems and prose together for social purposes.

Prose. Texts of various kinds may be used for group recital and choral reading. The first prose that children memorize will usually be in the form of the pledge to the flag or prayers. Some young children learn favorite story books "by heart" and can join in a rendition of *The Three Little Pigs,* at least on the huffing-puffing sequences. Other youngsters can be encouraged to learn passages from the Bible or other books that are important to them.

After they have learned to read well, children can do some group reading of prose. There may be some value in having them read important documents or famous speeches aloud and in unison: The Preamble to the Constitution, The Gettysburg Address, Martin Luther King's "I Have a Dream" speech, for example. Such reading may impress upon students the important values expressed in these materials and encourage them to memorize the entire statements or portions of them. Also, all of this will be exposure to some examples of the majesty of the English language.

Chants and Raps. Chanting has always been done by children—often as accompaniment to such play activities as jumping rope (*Teddy Bear, Teddy Bear, Turn Around*) or similar vigorous and rhythmical movement of the body. Other types of chanting include sports cheers (*Go Team Go, Go Team Go*) and work chants (*Yo, Ho, Heave Ho*), again with appropriate body movements. Raps are usually rapid chants with strong rhythmical support from instruments or sound synthesizers and some rhyming pattern (*I like it here at Watson School/ No one treats me like a fool/ And that's the way I want to live*). Reciting raps and chants readily leads to performances and to the children's writing of their own versions.

Poetry is discussed in Chapters 11 and 15.

Songs and Poetry. Many poems (*Battle Hymn of the Republic*) have been transformed into songs and some songs (*Sunshine on My Shoulders*) have lyrics that can stand as poetry. Clearly, there are close connections between songs and poems. Singing is a very important activity in the elementary classroom and should be done frequently and in addition to any separate class in music that may be scheduled. (If you are not especially musical, aids such as audio- and videocassette recordings of children's favorites are useful.) Singing together helps to create a positive group atmosphere and provides opportunities for language arts experiences (writing new verses for well-known songs such as *She'll Be Coming Around the Mountain,* for example).

Poetry should also have a prominent place in the classroom program, and one way to encourage this is to have group recitations of appropriate selections. Young children begin with nursery rhymes they have memorized and then go on to shared reading of big books that have also usually been committed to memory by most of the class. As they move through the primary grades, children can do choral reading of short poems and then, as they grow older, longer and more complex ones.

A poem such as *Poor Old Woman* (it's a song, too) appeals to children because it can be done in several different formats, with the entire group reciting or reading it or different small groups or individuals taking responsibility for various parts. When introducing this poem to the class, you can make it more appealing by displaying pictures of each thing that is swallowed. Used to make a delightful bulletin board, these pictures can sharpen imagery and highlight meanings.

POOR OLD WOMAN

(slowly and deliberately):

SOLO:	There was an old woman who swallowed a fly.
ALL: *(dramatically)*	Oh, my! Swallowed a fly!
(slowly)	Poor old woman, I think she'll die.

SOLO:
(slowly)

There was an old woman who swallowed a spider.
Right down inside her, she swallowed a spider.
She swallowed the spider to kill the fly.

ALL: *(dramatically)*
(slowly)

Oh, my! Swallowed a fly!
Poor old woman, I think she'll die.

SOLO:
(said in an aside)
(more quickly)

There was an old woman who swallowed a bird.
How absurd to swallow a bird!
She swallowed the bird to kill the spider,
She swallowed the spider to kill the fly.

ALL: *(dramatically)*
(slowly)

Oh, my! Swallowed a fly!
Poor old woman, I think she'll die.

SOLO:
(slowly and deliberately)

There was an old woman who swallowed a cat.
Fancy that! Swallowed a cat!

ALL:

She swallowed the cat to kill the bird,
She swallowed the bird to kill the spider,
She swallowed the spider to kill the fly.
Oh, my! Swallowed a fly!
Poor old woman, I think she'll die.

SOLO:
(as if telling a secret)

There was an old woman who swallowed a dog.
She went the whole hog! She swallowed a dog!

ALL:

She swallowed the dog to kill the cat,
She swallowed the cat to kill the bird,
She swallowed the bird to kill the spider,
She swallowed the spider to kill the fly.
Oh, my! Swallowed a fly!
Poor old woman, I think she'll die.

SOLO:
(slowly and carefully)

There was an old woman who swallowed a cow.
I don't know how, but she swallowed a cow.

ALL:
(with increasing momentum)

She swallowed the cow to kill the dog,
She swallowed the dog to kill the cat,
She swallowed the cat to kill the bird,
She swallowed the bird to kill the spider,
She swallowed the spider to kill the fly.

(slowly and deliberately)

Oh, my! Swallowed a fly!
Poor old woman, I think she'll die.

SOLO:

There was an old woman who swallowed a horse.

ALL:

She died, of course.

Drama

Plays: The Drama Magazine for Young People is available from this address:
120 Boylston St.
Boston, MA 02116

Drama is storytelling by people who perform for their own enjoyment or for an audience—either in person or indirectly through electronic transmission. Oral language is involved, although sometimes there is minimal speech, and pantomime may be thought of as drama. Most children very much enjoy being a part of a dramatic production, whether it is a pantomime, a play, or one of the several other forms. Drama promotes personal and social growth among children. Some of the benefits are

Dramatize moods and reactions—surprise, excitement, happiness, sorrow, pain, and so forth.

- using imagination and creative thinking to explore ideas and feelings
- helping students to gain self-confidence
- encouraging participants to experiment with their modes of expression, including body movements as well as tone of voice, rate of speech, and so forth
- gaining better understanding of others by pretending to be someone else

Pantomime. Pantomime, or just "mime," is communication without speech (although narration may be done simultaneously). It is included in this chapter because much oral language is used in discussing pantomime before and after it is done. Mime follows rather naturally and easily from the creative play and beginning dramatization described in Chapter 4. Familiar experiences are easy for children to mime. They may imitate a parent driving a car, caring for a baby, or watering the lawn. Producing facial expressions for someone who is happy, frightened, angry, or surprised is another useful exercise.

In pantomime the entire body is brought into use when students pretend to be a rag doll, a marching toy soldier, a monster, or a tree on a windy day. Such full body movement, often in conjunction with music, might be used to portray a science process, as when seeds sprout, send out their first leaves, and then grow into fully developed plants.

Pantomime activities may also be used to develop sense awareness. A child might pretend to put a foot into a pail of ice water or might look at an apple with anticipation of its good taste, take a bite and chew it—only to find half a worm! Another could mime smelling something bad and then finding the source on her or his own shoe or waking up to hear scary noises in the night and then discovering the cause.

Mime activities provide good opportunities for thinking and talking as children suggest possibilities and then discuss what might be done and how problems could be dealt with. A full-length mirror is useful for working out the plan and rehearsing. Videotapes help to show how the development of a sequence is progressing and viewing the final outcome.

Pantomimes to try:

opening birthday presents
playing a video game
getting dressed in the morning
diving from the high board
practicing the violin
wrestling with an alligator
eating spaghetti
roller skating
walking an unruly dog

Puppetry. Most children are quite familiar with puppets on television but have not used them much themselves. Manufactured puppets abound, but there is value in having the children make their own. Making puppets and putting on a puppet show are excellent creative experiences that also teach children to follow directions and find new ways to use their language abilities. Students will probably need assistance in using puppets, but they will enjoy the experience immensely. When making puppets, start with simple ones and then move on to more elaborate types.

Stick puppets are easily created by making a face or figure and fastening it to a foot ruler or similar piece of wood. Children may then use the stick for a handle as they hold the puppet. The face or head may be as simple as a paper plate with eyes, nose, and mouth drawn on it and yarn or colored paper attached for hair. Puppets can be clothed with either cloth or paper. Old wallpaper, leftover gift wrappings, or even colorful shelf paper can be useful for making attractive paper clothes, and remnants or scraps of cloth can provide materials for cloth garments.

For puppet information, write
  The Puppet Place
  245000 Glenwood Highway
  Los Gatos, CA 95030

Styroform Stick Puppet

Paper Bag Puppet

Sock Hand Puppet

Box Puppet

Using puppets is fun and helps develop speaking skills.

Empty-bag puppets involve the use of small paper bags. Children can make and use empty-bag puppets if the bags are not too large for them to handle. Place the bag flat, with the folded bottom part up. Draw or paint the upper part of a face on the bottom of the bag, and the lower part of the face on the side. If you want the puppet to have a moving mouth, the upper part of the mouth should be on the bag bottom, and the lower lip on the side. If the eyes are to move, the lashes should be on the bottom, with the lower part of the eyes on the side. Yarn, crepe paper, or cotton can be glued on for hair. The puppet is operated by placing fingers in the bag so that the folded-down bottom can be moved up and down to move the mouth (or eyes, eyelashes, or eyebrows).

More complex puppets can be made by older students, using socks with buttons sewed on for eyes and with crayons or paint used to make other features. Also, the stuffed-bag puppet is a modification of the empty-bag puppet. The bag is filled about halfway with crumpled paper. (This simply fills out the bag, which is used in about the same way as for empty-bag puppets.) If the bag is large, it can be partly drawn together with a string so that the bottom represents a neck and shoulders below the face; then other bags can be added to form arms and legs. These stuffed-bag puppets can be decorated or dressed to achieve delightful effects.

A puppet stage of some sort will be useful. Of course, hand puppets are good for storytelling, getting children's attention, and just talking, but to get full value from the puppets children make, dramatization is needed.

The puppet stage should be inexpensive and easy to make. Tip a card table on its side; the children can sit behind it and raise puppets above the table edge.

A large box or carton—the kind refrigerators or stoves are shipped in—also works well. Part of a side is cut out and the part visible to the audience is painted. The children sit inside and raise their hand puppets to the "stage floor" level.

Almost any situation can be dramatized with puppets. They can be used to:

- deal with common problems at school or home—handling conflicts, completing tasks, and so forth. Children write their own scripts and operate the puppets
- demonstrate appropriate behavior in social situations
- dramatize traditional stories (*The Three Bears* or *Hansel and Gretel*)
- perform some of the scenes typical of *Sesame Street,* using the familiar puppets
- have a puppet zoo or circus

A problem with puppet performances is that the children actually operating the puppets cannot see the results of what they have done. Use of a video recorder preserves a record of the show so that they can view it.

Readers' Theater. Readers' theater involves oral reading of poems or other texts. Individuals perform alone or members of a group collaborate to read a play or other material requiring several participants. The reading may be done simply for enjoyment or for a listening audience. Readers' theater also lends itself to recording on audiotape, since it is very much like a radio broadcast.

The readers' theater approach has several important features. First of all, there is no necessity to memorize lines; those involved simply practice reading until they reach a satisfactory level of proficiency. Much reading is encouraged as children search for appropriate materials, and they thus become acquainted with a variety of types of literature. Also, learning in other subjects can be furthered when content is adapted for a readers' theater experience (a radio commentary from undersea explorers). Imagination and listening both receive attention as students consider making revisions to the text being used and their manner of presenting it.

Readers' theater activities should be selected according to what is appropriate for your class. Plays specifically for children may be located (a librarian is a good source of suggestions), or scenes may be written based on real events or sequences from popular books such as the *Little House* series by Laura Ingalls Wilder. Taking a tale such as *Stone Soup,* adapting it for readers' theater, and adding a narration can be a very productive language arts activity, with thinking, writing, reading, listening, and speaking all significantly involved.

Readings may be done in the classroom, with or without audio recording. When an audiocassette recorder is available, readers can rehearse, record, listen, make changes, and record again. For best results taping needs to be done in a quiet setting. The production may be enhanced with music and sound effects, of course.

Readers' theater activities may be repeated with different casts so that all students have the opportunity to read any part. Practice with different voices will enable anyone, boy or girl, tiny or big, to pretend to be the giant in *Jack and the Beanstalk* or the fairy godmother in *Cinderella.*

Plays. Plays involve actors who memorize a script and perform a scene or series of scenes that tell a story or part of one. Often the actors have costumes

Children's Story Scripts are available from
   Baymax Publications
   2219 W. Olive Ave.
   Suite 130
   Burbank, CA 91506

Children who have had the opportunity to be in plays or other productions remember those experiences all their lives.

and there is a stage with furnishings. Only occasionally—once a year, perhaps—will it seem appropriate for elementary-age children to become involved in a full-scale play.

There have been short plays written especially for elementary students, though, and, because they require less preparation, these can be done in the classroom occasionally. (In many cases the plays appropriate for readers' theater activities can be used.) As with readers' theater, students may develop their dramatic version of well-known stories such as *Charlotte's Web.*

Again, roles should be performed by different children so that all have varied opportunities, and there should be no parts reserved for either boys or girls. Video recorders may be used to assist children in practicing their parts. Also, a video record of a play may be made so that it can continue to be enjoyed from time to time.

Creative Dramatics. Creative dramatics involves many types of activities, including the dramatic play of young children pretending to be zoo animals and the movement and gymnastics experiences offered in physical education classes. In some situations it is possible for classroom teachers and specialists in physical education and music to cooperate in a comprehensive program of dance, drama, and music to provide the students with many valuable creative experiences. For instance, a unit on Ancient Egypt might have a sequence on the building of pyramids that would involve music, movement, drama, and other ways of interpreting and expressing what occurred thousands of years ago.

Situations that may be dramatized:

- introducing a parent to a school friend
- introducing one friend to another
- a parent introducing her or his child to a guest
- introducing oneself to a stranger
- introducing a visitor to the class

In the classroom creative dramatics may involve several less comprehensive types of experiences, including role playing, improvisation, and interpretation. As was mentioned in the discussion of courteous behavior, children can role-play situations that they are likely to encounter in real life. In addition, they can take the role of one person in an argument or other realistic situation and act out what might happen (no script is provided; they must decide what to say by working it out).

Improvising in the classroom usually involves providing several children with some objects and asking them to devise their own story using the materials and then dramatize it. Children might be given a stuffed dog, a cow bell, a red tablecloth and a balloon, for example, and asked to devise and present a story for the class. Interpretation is likely to involve spontaneous movement and vocalization in response to some stimulus such as watching dolphins at an aquarium, listening to *Carnival of the Animals,* hearing a ghost story, or touching a large piece of sculpture.

ORAL LANGUAGE AND LEARNING ACTIVITIES

Close connections exist between language and thinking. As children discuss concepts and ideas and formulate what they wish to say about them, they are putting their thoughts in order. They use many different sources as they collect information, and they express their ideas through various media. Oral language is important in all the processes needed to prepare a report and present it. (Related matters are discussed in Chapter 13.)

Reports. An extension of the "Show and Tell" activity of young children, the giving of oral reports should have many of the same characteristics: that is, the content of the reports should be organized and the reports limited in scope rather than being rambling accounts. Many should be given because the children will be eager to give them. Children beyond the primary grades will volunteer to show something or to tell about personal interests and events. This volunteering, if encouraged, can lead to effective reporting on social studies and other subject-area topics, even if these report topics are assigned.

Guidelines for Reports

1. Pick an interesting topic and stick to it.
2. Have a good opening and closing.
3. Organize your information carefully.
4. Look at the audience.
5. Make your voice loud enough to be heard.
6. Use good sentences and interesting words.

Good reports don't just happen; they must be planned and students must learn how to give them. An effective report communicates to an audience something that is important to them. Thus, children will need to develop the ability to select material appropriate to classroom topics and to the audience, the ability to collect and organize material (this will require skill in reading critically, taking notes, summarizing, and outlining as discussed in Chapter 13), and the ability to face the group and give the oral report with accuracy, interest, and effectiveness. They also need to recognize that a report can often be made more meaningful to the audience through the use of a map, diagram, chart, overhead projector, or flannel board.

Oral reports should not be routinely assigned to children; they ought to grow from other classroom learning activities. (Children should not have to give reports at all, however, if they need to develop more security in speaking by other means first.) Instruction is generally needed in the location of information, preparation of notes, and avoidance of plagiarism. Children will also need help in judging the amount of time available for the report, developing a good beginning and ending for it, and selecting visual aids.

A bulletin-board display that gives steps for children to follow in preparing reports may be useful. Here is one example:

Steps in Preparing a Report

6. Develop good opening and closing sentences.
5. Think: Is this report too long? Should it be cut?
4. Choose interesting vocabulary and illustrations.
3. Review your notes and outline the report.
2. Check the encyclopedia and other references. Take notes to answer your questions.
1. What questions might be asked about this topic? List them.

There are many opportunities for genuine and useful reporting. Following are some suggestions:

- Topics related to social studies or science are suitable. See suggestions at the end of each chapter in student textbooks or teachers' editions.
- Reports may be an extension of reading. Perhaps the class has read a story about a Nigerian family and the children want to know more about Nigeria. The more able readers could be asked to give reports on the country to the class after they have consulted additional resources.
- New plans or rules of the school can be examined and reported on.
- Extensions of current-events topics may be the subjects of reports. For example, conflicts between countries as described in different newspapers and magazines

would supply interesting topics for reports during a study of propaganda techniques—detecting possible bias in a writer's viewpoint, the use of "loaded" words, and so on.

- Other opportunities for group or individual reports include interviews, trips to places of interest, and reviews of movies, books, or television programs.

When the children give their reports, you should be a model listener in the audience. But you should mentally note, and perhaps jot down, observations about speech and delivery that probably require attention. Such information can be included in students' language arts portfolios. And videotapes of the reports can also be used by children as they critique their own presentation.

Interviews. An interview is a good method of securing information and provides the interviewer with the opportunity to use speaking skills, organize his or her thinking, and develop listening ability. And not to be overlooked is the fact that the results of an interview can be written down and prepared for publication in the school or classroom newspaper. In fact, interviewing is an activity that makes possible the use of all of the language arts areas.

Many situations occur that give children the opportunity to conduct interviews. Intermediate-grade children studying another country may wish to talk with someone who has lived in or visited there. The children themselves may know of such a person, possibly a parent, a relative, a friend, or even a child in another class.

Interviewing parents and other adults about their occupations or hobbies will also enrich the curriculum. In planning for such interviews, emphasize the

The use of charts improves oral reports.

Note-taking and outlining can be taught with interviewing; see Chapter 13.

importance of the job or avocation to the community, its uniqueness, or its relation to subjects being studied. It is amazing how unaware both children and adults are of services that are provided in communities. For instance, when children drop money into a soft-drink machine, do they think about how the machine got there or who keeps it running? Have they ever thought that someone earns a living this way?

What is necessary for an interview experience? First, prepare some questions that the class or individual would like answered. Develop enough knowledge of the topic that sensible questions can be asked in following up on what the interviewee says. This often means that the children will need to do some library research. Above all, it is important that an interview have some purpose other than simply giving the child experience in interviewing.

Those who cannot meet with the children in person may agree to a telephone interview.

Some people will be able to come to school for an interview, but others will not, and plans will have to include arrangements for these interviews. In addition, plans should include ways the information gained may best be utilized. Children may want to use a cassette recorder for an interview if one is available. They should know, however, that if an interview is to be recorded, permission should be obtained from the person being interviewed.

Standards that could be developed for interviewing include the following:

1. Introduce yourself and state the purpose of the interview.
2. Avoid sentences like "The teacher says we have to ask you about _____."
3. Remember that the interviewer should open and close the interview.
4. Have the questions to be asked firmly in mind or on paper so that you stay with the topic.
5. If it seems advisable, give the person to be interviewed a list of the questions to be asked. This can be done when the appointment is made, thus giving the person time to consider his or her answers.
6. Identify appropriate times for an interview appointment.
7. Give the person being interviewed some idea of the amount of time the interview is to last.
8. Take notes during the interview (see Chapter 13).
9. Find a way to end the interview other than "Well, our time is up, so we have to quit."
10. Always be courteous, listen carefully, and express appreciation for the opportunity to conduct the interview.

Video Activities. Many elementary students are quite familiar with video cameras from home experiences, and video equipment is available to some extent in nearly every school. As mentioned throughout this chapter, videotaping is a way to provide feedback to speakers to let them know how their presentations look and sound as well as a means of preserving a record of a panel discussion or an interview. Puppetry and creative dramatics are also excellent opportunities for such recording.

Obviously, there is ample opportunity to use video equipment in class situations. A science demonstration may be seen better by the whole class if it is shown "live" while at the same time being taped and commented on by a student. In social studies the camera and recorder may be taken on a field trip, and the

Doing the news "on TV" is an excellent oral language activity.

videotape can be used later back in the classroom. Very often such productions require scripts, and, of course, these have to be written, so the experience actually involves all of the language arts areas.

Videotaping by elementary-school children has proved to be highly satisfactory. Cameras are easy to operate; the sound quality is generally good; the tape is immediately available for viewing; and copies can be made. Parents may even want to have videotapes of some classroom activities.

Preparing a television production and recording involves several steps:

1. Have the main goal of the videotaping clearly in mind and identify the audience.
2. Outline the content to be included and note any requirements for narration, music, or other production features.
3. Make a series of "story boards" that state precisely what will be done and said by participants and what the camera operator will do in each successive shot.
4. Rehearse with the story boards but without the camera until the production goes well.
5. Videotape as many times as necessary to obtain the desired result.

Videotaping responsibilities should be shared so that all class members can become proficient.

Children seem to require very little experience before becoming highly proficient with video recorders.

TV Story Board

DIALOGUE/ACTION	CAMERA DIRECTIONS
Girl #1:	long shot of two girls seated on stools at science table
Today we will introduce you to Emma, our gerbil	zoom in on gerbil

ASSESSING PROGRESS IN ORAL LANGUAGE

In one sense a child's oral language is the easiest area in which to see progress: talk goes on all the time in the classroom. Other opportunities to observe a student's development will depend on what sorts of oral language activities occur. A very important consideration is that a student's willingness to participate in self-evaluation will largely determine how much progress he or she makes. There are ways to promote such self-assessment, however, through the development of checklists and guidelines based on the information in this chapter and from such sources as those listed at the end of the chapter.

At several points we have mentioned that electronic records may be made of children's oral language behavior. Clearly, the practice of having a youngster watch a videotape of her or his report, oral reading of a poem, or performance in a play is the best possible means of promoting self-assessment. A checklist would assist students in identifying their strengths and locating areas that might need attention. The great advantage (and motivator) is that the learners can analyze their own progress and make plans for further development.

Checklists, evaluations, and audio- and videotape recordings should also be collected and accumulated from year to year in a child's language arts portfolio, along with other records and work samples. Such materials would present the best possible record of accomplishments and progress in specific areas.

A FINAL WORD

There are many ways in which effectiveness in using oral language enhances a child's life. As children speak, they use new words they have learned and make them their own; they also experiment with sentence patterns and may even try one that they have never heard before. Talking also improves thought processes; elementary-school children often work out what they understand and believe as they talk about a topic. Using oral language well is crucial to academic development and to social and emotional growth. People who are confident when speaking have a definite advantage over those who are tentative or halting. In discussing the goals of instruction and learning activities in reading, writing, and the other language arts, we will point out the extent to which their full realization depends on students' oral language abilities.

References

Considine, David M. "Visual Literacy and the Curriculum," *Language Arts* 64 (October 1987), pp. 634–640.

Cottrell, June. *Creative Drama in the Classroom, Grades K–3*. National Textbook Company, 1987.

———. *Creative Drama in the Classroom, Grades 4–6*. National Textbook Company, 1987.

Goldenberg, Claude. "Instructional Conversations: Promoting Comprehension through Discussion." *The Reading Teacher* 46 (December 1992/January 1993), pp. 316–326.

Heining, Ruth. *Improvisation with Favorite Tales*. Heinemann, 1992.

Hynds, Susan, and Rubin, Donald, eds. *Perspectives on Talk and Learning*. National Council of Teachers of English, 1990.

Kimeldorf, Martin. *Teaching Is Dramatic*. Endick Communications, 1985.

Kohl, Herbert R. *Making Theater: Developing Plays with Young People*. Teachers and Writers Collaborative

Language Arts 65 (January 1988), pp. 14–55 (issue on drama).

Laughlin, Mildred; Black, Peggy; and Loberg, Margery. *Social Studies Readers Theatre for Children: Scripts and Script Development*. Libraries Unlimited, 1991.

Lenz, Lisa. "Crossroads of Literacy and Orality: Reading Poetry Aloud." *Language Arts* 69 (December 1992), pp. 597–603.

Marling, Curt, and Searle, Dennis. *When Students Have Time to Talk*. Heinemann, 1991.

McCaslin, Nellie. *Creative Drama in the Intermediate Grades*. Longman, 1987.

McTear, Michael. *Children's Conversation*. Basil Blackwell, 1985.

Nilson, Allen Pace. "Children's Multiple Uses of Oral Language Play." *Language Arts* 60 (February 1983), pp. 194–201.

Nugent, Susan Monroe. *Integrating Speaking Skills into the Curriculum*. National Council of Teachers of English, 1986.

Ontario Ministry of Education. *Drama in the Formative Years*. Ontario Ministry of Education, 1984.

Seiler, William J.; Schuelke, L. David; and Lieb-Brilhart, Barbara. *Communication for the Contemporary Classroom*. CBS College Publishing, 1984.

Sklar, Daniel J. *Playmaking: Children Writing and Performing Their Own Plays*. Teachers and Writers Collaborative.

Sloyer, Shirlee. *Readers Theatre: Story Dramatization in the Classroom*. National Council of Teachers of English, 1982.

Stewig, John Warren. *Informal Drama in the Elementary Language Arts Program*. Teachers College Press, 1983.

Thomas-MacKinnon, Pat. "Conversations as Contexts for Poems, Stories, Questions." *Language Arts* 69 (December 1992), pp. 588–596.

Young, Terrell A., and Vardell, Sylvia. "Weaving Readers Theatre and Nonfiction into the Curriculum." *The Reading Teacher* 46 (February 1993), pp. 396–406.

Teaching Resources

BOOKS

Anthony, Rose Marie. *Fun with Choral Speaking*. Teacher Ideas Press, 1990.

Andersen, Yvonne. *Make Your Own Animated Movies and Videotapes*. Little, Brown, 1991.

Black, Kaye. *Kidvid: Fun-damentals of Video Instruction*. Zephyr Press, 1989 (grades 4–8).

Brown, Marc. *Finger Rhymes*. Dutton, 1980.

Burns, Marilyn. *The Hink Pink Book*. Little, Brown, 1981.

Carlson, Dale, and Fitzgibbon, R. *Manners That Matter*. Dutton, 1983.

Cole, Joanna. *Anna Banana: 101 Jump-Rope Rhymes*. Morrow, 1989.

Detz, Jane. *How to Write and Give a Speech*. Dale Seymour (grade 7).

Dunn, Sonja. *Butterscotch Dreams: Chants for Fun and Learning*. Heinemann, 1987.

Dunn, Sonja. *Crackers & Crumbs: Chants for Whole Language*. Heinemann, 1990.

Friedenberg, Alan. *Stand Up and Speak! Public Speaking for Students*. Curriculum Associates (grades 4–8).

Glazer, Tom. *Eye Winker, Tom Tinker, Chin Chopper: Fifty Musical Finger Plays*. Doubleday, 1973.

Hand Rhymes. Dutton, 1985.

Katz, Michael. *Ten Potatoes in a Pot and Other Counting Rhymes*. Harper and Row, 1990.

Kinghorn, Harriet R., and Pelton, Mary Helen. *Every Child A Storyteller: A Handbook of Ideas*. Teacher Ideas Press, 1991.

Livo, Norma J., and Rietz, Sandra A. *Storytelling Activities*. Libraries Unlimited, 1987.

———. *Storytelling: Process and Practice*. Libraries Unlimited, 1986.

Maestro, Guilio. *Riddle Roundup*. Clarion, 1989.

Playmakers. Cambridge University Press (grades 2–6).

Reader's Theater Plays. Curriculum Associates (grades 3–8).

Renfro, Nancy. *Puppet Shows Made Easy.* Watch Me Blossom Theatre Works.

Ring A Ring O'Roses. Flint Public Library, 1026 E. Kearsley, Flint, Ml 48502 (finger plays).

Roets, Lois. *Public Speaking.* Dale Seymour (middle grades).

Rosenbloom, Joseph. *World's Toughest Tongue Twisters.* Sterling, 1987 (grades 2–8).

Swanson, June. *That's for Shore: Riddles from the Beach.* Lerner, 1991.

Thompson, Gare. *Classroom Drama: Act It Out.* Scholastic, 1988.

Walker Plays for Oral Reading. Curriculum Associates (grades 3–6).

Williams, Mary Young. *Let 'Em Talk: Oral Language Activities for the Classroom.* Dale Seymour (K–grade 8).

Young, Karen Romano. *Please Come to My Party.* Children's Press, 1986.

VIDEOTAPES

Communication Fundamentals—Five Basic Skills. Phoenix/BFA (primary–intermediate).

How to Make a Speech. Greenleaf.

Persuasive Speaking. Greenleaf.

Your Communication Skills—Speaking. Coronet Instructional Films (grades 1–6).

OTHER RESOURCES

Challenge Boxes. Dale Seymour (fifty projects in creative thinking; grades 4–8).

The Storyteller. Educational Activities, 1986 (computer software; grades 4–6).

Talking Time Series. McGraw-Hill (two sets of eight filmstrips each; grades 2–6).

Perform! Developing the Natural Language of Every Child. Scholastic (theme-based plays; grades 1–6).

Plays and Musicals Catalog. Dramatic Publishing Co., P.O. Box 109, Woodstock, IL 60098.

Activities for Preservice Teachers

1. With a group of classmates, develop a video production: a commercial, sports commentary, travelogue, or skit. Focus on what you can learn that will help you use video equipment with children.

2. Plan some creative dramatics activities for a specific grade level. Collect simple props (such as hats, dolls, badges, telephones, luggage) that are likely to stimulate children to come up with ideas.

3. Learn several stories well enough to tell to children. Try your storytelling skill with neighborhood children or those at a nearby school. You may want to practice with peers first.

4. Make a list of the ways in which audio and video recorders might be effectively used in elementary classrooms. Discuss your list with classmates; ask for their reactions.

5. Start a collection of poems that are appropriate for choral speaking. Determine the type of choral activity each poem is best suited for.

6. While observing in a classroom, try to identify a child whose shyness or lack of confidence seems to be inhibiting her or his full participation in oral activities. Think of particular activities and experiences that could be used to give that youngster a gradually increasing sense of confidence in such situations.

7. Develop a plan for moving from pantomime to dramatization with children. Show how, over a period of a few weeks, it might be possible to do group pantomimes, rehearsed individual pantomimes, and, finally, dramatizations. Some subjects might be "The Cafeteria Line," "Riding on the Bus," and "Cheering for the Team."

8. Interview a speech therapist who works for a school district to find out what kinds of speech problems he or she encounters and what kinds of remedial procedures are used.

9. Observe a class during some oral activity, and use a checklist to assess the group and individuals. Decide which skills, attitudes, or abilities should have instructional priority.

10. As you prepare a report for one of your own classes, apply the suggestions presented in this chapter.

Activities for Inservice Teachers

1. Videotape a particularly vigorous and expressive speaker (in person or from a television broadcast). With your class, analyze what this person does and how well the techniques seem to work.

2. Assist the children in your class in forming a club based on some interest shared by many (a fan club for a local sports team, perhaps). Along with the many possible language-related club activities, see that they learn about and use some parliamentary procedures.

3. Plan a choral speaking activity that your class might present to another group. Videotape a rehearsal, and use the tape as a basis for group evaluation.

4. Plan to make puppets with your class. Get the students involved in the planning—deciding what purpose the puppets will have, what kind to produce, the materials needed, the procedures to be followed, and so on.

5. Prepare a card file of books of jokes, riddles, and word games that children may use.

6. Develop a lesson that uses creative dramatics in science, social studies, or math. Did it seem to promote understanding of the content? Would you try something similar again?

7. Arrange for your students to interview various people within the school (custodians, cafeteria staff, etc.) after reviewing with the children the suggestions made in this chapter.

8. Start a drama book shelf that holds books containing good stories to dramatize. Criteria for selection of stories should include simple sequences, clear-cut climax, significance of content, and varied characterizations.

9. Organize a field trip to a local TV station. Afterward ask one of the announcers (the weather reporter, for instance) to visit your classroom and perhaps be videotaped by the children.

10. Have children plan a program in which they announce various things: what they have to sell or buy, events of interest, or plans for a class activity, for example. Make sure that standards are developed and observed.

Activities for Children

1. Two children may work together to plan a play to demonstrate good manners. For example, one might be a guest visiting the classroom and the other could greet and introduce her or him, or they might illustrate ways to disagree in a conversation without being discourteous.

2. Have individual children plan skits for special days (Citizenship Day, the anniversary of the Boston Tea Party, Earth Day, Flag Day, etc.). The planning may include writing a script, getting props, researching, and selecting participants. A child may get help from other children with the planning.

3. A child can relate to a small group an incident in a story he or she has read, telling it as though he or she had been one of the characters. (The child may wish to rehearse this before a mirror or record it on tape before presenting it to the group.)

4. Assist children in selecting a "visitors' committee" who will take turns greeting guests to the classroom, explaining activities of the class to them, and otherwise acting as hosts. Ask school personnel and others to visit regularly in order to provide practice for the hosts. New members should be appointed at regular intervals.

5. Children can make puppets independently if they are provided with a place and materials—paper bags, paint, scissors, socks, sticks, stapler, and so on. Have a few puppet models, but encourage children to do more than merely copy these.

6. Stories can be made up to tell with puppets. Children may make up these stories and practice them in front of a mirror or on videotape before telling them to the class or to a small group.

7. Paper figures and their costumes can be cut out and used for dramatic play. Children should do the cutting, of course, and may create plays for the figures.

8. Children may write the material for "commercials" to "sell" the idea of reading a particular book to their classmates. The presentations could be made directly or videotaped for later showing.

9. Using a "talking computer," students can type in directions for doing something and then listen as the computer gives back the directions. As they attempt to follow these, the students may discover that what was typed needs revision.

10. Give a child a list of words that are sometimes not pronounced correctly or that are not clearly enunciated so that they are confused with other words. Have the child record these and listen to herself or himself. You may also check the recording or have two children do this together so that they help each other. Some pairs are *wrench–rinse* and *partial–parcel*.

11. A child can prepare a talk to give to the class on a topic such as

How to make a kite
How to build a snowman

How to build and care for an aquarium

How to begin a stamp collection

12. Give a child a collection of pictures from magazines and ask him or her to record on tape a story based on these pictures.

13. Children may also record original stories on tape. At a special time, such as once each week, tapes may be played to the class for practice in listening and discussion.

14. Have children keep a file of pantomime ideas. Provide a mirror in a corner of the room where they can experiment with pantomimes and prepare to present them to the class or to small groups.

15. Individual children may prepare and present announcements at school assemblies or over the school public-address system.

Chapter 6

Listening, Thinking, and Learning

*I*n Chapter 2 we presented our conception of language arts instruction and discussed *information processing* as one component of effective teaching, along with developmental programs and embedded lessons. Information processing was defined as a set of procedures used to conceptualize experience and analyze content. Conceptualizing, analyzing and other similar mental activities may be considered modes of *thinking,* which we have said should be viewed as one of the language arts. In this chapter on listening we also discuss thinking, not because thinking occurs only when we listen but because it certainly does happen then. This means that children probably find it easiest to discuss and examine their own thinking processes when they are involved in listening.

Helping students to consider their own thinking abilities as they listen will improve their learning, not only in language arts areas but in all other school subjects as well. What is learned in listening will, with some additional thought and teaching, be available for use when dealing with concepts, generalizations, and understandings in such fields as math, science, and social studies.

Of course, listening is done for other significant purposes, too, and these usually relate to certain aspects of the school program. For example, there is the very practical matter of being able to give attention and listen carefully to teachers when asked to. Children need experiences in listening for aesthetic reasons, too; they learn about the world through beautiful sounds such as the songs of birds and human voices reciting poetry. In addition, we need to listen to other people to establish a basis for sharing their concerns and understanding their way of seeing situations and events.

THE SIGNIFICANCE OF LISTENING

Of course, we listen for many different purposes in addition to language communication. Sounds convey meaning and cause emotions. From birth, the human is aroused by sounds, frighteningly loud ones and soothing soft ones. Other reactions are possible, of course; athletes can be stimulated to greater efforts by loud noises generated by bands and cheering spectators. However, not everyone hears well and some people do not hear anything or much at all, something that has significant ramifications in their lives.

Listening to the World

Besides speech, there are many other sounds that have meaning for us, such as the sounds of practical daily life—a telephone rings, someone knocks at the door, a car horn or siren issues a warning. New sounds are constantly being introduced:

Listening for Sounds Around Us

Street sounds—horns blowing, brakes screeching, dogs barking, car doors slamming
Shopping sounds—carts rattling, bottles clinking, registers whirring
Game sounds—crowd cheering, balls pounding, feet running, official whistling

telemetry signals from space, for example, or the "beeps" from a computer, some of which carry a sinister message.

There are sounds that many people enjoy listening to: music of all kinds, certainly, but also the buzz of a bee, the purr of a cat, rain on a roof, and other natural sounds. There are mechanical sounds that may also be considered pleasant—those made by sewing machines, high-performance auto engines, egg beaters, or push-style lawn mowers.

Students equipped with audiotape recorders can record sounds they make or those they hear around the school, at home, in their neighborhoods, and on television programs. They can then challenge classmates to identify the source of the sound. This is a good opportunity for youngsters to be inventive—by combining sounds from different sources and even using ones they produce with their own bodies—without their voice—as they clap hands, "pop" fingers out of the sides of their mouths, cluck their tongues, and whistle.

Hearing and Listening

Assistance for those who don't hear well or at all is discussed in Chapter 16.

Listening is affected by the acuity with which a person receives sound waves of various frequencies (tones) at various intensities (levels of volume). An inability to respond to normal frequencies and intensities represents a hearing loss, which may range from slight to serious. Although a hearing loss affects an individual's ability to perceive sounds and discriminate among them, it is possible for a person to have normal hearing and yet have difficulty with sound perception and discrimination. This is particularly the case with those who have speech problems or who may be unfamiliar with a language or particular dialect. There should be minimal difficulties with children who speak the same kind of language they ordinarily listen to and have no speech or hearing problems. Many children who seem to have difficulty with perception and discrimination are probably exhibiting a lack of understanding of what they are being asked to do, unfamiliarity with aspects of the language (the vocabulary, for instance), low motivation to retain what was heard, or lack of attention.

Hearing is also affected by *masking,* which is a failure to hear adequately because of the superimposition of sounds that interfere—the many voices at a party, for example. Related to this, but with a physical basis, is inadequate binaural hearing. *Binaural hearing* may be thought of as similar to depth perception in vision; that is, without adequate binaural hearing the individual cannot locate a particular speaker among several talking at once. A number of other factors may interfere with speech reception:

I can't understand a word she says!

I wish he would get it out!

What a mish-mash!

I didn't come here to listen to this!

What they are speaks so loudly I can't hear what they say!

Speech may be too rapid for adequate hearing (usually because the listener is unfamiliar with the topic or the speaker's dialect).
Speech may be very soft, slow, halting, or have unpleasant tonal qualities that make hearing difficult.
What is being presented may be poorly organized or inappropriately presented.
The message may be so emotionally distressing that hearing is interfered with.
Those listening may reject the speaker because of his or her appearance, mannerisms, or identification with a disliked group.

Some children with significant hearing difficulties are placed in regular classrooms. Chapter 16 discusses ways of helping such children to function with greater facility.

LISTENING AND THINKING

Discussions of thinking involve examination of how language is used when messages are received and processed in various ways (understood, remembered, related to other information, analyzed, etc.). Whether we are listening, reading, writing, or viewing, we will think about the content of the messages we are receiving either carefully and fully or perhaps only slightly or superficially. How deep the thinking goes depends on the individual's motivation and abilities.

Children often distort what they hear to make it somehow understandable to them; mature thinkers are more likely to realize that they do not comprehend. An example of a child's thinking is the story about the girl who told her father that her class was studying "gazinta" in arithmetic, "3 gazinta 12" being the type of problem receiving attention. Such instances clearly indicate that youngsters are thinking as they listen and trying to make sense of whatever is presented to them. As a teacher, you must check regularly to see what sorts of thinking the learning activities are promoting.

As thinking proceeds students use many different strategies for processing information. A number of these are closely related to listening.

Making Comparisons and Seeing Contrasts

Children, like adults, find it very helpful to examine whatever is presented to them as new to see if it has associations to something already known. A storyteller describes a small cottage in a forest and those listening think of it as possibly resembling the witch's house in *Hansel and Gretel*. A classroom guest being interviewed about mountain climbing says that Mt. McKinley is much taller than the children's favorite sledding hill, and this helps their thought processes.

Classifying

Learning new words and concepts depends on the ability to see relationships and apply labels. While viewing a television report, students hear the narrator say that the platypus has characteristics of both birds and mammals, which alerts them to the possibility that their existing classification system won't always work perfectly. Other problems could involve seeing distinctions (between brown eggs and white ones, perhaps) that some adults recognize as significant.

Making Predictions

Young children, having heard certain nursery rhymes frequently or participated in group reading of easily memorized books, learn what to expect next when listening and can act accordingly. As students gain further experience, they can think ahead; they know what the elements of a story are, how a three-act play unfolds, what occurs in a scientific experiment, and so forth. This ability to know what is coming (or have a rather good idea) can be an important aid to learning of all kinds.

Identifying Important Ideas

Listening to (or reading) material and then deciding on a statement that would effectively summarize it is not always easy for adults to accomplish with much

People find different meanings in the same content.

agreement. Such a task is nearly impossible for children unless they receive substantial assistance. When youngsters confront a complex situation, they often focus on specifics (the story has a kitten in it, the old lady wore a long dress, the king was angry). If they are going to get beyond these to see a theme or a problem-solution pattern, you must encourage them to formulate interpretations and gradually revise them as they listen to what others believe. This is a step in the direction of learning to think.

Making Inferences

Going beyond what is actually stated to think of what else might very likely be true, known as making an inference, occurs frequently as we listen to a speaker. "She hasn't said that the story is about adults; maybe children are involved," or "He reports all these charges, but I'll bet that he eventually says they aren't true" are examples of inferences that might be made while listening to speakers.

Teachers who listen carefully promote thinking.

Inferences are arrived at as we read, too (often called *reading between the lines*). Children who are encouraged to speculate as they listen should begin to make inferences in listening and reading.

Many additional examples of types of thinking might be given here and some are included in the discussions to follow. Whatever the specifics, it is apparent that children do have opportunities to think while listening. By making plans to capitalize on these instances, you should be able to help them develop strategies, ways of dealing with particular kinds of intellectual and academic tasks. Of course, it is important that they have some part in planning and defining what is to be done. By reviewing such challenges through listening and discussion, children have the opportunity to learn ways of processing information that can be used across the curriculum—in reading, speaking, writing, and dealing with content in social studies, science, mathematics and other fields of study.

GUIDING THE LISTENER

It is accepted by most authorities that we listen at an efficiency level of about 25 percent.

Students have different types of listening experiences and, with proper guidance from you, they can learn a great deal from each. Children can develop appropriate listening habits and attitudes if they have good experiences, particularly in the early years. Often in the preceding chapters we have stated that parents and teachers should talk frequently with young children, encouraging them to participate in conversations on many topics.

Reading storybooks and poems to children and discussing these also provides valuable listening experiences. In the case of television viewing, we have pointed out that such an activity can be more productive in children's lives if adults watch with them, talk about what is on the screen, and organize related follow-up activities.

In this chapter we have also mentioned that there is much else in the environment for children to listen to with pleasure—weather effects, music, animal calls, as well as sounds made by machinery and electronic devices. As they grow older, they can even go on to produce interesting sounds themselves—playing instruments, writing songs, reciting poetry, and performing plays that others might like to attend.

It is clearly possible, then, to encourage positive attitudes toward listening and help youngsters to see what sorts of contributions listening can make to their learning and their life.

Purposeful Listening

That we listen in different ways at different times and in different situations needs to be taken into account in a classroom program. Although listening is an active, interacting process, the level of involvement on the part of the listener varies. Interest in what is being heard influences this level, as do emotional and intellectual factors.

Children should learn to identify signal words and expressions such as: *next, at the same time, after, my next point,* and *thus.*

We should, of course, make it clear to children that listening well is *their* responsibility; no one can do it for them. You can help them see what their purposes for listening might be, however. Purposes *for* listening should be suggested or developed with the class; you should not simply demand that they listen *to* something. Listening should be done *for* information that can be gained, *for* appreciation of the language in a poem, *for* propagandistic words in a television or radio commercial, *for* directions, and so forth. Establishing standards, inviting class reactions, and discussing listening behaviors will all help students see the need for and the importance of careful listening.

Finding Meanings

Some Reasons for Listening

1. *to appreciate and enjoy*
2. *to look for propaganda, bias, or prejudice.*
3. *to experience unusual or especially appealing language*
4. *to show courtesy*
5. *to identify important ideas*
6. *to identify specific details*
7. *to determine a speaker's objectives*
8. *to gain information*
9. *to evaluate in terms of some criteria*
10. *to gain a visual image*

The process of listening requires identification of something that is meaningful to the receiver. Although messages are made up of speech sounds, words, and sentences, these seldom communicate much by themselves. It is the total context that conveys meaning and is thus "heard." The language that is listened to comes in "chunks" that have significance for the listener: a few sentences that describe a pollution problem in the community, a passage of several hundred words praising the work of Mother Teresa, or the text of a play such as *Death of a Salesman.*

Students can benefit from teaching that helps them gain meanings that are significant for them. The listener must construct her or his own meanings and then compare these to ones constructed by others. Making such comparisons leads to interesting discussions and thoughtful writing experiences, as discussed in Chapters 10 and 11.

When listening to a visible speaker, the listener can gain meanings from observing facial expressions and gestures or visual aids of various kinds. Whether or not the speaker can be seen, other clues to meaning are also available:

1. The context of what is heard. (A political speech by a candidate in a noisy hall full of her or his supporters usually generates more emotion than reasoned argument.)

2. The organization of the content. (The experienced listener is able to recognize such types of presentations as narratives, internal debates, attempts to persuade, and use of rhetorical questions.)

3. Use of repetition and redundancies. (A major difference between listening and reading is that speakers often try to make their points by repeating them nearly exactly or restating them in different terms, techniques that sometimes help listeners "catch up" by giving them a little extra time to think—something they can do for themselves when reading.)

4. Use of voice inflections, especially tone, rhythm, and volume. (Speakers may express anger by speaking loudly in a rasping tone of voice or excitement through rapid speech or disgust by sounding sarcastic.)

5. Use of such language signals as *"on the other hand," "but most importantly,"* or *"There are three reasons."* (Such signals provide information that helps listeners organize what they are hearing.)

As they listen to effective speakers make use of these various techniques, students may be helped to see how they might improve their own oral language competencies. Indeed, there are many important relationships between listening and speaking.

Much can be learned by interviewing someone from another country.

Teachers' Listening

In planning instruction for children, teachers should first give attention to their own listening. They should genuinely "pay attention," "be courteous to speakers," and manifest all the other behaviors that they expect to instill in their students. Doing so will avoid such unfortunate events as that which occurred with a teacher who responded, "That's nice. Now go finish your work," after a child told her that his grandmother had died the night before.

Active listening means having empathy with the speaker and viewing the situation from that person's point of view while she or he is talking.

Certainly you may find yourself at a loss for words when a child shares a confidence of doubtful significance, telling about her family's new VCR, for example. Commonplace as the event may be, and even a waste of time, as far as many adults are concerned, it is something of importance to the youngster and should be so recognized by you. It requires little effort to talk a bit about movies that may be rented and shown on the new machine. By sharing that moment, you have conveyed to the child the message that others value her contributions to the discourse that takes place in the classroom.

LISTENING AND SCHOOL PROGRAMS

Much listening takes place in elementary classrooms. Some studies indicate that in the average schoolroom someone is talking more than 60 percent of the time, mostly the teacher with the students listening.

The planning of a classroom listening curriculum ought to include a *developmental* component, *information processing,* and *embedded lessons,* as discussed in Chapter 2. The developmental sequence should incorporate many of the components that have been referred to in this chapter, including sounds other than speech, of course, but concentrating on literature (stories, poetry, and drama) and the types of oral language described in Chapter 5. Information processing has been described in the preceding section Listening and Thinking, indicating the importance of the relationships between hearing something and thinking about it. Embedded lessons could involve teaching about many specific applications of listening—from recognizing classmates' voices to seeing the patterns of specific kinds of poetry. Ideally, you are quite consistently giving embedded lessons on listening, at least several times a day.

Listening and Attention

Listening is important to information processing and its significance ought to be stressed in all subjects through the offering of good examples.

To listen attentively students must be able to consciously focus on what is being presented. When children are successful in giving attention to speakers, the likelihood is that they also will be able to do the same when they are reading and viewing. It is sometimes said that elementary-school students have developed habits of not paying attention. Excessive television watching is cited as a cause of this problem, since many children grow up in households where they routinely watch as much as 25 to 30 hours per week. The argument is that television viewing, combined with listening to popular music, teaches children to accept background sound, give little attention to it, and half-listen until something they hear captures their attention. When what teachers say becomes "background sound" and is therefore easily ignored, the results constitute a significant school problem.

Factors in attention include the ability to concentrate. The will to give attention when and where it is called for and for a substantial amount of time

Cooperative learning activities require all participants to listen carefully.

A teacher can improve students' listening by:

1. Discussing possible purposes for listening
2. Stressing that all should listen courteously
3. Making listening easier through clear enunciation and accurate pronunciation
4. Organizing material presented orally so that it is systematic, explicit, and brief.

may be restricted because of many physical and social problems. When all the problems that can beset a classroom situation are considered it is easy to become discouraged about sustaining a high level of concentration. No doubt improvement is possible, however, and we must be aware of ways in which attention may be promoted:

1. We should be sure that messages are worth listening to. Teachers should not talk constantly, repeating themselves and giving much time to general instructional and behavior guidelines that are needed by only a few members of the class.

2. Teachers should develop a way to signal to students that it is time to give particularly close attention to what is going to be said, whatever the source (morning announcements over the school intercom, directions for taking a standardized test, explanations by classmates about how they used a particular computer software program). Some teachers have catch phrases that they use at such times, often combining these with a physical action: "Put your brain in drive"; "Clean out your left ear, now the right one"; "Wake up and smell the coffee." For some children these sorts of reminders may help them gain better control over their listening behavior.

3. It should be recognized that rules about sitting up straight, looking directly ahead, and having nothing in your hands are not as helpful as it might seem. There is evidence that good listeners ordinarily shift the focus of their attention two or three times a minute. This means that a listener staring unwaveringly into the eyes of the speaker is not necessarily paying close attention. (Teachers often find to their surprise that students twisting pencils or gazing out the window are actually listening quite well.)

4. The emotional factor in paying attention is highly significant. Children have needs just as we all do—for acceptance by others, success experiences, feelings of security, and the desire to be in control of our lives. It is difficult to listen when one's emotional needs are not being met. On the other hand, if children see that their concerns are related in a positive way to what is going on in the classroom, they may be happy to pay attention.

Listening and Speaking

In Chapter 5 several kinds of oral language were discussed and their relationship to listening explored to some extent. You should make it explicit to students that listening and speaking are closely connected and that progress in one is often dependent on improvements in the other.

Oral language situations differ in terms of the listener's access to the speaker. There are many circumstances in which the speaker and listener are in a reciprocal relationship, alternating between being one or the other. These may be thought of as *face-to-face* situations, including conversations, discussions, and informal interviews involving a small number of participants. In other cases, the listener may not be of equivalent status with the speaker at all times, but the situation does allow for face-to-face exchanges at certain points. If announcements are being made, for example, or directions or reports given, listeners will ordinarily have *limited access* to the speaker and be able to ask questions or make comments. In most of our listening and viewing experiences, we have no access to the speaker who is *remote* from us and may be addressing an audience of 500 people, including ourselves, or who may be a stage actor and not likely to converse with anyone except the other actors. Even more likely, what we are listening to, or viewing, is someone on television, perhaps speaking live but thousands of miles away. We do, as listeners, have to understand what our roles can be in these various types of relationships to speakers.

Listeners in face-to-face situations. In face-to-face experiences such as conversations and discussions, where the individual is likely to be both listener and speaker, he or she has the opportunity to continuously assess how well what is heard is understood. As they strive for a good level of comprehension, listeners may ask themselves such questions as:

> Am I sure of what she is saying?
> How is he using that word?
> How can I find out what others think about this?

To assist students in increasing their ability to do such active listening, you can teach them particular strategic questions or statements that might be used to engage speakers in clarifying exchanges:

> What do you mean when you say . . . ?
> What does _____ mean to you?
> But I think that. . . .

When there is a face-to-face situation but with only limited access to the speaker, listeners should continue to formulate questions that they would like to ask or statements they want to make if there is an opportunity. These can be directed at securing clarification, raising related points not yet discussed, setting forth alternative explanations, and so forth. Again, this is thinking combined with listening. The listener must organize her or his own thoughts and not simply sit and wait to ask a question while ignoring all that is being said. Note paper and pen or pencil may be effectively used in such situations, even by elementary-school students.

Listeners in situations where the source is remote. In most audience situations, the listener is unable to assess understanding through direct referral to the source. Though such questions as "What did she say?" or "What did he mean by that?" come to mind, they cannot be directed to speakers. Also, in a live situation there is no way to stop the flow of speech while listeners discuss what they heard or ask for repetition so they can review the content.

Students need assistance in drawing on what they have learned from face-to-face listening experiences and applying these strategies to remote experiences, whether live plays and speeches, television programs, radio interviews, or sports broadcasts. They should have practice in noting what seem to be important points and then later thinking more about these or discussing them with someone else. With the availability of electronic equipment it has become possible to make audio and video tape-recordings of particularly significant speech events and later listen to them in part or in their entirety.

> Elementary-age students do not learn simply by "taking it all in"; they need to interpret meaning for themselves by talking, writing, drawing, singing, dancing, and otherwise exploring and communicating.

Listening and Reading

Since listening and reading involve receiving messages, there are many similarities between them. Both require that the individual be motivated to try to get meaning from what is spoken or read. Lack of attention, absence of interest, concern with personal difficulties, and similar problems will prevent listeners and readers from being successful.

Listening and reading also depend on the ability of the student to recognize a wide variety of words and other lexical units and to make useful guesses and approximations where necessary. The person who knows what *house* and *town* mean can, perhaps, come very close to understanding what the new word *townhouse* refers to whether it is seen or heard.

Comprehension in both reading and listening requires relating what is read or heard to past experiences so that the content can be thought about and examined creatively and critically. (This is yet another example of how thinking at high levels is of extreme importance.) As a teacher you need to be concerned with helping students to activate what they already know when they are listening to a presentation. The more they are able to construct meanings that integrate what they know with what is heard, the more successful the learning experience will be. The same is true for reading. If they come to the reading situation knowing how the content is likely to be organized and how the text relates to knowledge in their possession, a good level of comprehension will be reached.

Specific listening activities can be modeled after similar reading experiences. You can read passages to students and ask them to

* identify important ideas
* find significant details
* speculate about what will happen next
* give the meaning for a particular word
* identify irrelevant information

A Listening Tip

Before reading to the children ask them to look at the book cover, note the title, think about who the author is, and then discuss what the book might be about. Then they can listen to see if their expectations are met.

Listening and Learning

Much that is presented for children to learn is in the form of something for them to listen to. We know a great deal about how advertising is designed to convey messages and it is appealing to draw parallels between commercial products and teaching goals and how they ought to be packaged.

Unpleasant messages are turned off. Whether it's a question of bad news on the radio or a new TV series about a nasty character, we know that lots of people simply refuse to be a member of the audience. Students also need positive, attractive listening experiences. They don't want to be criticized, scolded, and lectured to constantly. If they need to be put on the right track concerning some problem, this can often be done in a friendly, humorous manner.

Messages should come by means of the most effective channels. You must consider what is interesting to students when planning a presentation. In general, children like color, movement, and variety. They like sports and popular-music figures and the characters they know from television and comics. A steady diet of drab, dull sameness will be, quite rightly, termed "boring."

Students whose basic needs are not met cannot listen effectively. It is not likely that a child who needs a hearing aid or is hungry, sleepy, ill, or anxious about personal and family problems is an efficient listener. Teachers cannot take care of all such pro- blems, but the school can marshal the sorts of community support that is needed to assist large numbers of children and make them more efficient listeners and learners.

Messages need to be structured for effective listening. If students are to become better listeners, their efforts must meet with success. All that they hear cannot be controlled by you, but what goes on in the classroom can be influenced by how you organize presentations. You can assist them by telling them about the pattern that will be followed—in a discussion of three reasons why trees are important to the ecological system, for instance—then making that presentation and asking them to summarize it.

Listening for Enjoyment

A considerable amount of listening in the classroom should be focused on experiences that are primarily enjoyable, even though they also have a significant learning component. We have, of course, stressed the value of reading stories aloud to children. Other possibilities exist as well.

Spoken Language and Speeches. Simply listening to varieties of human speech is enjoyable. Children should have the opportunity to hear English speakers who use different dialects. Such speakers may be found locally, and they may enjoy coming to the school to demonstrate aspects of their speech or participate in the making of a recording. Some of this can be accomplished by making videotapes of television programs set in different parts of the country, in other historical periods, or in some other English-speaking country. (Dialects are further discussed in Chapter 7.) You should exercise judgment in using such tapes or additional available recordings, since there should be no possibility of ridiculing those who speak in a particular way.

Inexpensive video equipment makes it possible for children to make tapes and then look at and listen to them.

Figures of speech and idioms contribute to making conversations enjoyable.

Related to dialects are figures of speech ("She's the queen bee over at the shop") and idiomatic expressions ("Something went wrong right off the bat") that different speakers may use. Equipped with audiotape recorders, students can ask people what they know about expressions like the ones on a list they have prepared and then bring these in to listen to and discuss. (Senior citizens are often good sources for information about why some people say, "That dog won't hunt," or "He went off half-cocked," even when they are not discussing hunting.) These could be embedded lessons when occupations are being studied, since each type of work often has its own language features.

Speeches by famous figures such as Winston Churchill or some of our presidents could be listened to as examples of how the spoken word can be effective at particular times. Also, recordings of dramatic readings by actors and sermons by famous preachers might be used to increase students' appreciation of the beauty and power of spoken English.

Other languages are important, too, and for some of your students the language spoken at home may not be English. The status of such children will be enhanced if they are given the opportunity to teach their classmates a greeting or a few words in the unknown language. Even if they do not understand much of what is said, students should listen to several languages, in person or on videotape. This should promote interest in learning more about languages.

Poetry. Poetry is often best appreciated when read aloud or spoken from memory. Whether it's a matter of two-year-olds sitting in their fathers' laps or several hundred adults in an audience listening to a poet reading her own work, humans enjoy the rhythms, rhymes, intonations, words, and images of poetry. Early experiences are important, but many of those who started out in life enjoying *Mother Goose* end up as somewhat older children who only tolerate or even detest listening to poems. It is important for teachers in the elementary school to read and recite poetry regularly so that pupils have positive experiences throughout the years. There are poems about activities (*The Swing* by Robert Louis Stevenson), as well as seasons, feelings, holidays and people. These are all good places to begin. Additional poetry appropriate for elementary classrooms is discussed in Chapter 15.

Music. Music is an important aspect of the school program and should be included in every classroom. In Chapter 5 we stressed that singing should be thought of as one of the necessary aspects of oral language, and certainly songs are to be listened to as well. Instrumental music is important, too. Again, early experiences are significant. Young children listen to band music and such concert pieces as *Carnival of the Animals*. In the middle and upper grades students can listen to popular music, of course, but also jazz, old ballads, and symphonic selections. For them, after they have had some experience, music can be listened to for its organization and structure as well as its inspiration and beauty.

Listening Critically

As with music, there are instances when children are able to listen to speech in ways that cause them to not only understand the message but also to note the way in which it is being presented. At a minimum we can expect them to examine how a speaker may be trying to establish a relationship with them and thus make them more likely to accept what they are listening to. The techniques most commonly used are simply good advice, and pupils can learn more about what a good speaker does by watching one. Some common concerns of speakers are

Invite a salesperson to class to discuss these points.

- making a good appearance—being neat and suitably dressed
- being pleasant and friendly and showing that they are enjoying the experience of speaking themselves
- speaking enthusiastically and in a way that shows genuine interest in their topic
- telling jokes or stories that are on their topic and also entertaining
- showing connections with the audience—knowing what their interests and concerns are and touching on them
- building positive associations between their topic and what the members of the audience already know and believe

Certainly there is little to criticize in such speaker behavior, but it is important for students to become conscious of what speakers do in trying to be effective. Then, when and if a speaker crosses the line from being particularly pleasant to beginning to use what might be thought of as faulty thinking or propaganda techniques, students will have some chance of understanding what has happened. (Use of such techniques is discussed in connection with reading in Chapter 13.)

Of course, watching television commercials is good preparation for examining the form of the message and the techniques being used to "sell" the product. Many youngsters have already been disappointed by the gap they sometimes find between what is said in commercials and the reality of what is actually obtained.

LISTENING ACTIVITIES

A teacher can improve listening in the classroom by:

1. Reminding students of possible purposes for listening
2. Stressing that all should listen courteously
3. Asking that students make listening easier by organizing what they are going to say and speaking clearly

Improvement of listening abilities should be a concern that permeates the classroom program. In the way you organize and supply the room, the stress you place on understanding directions, your attention to reading good literature to the class, your attempts to use educational television effectively, and the connections you make between speaking, listening and thinking, you will guarantee students' progress in the area of listening. Specific listening activities also make contributions to the program. Few specific instructional materials on listening have been prepared for use in schools, although English and reading textbooks do usually contain some lessons that make use of listening skills and strategies.

Activities for Young Children

As discussed in Chapter 4, children in the early grades are involved in listening for many purposes: picking out rhyming words, discriminating among speech sounds, relating sounds to alphabet letters, and identifying nonspeech sounds. They often listen to music and rhythms and experience listening as a stimulus for imaginative thinking and movement or other interpretive activities.

Young children should also be encouraged to listen for meaning. For instance, they can respond to stories read to them by discussing the characters, the ending, or what a particular story reminded them of. Also, as described in other chapters, they should give attention to the courtesy and listening aspects of such activities as "Show and Tell" and the reading of books they have written themselves.

Word Play. Word play is important for young children because they are constantly refining their pronunciation, increasing their vocabularies, and becoming aware of how words relate to one another and are put together in sentences. Experiences may include asking children to think of pairs of words that rhyme (*cold* and *told, fast* and *last,* etc.), to identify the rhyming words in Mother Goose or even think of substitutions ("What if the line were 'Little-Bo-Peep has lost her *dog*'?"), and to think of answers to rhyming riddles ("I rhyme with sled and you sleep in me"). Particularly able children may enjoy such challenging activities as providing a sentence whose last word rhymes with the final word of a previous line, for example:

Word play may lead to poetry writing (see Chapter 11).

TEACHER:	I baked a cake.
PUPIL 1:	You baked a snake?
PUPIL 2:	No, she backed into a lake.
PUPIL 3:	She baked a snake and stepped on a rake.
PUPIL 4:	My goodness sake!

A related activity would also involve providing a common word ending and having students supply consonants that make words (for example, *end* becomes *send* or *blend*). Lists made in this way can then be used to create silly rhymes such as:

There was a red hen
That lived in a pen,
Could count to ten,
And chase old men.

These may be collected and put into class books for children to illustrate and read.

Sentence Completion. Sentence completion involves paying attention in order to be able to complete sentences when the beginnings have been given ("Puppies are . . ."). These may be simple at first, with one- or two-word additions ("Puppies are funny," "Puppies are funny and wiggly"), and then longer completions can be tried ("Puppies are funny when they try to run and fall down").

Listening to Directions. Listening to directions is something frequently required of young children. It is helpful occasionally to put them in the position of being the one giving directions. This provides the student giving directions (about how to fold a paper airplane, for example) a different orientation and requires the other children to follow directions given by a classmate.

Following Directions. Following directions can involve accepting responsibility for carrying out an errand for the teacher. Students usually enjoy going to the school office, to the custodian, or to another classroom to deliver a note, collect something, or ask a question. There is always strong motivation to listen carefully to be sure to do what is needed.

A few minutes devoted to a listening activity may be especially significant for an individual child. If Allie is a class member who is shy and withdrawn, she would likely be terribly pleased if one day you were to tell a story about how much an elderly lady was helped by a wonderfully thoughtful and polite girl whose name happened to be Allie.

Activities for Older Children

Most of the listening activities that are appropriate for young children can also be adapted for use with older students. Also, listening experiences for students in middle and upper grades can include embedded lessons related to curriculum content from the classroom program. Possibilities could include the following:

- In mathematics students can attempt to convert spoken number words into numerals: one student (or a tape recorder) says, "One hundred twelve thousand six hundred seventy-five," and pupils attempt to write 112,675.
- An interesting social studies experience involves videotaping political debates such as those shown on public-affairs networks and then listening to them several times to note the kinds of issues involved in questions such as pollution control or raising the price of gasoline to encourage the use of smaller cars. (Emotion-laden topics should probably be avoided in the elementary school.)
- Students can listen, live or on tape, to communications between astronaut crews and ground control personnel during space flights. A great deal of the content—elapsed time for transmittal of messages and the conversion of electronic data into photos, for example—can be the focus of class science study.
- Interviews with retired nurses and doctors can be conducted to discover the ways in which medical treatment has changed during their years of service.
- Computer experts can be invited to class to give demonstrations and help students understand how computers operate.
- Children can dramatize scenes from their favorite works of literature (*The Wizard of Oz* or *Sounder,* perhaps) and record these for later listening. They could offer some parts to the principal or other teachers.
- Students learn most new words through encounters with them in reading and listening. Occasionally you may wish to deliberately use words that some students may know only vaguely or not at all (*contraption, erstwhile, fluctuate*) and then stop for a minute or two and repeat what was said or read so that they can attempt to grasp the meaning from the context.

AIDS FOR IMPROVING LISTENING

Several sources are available to aid in the teaching of listening. These include conventional learning materials such as records and books as well as electronic devices. In some classrooms there are "listening centers" where students may use earphones when listening to various kinds of recordings.

A Bulletin Board Idea

A GOOD LISTENER

1. Has a purpose for listening.
2. Thinks while listening.
3. Is not distracted from listening.
4. Controls his or her emotions.
5. Recognizes his or her responsibility to the speaker.
6. Prepares to react to what is heard.

Issues children can relate to:

- use of plastic in the lunchroom
- school dress code
- age limits for movies
- curfews
- acceptable TV programs

For information on obtaining tapes of educational radio programs write to:
National Public Radio
2025 M Street, N. W.
Washington, D. C. 20036

Listening Centers

A "listening center" consisting of cassette players on a table can provide a variety of valuable experiences.

Classroom listening centers are usually tables holding several playback machines equipped with earphones. In most situations four or five students can each listen to a separate disk or tape recording, although some arrangements permit several youngsters with headsets to listen to the same record simultaneously.

Recordings

Recordings of all kinds can be used in connection with listening experiences. This chapter has emphasized how teachers and students can make and use their own recordings. In addition, of course, many suitable commercial recordings are available and can be used effectively in the elementary classroom.

Music. Music is not only enjoyable for its own sake but is also relevant to the classroom program for other reasons. Some kinds of music tell stories themselves, and these should be introduced to children, *Peter and the Wolf* being a good example. Selections are sometimes effective because they associate important events in children's lives (Halloween) with music (*Danse Macabre*) that evokes related sounds and images (cemeteries and skeletons). Such selections may be placed in the classroom listening center, along with less well-known works—an opera or two, perhaps, since there may be children who would like to listen to one.

Listening centers may be used in many ways.

Poetry. There are recordings of poetry suitable for use in the elementary school. These include collections by particular poets and recordings related to the same topic. Of course, you can make recordings of poems for your own class, or they can.

Books. Full-length book favorites available on audiocassettes include, for young children, *The Tale of Peter Rabbit, Frog and Toad, Amelia Bedelia,* and *The Little Engine that Could.* Those for older students include *Nothing's Fair in the Fifth Grade; Are You There, God? It's Me, Margaret;* and *Where the Red Fern Grows.* Many of these are of such length that they might be loaned out for home use by some children who could listen to them while following along in the text.

Audio Recorders

Inexpensive audiocassette recorders provide many opportunities for classroom listening activities. You can record directions, study questions, practice exercises, and stories, leaving you free to provide more individual assistance to pupils. Some teachers record spelling lists and vocabulary exercises, as described in Chapter 8.

Video Recorders

Several possible uses of the video recorder in developing oral language were mentioned in Chapter 5, and this aid is equally relevant to listening. Many of the activities suggested for the audiocassette recorder will be even more effective if video equipment is available. Of particular value are recordings made of guest speakers. (A television weather commentator may be willing to come to a class and discuss both weather forecasting and television newscasting.) Students can watch such a tape several times to see how a "pro" tries to make sure that the audience hears a message.

Computers and Related Media

Some computers are equipped with voice synthesizers so that they can combine speech with visual presentations. Software programs that are useful in this regard permit the computer operator to type letters, words, and whole stories and then have these read back by the computer.

Multimedia presentations on compact disks permit students who are interested in a particular topic to view video selections, animations, and still pictures related to the subject and also to listen to sound recordings. A pupil interested in the Erie Canal can, for instance, while seated at a computer, look at pictures and maps related to the construction of the canal and read text displayed on the screen. Listening would involve the sound track on the video, oral history segments recorded by those who once traveled on canal boats, and songs such as *The Erie Canal.*

Children who wish to listen to familiar English materials spoken in other languages may use audio or video recordings to do this. Also available are hand-held electronic devices that pronounce the foreign-language equivalent of English words typed into them. Such experiences are likely to increase children's enjoyment of languages.

ASSESSMENT OF LISTENING

Am I a Good Listener?

1. *Do I pay careful attention and avoid doing anything distracting?*
2. *Do I show appreciation without calling attention to myself by commenting or laughing too loudly?*
3. *Do I jot down questions or notes for later discussion with the speaker?*

Taking into account the goals selected for the program, you can best determine whether a classroom group is making progress in the area of listening. If, for example, you have decided to give directions only once and then require those who don't know what to do to wait until a classmate has time to help them, you may see that, gradually, fewer pupils need such assistance. The same may be said of individual youngsters. Perhaps you realize that Donna, whose important needs are emotional, listens better if you are close by. This you can do for her while at the same time formulating a plan to help her to gain better control over her ability to attend and listen.

Standards

Setting guidelines for specific types of listening situations is a helpful activity because students need to develop listening standards. This experience gives them guidance as listeners and helps them evaluate how well they and other members of the audience meet their responsibilities. As they become increasingly adept at discerning what is important in a listening experience, they can outline their objectives in advance and then use them to assess the degree to which they achieved what they set out to do. For example, questions such as

Do I keep in mind the main idea of what I'm listening to?
Am I courteous in my listening?
Do I reserve judgment until the end of a presentation?
Do I try to understand how the presentation is organized?
Am I aware of transitional phrases and what they mean?
Am I aware that there may be bias on the part of the speaker?
Do I keep in mind what it is that I am listening for?

could be reviewed before an informational listening activity and then checked afterward to determine what actually occurred.

Portfolio Materials

Samples of students' listening performances at successive age levels can be taken and kept by means of audio- and videotaping. A child may be taped while listening to something spoken or read (live or on a record) and then respond by discussing and answering questions. A youngster could also be asked to write in response to what he or she has heard. Tape recordings and written work may be placed in the language arts portfolio along with, perhaps, the student's and the teacher's rating of how well the listening was done.

A FINAL WORD

In many ways listening has become more important in the modern technological world than it was in earlier times. Not only do we continue to have numerous face-to-face speech encounters each day (an experience shared with previous generations), but we also talk on the telephone a great deal, often to individuals located hundreds or even thousands of miles away and sometimes to people we have never met and will likely never meet. In addition, we listen to radio and television broadcasts and to much electronically recorded content.

Clearly, learning to listen well and for specific purposes is an increasingly important activity. Helping children to master these strategies must be viewed as an important function of the elementary-school program.

References

Basic Listening Skills. Illinois State Board of Education, 1982.

Costa, Arthur L., ed. *Developing Minds: A Resource Book for Teaching Thinking.* Association for Supervision and Curriculum Development, 1985.

Devine, Thomas G. *Listening Skills Schoolwide.* National Council of Teachers of English, 1982.

Dunleavy, Deborah. *The Language Beat.* Heinemann, 1992.

Duthie, Christine, and Zimet, Ellie Kubie. "Poetry Is Like Directions for Your Imagination!" *The Reading Teacher* 46 (September 1992), pp. 14–24.

Friedman, Paul G. *Listening Processes: Attention, Understanding, Evaluation.* National Education Association, 1986.

Lundsteen, Sara W. *Listening: Its Impact on Reading and the Other Language Arts.* National Council of Teachers of English, 1979.

Oregon Listening Curriculum, Primary and Intermediate Units. Oregon Teaching Center, 1976.

Parsons, Les. *Poetry, Themes, & Activities: Exploring the Fun and Fantasy of Language.* Heinemann, 1992.

Seiler, William; Schuelke, David; and Lieb-Brilhart, Barbara. *Communication for the Contemporary Classroom.* Holt, Rinehart and Winston, 1984.

Steid, Lyman et al. *Listening: It Can Change Your Life.* McGraw-Hill, 1987.

Thurber, Marshall. *The Listening Road to Literacy.* Literacy Publications, 1990.

Ur, Penny. *Teaching Listening Comprehension.* Cambridge University Press, 1984.

Upitis, Rena. *Can I Play You My Song? The Compositions and Invented Notations of Children.* Heinemann, 1992.

Wisconsin Department of Public Instruction. *Classroom Activities in Listening and Speaking.*

Teaching Resources

Listening Between the Lines. Alfred Higgins Productions (video; intermediate).

Listening Comprehension Skills Kit. Curriculum Associates (two levels; cassettes and other materials).

Listening Corner. Houghton Mifflin (manual, worksheets, cassettes, K–grade 3).

Listening Skills Unit. Aquarius People Materials, 1983 (grades 1–6).

Listening with a Purpose. Random House (twelve audiocassettes, response books, manual, and guide; grades 3–7).

Scholastic Listening Skills. Scholastic (kit).

Your Communication Skills—Listening. Coronet (video; grades 1–6).

Activities for Preservice Teachers

1. Obtain the instructor's permission to read a news article aloud to one of your classes and then give a comprehension test. How much variation in listening ability is there in the group? Do you believe that the best listeners are also the best students? (Repeat the test a week later and see what happens.)

2. Examine basal series in reading and language and identify "lessons in listening." Do you find any? What do they consist of? Report your results to the class.

3. Try to improve your own listening. Anticipate what speakers are going to say by looking for clues as to how the material being presented is organized and paying particular attention to summaries and conclusions. Do you notice any improvement in your comprehension?

4. Plan an activity for which specific directions must be given. Go over what you have prepared very carefully, noting where you have been incomplete or vague. Then try out the directions to see if someone can follow them exactly.

5. Add to the list of "listening books" given in this chapter.

6. With the permission of the speaker, record a lecture using both audio- and videocassettes. Play both tapes several times, noting differences between the two formats.

7. Talk with several teachers about what they do to teach listening. Do they relate teaching of listening skills to teaching in the content areas of the curriculum? Do they use audio recordings they make or ones marketed commercially?

What do they do about listening that is related to their teaching of reading? Report to the class on your findings.

8. Examine publishers' and distributors' catalogs for materials useful in teaching listening. Also check sources that review such materials (for example, *Language Arts, The Reading Teacher*, and *The School Library Journal*). Give particular attention to materials that relate listening to other aspects of the curriculum.

Activities for Inservice Teachers

1. Find out how many of the children in your class have their own audio cassette recorders. If several do, begin to plan some ways in which they could use the recorders to contribute to their class work.

2. Review expectations for listening in your daily program. What changes might be made with respect to the amount of listening expected of the children and the amount of guidance in how to improve their listening? Discuss this with the children.

3. Consider establishing a "listening center" in your classroom. What materials will you need? What space can be used? What sorts of activities will be emphasized?

4. Talk with a curriculum consultant or supervisor about some activities you might try that combine listening, thinking, note taking, and other study skills. (See Chapter 13 for further information.)

5. Try out different physical arrangements in your classroom and see if any seem to have a positive effect on listening behavior.

6. Visit the instructional media center of your school or district to determine what materials are available (such as video and audio recorders and players, prepared tapes, and activity kits) that might be used in teaching listening.

7. Tape discussions of small groups and then permit children to listen to them to see how much of what was said was actually listened to.

8. Tape directions for games. While the children are listening and following the directions, you can observe how well they listen.

9. Examine state or district curriculum guides in language arts to see what they recommend concerning listening. Discuss the need for attention to listening with members of a curriculum committee or an appropriate supervisor.

10. Prepare sets of listening lessons of the types discussed in this chapter for use with your children. Try these lessons, and report the results and your observations to the class.

Activities for Children

1. Tape-record various sounds—street traffic, children playing, sports crowds, and animal noises, for example— and ask children to listen to these and write as many associated words as they think of. The children can then write stories and poems based on these words.

2. Have pairs of children use "walkie-talkies" to practice taking messages and making notes (they can pretend to be secret agents or police on a stakeout).

3. Tape recordings of stories can be useful in many ways. For example, one child could listen to the story and select the best title from a list of possibilities provided on a card. Another could listen for the main idea or the se-

quence of events. A third could listen to discover the feeling or mood or to find words that bring to mind particular pictures: tall house, round face, worn shoe, and so on.

4. Have a child perform an experiment or construct an object after listening to directions only once. Directions may be taped, or they may be read by another child. Taped directions should be spaced to allow time to perform each step; the tasks might be simple ones, such as folding paper to make a hat. Oral directions for three to five simple tasks could be given all at once, for example: "Go to the window and raise the shade about two inches. Then come back, sit down in your chair, and fold your arms." Chil-

dren will enjoy thinking up unusual directions and attempting to perform tasks accurately.

5. Record tests such as those in *Weekly Reader* for children to take individually.

6. Have a child listen to a recorded story or description and then draw a picture of the scene described or an episode in the story.

7. A child can listen to a recorded story and then prepare cutouts to use with a flannel board while telling the story to other children. Listening individually permits the child to relisten to parts of the story in order to develop the sequence and to decide what illustrations she or he needs.

8. Have a child make a list of all the sounds heard in a particular place—for example, in the lunch line, on the playground, or at a certain street corner on the way to school. As an added bonus, the child might use the list to write a "sound picture" of the spot or try to find the best words to describe each sound.

9. As a variation of the preceding activity, a child can sit quietly in a corner of the room listening for sounds such as a clock ticking, a car going by, a whistle, a buzzer, a dog barking, or walking in the hall. He or she should write down a word or two for each sound heard. Or two children

can listen for the same period of time and compare the number of sounds they have heard.

10. Children can work in pairs, with one child reading a sentence and the other listening for words that sound alike. Sentences such as the following might be used:

> Jane knew that her mother would bring a new dress.
> The whole class saw the hole in the fence.

11. A child can listen to the weather report on radio or television and be prepared to present a forecast to the class, including expected temperature range, probability of precipitation, and so forth.

12. Newscasts can be listened to for the major topic reported, the name of the newscaster, the name of a public figure mentioned in the newscast, and so on.

13. Have a child take notes on an assembly program or a program presented to the class for the purpose of preparing a written summary for the class diary.

14. Oral presentations may be improved if a child tapes a poem or story she or he is going to read to the class and then listens to it several times to discover ways to improve the reading.

Chapter 7

Grammar and Language Usage

*U*ntil relatively recently what we call the elementary school was often generally known as the *grammar school,* and still is in some speech communities. The name reflected the expectation that children attending such an institution would be concentrating on learning to speak and write according to certain rules—what some commonly think of as the "grammar" of English.

In such schools much of the curriculum was indeed devoted to learning grammatical terminology, diagraming sentences, memorizing rules, and doing related exercises. It was presumed that these activities would teach children to speak and write well, certainly an admirable goal, not only then but now. But the presumption was not then and is not now valid. However, despite evidence provided by both research and experience, the tradition of emphasizing classification of words as *nouns, verbs,* or some other *part of speech* and putting *phrases* and *clauses* on patterns of straight and diagonal lines continues in some schools, with the teaching often just as formal and unproductive as it was in the past. Every day, however, many schools and teachers are demonstrating that the best way to help children learn to speak and write effectively is to encourage them to speak and write to the best of their ability while providing the kinds of assistance recommended in these chapters.

The chapter also deals with *usage,* the ways in which we customarily talk and write, language habits that have been developed unconsciously for the most part. "Usage" is, in fact, what many people mean when they say "grammar." Whether someone says "It was I" or "It was me" has to do with her or his background and, perhaps, the situation in which a conversation is taking place. This chapter discusses these matters in the context of the elementary school.

LEARNING AND TEACHING GRAMMAR

To many people the word *grammar* means "the rules" of sentence construction for speaking and writing correctly, including rules about punctuation, spelling, and handwriting. Less common, particularly outside of schools, is the term *usage,* which refers to the form of expression or choice of words a person makes when writing or talking. Saying "We was going" instead of "We were going" is a usage choice. Grammar, on the other hand, refers to the system of word structures and word arrangements in expression. Both of the examples just used are grammatical; however, expressions such as "Were going we" and "All the boy and girl are going" are ungrammatical—they are not valid in the English language.

Development of Grammar

Native speakers of English have the ability to judge whether or not a string of words is arranged in an acceptable manner, "acceptable," that is, in the sense of conveying meaning without regard to appropriateness of use in all social and business situations. Native speakers know the grammar of the language, at least in a general sense; they learn it at the *intuitive* level by communicating thoughts and acquiring meanings as they grow up. They would possess such knowledge even if they never went to school.

This learning of grammar begins to be apparent at the age of eighteen to twenty months when babies put together two-word combinations. Most of these early expressions involve a few words used in a particular position with a variety of other words. This type of experimentation lasts only a short time, but it is an important step. The child who says "Chair mama," "Chair dada," and "See chair" is trying out word order. Very young children gradually become aware that some types of words come first and others second. Compared to that of an adult, the child's understanding is sometimes faulty but, even so, it provides evidence of the development of a language system, or grammar, characteristic of the child's level of maturity.

Children learn the classes of words early (although not, of course, the grammatical terminology) and demonstrate this in using many of their first words in different contexts. The repeated words are likely to be nouns and verbs or, less often, adjectives. At this stage the meanings expressed are largely dependent on the context. The child who says "Mommy sock" may mean "Mommy, put on the sock" or, perhaps, "This is mommy's sock." Toddlers continue to talk mostly about the here and now but begin to use longer utterances, such as "Me push truck" or "Go outside swing now." Various sentence types appear: "He no hit you" and "Where Daddy go?" Pronouns begin to be used: "I go bed" and, of course, "Mine! Give me!"

This early development shows that children attach meanings to the words they use, that they know that the functions of these words may differ, and that they realize conveying meaning depends on the order in which the words are spoken. Their utterances provide clear evidence that young children develop an early understanding of the language system. Although this grammar is not the same as that of a mature speaker, it is a definite step toward it. Young children have not yet learned how elements such as auxiliary verbs, prepositions, and inflectional endings work, but as their experimenting continues, they do learn to use them. In fact, they begin to try out noun and verb endings with such constructions as *foots, goed, mines,* and so forth. Using these overgeneralizations, they gradually learn from the responses of others that some ways of saying things are widely used by speakers and some are not. As they mature, children learn how to make many generalizations about language use, but some of this learning takes a while.

Children entering a nursery school or even kindergarten or first grade are not yet literate in the generally accepted sense of the word, but they understand rather complex sentences when they hear them and know if a part of a sentence has been omitted or is in the wrong place. They speak in phrases and sentences that reflect their knowledge of language patterns. They know many words, and they know the language system well enough to realize that struc-

A four-year-old knows, without being taught, that we say "two red balls" but not "red two balls."

The examples of utterances are from Chapter 4 of Bryen's *Inquiries into Child Language.*

Most three-year-olds have the language under good, if not perfect, control.

tural changes can be made in certain words to achieve particular purposes and meanings (for example, adding endings such as *-s*, *-es*, *-er*, and *-ing*). Some children of this age occasionally confuse word order, add the wrong ending, or fail to add an ending at all, or have problems with tense or person, but basic comprehension of the system is present and developing. If it were not, the children would not have been able to communicate during their preschool years.

What is important to recognize is that children have reached quite an advanced level of language development by the time they enter school. However, since not all children are at the same level at this or any other point during their school years, language development must be a concern of the school. This concern should focus on the individual child as much as possible, since further development is likely to be sporadic: some children will only be able to grasp the basics; others will soon be ready to learn about placement of modifiers, using the passive voice, and developing complex sentences.

The Place of Grammar Teaching

As was stated earlier, the teaching of grammar—of any type or description—is supposed to help people write and speak more effectively. However, elementary-school children (and secondary-school students as well) do not appear to improve in expressive abilities by learning abstractions and applying rules. They gain communicative competence from direct experiences and attention to such specifics as variation of sentence patterns, vocabulary development, and use of language that is likely to be most effective in a given situation. Children learn to *write by writing* and to *speak by speaking* (and to *read by reading*), while receiving ongoing guidance from teachers who are sufficiently sensitive and knowledgeable to see where progress can be made.

For years elementary-school teachers have been prodded into teaching grammar by complaints, both real and imagined, from secondary-school teachers that pupils come to them unable to identify the parts of speech or tell a subject from a predicate. Of course, such ability has no direct bearing on developing effectiveness in speech or writing, and there is no evidence that the teaching of grammar in the secondary school has any more influence on language performance than it does in the elementary school. Pressure has also come from secondary-school foreign language teachers. Complaints from these teachers about students not "knowing" grammar reveal an apparent lack of awareness that there is no "universal grammar" and that many years of research evidence shows that the teaching of English grammar—of whatever type—has no bearing on the learning of a foreign language.

However, if the kinds of informal teaching procedures suggested in this book are followed, pupils entering junior or senior high school will very likely be able to identify subjects, predicates, and parts of speech. Certainly, if a teacher says to a student "Can you think of a better adjective to use?" it is legitimate to expect the student to know which word is the adjective. And the same may be said for the other major grammar items. But such knowledge can and should be taught as a corollary to actual speech and writing, not in isolation or as something of value in and of itself.

Hillocks (see References) has reviewed the evidence accumulated from research over many years and concluded that studying grammar has no effect on ability to write well.

Weaver (see References) provides an overview of grammar and grammar teaching.

Many teachers, even though they know that it is not a good use of their students' time, succumb to the pressure to use language textbooks and teach parts of speech through drill and practice.

Examining Grammars

Grammars, defined as "descriptions of the structure of a language," have developed and continue to develop in different forms as linguists seek better explanations for the workings of the complex phenomenon that is language. The following discussions of the grammars most commonly identified are necessarily brief and not intended to provide a thorough understanding of any one. Nor are they intended as something to be taught to elementary-school children. But as a teacher of language arts, you should have a solid understanding of your language and its workings. If you lack such knowledge, you should seek it out through further study, so that you may be better prepared to teach children "about English" as discussed in Chapter 1.

Traditional Grammar. **Formal traditional grammar** is a description of English that is based on the system of the Latin language. Historically, it was called simply grammar; the modifier *traditional* was added only recently, when other grammars began to appear. This description first arose about four centuries ago in an effort to explain why particular words were used or certain sentences constructed, and, since Latin was at that time the language of scholars, it was natural to choose Latin as the basis for the description. Words were classified into eight categories—nouns, verbs, pronouns, adjectives, adverbs, prepositions, conjunctions, and interjections—and there were subclasses for most of these (for example, common and proper nouns, transitive and intransitive verbs). Rules and definitions were formulated to show how these categories are related to one another and how they can be combined into "correct" sentences.

The problem with this description was the assumption that all languages have the same system (and all do, of course, have some sort of system). But English is a polyglot language. It descends to some extent from Latin but also has origins in the Germanic languages. Thus, it was—and still is—difficult to formulate rules that accommodate the many irregularities of English. Consider, for example, the formation of plurals: a majority of nouns form their plurals by the addition of *-s* or *-es,* but that "rule" does not cover the question of whether a final *-s* should be doubled before the *-es* is added or the multiplicity of exceptions, such as *knife* and *knives, foot* and *feet,* and *child* and *children.* Furthermore, there is great irregularity in the conjugation of some commonly used verbs; even people who think they know English grammar fairly well may sometimes have to consult a dictionary to make sure of the correct past tense or participle.

Despite these problems, traditional grammar was for years (and too often still is) taught formally, in the belief that learning its rules and definitions would assist children in their writing and speaking. Perhaps because of being taught so formally, traditional grammar has become *prescriptive* (emphasizing what is "right" and "wrong") rather than *descriptive* (emphasizing what speakers and writers actually do in real situations) and has not recognized that there are different levels of usage and that so-called correct usages that are awkward or difficult to learn are likely to disappear. Children have spent many hours learning to say "It is I" or "The stranger was he," but this type of structure is seldom used in writing and is today considered stilted in speech. Similarly, much time has been wasted in doing exercises that involve selecting *who* or *whom* (often in badly constructed sentences), even though an examination of much current

Some words will fit in several categories:
Brown is a dark color.
(noun)
She has *brown* hair.
(adjective)
He will *brown* the meat.
(verb)

writing would demonstrate that *whom* has virtually disappeared from our language (or, worse yet, that people trying to sound sophisticated will use *whom* at every opportunity, whether it is appropriate or not).

It should be noted, of course, that those who attempted the first description of English made a contribution. There may have been some flaws in their description, but their classification of words is still valid. Words such as *the* and *my* are now often called noun markers rather than articles or possessive pronouns; conjunctions and prepositions may be called connectors, clause markers, or phrase markers; but the four major classifications—noun, verb, adjective, and adverb—are still recognized. The important thing to remember is that English is a hybrid, complex, growing language, yet children have learned to use it well enough to satisfy their needs. They will learn to use it more effectively not by studying grammar, either traditional or modern, but by having many and varied experiences involving reading, writing, speaking, and listening.

Structural Grammar. A product of the scientific study by linguists of the way English is spoken and written, **structural grammar** does not prescribe what is "correct" but simply reports the language as it exists. The ways words are being combined with one another by writers and speakers are categorized, producing certain principles and patterns. These include basic sentence patterns, a rather small number in English, as shown here:

1.	Birds fly.	Only two words, one the subject and the other the verb
2.	Birds eat seeds.	Subject, action verb, and the recipient of the action
3.	Birds are animals.	Subject, linking verb, and a noun that completes the meaning
4.	Birds are beautiful.	Subject, linking verb, and an adjective that completes the meaning
5.	Birds give me pleasure.	Subject, verb, indirect object, and direct object
6.	Birds make people happy.	Subject, verb, direct object, and an adjective that completes the meaning
7.	They called birds vampires.	Subject, verb, direct object, and a noun that completes the meaning

In traditional grammar a word is described in terms of its meaning: *A noun is the name of a person, place, or thing* or *A verb expresses action or state of being*. In structural grammar, on the other hand, words are described in terms of form and function. As mentioned previously, the four major classes of words are called by their traditional names, but words such as *the, my,* and *some* are called determiners or noun markers; they signal that the word that follows is a noun. There are also verb markers (such as *can, could, might*), clause markers (*because, if, how*), phrase markers (*in, down, toward*), intensifiers or qualifiers (*very, just, less*), and connectors or conjunctions (*and, but, for*).

This system also has its problems, however. One way to illustrate some of them is to examine a nonsense statement: *Ra jerfuls buked ra vaky marm pugly* and classify the wordlike forms. To begin with, *Ra* is almost certainly an article, or noun marker, since it appears twice in a position where these are usually found. *Jerfuls,* then, is probably a noun (it also ends in *s,* an indication that it may

Children may create nonsense words and make sentences with them. This activity may be enjoyable, but there is no evidence that it does more than provide an opportunity to discuss clues furnished by word structure and word order.

be a plural form of a noun), and it occurs in the place where the subject is found much of the time; so tentatively *jerfuls* can be identified as the subject. *Buked* appears to be the verb, since it is in a typical position for a verb (this also confirms *jerfuls* as the subject, since the verb usually follows) and ends with *ed,* indicating past tense. At first glance, *vaky* might be the direct object but *marm* is more likely to be, since *vaky*—because of its position and *y* ending—is probably an adjective describing *marm.* And *pugly* must be an adverb because of its position in the sentence and *ly* ending.

Although this is a logical way to go about examining and explaining the way the language works, again the hybrid nature of English creates problems. Consider how many times the word *probably* or its equivalent was used in the preceding description. There is a very good reason for this. Suppose, for example, that the translation of the nonsense sentence is *The girls called the expensive dress ugly* or *Our enemies found our ally most unfriendly.* Then, neither its ending nor its position makes *pugly* an adverb or *vaky* an adjective, and we must fall back on meaning to make a determination. Other possibilities exist, of course, but these are sufficient to illustrate the problems faced by the linguist.

Another difficulty lies in the fact that not everyone speaks the same way; that is, there are social and regional differences in usage and pronunciation. Furthermore, English is spoken and written at different levels, something often influenced by the social situation. All of these problems make the scientific examination of the language a challenge. Of course, these difficulties also affect other grammars, but since the basis of structural grammar is its scientific determination, such problems raise questions as to the usefulness of this type of description of our language system.

Transformational Grammar. **Transformational grammar,** sometimes called **generative** or **transformational-generative grammar,** came into being after the development of structural grammar, as a result of the recognition by some grammarians of the impossibility of securing factual information on all possible sentences the speakers of a language may use. Transformational grammar has a theoretical base rather than an observable base such as that of structural grammar. To avoid the problems associated with examining actual utterances, transformational grammar assumes the existence of a *deep structure* system (the meaning) that leads to a *surface structure* (the sentences actually said and written). There are two basic types of sentences: kernel and transformed. *Kernel sentences,* of which there are a relatively small number, are the core of the system. They are sentences that cannot be derived by analysis from other sentences. The basic patterns for kernel sentences were illustrated in the preceding section, but these may be changed by speakers and writers to provide a great diversity of sentences, or *transformed sentences.* If the kernel sentence is *Birds eat seeds,* for example, several kinds of transformed sentences are possible. Three of the most common transformations are the following:

Birds do not eat seeds.	Sentence changes to give opposite meaning.
Do birds eat seeds?	Sentence changes to a question.
Seeds are eaten by birds.	Sentence changes so that the direct object becomes the subject.

See suggestions in Chapter 10.

Other kinds of transformations are possible. In writing, sentence combining and sentence expansion are especially significant. In sentence combining, two or more sentences are restated as one. For example, *Birds eat seeds* and *Birds eat worms* become *Birds eat seeds and worms*. Through sentence expansion, kernel sentences are made more informative and interesting by adding words (such as *many* and *yellow*), phrases (*from my garden*), and clauses (*when I am not at home*): *Many yellow birds eat seeds from my garden when I am not at home*.

Transformational grammar makes use of terminology similar to that used in structural grammar. Like structural grammar, it is not prescriptive, except in the sense of indicating whether or not a sentence is grammatical. There is no ruling as to correctness of the words used. However, transformational grammar can be taught as formally as traditional grammar, and this often is the case. Teaching it (or structural or any other grammar) can have the same emphasis on rules, relationships of words and phrases to one another (usually by a new kind of diagraming), isolation of the study from the expression of children, and activities that have little interest or meaning for children.

A Functional Approach to Teaching

There is no place in elementary schools for formal, direct, sequential instruction in grammar. This includes memorizing definitions (*An adverb modifies a verb, an adjective, or another adverb*), picking out parts of speech (*Is* for *a preposition or a conjunction in sentence number three?*), and explaining errors (*Find the wrong word and tell why it is wrong in the sentence, "Mom and me went shopping"*).

Most children have learned to understand and use the language spoken in their homes and neighborhoods without necessarily being able to respond to such questions correctly nor able to draw a diagram for either of the sample sentences. If a child comes from a home where the language spoken is not English, as a large number do in some communities, there is even less reason to teach English grammar in any kind of formal way. But teachers certainly have the responsibility for providing good language models and should take advantage of opportunities to use grammar-related terms such as *sentence* and *verb* (as well as *period, comma*, etc.) to build readiness for more sophisticated understandings.

Teachers also need to know the research evidence concerning grammar teaching, to understand and be able to explain the difference between grammar and usage, and to do what will improve youngsters' speaking and writing. They must also know a good deal about the kind of language study that appeals to children.

Children are not likely to feel much enthusiasm if the program is centered around a textbook that insists it is wrong to say, "Don't go in the house," and that it is normal and proper to say, "The team is we, the athletes." Children like to talk and they like to write; they want to tell what they have discovered and what they think about something. Thus, the program should focus on *using* language—speaking, writing, reading, and listening.

A language textbook may present ideas for using language appropriately. It also may be a source of examples and explanations (as noted in Chapter 2). The material on grammar need not be taught in the sequence used in the book, however, nor should the exercises provided be routinely assigned. Rather, your emphasis should be on *functional* teaching, on the examination of grammar as one aspect of expression.

Infusion of grammatical terminology into teaching of writing, speaking, and reading is mentioned in several chapters of this book.

Questions related to the structure of sentences come up in discussions of writing.

Teaching Grammar Functionally. Teaching grammar, then, must be related to actual use. In the terminology employed in this book, grammar should be taught mostly in conjunction with information processing activities and embedded lessons. For instance, information-processing activities such as teaching about the actions of historical figures and what they *could have* or *should have* done would provide an opportunity to teach an embedded lesson about the "helping words" as verbs and the problems involved when students write *could of (could've).*

You can, of course, include a grammar-related developmental program in your teaching. The aim should be gradual development, of course, and you must know what you want to emphasize and what your group is able to do. Certainly the classroom program itself will provide many opportunities for teaching grammar. The kindergarten or first-grade teacher who says "Let's give the names of things we saw at the bakery" is teaching grammar. So is the teacher of fifth graders who plans to use the word *adjective* in conjunction with science content on animal camouflage and a social studies activity involving transportation before emphasizing descriptive words during the writing period.

If your students construct sentences well and thus convey the messages they intend, there is no need to spend time on grammar. On the other hand, if a child says "The boys is going," the opportunity *may* be present to teach about agreement of subject and verb. Of course, the pupil can be taught that *is* should be called a *verb*, not just something referred to as "this word." In a similar way, if a pupil describes the bear that appeared in a videotape shown in class as simply a "black bear," a functional situation is present for teaching about using other adjectives (*big, quick,* etc.) to give a better word picture of what has been seen.

It is relatively easy to do such one-on-one teaching in a writing conference (see Chapter 10).

There is no need to avoid using grammatical terminology when it seems natural to use it. A verb is more properly called by that term than by "action word," and it is no more difficult to learn than many other words that children readily use. We don't call a television a "box that shows pictures" or a wheel "something that goes around," and children have no trouble with these words or the basic concepts they represent.

In the middle and upper grades, as students learn to combine their ideas into longer and more complex sentences, it is reasonable for a teacher to begin to use terms such as *phrase, clause,* and perhaps even *antecedent of the pronoun,* but these should *always* be introduced in relation to actual expression. Any definitions should come only after students have had a substantial amount of direct experience related to the concepts and terms involved.

Learning Activities. As indicated in the preceding section, you should consider ways in which grammar-related content can be taught within the context of normal classroom activities. These may relate to writing, oral language, or learning experiences in other subject areas. Activities should be developed with a specific group of children in mind and ought to be thought of as part of their continuum of learning in the language arts.

Expanding basic sentences: this activity can begin with simple forms such as *Birds sing.* Younger children may think of adjectives to describe the birds—*yellow, angry,* and so on. Then they can go on to consider sentence structure, making the sentence more complex and varied by turning the adjectives into phrases, clauses, verbs, or adverbs. For example, *the angry screeching yellow birds* might become *the angry yellow birds with the screeching cries* or *the yellow birds that screeched at us with angry cries* or *the yellow birds screeched angrily at us.* This kind of learning activity can also involve discussions of how words change form and position when used differently and, if done often, should lead to much greater variety in students' sentences.

Word order: this activity can involve presentation of simple sentences in jumbled arrangements, for example, *had many about airplanes Joe books read.* Children will have little trouble putting this sentence in order, but if phrases or clauses are added (*in the fourth grade* or *which were used in wars*) they will soon discover that word order is important to sentence sense. This kind of activity should be helpful to children who misplace sentence parts: "Having just eaten a rat, John saw that the snake was going to sleep." By using some of the children's own sentences noted during writing conferences, you will be able to help them see how the way a sentence is put together can contribute to meaning and effectiveness.

Sentence structure: this aspect of grammar can be explored in a variety of ways. One involves use of the overhead projector to show a paragraph in which all sentences are simple ones with the same structure (for instance, *subject–verb–direct object*). To demonstrate the need for variety, have them rewrite each sentence in the paragraph in the same way, and do this several times. Depending on the maturity of the students, they might first invert word order and make every active verb passive (*Children threw snowballs* becomes *Snowballs were thrown by children*), add an adjective before each noun in the subject position, begin each sentence with a prepositional phrase, or make all sentences compound by connecting pairs with the word *and.* After redoing each sentence in several ways, have the students select one new sentence from each rewritten paragraph to make another paragraph, and then another, perhaps experimenting with several differ-

Hearing good literature read aloud on a regular basis gives children a background for considering ways in which sentence structure may be altered.

"Clotheslines" with words fastened to them, magnetic display boards, and word charts with slots are all good devices for experimenting with word order in sentences.

Brief lessons on word order may be taught as an aspect of editing conferences.

One advantage of writing with word processors is that it is relatively easy to move sentence parts around and try different types of organization. Most students are not likely to do such rewriting by hand.

ent combinations of sentences. Evaluate the results by reading several paragraphs aloud and comparing them with the original.

In the upper grades the value of variety in sentence structure can be illustrated by rewriting a famous speech such as the Gettysburg Address or Patrick Henry's "Give me liberty, or give me death" oration, keeping vocabulary the same, insofar as possible, but structuring all the sentences in the same way.

Staying in tense and dealing with number and person: these are all concerns as students in the middle and upper grades deal with more complex speech patterns and writing tasks. Activities such as those suggested in the preceding sections can be changed to develop better understanding of the way language works in the areas of tense, number, and person as well. For example, if sentences are being rewritten and rearranged, try including various tenses of the same verb, both singular and plural forms of nouns, or a selection of pronouns (definite and indefinite; singular and plural; first, second, and third persons). Or play a game in which no one is allowed to use plurals, past tense, or a particular pronoun (first person singular, perhaps) for a certain period of time.

USAGE AND DIALECTS

This and earlier chapters have emphasized that the language anyone uses is largely a matter of early environment, although by the time a person is an adult he or she has learned a great deal about choosing language appropriate to the communication situation. Such choosing does not mean that a person invariably changes the pronunciation of words or modifies the expressions learned in childhood, but most people do pick up the jargon of their profession and social group and, in some situations, will try to avoid language that might be labeled nonstandard.

As students respond to questions about their reports, a teacher may note usage problems.

We suggest that there are levels of language, and differences in usage are sometimes viewed as being on various levels, such as *formal, informal,* and *colloquial,* and sometimes—in an attempt at finer distinctions—*illiterate, homely, informal standard, formal standard, literary,* and *technical.* An individual uses the language of one of these levels all or most of the time. We know that each person's language usage varies. However, usage is still largely termed *standard* and *nonstandard,* even though these terms are difficult to define.

Acceptable Usage

Deciding what the school should do about teaching usage is a major problem. In the first place, determining what usage is unacceptable is difficult at best. A textbook is only a partially satisfactory guide, as it is directed at a hypothetical classroom rather than an actual one, and the focus is often on grammar rather than on usage. Also, the items that textbook authors list as unacceptable are often not realistic. For some years language scholars have been recommending that only a very few usage items should receive instructional attention in elementary schools. In support of this position, one authority has stated:

1. The constant repetition of a relatively small number of deviations constitutes over 90 percent of the nonstandard usage problems in the elementary grades.

2. A large number of "errors" listed in textbooks and language workbooks are not errors at all but standard colloquial English appropriate to the speech and writing of children and adults alike.

The reluctance of many teachers to accept certain usages is the major reason why the number of usage items identified here and in most textbooks is not more limited. A study done several years ago showed that only about half as many teachers were accepting of *"Can* I have another helping of dessert, please," "Everyone put on *their* coats and went home," "Go slow," and "It is *me,*" as were editors and writers. A later study by Johnson (see References) showed that five items of usage identified as acceptable by linguists were regarded by teachers as incorrect (particularly in writing, but also in most cases in speech). The Johnson study dealt with the following examples of "incorrect" usage:

1. Everyone put their name in the upper left corner of the paper.
2. I will go to the store tomorrow.
3. The reason the page is missing is because Johnny tore it out.
4. They invited my friends and myself.
5. Who did you see?

Even more startling, this research also showed that 99 out of the 100 teachers participating in the study actually used at least one of the "incorrect" usages in either their own writing or speech, or both!

The list below is intended to be a guide to the kinds of usages that should receive attention in the elementary school. It is not likely that the children in any one class will use all of them—and of course the items should only be focused on if the need is present. In no case, however, should all of them receive direct

In some dialects speakers say "anyways." Is this acceptable as standard English? What does your dictionary say?

What could possibly be wrong with number 2?

teaching effort in a single year. If the children use a large number of them, it is best to select those that occur most frequently and focus on these few so that your teaching effort is concentrated in significant areas.

ain't or *hain't*	*hadn't ought*	where *it* at?
yourn, hern, ourn	he *give,* he *walk*	where *is* she *at?*
hisen, theys	*me and Mary* went	he *run*
youse	she *taken*	have *saw*
onct	I *likes* him	I *says*
hisself, theirselves	I *drunk, drunks*	he *seen*
hair *are*	*can't hardly*	*them* books
a orange	*does* we have	*this here*
have *ate*	my brother, *he*	*that there*
they *eats*	*her* and *me* went	*us* boys went
was *broke*	there *is* four	we, you, they *was*
he *brung*	there *was* four	with *we* girls
he *come*	they *knowed*	have *went*
clumb	I, they *growed*	have *wrote*
had, have *did*	haven't *no,* isn't *no*	the *mens*
she, he *don't*	*leave* (for let)	*learn* me a song
it *don't*	haven't *nothing*	
didn't ought	that's *mines*	

Because language does change and because the studies cited suggest that teachers and textbooks are often slow to recognize this, you may need help in deciding what to teach. Two ways to obtain this aid are to listen to the speech of educated people and to read current newspapers and magazines; doing these with particular usages in mind can be very revealing. For instance, some young people say "like" and "y'know" at every pause in their speech. Keeping current about language that is acceptable (and those two examples are not) is important for teachers who wish to help students drop such speech habits. Of course, appropriateness of words and expressions can be checked in reference books such as dictionaries, but sometimes these are not really current and may largely reflect the point of view of their authors.

Dialect Differences

It is certainly true that the pronunciations, vocabulary, and language structures of some children are such wide departures from the standard language or prestige dialect of the community that they cannot be ignored in the classroom. On the other hand, the dialects of other children may differ from the prestige dialect yet not depart widely from the language found in the community. Thus, the attention that must be given to various usages may be minimal, since many of the differences cause no real communication difficulties and do add color and individualism to expression.

Dealing with dialect differences can be important, however, if a youngster consistently communicates in a way that others consider inferior. There is a possibility that he or she will have social and academic difficulties, and you should be prepared to deal with these. For the most part, however, at the elementary level students' dialects do not require much attention.

The teaching of children who are learning English as another language is discussed in Chapter 16.

Teachers should be well informed concerning dialect differences in a community so that they can judge which characteristics are worthy of attention. The following are the principal types of distinctions often observed:

1. absence of inflectional endings (*-s, -es, -'s, -s', -en, -ed, -ing*) ("I need twenty cent," "That Bill shirt," "Yesterday we climb a tree")
2. analogical forms such as *hisself* or *theirselves* and possessives such as *ourn, yourn, hisn, hern,* and *theirn*
3. double comparatives and superlatives, such as *more prettier* and *most lovingest*
4. Omission of the copula *be* (usually *is,* for example, "She a bus driver")
5. *be* as a finite verb ("He be fast" for "He runs fast")
6. differences in the principal parts of verbs, such as *growed* or *drawed* as past tense, *rid* as the past participle of *ride,* and *clumb* as the past tense or past participle of *climb*
7. use of *youse* as a plural (or even a singular) pronoun

It is important to recognize that a child using such expressions is not being careless. Attentive listening will reveal that there is a system to the sentence construction as well as to the pronunciation and the vocabulary used. The child is using language that is familiar and that has worked well in meeting his or her communication needs.

In addition, no teacher should overlook the fact that his or her speech may not be fully understood by a child. Not only may the teacher use words unfamiliar to the child, but the pronunciations or the names given to objects or actions may be new as well.

Standard English

Which is the more acceptable past tense of:
  drag: dragged or *drug?*
  dive: dove or *dived?*

Parents and others in our society expect schools to teach "good English," meaning that they want children to learn the English that "important" people in the community use. This is the **standard English** referred to earlier that is so difficult to define. In fact, it simply cannot be defined in terms of specific words or pronunciation. However, it can be thought of as expression that is appropriate to the purpose of the speech or writing, that is consistent with the system of the language, and that is comfortable to both the expressor and the audience. It is language that is natural and uncramped by rule, reflecting custom that is widely accepted by society because it serves the needs of society. It changes with the communication needs and other alterations in society.

This definition is based on criteria that the National Council of Teachers of English has long urged teachers to observe. According to these criteria, acceptable usage

1. is determined by the living language of today
2. recognizes dialectal, geographical, and vocational variations
3. is judged by its appropriateness for the purpose intended
4. recognizes that there are situational levels of speech
5. takes into account the historical development of the language

TEACHING ABOUT USAGE

Judgments about adults are frequently made on the basis of the language they use. Fair or not, this is a fact. Thus, even though the way a child uses language at home and in his or her neighborhood is satisfactory for immediate communication needs, it may not serve lifetime needs, and the child may later be at a disadvantage if the school has not attempted to teach a more widely acceptable dialect. It is important, therefore, to help each child to see the advantage of learning and using standard English, but it is equally important to do this without condemning his or her original dialect.

Procedures for teaching language usage are not as well defined as would be ideal. However, the following sections suggest instructional principles and practices that appear to have the best foundation in research evidence and learning theory and to have received the greatest acceptance by teachers. These should help teachers who are frustrated by the failure of efforts they have made to bring about changes in the language children use. Many teachers do not modify their procedures in spite of being aware that what they have been doing is often fruitless, possibly because they do not know how these procedures might be changed. It is also possible that they do not appreciate the fact that language habits are really that—habits—and habits are not easily changed.

Point out to children that we don't wear the same clothes to church and to play outside. Neither do we talk the same way in those two situations.

To expect children to change their language usage because a teacher or a textbook says they should is unrealistic. What is realistic is to recognize that the daily program in every classroom presents numerous opportunities for children to use a more generally acceptable language for genuine communication purposes. What is also realistic is to realize that pupils learn by doing. If children are to speak and write a standard dialect, they must have practice in speaking and writing it. Rules and exercises are too far removed from genuine communication to have much value.

Determining Usage Problems

It is not possible to indicate the specific items of usage that you may need to teach, since the language backgrounds of children vary widely. The usage items suggested earlier in this chapter are a guide, but the specific needs of the children in a class must be determined by a survey of the oral and written usage of the children in that class.

On the following page are examples of survey forms you can make and use to record usage items that very likely need instructional attention. Listening to the children in the classroom and on the playground and observing their writing will provide the information for the first form. Note language patterns (grammatical structures) as well as individual words.

The form at the bottom of the page may also be useful. This one focuses on items previously selected; if filled in at regular intervals, it provides a simple means for noting particular improvements by the children.

Teaching Procedures

The most vital factor in teaching acceptable usage is motivation. Therefore, every possible device must be utilized to relate the activities of the classroom to

	Usage survey for _____			
	verb forms	pronouns	redundancy	illiteracies
Michael	he growed			yourn
Amanda			John he	
Scott			this here	
Toni	be tall			yourn
Debra	axt			
Brian				
Jeffrey		it's		
Julie	has took			

	Chris	Kelly	Jill	Todd	Kurt	Miguel	Danielle	Rosalita	Linda	Barbara
I goes	✓		✓	✓				✓		
brung	✓	✓		✓						✓
he don't				✓		✓	✓			
hisself	✓	✓								
me and ____			✓		✓		✓			
drawed	✓	✓				✓				
he be late	✓		✓	✓						
he a tall boy	✓									
rid for rode		✓								

the basic goals of each pupil. Children must be made to feel that standard English is actually in widespread use (thus, as suggested earlier, the items taught must be realistic ones) and that learning it will benefit them personally. They must be shown that their communication is, at least in many situations, more effective when they use standard English.

Acceptance of children and the language they use is the most important aspect of teaching usage. Finding fault doesn't work; all adults recognize this through their own experience. Acceptance means more than simply recognizing that children can and should use their own dialect when it is appropriate (on the school bus, for example). It means also accepting each child's cultural heritage—family, neighborhood, style of living, and so on. It means encouraging children to talk and write about their experiences and the things that are important to them.

Begin by surveying your class early in the year and at intervals throughout the following months. From these surveys choose only a few usage items for concentrated teaching effort. A few items will probably apply to the entire class, and these may receive total class instruction. Items needed by only a few may be worked on individually or in small groups. Only the most frequently used and grossest departures from acceptable usage should be selected for teaching—perhaps by comparing the children's speech with lists of divergent dialect features or misused words such as those presented earlier in this chapter. After usage items have been selected, identify them for the children, along with the reasons for their selection, without making any child feel inadequate because he or she employs a particular usage.

Usage items may be dealt with in two ways. First, and most important, opportunities must be provided for the children to use accepted alternatives to the particular items being emphasized in natural communication. The focus should always be on communication rather than on usage, but teaching directed toward identifying the particular items need not be minimized by this focus. Simply encourage the children to use the accepted forms selected ("We have decided to say _____ here in our room"), and do so without fault-finding or placing undue stress on them. Second, continue to work toward building interest in words and expressions and in language generally. This is done principally through providing experiences with language of many kinds. Read to children regularly from both imaginative and factual materials and call attention to the pictures created by words, as well as to the emotional reactions they call forth. Particular attention should be given to variations in language used for different purposes—for example, a science lesson and a story containing conversation.

This kind of activity can be combined with discussions about dialect, colloquialisms, and differences in situational usages. Children might collect sentences heard on the playground and revise them into language appropriate for an assembly announcement or a social studies report. Activities such as those suggested earlier in this chapter for teaching grammatical concepts (see Learning Activities) can also be adapted for usage practice. For example, tagboard strips containing noun and verb phrases can be combined, with children saying sentences aloud as they are formed. Both seeing and hearing the accepted forms will help to provide reinforcement.

As much as possible, the children themselves should assume the responsibility for making changes. Encourage them to work independently, both individu-

If you have a particularly good relationship with a class, you may be able to get them to use a signal (buzzing like a bee, perhaps) whenever anyone hears a particular form of usage the group is trying to avoid.

Elimination of a particular speech item (for example, "Me and him played") begins only when the child recognizes it in his or her own speech.

ally and in groups, keeping their own lists of individual problems and charting progress they make in learning new forms. This will help to focus their attention on their own particular problems and provide motivation by concentrating on improvement.

In short, then, providing for much use of language (both oral and written) in meaningful situations, presenting many opportunities for children to see and hear language that is well used (through books, records, films and filmstrips, and your own language), and including frequent, *brief* drills on a limited number of items that have been selected for your particular pupils, should result in some measure of success in teaching children to use language more effectively.

A FINAL WORD

Grammar and usage are two aspects of the language arts for which instructional decisions must clearly be made by the teacher rather than taken from textbook materials. For this reason you need to understand the English language as thoroughly as possible, including the usages that are acceptable or unacceptable in particular situations, and to appreciate and have some knowledge of various dialects. You also need to understand and be able to use the techniques suggested here for teaching your students about our language, its structure and usage, and how it may best be employed in communicative situations. The extent to which a class needs help with standard English or is interested in or ready for examination of sentence structure can only be fully understood by a knowledgeable teacher who interacts with students daily. Much time and effort will be wasted if, instead, teaching of grammar and usage is based on textbooks or duplicated worksheets.

References

Baron, Dennis E. *Grammar and Good Taste.* Yale University Press, 1982.

Bryen, Diane Nelson. *Inquiries into Child Language.* Allyn and Bacon, 1982.

Daniell, Beth. "Rodney and the Teaching of Standard English." *Language Arts* 61 (September 1984), pp. 498–504.

Hillocks, George, Jr. "Grammar and the Manipulation of Syntax," in *Research in Written Composition,* pp. 133–151. National Conference on Research in English/ERIC Clearinghouse on Reading and Communication Skills, National Institute of Education, 1986.

———. "Syntheses of Research on Teaching Writing." *Educational Leadership* 44 (May 1987), pp. 71–82.

Holbrook, Hilary Taylor. "ERIC/RCS Report: Whither (Wither) Grammar?" *Language Arts* 60 (February 1983), pp. 259–263.

Johnson, Robert S. "A Comparison of English Teachers' Own Usage with Their Attitudes Toward Usage." Doctoral dissertation. Teachers College, Columbia University, 1968.

Lindfors, Judith Wells. *Children's Language and Learning.* Prentice-Hall, 1980.

Noguchi, Rei R. *Grammar and the Teaching of Writing.* National Council of Teachers of English, 1991.

Non-native and Nonstandard Dialect Students. National Council of Teachers of English, 1982.

Pooley, Robert C. *The Teaching of English Usage.* National Council of Teachers of English, 1974.

Temple, Charles, and Gillet, Jean Wallace. *Language Arts: Learning Processes and Teaching Practices.* Little, Brown, 1984.

Weaver, Constance. *Grammar for Teachers: Perspectives and Definitions.* National Council of Teachers of English, 1979.

Teaching Resources

COMPUTER SOFTWARE

Dragon Games. Educational Activities (disk and guide; grades 3–6).
Grammar Gremlins. Scholastic.
Group Grammar. Tom Snyder Productions (grades 5–8)
Kid Bits Words Fair. Potomac MicroResources, 1982 (K–grade 4).
Microcourse Language Arts. Houghton Mifflin, Software Division (diskette; grades 3–8).
Noun Bound. Scholastic.
Parts of Speech. Hartley (grades 4–6)
Usage. JMH Software of Minnesota (tape and diskette; grades 3–8).
Verb Usage Multi-Pak. Hartley (grades 3–5)
VERBatim. Scholastic.
Wally's Word Works. Sunburst, 1985 (guide, three disks, and record sheet; grades 4–6).

VIDEOTAPES

Basic Grammar Series. Society for Visual Education.
Grammar As Easy As ABC. Greenleaf.
The Search for the Stolen Sentence. Society for Visual Education.

OTHER RESOURCES

Baten, Linda. *Grappling with Grammar.* Children's Story Scripts (dramatizations).
Bell, Sandra M., and Wheeler, James B. *Learning Grammar through Writing.* Educators Publishing Service (grades 3–8).
Goffstein, Marilyn B. *School of Names.* Harper and Row, 1986.
Morley, Diane. *Marms in the Marmalade.* Carolrhoda Books, 1984.
Page, Mary; Guthrie, Peter; and Sable, Sloan. *Rules of the Game: Grammar through Discovery.* Educators Publishing Service. (grades 5–9).
Terben, Marvin. *Your Foot's on My Feet! And Other Tricky Nouns.* Houghton Mifflin, 1986.
Treanor, John H. *Exercises in English Grammar.* Educators Publishing Service.
Goffstein, M. B. *A Writer.* Harper and Row, 1984.
Heller, Ruth. *A Cache of Jewels and Other Collective Nouns.* Grosset and Dunlap, 1987.
Heller, Ruth. *Kites Sail High.* Grosset and Dunlap, 1988. (verbs)

Activities for Preservice Teachers

1. Ask others in your classes to define terms such as *adjective, reflexive pronoun, weak verb,* and *subordinate clause.* What do they say? Do they recall studying definitions for these in school? If they recall the school definitions, ask them how frequently they've needed to know them. For what purposes?

2. Videotape television programs that make extensive use of characters with strong dialects (don't forget British, Irish, and Australian productions on the Public Broadcasting System's stations). Pick out particular characters and play their scenes several times. How do their dialects differ from yours? Try to speak as they do. Ask others to tell you how you do.

3. Compose a paragraph using only simple sentences and plan the kinds of sentence-structure revisions you might ask a particular group of students to make.

4. Observe a particular class over several days, and listen to their use of language. Make a record of nonstandard items that require attention. Based on your observations and record, to which items would you give teaching priority? Why?

5. Work out some techniques that you might use for the items you identified in the preceding activity.

6. Note differences in usage that you hear on television and radio and among your associates. Divide those you find into examples of dialect differences and examples of nonstandard usage.

7. Examine several elementary-school language textbooks to see how much attention they give to grammar definitions and rules. To what extent is there a balance in emphasis between such material and functional language use? Which, if any, of the textbooks would you want to use?

8. Consider several common usages that some would classify as "poor English": *Who do you want to speak with? I'm feeling very good. Help each child with their work. We don't have hardly any.* Do you use any of these? If so, do you see any reason to change?

Activities for Inservice Teachers

1. Ask the teachers in your school to estimate the proportion of pupils who speak standard English. What do they think? Is there agreement? What kinds of definitions do they seem to be using? Ask some secondary-school English teachers the same question.

2. Find out from supervisors or members of a curriculum committee how much attention is being given to the teaching of grammar and usage in your school system. To what extent is the emphasis on "correct" grammar as opposed to language use?

3. Carefully examine the writing of one of your favorite authors (King or Oates, for example). Do you find any sentences that do not meet the definition of a sentence as given in many elementary-school language textbooks? Do you find any other constructions that seem to break traditional grammatical rules?

4. Videotape some programs that have characters who do not speak standard English. Being careful to avoid racial stereotypes, discuss some examples with your class, and use this discussion as a departure point for sensitizing them to the issue of appropriate language for given situations.

5. Prepare a survey form similar to one shown in this chapter, and assess your class. Then plan with the students a campaign to eliminate a few common problems.

6. Have an oversized stuffed animal (*Fuzzy Bear*) announce which usage form the class is working on by hanging a sign around the bear's neck with the item written on it (*WE WAS*, for instance) and the symbol for *NO* (red circle with diagonal line) superimposed on it. From Fuzzy's legs and ears hang signs with acceptable alternatives written on them: *WE WERE, THEY WERE, YOU WERE, I WAS, SHE WAS, HE WAS*. As with any advertising campaign, everyone can help Fuzzy rid the room of what is seen as undesirable.

7. Devise patterns to help students analyze usage situations. If they say "Her and me went," break it down into: "Her went" and "Me went." When students reject these because they sound like "baby talk," lead them to make substitutions and then combine these into, "She and I went." (Also point out why *she* ought to come first.)

8. Evaluate your own ability to identify parts of speech. Assess your situation in terms of your need to use such knowledge in working with children in writing. Are there some matters you need to clarify?

Activities for Children

1. Have pupils make individual checklists of expressions to try to avoid in their writing. For example, someone might list these in two columns:

Words I Use with Friends	Words I Use in Writing
I ain't gonna do it.	I am not going to do it.

Only a few expressions should be worked on at a time. When these have been mastered, the child can add others.

2. Tape-record children using nonstandard and standard forms, and then let them listen to themselves. The contrast will help them identify the differences. Expressions to start with might include these:

have ate	have went	was broke
she give	he brang	them books

3. Write on cards sentences in which the child is to substitute phrases. For example, a sentence such as *He wanted to go to the store* might be used with directions to the child to substitute other words or phrases at the appropriate point in the sentence: *to the playground, come with us,* or *game.*

4. Prepare a set of cards with a two-word sentence on each (*Cars raced; Dogs barked; Snow fell*). Adding one or a few words at a time, the child is to expand each into a series of sentences, for example:

> Snow fell.
> Snow fell steadily.
> Snow fell steadily all day.
> Snow fell steadily all day long.

5. To help individual children with word order, make cards with simple instructions, such as the following:

> Write a simple sentence. Then add an adverb to make your sentence more specific. Tell how, when, or where. For example:
>
> The horse jumped.
> The horse jumped *suddenly.*
>
> Rewrite the sentence with the adverb in another position. Add your adverbs to your personal dictionary.

6. Prepare cards or duplicated sheets from which students can select sentence exercises such as the following:

Put in missing words.

The _____ man _____ scolded the _____ boy.

There was a _____ storm _____ night.

Directions may include listing as many words as possible that would "make sense" for each blank.

7. Give the child cardboard strips containing noun and verb phrases. Have her or him see how many can be matched so that they make meaningful sentences. As an extension of the activity, you could write coordinating conjunctions (*and, but,* etc.) and subordinating conjunctions (*if, because, when,* etc.) on other strips that could be used to form compound and complex sentences.

8. Using cards of various colors, make stacks of different classes of words and phrases: determiners, nouns, verbs and verb phrases, adjectives, adverbs, prepositional phrases, and conjunctions or clause markers. Pupils may experiment with word order and structure by making sen-

tences from these. As an enrichment activity for especially able students, gerunds (*running* as a noun) and participles (*running* as an adjective) may be added.

9. Using the letters in their own names, children can list adjectives they believe describe themselves:

> JOAN joyful, obedient, active, nice
> TOM terrific, organized, mighty

Or they can do the same with verbs that tell what they do:

> DIANE dives, investigates, announces, nails, enjoys
> SAM skates, argues, moves

10. Individual children can make lists of incomplete sentences to share with the class at a later time. Other children then try to think of words and/or phrases that fill the blanks and make interesting sentences.

> I looked out the window and saw _____ .
> Sitting on the front doorstep was _____ .
> He _____ the cake _____ .

Chapter **8**

Learning about Words: Vocabulary, Spelling, and Dictionary Use

*T*he English language is rich in words and more of them are being added every day; in addition, new definitions for existing words are being established. Space travel, computer technology, and the vibrancy and creativity of cultural groups within our own society are among the influences causing new words and meanings to appear and be adopted. As was pointed out in the first chapter, many words in English are borrowed from other languages, and this process is continuing as international contacts increase.

When students encounter a new word, questions about its pronunciation, spelling, and possible meanings inevitably occur. Certainly, the elementary school program must be concerned with areas such as vocabulary growth, meanings of words, and correct spelling. All of these make a significant contribution to the pupil's understanding of our language.

WORD STUDY IN THE CLASSROOM

Organize classroom spelling challenges. Anyone can bring in an unusual word for others to try to spell.

It is important that the entire classroom program involve significant concern with words. Students ought to be exposed to a large number of spoken and written words and this should be a significant goal for all of your teaching. Attention needs to be given to meanings, word selection, pronunciations, spellings, and relationships to other words. Daily teaching activities should stress all aspects of word learning. If the environment is rich in potential vocabulary items and you and the class members enjoy using a variety of words and talking about their meanings and appropriateness, a very good learning climate has been established.

Word Lists. Students should keep personal word lists, including new ones encountered in reading and needed in writing, their own particular spelling difficulties, and words from curriculum areas such as social studies and science. If there are computers available to the children, they can easily use these to keep records of words in several categories.

Library Resources. Classrooms and school libraries ought to be supplied with word-related resources such as dictionaries, thesauruses, writing guides, and books about word origins and related matters.

Electronic Devices. The school and classroom environment ought to include equipment such as typewriters, audio- and videotape recorders, microcomputers with software programs related to spelling and other areas, and word processors with provision for automatic checking of spelling and using built-in thesauruses. Electronic dictionaries are also discussed in this chapter.

196

Word Games and Puzzles. Games played directly or indirectly with alphabet letters and words should be encouraged. Popular ones are hangman, Scrabble, anagrams, searches for words in matrices, crossword puzzles, and riddles. Many of these as well as dozens of others are available in the form of computer software.

Literature. In addition to books about words, include poems (*The Walrus and the Carpenter,* for instance), stories that make imaginative use of words (*The BFG* by Roald Dahl), and even songs with special attention to words (*Supercalifragilisticexpialidocious*) in the classroom program. Books involving play with words are popular: Fred Gwynne has written *The King Who Rained* and there are several about an often confused Amelia Bedelia.

VOCABULARY

A 1972 study by Thomas showed that 1,000 words account for 83 percent of all words used in children's writing; 2,000 account for 89 percent.

Another study found that the following words account for 36 percent of all words written:

the	of	on
I	is	they
and	was	that
to	have	had
a	my	she
you	are	very
we	he	will
in	for	when
it		

Knowledge of words is very important, enabling us to express what we mean with precision (we can say that a person is "happy," "pleased," "overjoyed," "blissful," "ecstatic," "over the moon," or whatever). Words are basic to our understanding and the ability to express ourselves. Much of the capacity to think depends on having an extensive vocabulary, and vocabulary is an important factor in assessment of intelligence.

Clearly, the school has an important role to play in increasing the student's stock of usable words—generally and in specific fields such as biology, mathematics, and geography.

Growth of Vocabulary

As was described in several of the preceding chapters, beginning speakers normally develop their vocabularies very rapidly. Although there are problems in defining exactly what it means to *know* a word and in precisely determining the size of a person's vocabulary, there does appear to be substantial evidence that the average three-year-old child knows as many as 2,000 words and the high-school student has a vocabulary of 40,000 items. This indicates that the individual adds approximately 3,000 words per year to her or his vocabulary, which means, on the average, *8 to 10 words per day.* (Some authorities believe that young children may go through periods when they learn as many as *20 new words per day.*)

Data in this table are adapted from *The Nature of Vocabulary Acquisition* (see McKeown et al. in References).

Estimates of Vocabulary for Ages 3 to 11

AGE	VOCABULARY ESTIMATE
3	2,000
5	7,000
7	13,000
9	19,000
11	25,000

Learning Vocabulary

Studies of vocabulary development generally show that direct teaching of words is possible in the elementary school but isn't very practical. Therefore, we do not usually think of a developmental program in vocabulary. This is not done, first of all, simply because of time. It appears from research results that, for a child to learn a word, she or he ought to spend about 20 minutes studying it and then would need to find it used 20 or more times before it became part of her or his vocabulary. Even if you did nothing but teach words all day long, only a few hundred could be presented in a year.

If having a good vocabulary is important (and we can agree that it is), but doing a lot of teaching about words (with, perhaps, regularly scheduled classes, workbooks, testing, and all the rest of what ordinarily goes with routine teaching) doesn't seem to be an efficient procedure, the question remains as to how schools can best help students develop their vocabularies. The only reasonable assumption is that we learn words naturally, through hearing them used, trying them out, seeing them in print, studying them as we need to, and so forth. Those who have very large vocabularies—100,000 or more words—evidently learned them that way. Fortunately, these are the very activities found in a lively and well-run classroom. Thousands and thousands of words have been encountered, used, and very often learned as a consequence of information processing in classroom activities.

There is evidence that the average fifth grader reads a total of one million words in a year.

In this chapter we do recommend that you occasionally take some time to teach embedded lessons in vocabulary or word study, however. There will be times when unfamiliar words appear in news reports and in discussions of neighborhood events—*effluent,* perhaps, in connection with a public health problem—and this may become the focus of a brief lesson, without the expectation that every student is going to immediately understand and retain what is heard. It is also desirable that the children have some enjoyable experiences with words in school, and this can best be accomplished through use of games, puzzles, contests, and other enrichment activities that do teach but are also simply fun for students and the teacher.

Whatever word study is done should be carried out in conjunction with academic work in, especially, social studies and science, although important vocabulary items also appear in mathematics, music, physical education, art and other special subjects, depending on what is included in the school program.

Vocabulary and School Subjects

There are many ways in which vocabulary learning is advanced through reading and the other language arts, of course. But studying of all kinds involves the examination of word meanings.

Reading. Studies indicate that the single most important influence on vocabulary development is wide reading, in school and at home. Those who read much and read widely will eventually have large vocabularies. As with vocabulary study in any field, though, the reading program should not be dominated by the study of "new words" in isolation. (See Chapter 12 on reading.)

Writing. Effective writers use words carefully and it often happens that they need to find just the right one for the piece that they are working on. They will, of course, be in an advantageous position if they already know many synonyms

Extensive reading builds vocabulary.

for *bright* when they want to describe the effect of the moon on the beach. If the right word doesn't seem to come they need to go looking for it—in their own word list, in a thesaurus, or in lists stored in computers and available at the click of a few keys. It is a happy result if they find not only the word that helps in this situation but learn two or three others in the course of the search.

Science and Social Studies. In Chapter 1 we stated that elementary teaching should be composed, in part, of work on large-scale units or themes such as "Jets and Rockets" or "Ancient Greek Civilization." An important aspect of such study is learning concepts, some of which may be entirely new to students. If the topic is rockets, for example, vocabulary items likely to be acquired will include *thrust, vanes,* and *trajectory.* Studies of word clustering indicate that a topic such as farming will provide the opportunity for children to learn as many as 40 new words and, very likely, several new meanings for known words.

> A *glossary* is a mini-dictionary for a particular book. Usually found in the back, it provides a list of important words together with their definitions and pronunciation aids.

Other Subjects. Whether mathematics (*trapezoid, reciprocal*), music (*sonata, percussion*), art (*tempera, perspective*), physical education (*aerobic, biceps*), computers (*byte, software*), foreign languages (*case, inflection*), or library (*atlas, fiction*), special subjects available in elementary schools offer countless opportunities for learning words and meanings.

Vocabulary Activities

Although the best opportunities to develop vocabulary occur in connection with free reading, studying in content fields, and lessons that naturally occur, a number of activities can occasionally be undertaken simply for interest or because a specific experience represents a kind of embedded lesson in one area or another.

Synonyms. In addition to opportunities in writing, possibilities exist for taking a few minutes occasionally to consider how words can have similar meanings but still be distinctive. With regard to synonyms, students can be asked to find replacements for such overworked words as *awesome, cute, nice, good,* and *real* and more descriptive alternatives for *little, hot, pretty* or *sad.* Children can be challenged to be alert for the appearance of words that do not express much meaning and think of ways to replace them. A list of "target words" can be posted and one or two focused on from time to time, along with a list of alternatives.

Antonyms. Antonyms or opposites are of less significance than synonyms in classroom activities, but there is some value in knowing them when writing, since thinking of opposites can sometimes be helpful in finding just the word needed.

Also, it can be an interesting exercise to think of antonyms. Children can begin with those that are relatively easy (*hot–cold, young–old, bottom–top*), whereas others can be fairly difficult (*start–finish, smooth–rough, seldom–frequently*). A chart may be made of all the opposites class members find in order to see what some of the more unusual ones might be. Students in other classes, members of the school staff, and parents can be invited to join in the search.

Compound Words. Children can also formulate lists of compounds that have been formed by two other words—*sidewalk* and *breakfast,* for example. They can begin with a list of possible component words (*day, news, hall, base, stand, light, band, paper, ball,* and *way*) and see what compounds they can form (including, perhaps, inventions such as *paperday* or *standball,* which then obviously require defining and illustrating).

Word Origins. Children can become quite interested in words because of their origins, their forms, or changes that have occurred in their spelling and use. For example, they might like to try to find the origins of such words as *braille, boycott, vandal, cologne,* or *nicotine.* They could find it challenging to trace some from other languages: *cipher, kimono, oasis, parka,* or *pretzel,* for instance, and then find out if the pronunciation in the two languages is identical.

Varieties of English. Native speakers of English may be found in several countries, and they often use different words for common objects and events. (The British say "lift" and "lorry"; residents of North America say "elevator" and "truck." What do Australians say? New Zealanders?) Students will need to do some detective work to formulate such lists.

Puzzles and Games

Some children very much enjoy games and similar activities that also teach them about words.

Names. Many last names and place names mean something in English (*Baker, Cambridge*) or some other language (*Schwartzkopf, Baton Rouge*). Searches for such words increase interest in vocabulary and other languages.

Find another name for
humorous rabbit
(*funny bunny*)
lives in a basement
(*cellar dweller*)

A collection of synonyms is called a *thesaurus.* There are computer word-processing programs that include thesauruses.

Some prefixes that change a word to its opposite are
in-
un-
dis-
mis-
But *flammable* and *inflammable* are synonyms.

Food words that have other
meanings:
  plum
  nut
  lemon

Food Words. *Hamburger* is a word and so are *sorbet* and *escargot.* Children may be surprised by the meanings of some food words, as well as by what is sometimes eaten!

Word Mysteries. The teacher or a student gives a clue: "I'm thinking of a word that rhymes with *blue* and you can buy it at a store." The challenge is to find many possible answers and one that no one else thinks of.

Drawings. Students may make drawings with the intent of causing you or classmates to think of particular words. Charades, acting out words, is also an enjoyable activity.

Filling Grids. A two-dimensional grid with columns and rows is created, with alphabet letters at the top and categories (food, clothing, and games, for instance) down the side. Teams or individuals race to fill in the grid.

	R	*H*	*S*
Foods	rhubarb		
Games		hockey	
Clothing			skirt

SPELLING

Some words used in the finals of a national spelling contest:
  heirolatry
  micaceous
  propylaeum
  taknonymy

Spelling has had a prominent place in the classroom program for many years. Indeed, because of a national contest that produces a "spelling champion" each year, it has a place in the annual calendar of newspapers and television news broadcasts. But spelling is not important because it gains national attention for a few days in the spring of the year. Spelling makes a significant contribution to a person's ability to write effectively, and this should be the focus of instruction in the elementary school.

It is also significant that knowledge of how words are spelled, and why, contributes to a fuller understanding of our language. Spelling is a subject worthy of study in the elementary school.

Goals of Spelling Instruction

The basic goal of spelling instruction, then, is to teach children to spell the words they use in their writing. This means the writing they do in school *and* the writing they will do after their school years. Of course, it is impossible to determine all of the words any person may need to spell in a lifetime, but everyone should learn to spell the words that are most frequently written. It is also important to encourage children's increasing awareness of the structure and history of their language and how aspects of these relate to the spelling of specific words. Finally, a positive attitude toward spelling correctly and habits that support this attitude need to be developed.

Since spelling requires putting into written form words that are familiar from speaking, reading, and listening, two important abilities are needed. One of these is the ability to **recall the appearance of words**—the words that the child has studied and those that have frequently appeared in materials he or she has read. The other basic ability involves **associating letters and sounds of speech.** These two abilities become closely allied in the spelling efforts of most children, and both are influenced by the children's understanding of the language.

Of course, a child should possess many spelling-related abilities treated in other chapters of this book. For example, good handwriting will reduce the likelihood of confusion about how a word has been spelled. In this chapter we consider what pupils need to understand alphabetical order and use this knowledge to find the spelling of words in dictionaries and glossaries. They should be able to pronounce words clearly and accurately and understand the diacritical markings and key words in a dictionary, as well as phonetic and structural aids, to help with pronunciations.

A person who spells well shows a concern for doing so by proofreading his or her own writing, by looking up the spellings of unknown words, and by establishing a specific study procedure for learning to spell new words. Thus, teaching the child habits of proofreading, studying, and using the dictionary properly is very important.

These basic objectives should be kept in mind as you read the remainder of this section on spelling, as you plan your program, and as you select and use instructional materials.

The Nature of Spelling

For children, learning to spell begins with their first writing efforts, as described in Chapters 3 and 4. Learning to spell continues throughout the school years and into adulthood for most of us, with the rate and extent of such learning varying greatly from one person to another.

As with other skill areas you need to know something of how spelling ability develops and how to support such growth by providing appropriate experiences and instruction. The ability to spell correctly is largely contingent on the effectiveness of two processes: *impression* and *recall*. Impressions come from *recognizing* letters, noting their sequence in a word, and associating them with sounds and knowledge of word structures. (Someone may be successful in learning to spell *reflection* because he or she can focus on the three parts, two, *re* and *tion,* that are commonly found in the language and one that has to be studied until it becomes apparent that it resembles the word *fleck* but doesn't require the *k*.) Recall requires *remembering* the sequence of letters or any associations that may help the individual to spell a particular word. (Remember that there is *a rat* in *separate* and you can avoid the common misspelling *seperate*.) Spelling instruction should include activities that give attention to assisting students in developing these types of learning strategies.

Fostering Positive Attitudes

A good speller has concern for correct spelling and has also developed strategies for learning to spell a new word, obtaining assistance in spelling unknown words, and making the best use of the word knowledge she or he possesses. It helps if students are in classrooms where words are an important area of interest, where vocabulary-related activities are common, where dictionaries are routinely con-

---

Are you a good speller?

Do you believe that correct spelling is important?

Do you proofread for spelling errors?

Do you know several ways to find out the correct spelling of a word?

Do you know a good way to learn to spell a new word?

Learning to spell is a series consisting of

impression
↓
recall
↓
impression
↓
recall

sulted, and where students do much writing and therefore have a need for spelling a variety of words.

Showing the children that what they are learning is helpful when they write also contributes to the development of positive attitudes. You may, for example, find that students are interested in making word counts in their reading materials and their own writing products and then tabulating answers to such questions as:

Children can tabulate and graph their findings for comparisons.

> Which letters of the alphabet appear most in words?
> Which words most often begin sentences?
> What is the average length of sentences?
> Which words are most commonly used?
> Which are most often misspelled?

Such investigations provide opportunities for authentic learning experiences in both mathematics and language arts.

Encouraging efficient study methods also serves to develop good attitudes. Proficient spellers should devote attention to lists of challenging words or should simply give more time to reading and writing and less to the study of spelling. At the same time, those with serious spelling problems ought to concentrate on a small number of important words and on those chosen from their own writing and other class materials. There is no value in having them give a substantial amount of attention to words that are obviously too difficult for them.

Using word processors focuses attention on spelling.

Many cooperative learning activities are possible.

Every effort should be made to develop a cooperative classroom spirit with regard to spelling. Students may proofread one another's writing, pronounce spelling lists to partners, come together in small groups to study selected words, and make records of the words the class needs to study. Particularly good spellers may enjoy challenging one another with quite difficult words (an activity that may well lead to increasing of vocabularies, too).

Developing Desirable Habits

The desire to do well in spelling should be complemented by the development of appropriate habits. Several of these are particularly important:

Correct spelling is a concern of parents. Make sure that they understand "invented spelling" as used in early drafts of students' writing.

- *Being concerned about the spelling of words used in written expression.* First-draft writing does not require perfect spelling, but when a piece is to be read by someone else, the writer should realize that misspelled words will interfere with communication. The habit of being concerned about correct spelling is established by the development and maintenance of standards and by the concern shown for correct spelling in finished products. (See Chapter 10 for a discussion of spelling within the writing process.)

- *Proofreading systematically.* Writers must accept responsibility for examining their drafts carefully. Anyone can spell a word incorrectly through carelessness or temporary confusion, and less than perfect skills in handwriting or typing may also be the cause of difficulty in some situations. (Even those who use a word processor with an automatic spell-checking feature are not protected from such errors as using *their* when they need *there*.)

- *Checking the spelling of all words about which there is any doubt.* Writers should be conscientious about checking words if there is any question in their minds about them. Children ought to know how to use a variety of sources—human and print—and should be willing to continue the search until verification is made.

Students learn in different ways.

- *Using a specific procedure for learning the spelling of new words.* Although the specifics of study procedure will vary somewhat from student to student, there are steps in studying that are important, and each child should understand these and use what works best for her or him. (See the section in this chapter on Pupils' Study Procedures.)

- *Using time efficiently.* Students should be aware of how to study spelling without wasting time and effort. Several principles are important: study only the verified correct spellings of words, don't invest time in words that are already known, and use the study method that works best for you.

Components of a Spelling Program

The classroom program in spelling should consider developmental aspects of spelling, spelling as part of information processing, and embedded lessons involving spelling.

Developmental Aspects of Spelling. As was pointed out in Chapter 4, young children begin by thinking of writing as the making of letters without any concern about spelling. Gradually youngsters begin to grasp the *alphabetic principle,* the idea that there is a relationship between letters and speech sounds. As they use combinations of the names and sounds of letters in their writing, they begin to refer to this as spelling, asking the question, "How do you spell _____ ?"

As children use spelling inventions (or *temporary* or *kids'* spelling) major changes occur. Kindergartners and first graders may begin to write by using initial sounds only (*S* for *sun*) and by using initial and final sounds (*MN* for *moon*). They then go on to writing consistently spelled three-letter words accurately (*cat, hot, sit, pet,* etc.) and to understanding and using strategies such as how to add *-ing* to different types of words and when to double consonants (*dinner vs. diner*). It is important for you to understand how spelling develops so that appropriate assessments of students' progress can be made. (If a third grader writes *palushun* in a first draft, that is much more acceptable than if a sixth-grade child does.)

If they write extensively and make good progress in reading, many middle-grade students will be able to spell hundreds of words correctly. (You should keep it in mind, however, that spelling success is not perfectly correlated with reading ability; at all age levels there are some individuals who are good readers but only average or even poor spellers.)

Information Processing and Spelling.

As with vocabulary, spelling performance is in part based on what students learn as they pursue study of the content areas of the school curriculum. Certainly children write in order to learn (see Chapters 11 and 13) and part of that writing will involve learning to spell the words that make up the vocabulary of the subject field.

Certain words in informational books will be quite different from others encountered by students, and spelling patterns may be unusual. In mathematics and science, for instance, children may be expected to use metric measures, and this will involve such terms as *liter* (or the French spelling, *litre*) and *kilogram.* In social studies there will be new words to spell, too: *longitude, parliament,* and many more. Words from other languages sometimes present difficulties (*koala, chocolate*) as do British spellings (*gasolene, colour, recognise*).

When students use learning logs in such areas as social studies, they may keep lists of new words they encounter, for reasons having to do with both vocabulary and spelling. As they write in response to literature reading, similar opportunities will present themselves, of course. Though studying content and enjoying literature should not be interfered with by overconcern with the spelling of words, these experiences do make a contribution to understanding of content.

Exposure to words in such fields as biology, botany, economics, and geography present many opportunities to consider what roots, prefixes, and suffixes mean and how they are related to spelling. Examples likely to be available in the upper elementary grades are *thermometer, unincorporated, immigrants,* and *revolution.*

Embedded Spelling Lessons.

As thousands of words are used in your classroom, you will have many decisions to make regarding selection of those to be added to the spelling program. In discussing the day's news, numerous place names will be used, and certainly children should be able to spell *United States of America* and *Washington, District of Columbia,* as well as the name of their state and its capital city.

Adams has reviewed some of the evidence and concluded that children who began by using invented spelling are often doing very well in spelling by third grade. (See her book listed in Chapter 4 References.)

The word *intension* would be a misspelling in most elementary classrooms but is a valid term in philosophy.

Sometimes orthography depends on geography.

Which is larger—the *capital* or the *capitol?*

Students should also know the spelling of local names—their school and their town or nearest city, for example. They very likely have many interests (names of athletic teams, television performers, popular music numbers, sports cars) and they may want to write about them and in some cases to send letters. There is much here for you to capitalize upon, including embedded spelling lessons in which you teach important items of content to the entire class or individuals.

Identification of the Words to be Learned

In organizing the spelling program, you must decide which words to emphasize most.

A Basic Word List. The words that must be included in every spelling program are those known to be used most often. The approximately 300 words given below have been found to be extremely important in the elementary-school classroom. Nearly all students should be able to spell them by the time they reach the middle grades.

a	boy	don't	glad	into	morning
about	boys	door	go	is	most
after	bring	down	going	it	mother
again	brother		good	its	much
ago	but	each	got		must
all	buy	eat	grade	just	my
along	by	end	great		
also		even	grow	know	name
always	call	every			never
am	called		had	land	new
an	came	fall	hand	large	next
and	can	far	happy	last	nice
another	car	fast	hard	let	night
any	cat	fat	has	letter	no
are	children	father	hat	like	not
around	close	feet	have	line	now
as	coat	few	he	little	
asked	cold	find	hear	live	of
at	come	fire	heard	long	off
away	coming	first	help	look	old
	could	five	her	looked	on
baby	country	for	here	lost	once
back	cut	found	him	lot	one
bad		four	his	lots	only
ball	daddy	friend	hold	love	open
be	day	from	home		or
because	days	fun	hope	made	order
bed	dear		hot	make	other
been	did	game	house	man	our
before	didn't	gave	how	many	out
best	do	get		may	over
better	does	getting	I	me	
big	dog	girl	if	men	part
black	doing	girls	I'm	milk	people
book	doll	give	in	more	place

play	saw	stop	things	use	while
played	say	such	think		white
please	school	summer	this	very	who
pretty	see	sun	thought		will
put	seen	sure	three	walk	wish
	send		through	want	with
rain	she	take	time	wanted	work
ran	should	teacher	to	was	would
read	show	tell	today	water	write
red	side	than	told	way	
rest	sister	that	too	we	year
ride	sleep	the	took	week	years
right	snow	their	top	well	yes
room	so	them	town	went	yet
run	some	then	tree	were	you
	something	there	two	what	your
said	soon	these		when	yours
same	started	they	until	where	
sat	stay	thing	up	which	

These words represent approximately 90 percent of all those used in the elementary school. Other words are important, too, of course, and it is the responsibility of teachers and other school personnel to decide how they wish to add to the list. Published spelling series usually contain about three thousand words that have been identified in various ways.

Identifying Other Spelling Words. For the most part, elementary-school students need to spell the most common words (those we have listed) and those they encounter in their school subjects. The average vocabulary of a sixth-grade pupil will approach 25,000 words and perhaps half of these will be needed in writing.

At the beginning of the year in third or fourth grade, the spelling performance of each student ought to be assessed. You should take samples of words from various lists—the basic one and that of the "demons" presented in this chapter (see Special Spelling Problems), a list used by a publisher of spelling books, and words from the textbooks used at the grade level. Tests, perhaps two of them with 25 words each time, should be administered to the children and the results examined so that you will have a general idea of the status of the group and detailed information about individual students.

On the basis of the testing, you might discuss students' spelling with them as individuals. (If you schedule writing and reading conferences as described in Chapters 10 and 12, spelling and handwriting can be covered in those.) You can help each child assess his or her spelling status and provide general guidance concerning directions study might take.

Learning to Spell

Students are responsible for improving their own spelling; no one can do it for them. You can make spelling a priority and provide activities intended to support students' learning, but effort—often substantial on the part of some children— will have to be expended. ("Everyone in our family is a terrible speller" is a statement that cannot be accepted as a substitute for care and persistence.) Pupils do need to know what your expectations are and how they can be met, however. Following are suggestions that will help.

Pupils' Study Procedures. Conferences with students may be used to develop a trial plan for finding out which spelling study procedures would be best for each youngster. There is general agreement among authorities that the spelling of a word is learned through a series of steps involving impression and recall (as mentioned in a preceding section of this chapter).

The *impression*, or image, step generally includes visual, auditory, and kinesthetic sensations. The *recall* step usually involves *visualizing* the word in the mind and then writing from memory. Children who are proficient at spelling can often learn a new word after seeing it only once; for them, any additional steps may not be necessary. The less able spellers need help and encouragement in learning the steps and putting them into practice.

The method of study presented is suggested as suitable for most children. You may choose to modify it in some manner for your class.

1. Look at the word carefully and pronounce it correctly. Say it slowly, naturally, and clearly, looking at it as you say it.

2. Cover the word with your hand or close your eyes. Say the word and think how it looks. Try to visualize exactly the way the word is written as you say each letter in sequence to yourself.

3. Look at the word again to be sure that you said it and spelled it correctly. If you did not, start again at step 1.

4. Cover the word and then write it, thinking carefully about how it looks.

5. Check your spelling. If you misspelled the word, begin again at step 1. If you spelled it correctly, look at it again and then go on to another.

Children need to see that they are making progress in spelling as in other areas of the classroom program.

If your students keep personal lists of words they need to learn to spell, you should review these occasionally and ask them to try a few they believe have been mastered. Mark these in some way so that the child will have a sense of accomplishment and progress.

Using Generalizations. There are regularities in English spelling and you may point these out as embedded lessons. (Learning "rules" apart from actual use isn't very effective.) Of course you should be alert to identify instances where the generalization may be usefully applied, but you ought to give examples of exceptions, too, if there are any.

Particularly important generalizations with few exceptions are the following:

Use rules cautiously. Will rules help you spell these?

birch	curse	beard
church	hearse	weird
perch	terse	feared
search	worse	leered

1. Words ending in a silent *e* usually drop this *e* before a suffix beginning with a vowel (*make–making*) but keep the *e* before a suffix beginning with a consonant (*time–timely*).

2. For words ending in a consonant and *y,* change the *y* to *i* before adding a suffix, unless the suffix begins with *i* (*candy–candies, baby–babying*).

3. For words ending in a vowel and *y,* do not change the *y* to *i* when adding a suffix (*play–played, enjoy–enjoying*).

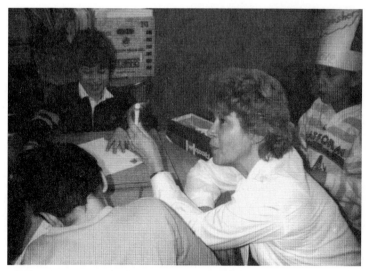

Teacher and students discuss the spelling of a word during an editing session.

4. For words of one syllable or accented on the last syllable that end in a single consonant preceded by a single vowel, double the final consonant when adding a suffix beginning with a vowel (*run–running, begin–beginning*).

5. The letter *q* is always followed by *u* in common English words (*quite, quart*).

6. English words do not end with *v* (*believe, give*).

7. Proper nouns and some adjectives formed with proper nouns begin with capital letters (*France, French*).

Rules concerning the use of the apostrophe also deserve attention, since improper use of the apostrophe is the cause of many spelling errors. The following rules are helpful:

1. The possessive of a singular noun (including those ending in *s, z, ss,* or *x*) is formed by adding an apostrophe and *s*.

   Sue's idea   Congress's action
   father's hat   box's top
   Ms. Jones's house   Buzz's pitch

2. The possessive of a plural noun ending in *s* is formed by adding an apostrophe.

   girls' coats   Matthewses' relatives
   Smiths' house   states' rights

3. The possessive of a plural noun not ending in *s* is formed by adding an apostrophe and *s*.

   women's hats   data's use
   teeth's whiteness   children's books

4. Pronouns do not take the apostrophe to show possession.

   his   theirs
   hers   whose   its

5. Pronouns that are not ordinarily possessive show possession by adding an apostrophe and *s*.

someone's coat	each other's dog
everyone's house	another's name

6. An apostrophe is used to indicate missing letters in contractions, letters omitted to show speech, and numbers left off the beginning of the year.

don't (do not)	we'll (we will)
it's (it is)	you're (you are)
'ere's to you	your 'ome
the winter of '92	the class of '72

With its and it's the spelling error rate is over 50 percent. (Remember that the one with the apostrophe is a contraction for it is.)

A number of rules about the formation of plural forms that are also useful include the following:

1. Plurals of most nouns are formed by adding *s* to the singular.

    girl–girls   book–books

2. When a noun ends in *s, x, sh,* or *ch,* the plural is generally formed by adding *es*.

    buses   foxes   bushes   churches

3. A noun ending in *y* preceded by a consonant forms its plural by changing the *y* to *i* and adding *es*. Words ending in *y* preceded by a vowel do not change *y* to *i*.

    body–bodies   boy–boys

4. Plurals of a few nouns are made by changing their forms.

    woman–women   mouse–mice   scarf–scarves

Special Spelling Problems. Some words are frequently misspelled (these are the "demons" that most teachers know about) and will require persistent effort from you and your students. There are reasons for their difficulty, though and knowing about these problems may help children.

Many words are misspelled because the children do not know or do not apply the rules that are workable, do not understand the use of the apostrophe, fail to capitalize properly, or do not have the linguistic knowledge they should have (for example, how compounds are formed). Here are some that are frequently misspelled, apparently for one of these reasons:

coming	I'll	it's	studying	tried
didn't	I'm	getting	Sunday	truly
don't	its	sometimes	that's	writing

Learnings support one another. In reading a child may encounter a new word—hew—and then discover that there is a homonym, another new word—hue.

Homonyms also often cause difficulty. For pupils to learn which spelling to use when requires that meanings be fully understood and that visual images be well established. Spelling authorities disagree about whether homonyms should be taught together. For the first instruction it seems better to present them separately. However, because much review of them is necessary, they should be presented together from time to time to emphasize the differences:

there	hear	your	know	some
their	here	you're	no	sum
they're				

two	four	write	buy	piece
to	for	right	by	peace
too	fore	rite	bye	

Improper pronunciation is a frequent cause of errors. Words such as *and, going, third, ask, today, Saturday, pretty, hundred, kept, been, library, children,* and *desk* pose both pronunciation and spelling problems for some children.

Phoneme-grapheme irregularity that results in misspelling because of the misapplication of a generalization is also a problem. Commonly written words that fall into this category include the following:

ache	believe	enough	thirty
across	birthday	friend	though
afraid	build	guess	thought
again	color	heard	tonight
among	could	one	very
answer	cousin	sure	were
beautiful	decide	the	when
because	does	they	women

The following list of spelling "demons" has been developed from studies of misspellings of elementary-school children. These words are important and should be studied by every pupil.

about	boy	every	has
address	boys	everybody	have
afraid	brother		haven't
afternoon	brought	father	having
again		February	he
all right	can	fine	hear
along	cannot	first	hello
already	can't	football	her
always	children	for	here
am	Christmas	fourth	his
an	close	Friday	home
and	clothes	friend	hope
answer	come	friends	hospital
anything	coming	from	house
anyway	couldn't	front	how
April	cousin	fun	how's
are			hundred
arithmetic	daddy	getting	
aunt	day	goes	I'll
awhile	December	going	I'm
	didn't	good	in
baby	different	good-bye (good-by)	isn't
balloon	dog	grade	it
basketball	doing	guess	it's
because	don't	guest	its
been	down		I've
before		had	
birthday	Easter	Halloween	January
bought	enough	handkerchiefs	just

knew	one	sometimes	toys
know	our	soon	train
	out	stationery	truly
lessons	outside	store	two
letter		studying	
like	party	summer	until
likes	people	Sunday	
little	play	suppose	vacation
lots	played	sure	very
loving	plays	surely	
	please	swimming	want
made	pretty		was
make		teacher	weather
maybe	quit	teacher's	well
me	quite	Thanksgiving	went
Miss		that's	we're
morning	receive	the	were
mother	received	their	when
Mr.	remember	them	whether
Mrs.	right	then	white
much		there	will
my	said	there's	with
	Santa Claus	they	won't
name	Saturday	they're	would
nice	saw	think	write
November	school	thought	writing
now	send	through	
nowadays	sent	time	you
	sincerely	to	young
o'clock	snow	today	your
October	snowman	together	yours
off	some	tomorrow	
on	something	tonight	
once	sometime	too	

The Weekly List. The spelling of a word used often in writing should be taught whenever the opportunity to do so occurs, and each youngster should have his or her own list of words to work on. These procedures will provide most of the spelling instruction that students require, as long as word study in general is a prominent feature of the classroom program.

In many schools. though, it is expected that each class should have a common list of words to work on, usually for the week and presented in a set of lessons in a commercially published spelling book. If you have such a weekly list you should adopt the *test-study* rather than the *study-test* approach. That is, the better spellers should be given an opportunity to demonstrate by means of a pretest that they know the words at the beginning of the week and can therefore be excused from studying them and allowed to devote their attention to their own words or some other activity. Also, those who know some of the words but not others can use the test results to see which words they should concentrate on. The study-test approach is a poor use of students' time because many of them would be spelling words they either already know or have little hope of spelling correctly. (Very poor spellers probably should not take the pretest at all but simply study their own list of easier words.)

Another possibility, especially when most of the class members are at least reasonably good spellers, is to reduce the amount of time to three days for the weekly list. The five-day pattern will usually look something like this:

> *First Day.* Administration of a pretest of the words in the lesson (pronouncing the word, using it in a sentence, and pronouncing again); checking the test (each pupil checking his or her own); making individual study lists of words misspelled; discussing the words as necessary—their meanings and use, any unusual spellings, the application of any rules, or etymological matters that are appropriate and of interest.
>
> *Second Day.* Visual and auditory study of structural and phonemic elements in the words; direct study of the words on individual spelling lists.
>
> *Third Day.* Administration of a test (usually including all the words in the lesson as a means of ensuring that guessing did not account for some correct spelling on the pretest); checking the test again, with each pupil checking his or her own; studying the words misspelled.
>
> *Fourth Day.* Continued practice in visual and aural analysis of the words; learning new meanings for the words; extending word knowledge through practice in using linguistic principles; studying words misspelled on the third-day test.
>
> *Fifth Day.* Administration of the final test; checking the tests, with each pupil again checking his or her own; writing words in a review list; marking achievement on a progress chart.

In addition, time may be given as it is available to practice in using the dictionary, to use of vocabulary building exercises, and to participation in games and enrichment activities. Some study of language, particularly of word origins, is also appropriate for inclusion in the lesson as time permits.

Electronic Aids. Audiovisual equipment and computers offer many possibilities for spelling practice. Word lists may be put on audiocassettes, and children can listen to the words pronounced and test themselves by writing what they hear. This is particularly effective for an individualized program since several lists at different levels of difficulty can be produced by the teacher and used repeatedly by the students. Students should keep track of their progress and the words they need to study; this will promote acceptance of responsibility for their own learning.

Overhead projectors are sometimes helpful in gamelike spelling activities. Writing on the platform of a projector more closely approximates the usual spelling environment than does writing on a chalkboard. Some projectors have the very useful capacity of projecting on a screen what is typed on a typewriter or computer keyboard.

It seems likely that typing and word processing will have a positive effect on students' spelling: interest is heightened, what is produced looks like real print and so is more easily recognized, and changing the spelling of a word may be relatively simple on an electric typewriter or word processor. At a basic level, a computer can flash a word on its screen and then remove it, giving the student a few seconds to type the correct spelling before signaling "right" or "wrong." A variety of software programs offer other spelling experiences. Some programs permit a record of each child's success rate, achievement level, and problem words to be kept on the computer.

Although word processors with spell-checking features don't teach children much about spelling, some hand-held electronic devices do. One of these permits a child to type in a possible or approximate spelling and then look among the displayed words for the one that seems to be the target.

Games and Exercises. The spelling program can be enlivened through the use of games and other activities directed at learning the words in the spelling lessons and at building vocabulary. Activities and games are useful for motivating pupils, allowing for individual differences, and providing variety in the program.

As in other curriculum areas, spelling activities that resemble games, puzzles, and quiz shows interest children and build class spirit. It is important, though, that such activities in spelling call for writing the words or seeing them in written form (reinforcement of visual impression) rather than spelling them orally (a nonrealistic experience). Writing may be done on the chalkboard, the overhead projector, chart paper, or individual "slates" made by painting hardboard black or green (these, written on with chalk, are also useful in handwriting, mathematics, and other subjects and so are worth making or purchasing).

Races or other forms of competition may add to the frustration of poor spellers, so they should be used with discretion. Many of the activities described here (and at the end of the chapter) are noncompetitive or can be adapted to eliminate the competitive element.

Palindromes are total reversals:
    noon
    evil

1. *Jumbled Words.* Individuals or groups are given a specific selection of plastic letters or letter cards and instructed to make a word. Clues such as "name of an animal" or "something related to music" may be given. All the letters have to be used, and the word must be spelled correctly.

2. *Plurals.* The singular form is pronounced, and students write the plural (or the reverse). Use common (*mouse*) or uncommon (*sister-in-law*) words, depending on the maturity of the group.

Anagrams are rearrangements:
    tops
    spot
    stop
    pots

3. *Team Spelling.* Each of four children is given a large card on which one of the letters *S, T, O,* or *P* is written. The children are told to arrange and rearrange their cards in a line to spell as many words as they can, using all four letters (many variations on this are possible: three children and *R, A,* and *T* or *E, A,* and *T;* five children with *E, A, S, T,* and *L;* etc.).

4. *Concentration.* Target words are written on cards turned face down. On a small chalkboard a child writes a word from memory and then tries to turn over the corresponding card for a match. To win a point, the spelling must be correct.

5. *Contractions.* The teacher or a student pronounces two words for which a contraction exists. The rest of the class or group try to write the contraction. (This activity may be reversed, with the contractions being pronounced.)

6. *Add-a-Letter.* Teams are given the same word to spell. Each team member goes to the board to write a single letter and then gives the chalk to a teammate (who has until then remained seated) to write the next letter. A judge—either child or adult—rules on the accuracy of the spelling. Coaching of teammates may or may not be permitted.

7. *Pyramids.* Children can make pyramids by starting with any letter, adding another to make a word, and continuing to add one letter at a time, always making

a correctly spelled word with each addition. The objective is to make the longest list of correctly spelled words.

t	o	m
at	on	am
ate	one	ham
late	tone	sham
plate	tones	shame
plated	stones	ashamed

8. *Roots and Affixes.* The children start with a root word such as *happy* and make other words by adding prefixes and suffixes: *unhappy, happier, happiness,* and so on. The object is to see how long a list of correctly spelled words can be made.

9. *Baseball.* Movable markers on a chart or chairs can be used as bases; children get a hit if they write the correct spelling for a word that is pronounced or make an out if they misspell it. A variation involves using lists of increasing difficulty for singles, doubles, triples, and home runs, with players selecting the level they want to try. Better spellers may then make "outs" more frequently.

10. *Filling Grids.* A two-dimensional grid is created that has columns headed by alphabet letters (*E, H, T,* and *S,* for example) and rows labeled by categories (Foods, Games, Clothing, and TV Shows, for example). Teams or individuals compete by filling in the grid row by row. All words must be spelled correctly.

	E	**H**	**T**	**S**
Foods	*egg*	*ham*	*tomato*	*soup*
Games				
Clothing				
TV shows				

USING DICTIONARIES

At several points in this chapter, and in others, references have been made to the use of dictionaries in the elementary classroom. Elementary dictionaries should be thought of as important resources for the classroom program. Several types are available.

Picture dictionaries are designed for young children. They usually have from several dozen to a few hundred words, with a picture for each. They may not be arranged in alphabetical order but, instead, have words organized into clusters around a topic such as toys or farm animals.

Beginning dictionaries are intended for the primary grades and may contain as many as 3,000 words in alphabetical order. There will be many color illustrations and definitions will probably include one or two meanings. Guide words will be located at the tops of pages. Other features include letters for each of the 26 sections printed close to page margins so that users can "find the *T*s" more easily, plural forms given in sentences for nouns and inflected forms for verbs (parts of speech not usually given), and phonetic respellings sometimes included (but not diacritical marks).

Advanced dictionaries for the intermediate and upper grades are similar to those for adults. The total number of words will be 30,000 or more; several

Alphabetical order receives attention in Chapters 4 and 13.

meanings and synonyms will be given; words will be separated into syllables with diacritical marks and key words given to aid pronunciation; and very likely parts of speech will be noted. Illustrations will be plentiful and in black and white, with the actual size indicated.

Other possible features are: notes on word origins may be included, and there will sometimes be information sections at the back with lists of presidents, states and their capitals, and so forth.

Learning to Use a Dictionary

With simple and more complex dictionaries available, a student should be able to find one that is appropriate for her or him. Of course, as pupils grow older they develop skills and understandings and encounter new situations that require more sophisticated dictionaries. The young child wants to know how to write a word and the older student needs to see how it may be divided between syllables when there is a need to have a hyphen at the end of a line. Inexperienced pupils can use only the first letter when considering alphabetical order; more mature ones will be able to consider the second and even the third letter.

As far as definitions are concerned, the beginner may need only a picture or a synonym (*shop* means "store"). Later that same child will be able to choose from several alternative meanings (*shop* also means "to look for something to buy"). Older students will see that a word may be both a noun and a verb (*tack,* for instance).

It is important that dictionaries be readily available to students. Only regular use and much modeling of when to do what by you will enable students to make the sort of progress that is required to become proficient with the dictionary. Most learnings, then, will likely come in the form of embedded lessons as you guide the class and individuals.

Finding words requires practice. Provide students with a stopwatch and have them participate in pairs, with one child giving a word and timing how long it takes for the partner to find it in the dictionary.

Electronic Dictionaries

Two principal difficulties are common for children who want to use a dictionary: the word has to be found and its pronunciation deciphered. Both of these skills are important but are often such a problem that young children are unnecessarily prevented from following through on their interest in words. For these reasons electronic devices may be used to provide direct access to the target word.

Word Processors. Not only thesauruses but also dictionaries may be part of a computerized writing system. If a student encounters an unknown word while doing research or wants to know the definition or pronunciation of a particular word, it may be typed into the computer and the definition will appear on the screen. If a printer is available, the entry may sometimes be printed and added to the student's personal dictionary. Some computers can pronounce words when signalled to do that.

Hand-held Electronic Dictionaries. Small electronic dictionaries permit the student to type in the word and read the dictionary entry from a small screen. Other models have a sound feature and can pronounce the word.

EVALUATION AND WORD STUDY

Many school systems have adopted reporting methods that reflect a developmental view of learning in the language arts.

Vocabulary, spelling, and dictionary use are integral to many aspects of a child's literacy development. A youngster who is developing an extensive vocabulary may be expected to make excellent progress in oral language, listening, writing, studying, and reading. Spelling is, of course, closely connected with writing. When youngsters are engaged in studying and research, they have many opportunities to assess their ability to use dictionaries as well as other reference sources. Clearly, then, appropriate evaluation should emphasize actual use in realistic situations.

Spelling skills do logically separate into such areas as competence with basic lists, use of sources to find out how to spell a word correctly, and knowledge of language characteristics and generalizations about English spelling. Even though it is possible to assess children in these various areas, the basic concern should be with use. Sometimes that use is immediate, however, so nothing really substitutes entirely for knowledge of how a particular word is spelled.

Checklist of Spelling Behaviors

November Name	Uses Many Resources	Makes Good First Attempts	Edits All Writing For Spelling	Has Well-Developed Study Procedure	Identifies Own Spelling Needs
Bill	*no*	*no*	*no*	*no*	*sometimes*
Roy	✓	?	✓	*no*	✓
Mary	✓	✓	✓	✓	*no*
Julie	✓	✓	*sometimes*	✓	✓

In constructing a language arts portfolio, students should maintain lists of new vocabulary items they have learned and lists of words they are working on in spelling. Copies of standardized spelling tests and classroom tests that have been taken might also be included, as well as a videotape showing how the youngster uses the dictionary.

A FINAL WORD

The material covered in this chapter is especially relevant to the following chapters on writing and reading. As students confront the task of making their own meanings clear and considering how their ideas relate to what others have to say, the essence of literacy becomes apparent. Words are often the keys that unlock meanings and they will be acquired and understood best only in classrooms where they are valued as summaries of experience, the most effective of communication tools, and as objects of delight.

References

Anderson, Kristine F. "The Development of Spelling Ability and Linguistic Strategies." *The Reading Teacher* 39 (November 1985), pp. 140–147.

Betza, Ruth E. "Online: Computerized Spelling Checkers: Friends or Foes?" *Language Arts* 64 (November 1987), pp. 438–442.

DiStefano, Philip P., and Hagerty, Patricia J. "Teaching Spelling at the Elementary Level: A Realistic Perspective." *The Reading Teacher* 38 (January 1985), pp. 373–377.

Downing, John; DeStefano, Johanna; Rich, Gene; and Bell, Aula. "Children's Views of Spelling." *The Elementary School Journal* 85 (November 1984), pp. 185–198.

Fitzsimmons, Robert J., and Loomer, Bradley M. *Spelling Research and Practice.* Iowa State Department of Public Instruction and the University of Iowa, 1977.

Gentry, J. Richard. "Learning to Spell Developmentally." *The Reading Teacher* 34 (January 1981), pp. 378–381.

Hall, Susan, and Hall, Chris. "It Takes a Lot of Letters to Spell 'Erz'." *Language Arts* 61 (December 1984), pp. 822–827.

Henderson, Edmund. *Teaching Spelling.* Houghton Mifflin, 1985.

Hodges, Richard E. *Learning to Spell.* Clearinghouse on Reading and Communication Skills and the National Council of Teachers of English, 1981.

Holbrook, Hilary Taylor. "ERIC/RCS Report: Invented Spelling." *Language Arts* 60 (September 1983), pp. 800–804.

Horn, Ernest. "Phonetics and Spelling." *The Elementary School Journal* (May 1957), pp. 431–435.

Kamii, Constance, and Randazzo, Marie. "Social Interaction and Invented Spelling." *Language Arts* 62 (February 1985), pp. 124–133.

Marzano, Robert J., and Marzano, Jana S. *A Cluster Approach to Elementary Vocabulary Instruction.* International Reading Association, 1988.

McKeown, Margaret G., and Curtis, Mary E., eds. *The Nature of Vocabulary Acquisition.* Lawrence Erlbaum, 1987.

Middleton, Mildred L. *Improving Spelling Performance.* Kendall/Hunt, 1981.

Petty, Walter T. "The Teaching of Spelling." *Bulletin of the School of Education* (Indiana University) 45 (November 1969), pp. 79–98.

Sears, Nedra, and Johnson, Dale. "The Effects of Visual Imagery on Spelling Performance and Retention Among Elementary Students." *Journal of Educational Research* (March/April 1986), pp. 230–233.

Thomas, Ves. *Teaching Spelling, Canadian Word Lists and Instructional Techniques.* Gage Educational Publishing, 1974.

Wilde, Sandra. *You Kan Red This!* Heinemann, 1991.

Teaching Resources

COMPUTER SOFTWARE

Alphabet, Sequences, and Alphabetizing. Random House School Division (grades 2–4).

Computer Scrabble. The Writing Company.

Customized Flash Spelling. Random House (grades 2–6).

Fundamental Spelling Words in Context. Random House, 1982 (grades 1–8).

Let's Alphabetize. Unicorn Software (K–grade 3).

Magic Spells. Scholastic.

Maze-O. D. C. Heath (grades 2–6).

See It, Hear It, Spell It! MultiMedia Software (all grades).

Spellagraph and Spellakazam. Silver-Burdett (grades 2–8).

Speller Bee (Talking Notebook Series). First Byte (preschool and up).

Spell It. Davidson.

Spelling Wiz. Developmental Learning Materials, 1983 (guide and record sheets; grades 1–6).

Webster: The Word Game. Spoken Arts (grades 1–5).

Wizard of Words. Computer Advanced Ideas, 1983 (grades 2–7).

OTHER RESOURCES

Dictionary Skills. Curriculum Associates. (grades 3–6).

The Dictionary. Society for Visual Education (videotape and ancillary materials).

Ellyson, Louise. *Dictionary of Homonyms: New Word Patterns.* Amereon, 1979.

Espy, Willard. *A Children's Almanac of Words at Play.* Dale Seymour Publications (grades 4–6).

Exploring Language with the Dictionary. Schoolhouse Press (workbooks; intermediate grades).

Grant, Niels, Jr. *Vocabulary and Spelling Activities.* Fearon Teaching Aids.

Manchester, Richard B. *The Mammoth Book of Word Games.* Hart Publishing, 1976.

My First Thesaurus, McDougal, Littell and Company, 1988 (Grades 1–4)

Young Writer's Thesaurus, McDougal, Littell & Company, 1990 (Grades 5–9).

Spelling Wordfinder. Curriculum Associates (book).

Tompkins, Gail E., and Yaden, David B. *Language, Answering Students' Questions about Words.* National Council of Teachers of English, 1986.

Vocabulary Building. Zaner-Bloser (kit).

Activities for Preservice Teachers

1. Try some of the spelling-related computer programs listed in the resources section (or other programs to which you have access). What are the advantages and disadvantages of the ones you examined? Be prepared to discuss in class whether or not you would use one of these programs and why.

2. Attempt to spell the "demons" listed in this chapter. Be sure that you have mastered all of them. Then begin to compile a list of your personal "demons"—words you know give you trouble.

3. Examine beginning, intermediate, and advanced dictionaries and consider how they differ in respect to the number of words contained, types of illustrations, comprehensiveness of definitions, information supplied on words, and so forth.

4. Study teachers' manuals and advertising materials for several sets of spelling books to find answers to the following questions: How were the spelling words selected? What is the total number of words for each grade? Does the series use the test-study or study-test method? Are provisions made for both good spellers and poor ones? What activities are provided other than tests and direct study of words? Are study steps suggested?

5. Select a spelling book for a particular grade level, and plan a spelling program for a week, basing it on one of the weekly lists in the book. Show how you would use an individualized approach. How would you modify activities in the book to make them more effective? What enrichment activities would you add? How might learning experiences be integrated with other subjects or other areas of the language arts?

6. Assess several children's vocabularies by taking a sample of 20 words from an adult-level dictionary and interviewing each child about what these mean. Discuss your findings with someone who is knowledgeable about language development or intelligence testing.

7. Interview several classroom teachers and ask them to tell you what they do about teaching vocabulary—general vocabulary and reading vocabulary.

8. Discuss children's spelling with several elementary-school teachers to determine (a) what they consider to be children's chief problems, (b) the range of abilities in their classes, and (c) if they use practices advocated in this chapter.

9. Check your own dictionary skills. Identify words you are not entirely sure of in magazines and textbooks. See how quickly you find them in a dictionary; try to pronounce them from the information given; examine the possible meanings; and find out what else the dictionary tells about them.

Activities for Inservice Teachers

1. Parents and other concerned citizens sometimes believe that children may be negatively influenced by objectionable words and meanings found in school dictionaries. Examine several dictionaries for different age groups (including adults) and compare them with respect to what words related to sexuality are included and how these are defined.

2. Assume that a decision has been made to emphasize homework in your building, and your grade level is to concentrate on spelling. What activities could you justifiably use? What problems would you expect to encounter?

3. Be prepared to discuss in class several aspects of teaching spelling in your school or district. For example, is there a requirement that a certain amount of time be devoted to teaching spelling? Are spelling materials specified for each grade level? Is there a policy against displaying writing that contains misspelled words?

4. Bring to class samples of invented spelling from the children in your room or from younger children to whom you have access. Analyze these attempts to determine the extent to which what the children have done "makes sense" and/or conforms to correct spelling. If possible, include in these samples examples that show progress toward standard spellings.

5. Start a file of spelling games and puzzles, including the ones described in this chapter. Get ideas from other teachers, professional magazines, and textbooks.

6. Try out some spelling-related computer programs that may help you solve a particular problem you have in teaching (record keeping, providing individual practice, providing enrichment activities, etc.).

7. Develop a schoolwide list of words on which children at every grade level above second are tested each year. Plan a way to determine if there is steady progress in learning these words from one grade level to the next. Are there words that need particular teaching attention? How might you determine if the yearly testing of basic words has a positive effect on spelling performance?

8. Review the reading levels of children in your class. Consider general performance and strengths and weaknesses in vocabulary. Give a word-recognition test (*The Wide Range Ability Test*) and a test of receptive vocabulary (*The Peabody Picture Vocabulary Test*). Then interview students concerning the meanings of some fairly difficult words. What do you note? Are children likely to be equally strong on all measures?

9. Examine some standardized achievement tests in spelling (or the spelling sections of more inclusive standardized tests). How were the words selected? What is the task—identifying correct or incorrect words, actual writing of the words, or something else? Administer one or more of the tests to a few children. Compare the results of this testing with your assessment of their spelling abilities.

10. Examine the glossaries of science and social studies textbooks for a particular grade level. Which words are so important that you would want every child at that grade level to know them? Which seem too difficult for many? Which are more technical and less generally useful?

Activities for Children

1. Children, particularly those who are good spellers, will enjoy looking for misspelled words on supermarket windows, on hand-lettered notices on bulletin boards, in newspapers (perhaps those from local colleges), and in advertisements. Have an award ("Spelling Spy") for those who find errors made by adults.

2. Have a child prepare a chart for the bulletin board listing the most commonly used contractions: *don't, aren't, can't, I'll,* and so on. Another child might make a chart giving the use of the apostrophe (other than in contractions).

3. Two children can in turn take letter tiles from a supply of several dozen that have been turned over so that the players do not know what the letters are. The first player to make a predetermined number of correctly spelled words is the winner.

4. Each child should keep his or her own list of spelling "demons"—words consistently misspelled in writing activities. He or she may study these independently or with a partner and then confer with you concerning progress made.

5. Word-study cards can be prepared with questions, directions, and spaces for the child's responses. Activities such as the following might be included:

   a. Change the first two letters of *fright* and write the new words (*bright, slight, flight*).

   b. Put prefixes before the words so that antonyms are formed:

_____	clear	_____	true
_____	spell	_____	correct
_____	patient	_____	sense

   c. Write synonyms for these words:
     throw (hurl, cast, pitch, toss)
     shut (close, bar)

   d. How many compound words can you make by adding words to these words?
     fire (fireworks, fireplace, fireside)
     ball (baseball, football, basketball)
     door (doorway, doorbell, doorstop)

6. Put a series of compound words on cards, one word on each card. The child may add as many other compounds as possible that include one of the words in the given compound word. Some compound words to use are *playground, bathroom,* and *mailbox.*

7. Have students identify vocations (plumber, nurse, bookkeeper) and leisure activities (bowling, fishing, gardening) that are common in the community. Then, using adults as sources, list some of the vocabulary items associated with these activities. See who can find some that no one else does. Examine their entries in a dictionary.

8. Make a list of words commonly misspelled in children's writing, and have children make crossword puzzles from it. Children's puzzles then can be exchanged. (There are computer programs that will produce a puzzle for any list of words typed in.)

9. Have the children look in dictionaries (adult ones) for variant spellings of words (*theater* and *theatre*, for example). These can be put on a chart, which can then be used in a group discussion of why differences arise.

10. Children can find and list pairs of homonyms. A variation of this would be to make a list of words that the children then match by sound with other words, for example: *plain, weigh, write, cent, feet,* and *mist.*

Chapter 9

Writing by Hand and Machine

*F*or several understandable reasons handwriting has declined in importance in the schools and in society. First of all, the typewriter has been the principal means for written communication in business over many years and is now commonly used for personal writing as well. In addition, telephones are used to conduct business activities that were formerly done by mail and have in some cases all but replaced letter writing between relatives and friends. Another significant development influencing both personal and business communication is the growing availability of electronic devices. For example, some families regularly exchange audio- or videotape recordings and find these much more satisfying than letters. Photocopying machines have reduced the need to take notes from print materials (or even entirely recopy by hand). Typing by means of computerized word processors has also become increasingly popular.

But writing by hand continues to be done, too. A typewriter or word processor is not always available, of course, and is inappropriate for many tasks anyway. People often need to take messages, make lists, leave notes, and send greeting cards, and such writing is generally done by hand. Students are able to make photocopies of one another's class notes, but first someone has to take them in readable form. Even for material that is typed the preliminary work is sometimes handwritten and often has to be good enough to be read by someone else. Also, many people simply feel that a handwritten letter or note is more personal than a typewritten one and that more careful thought can be given to what is said in a handwritten letter than is usually possible during the give and take of a telephone call.

The elementary-school program must give attention to both handwriting and writing by machines. Much of this attention can be incorporated into work in the subject areas, but writing itself also deserves specific instructional attention. Beginning writing was discussed in Chapter 4, where it was emphasized that the manuscript form meets the criteria of legibility, ease of execution, and similarity to the print that children of that age are learning to read. This chapter describes instruction in hand and machine writing and suggests activities that should be a part of an effective elementary-school language arts program.

HANDWRITING IN TODAY'S SCHOOLS

The major rationale supporting handwriting instruction is that handwriting is still important and that it must be legible and done with reasonable speed. Therefore, instruction—in letter formation, instrument position, and movement—and practice are needed. Handwriting should be viewed as a complex skill involving both mind and muscles and the coordination of the two.

Children's handwriting improves when they are motivated to diagnose their own handwriting needs, to evaluate their own progress, and to respond positively when assistance is offered. This motivation is largely based on their doing purposeful writing. Thus, handwriting should be taught throughout the day rather than being relegated only to instructional periods, although specific times should occasionally be reserved for working on problems or for teaching forms and movements.

Certainly, handwriting must be legible. Letters should be well formed and of the proper relative size, with adequate and uniform spacing between them. There should be consistency of slant of the letters (or a lack of slant in the case of manuscript letters) and adequate and uniform spacing between words.

The best handwriting is done with ease rather than laboriously. To write easily the writer must have a comfortable posture (body, arms, and hands), with writing instruments and paper properly positioned, free movement of the arm and hand, and an appropriate rhythm to the writing movements.

Finally, your own handwriting, your understanding of the developmental nature of handwriting skill, the knowledge you have of effective teaching procedures, and your skill in using these procedures are important factors in creating a successful program for children.

Manuscript Writing

Some published handwriting materials provide for practicing manuscript forms at every elementary-school grade level.

Although manuscript writing is usually taught only in the first years of school (as discussed in Chapter 4), it is becoming accepted as a valid form of writing for personal use. There are clearly several good reasons why children should continue to practice and use manuscript writing throughout the elementary-school years and beyond. When the need arises to label drawings, make signs, or fill in forms, those who can write manuscript have a distinct advantage. Also, if the legibility of the writing done by many adults is any indication, children's manuscript is much easier to read than their adult cursive is likely to be.

In *Handwriting: Basic Skills for Effective Communication,* the authors report on studies demonstrating that manuscript writing is easier for children to do, just as fast as cursive, and more legible.

It is particularly unfortunate that, just as children begin to master manuscript after two years or so of experience and to use it effectively for writing stories and other texts, instruction stops, and in some cases the school even begins to require that all the children's work be done in cursive. A better practice is to provide for the maintenance of acquired manuscript skills. This can be done with little instructional time; as suggested above, manuscript use can be encouraged when children are labeling posters, filling in forms, and so on.

Transition to Cursive Handwriting

Children themselves are usually the ones most insistent that they learn to do "big people's writing."

Learning to do cursive, or "real" writing as children often refer to it, usually occurs in the third grade, although some schools teach it earlier and a few do not teach it at all. Cursive can be difficult for children to execute since there are many upward movements, some awkward connections of letters, and the need to keep a consistent slant to the letters. There seems to be an advantage in beginning instruction by showing the children that the new way of writing is similar to the old. This is done by connecting manuscript letters and tracing cursive forms over manuscript equivalents where possible. Letters such as lowercase and uppercase *G* can then be taught as exceptions.

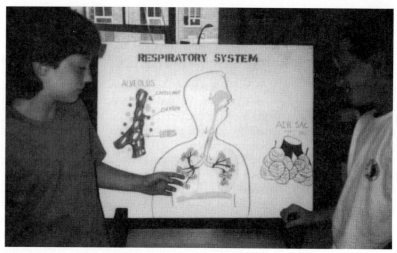

Manuscript writing is needed for labeling charts.

Published handwriting systems include instructions for teaching cursive forms, and it is generally a good idea to follow the directions provided with the materials to be used. However, the following suggestions may also be useful.

- Show the relationships of cursive forms to manuscript forms by illustrations such as these:

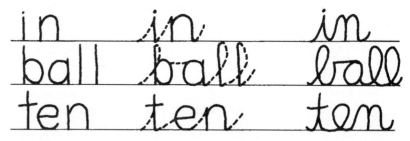

- Move from the simple to the complex. Introduce lowercase letters first, starting with the ones that are easiest to make: *l, e, i, t* (undercurve and slant strokes).

Slant can be taught as part of manuscript writing or introduced with cursive.

- In introducing letters, use parallel guidelines on the board to show how each straight line slants the same way as the others. The parallel lines will also help in showing spacing between letters, the width of humps in *m*s and *n*s, the width of the loop in an *l*, and so on.
- Introduce letters in words on the chalkboard or overhead projector, calling attention to the strokes, to the way the word begins, to the way the letters join, to the size of the letters, and to the ending stroke of the word.
- Introduce new letters in several words so that a new letter will appear in various positions—at the beginning, in the middle, and at the end of a word.

Handwriting in Intermediate and Upper Grades

After cursive handwriting has been introduced and adequately learned, practice continues to be important if children are to maintain their skill. As more and more writing is done in science, social studies, and literature, students need to increase their competence so that handwriting will be a tool to serve them rather than something that takes up a great deal of time and attention. Further, as speed increases, legibility often declines, so teachers in the intermediate and upper grades must be prepared to assist students in evaluating their handwriting and taking steps to improve it. You should focus attention on helping students achieve these specific objectives:

- to write all letters legibly in both manuscript and cursive forms and in upper and lower case
- to understand how the terms *shape, size, spacing, line quality,* and *alignment* apply to evaluating their own handwriting
- to be aware of posture, hand position, and movement when writing
- to evaluate their own handwriting in terms of class standards, commercial models, and diagnostic materials

Emphases in Handwriting Instruction

The preceding section discussed the transition to cursive writing, showed the need for maintenance of manuscript after the transition, and presented an overview of handwriting in the intermediate and upper grades. This section discusses specific aspects of handwriting instruction.

Practice. In addition to teaching handwriting directly and maintaining skills through the use of teachers' and pupils' guides and textbook materials, you should capitalize on opportunities to give attention to handwriting in all of the pupils' writing. Handwriting skill will diminish unless it is practiced, and this practice must include corrective work on factors that cause the writing to be illegible or cause it to be done awkwardly or in a tiring fashion.

Keep a checklist for recording individual problems that need correction. Search for the causes of handwriting difficulties as well as for the faults or errors themselves: check for poor posture, improper paper position, poor lighting, a too tightly held pen or pencil, or a writing instrument that is too large, too small, or too short. In addition to the checklist, it is a good idea to keep samples of the children's writing collected at intervals throughout the year and compare them as a means of evaluating progress.

Children should also evaluate their own writing. They can make comparisons with levels of performance shown on published scales as well as with their own previous writing efforts. Their attempts at improvement may be encouraged by displaying samples on the bulletin board, holding a writing clinic with several of the best writers acting as "consultants" for specific problems, having children report on their handwriting (each child identifying or describing his or her best letter, the most difficult letter to make, why his or her handwriting

Discuss expected difficulties (as shown in the chart on page 231) and determine the extent to which any appear in the students' writing.

is improving, etc.), and giving emphasis to handwriting in all areas of the curriculum.

Opaque and overhead projectors are useful for examining children's writing. (No student's handwriting should be used for group discussion without her or his permission, however.) In such sessions do not stress details too much: dwelling on "the tail of the *q* is too long" or "the *o* is not round enough" will focus attention on specifics rather than overall appearance and lead students to believe that their task is to satisfy you. Instead, have the children refer to handwriting charts to form their own judgments.

Some general discussion of handwriting will help in directing the students' attention to important features. For instance, on one day talk about the effect of the slant of letters on speed and legibility. On other days attention can be given to uniformity of letter size, spacing, formation of letters, and so on.

Handwriting practice should grow out of the needs that arise as the children write stories, poetry, reports, summaries, diaries, minutes, letters, notes, announcements, signs, and whatever. When there are genuine communication situations (sending an invitation to someone the child cares about), an appreciation of the importance of good handwriting will develop. It is sometimes helpful to set up one main objective for the class each week, with each pupil paying particular attention to any personal handwriting faults that are relevant to that objective. The objective might be maintaining parallel slant, gaining uniformity of letter size, closing letters properly, maintaining good margins, or having good posture when writing.

Instruction Time. Most primary-grade teachers will find occasion and need for daily handwriting periods, whereas perhaps no more than a five-minute

Using an overhead projector involves particular writing skills.

Handwriting maintenance in the intermediate grades requires only some self-evaluation and a few minutes of practice each week.

Paper Position for Cursive

The relaxed angle of the forearm across the desk and the maximum convenience of the forearm and fingers to the paper decide the position of the paper. Usually the angle of the bottom of the paper with the edge of the writing surface should be 30 degrees. For the left-handed writer, the paper should be angled in the opposite direction.

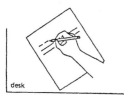

lesson on alternate days will be expected at higher grade levels. The use of less frequent and shorter periods presupposes, of course, that attention is being given to individual diagnosis and practice.

In addition to having handwriting periods, devote attention during the day to handwriting skills in all areas of work in which writing is involved. Pupils must feel responsible for legibility in all their writing that is to be read by others. The way to eliminate poor handwriting is not to spend more time in handwriting periods but to better utilize the time that is devoted to its teaching and practice.

Position and Movement. A child's handwriting is affected by the fit of the desk and the child's position in relation to it. Handwriting is also influenced by the position of the paper, the way the writing instrument is held, and the movements of the arm and hand. If attention is given to each of these factors in the proper way, both the child and the teacher will save much time and energy.

A child should sit comfortably, with both feet touching the floor and both arms resting in a relaxed position on the writing surface. The writing instrument should be held lightly, and the index finger should be placed nearer to the point than is the thumb, with both at least one inch above the writing point. The writing movement should involve smooth coordination of the whole arm, the wrist, and the fingers.

Speed of Writing. Attention to speed is not only useless but harmful if it begins before letter formation is spontaneously good. No end is served by making letters, words, and sentences rapidly and illegibly. Speed is important once letter formation has been properly established, since we all need to write rapidly at times. However, pupils usually make their own adjustments according to the nature of the work—pressure work, personal writing, or work that needs to be particularly neat and pleasing in appearance. Speed norms (see the scale samples presented later in Evaluating Handwriting) are only rough averages and should not be used as arbitrary standards for all children or for every product of a child's writing.

Differences in Letter Forms. A common instructional problem, particularly in the intermediate grades, is that different children in a class will write a number of different forms of the same symbol. These differences are particularly apparent for many capital letters, and they usually simply reflect the fact that the teachers the various pupils have been instructed by in earlier grades have used different commercial materials. Since there seems to be no conclusive evidence to demonstrate the superiority of a given letter form over other ways to make the same letter, it is reasonable to permit pupils who have learned different forms to continue to use these so long as they are legible and can be made with sufficient ease and speed. However, it is a good idea for a school to adopt a single system so that teachers will not confuse pupils by advocating their individual ideas. Before adopting a system, a school may want to simplify some letter forms (removing loops and swings, perhaps).

Handwriting Materials. Materials for handwriting include chalk, chalkboard, paper, crayons, pencils, pens, and usually commercial handwriting books. There is great variation in the use of these materials in different programs. Most programs call for the use of chalk and crayons in the primary grades, and many use large beginners' pencils. There is less emphasis today on a larger than normal

Don't force children to attempt to make letters of a size they can't comfortably handle.

pencil diameter, but the lead should be thicker, since the essential requirement is that the beginning writer be able to make a line that is easily seen.

There is also variation in what paper is advocated for the various grade levels. You should insist that several types of paper be available to the children in your classroom—not all paper in grade 2 should have lines that are a half-inch apart, for example. In addition, there should be stationery available for letter writing. The following is a guide to appropriate paper for practice and instruction.*

Grade 3	9 × 12, lined the long way with lines 1 inch apart
	9 × 12, with lines $\frac{1}{2}$ inch apart, alternating light and heavy
	9 × 12, with lines $\frac{1}{2}$ inch apart
	8$\frac{1}{2}$ × 11, with lines $\frac{5}{8}$ inch apart
Grade 4	8$\frac{1}{2}$ × 11, with lines $\frac{1}{2}$ inch apart
	8$\frac{1}{2}$ × 11, with lines $\frac{3}{8}$ inch apart
Grade 5	8$\frac{1}{2}$ × 11, with lines $\frac{3}{8}$ inch apart

Three of our recent presidents are left-handed.

The Left-handed Child. In a classroom 5 to 10 percent of the pupils are likely to be left-handed. These pupils are in a right-handed world and are probably taught by a right-handed teacher. If the pupil cannot imitate the teacher as the right-handed pupils do, he or she starts off with a problem. It is important, therefore, that you be aware of the left-handed pupils in your classroom, since their need for instruction is at least equal to that of right-handed pupils. First of all, it is necessary to recognize that left-handed children can be taught to write as well and as quickly as the right-handed ones. On the other hand, the time needed for development of particular skills is not necessarily the same for the left-handed

A left-handed child does manuscript writing.

*Paper varies in size. Some beginning-level lined paper, for example, is 8$\frac{1}{2}$ × 11 inches, with the lines running the long way.

pupils as for right-handed ones. In any case, it is important to avoid the implication that a child needs special attention because he or she is left-handed; simply pay attention to this child's individual needs as you do to those of other children.

Attention does need to be given to special instructional problems. For example, there should be much writing at the board in the early years, because when a child is writing at the board, it is practically impossible to use the upside-down style emphasized by some left-handed writers who were improperly taught. The best way to prevent the acquisition of this habit is to make sure that the paper is angled in the opposite direction from that suggested for the right-handed child. In addition, encouraging the left-handed child to hold the writing instrument slightly farther from the point helps, as does making sure that the top of the pen or pencil is pointed toward his or her left shoulder.

It is possible that some left-handed pupils will have developed the upside-down writing habit before they come into your classroom. Whether or not a teacher should attempt to change this habit after about the fourth grade depends on a number of factors. The pupil may not be psychologically or emotionally responsive to a change. In such cases, if the handwriting is reasonably legible and can be done with adequate speed, no attempt to change it is advised.

Left-handed writers should not be expected to write with the same slant as the right-handed ones, although some may do so. If the paper is placed properly and the writing instrument held correctly, it is possible that the left-handed child's writing will slant in the direction of the writing movement—that is, to the right.

Maintaining Interest. Young children are eager to learn to write. Later, they are also highly motivated to learn the cursive form. However, interest in practicing handwriting may lag. For a program to be successful special attention must be directed toward creating interest in handwriting and providing a freshness to instruction. Try using some of the following activities to supplement the suggestions already made and furnish motivation:

- Combine spelling and handwriting practice by having the children compose sentences using the spelling words from their individual list. They can thus give attention to their particular needs in both areas at the same time.

- Children can use bags or envelopes to make individual mailboxes. These mailboxes are then placed beside the pupils' desks, and the pupils may use them to send daily notes to one another. Legibility is very important for successful delivery.

- Pupils may do research on the history of handwriting, kinds of paper and how paper is made, the handwriting of famous people, kinds of handwriting tools, italic writing, graphology, or the handwriting of pupils in other grades.

- Children may report on writing they do at home, for example, letters, thank-you notes, shopping lists, and telephone messages. To help show the importance of writing, they may also report on writing their parents do.

Novelty can be added to practice through the use of such sentences as the following:

Zillions of zebras zipped by.
Well, Willie works willingly.
Buzzy, a busy bee, buzzed by.
A snapping turtle snapped at the stick.

To provide further variety in practice, tape-record a paragraph or two, speaking slowly but evenly and paying attention to the number of words per minute. If you have several tape recorders with listening stations, different children can practice writing different paragraphs (varied content, varied speeds, etc.).

Planning a handwriting project with another teacher of the same grade level can also provide motivation for practice. Pupils can write selections (without names on papers) to be exchanged between classes for other children's assessments of legibility. A variation of this is to exchange letters with pupils in a more advanced grade or some other part of the country.

If a child's handwriting remains poor, consider the possibility that he or she may have a physical or an emotional problem. If so, it would probably be wise to forget about any intensive effort to help the child improve. Instead, try to give support and look for ways to help with the problem. Persistently poor handwriting may be caused by poor visual-motor control. Vision should be checked, of course, but sometimes readiness activities merely need to be continued.

Evaluating Handwriting

Handwriting can be evaluated either formally through the use of published scales or less formally by the teacher and the pupils. Since evaluation should lead to corrective practice and remedial teaching, the latter procedure is recommended. This evaluation should be pupil-focused and systematic and should be used as the basis for further teaching.

Diagnosis and Attention to Needs. Most publishers of commercial handwriting materials can supply instruments helpful in locating handwriting faults. Some extracts from one handwriting chart, "Handwriting Faults and How to Correct Them," are given below.*

[This chart] is designed to reveal whether or not the pupil's handwriting violates one or more of the following essential qualities: (1) uniformity of slant, (2) uniformity of alignment, (3) quality of line, (4) letter formation, and (5) spacing. Three levels of quality—excellent, mediocre, and poor—are shown for each trait. In addition to illustrating these qualities, the chart contains excellent suggestions on ways to test a pupil's handwriting for each quality. The chart is particularly helpful because it enables both the teacher and the pupil to discover specific handwriting weaknesses that are in need of remedial treatment and makes helpful suggestions for correcting the defects.

How to test legibility: Make a letter finder by cutting a hole a little larger than the letter in a piece of cardboard. Place the hole of this finder over each letter in turn and mark the letters which are illegible. Have the pupils practice these letters separately, then write the word again and test as before.

*Chart published by Zaner-Bloser Company in 1937 and periodically revised. Used by permission.

How to test slant: Draw slanting lines through the letters and mark all letters which are off slant. If the slant is too great, the paper is tilted too much. If the writing is too vertical, the paper is too upright, and if the slant is backward, the paper is tilted the wrong direction.

How to test for spacing: Draw parallel lines between letters (see diagram). Place the paper in front of you and mark all letters and words which are unevenly spaced.

How to test alignment: Alignment and size are closely integrated and should be studied together. Use a ruler (a diagnostic ruler is best) and draw a base line touching as many of the letters as possible. Also draw a line along the tops of the small letters. Mark the letters above or below these lines.

How to test size of letters: Draw lines along the tops of the letters. Remember the minimum letters, i, u, v, etc., are ¼ space high; t and p are ½ space; capitals and l, h, k, b, d, are ¾ space high. All the lower loop letters extend ½ space below the line.

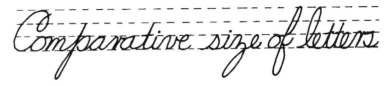

How to test for quality of line: Make a letter finder by cutting a hole a little larger than the letter in a piece of cardboard. Place the hole of this finder over each letter in turn and mark the letters which are illegible due to the quality of line.

Have pupils practice these letters from their writing books separately until the letters are perfectly legible. Then have them write the whole word again and test as before.

Handwriting Scales. Handwriting scales are often not used because of the feeling that children will attempt to copy the handwriting on the scale and thus lose the individuality of their writing. However, scales do not have to be used for *grading* pupils' handwriting; they can simply be bases for the pupils to use in making their own judgments about the legibility of their handwriting.

One commercial instrument, *Guiding Growth in Handwriting Evaluation Scales,* provides five specimens of handwriting for each grade level and suggests that samples comparable to these specimens be rated.* Two of these specimens are reproduced below.

Specimen 3—Medium for Grade 5. Similar cursive handwriting may be marked "good." The standard speed for this grade is about 60 letters per minute.

> *I live in America. It is good to live where you have freedom to work and play. As an American, I support my country and what it stands for.*

Specimen 5—Poor for Grade 5. Similar cursive handwriting may be marked "needs improvement."

> *My name stands for me. I want to write it well.*

Checklists. Procedures for evaluating handwriting were suggested in the section on handwriting practice, since practice should grow from diagnosis and evaluation. You can make a legibility checksheet such as the one shown on the next page, but be sure to list only the letters causing difficulty for your class. The checksheet can be added to if new problems are noted.

WRITING BY MACHINE

Handwriting has advantages, not the least of which is that the equipment needed to do it is simple and completely portable, so it can be done nearly anywhere.

*Scales published by Zaner-Bloser Company in 1966. Used by permission.

	NOT THIS	BUT THIS
Straight back stroke for e, l	*e, l*	*e, l*
Avoidance of loop in a, i, n, t, u	*a, i, n, t, u*	*a, i, n, t, u*
Points on r and s	*r, s,*	*r, s,*
Well-rounded curves on m, n, u	*m, n, u,*	*m, n, u*
Carefully crossed t	*t, t, t*	*t, tt*
Open loops on b, f, h, k	*b, f, h, k,*	*b, f, h, k,*
Avoidance of lazy ending on h, m, n	*h, m, n*	*h, m, n*
Open loop on g, p, y, q	*g, p, y, q*	*g, p, y, q*
Dot over i, j in line with letter	*i, j*	*i, j*
Closing of f on the line	*f, f*	*f*
Careful closing of a, d, g, q	*a, d, g, q,*	*a, d, g, q*

Handwriting is highly personal, too. You can probably recognize that of several relatives and friends, and some people even claim to be able to deduce much about the personalities of writers from samples of their penmanship. Also, the use of handwriting conveys feelings; lovers do not ordinarily type intimate messages, and an angry note executed with emphatic graphic flourishes has a certain impact.

However, notwithstanding all these uses, machines are taking over most writing functions. Typewriters and computers have advantages of speed, accuracy, legibility, and storage capability, which are highly important in commerce and communications. A practical consideration for schools is that computers are found in more and more homes, and large numbers of children are learning to use them to write. It seems clear that the elementary-school program must include writing with machines as a part of the language arts curriculum.

Typing

Time spent perfecting cursive handwriting might better be used in practicing keyboarding.

The advantages of being able to type are obvious. Students may benefit from possessing this skill at any level but, at the secondary level and above, they may be required to submit typewritten assignments. Those who cannot type for themselves must either pay for the service or make arrangements to have it done at times that are not necessarily convenient. Even if an instructor accepts handwritten assignments, there is always the likelihood, supported by some evidence, that typed materials receive a higher evaluation.

In his article listed at the end of the chapter, Hoot mentions some of the studies which show that typing seems to improve the academic performance of elementary-school students.

Typing has not been widely used in elementary classrooms but available results indicate that those students who type produce longer texts, spell and use punctuation more accurately, and write better in other ways. Routine typing may be difficult for children, however, and although electric typewriters have been a big improvement over the manual kind, it was not until the appearance of word processors that writing by machine became common in elementary classrooms.

Computers and Word Processing

As discussed in Chapter 16, computers have been a major aid to children with special needs.

Personal computers are used in many ways, and one of the most common is for word processing. The computer is much more than a typewriter, of course. One principal difference is that what is written is displayed on a television screen rather than being directly typed on a piece of paper. While the text is on the screen, deleting, changing, and adding of material may be accomplished very easily and this is why writers find using computers to be a very advantageous method of composing. Also, when a printer is connected to the word processor, the writer may have the text typed onto paper. (When there is no printer the writer may create a *file,* a computer-disk copy of what was written and then take that to a location where a printer is available.) What is typed may be the text in final form or a draft that the writer can change further at a later time. The computer is also able to store what has been typed. Its own memory can hold relatively short texts, and longer ones can be stored on magnetic disks.

The keyboard used with the computer is quite similar to that on an ordinary typewriter. There are some additional keys and other controls, and the locations of keys for certain characters or functions may not be the same as on a typewriter. The computer keyboard is likely to be the first encountered by most children.

Procedures for Using Word Processors

Each word-processing program is somewhat different from the others, but there are some general procedures common to nearly all of them. Going through a simple writing activity step by step demonstrates what happens when children begin to use a word processor.

1. Select a program disk and place it in the disk drive. In a a matter of seconds the program is "booted up," or transferred to the memory of the computer. The system is then ready to be used for writing.

2. Type the text, correcting errors that occur along the way, if desired.

3. Read the text and make any necessary changes, in anything from the spelling of a word or the placement of a comma to the location of a word, sentence, or several paragraphs.

4. When the writing is finished, activate the printer to obtain a copy typed on paper (the "hard copy").

Children's computer disks are most conveniently kept in a covered box near the computer (although those with computers at home may want to take disks with them sometimes).

Many other procedures are possible, too. Making a file for later revision or printing has already been mentioned. In addition, certain program features permit the writer to decide how lines will be spaced when the printing is done, whether or not there will be an even margin on the right-hand side of the page, which words should be changed each time they appear in the text, and more.

Word Processing in the Classroom

In order for computers to be available to pupils on a reasonable basis, there should be one or more in each classroom. Several are probably needed if word processing is to become a really effective teaching tool.

Significant numbers of elementary-school teachers are using word processing in their classrooms, and the ones with the most experience have identified and at least partially solved the problems encountered in implementation. They are convinced that the major difficulties can be overcome and that the contribution made by word processing is valuable enough to be worth the effort. Several factors that seem to be particularly important to the effective use of word processing in the classroom are discussed in the sections that follow. (This discussion emphasizes the use of word processing as an alternative to handwriting. The actual process of composing with the computer is a separate concern discussed in Chapters 10 and 11.)

Placement of computers in library media centers is discussed in Chapter 14.

Availability of Computers. In elementary schools computers may be located in separate "computer rooms," in library resource centers, or in regular classrooms. When a computer room serves an entire school population, its use usually involves taking a whole class there on a regular basis to acquire "computer literacy," or general knowledge about computers, and to get some experience in operating them. In such circumstances it is not likely that students will be able to use the machines to learn word processing; there simply will not be enough time for them to do so unless the school is quite small. When computers are located in a library or resource center, it is sometimes possible for individuals or small groups to use them for a variety of purposes, including writing activities. Generally, the students who do this will have to be those who are able to work without much supervision, however.

When computers are in classrooms permanently, or at least for large blocks of time, doing word processing is quite feasible. Much can be learned even if

Children can teach one another how to use a word processor.

there is only a single unit in a classroom, but the availability of three or four makes a big difference. The reason even a single unit is advantageous is that word processing is not necessarily a solitary activity. Because the text is on the screen and easily seen by anyone in the vicinity, others can observe the writer, and comments about everything from spelling to content may be expected. Some teachers have children work in small groups; one child may be making notes and another reviewing hard copy while others are composing on the screen and still others are reading the story or other composition to themselves or aloud as it is being written. In such a situation the sense of writing for an audience is immediate.

Keyboarding is a skill, and the skill-related learning generalizations apply. For example, there should be frequent, brief periods of meaningful practice.

By fourth grade some students are quite competent, typing forty words per minute or more.

Learning Keyboarding. When children are introduced to word processing, they should become acquainted with the keyboard but not necessarily be required to learn adult-level touch typing. It is probably best that elementary students begin by using both hands on the keyboard, even if they need to look at the keys and don't necessarily conform to any particular pattern of matching fingers to particular keys. They should *not* develop the habit of using one or two fingers at a time for typing.

There are some very good devices for teaching keyboarding, including several computer programs that have been developed specifically for elementary students. Several principles guide such instruction for elementary-level students:

- The school or school system should adopt a consistent policy and program for introducing and teaching word processing to all students.
- Classroom teachers should have at least general knowledge of the methodology of keyboarding instruction.
- Emphasis should be on accuracy rather than speed.
- Keyboards (even in the form of hand-me-down typewriters) should be readily available for individual practice.

Selecting Appropriate Programs. Word-processing programs vary in their possibilities, capacities, and complexity of operation, so choosing which one to use is a difficult decision. An elementary-school student should usually concentrate on learning only one, which means that a school ought to plan to designate a particular program for use by everyone. This choice should be made with several criteria in mind, including ease of use by beginners as well as potential for providing assistance to advanced writers. If you, as teacher, must select a program for a class, you should consult with several experienced people who know computers and have worked with students of the same age group as the class.

Teaching Word Processing. When elementary-school children are being taught to do word processing, several important considerations apply. As with any other learning there should be opportunities for the children to explore use of the computer, and this should include writing as well as operation of instructional software programs.

Once students begin to write on the word processor a decision needs to be made about what the procedure should be. If there is one word processor in the classroom it may be reasonable to ask students to do their initial draft by writing on paper and then type in their text for revision. (Some will revise as they type

```
                            THE PANDA
        One sunny day panda was sitting in her dreaming tree. She  was
    dreaming  of  being in a panda moveie all of a  sudden  she  woke
    up.OH my I have to get up and cook again time just go's so  fast.
    So  she got up and went to the kitchen. The frist customer was  a
    littel panda he got soup. The next customer looked like a  ROBBER
    .he  got hot coco while she was in the kitchen she took a peek  at
    the newspaper sure enoughhe was in there for most wanted. So  she
    called the police when they got there they took him away and gave
    panda a free trip.The next day while she was on her trip her  car
    broke down. Soshe was in the middel of nowhere so she got out  of
    her car and started walking.After a while it was darke so she sat
    down  to  rest.She woke up she heard peopole  talking  they  said
    let's  go  robb the bank. So panda ran to the nearst  police  and
    toled them they founed the robber's and took them to jail.And for
    panda she became a police panda.


                                              THE END
```

A story typed on a word processor by a third grader.

Copying over work in "your best handwriting" almost always represented a huge burden before word processors came into use.

it in.) Typing a familiar text provides valuable practice. Alternatively, an older student or adult may do the typing for a beginner. Once the text is in the computer, the writer may take over, however, and give attention to revision.

After students have become proficient in word processing, they should be introduced to a desk-top publishing program. With this they will be able to use various formats and graphics to produce quite sophisticated newspapers, magazines, signs, and books.

Evaluation of Word Processing

If there is ample time to practice using the word processor, children will make very good progress with it. You can, of course, take steps to encourage self-assessment and goal setting. With regard to language arts portfolios, samples of students' work can be placed in these from time to time. More important, sequences of drafting and revising can be collected (see Chapter 10). Also, videotapes can be made of students actually using the word processor, and these can be reviewed regularly for indications of increased knowledge of the process and growing skills in all the areas involved.

A FINAL WORD

Years ago the principal tools for writing were pencils or pens to be dipped in ink. School children worked on their "penmanship" for hours each week, and some went on to work in occupations requiring that they be able to "write a good hand." Now there are many means for written communication, and people who do the most writing use machines much of the time. In many school systems all students learn how to use a word processor, often in the elementary school.

Handwriting—manuscript, cursive, or both—should be taught with an emphasis on legibility and speed, but written forms do not have to be identical for every member of the class, nor does the writing need to be a work of art. Given that innumerable blank forms must be filled out in the modern world and that machines are not always available, students should be encouraged to maintain and use manuscript writing.

Because manuscript is at least an adequate form of handwriting, the time taken to teach cursive could very likely be put to better use in practicing keyboarding and word processing. Cursive could then receive a minimum amount of attention. It might be argued that enough time should be given to enable students to read the cursive writing of others but, considering the nature of the handwriting produced by many adults (some of whom say that their cursive was quite good when in school), it might be unwise to offer such a guarantee.

References

Barbe, Walter B.; Lucas, Virginia H.; and Wasylyk, Thomas M., eds. *Handwriting: Basic Skills for Effective Communication*. Zaner-Bloser, 1984.

Chandler, Daniel. *Young Learners and the Microcomputer*. Open University Press, 1984.

Handwriting Resource Book, Grades 1–7. Ministry of Education, British Columbia, Canada, 1981.

Hoot, James L. "Keyboarding Instruction in the Early Grades: Must or Mistake?" *Childhood Education* 63 (December 1986), pp. 95–101.

Hoot, J. L., and Silvern, S. B. *Writing with Computers in the Early Grades*. Teachers College Press, 1988.

Kaake, Dianne M. "Teaching Elementary Age Children Touch Typing as an Aid to Language Arts Instruction." *The Reading Teacher* (March 1983), pp. 640–643.

Teaching Resources

Elements of Legible Handwriting. Zaner-Bloser, 1974 (pamphlet).

Evaluating Handwriting. Zaner-Bloser, 1977 (pamphlet).

Fry, Edward. *Computer Keyboarding for Children*. Teachers College Press, 1984.

Handwriting Evaluation Scales. Zaner-Bloser (kit).

Keyboard Cadet. Mindscope (software).

Learning the Keyboard for Children. Random House (six cassettes, keyboard fingercharts with colored key stickers, and lesson sheets; K–grade 6).

New Links to Cursive: A Power Approach to Handwriting. Curriculum Associates (kit).

The Print Shop. Scholastic (software).

Rainbow Keyboarding. Scholastic (software).

SRA Lunchbox Handwriting Kits (separate kits for manuscript and cursive; K–grade 4).

Success with Typing. Scholastic (software).

Touch N' Write Palmer Manuscript Penmanship. Sunburst Communications, 1986 (grades 1 and 2).

Activities for Preservice Teachers

1. Practice your handwriting, manuscript and cursive, on many surfaces and with all kinds of writing instruments. Evaluate what you write in the ways suggested in this chapter. Keep in mind that some people judge a teacher by the quality of her or his handwriting. (And, of course, the children have to be able to read it!)

2. Obtain handwriting samples from college students (preferably class notes, not something for display). How is the legibility? Are letters similarly made? Do those from the same schools write similarly? Can you tell who is left-handed?

3. If you do not type, take steps to learn. Typing classes are offered by adult education departments of public school systems, by community colleges, and by commercial schools, and many individuals have learned touch typing on their own, using a high-school typing textbook. As you learn typing, examine computer programs developed to teach children keyboarding.

4. Observe handwriting lessons at several grade levels. Note differences in posture, hand and arm movements, quality of handwriting produced, degree of insistence on uniformity throughout the class, and so forth.

5. Examine samples of commercial handwriting materials for a grade level or levels of interest to you. Decide which you would choose if the decision were up to you.

6. Obtain several samples of children's handwriting and evaluate them, using a handwriting scale.

7. Visit a classroom, computer room, or resource center where elementary-school children are learning keyboarding and word processing. Do they seem interested? What difficulties do there seem to be? What software is being used? Is the teacher an expert in typing and/or computers?

Activities for Inservice Teachers

1. Ask a colleague to do a critique of your handwriting—on the board, on the overhead, and on children's papers. Are there areas in which you could improve? What specific plan can you devise for improving?

2. Have children at one grade level write the same paragraph and then identify three or four levels of quality among the samples. Offer these to your colleagues as the beginning of a handwriting scale for the building. What reaction do you get?

3. Start a file of examples of good and poor handwriting by adults. Try to get examples that are not signatures. With the children, examine the poor examples to determine why they are illegible (bad letter formation, spacing, slant, etc.).

4. Ask college professors, administrators, and parents what they think about eliminating cursive writing from the school program and concentrating on manuscript, typing, and word processing. What do they say? What reasons do they offer in support of their positions?

5. Find out what your school or district policy is on teaching word processing. What provision is there for helping teachers to learn how to do word processing?

6. Try several computer programs that teach keyboarding to elementary-school students. Which one seems best to you? What recommendations would you make to those responsible for purchasing such items?

7. Prepare activities for the children in your class to do individually to improve their handwriting.

8. Make an informal survey of the handwriting in your school. Collect papers and analyze them for specific handwriting faults. Note the amount of writing done, types of assignments, and so on, and see if you can relate such factors to handwriting ability.

9. Make a survey of local school systems to see how computers are being used by students at various grade levels for their written work. What do you conclude? What are the opinions of the most experienced teachers regarding computer use by students?

10. Acquire some books on graphology. Use the study of graphology to stimulate interest in handwriting among upper-grade students.

Activities for Children

1. Each child can keep a personal handwriting improvement record by filing dated samples of writing and reviewing these periodically, using some of the diagnostic and evaluative suggestions in this chapter to see where improvement has been made and what needs to receive attention.

2. Encourage pupils to use a diagnostic chart such as the one presented in this chapter to examine their handwriting for common problems.

3. Make available a device for determining the legibility of a single letter in a word. An easy device to make is a piece of tagboard about one inch wide and three inches long; near one end punch a hole with a hole punch. The child places the hole over individual letters and practices making those that are illegible.

4. For individual practice, prepare a folder with a pocket on one side and a sheet of acetate on the other (fasten it to the folder on one long side and on the bottom). In the pocket, place cards containing directions for the formation of letters and lists of words using those letters. A child selects a letter to work on and places it under the acetate. Using a marking pencil and with the card as a guide, the child first traces the letter, then writes it without tracing, and finally writes the words, comparing them with the model.

5. Some attention to speed is necessary in the middle grades, although legibility must remain paramount. To practice speed, individual children can copy short paragraphs and time themselves. Prepare materials that should take about a minute to copy (about forty to sixty letters) at first.

6. As an incentive to improve, suggest that a child prepare a sample of his or her handwriting (enough so that most letters—uppercase and lowercase—and numerals are included) and write a letter to a pupil in another part of the country to send with the sample, suggesting an exchange several times during the year.

7. To encourage the learning of touch typing, provide keyboard shields or color-coded keys (with corresponding stick-on finger dots) for children whose hands are large enough and who have adequate eye-hand coordination.

8. Children who have learned to use a computer program such as *Print Shop* by Scholastic can make attractive book covers, posters, and banners for special events in the class or school.

9. Arrange for children who are doing very well in touch typing to see a local speed-typing champion in action. Such a visit should be a real treat for them, since they have some appreciation of the skill involved.

10. Children can collect samples of writing by adults and older children and practice identifying illegibilities in this writing. In some instances, if it can be done without offending, they might point out to the writers (perhaps their parents) the illegibilities.

11. Have a child find examples of early picture writing or other alphabets—hieroglyphics, Native American picture writing, the Greek alphabet—and prepare a demonstration for the class. As a part of the demonstration, several children might develop symbols depicting an activity with which the class is involved and have the other children try to "read" what they have written.

Chapter 10

The Writing Process

Writing compositions has been a part of school programs for many years. Results have seldom been encouraging, though, possibly because instruction so often emphasized everything but writing itself. Activities receiving the most attention were identifying parts of speech, diagraming sentences, filling in blanks with the "right" word, and providing punctuation for sample sentences. When students actually wrote compositions, teachers or textbooks supplied such stereotyped topics as "What I Did on My Summer Vacation" or "A Funny Mistake." Teachers' expectations usually focused on neat handwriting, accurate spelling, and "complete" sentences, each beginning with a capital letter and ending with the appropriate punctuation mark. Very often, the products fell short of the expectations, and the teacher had to "correct" them for rewriting in approved form. Quite understandably, under this sort of regime not many children enjoyed writing. Getting their compositions back all marked up with red pencil and receiving instructions to do them over again caused most children to dread the entire procedure.

Books by Elbow, Murray, and Graves (see References) contain good discussions of the writing process.

Now, many teachers work in a different way. They teach writing as a process, as briefly described in Chapter 4. The first section of this chapter further describes that process and focuses on the writing done in the middle and upper grades. The value of the process is that it encourages children to write, develops writing confidence and ability, and has applicability to all types of writing. Furthermore, children like it and can easily do it if they are properly taught and the teacher encourages its use.

COMPOSITION AS A PROCESS

There are several advantages to emphasizing the process of writing in your teaching. One of the more important benefits is that attention is directed away from the finished product and to the act of writing. A piece of writing is not simply done and then given to someone to read; much has to be accomplished before there is any reason to be concerned about preparing the text to be read by others. Another advantage is that the student who develops a real understanding of the writing process learns about procedures that can be applied to many tasks. Techniques and terminology associated with the writing process also become familiar, and, as a result, students and teachers are able to talk with one another about such matters as drafting, having conferences, and editing. The process becomes an internalized one that writers can use on their own for the rest of their lives.

Many professional writers use these same procedures.

The major process stages are *prewriting, writing,* and *postwriting,* with each of these having substages. For young children, depending on their maturity and writing experience as discussed in Chapter 4, stages are rather brief and simple. For example, the child may draw a picture (prewriting), write a related text (writing), and then read that to the teacher or a friend (postwriting).

Some well-known writers say that writing is "a process of discovery," meaning that they sometimes don't know what they are actually going to write until they write it. Some even say that they are occasionally surprised or even shocked at what appears.

As children gain more experience and maturity, each stage becomes richer. Before writing, the child usually decides on a topic, thinks of some ideas related to it, and begins to develop some enthusiasm for writing. As he or she begins to write, the first necessity is to get ideas down on paper, recognizing that what is being done is a draft, an attempt that can be discarded entirely or extensively modified. The draft may be reread, discussed with others, and revised during the postwriting stage. A final step is publication, sharing what has been written by reading it to others or preparing it for them to read for themselves, if that seems appropriate.

Prewriting Activities

When you have a major writing task, it is most likely connected with academic work, a term paper perhaps. If the end result is to be successful, much preparation is required; you read, talk with others, use several resources, take notes, and possibly make an outline. This is all a rehearsal for writing, and elementary-school students need to go through a similar process, deciding what to write about and collecting their thoughts. They must talk with the teacher and the other children, because, as they hear responses to the ideas they express, their thinking will be stimulated. Reflection on these interchanges will put them in a much better position to begin writing. Time spent on prewriting activities is time well spent.

Children get input from:

reading and being read to
observing nature
listening to music and poetry
examining word meanings
attending dramatizations
and much more

Selecting Topics. Subjects to write about come from various sources. The best ones are those that are important to the writer. If children keep journals as described in Chapter 4, they will have been writing about trips, play activities, experiences with their friends, and other events important to them. Journal writing is a means of exploring experiences and thoughts about important subjects, some of which may be interesting enough to be treated more fully. Older students can be introduced to writers' notebooks (described in Chapter 11). To help children select topics for further development, ask them to look in their journals or notebooks.

It is much better for students to decide on their topics themselves. You should resist entreaties to "Tell me what to write about." You can be prepared with a list of comments that encourage without giving direction: "Just start writing"; "Think of something no one else will write about"; "Draw a picture—that may help." Specific activities may be planned for the purpose of helping children to think of topics and clarify them.

Discussions among children can promote the generation of ideas about subjects to be written about. This approach is best used by older students, however, since young children are likely to copy the ideas expressed by classmates. Opportunities to talk about broad topics such as animals, sports teams, television programs, hobbies (and others mentioned in the Conversation and Discussion sections of Chapter 5) will usually generate sufficient exchange of ideas to permit everyone to identify a promising topic for writing. After several months of experience with the writing process, most students can discuss a variety of

Talk is basic to all communication.

topics among themselves and give and receive advice about the ones that will likely be most interesting to try.

Conferences between you and an individual child concerning topic selection may be very brief when the child has a definite idea and you see good possibilities in it. Such conferences may also be rather brief if you have doubts about a choice but believe it is advisable to encourage the child to go ahead and try. In such cases, though, be sure to watch for the development of any difficulties as the child proceeds. Other conferences may involve some discussion to help writers clarify their thinking about possible topics. Many times teachers find that such conferences are not only productive for the writing program but also worthwhile in establishing relationships with children, since they provide excellent opportunities for talking with individuals about what interests them.

Lists of possible topics can be kept by individual children for use as needed. Students can be encouraged to add items to such lists in their journals and notebooks and you may use these in conferences with them. A classroom list may be used, too, but only when it seems likely to be helpful to a large proportion of the class. It might have a heading such as "Why doesn't someone write about _____?" Classroom lists should reflect local concerns so that writing remains close to the children's experiences.

Exploring a Topic.   Once children have decided on their topics, it is helpful to make them aware of ways of generating related ideas. Too often, when a topic is assigned by the teacher or taken from a textbook and there is little or no exploration of what it means to them, children will write a few perfunctory sentences and announce that the assignment is completed, or they will ask how much writing is required. Whatever the source of the topic, writing about it can be made easier and better if writers learn how to use drawings, diagrams, and topic webs (introduced in Chapter 4), how to do brainstorming or free writing, how to consult books and other resources, how to conduct interviews and conferences, and how to take notes. These you should describe and demonstrate when there are good opportunities as you work with the total class or with individuals.

Pictures and drawings can be used by younger writers as described in Chapter 4, and the same idea may be appropriate for older children. Although they may not be interested in drawing a picture, certain types of writing may be aided by making sketches or diagrams. When writing about ballet or figure skating, for example, a child may wish to draw stick figures in various body positions before trying to write descriptions of particular leaps and movements. A student interested in aircraft or rockets will often make elaborate drawings of individual pieces or scenes before writing about them. Of course, making such sketches usually requires some research by the pupil.

Brainstorming is the process of coming up with many ideas that might be related to a topic. This should be done as a group experience at first, involving either the whole class or a subgroup. Once the process has been demonstrated, individuals may use it, although group results are usually more satisfactory. In brainstorming the goal is simply to generate ideas, whether they are good, not so good, or useless. During the procedure, participants are not supposed to criticize the ideas of others but should only produce new ones or expand on one that has been presented. Ideas can be represented by isolated words, short phrases, or sentences. After a dozen or so have been produced, related ones may be grouped together. From a list of brainstormed ideas a writer will likely be able to see what

In The Art of Teaching Writing, Calkins presents very interesting accounts of what can be accomplished in conferences.

Webs can be thought of as networks of information— clusters of ideas related to a single topic and connected by lines to that topic and to each other.

can be used to get the writing started. Ideas that do not appear to be helpful can be ignored.

Even experienced writers sometimes find it necessary to write "just anything" in order to get started.

Free writing is similar to brainstorming in that the writer permits ideas to flow without exercising much control. Usually only older children can do this with any success, because it requires writing as fast as possible in an attempt to keep up with thinking. The child simply writes about a topic for a few minutes without stopping and without really thinking about what is being put down on the paper. There should be no going back to read or any attention to corrections, changes, or punctuation. (However, the writing does have to be legible enough to be read later by the writer.) Through using this technique, the writer explores ideas and feelings and, very likely, discovers something worth keeping and developing.

Teacher conferences for the purpose of getting started provide an opportunity for you to ask questions that may help a writer focus on the chosen topic and explore it, looking for aspects that have the most personal significance. The child should also be led to examine his or her reasons for writing and to consider what audience might be interested and what that individual or group will already know or might want to know. During these conferences, intrude as little as possible. Resist any temptation to tell a child how the writing might begin or even to offer hints and suggestions. Instead, follow the lead of the child, bearing in mind whose piece it is and the importance it might have to the author. This kind of conference is an opportunity to point out the value of making notes as a means for reminding the writer of the need for information from another person, a book, or some other source.

Peer conferences put children in the role of a teacher as they help classmates think about their topics and what they might mean to others. Children will learn to employ the same techniques they have observed the teacher using: they will

Asking classmates questions may help them with their writing.

ask how interest in the topic came about and other appropriate "when," "where," and "why" questions. You may want to listen in on some peer conferences (but only infrequently) to encourage the most beneficial lines of discussion. Another benefit of having such conferences regularly is that children will begin to ask themselves questions as they write, anticipating what their classmates are likely to want to know about in the conferences.

Webs, or *semantic maps,* are tools a writer may use for jotting down ideas or information related to a central topic. Writing the items in a schematic form such as a web gives a focus to the central idea and is helpful for remembering related or supporting items and how they are related. The first webs used are usually relatively simple, but they should become more complex. For example, a simple web used by a student named Val to write about her dog Ollie was shown in Chapter 4. If Val were more experienced, she would number the related circles within a web to help her decide what to write about first, second, and third. And, in the middle grades and beyond, she would put in a third set of circles to support or describe the second, as shown in the example on the following pages.

As webs become more complex, they are very useful as a first step in outlining. Nearly all effective writers will jot down words or phrases, often in a sort of map that shows how ideas are related to a topic and to one another. They do this so that what they have thought of won't be forgotten but will be retained as notes that can be examined, added to, put in order, and possibly used as a basis for writing. Writers may also go on to arrange the parts of the web in an outline form. This doesn't have to be a formal outline, even though it can later be turned into one if the writer chooses; but it should show some order and reflect the relationships among the ideas.

Writing

The writing stage involves getting an organized text on paper so that the writer (at least) can read what has been written. For some types of writing there will be only one draft, especially for writing done by younger children and for journal writing in the upper grades. As writers gain in confidence and experience they will come to see their initial efforts as first drafts that will be changed, extended, and improved at a later time. Such an attitude permits them to take risks in trying challenging topics, in exploring their thinking about a subject, or in simply dealing with the subject as accurately and completely as possible.

When sitting down to actually write, the writer should call on all that she or he has done in preparation, including notes from brainstorming, free writing, conferences, reference sources, and a web or outline. The sources and the organizational aids provide the basis for "getting something down" on paper. As thoughts begin to come to mind, the writing must be done fairly rapidly so that ideas are not lost. Giving too much time to selecting just the right word or worrying about spelling is not advisable at this point. Building momentum and seeing what there is to be said about the topic should occupy the writer's attention.

The following guidelines may help to clarify for children what should be emphasized during initial writing:

- Use scrap paper for first drafts. Writing on something other than "good" paper reinforces the transitory nature of these initial attempts. Backs of printed materials

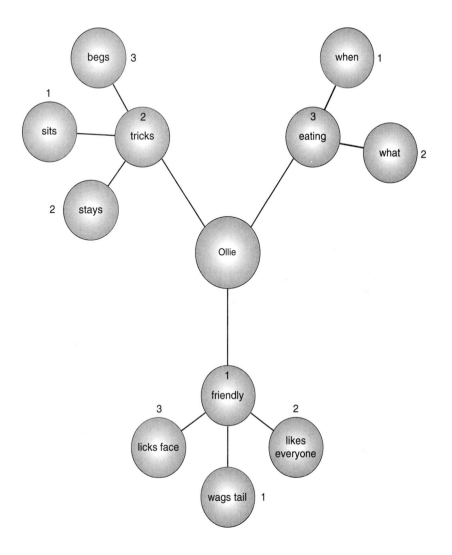

and worksheets and paper that might otherwise be discarded, such as computer printouts, serve very well for drafts.

- Try different "leads," or beginnings. Getting started may require that several approaches to a topic be tried until the writer finds one that is effective in keeping the ideas coming.

- Cross out rather than erase. Drawing a line through what is being changed or discarded is faster and easier than erasing it. Also, text that has been crossed out can still be read; it might turn out to be the better alternative after all or useful in another place.

- Use arrows and other marks to show how sections of the text relate to one another. During the writing of a first draft some additions and transpositions may be

Speaking and Writing K-12, edited by Thaiss and Suhor, gives attention to how thinking, talking, and writing are related.

A ten-year-old student may have a "writer's block" just as an older and more experienced writer does.

necessary. These can be done with notes and other markings that indicate what comes next. It doesn't matter how messy the text is as long as the writer can read it to someone else.

- Do not be concerned about handwriting, typing, spelling, or punctuation. During initial writing, concentration should be focused on ideas, not on mechanics. Children need to be cautioned that the handwriting should not be so bad that they cannot read it themselves, of course. Other matters will receive attention later.
- While writing, also read, think, and talk. Writers must shift among reading over what has been written, writing some more, thinking about the ideas to be expressed, and talking with others. One activity leads to another, and this interaction will keep the writing flowing.
- Recognize that sticking points will sometimes occur. Even when they are familiar with many techniques for maintaining the momentum of writing, children will occasionally be unable to make progress. At these times the best solution is often to put the piece away and come back to it later. A fresh look may then bring new ideas.

Writing first drafts will become easier as children have more experience with the writing process. As they gain in experience, concern about mechanics or even word choice or the awkwardness of sentences will lessen. They will know that all of these aspects can be dealt with later, perhaps when they reach a point in first-draft writing when they need to review what they have done, or even when the draft has been completed. In addition, they probably will have learned how to anticipate the questions that you and their classmates are likely to ask (What does that mean? Can you tell more about this part?), and such knowledge will enable them to think about these points as they write. All of this will gradually lead them to produce more successful first drafts.

Postwriting Activities

After the first draft of a piece of writing has been completed and, perhaps, read to others, the writer needs to decide whether or not anything further should be done with it. Acknowledgement of children's rights to have some control over their own products means that a decision by a student to stop working on a piece has to be respected. On the other hand, you should encourage students to keep much of their writing in folders for a time, probably several weeks. Something that wasn't satisfactory when first written may be returned to later with a different result.

Children should be encouraged to examine their first drafts and select those that seem good enough to warrant revision. It is through reading and considering their own writing products and deciding what changes will improve them that they will learn to write. Beginning in the first grade, nearly every child will be able to revise something he or she has written and make it better. As children learn various strategies, an increasingly higher proportion of their writing will be taken through the postwriting steps of revision, editing, and sharing, including publication.

Learning about Revision. Once students have been through the writing process a few times, they will understand the difference between writing a first draft and making a revision. In the early grades, however, or when the process is being introduced to older children for the first time, you will need to take specific steps to familiarize them with revision procedures.

Most important, writers will need guidance in learning how to see the difference between what they wanted to express and the actual products that resulted. Of course, total satisfaction with a product cannot always be achieved, but it is extremely important that children learn to identify problems in their own writing. With experience they will begin to find ways to express themselves more effectively. Beginners generally think of revision as a process of adding more to the text or correcting spelling and punctuation. More experienced students realize that major changes in organization or even switching to an entirely different form of writing are sometimes necessary.

What seems an unsatisfactory story might evolve into a really good poem.

Reading a first draft and revising it as a group activity is helpful in demonstrating what revision involves. You may present a sample piece of imperfect writing (not the writing of a class member) on a chart or overhead projector, read it with the children, and discuss how it might be changed for the better. Changes should actually be made, based as much as possible on the children's suggestions. Cross out parts, make insertions, and use whatever revision strategies seem to be appropriate, while encouraging the class members to discuss these and their effectiveness. After children have participated in several such group activities, some will be able to apply the revision techniques to their own work; others will need to be helped further. You can help them by going over their texts with them privately but in a way similar to that used with the group.

Revising a First Draft. After children have participated in group revision activities, they should be encouraged to examine their own drafts and identify at least some features that require attention. As a first step, they should read what they've written aloud to themselves (softly, of course) and apply questions like those suggested in the group sessions: "Is this what I wanted to say?" "Does it make sense?" "Could I say it better?" Since many students soon begin to realize that

Reading aloud what he or she has written (or listening to a recording of it) will usually help the writer see where improvements could be made.

Revision is an important step in the writing process.

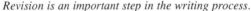

they are writing for an audience, perhaps a particular one, you can suggest other points they should keep in mind during their reading: "Will anyone want to read this? What more will they want to know? How can I make it more interesting?" Attempts to answer such questions will produce helpful ideas for revision.

Some written guidelines for revision should be provided. Posting a chart that summarizes the writing process will help children to remember the distinctions between first-draft writing, revision, and editing. Also, a checklist of basic, specific writing features to be examined when revising may be duplicated and handed out to the class, or perhaps a language textbook may contain one that is applicable. Such a list should not be overly long and ought to be updated from time to time as writers gain in proficiency. Once a particular writing feature has been discussed by you and the children, it may be added to the list. The emphasis should be on meaning and ideas, although checklists certainly need to cover punctuation and spelling, particularly if the meaning of what the children compose is not clear because of problems with these aspects of writing.

A checklist of writing features should direct the children to read their drafts and then respond to the questions on the list. A beginning checklist might contain the following questions:

> Does the piece begin in an interesting way?
> Does it tell enough?
> Is there something that isn't needed?
> Does each sentence make sense?
> Could better words be used?

For more advanced writers other questions can be added:

For suggestions on how to help upper-grade children with their writing, see Atwell's book, listed at the end of the chapter.

> Is the topic developed in an interesting way?
> Does each sentence fit in with what comes before and after?
> Are there gaps that need to be filled in?
> Are synonyms or more expressive words or phrases needed anywhere?
> Could some sentences be combined?
> Does any sentence need to be divided into two or more?
> Is each sentence really a sentence?

Conferences with the Teacher. You should be available to confer with children about their first drafts. As what they write becomes longer, more time will be required for them to read the drafts to you. Once peer conferences begin, however, this demand on your time will be at least partially alleviated because they will read to one another. A conference may require only a few seconds for a discussion of word choice or several minutes for consideration of text organization.

During such a conference you should be giving direct assistance—but not specific directions—as well as demonstrating a procedure that the children will be able to use with one another and by themselves when working alone. Try to keep the following considerations in mind:

- *Ask questions that encourage children to talk.* You will learn a lot by listening, and the students will explore their ideas more fully.
- *Respond honestly but with discretion.* Finding something good in the piece and mentioning that should be the goal.

Conferences are very important in the writing process.

- *Ask the writer to identify something that needs attention.* Work on what the writer identifies, holding your own questions until later.
- *Deal with only a small number of concerns at any one time.* Too much attention to problems creates the wrong kind of atmosphere.
- *Encourage children to react to what they have written.* Remember that the child's opinion of something she or he has created is more important than the opinion of anyone else.

Pose questions that direct the writer's attention to the text:

How is this piece going?
What do you like about it?
What part are you going to work on first?
Who will read this?
What else might readers like to know?
How do the parts fit together?
Does the beginning do what you want it to?
Are there problem places?

If children ask questions or otherwise indicate readiness for a particular learning experience, conference time can be used for direct teaching. This is an effective means for promoting growth in writing.

Conferences with Peers. After you have demonstrated the conference procedure in class and individual sessions, children should begin to meet in pairs or small groups to read and discuss their drafts. Emphasize to the children that their remarks ought to concern positive aspects of what a peer has written and they should concentrate on productive questions and suggestions rather than on negative criticism. When a positive atmosphere prevails, writers feel more free to express in writing what they really believe is important to them.

Beginning to think of the reader is a major step for a writer.

Reading one's work to peers also creates a genuine audience situation. Children should begin to realize that they do not write only for themselves or the teacher, but also to produce writing that will hold the attention of their classmates. Who the audience is for a particular piece needs to be thought about during the revision of almost every type of writing.

Writing Additional Drafts. In the elementary school a second draft is usually sufficient to make a piece satisfactory to the writer, although occasionally a child will be so caught up in a topic that she or he will want to do a third or even fourth version. Such enthusiasm is not common, but it certainly deserves encouragement. All writers must know that perfection is seldom achieved, however; those who write must come to accept that they will often have to stop working on something they don't feel is "finished" yet.

As children prepare to do second drafts, they should begin by working directly on the first—replacing words, making insertions, and even cutting up pages to move sections around. In general, the more mature the writer, the greater the extent of revision. More experienced and interested students will occasionally revise a piece of writing so that it is quite different from the original text. All drafts, even those that have been changed a good deal, should be kept in each child's writing folder; then, during conferences, you and the child can review and discuss what occurred at each step in the revision. This should help the child to

A student refers to an edited earlier draft to write a final draft.

understand her or his development as a writer as well as giving you some hints about what needs to be taught.

Editing. When children read their own writing to classmates, teachers, and parents, there is little reason to be greatly concerned about handwriting, spelling, punctuation, and usage. (But do make sure that parents understand what your teaching procedure is.) However, if a piece is being prepared for others to read, different standards prevail and children should understand this. Common sense and courtesy require that writers adhere to accepted conventions, and discussion of these will be the basis for much skill teaching in the language arts.

Every teacher has had the experience of attempting to read something that was difficult if not impossible to decipher because of improper punctuation (or lack of punctuation), poor handwriting, and incorrect spelling. Even though a reader may be able to see value in content that is poorly presented, a writer who wants a piece to receive the attention it deserves must be concerned with readability. This includes, even for elementary-school children, at least basic punctuation, the correct spelling of common words, and evidence that thought has been given to organization.

It is not necessary to insist on perfection during the editing stage; even the best newspapers and magazines sometimes contain misspellings or inappropriately placed punctuation marks. Ownership should be kept in mind, too; it is the child's piece that is being put into good order, not the teacher's. If you take over during the editing process, much of what has been accomplished in the teaching of writing may be undermined. The child has identified the topic, explored it, done the writing, and made revisions; the work is his or hers in a very personal way. No one, not even the teacher, should step in at this point and make numerous "corrections."

Skills need to be taught and learned, of course, as is discussed throughout this textbook, but such skills should not receive much attention in isolation from the writing process. In the revising and editing stages it is especially important to establish classroom procedures that encourage children to check their own texts carefully when preparing them for reading by others. These procedures should include assessment of legibility, spelling, usage, vocabulary, and punctuation. Several steps ought to be taken in each area of concern.

Handwriting or typing will require attention before a piece is ready for publication. The writer needs to be sure that the best handwriting possible has been done or that the typing has been well executed. If a piece is to be published in handwritten form, this is the time to give attention to individual handwriting problems as described in Chapter 9. With respect to typing, others may type for the children, but it is preferable for students to have access to typewriters or word processors (classroom procedures for these are also discussed in Chapters 9 and 11).

Spelling errors are usually the first thing noticed by a reader who is examining a written product. Therefore, a writer needs to check for correct spelling before publishing. There are a number of steps that may be taken to help young writers with their spelling. First, spelling should be properly taught, as described in Chapter 8. Second, dictionaries of varying degrees of inclusiveness should be available, as well as lists of the most used words and common spelling errors. Third, children ought to maintain individual lists of words they have trouble with, and, fourth, the most expert spellers in the class can be used as resources.

It is important for young children, especially, to feel that they *own* what they have written.

Developing a "Writers' Handbook" of forms and conventions for a classroom (or an entire school) will help both teachers and students (and is a good exercise in itself).

Christy Brown

Could he ever communicate with the people around him ? Would he
ever be able to lead a normal life ? All these thoughts whirled in
the mind of crippled Christy Brown. Christy Brown was diegnosed as
having cerebal palsley since he was an infant. Christy had no control
over his body except his left foot which he soon became very
dependant on. Christy was not able to talk and all his doctors and
almost every one around him had given up hope, all except his mother.
No one had discovered the use of his left foot. yet until one
afternoon in december when he picked up his younger sister's chalk
and wrote the letter "A". he was 5 years old when it was
   Christy Brown was born in Rotunda Hospital on June 5th ,1932 in
Dublin, Ireland. He was the tenth child out of seventeen born to
Paddy and Mary Brown. At age eighteen Christy attended Lourdes, a
sorts of healing hospital-church in London. Dr. Collis soon came in
to Christy's life with a sugestion, his sister a medical doctory in
England had found some treatments for cerabal palsley. He was to fly
to London with his mother and meet with the doctor and she would
determine how the rest of his life would develop. If she thought he
was to advanced for the treatment, he had come a long way with his
left foot, he would go back to his life . On the other hand if she
thought him needed for the treatment he had a chance at a semi-normal
life ahead of him. She decided he would be perfect for the treatment
and she soon had planned a personalised program for him to start
right away at home. However, there was one flaw to the treatment
Christy was not allowed
course, if Christy coul
more to use his other p
alright to the doctors
would fall apart. He wo
world. It also ment he c
become so fond of inall
while everyone else was
to his home for childre
four sucessful years at
not fully. exp
   Christy Brown is a
many things an ordinary
acheived many victorys
Christy Brown strived t
insperstion to everyone
just as Christy had pra
person and we will neve

Christy Brown

Could he ever communicate with the people around him ? Would he
ever be able to lead a normal life ? All these thoughts whirled in
the mind of crippled Christy Brown. Christy Brown was diegnosed as
having cerebal palsley and his parents were told to put him in an
institution. Christy had no control over his body except his left
foot which he soon became very dependant on. Christy was not able to
talk and all his doctors and almost every one around him had given up
hope, all except his mother.
   Christy Brown was born in Rotunda Hospital on June 5th ,1932 in
Dublin, Ireland. He was the tenth child out of seventeen born to
Paddy and Mary Brown. When he was five years old it was discovered
that he could use his left foot. One afterrnoon in december he
picked up his younger sister's chalk and wrote the letter " A".
   When he was eighteen Christy attended Lourdes, a sorts of
healing hospital-church in France. This did not help Christy's
condition. A Dr. in Christy's home town by the name of Dr. Collis
had seen Christy when he was young and also years later in a movie
theater with his brothers. Dr. Collis soon came in to Christy's life
with a sugestion, his sister-in-law, a medical doctor in England
had found some treatments for cerabal palsley. Christy was to fly to
London with his mother and meet with the doctor and she would
determine how the rest of his life would develop. If she thought he
was too advanced for the treatment, that he could not benefit from
the treatments, he would go back to his life . On the other hand if
she thought he needed the treatment then he had a chance at a
semi-normal life ahead of him. She decided he would be perfect for
the treatment and she soon had planned a personalised program for him
to start right away at home. However, there was one flaw to the
treatment, Christy was not allowed to use his left foot. This all
made sense of course, if Christy couldnt use his left foot he would
have to try to use other parts of his body to do things. This all
seemed alright to the doctors but to Christy it was as if his whole
world would fall apart. He would have no communication to the
outside world. It also ment he could not draw, paint, or write. These
things he had occupied himself with all those years he had spent
alone in his room while everyone else was outside playing. A new
clinic soon opened up near to his home for children with cerabal
palsley. He spent four sucessful years at the clinic and he improved
tramendously. He learned to improve his speech, get around quicker
and better and also wrote a autobiography about his life.
   Christy Brown is a well known man in Ireland. He acheived many
victorys and lived through many disappointments. Christy Brown
strived to be a better person inside and out. He is an insperstion
to everyone to keep on living and learning even when it seems that
they have very little in life. He was a truly wonderful person and
will be remembered through his books and the movie about his life, "My
Left Foot".

Editing on a word processor by writing directly on a draft, typing changes, and printing the next draft.

Marks Used by Proofreaders			
≡	Make a letter a capital.	ℐ	Take out a word or phrase.
/	Make a letter lowercase.	∧	Insert a word or phrase.
⊙	Put in a period.	(SP)	Fix the spelling.
⌃	Put in a comma.	⌗	Indent to begin a paragraph.

A Bulletin Board Idea

THINGS WE AVOID IN OUR WRITING
1. Overworked words
2. Inactive verbs
3. Vague references
4. Misplaced modifiers
5. Stale, worn-out phrases
6. Inaccurate expression
7. Sweeping generalizations

Usage and *vocabulary* problems must also be considered in the editing stage. The choice of words can be particularly important for more experienced writers. With respect to usage, whatever specific items have been identified for attention in the classroom should be checked for in editing (refer to lists presented in Chapter 7). This concern in writing will support general usage learning in a significant way. Vocabulary may receive attention through the use of lists of synonyms for overworked words and lists of imprecise words that ought to be avoided. Older students or the most proficient younger ones can be encouraged to use a thesaurus when editing.

Punctuation items are discussed in the section Form and Convention in Writing. From the chart included there you can formulate a checklist that will be appropriate for your class. Initially, such a list should be fairly brief; add to it gradually as class members are expected to be aware of and properly use additional items.

As one element of editing and proofreading procedures, a system of symbols should be introduced and used by everyone in the class. This saves time, promotes communication, and gives students a sense of being involved in adultlike activities. Lists such as the one shown below are often found in language textbooks.

Publication

Publication, the final stage in the writing process (and a stage not reached for more than a few samples of what a child has written), involves sharing a finished product with classmates, other students, teachers, family members, or even people in the community. (Of course, the final product can be a play, a videotaped reading, or some other type of performance, but *publication* generally means producing a text for someone to read.) For younger children such sharing often consists of taking a single page written in careful handwriting and placing it on a special shelf, displaying it in the corridor, or carrying it home in a transparent folder. For older writers a fairly lengthy book may be the product of the writing process, with typed copy and illustrations. Such books might be placed in the classroom, school, or even public library. A few children may write well enough that their work can be submitted to a magazine that publishes children's writing.

See *Market Guide for Young Writers* by Kathy Henderson for information concerning publication outlets for children's writings.

In addition to those just mentioned, there are many other ways for children to share their finished writing. Some are listed below, but you can probably think of others.

- Read a piece to younger children in the school or place it in their classroom for them to read.
- Set up displays of writing in stores, banks, libraries, or shopping centers.
- Read the writing products to community groups such as senior citizens.
- Have a schoolwide "Young Authors' Day" when children read and display their work for other students and guests.
- Encourage the children to submit their writing to the school newspaper or magazine.
- Invite an author to come to school to discuss writing and to look at what the students have written.

Publication fulfills several important functions with respect to the writing process. Most significantly, it demonstrates to the children the validity of questions about audience and purpose. When you ask a child "What will others want to know about your story?" or "How can you tell what you felt like when that happened?" the idea of writing for an audience will have more meaning to the writer. When you inquire about the reasons for selecting a particular topic or treating it in a particular way, a child who has been through the full writing process a number of times will be better able to discuss the type of writing he or she is attempting to produce.

Older children can produce high-quality illustrations for their writing.

SUPPORTING THE WRITING PROCESS

In *The Art of Teaching Writing,* Calkins calls for an hour of writing each day—and she doesn't mean writing words in blanks on ditto sheets!

Use of the writing process provides students with a framework in which to carry out their various writing activities, and the process can be used by them throughout their years in school and on into adulthood. In a similar way, much of what has been covered in other chapters of this book—oral language, listening, grammar, and usage, as well as spelling, handwriting and the other "writing" areas—is most readily developed and strengthened as one of the aspects of the writing process.

Learning activities related to writing clearly include developmental, information-processing, and embedded-lesson experiences. As you help students gradually expand their abilities to use the writing process you are implementing a *developmental program* in writing. *Information processing* is a significant aspect of writing, since much is learned about a topic when children write about it (see Chapter 11 for examples). Also, as we have pointed out, many *embedded lessons* concerning nearly every phase of the language arts will be included in writing.

Inclusion of a variety of strategies and skills in writing activities means that you need to be concerned with appropriate teaching procedures. Although it is tempting to believe that you can teach something and then the children will use it in their writing, that's usually not what occurs. As discussed more fully in Chapter 13 in the section Teaching Study Strategies, you need to have a plan for (1) making students aware of writing abilities, (2) demonstrating these, and (3) providing guidance in their use. When this is accomplished, a student will have a good chance of becoming a writer who easily and independently employs effective techniques.

Important writing strategies involve organizing content for writing, developing and modifying sentences, making good word choices, and following accepted conventions in writing. The following sections discuss these strategies.

Organizing Content

The best way to present a thought effectively is to organize the expression of that thought so that it sticks to the point and presents the information interestingly and in a suitable sequence. Attention to organization is reflected in the construction of sentences, paragraphs, and the entire text. No expression—one sentence or much more—is effective unless it is well organized and thoughtfully composed.

When a child begins to recognize relationships, he or she is beginning to organize. Activities such as the following apply organizing skills and begin to help the child learn how to organize thoughts in written form:

- putting pictures related to a story into proper sequence
- telling in sequence the items or events seen on a trip
- deciding what classroom tasks should be done and when
- telling how to play a game
- thinking of words that are associated with special days or events

Guidance in helping children organize their expression should begin as they tell about experiences and continue as they dictate more than a single phrase or sentence and write independently. Organization is a thinking skill that develops through guided practice; therefore, early guidance in oral expression (as considered in Chapters 4 and 5) is particularly important to organized writing. This guidance should be subtle so that free expression is not stifled, but it does need to be present. Dictation by children to the teacher who then writes for them provides especially good opportunities for such guidance, and this is the major reason that such dictating should not stop just because children have begun writing themselves.

As children engage in the writing process, it is important to help them focus on organization of content. Some of the speaking and listening experiences suggested in Chapters 5 and 6 can be utilized effectively. Activities such as the following may also be helpful:

1. Display a paragraph on a transparency projector or duplicate it. Have the children attempt to give the main idea of the paragraph in one sentence. The paragraph may be taken from a social studies or science book.

2. Have children look at and discuss the content of a picture and then state in one sentence the message conveyed by it. A variation of this activity is to choose a title for the picture (without regard to whether it is a sentence).

3. Write several sentences on the chalkboard, and have the children select those that could be put together into a paragraph.

4. Provide the children with paragraphs in which there are one or two sentences unrelated to the main idea. Have the children identify the unrelated sentences.

5. Provide the children with a paragraph in which the sentences have been scrambled, and have them rearrange the sentences in the most reasonable order.

6. Give children paragraphs in which the beginning or ending sentences are missing. Have them compose appropriate sentences to make the paragraphs complete.

7. Provide opportunities for pupils to discuss ideas and information on a topic and make lists of these before they begin writing. This should be done regularly at all grade levels; it is one of the most valuable ways in which you can help children learn to organize their thinking.

8. Discuss use of paragraphs and ways authors employ them to put content in sequence, move from one topic to another, or write dialogue.

The book by Hansen listed in the References gives many good examples of activities involving reading and writing.

Developing Sentence Sense

Much written expression is not as effective as it might be because of problems with sentences. Although there are no shortcuts to developing skill in constructing effective sentences, there are some things teachers can do to help students, as well as some that are often done that probably do not help. (In the latter category are teaching a grammatical definition of a sentence, identifying parts of speech in sentences, and having children do sentence construction, punctuation, and capitalization exercises totally unrelated to their interests and their own writing.) Basically, children need to learn that a sentence is a means of expressing an idea. The focus is on the idea and on expressing it in a way that is clear and exact, a way that makes sense.

As has been mentioned frequently, children should have many opportunities to express themselves orally and receive encouragement to present their ideas clearly. This does not mean that every response has to be a "complete" sentence in the sense that most of us have had drilled at us in grammar study. However, questions may be asked or issues and problems advanced that require more than a "yes" or "no" answer.

The development of sentence sense is greatly helped if children frequently hear well-constructed sentences. A major way to accomplish this is to read high-quality material to them in a voice that carries "sentence feeling." Sometimes it is helpful to have children listen to recordings of their own speech, noting how the voice tends to drop at the end of a group of words—that is, at the end of statements (not questions or exclamations). Another way to illustrate good sentence structure is to write two stories in contrasting forms: one in which good sentence sense is evident and one in which the sentences are poorly or improperly constructed. Then have the stories compared and evaluated and the poorly written ones reconstructed.

You may also want to try activities such as those suggested below. They are listed in an order that reflects increasing difficulty, but many can be varied to suit different ability levels.

Don't overlook opportunities presented by conferences and other feedback situations for encouraging children to focus on creating sentences that *make sense*.

1. Display a large picture to the class and ask, "Who can give us a sentence about this picture?" A picture of a firefighter, for instance, might elicit responses such as these:

   "The firefighter has a big hat."

   "She is holding a hose."

   "We had a fire on our street."

   Write the sentences the children give you on a chart. Do not write a child's response unless it is a sentence. Don't be negative about this, though; simply suggest that the thought be rephrased and the chances are good that someone will come up with a useful alternative.

2. On a chart write sentences from a story the children have heard, scrambling the order of words. Have individual children or small groups rearrange these so that sentences are formed.

3. Give each child an envelope containing words printed on small pieces of durable paper. These may be words taken from various class activities. Each envelope should contain nouns, verbs, adjectives, adverbs, connectives, determiners, pronouns, and so forth, so that sentences can be made. Have students see how many sentences they can compose, making sure that each sentence makes sense.

4. Write sentences on the overhead projector, asking students to add phrases to make the idea clearer. A variation is to add adverbs and adjectives rather than phrases.

5. Write on the board several phrases that elicit mental pictures, for example: a pile of clothes on the floor, wet leaves on the window pane, the smell of bananas. Have pupils combine or add to the phrases to make sentences.

6. Have students revise sentences in which time relationships are expressed; for example: *When Edith's father came to the door of the kitchen, all of the children were exclaiming about the dessert* might be revised in one of these ways:

   The children were exclaiming about the dessert as Edith's father came to the door of the kitchen.

   Edith's father came to the door of the kitchen just in time to hear the children exclaiming about the dessert.

7. Write a sentence such as *She will play* on the board. Have the children add details that provide more information; they can do this by asking themselves such ques-

tions as "Who?" "What?" "How?" "When?" "Where?" "What kind?" whereby the sentence evolves:

She will play with Billy.
She will play catch with Billy.
She will play catch with Billy on the playground.

Remedying Sentence Faults

In their writing children, like many adults, typically make several types of errors:

1. Run-on sentences: *We went to the movie it was good and we bought popcorn so Susan got mad and she has braces and it was awful.*
2. Sentence fragments: *Not after school.*
3. Confusing placement of sentence parts: *We saw four live ducks on the way to the market.*
4. Absence of needed punctuation: *Tony said I won't go with them.*
5. Use of extraneous words: *Well, I went to see my friend, you know, and well, you know, he wasn't home.*

Activities such as those suggested for developing sentence sense will help to remedy these faults. The idea of "making sense" causes children to realize that such problems interfere with clarity—that they make communication less effective and sometimes even impossible. Exercises that provide practice in distinguishing between fragments and sentences, in correcting run-on sentences, in using punctuation marks appropriately, in adding or deleting words to make sentence meaning clear, and in making sentences out of non-sentence groups of words may also be helpful.

Sentence-Combining Activities

One difference between writing done by younger children and that done by older students and adults is that the more experienced writers use sentences that contain more and longer clauses. Since readers tend to prefer a style that has fewer and somewhat longer sentences rather than numerous short ones, a useful revision strategy is for writers to look for places to do sentence combining, to make two or more sentences into one. Ability to do such combining may be improved to some extent by having children do exercises that require several sentences to be replaced by a single one through compounding, subordination, or substitution.

It is best to present sentences related to matters the children are studying, talking about, or writing about, and then let them experiment with combining to achieve greater clarity, emphasis, focus on the image the writer desires the reader to have, ease of reading, or variation in style.

You might simply write two sentences such as the following on a chart and ask the children whether they can be combined into one sentence:

The fifth-grade classes are having a party.
The party will be in our room.

The students should easily find several ways to combine such sentences, and then you can move on to asking them to combine three or even more sentences into one. (As with any other complex activity, expect that there will be wide variation in class members' abilities to do this sort of thing.) Emphasize that the ideas from sentences can be combined in different ways. For instance, pupils could consider the following sentences:

The children got off the bus.
Jan got off the bus first.
As soon as the bus emptied, the driver closed the door.

These sentences are *examples.* Use those relevant to your children and their activities.

These might be combined in two ways, at least:

Jan was first as the children got off the bus, just ahead of the closing door.
Jan got off the bus first, and after the other children followed him, the driver closed the door.

You may want to emphasize combining in particular ways to show how style may be changed. For example, sentences such as

The girl played hard.
The girl won the game.

can be combined in several ways by

1. using a connector:

   The girl played hard, and she won the game.

2. not using a connector:

   The girl won the game by playing hard.
   By playing hard, the girl won the game.

Still another activity is to present words such as *when, after, until, there, where, if, because, then,* and *since* along with pairs of sentences such as these:

Everyone sat down to dinner.
The children came in from playing.

We will go to the airport early.
My grandmother is coming from Philadelphia.

Have pupils combine the sentences in each pair using one of the words supplied, for example:

After the children came in from playing, everyone sat down to dinner.

Sentence-combining activities may not be of interest to some students. You may, however, take a few minutes during the writing period (see Chapter 11) for the sorts of exercises described here and, of course, some students in their conferences with you will be receptive to seeing how they can use sentence combining in revision of their drafts. Also these sorts of experiences provide good opportunities for introducing discussions about grammatical features such as clauses, compound sentences, complex sentences, and related matters.

Improving Word Choices

Change "the picture" by changing the sentence:

The bear came down the road.
The bear ambled down the path.
A brown bear shuffled along under the trees.
A small brown bear loped down the path.

Some Noise Words

thump
thud
sigh
slurp
murmur

As discussed in Chapter 8, the precision and vividness of words are aspects of language to be especially valued, and this certainly applies to writing. Children should be encouraged to replace words such as *thing, something,* and *a man* with the name of the object or person. Replacing, for instance, *made a face* with *scowled* or *frowned, slowly walked* with *sauntered,* or *got away* with *escaped* will improve exactness of expression and be more appealing to readers as well. Thus, vocabulary building is vital, since choosing better words is possible only if the writer has a storehouse of words to choose from. Selecting can be made easier, though, if the writer knows how to use a thesaurus and other vocabulary aids.

Writing is also improved by strong verbs, for example: *amble, trudge, march, slink,* or *pace* rather than *walk.* Similarly, adjectives should be carefully chosen; such words as *bulky, enormous, huge, vast,* and *burly* convey meaning much more accurately than *big.* With expanding vocabularies children will know better, more vivid verbs and descriptive adjectives, and they will be interested in learning even more and using them more often as they realize that carefully selected words add clarity and appeal to their writing.

In their reading, children are likely to encounter figurative language, including *personification, similes,* and *metaphors,* and may wish to try these in their own writing. *Personification*—the assigning of human characteristics to nonhuman referents—is no stranger to children who know the Gingerbread Man, Miss Piggy, Cookie Monster, Little Toot, and so on. Perhaps they are less familiar with the *simile,* an expression that makes a direct comparison, such as *slow as molasses in winter* or *fought like a tiger,* although many will surely have heard a cake described as being *light as a feather* or of something happening *quick as a flash.* Children also may have heard metaphors such as *She has a finger in every pie* or *He blew his stack;* in these a comparison is implied, not directly stated. Children may also know about *onomatopoeia,* the use of words whose pronunciation imitates or suggests specific sounds; from their earliest years they've been delighted by such words as *tinkle, boom, pop, purr,* and *zoom.* These forms shouldn't be taught formally, with definitions and applications, but children ought to be encouraged to look for them in their reading and try them in their writing.

Form and Convention in Writing

Writing conventions—punctuation, page appearance, capitalization, and the other agreed-upon customs of putting language symbols on paper—are important but must be kept in proper perspective. They are aids to communication, not ends in themselves. As suggested earlier, during first-draft writing the primary concern should be getting ideas recorded. Yet even at this stage, if absolutely no attention is given to conventions, meaning could sometimes be lost to the writers themselves.

Form and Appearance. A neat and attractive-looking document, whether a letter, a report, an announcement, or a story, constitutes a courtesy to the reader and helps make the writing more effective. Although there are few strict rules about matters of form, some generally accepted guidelines cover such matters as leaving margins at the top, bottom, and sides of the paper, indenting the first line

Keep the focus on *content.* Teach *form* and *appearance* in the context of the children's writing.

of a paragraph, placing a title, avoiding crowded writing at the end of a line, and eliminating messy erasures and other types of untidiness. Children should learn about these and know what is expected of them.

It is a good idea to work with the children early in the year to establish standards of form and appearance for written work once it reaches the stage of being submitted to the teacher or someone else who needs to read it. These standards should be simple and should include only items needed for identification, neatness, and correctness. Items to cover might be position of name and date on papers to be handed in, the extent of margins, regulations about writing on one or both sides of the paper, types of paper to be used for written work, and so on. By all means, let the children themselves participate in setting these standards. Discuss the reasons for having such standards, and then post them until habits become established. Also, make sure everyone adheres to the standards consistently to avoid confusing the children.

Punctuation practices vary. For example, a comma may or may not precede *and* in sentences containing words in a series.

Punctuation. Punctuation can be overemphasized, but it does have an important place in writing: it helps to convey meaning. Simply stated, punctuation is a means of showing, by the use of a number of specially designated marks, meaning that cannot be shown or is only partially shown by words and their positions in sentences. In speech these meanings are usually transmitted by the rising and falling tones of the voice, by emphasis or stress on certain sounds, and by pauses in or the breaking off of the stream of speech.

As indicated in Chapter 4, punctuation instruction begins early in kindergarten and first grade. The first sentences seen in a book or written under a child's drawing provide opportunities for learning about punctuation. Also, children have many opportunities to see how capital letters, periods, question marks, and exclamation points are used when teachers discuss these briefly while doing chart writing with them. There should be little or no emphasis on direct teaching during chart writing.

It is through reading that older students will most readily learn about punctuation, as well as other conventions, but this learning should not be left entirely to such experiences. You should provide brief lessons on selected aspects of punctuation during the writing period and note the progress students make in their own writing. The best type of learning experience is always one that grows out of a child's questions, interests, or thoughts. The following sections discuss the most common punctuation marks, the ones that are first taught, and how they should be taught.

The Period. As children begin their own writing, remind them of the need to signal the end of each statement they write. Early in children's experience they will also encounter three other uses of periods:

- abbreviations of titles of persons and of place names
  Dr. Jones
  Hill St.
- initials in proper names
  H. O. Smith
- after numerals in lists
  1.
  2.
  3.

A Punctuation Guide

ITEM	USE	K	1	2	3	4	5	6	7	8
Period	At the end of a statement	*	*	†	'	'	'	'	'	'
	After initials	*	*	†	'	'	'	'	'	'
	After abbreviations	*	*	*	†	'	'	'	'	'
	After numerals in a list	*	*	†	'	'	'	'	'	'
	After letters or numerals in an outline				*	*	†	'	'	'
	In footnotes and bibliographies						*	*	†	'
Question mark	After an interrogative sentence		*	†	'	'	'	'	'	'
	After a question within a larger sentence				*	†	'	'	'	'
Comma	Between the day of the month and the year	*	*	†	'	'	'	'	'	'
	Between city and state	*	*	†	'	'	'	'	'	'
	After a salutation in a friendly letter		*	†	'	'	'	'	'	'
	After a complimentary close		*	†	'	'	'	'	'	'
	To separate parts of a series			*	†	'	'	'	'	'
	To set off words of direct address				*	*	†	'	'	'
	To separate a direct quotation					*	†	'	'	'
	Before and after appositives					*	*	†	'	'
	After introductory clauses					*	*	†	'	'
	After introductory words: yes, no, interjections					*	†	'	'	'
	Before the conjunction in a compound sentence						*	†	'	'
	Before and after a nonrestrictive clause						*	*	†	'
	Before and after parenthetical expressions						*	*	†	'
	In footnotes and bibliographies							*	†	'
Apostrophe	In contractions			*	*	†	'	'	'	'
	To show possession			*	*	*	†	'	'	'
	To show plurals of figures and letters				*	*	*	†	'	'
Quotation marks	Before and after a direct quotation			*	*	†	'	'	'	'
	Before and after titles (other than titles of books)				*	*	*	†	'	'
Exclamation mark	At the end of an exclamatory word or sentence			*	*	*	†	'	'	'
Colon	After the salutation of a business letter					*	*	†	'	'
	To separate the hour from minutes				*	*	*	†	'	'
	Before a long series or list						*	*	*	†
	To denote examples						*	*	*	†
Hyphen	At the end of a line to show a divided word			*	*	*	†	'	'	'

*Introduction   †Suggested teaching   'Maintenance

The Question Mark. First-grade children should be introduced to the question mark. Often you will find opportunities to place a question mark *at the end of a direct question* in a story being written cooperatively. It is also likely that some of the children will want to include questions in their stories and use the question mark if it has been introduced. In fact, some will appear to be including questions just to have a reason to employ the appropriate punctuation. A second use of the question mark is *after a direct question in the context of a larger sentence,* as in

> *"Are you going to the store?" Billy asked.*

This is more difficult for children to understand and should not be introduced until the late third or early fourth grade.

The Exclamation Point. Children readily recognize the exclamation point because it is identified with exciting and funny incidents in stories. Many library books for young children make much use of exclamation marks. (Of course, textbooks do not present many opportunities for such use, but you can be sure to include chart sentences that call for them: *Boo! There are only four days until Halloween! Boo!*)

The Comma. There are many uses for the comma, but children should be directly taught only those they are most likely to need in their writing. In the primary grades, as you write experience stories children dictate and notes that the children may copy to take home, and as they begin writing themselves, some uses of the comma will, of course, be introduced. These may include the comma between the date and the year, between city and state, after the salutation in a friendly letter, and after the complimentary close of a letter. The need to teach these is dependent on the emphasis that is being given to letter writing. In much of the writing that children do independently, they become aware of the comma used to separate words in a series; direct teaching of this is usually done in the third grade.

Quotation Marks. Children in the primary grades will encounter quotation marks in their reading and will naturally have questions about them. This is the right time to discuss them. A good way to do this is to have students take the parts of characters in stories in which the speech is set off by quotation marks. They will learn that this type of punctuation signals speech ("talk marks," they may be called as you demonstrate their use in cooperatively written stories). Quotation marks are then likely to appear frequently in the children's writing.

The punctuation marks and their uses discussed in this section are not all of the marks and not all of the uses that should receive attention in the elementary school. The punctuation guide suggests grade levels for the introduction, direct teaching, and maintenance teaching of the various punctuation marks usually taught in the elementary school. Keep in mind, however, that these are approximations only; each student progresses at her or his own rate. If punctuation is taught in connection with situations where there is a genuine need to communicate, students will make steady progress.

Capitalization. Capitalization is another convention of written expression about which a great deal is known in relation to children's writing needs. These needs can be determined by examining the children's writing. Textbooks and course guides often give recommended grade levels for introducing and teaching

Such activities as having students memorize "the 18 ways to use a comma" are a waste of time. A child learns how to use punctuation by writing a great deal over several years.

Capitalization Chart

WORDS TO CAPITALIZE	K	1	2	3	4	5	6	7	8
First word of a sentence	*	*	†	′	′	′	′	′	′
First and last names of a person	*	†	′	′	′	′	′	′	′
Name of street or road	*	*	†	′	′	′	′	′	′
The word I		*	†	′	′	′	′	′	′
Name of a city or town		*	†	′	′	′	′	′	′
Name of a school or special place	*	*	†	′	′	′	′	′	′
Names of months and days	*	*	†	′	′	′	′	′	′
First and important words in titles	*	*	*	†	′	′	′	′	′
Abbreviations: Mr., Ms., Mrs., St., Ave.	*	*	†	′	′	′	′	′	′
Each line of a poem[a]			*	†	′	′	′	′	′
First word of a salutation		*	†	′	′	′	′	′	′
First word of a complimentary close		*	†	′	′	′	′	′	′
Initials		*	*	†	′	′	′	′	′
Titles used with names of persons		*	*	†	′	′	′	′	′
First word in an outline				*	*	†	′	′	′
First word of a quoted sentence			*	†	′	′	′	′	′
Names of organizations			*	*	†	′	′	′	′
Sacred names			*	*	*	†	′	′	′
Proper names generally: countries, oceans, etc.			*	*	*	†	′	′	′
Proper adjectives					*	*	†	′	′
Titles of respect and rank and their abbreviations			*	*	†	′	′	′	′

*Introduction   †Suggested teaching   ′Maintenance

[a]Be sure to point out that there are exceptions to this, particularly in modern poetry.

capitalization (see the capitalization chart above), but, as always, such lists are only guides, not firm requirements. The best guide is the writing the children actually do.

Capitalization can be introduced to children at a fairly young age. When they first begin to learn about letters in the preschool years and kindergarten, they discover that each has two sizes. Later, when they see words and sentences written on charts or on the board or printed in their storybooks and textbooks, they encounter many words that are capitalized. The experience stories children dictate to you provide opportunities to point out capital letters as they are written: "Notice that I am beginning the sentence with a capital letter" or "*Bruce* begins with a capital letter because it is someone's name." Learning keyboarding also requires students to change procedures when they wish to switch from upper- to lowercase letters or the reverse.

When young children first begin to do their own writing, they apply what they have learned from watching you write. They capitalize the letter *I* when referring to themselves, the word that begins a sentence, and the first letters of people's names. When many members of your class indicate that they are aware of these uses, you can gradually note others, perhaps beginning a classroom chart that lists those that have been discussed. The students can then compare their writing to models that illustrate capitalization and make needed corrections. Group examination of writing, with special attention to capitalization, is possible if an overhead projector is used. Remember that forming good habits at the very beginning and teaching children to revise and edit their writing will generally accomplish more than any amount of direct teaching.

Punctuation and Capitalization Activities.

In the lower and middle grades, the teaching of punctuation may be enlivened by making cardboard stick puppets representing various punctuation marks. You can give puppets names such as Rollo Period, "Slim" Exclamation Mark, and Paula Apostrophe or let the children choose names they like. Each character can tell what he or she does and from time to time be used to remind pupils of what they may have forgotten.

Children can also play matching games, matching punctuation symbols with their uses. Make tagboard cards, printing a symbol or a use on each one. For example, make a period on each of four cards; then on four additional cards print the words *at the end of a sentence, after an abbreviation, after initials,* and *after a numeral on a list.* A symbol card is needed for each use. If desired, an additional set of cards can show illustrations of the uses.

The importance of punctuation and capitalization can be shown in many ways. One is to have pupils find examples of specific punctuation and capitalization uses in books, newspapers, and magazines. For instance, they might look for sentences in which commas set off words in a series, a period is used after an abbreviation, a word is divided by a hyphen, or parentheses are used to enclose material that is not part of the main thought. These examples can be used to make charts or a bulletin-board display. (Students will likely find that adults' uses of punctuation are inconsistent.)

Another way to emphasize the value of punctuation and capitalization is to present the children with a paragraph that has none. Choose such a paragraph carefully, selecting one in which meaning is actually obscured by the lack of signals. Or let the children try reading some of Don Marquis's *Archy and Mehitabel*—something that will amuse them and probably be convincing. There are also computer programs that present unpunctuated materials; with these students can act as "editors" and make changes on the screen.

It is fun occasionally to present "trick" sentences for pupils to punctuate. Sentences such as these can be used:

Sixty, three, and eleven are the numbers.
Sixty-three and eleven are the numbers.

No water is coming through the pipe.
No, water is coming through the pipe.

Bill, said Joe, is very noisy.

Bill said Joe is very noisy.

An important aspect of teaching any skill is helping children to become aware of their own errors. Checklists for punctuation may be supplied to each student or posted in the classroom. Writers preparing a piece for publication may then use these during revising and editing stages. If pages of writing are dated with a hand-held stamp, students can readily see their progress with writing conventions over several weeks, and this is good motivation.

Exercises can be made up from the children's own sentences if this can be done without embarrassing anyone (perhaps you will want to use writing samples from a previous year). Going over someone's actual writing and "editing" it provides a realistic learning experience. Photocopies can be made and used for a few students or transparencies can be projected for a class activity.

Dictation exercises can furnish variety, and they can be used in several ways. Children can dictate several sentences to each other, or dictation can be recorded and used by individuals who need practice on particular items. Spelling words that need review can even be included in dictation drills, and, of course, hand-writing is thus practiced. You can also give dictation when a large group or the entire class needs practice on a specific skill or as a general review. When dictating, read the selection three times: once so pupils will know the length and get the gist of what is said; a second time, very slowly, so they can write it; a third time, more rapidly, so the writing can be checked. A duplicated paragraph provides a general review of punctuation and capitalization, again with specific directions as to the number of items to be supplied.

> *Directions:* Rewrite the following paragraph, using eight capital letters, three periods, and four commas.

> no one was allowed to leave boston and this could have been disastrous for paul revere had he not known the city so well in the darkness he was able to reach the charles river where he had hidden a rowboat a few days before and two friends were waiting to row him across it would be a very dangerous mission for their boat would have to pass near the enemy

It is a good idea to have a generous supply of practice materials of all types for individual children or small groups to use as needed. These can vary in difficulty according to the grade level and the needs of the particular children in the class. Computer software programs that might be used are listed at the end of the chapter.

A FINAL WORD

The introduction to this chapter pointed out that the teaching of writing was for a long time dominated by an overemphasis on handwriting, mechanics, and grammatical rules. A high level of awareness of the significance of the writing process has now largely redressed this imbalance. Many elementary teachers are giving the necessary attention to how children express what they want to say and are carefully guiding the children so that this expression is successful. Of course, this approach does not mean that matters such as organization of content, sentence construction, spelling, and punctuation are unimportant; these elements should be focused on at the appropriate points in each child's learning. This is the challenge you face as a teacher—asking the right questions and making useful suggestions during the writing process when these will be of the greatest benefit. Children will be stimulated and encouraged by their growing mastery of the process, and well-written, attractively presented texts will be one of the outcomes, too.

References

Asher, Sandy. *Where Do You Get Your Ideas? Helping Young Writers Begin.* Walker, 1987.

Atwell, Nancie. *In the Middle: Writing, Reading and Learning with Adolescents.* Boynton/Cook, 1987.

Baskwill, Jane, and Whitman, Paulette. *A Guide to Classroom Publishing.* Scholastic, 1986.

Calkins, Lucy McCormick. *The Art of Teaching Writing.* Heinemann Educational Books, 1986.

Calkins, Lucy M., and Harwayne, Shelley. *Living Between the Lines.* Heinemann Educational Books, 1990.

Collins, James L., and Sommers, Elizabeth A. *Writing On-Line: Using Computers in the Teaching of Writing.* Boynton/Cook, 1985.

Elbow, Peter. *Writing with Power: Techniques for Mastering the Writing Process.* Oxford University Press, 1981.

Fletcher, Ralph. *What a Writer Needs.* Heinemann, 1992.

Graves, Donald H. *Writing: Teachers and Children at Work.* Heinemann Educational Books, 1983.

Hansen, Jane. *When Writers Read.* Heinemann Educational Books, 1987.

Harste, Jerome C.; Short, Kathy G.; and Burke, Carolyn. *Creating Classrooms for Authors.* Heinemann Educational Books, 1988.

Hillocks, George, Jr. *Research on Written Composition.* National Council of Teachers of English, 1986.

Huff, Roland, and Kline, Charles R., Jr. *The Contemporary Writing Curriculum.* Teachers College Press, 1987.

Langer, Judith. *Children Reading and Writing.* Ablex Publishing, 1986.

Lane, Barry. *After "The End": Teaching and Learning Creative Revision.* Heinemann, 1992.

Murray, Donald. *A Writer Teaches Writing.* Houghton Mifflin, 1985.

Olson, Carol Booth, ed. *Practical Ideas for Teaching Writing as a Process,* rev. ed. California State Department of Education, 1987.

Parsons, Les. *Writing in the Real Classroom.* Heinemann, 1991.

Proett, Jackie, and Gill, Kent. *The Writing Process in Action.* National Council of Teachers of English, 1986.

Richards, Meredith. *Scholastic Software's Guide to Classroom Publishing.* Scholastic, 1988.

Stewig, John W. *Read to Write.* Richard C. Owen, 1986.

Thaiss, Christopher, and Suhor, Charles, eds. *Speaking and Writing K–12.* National Council of Teachers of English, 1984.

Tiedt, Sidney W., and Tiedt, Iris M. *Language Arts Activities for the Classroom.* Allyn and Bacon, 1978.

Tomkins, Gail E. *Teaching Writing: Balancing Process and Product.* Merrill, 1990.

Wilde, Sandra. *You Kan Red This! Spelling and Punctuation for Whole Language Classrooms, K–6.* Heinemann Educational Books, 1991.

Wresch, William. *A Practical Guide to Computer Uses in the English/Language Arts Classroom.* Prentice-Hall, 1987.

Teaching Resources

COMPUTER SOFTWARE

The Children's Writing and Publishing Center. The Learning Company.

Bank Street Writer. Scholastic.

Cap'n Punc. Hartley Courseware (grades 4–6)

SRA Writing Skills: Punctuation. Science Research Associates (diskettes, guide book, and back-up disks).

Writer Rabbit. The Learning Co.

The Writer's Assistant. InterLearn, Inc.

The Writing Adventure. Developmental Learning Materials.

The Writing Workshop. Milliken.

VIDEOTAPES

The Authoring Cycle: Read Better, Write Better, Reason Better. Heinemann.

Celebrating Children's Writing. National Council of Teachers of English, 1985 (includes mini-lessons on grammar, punctuation, and spelling).

Prewriting. National Council of Teachers of English, 1984 (grades 4–6).

Teachers Teaching Writing. Association for Supervision and Curriculum Development (six videos and discussion guides; grades 3–12).

Teaching Writing: A Process Approach. Maryland Department of Education (nine half-hour videos; elementary through secondary level).

The Writing and Reading Process. Heinemann.

The Writing Conference. National Council of Teachers of English, 1984 (middle grades).

Writing as Discovery. National Council of Teachers of English.

OTHER RESOURCES

Basic Writing Skills. Society for Visual Education (two groups of six filmstrips and six audiocassettes each; intermediate and upper grades).

Henderson, Kathy. *Market Guide for Young Writers*. Shoe Tree Press, 1988.

Lessons in Proofreading. Curriculum Associates (kit).

Sebranek, Patrick, and Kemper, Dave. *The Write Source*. The Write Source, Burlington, Wisconsin, 1987.

Suid, Murray; Lincoln, Wanda; and Gatheral, Maryann. *For the Love of Editing*. Scholastic (grades 2–6).

Activities for Preservice Teachers

1. When doing the next assigned paper for a course, make a conscious attempt to use the writing process described in this chapter. Does using it seem to help? If so, in what way? How different is the process from what you would have done anyway? What modifications to the process, if any, would you suggest?

2. Select one of the items listed in the references section of this chapter and report on it to the class. Make sure that your report conveys the substance of the book or article and include your personal reactions to the content.

3. Report to the class on what one language textbook series does with respect to teaching sentence sense, organizational skills, and making word choices in order to improve children's writing. (Several students could each analyze a different textbook series.)

4. Make a checklist to use in assessing children's writing. Include such factors as vividness of language (intensity, freshness, vigor), picturesqueness of dialogue, involvement of feelings, element of surprise, and so on. Decide on the range of points you will assign each item. Check out your list and the points awarded for each item with someone who is now teaching.

5. Prepare a set of transparencies to be used for group practice in proofreading at a particular grade level.

6. Plan a bulletin-board display of ambiguous sentences in which the meaning is altered by changing the punctuation.

7. With you acting as the teacher, have a conference with a friend who is writing a paper for a course. Can you help just by listening? Try to ask helpful questions. Resist the temptation to step in and "take over."

8. Observe some writing activities in elementary classrooms. Are the teachers using elements of the writing process as described in this chapter? What kinds of problems do the children have, and what does the teacher do about them? What happens to the children's writing when they are "finished"?

9. Find out if there are any writing competency tests for prospective teachers in your state. When are these taken? What are they like? Are you preparing for them?

10. Report to the class your assessment of what the average person, the public media, and the professional literature in education believe to be "basic" to teaching children to write effectively.

Activities for Inservice Teachers

1. With the children in your class, prepare a bulletin board display on editing. The editing signs (*sp* = spelling error, *lc* = small or lowercase letter, etc.) will interest children.

2. If you do not already hold regular conferences with the children in your class about their writing efforts, try it for a few weeks. Does it seem worth the effort and time? Do you find that you understand individual children better?

3. Visit a newspaper office with your class or have a newspaper staff member come to school to talk about how stories get edited. Get copies of edited material if available (more and more newspapers do everything on word processors). Put up a bulletin-board display that summarizes the newspaper production process, including proofreaders' marks and their use.

4. Inventory the types of writing the children do in your class: making class books, keeping journals, trying fiction, preparing reports, contributing to the school newspaper, and so on. Develop a plan for adding two or three additional types over the next several months.

5. Start a newsletter for parents. Children can write stories about what is going on in the classroom. If you have access to a photocopier, they can include drawings, pictures, and cartoons. One of the early issues should be about the writing program so that parents can see what is being done about sentence construction, spelling, punctuation, and so forth.

6. Review the writing of the children in your class, making notes on common punctuation and capitalization problems. Share the list with the children, and ask for their assistance in planning activities or procedures that might help reduce the number of problems.

7. Call attention to the relationship between oral reading and some forms of punctuation. Have children read their own writing and decide where periods, question and exclamation marks, and commas are needed. Depending on the maturity level of the children, follow up by examining punctuation marks that usually are not evident from oral reading.

8. When the children are writing, join them by writing yourself. You will need to be brave enough to share what you've written if you ask the children to share theirs. Most children will especially appreciate stories about the times you got into trouble when you were their age.

9. Report to the class your reactions, based on your teaching experiences, to the content of this chapter, especially the description of the writing process.

10. Investigate different ways for children to manufacture their own books and then try them in your class. (Tiedt and Tiedt, in *Language Arts Activities for the Classroom,* offer several suggestions.)

Activities for Children

1. Provide bulletin-board space for an "Announcement Center." Children may post sign-up sheets for use of classroom facilities such as the computer or materials such as the unabridged dictionary, notices of scout or club meetings, advertisements of articles for sale, and so on. Announcements should be carefully prepared and well displayed, and someone should be in charge of removing out-of-date materials periodically.

2. Provide time for journal writing, preferably at the beginning of each day. In general, the older children are, the less they will want to read aloud what they have written, a feeling that should be respected. But you can circulate to see that they are writing *something* and express your interest in reading whatever they want you to see.

3. Encourage children to write about classroom activities: how the plants are growing, what the gerbil did, the best things that happened this year, the play the fifth graders did, the trip to the zoo, and so on. Plan activities that are likely to produce good writing opportunities.

4. Videotape short sequences from TV programs, and play them back with the sound turned down. Ask pupils to write a script that could be associated with the action on the screen.

5. Children who have pets can write about them, or they might want to write a daily journal as though the family dog or cat were keeping it.

6. Have a child adapt a story for dramatization and videotaping, writing a script with dialogue and staging and camera directions, perhaps including recommendations for musical background, too.

7. Editing checklists, punctuation charts, and lists of usage forms to be avoided in writing can be made by children working in groups. This can be followed up by the groups deciding how the lists and charts will be used.

8. Invent an imaginary character called, perhaps, "Ralph the Rotten Reporter," who publishes a newspaper with all kinds of mistakes in it: punctuation and spelling errors, gross usage problems, jumbled paragraphs, and so on. Anyone who wants to can act as Ralph's editor. Those who are really interested may want to be Ralph and write something with many deliberate mistakes. Make sure the editor does his or her job so that the ones acting as Ralph aren't establishing bad habits.

9. "Pattern" books of fill-in sentences are sometimes useful in getting a pupil started in writing. These can

be only a few pages long. Possibilities for sentences include:

    I like _____ but I don't like _____ .

    The good news is _____ ; the bad news is _____ .

10. Encourage children to share good ideas. In the writing corner, place a suggestion box in which pupils can place notes about what they think would make a good story. Children can then go to the box for ideas when they are "stuck" and don't know what to write about.

11. Have the children make a chart showing commonly used abbreviations. The chart can be illustrated with pictures of a street, an army officer, a medical doctor, and so forth.

12. One child can prepare a set of sentences with different punctuation marks at the ends. He or she can then read them to a friend, giving the necessary (but natural) inflection. The second child guesses what the punctuation mark is. This activity can gradually be extended to punctuation marks other than those that go at the ends of sentences.

Chapter 11

Writing in the Classroom Program

*D*iscussion of the writing process in Chapters 4 and 10 stressed what occurs as a child decides to write about a topic and then, in some cases, carries that activity on through several stages, culminating in publication. The focus of this chapter is a consideration of how this process fits into a classroom program where youngsters are using writing for many different purposes and how you as the teacher can assist them.

It is, of course, one thing to help an individual student use the writing process and quite another to implement such an activity for a classroom group. Students vary in their writing competence and interest, perhaps more than in most other areas of the school program, so planning a class period for writing will require careful preparation on your part. In this chapter we provide some guidance.

THE CLASSROOM PROGRAM

The elementary classroom should provide many opportunities for writing, and several of these will be discussed in this chapter. How they are related to the way you teach writing (and the other language arts) is largely up to you—whether you present such content separately from other material or seek to include it as part of more comprehensive teaching-learning activities such as science or social studies thematic units. As with the other aspects of program planning discussed in this book, you need to consider developmental, information-processing, and embedded-lesson types of teaching in writing.

Developmental programming basically involves increasingly sophisticated use of the writing process. A kindergarten child draws a picture and labels it with a few alphabet letters that do not spell any words that someone else would recognize. Six years later that same student may complete a ten-page report based on several sources and type it on a word processor. In the intervening years, as a result of maturity and learning, elementary pupils are expected to have developed many skills and strategies. Which learnings are taught when and how must be the focus of attention for each succeeding teacher.

Much of what is learned will be the result of information processing as the student reads and writes in connection with work in science, social studies, mathematics, and literature. Also, embedded lessons are taught as opportunities present themselves, whether you are involved in teaching the whole class, a small group, or an individual student.

Program Guidelines

Effective teaching of writing must be based on a comprehensive and well-conducted classroom program. Several guidelines have proved to be very important.

Students learn a great deal during their years in the elementary school.

1. Organize the day so that large blocks of time are available rather than scheduling many brief periods. Remember that writing involves handwriting, spelling, usage, and vocabulary, so it is reasonable to think of adding the time allocated for those to the writing period.

Thinking aids writing and the reverse is also true.

2. Use the writing process in all subjects. Writing relates to learning and also to exploring and extending thinking.

3. Provide for a wide variety of oral expression: sharing, discussing, dramatization, and other activities mentioned in this book. Listen to the children, encouraging them to put their ideas into written form.

Good writers are observers.

4. Guide children toward being observant of the world around them, from spellings used in some advertisements, to how a snake crawls, to how an author "paints a picture" of a character.

5. Stimulate children with stories, poetry, field trips, and class visitors; bring in curious objects and pictures of unusual events; discuss movies and television programs.

6. Encourage children's curiosity and creative thinking. Explore possibilities for having them engage in creative problem solving or *Odyssey of the Mind* activities.

7. Have a comprehensive writing program, one that includes the various forms of written expression described in this chapter, along with any others that you and the children may think of.

8. Respect the children's privacy by not showing their work to other students without permission, and do not insist on reading everything students write. Remember that adults would not want to share all that they write.

9. Set up a writing center that includes all kinds of paper and writing tools, dictionaries and thesauruses, charts on the writing process, editing checklists, word lists, and so forth.

Selections from the writing folder may be added to the student's language arts portfolio.

10. Each child should keep a writing folder including current work, first drafts that were not revised, and lists of ideas for possible writing topics. Such folders can be used to review a student's progress on a regular basis, with some items discarded, others retained.

Opportunities are provided through much reading aloud.

11. Show that you value ideas, originality of expression, and effective use of language by calling attention to examples in literature and in the children's writing.

All classmates are potential teachers.

12. Encourage students to use one another as resources. They can respond to a classmate's writing, spell for each other, help with illustrations, and even write collaboratively.

Plateaus often serve as launching pads.

13. Accept that growth in writing ability occurs in spurts. Performance will vary among members of the same class and even for the same child. Writing is influenced by many factors that affect the child and is itself complex, so you should not expect that progress will be steadily upward.

14. Use textbooks in spelling, English, and handwriting as resources for writing. English language books often contain writing manuals and thesauruses.

Writers' Choices

The classroom program should be based on children's full participation in the writing activities. Such participation is best secured when students have maximum control over the various aspects of their writing.

What to Write About. For the most part children should determine their own writing topics. You should expect that they write every day but should not tell them what they ought to write about or even give suggestions. Writing is a personal process of discovery and should be so treated. Even in such areas as science and social studies you should attempt to provide latitude for choice in the students' writing.

What Genre to Write In and When. Whether to write poetry, mystery stories, plays, essays, or whatever, should also be the choice of the writer. Certainly you should read many types of literature to the class, and such exposure will provide motivation for students to try a particular kind of writing. However, there should be no time when every member of the class is required to write a poem, submit an essay, do a book report, or perform some other such assignment and, furthermore, do that by a certain date. Instead, rely on your ability to build the kind of classroom climate that will bring each youngster to the point of wanting to try every genre.

Stress opportunities and invitations rather than requirements.

How to Say What They Want to Say. As we said in Chapter 10 an important matter is that of *ownership*. What the child is writing belongs to her or him. (This is another reason for insisting that they think of their own topics; being told what to write about demonstrates to them that someone else is in charge from the beginning.) Certainly, ownership means that the writer will decide what words to use and what kinds of sentences to put together. You may think of your contribution as minor as you suggest a better word, but some students will view that as a major intrusion. ("Mrs. Johnson ruined my story," one young author tearfully charged when the teacher changed only one word.)

Identifying and Writing for an Audience. An important aspect of writing is deciding who will likely be reading the piece and what their response could be. Only very exceptional young children will be able to think of others as potential readers of what they are writing, but it is likely that by second or third grade many will have that ability. In fact, growing awareness of audience, along with experience in responding to classmates' questions about written products, will aid a young writer in taking a critical view of her or his own writing.

What Revisions to Make. To the young child, and often older students as well, revision usually means nothing more than adding to the length of what has been written. However, revision should mean much more, as discussed in Chapter 10. Learning to revise is an important aspect of a writer's development and can best be done as the writer gets feedback from others and confers with you, the teacher.

The Teacher's Role

As the teacher you are responsible for making the writing program work without being the center of all activity yourself. You should concentrate on teaching by example and by doing demonstrations that will help students see skills and strategies in use. At the same time, you ought to encourage children to rely on their own judgment and to use other members of the class for response, advice, suggestions, and questions. In addition, you should follow procedures that keep you directly involved with students and their writing.

TV scripts must be talked about, written, and revised before use.

Be a Writer Yourself. As a teacher of writing you should also write. You may do this outside of school or, at least occasionally, while the children are writing. They will enjoy hearing what you have written (particularly if the content involves them!) and you will receive many direct benefits from the experience.

Gradually expand the length and complexity of the writing when you are acting as the students' scribe.

Write Cooperatively with Students. Teachers of young children often act as "scribes" with responsibility for recording what the pupils want written. When doing the "Morning News," for example, you will likely find yourself writing sentences such as, *On Saturday Sonya slept at her grandmother's house,* and *Billy has a new baby brother and his name is Dexter.* With older children cooperative writing can involve group composition of an invitation to parents to visit or a thank-you letter following a field trip. Such cooperative writing builds good attitudes toward group work and provides demonstrations of how to carry out a writing activity.

Demonstrate Skills. When writing cooperatively or engaging in similar class activities, you will find many opportunities to teach embedded skills in areas such as spelling, phonics, punctuation, word selection, and organization of material. In the sentence about Sonya, for instance, it would be possible to emphasize several learnings: why some letters are capitalized, why there is a period at the end, and why there is an apostrophe in *grandmother's.* For pupils in later grades you can demonstrate how to check the spelling of a word, how to use a *caret* (^) to show that a word is being inserted, or how to decide when to start a new paragraph.

Make Effective Use of Conferences. When conferring with students, use the opportunity to find out more about individuals, what their writing interests are, what understandings and skills they already have, and how best to help them evaluate their writing and keep records of what they are working on. Also, you may gain some insights about how they prefer to write—whether alone or cooperatively, after much planning or little, using or not using drawings or webs, and so on. Conferences present important opportunities to listen as students read what they have written and discuss what changes might be made. Your questions are likely to be very helpful.

You will likely do some of your best teaching during conferences.

Write in Response to Student Writing. Children's writings, particularly their journals, make it possible for you to write in reaction to what they have written. For example, Anna writes about the approach of her birthday and you respond by acknowledging that it is an exciting time to speculate about presents and a party. Of course, children sometimes write about less happy matters, and a teacher may be able to supply some comforting words. Such exchanges sometimes evolve into a "dialogue journal" comprised of writing done by both people over a lengthy period of time.

The Writing Period

Children's writing improves best when there is time to write and they write regularly. Their progress will be sporadic, of course, and sometimes only apparent from a perspective of several weeks, but if they are continually seeing other students' writing, hearing those pieces read, listening to you read high-quality literature, and writing in a supportive environment, their own writing will increase in amount, will gradually become more fluent and interesting to read, and will be freer of mechanical problems.

The period ought to be of appropriate length. Kindergartners and beginning first graders may do best with about fifteen minutes; thirty minutes ought to be a minimum for older first graders and those in the next few years. Middle-grade classroom schedules should provide forty-five minutes or an hour for writing. Since much spelling and handwriting as well as language will be taught as part of the writing program, scheduled time for these can be reduced substantially to create a large block of time.

Activities included in a fifty-minute writing period and approximate time allocations could be

These allocations are only guidelines. Elementary teachers are fortunate in that they may be flexible, devoting an hour to writing time if that seems advisable. (Avoid *departmentalization*, which separates writing from other subjects and restricts class sessions to 40 minutes, often with one person teaching writing and another teaching reading.)

Specific lesson	10 minutes
Student checkup	5 minutes
Writing	25 minutes
Sharing	10 minutes

Specific Lessons. Brief whole-class lessons may be taught as a part of the writing period; in these you can emphasize helpful and positive ways of responding to a piece someone has written. Other lessons might have to do with a

Even young authors need uninterrupted time to write.

specific aspect of writing—how to identify nouns and verbs that best convey what the writer wants to express, for example. Other concerns have to do with classroom management, such as where to store writing folders and what to keep in them. You may also use a few minutes to do something that not everyone really needs. Only a few say that they can't think of anything to write about, for instance, but a discussion in the class may help them see how others develop ideas.

Checkup time reminds students that they have the responsibility to follow through on their plans.

Checking Up. At the beginning of writing time it is a good practice to ask each student what she or he is working on and whether assistance is required. This can be done quickly and will provide you a quick impression of what each pupil is working on. Also, conferences you want to hold or those they request can be planned for at this time.

Students will respond by telling what their current writing activity involves in regard to content and where they are in the process. A developing weekly chart for status reports might look like this, in part:

NAME	M	T	W	Th	F
Tony	*finishing piece on parrots*	*writing in notebook*	*thinking of new topic*		
Beth	*sharing piece on buildings*	*making revisions*	*reading more about skyscrapers— needs conference*		

Checkup time will give you a quick overview of what is going on with the group as a whole and with individual students.

Writing Time. During writing time children will be carrying out many language activities. This means that one will be conferring with you while others are listening to a classmate explain her or his ideas or reacting to something written by another student. Some may be using the word processor or typewriter. With all this going on, writing time will be busy and not very quiet. This is why some teachers call it *writing workshop* and others make comparisons to the artist's studio. Depending on the age of the children, several different kinds of writing will be in progress during this time.

Journals. Journals were mentioned in Chapter 4 and discussed to some extent in Chapter 10. They are like diaries in that the students write mostly about what has happened to them. From these, longer pieces are often developed.

Notebooks. For some older students the journal falls into disfavor. They are no longer as self-centered as primary-grade children and may want to write about a very wide range of topics. A notebook is more like a scrapbook and may include newspaper clippings, magazine pieces, and other materials that are of interest and may promote some writing.

General Writing. Depending on how the classroom program is organized, various types of writing may be done during the writing period and may include:

> articles for classroom or school newspapers
> reports for science or social studies
> stories
> poetry
> letters
> reviews
> essays

The forms of writing students might do are discussed throughout the rest of this chapter and in Chapters 13, 14, and 15. As students use the writing process during writing time, they will be brainstorming ideas, writing first drafts, reading

Most professional writers keep notebooks. Have a newspaper reporter talk about this with children.

All stages in the writing process are likely to be represented in class activities. There should be no expectation that all writers are at the same point.

their pieces to one another, conferring with you, making revisions, doing final drafts, and making their own books.

Writing is seldom a solitary experience in the elementary classroom.

Sharing. Different kinds of sharing occur throughout the writing period. As part of a lesson a student may read a part of her or his story that appears to be a good example of some aspect of writing—how dialogue can tell about a character, for example. At class check-up time, students will tell everyone what they are working on and this, too, is sharing. Sharing in the form of reading writing products to one another can also be done with partners or in small groups.

In addition, the period can conclude with specific sharing experiences. For example, when a student has written a book it may be read aloud to the class by him or her before being placed in the classroom library. Someone else may wish to read a letter to be sent to a pen pal. Others may wish to read a draft and see what questions and suggestions others may have about the piece.

TYPES OF WRITING

Whether done during the writing period or at times scheduled for other curriculum areas, various kinds of writing or genres will be used in the elementary classroom. Writing is involved in learning activities for all subjects, is an impor-

Students are very proud of the books they have produced.

tant means of expressing personal beliefs and meanings, and is a useful tool in everyday life experiences in and outside of the school.

Writing for Public Purposes

Writing about a topic requires good understanding of it—and extends that understanding.

Writing is an important way to gain understanding. Thinking is involved as the student organizes what she or he knows regarding a specific task, identifies what needs to be added to the store of knowledge if some goal is to be met, gathers that information, and integrates it with what is already understood. Writing can be significantly involved in all of these steps.

Specific kinds of writing exemplify aspects of the process of seeking understanding and presenting what has been understood.

Reports. Often students write reports of what they have found out about an area of investigation, a science project, for example, or the results of an interview. Writing such a report helps in organizing and summarizing knowledge, identifying new material, learning vocabulary, and seeing what related areas might be investigated next. And, of course, many new skills and strategies are learned when doing a report (see the related content in Chapter 13 on studying and Chapter 14 on the library media center).

When children write for classroom or schoolwide newspapers or magazines, they will have numerous opportunities to prepare reports. There will be descriptions of school events—holiday programs, fundraising drives, class or school projects, and athletic events. There may also be community activities that involve the school or its students.

As they write for and publish newspapers or magazines (and, perhaps, make a trip to a local newspaper), children will learn about journalism. To their existing vocabulary related to the writing process they will add terms such as *copy, deadline, layout, reporter,* and *editor.* They will likely develop a better understanding of

Artwork adds to the meaning of written material.

certain kinds of writing, the *wh* words of a news story for example: *who, what, when, where, why.* (Newspapers and magazines present opportunities to do other kinds of writing, too—features, editorials, advice columns, advertisements, letters to the editor, jokes, poetry, and comics. And, of course, being involved in publication will make children better readers of newspapers, as discussed in Chapter 13.)

Ideas for specific brief written reports are

> an athlete in the news
> a hobby involving collecting something
> a baby animal at the local zoo
> how a holiday is to be celebrated in a different way

Such reports may be prepared for reading over the school public address system or videotaped and distributed for other classes to view and listen to.

Recommendations to improve mathematics teaching include using more writing activities.

Descriptions and Records. Study activities often involve keeping records and writing descriptions. For example, a mathematics experience might consist of flipping 5 pennies 100 times to see how often they all come up "heads" or "tails" (or any of the other possible combinations). Writing would be necessary in devising a record-keeping chart, making entries, describing the process actually used, and summarizing results. Students who develop a thorough description of a learning activity will gain valuable experiences in thinking, talking, and listening as well as writing. Furthermore, they are much more likely to understand and recall the content than if they only perform the procedure or, worse yet, just see it done.

Keeping a record of what occurred at a meeting (usually called the minutes or the secretary's report) is a very specific kind of writing that often needs to be done. Club and other kinds of meetings are discussed in Chapter 5.

Other records kept in connection with classroom activities may include:

Use charts and models to show acceptable formats for friendly letters and business letters.

> weather calendars
> daily temperatures—highs and lows
> growth of plants
> number of students who have read the same book
> daily attendance
> weight of gerbil each day
> class members' height
> class members' favorite breakfast foods
> television programs watched

Finally, biographies are particular kinds of reports, descriptions of people's lives. Elementary students enjoy reading biographies and may want to try writing one.

Business Letters. Often elementary-school children need to send a business letter to companies, agencies, and officials. Common types of business letters include

Requests	To a company or individual for information
	To a place for permission to come for a field trip
	To an organization for free materials
	To a speaker who might make a presentation at school

Make a bulletin-board exhibit of copies of business letters actually sent and replies received. Stress the variety of formats but the commonality of information conveyed.

Thank-you letters	To those who have hosted a field trip
	To someone who has spoken at school
	To a business or an individual for making a gift to the school
Orders	To a publisher for a magazine subscription or book
	To a company for equipment
Applications	For a position on the school paper
	For membership in an organization
	For a position as helper in the school office or library
Complaints	About a program on television
	About a problem concerning the school buses
	About a product to an agency or company

In the middle and upper grades of the elementary school there are, of course, certain aspects of business communication that should be studied. But such learning and practice ought to culminate in sending an authentic business letter—and, hopefully, receiving a reply. Not many students will put forth their best effort if letters they write are never sent. (Whenever appropriate, students should use the school's stationery, too.)

Considerations to be emphasized are

Business writing is a specialized form of communication.

1. The proper form for business letters: inside addresses, formal salutations (followed by a colon), and appropriate closings (including the practice of both typing or printing and signing one's name). Dictionaries or other references may be consulted for information concerning forms to be used when writing to public officials.

2. Content and mechanics. What is included in a business letter and how well that content is presented are equally important. Overall organization is of significance; the letter should cover the important points without including duplications and extraneous material. Also important are spelling, choice of words, punctuation, and formal layouts.

3. Use of formal language. In general, slang and even some types of everyday language should be avoided in business letters. Making such choices presents you with opportunities to help students understand some of the usage distinctions discussed in Chapter 7.

4. Appearance of business letters. Because a messy letter may be considered an indication of lack of seriousness, special attention should be given to appearance. Children who are able to use typewriters and word processors can produce letters of the same quality as those done in many offices. Copies of several different examples of business letters should be available to students; these could be placed on a bulletin board.

Of course, students may receive replies to the business letters they send. This experience will enable them to see the different kinds of letters produced by businesses and agencies.

Announcements, Labels, and Forms. As students encounter more and more writing activities of a functional nature, they learn how to produce announcements of various kinds and labels for objects and materials. Attractive and effective signs and flyers can be made by hand-done lettering and drawing or by desktop word processing programs, but first their content must be drafted and revised. Labels for charts and diagrams may be written and then printed on a computer. Completing forms of various types often involves elementary students. Possibilities include

enrollment cards
questionnaires asking for name, address, and so forth
library loan cards
a money order
subscription blank
order blanks for free materials
application to participate in a book club

Invite students to conduct a survey of favorite children's books and then distribute an announcement of the findings.

Writing as Personal Expression

Writing, probably more than any other activity, provides the individual with opportunities to set forth what he or she thinks about something. When writing a personal letter or an essay, for example, we feel free to state our own views without necessarily acknowledging that others may think differently. Also, in doing something personal—producing a poem or a story, for instance—the writer is especially concerned to choose just the right words and make every effort to convey meaning and feelings fully. Several types of writing are especially personal.

Samples should be read aloud, of course.

Stories. Although adults often expect children to "write a story" rather easily, you should not assume that many of them can do so successfully unless provided with a great deal of guidance. Young story writers should have many sorts of experiences, including hearing and reading all kinds of stories—realistic ones as well as those that are highly imaginative. Discussion of stories will help students to see what the components are:

- setting (where the story takes place)
- characters (who is in the story)
- plot (what happens in the story)

Other considerations are:

- time (when the story takes place)
- point of view (who tells the story)

and what kinds of stories might be written:

- animal stories
- funny stories
- adventures
- mysteries
- science fiction

Children's ideas for writing stories may come from several different sources (those close to their own experiences are to be preferred over unrelated "story starters"):

- incidents from their own journals (a child learns to swim)
- their own story about a favorite character (Clifford or Curious George)
- story about a family member (how grandmother found her glasses)
- school-related story (a new boy or girl joins the class)
- spin-off from book read (*Little House on the Prairie*)
- seasonal idea (Halloween, water skiing)

Two students can write opposing reviews.

Reviews. The term *review* refers to a type of writing that expresses an individual's opinions and reactions regarding a book, music performance, movie, play, or other cultural event. Older elementary students have opportunities to read reviews of music concerts and television programs in local newspapers. (Reviews of films would have to be restricted to those appropriate for the age group.)

If there is a classroom or school newspaper, students can write reviews of television programs and other events that may be available to them. Most important, they can write reviews of books (see Chapters 14 and 15). It should be stressed that reviews are not restricted to summaries but are opportunities to share personal feelings, something which may require much careful thought and revision.

Local newspapers will sometimes publish "letters to the editor" submitted by children.

Essays. An essay is a statement by someone concerning either private or public matters. Essays are commonly found in daily newspapers and news magazines—editorials, columnists' contributions, and letters to the editor. Some magazines contain articles written in essay form. Essays may be submitted to a classroom or school newspaper or, perhaps, regional and national magazines that publish material written by elementary-school students. If there are no such local outlets you might consider collaborating with other teachers to establish one.

Read The Jolly Postman to a group of children.

Personal Letters. Personal letters and notes, though not so frequently sent as they once were, are still written. They are quite different from business letters in terms of the writer's purpose, the contents, style of writing, and choice of words. There are several reasons for sending a personal letter, the most common of which is to maintain contact with relatives and friends. Other types of personal correspondence include

Invitations	To parents to come to an activity
	To another class to see a program
	To the principal to visit the room
Replies	Accepting an invitation sent by another class
	Sending regrets at not being able to accept an invitation
Sympathy	To a sick classmate or adult
	To someone who has suffered a personal loss

Poetry. At several points in this book, poetry has been discussed as something to read aloud, recite, and listen to. As a result of such encounters with poetry,

Learning about the parts of a letter.

Much writing of poetry will usually be necessary before students' own voices begin to come through.

students may wish to try writing verses and rhymes. Of course, you should emphasize voluntary attempts and begin with activities that are easily accomplished by children of the age group you are teaching.

Important to poetry are words, visual and sound images, a sensitivity for feelings, and creativity, particularly the ability to notice relationships. Writing a class poem may be a good way to discuss how poems might develop. Very likely you should select a topic or even a title that would be appropriate (*The Bridge,* perhaps, if there is a bridge that is well known to the students) and utilize a format that is simple: perhaps four lines with the second and fourth lines rhyming (Robert Louis Stevenson's *The Swing* could be a model).

Discussion could then bring out some of the children's ideas. Jerry might point out that the full name is *Island Bridge,* and Susan could describe how beautiful the bridge lights look as they outline the towers and suspension cables. It then would seem a good idea to use a new poem title, *Island Bridge at Night.* Other images are mentioned: ferry boats moving under the bridge; the long lines of red tail lights on cars crossing the bridge; the roar of the wind through the cables during a storm; the feeling of having gotten safely across.

A student may put some of these images and ideas together: "It's like the bridge is a mother putting her arms around the cars," Terry says. Louann proposes a first line: "The cars come into the arms of Island Bridge." Others join in with suggestions about what lines could come next and what rhymes might be possible.

As with any other kind of writing, whole-class attempts can lead to efforts by small groups and individuals. A few successes will encourage further writing of other types of poems.

Some degree of success with any form of poetry will be important for a child.

Couplets and Triplets. Children's activities that call attention to rhyming words may stimulate their first attempts at making verses. Early attempts at rhyming should not be hampered by a concern with rhythm, although youngsters love rhythm and may well try to produce it (you can use this interest to help them develop the concept of *syllable,* too).

In making a couplet, it is usually sufficient to come up with one line and try for another that rhymes (The couplets in *Brown Bear, Brown Bear* can serve as examples.) Several of these can be gathered for a class book complete with children's drawings. Triplets can then be tried. The rhyming is enjoyable and occasionally provides some phonics practice.

Cinquain. The cinquain pattern is not difficult to use and is quite effective in helping children to become aware of the special quality of poetry: its appeal to the emotions and the senses. Cinquain has a very specific format:

First line:	one word, giving title
Second line:	two words, describing title
Third line:	three words, expressing an action
Fourth line:	four words, expressing a feeling
Fifth line:	one word, a synonym for the title

The cinquain form does allow some freedom in the choice of words and phrases, and almost any child can achieve a degree of success. An example shows how a simple topic can be used.

SAM

Warm, friendly
Licks my face
To show his love.
Puppy.

Free Verse. Free verse places no restrictions on total length and number of syllables or words to a line and prescribes no rhythmic pattern. The writer decides where to break lines or begin new stanzas and when the poem is complete. In a sense, free verse may be thought of as *free thought*. The length of the thought might be one sentence by a third grader or two pages by a talented sixth grader.

If children experience activities in which they talk about and use words and phrases that express their feelings about commonplace but important matters—family, friends, fear, happiness, suffering, and all the rest—then making notes on these and writing can follow. Prose is always acceptable, of course, but free verse may be more expressive for those who can best compose when there is very little restraint on their writing.

Limericks. Middle-grade students derive much enjoyment from reading and writing limericks, and certainly children should realize that poetry can be humorous. Limericks have a set form with which most of us are familiar: the first, second, and fifth lines rhyme; the third and fourth lines rhyme and are shorter.

Children should be helped to see that the "trick" is to find a number of words that rhyme and then see if several of them together suggest an idea. A couplet is needed to begin with and then experimentation with rhymes, synonyms, word order, and rhythm will produce the desired effect:

There was an old woman named Snow
Who couldn't get flowers to grow.

She planted some seeds
But got only weeds.
What happened I really don't know!

Other Forms. After a substantial amount of poetry writing, a few of your students may wish to try one of the challenging forms. They might be interested in *ballads,* long poems that tell a story (*Lochinvar,* for example) and may wish to compose music so that these become songs. The Japanese verse form *Haiku* is interesting because it must be composed of a total of seventeen syllables, with five in the first line, seven in the second, and five in the third. The central image is usually from nature, with the final line making an observation about life. There is no need for attention to rhyme or meter. Another form of verse is the *triante,* which calls for "sense" words as follows:

First line:	one word, giving the title
Second line:	two words, telling how it smells
Third line:	three words, telling how it feels
Fourth line:	four words, telling how it looks
Fifth line:	five words, telling how it sounds

Children may also enjoy the challenge of producing a poem in a particular shape—a Halloween poem in the form of a witch's hat, for instance.

Personality Sketches. Children may write descriptions of individuals, both real and imaginary. If there is a class newspaper a student may interview someone in the school (a cafeteria worker) or the wider community (a store operator) and write not only about these people's work responsibilities but also their family situations, their own school experiences, and their hobbies and travels. Students may also write sketches of their classmates and about characters from stories.

> Writing about people's jobs helps to inform a student about the world of work.

Plays. Children can begin to write plays, or at least scenes, if they have gained some preparation by participating in plays and reading stories with much dialogue. To create a play they need only identify characters, assign the lines of dialogue to them, and add stage directions. After they have written several scenes in this way and performed them, they may be ready to write dialogue from another story or even to create an original play. These first attempts should be based on familiar content such as fairy tales, legends, historical episodes, and television situation comedies. These may also be performed as "readers' theater" (described in Chapter 5).

> Youngsters can try writing a *Sesame Street* episode about their old friends Bert and Ernie.

WRITING AND THE WORD PROCESSOR

In Chapter 9 it was pointed out that writing in the elementary school can be done through the use of word processors. In some schools students have regular access to computers and printers, so they readily learn to use word-processing programs. (Several programs appropriate for the elementary school are listed in the references for this chapter as well as in Chapter 10.)

For children word processing is usually a cooperative activity.

Word-Processing Procedures

Solomon, in her book *Teaching Writing with Computers,* presents a thorough review of the subject.

Elementary students enjoy using a word processor for the same reasons many adults do: making corrections is easier and there is no necessity to recopy something entirely in handwriting before it is "finished." Depending on their age, children can write something in manuscript or cursive and then type it into the computer themselves or have someone do that for them. Then they can print it for later editing by hand or do their editing directly on the computer screen.

Word-Processing Programs. Though most elementary students cannot be expected to make maximum use of the writing possibilities offered by computers, adults are usually impressed by what children as young as kindergarten and first grade can do.

Children can use word processors in several ways. Preschoolers can type and often name letters as they appear on the computer screen (with some programs letters will be very large and even in color; when sound is available the computer will supply the names of the letters typed and even pronounce any words produced). Actual writing begins when children in kindergarten and first grade can type a few lines of enlarged print, and, using invented spelling, begin to write stories, just as they write in journals.

Older children who have had these kinds of experiences can go on to do a great deal with computers: first-draft writing, as much revision as desired (either by writing directly on the "hard copy"—pages that have been printed out—or by making changes on the screen), final editing, and then printing of the finished piece. Revision can be extensive, since the word-processing programs make it possible for the writer to store a draft on a disk and bring it back to the screen for further development.

Some elementary students become very adept at making substantial changes in a text. They move sentences, paragraphs, and even larger blocks of print to different locations. They decide what style of print they want a document to appear in (or even which words should be in a style that is different) and how large and dark the print should be.

Other Features.   Many features other than basic word processing may be available in various computer programs. For example, a computer may have a "spell checker" that prevents a writer from making certain kinds of spelling errors. If *seperate* is typed, for example, the machine will type out *separate*. Many word-processing programs also include built-in dictionaries so that a word may be looked up without leaving the machine. Thesauruses, lists of words that are synonyms for a particular word, may also be included in the program so that considering the replacement of a word is only a matter of typing a few keys.

Desktop Publishing

Some desktop-publishing programs can print images from television screens.

A special type of word processing is *desktop publishing,* which refers to use of computer programs that enable even rather young children to produce signs, notices, announcements, and pages for newspapers and magazines. Such products are in many cases just as attractive and effective as those done by highly experienced adults.

The principal difference between desktop programs and those for ordinary word processing is that desktop publishing has important capabilities that relate directly to rather complex types of productive writing. Desktop activities include laying out pages so that it is possible to have such features as print in several styles, bold headings, various kinds of borders for pages and sections of pages, and columns of different sizes. Students, then, can easily produce flyers, newspapers, and pages for magazines and books in the same manner that commercial publishers do. In addition, desktop programs permit the inclusion of cartoons, pictures, drawings, and graphics of all kinds (see the sample on page 292). Hall banners, posters, greeting cards, class stationery, bulletin boards, calendars, awards, and certificates are other possibilities.

ASSESSMENT OF WRITING

Many famous writers got low grades in "English."

Chapter 2 presented a discussion of how a language arts portfolio may be assembled for each student, including work samples, audiotapes, videotapes, checklists, teacher commentaries, and test results. Such a portfolio lends itself very well to assessment of children's writing—assessment done both by you and by students as they engage in self-evaluation. And, of course, when parents are presented with an opportunity to inspect their child's portfolio, they get much more information than could possibly be conveyed by a conventional report card.

In writing both the written product and the processes used in writing are major concerns. Both are discussed in the sections that follow.

Writing Products

In Chapter 10 it was stressed that in the elementary school attention should be given to the writing process rather than the assignment of marks or grades to particular written products. Evaluation should only involve examination of something that has been written in order to determine the extent to which it meets criteria that the writer understands and accepts. If a report has been completed, for instance, and a checklist such as that given in Chapter 10 under Postwriting Activities has been developed cooperatively with the students, you may give a child your assessment of how well the piece meets expectations. Of course, it is even better if the writer participates in the discussion and also points out apparent strengths as well as matters that need more attention. Evaluation should be for the purpose of helping the learner to make progress, not for gathering information on which to base marks.

A student's writing products should be gathered in a portfolio that is passed along from year to year and contains items selected according to some school-wide plan. (The portfolio might also contain computer disks that store nearly all the texts a child has written over several years.) By the time a student is in the later grades of the elementary school, her or his writing samples from different levels could include

Numbers of parents are making such collections themselves, usually because the child has done these sorts of things at home.

- *home and prekindergarten*: scribblings, drawings, and attempts to write name and other alphabet letters
- *kindergarten*: writings of name and alphabet, drawings accompanied by strings of letters, invented spelling attempts

A Student Using a Desktop Publishing Program Can Incorporate Illustrations.

**A HOCKEY STORY
BY JOSEPH WAHLER**

    ONCE UPON A TIME THERE WAS A PROFESSIONAL HOCKEY PLAYER BY THE NAME OF JOEY. HE WAS THE BEST AT HOCKEY. HE SCORED 4 GOALS IN A GAME. AFTER THE GAME THEY'D HAVE A BIG, BIG PARTY.

    ONE NIGHT DURING A GAME, JOEY GOT HURT. HE BROKE HIS JAW BECAUSE SOMEONE FROM THE OTHER TEAM HIT HIM WITH A HOCKEY STICK. JOEY FELT MAD BECAUSE HE COULD NOT PLAY HOCKEY FOR A MONTH.

- *primary grades*: sequential samples of invented spelling, completed books, letters to parents, story writing, research, and informational writing
- *intermediate grades*: research reports, essays about books read, stories in several genres, business and personal letters, television scripts, descriptions of science projects, math story problems, music reviews in newspapers, and self-assessment of own writing

Also, students could make annual reviews of their writing progress, perhaps in the form of written commentaries done in cooperation with that year's teacher. These could include statements explaining why particular items were selected for inclusion in the portfolio.

The Writing Process

The progress of the student in learning to use the writing process is best reflected by samples of first drafts, revised drafts, and final versions of the same piece that are retained for the portfolio. Other means of documenting progress are also possible.

Checklists and Checkups. Checklists accumulated over the years will furnish insights about student progress. In the primary grades (as described in Chapter 4) the concern may have been with the kinds of topics written about, the revision strategies favored by the writer, and what kind of publications were done. In the later years, sample writing-convention checklists can be examined to see how much and what sort of progress has been made at particular times. The same is possible if the students keep personal spelling lists. Information from daily teacher checkups during writing periods could be compiled to provide information concerning how many different pieces of writing a student worked on during the year, how many days were devoted to each, and what proportion of them were published.

A few good insights every month or so add up to a significant commentary.

Teachers' Comments. During your regular conferences with writers you should record (maybe on the inside of the student's writing folder) what was discussed regarding their use of the writing process as well as their progress in such areas as organization of texts and use of conventions. Every few weeks you should also make summary comments about the kind of progress each student is making. These may be written in the student's folder or placed in his or her portfolio. Of course, such information should be shared with students and their parents.

Videotapes. Videotapes of the child using the writing process are invaluable in showing progress. Specifics such as handwriting may be observed as the young child gradually gets it under control, reduces the size of letters, and so forth. When students are making revisions, a videotape can show how rapidly they work, what kinds of changes they make in what order, and how they read aloud to make word changes and punctuation decisions. If children use a word processor, only a videotape can reveal how much revision they do when texts are on the screen.

A FINAL WORD

This chapter and the one preceding it have both been devoted to writing. It seems clear that the writing component of the classroom program is extremely significant in determining how well your teaching is succeeding. This is where all language arts areas come together as students think and talk about their work, read their material to themselves and one another, and write in response to what they read.

At the same time you are assisting students in evaluation of what they have done and where they are as writers, you should be examining the program to see what needs to be done to make it more effective. Progress in your writing program will bring general improvement to the classroom offerings.

References

Atwell, Nancie, ed. *Coming to Know: Writing to Learn in the Intermediate Grades.* Heinemann Educational Books, 1990.

Church, Jean. "Record Keeping in Whole Language Classrooms" in *Assessment and Evaluation in Whole Language Programs,* edited by Bill Harp. Christopher-Gordon Publishers, 1991.

Denman, Gregory. *Sit Tight, and I'll Swing You a Tail: Using and Writing Stories with Young People.* Heinemann, 1991.

Evans, Christine Sobray. "Writing to Learn in Math." *Language Arts* 61 (December 1984), pp. 828–835.

Freeman, Evelyn B. "Informational Books: Models for Student Report Writing." *Language Arts* 68 (October 1991), pp. 470–473.

Fulwiler, Toby. *The Journal Book.* Boynton/Cook, 1987.

Grossman, Florence. *Listening to the Bells: Learning to Read Poetry by Writing Poetry.* Heinemann, 1991.

Hall, Nigel, and Duffy, Rose. "Every Child Has a Story to Tell." *Language Arts* 64 (September 1987), pp. 523–529.

Harwayne, Shelley. *Lasting Impressions: Weaving Literature into the Writing Workshop.* Heinemann, 1992.

Hollingsworth, Helen, and Eastman, Susan. *Teaching Writing in Every Class: A Guide for Grades 6–12.* Allyn and Bacon, 1988.

Kintisch, Lenore S. "Journal Writing: Stages of Development." *The Reading Teacher* (November 1986), pp. 168–173.

Mayher, John S.; Lester, Nancy; and Pradl, Gordon M. *Learning to Write/Writing to Learn.* Boynton/Cook, 1983.

McGinley, William, and Madigan, Daniel. "The Research 'Story': A Forum for Integrating, Reading, Writing, and Learning." *Language Arts* 67 (September 1990), pp. 474–483.

New York State Education Department. *Composition in the English Language Arts Curriculum.* New York State Education Department, 1986.

Newkirk, Thomas. *More Than Stories: The Range of Children's Writing.* Heinemann, 1989.

Parry, Jo-Ann, and Hornsby, David. *Write On: A Conference Approach to Writing.* Heinemann, 1988.

Parsons, Les. *Poetry, Themes, & Activities.* Heinemann, 1992.

Petty, Walter T., and Finn, Patrick, eds. *The Writing Process of Students.* Department of Learning and Instruction, State University of New York at Buffalo, 1975.

Phillips, Kathleen C., and Steiner, Barbara. *Creative Writing: A Handbook for Teaching Young People.* Libraries Unlimited, 1985.

Solomon, Gwen. *Teaching Writing with Computers: The POWER Process.* Prentice-Hall, 1986.

Smith, Carl B., and Dahl, Karin L. *Teaching Reading and Writing Together.* Teachers College Press, 1984.

Taberski, Sharon. "From Fake to Fiction: Young Children Learn About Writing Fiction." *Language Arts* 64 (October 1987), pp. 586–596.

Tiedt, Iris M. *Teaching Writing in K–8 Classrooms: The Time Has Come.* Prentice-Hall, 1983.

Wells, Gordon, and Chang-Wells, Gen Ling. *Constructing Knowledge Together: Classrooms as Centers of Inquiry and Literacy.* Heinemann, 1992.

Teaching Resources

COMPUTER SOFTWARE

Build a Book. Mindscope.
Explore-a-Story. D. C. Heath
Kidwriter. Spinnaker Software (diskette and guide; grades 1–5).
Letter Writer. InterLearn (diskette; grades 3–8).
Magic Slate. Sunburst Communications.
Story Builder. Random House (tape, diskette, and guide; grades 3–6).
Story Maker. Scholastic (four diskettes and guide; grades 2–6).
The Children's Writing and Publishing Center. The Learning Center.
That's My Story. Learning Well (two diskettes and guide; grades 3–8).
The Writing Adventure. DLM Educational Software (grade 4 and up).
Writing Skills. Milliken.

VIDEOTAPES

Think 'N Write. Society for Visual Education.

Write a Letter. Barr Films (grades 1–6; also available as a film).
Writing in the Content Areas. National Council of Teachers of English.

OTHER RESOURCES

James, Elizabeth, and Barkin, Carol. *How to Write a Great School Report.* Lothrop, Lee and Shepard, 1983.
Report Writing Skills. Random House (eight audiocassettes, worksheets, and guide; grade 4 and up).
Richards, Meredith. *Guide to Classroom Publishing.* Scholastic, 1988.
Urdang, Lawrence, and La Roche, Nancy. *Picturesque Expressions: A Thematic Dictionary.* Gale, 1983.
The Write Source. Knowledge Unlimited (handbook).
Writer's Workshop. Scholastic (kit).
Writing Is Reading. National Council of Teachers of English, 1985 (booklet).
The Young Writer's Handbook. Scribner's (handbook).

Activities for Preservice Teachers

1. Keep a diary for two or three weeks. What do you find yourself writing about? Is it easy to write every day? Do you think daily writing is beneficial?

2. Write a letter you "owe" to a relative or friend. Do you include anything you would not say in a telephone conversation? Do you express something differently than you might in speaking?

3. Plan writing activities for a fifth-grade class working on a unit in social studies or science. See how long and varied a list you can compile; ask others for their ideas. Consider also how similar subject area activities might be planned for.

4. Collect some magazine pictures and other materials that would be especially useful in teaching writing. Plan activities related to them, for example, generating word lists, formulating questions, creating original phrases, writing dialogue, and writing descriptions.

5. If you feel sufficiently confident of your writing skills and your college has a center where students may go for help with their writing assignments, volunteer to be a tutor. See what the directors of the center suggest to students to help them improve their writing. How does whatever is recommended compare with the content of this chapter and the preceding one?

6. For a specific grade level, plan an activity to encourage highly imaginative writing. For instance, have children write a TV commercial, conversations in "balloons" over the heads of cartoon characters, or a newspaper advertisement for a new kind of toy.

7. Write about a personal problem or an important decision you have to make. Does writing seem to help? Do you experience any sense of discovery?

8. Using overhead transparencies, prepare several poorly-organized paragraphs. Have some that are relatively easy to work with and others that will be more difficult to edit. Develop a plan that would involve projecting each of these paragraphs onto a screen and leading a group of fifth graders through the process of reorganizing them to make them more coherent.

9. Examine some free materials that children can secure by writing letters and requesting them. Prepare a class report in which you describe the materials and assess their appropriateness for distribution to middle-grade students.

Activities for Inservice Teachers

1. Identify two or three pupils in your class who write very little. Begin to confer with them frequently concerning what they might write about and how they might go about it. Be alert for any signs of interest and encourage all attempts. Assess the situation after a few weeks.

2. Conduct an interest survey in your class—or, better yet, have the children do it. Find out what sports, hobbies, reading materials, TV programs, music, and board games the children are interested in. Could any of these be used as points of departure for writing?

3. Collect samples of children's writing at one grade level. Devise a rating scale that covers such areas as organization, sentence variety, word choice, and mechanics. Rate some of the writings and discuss the results with other teachers.

4. Collect sports articles from newspapers and magazines, and have pupils look through them for colorful language and specific items such as metaphors or similes ("The Lions were toothless tabby cats last night" or "Rogers covered Smith like a steel sleeping bag"). Put examples on a bulletin board.

5. Parents often state that they have no idea what their children do in school. Plan a biweekly newsletter for reporting class activities to parents. Precede this activity with a study of newspapers and a visit to a local paper.

6. Survey your classroom program as objectively as possible to determine the degree of creativity fostered by the environment. Are children's ideas evident? Are there adequate stimuli for original thinking? Is the classroom yours or does it "belong" to the entire group?

7. Investigate the possibility of establishing a "post office" in your classroom or one for the entire school. Children can write letters to one another and to you (and to siblings and friends in other rooms if the whole building is involved). Letters can be picked up each day, sorted, and delivered. The importance of clear handwriting and correct spelling can be stressed.

8. With other teachers in your school, plan for publishing a schoolwide writing anthology. Decide what kinds of writing will be published: poetry, stories (consider limiting the length), jokes, riddles, and so on. Also decide on submission and publication dates, the form in which the writing should be submitted, who will decide which writing is accepted (the children should be involved in this), and so on.

Activities for Children

1. Children may collect letters from a variety of businesses and offices (including the school office). They can make displays of these, noting the various ways in which parts are arranged, the efforts to make the letters attractive, and the variety in content.

2. Contact a local nursing home or convalescent center and ask for names of people who might enjoy corresponding with children. The children can write letters telling about class activities, what they are interested in, plans for the future, and so forth. Possibly poetry or stories could also be sent from time to time.

3. If a child seems interested in an important public issue, encourage him or her to write a letter to the editor of the local newspaper. This should be well planned and done carefully. You may want to include a note to the editor, explaining the circumstances.

4. Ask businesses for out-of-date forms of any kind; many children will be interested in attempting to complete them. This is good practice in using legible manuscript writing.

5. For the child who can't think of a story to write or who doesn't believe his or her experiences are worth relating (or doesn't know how to relate them), keeping records about a window garden may be the answer. Have the child bring the soil and container (paper cup, egg carton, etc.), and you furnish the seeds.

6. Prepare collections of materials to spark children's writing. The collections (usually a box is needed for each) might include the following:

    Comic cartoons from newspapers

    Photographs of interesting places and events

    Cloth and other objects of different textures

    Newspaper stories

    Pictures from magazines

7. Children can write letters to their favorite TV personalities (and usually get some kind of response).

(Name of Star)
ABC-TV Public Relations
1330 Avenue of the Americas
New York, NY 10019

(Name of Star)
NBC-TV Information Services

30 Rockefeller Plaza
New York, NY 10020

(Name of Star)
CBS-TV Entertainment
51 W. 52nd Street
New York, NY 10019

8. Cut up workbooks to obtain pictures that tell a story in sequence. Fasten each group together with a paperclip or rubber band, and keep them in a shoe box covered with gift wrap or contact paper. A child selects a group, places the pictures in sequence, and then writes a sentence about each, thereby making a paragraph.

9. Children can write poems according to particular restrictions. For example, the first letter of each line spells a word:

Fair skies, but

Across the
Lake comes a
Long blast of cold air.

Or, there are only two words per line:

CLIMBING
Up faster;
Out farther
And farther;
Down quickly.

10. When children need to learn about the use of hyphens to divide words at the ends of lines, turn to the newspaper. Because newspaper columns are narrow, they contain many hyphenated words. Have the children look for these, cut out the columns, and circle the hyphens with red crayon. Put the articles on a chart or bulletin board. Using the display, help the children formulate generalizations about the use of hyphens to divide words.

11. A child or several children working together might do any of the following:

Make lists of colorful phrases

List adjectives describing objects in the classroom

Find good beginning sentences for stories

Collect objects that provide sensory feelings

12. Have children collect particularly striking similes, metaphors, and images. They might then work in groups to compile booklets of those they like best.

13. Two children can play a game with cards bearing various types of punctuation—periods, quotation marks, exclamation marks, and so forth. One child draws a card; he or she must compose a sentence that uses the mark on the card, giving the proper inflection. The other child guesses which mark was on the card. Individual children can play this game by drawing cards and then writing sentences using the marks correctly.

14. Two children can work together: one writes a question, using the correct capitalization, spelling, and punctuation, and the other writes a statement in reply to the question. The children can check each other. (This is also excellent practice in spelling, changing person and forms of verbs, etc.)

15. Suggest that children exchange stories or other writing with children in other schools. These may be children whose names were obtained from one of the sources for pen pals, or they may be children in a nearby school. Each child should write to another child, inviting him or her to exchange writing and reactions to that writing.

Chapter 12

Children and Reading

*T*he contents of Chapters 3 and 4 stressed that beginning-reading experiences should be closely related to activities involving the other language arts: speaking, listening, and writing. Schools have, however, usually considered reading so important an area of the curriculum that it is often taught in isolation with little acknowledgment of its connection to other aspects of language.

This chapter gives some attention to reading as a separate component of the classroom program but will emphasize its relations with each element, including not only the language areas but the other subjects as well. The approach to reading that is recommended will resemble, and should be an extension of, what has been described as best for younger students. This includes a great deal of literature; the provision of a variety of reading experiences; skill teaching within the context of meaningful reading; and, above all, an attempt to ensure that each child grows up enjoying reading.

READING AS A PROCESS

How many kinds of reading did you do yesterday?

Reading is not a separate school subject but a process that occurs in all areas of the classroom program. The nature of the process changes to some extent, however, depending on the particular kind of reading activity involved. For example, reading a story is different from reading a mathematics problem, an account of life in another country, or a description of a scientific experiment. All kinds of reading take place in an elementary classroom and each contributes to a child's education.

As was pointed out in Chapter 4, the pupil will learn to read best if the classroom program and the reading done as part of it are varied and likely to capture the learner's interest. Limiting a child's reading to a few pages of highly controlled material or a list of skills to be practiced day after day through the use of workbooks and duplicated worksheets will not do much to build good attitudes toward reading or establish a lifelong habit of reading.

The term *aliterate* is sometimes applied to those who can read but don't.

Reasons for Reading

People read for two principal reasons. The first involves reading for *satisfaction*, because the activity is an enjoyable one, and the second relates to reading for *information*. Both are significant in the elementary school.

Reading for satisfaction and personal involvement is significant for many pupils beginning in the early primary grades. They frequently read stories about characters and events that they find entertaining and interesting. When a well-stocked library is available to them, first and second graders will read dozens of

List some of the books you particularly enjoyed when you were a child.

story books in a few weeks. As they move into the middle and upper grades, these children who have come to find great satisfaction in reading animal books and humorous stories will add to their list of favorites and move on to legends, adventure, realistic fiction, and much else. Those who have not developed much interest in reading will, sad to say, do very little reading that they find satisfying.

Reading for information includes such activities as consulting television listings or studying an assigned textbook. Of course, reading about bees may be both informational and pleasurable if your hobby is beekeeping, but it is still a particular kind of reading done for a purpose other than the enjoyment of reading itself. And some types of purposeful reading are very unlikely to be considered enjoyable. Hardly anyone reads the telephone directory for the fun of it!

The Nature of Reading

In the discussion of early reading in Chapter 4 it was stated that three systems operate when a person reads: the *meaning* system, the *language* system, and the phonics or *graphophonic* system. As children continue through the elementary years, these systems continue to function, with each becoming more complex and relationships among the three becoming more involved.

Meaning is not *given* to the reader but must be actively striven for.

The Meaning System. Meaning is constructed by the reader as he or she interacts with the text being read. Individuals bring to the reading situation not only an attitude toward learning and reading in general, and an understanding of how to use certain skills and strategies, but also a degree of knowledge about the topic discussed in the text.

When students read material about which they know very little, the meanings they take away will often not be what the author had expected to convey ("The story we read was a myth about a man named Apollo who was one of the first Astronauts.") On the other hand, when reading a text about a familiar topic, a person's understanding might be so thorough that she or he not only easily grasps what the author has written but disagrees with all or parts of it (just as an advanced student of reading may believe that the content of these paragraphs is not quite correct).

If children are to be helped to read well they need to learn what to expect in particular situations. They should know the appropriate techniques to use when trying to deal with varied sorts of reading matter—newspapers, recipes, sports magazines, or encyclopedias, for a few examples. More important, you should help them to see that it is their responsibility to monitor their own comprehension, to realize when the content isn't making sense, and to decide what actions could be taken to meet that difficulty.

It's important to know when we "don't get it." Children have difficulty because they almost always believe that they understand.

The Language System. As a child becomes more familiar with the many aspects of language, his or her facility as a reader will improve. For instance, when sentence structure is well understood even the very young speaker of English expects certain kinds of words to follow others (see Chapter 7). This means that, confronted by the sentence *The dish was sitting on a credenza,* even a student who has very little hope of pronouncing the last word or knowing exactly what it refers to will understand that the dish is sitting on *something;* because that's how English works. (Of course, he or she may also anticipate that a credenza is a piece of furniture low enough for someone to place a dish on it, but that kind of anticipation has to do with the meaning system rather than familiarity with language structure.)

As the child hears more complex sentences (usually from being read to) he or she is better prepared to read what would have been too difficult a year or two previously. A reader begins to note, for example, that clusters of words often perform the same function as a single word. For instance, *Someone bothered her* is in the same sentence pattern as *A tall boy wearing a blue jacket and a red cap bothered her* and is understood in the same way. Also, such specialized language as that of some kinds of poetry (*The House That Jack Built,* for example) often needs to be heard a few times before it can be read easily by children.

The Graphophonic System. In the early grades children rapidly develop a rather large stock of words that they immediately recognize. They have learned these in several ways, including *decoding,* using the graphophonic system (letters and associated sounds) to try to identify an unfamiliar word by coming up with approximate pronunciations until one seems to fit. This usually occurs when the reader suddenly recognizes the word, realizing that it is in her or his listening or even speaking vocabulary.

In some cases using the graphophonic system doesn't work very well. If the unknown word is *chemistry,* for example, the reader may assume that it begins with the "ch" sound in *chair* and make little progress at first. When language and meaning systems are combined with the graphophonic, however, better results will usually be achieved. (Perhaps the text is about pollution and the reader has heard about the effects of dumping *chemicals,* which provides a significant clue about another sound related to *ch*).

As older children read, they are likely to encounter many words they do not immediately recognize, and they need to be able to use graphophonic knowledge where appropriate. Their understanding needs to be extended into such areas as separating words into syllables (*miscellaneous*), realizing that some words are not English in origin (*liaison*), and appreciating the importance of knowing the terminology of particular fields (*gastroenteritis*).

The act of reading involves putting all this information together in various ways until "something clicks."

Reading thus involves being able to, in a matter of seconds, recognize dozens of words, integrate the meanings of these into what the reader already knows about the material being read, extend and alter understanding of the text, and, to some extent, predict what content will be coming next. When the flow of meaning is interrupted, the proficient reader knows how to go back into the material and, coordinating meaning, language, and decoding systems, identify the difficulty and rectify the situation.

THE READING PROGRAM

National tests reveal that, in general, young children are doing well in reading.

The reading program for children in kindergarten and the early primary grades was described in Chapter 4. When students have experienced that kind of program, they may be expected to enter the middle grades reading rather well and displaying much interest in books and reading. Children not in such an advantageous position should, of course, be provided with opportunities that have not been made available at home and school. As described in Chapters 3 and 4, they need to have extensive oral language experiences; they should be read to regularly; they ought to be provided with drawing and writing materials; and so forth.

Reading in the Classroom

See Routman's book for a description of such classrooms.

Growth in reading performance occurs most readily in the kinds of classrooms where meaningful experiences and total literacy are emphasized. When your reading program supports children as they learn about and enjoy language, listen to good literature, study words, and do writing of all kinds, they have an excellent opportunity to read well and make use of reading in varied circumstances and for different purposes. In such a setting *developmental, information-processing,* and *embedded-lesson* aspects of reading instruction make important contributions.

Developmental reading involves providing experiences that assist children in recognizing and identifying words, seeing how various kinds of reading tasks are performed, and becoming proficient in reading many kinds of materials. Very often attempts are made to provide all this learning by means of a single set of published materials known as a *basal reading series,* but there are many ways in which necessary abilities can be developed, including effective use of information-processing and embedded-lesson experiences.

Many teachers have decided that they don't need a basal reading series to achieve their program goals.

Information processing in reading refers to what happens in such areas as literature, social studies, mathematics and science as readers attempt to construct meanings. Teachers are responsible for presenting an organized program designed to show their classes how to read history, how to study scientific words in a text being read, how to relate details when reading a word problem in mathematics, and how to analyze the type of literature they have been asked to read.

Children have not learned to read until they can comprehend the content of their textbooks and other non-fiction materials, including understanding concepts, directions, and questions.

Embedded lessons are brief lessons taught to readers in conjunction with actual reading situations. How to deal with an unknown word in the morning newspaper, what is meant by a phrase in a political cartoon, how to use an index in an encyclopedia, and why a book has a particular title are all opportunities for you to take a few seconds and do some high-quality teaching. There is often a multiplier effect, since students who know something can help others to understand it.

Reading Materials

A classroom reading program must be based on a wide variety of reading materials. Textbooks are read, of course, and reading and studying of them are discussed in Chapter 13. Other types of reading matter are also likely to be of use.

Literature. Literature—stories, poems, plays, and other writings by authors who write to express themselves—is important in the reading program because such writing is inherently interesting to children. When you make genuine literature available to students, you are introducing them to important aspects of their cultural heritage and providing them with much to think and talk about (see Literature and the Reading Program later in the chapter).

Magazines and Newspapers. A classroom collection of reading materials should include a rich variety of content, including magazines and newspapers.

A large selection of books should be available in the classroom.

Certainly, there should be several children's magazines in your room. These are costly, but sometimes families who have subscriptions can supply back copies. Classroom newspapers such as *Weekly Reader* should also be available.

Depending on the maturity of your class, daily newspapers and general magazines might be kept in the room. Again, some may be "handed down" to the group. Considering the sensitive nature of content appearing in popular magazines, you may have to exercise considerable care in making selections.

This is especially true if a school has no library or one that includes only storybooks.

Informational Sources. A classroom should be equipped with reference materials of all kinds—dictionaries, encyclopedias, atlases, telephone directories, almanacs, and books of facts about sports and other matters. In addition, there should be nonfiction books about animals, cities, art, oceans, and other topics likely to be of interest to your children. When the class has taken up the study of a topic in science or social studies ("Our Weather," for example) you should accumulate a variety of materials from the school and public libraries.

Basal Reading Series. In many classrooms the teaching of reading is based on published reading programs commonly referred to as *basal readers.* These are collections of reading selections with detailed guides for teaching skills in sequence. They are often used in conjunction with an organization that involves small ability groups that meet regularly with the teacher. Whether or not you use basal readers occasionally, regularly, or hardly at all, you may wish to have some available. A portion of the stories and other selections in them are quite good, and you may wish to have a group of youngsters all read the same selection and do the suggested follow-up activities. In addition, the lists of objectives at the various grade levels might provide guidance about what kinds of learnings you should be sure to offer in your program.

> Basals can be used as *part* of a reading program.

Computer-based Reading. If a computer is available in the classroom it will be fairly easy for students to use software programs intended to improve performance in reading. These include practice activities in areas such as phonics and word identification, and comprehension activities. (Several sample software items are listed at the end of this chapter.)

Miscellaneous Reading Aids. Reading materials include book-audio tape kits, collections of sequentially arranged reading exercises, word-matching games, skill-practice exercises, and other kinds of learning aids. You should give careful consideration to what is available in your classroom, however. Almost anything can make some sort of contribution, but occasionally you will find that there is an item that appears to be totally inconsistent with your goals (out-of-date materials may have illustrations demeaning to cultural groups, for instance).

> Books should be examined for possible bias against:
> the handicapped
> the elderly
> racial minorities
> religious groups
> girls and women

Directed Reading Experiences

Directed reading activities are the types of learning experiences commonly provided in basal reading series. (The "basal," as it is usually called, is developed as a means of delivering instruction in reading skills and understandings.) These experiences are almost always presented as lessons to a group of pupils of similar reading ability who meet every day. There is a total of three or four groups, a top group of the best readers and groups composed of successively weaker readers. Since groups meet for approximately twenty minutes each, the reading period requires about one hour. Most of the content read comes from books in one or more reading series, and the teacher's manual provides detailed directions as to how the lesson ought to be conducted. (Shortcomings of this approach to the teaching of reading were discussed in Chapter 4.)

Several steps make up the conventional directed reading experience:

1. *Preparation.* Students are introduced to the selection (usually a story) and new words to be encountered in it are presented.
2. *Survey Reading.* The selection, or a portion of it, is read silently in order to answer questions identified by the teacher (usually from the manual provided) and the group.
3. *Rereading.* In answering questions and discussing the new words and understandings presented in the lesson, individual students reread portions of the text, either silently or aloud.

Teachers' manuals often include "scripts" telling what the teacher should say and how students will likely respond.

4. *Practice.* The targeted skills and understandings are practiced (sometimes in the group session but more likely alone and in workbooks while the teacher is occupied with another group). Answers will be checked at the next group meeting.

5. *Extensions.* Though not essential, follow-up or extension activities are often included as an aspect of a directed reading experience. These activities may range from additional skill practice to creative interpretations of selections.

Depending on the abilities of the children involved and the teacher's preferences, the activities related to a particular reading selection will continue over two to three days or as many as five to six, with nearly everything done during the reading period.

It may be that you do not wish to devote much of your reading period to directed reading activities, but choose to do this occasionally to assure yourself (or a supervisor) that children's progress in basal-reader sorts of materials is being monitored.

Reading Logs

When students are using a variety of reading materials in several different situations during the day, it is best if each child keeps a record of whatever she or he has read and reactions to it. This record, called a *reading log,* is like a diary of reading experiences and should be the subject of regular conferences between you and the students.

Read Nancie Atwell's *In the Middle: Writing, Reading and Learning with Adolescents* (Boynton/Cook, 1987) for good examples of students writing about their reading.

The reading log should be a separate notebook or a section in a notebook. A page at the front or back ought to be reserved for making a list of all the books (and other longer texts) that the student has read. Dates of beginning and completion should be recorded.

Most of the entries in the log will refer to storybooks students have selected to read during the reading period, at other times during the day, and at home. Entries may also refer to information books, magazine articles, longer newspaper stories, poetry, books written by classmates, and other significant texts.

Reading Conferences

You should hold regular reading conferences with pupils (some teachers combine reading conferences with the writing conferences discussed in Chapter 10). During these conferences the student may engage in several activities:

Such a range of activities provides you with a valid basis for understanding a student's progress.

- going over his or her log, discussing what has been read, reactions to these materials, new words learned, and plans for additional reading
- reading silently so that the two of you can discuss what was read, providing you with the opportunity to gain insights into aspects of the student's reading comprehension
- reading orally from familiar material, giving you the opportunity to listen as the child interprets the text with voice tones, inflections, and so forth
- reading orally from unfamiliar material, providing you with the opportunity to note strategies of dealing with unknown words, deviations from the text, rereadings, and so forth

- undertaking any tasks (reading word lists, retelling stories, determining author's purposes) that you believe particularly important for her or him
- writing, at your request or voluntarily, in response to something that has been read and sharing that with you

The Reading Period

The daily reading period ought to be about an hour in length in the middle and upper grades but need not be organized in the same way every day. (In some schools basal series are used two or three days a week and literature selections on the remaining days. In other situations only literature is used.) Components of a literature-emphasis program would be as follows:

These goals are an indication of the significance of reading aloud for all aspects of language arts teaching.

1. *Reading Aloud* (15 minutes)

   You should read to your class every day for approximately fifteen minutes (more is preferred for older students). As has been stressed throughout this book, reading aloud from high-quality literature accomplishes several important goals: children hear the best books and gain an appreciation for them; they add many words to their vocabulary; they are exposed to countless sentences, which helps them develop a sense of what a sentence is; and they may be stimulated to think more about their own writing attempts. Most of all, however, being read to is highly enjoyable and builds good attitudes toward reading.

Select only crucial content for class lessons and repeat it in varied formats so that all students have ample opportunity to learn.

2. *Class Lesson* (15 minutes)

   For approximately ten or fifteen minutes you ought to give attention to skills, strategies, or understandings that you have decided to present to the entire class. As with teaching done during the writing period (discussed in Chapter 11), what you choose to work on ought to be influenced by what you have observed pupils doing during the times when they have been reading.

   Lessons will, then, cover a variety of topics. On a given day the focus might be on root words, prefixes and suffixes, or it could be on the differences between legends, fairy tales, and myths.

Of course, you can combine SSR or DEAR (Drop Everything and Read) with a basal reading program.

3. *Reading Time* (25 minutes)

   Depending on the maturity of your particular classroom group, you should plan to allot about twenty-five minutes to student reading. You may wish to reserve a portion of this time, or all of it, for SSR (Sustained Silent Reading) when everyone reads without interruptions. Or you may schedule SSR for two or three days a week so that activities during the reading period can include such nonsilent activities as conferences with you, meetings of literature response groups, and practice for readers' theater presentations.

4. *Sharing Time* (10 minutes)

   At the end of the reading period, some time should be reserved for students to share what they have been reading with the class or one or more members of it. (Some reasons for sharing are discussed in Chapter 15.)

Students' Reading Experiences

During the reading period (and at other appropriate times during the day) a student may have reading experiences as a member of the entire class, as a member of a small group, and as an individual. You need to plan for opportunities of each type since all will make several contributions to the child's growth in reading.

Periods of silent reading are a common feature of classrooms in many schools.

Whole-Class Experiences. As an entire class, students may have many different kinds of reading experiences. This is especially true in a classroom program where activities involve reading in conjunction with other areas of the language arts—speaking, listening, and writing.

- The class is read to by you or one of the class members.
- The class does choral reading.
- Students discuss favorite books and authors, reading excerpts they especially like.
- Students do oral reading of poetry.
- Students do a "readers' theater" production (as described in Chapter 5).
- You demonstrate a reading strategy for the class.

Studies have found that pupils in the low-ability reading groups spend most of their time completing workbook pages and other duplicated materials. *All* readers need involvement with meaningful texts as their major activity.

Small-Group Experiences. Groups of students may profitably meet for specified amounts of time to work together on a particular facet of reading. (They probably should not meet continually as an "ability group"; that practice too often has negative effects on motivation and attitudes.)

- Several children with a special need may receive help from you at the same time.
- Those with interest in stories of a particular type could come together to read several of them.
- Students who have read the same book might wish to plan a skit based on an episode in it.
- A group working on a mathematics, science, or social studies project will likely read some of the same materials.

- Those identifying sources for study of a particular topic could meet with the school librarian for suggestions.
- Those interested in a particular computer activity (*Where in the World is Carmen Sandiego?* for example) come together and read from the screen.

Individual Experiences. In most ways an individual activity, reading leaves no shortage of opportunities for individual experience. Variety should be sought, however, in order to meet individual needs.

- A student confers with you concerning selection of a book or other reading material.
- A child goes to the school library to confer with the librarian and select materials on a topic.
- A student selects something to take home and read to a family member.
- A child confers with you about his or her reading log.
- A student writes in her or his reading log.
- A student uses a computer program to check her or his ability to correctly answer comprehension questions.

Some teachers prepare special "take home" bags of reading materials.

READING ACTIVITIES

As you develop an increasingly effective reading program, you can benefit from using a decision-making framework to help guide your thinking. Such a plan ought to include a view of what the most important goals are and a conception of what is required to accomplish the major objectives you have in mind.

Guidelines for Teaching Reading

Several principal objectives should guide decisions regarding reading instruction.

Lifelong Reading. Your reading program must have the goal of helping every youngster to become a person for whom reading will be a significant activity throughout life. Reading instruction in our schools has commonly produced a large number of people who can read but do not, an outcome that is not good enough. Some of the blame for this result must rest with the use of reading materials that have been formulated primarily as vehicles for presenting long lists of skills and isolated words to be studied systematically. You should avoid these materials and teaching methods.

Millions of children have learned to read through use of basal readers—but some have not.

Learn to Read by Reading. In the initial chapters of this volume it was pointed out that very young children learn language by speaking and listening and learn to write by beginning to scribble. With all the attention given to the teaching of reading, the fact that youngsters learn to read mainly by being read to and reading themselves sometimes gets lost. As you make decisions about your reading program, it is very important to be sure that class time is not wasted on interminable skill drills. Real books and the whole act of reading must be involved if the best results are to be achieved.

The beginning of a lasting interest in reading.

Emphasis on Meaning. Too often reading programs include a high proportion of activities that lack meaning for children. Exercises involving the use of complex rules that have been memorized but do not apply consistently are examples of activities lacking in meaning for the student. Practice materials based on underlining the correct word and filling in the blanks mean little to students.

Components of Reading Performance

Some students learn to read easily and seem to require little direct teaching; they pick up skills on their own and have the ability to read almost anything that interests them. Others need more than experience, and teachers must be prepared to conduct instructional activities that cover necessary approaches to reading processes.

This section discusses procedures and activities for helping children learn how to read and for encouraging them to want to read. The topics included are ones you would find in teachers' manuals for published reading programs but you can provide needed teaching and practice within the type of reading program you prefer.

Good teachers match learning experiences with students' needs and characteristics.

Word Recognition. The ability to recognize, recall, or decode a word is basic to reading. Several interrelated skills are involved in such word recognition. No one of these alone always works, nor do all children need an equal amount of instruction in each of them. Several types of activities assist in gaining such skills.

Sight Recall. Adults generally recognize at sight most of the words they encounter in reading. Mature readers simply know the words and do not have to stop to figure out what they are. They have gained this ability through their experiences, having heard many words, seen them often in various print forms, and possibly written most of them at one time or another.

One of the principal goals of teaching in the early grades is the development of a beginning *sight vocabulary* (the importance of recognizing words in print was discussed in Chapter 4). These known words are used for reading and as a basis for learning unknown words (if you know *fast* you are likely to be able to figure out *fasten.*)

In the middle- and upper-elementary grades, most students will have very large sight vocabularies—hundreds or even thousands of words. Less frequently occurring words will be in their listening and speaking vocabularies and will be quickly recognized because of the contexts in which they appear. Children who require specific assistance with development of sight vocabularies will be helped most by extensive reading of easy but interesting material. (Consult a reading teacher for advice.)

Context Clues. An important strategy for identifying words not immediately recognized involves use of context, the sentence in which the word appears, as well as the larger context provided by the story or other form of reading material. Context clues become available to readers as products of the meaning and language understandings described in a preceding section of this chapter. If there are pictures, as there often are in books at the elementary-school level, those will be part of the context too.

Thus, the reader draws on many types of information in making an "informed guess" as to the indentity of a particular word. If the guess is accurate and meaning is advanced and if the word is seen a few more times, it will likely become part of the reader's stock of sight words.

Some youngsters will spend time practicing skills if the activity involves operating a computer.

Skill in use of contexts depends to a great extent on students' knowing many words, synonyms for words, figures of speech, and other aspects of language. Activities such as the following can help develop the ability to use the context in which a word appears:

1. Put a paragraph on chart paper and cover several words—nouns one time, verbs another, and so forth—with small gummed pieces of paper. Have students use the context to determine possibilities for the hidden words. (As an alternative, cover all letters of the word except the first.)

2. Present homonyms (*bear, fair,* etc.) and illustrate their meanings with sentences:

   I cannot *bear* to see you suffer.

   The *bear* ran down the road.

3. Write numerous sentences showing different meanings of common words. Try *run, walk, back,* and *step.*

4. List synonyms for words in a story. Discuss shadings of meaning and determine which words might be more acceptable than others.

5. Ask students to circle the clues to the meanings of the underlined words in sentences such as these:

   The <u>submarine</u> is a reliable underwater craft.

   After Sue bought the groceries for her mother, she <u>purchased</u> candy with the change.

Structural Analysis. Structural analysis involves looking for known parts within unknown words. When a reader knows component parts of a word that has not been immediately recognized, he or she can often successfully analyze it. Some words are compounds, and a reader may know the meaning of one of the words forming the compound (*campground,* for example). This may be enough of a clue (especially if other word-recognition skills are used) for the reader to succeed in identifying the word.

Further structural analysis clues are provided by other word elements:

inflected endings: (*-s, -ed, -ing, -ly,* etc.)
prefixes: (*un-, re-, con-,* etc.)
suffixes: (*-tion, -al, -ness,* etc.)
roots: (*vert, kind, tal,* etc.)

Knowledge of how contractions and plurals are formed and how words may be divided into syllables is also helpful in structural analysis (and in spelling as discussed in Chapter 8).

The ideal approach for teaching about structural analysis involves embedded lessons for individuals or small groups. The teaching should be done to meet students' immediate needs if you believe that motivation is high and the flow of reading will not be significantly interrupted (when the word is part of the title of a heading, for example). Otherwise, you should supply the unrecognized word and then come back to it later.

Activities useful in teaching about structural analysis include the following:

1. Present students with inflected and derived forms of words (for example, *happier, making, shorter, carries, flies*) and have them identify the root word of each.

Some of these exercises can be put into a game format.

2. Ask class members to find the root common to a group of words—*reporter, portable, import,* and so on.

3. List words that have the same suffix (*helpful, tearful, hopeful,* for example) and ask pupils to infer the meaning of the suffix.

4. Have pupils make lists of compound words or put words together to make compounds.

5. Provide lists of words to be divided into syllables.

6. Write prefixes on cards and place them in a box. Have students draw a card and supply a word that begins with that prefix.

7. Provide lists of contractions (*shouldn't, can't, I'll, won't,* etc.) for pupils to change to the contracted words.

Many such structural analysis exercises are available as computer software programs if you have students who could profit from using them.

Phonics. A shortened version of the term *graphophonic system* is *phonics,* referring usually to the use of letter-sound associations in reading. Phonics is quite important in reading, of course, as has been pointed out in this text. We have also noted in Chapter 4 that there is a controversy concerning the use of phonics as the principal way of teaching young children to read. Our position is that reading to and with children is what should be considered most important in beginning reading and that phonics is best learned through a variety of embedded lessons:

- Teacher writes on charts and chalkboard, asking for spelling suggestions, showing that children's names begin with the same letters and sounds, and so forth.
- Children do shared reading of large-format books, looking at beginning letters of words and hearing how they are pronounced.
- Children look at predictable and other memorized books, noticing that rhyming words often have the same endings.
- Children copy words they want to use, paying close attention to the sequence of letters.
- Children practice keyboarding, giving attention to the sequences of letters.
- Children use invented spellings as they write, searching for the alphabet letters likely to spell the sounds they need.

The major question in phonics teaching is how to make sure that the reader has enough knowledge and skill in that area without burdening him or her with an extensive body of "rules" that do not help much or at all. You should decide how much your own students need and find opportunities to determine which associations are well developed. One such list might well include:

Beginning to Read by Adams (MIT Press, 1990) includes a comparison of the contents of several phonics programs.

beginning consonant sounds: t, s, b, c, p, f, d, h, r, m, w, l, j, y, k, w, v, z, j sound of g, qu
final consonant sounds: t, s, b, p, d, g, r, m, n, w, l, z, x, ck
vowels—short sounds: a, e, i, o, u
vowels—long sounds: final e pattern; digraphs ee, ea, oa
consonant digraphs: ch, wh, sh
consonant blends: bl, st, tr, dr, pr, str

There are many ways to assist children who seem to require additional practice in using phonics understandings and skills:

1. Think of words that rhyme, write them, and discuss why they rhyme, or seem to.
2. Think of words that begin with the same sound, write them, and discuss why they begin the same way, or seem to.
3. Try "phonics riddles" such as "Think of something in the kitchen that rhymes with *pink*" or "Think of something in the bathroom that begins like *toy*."
4. List "families" of words (*cake, take, make, lake,* etc.)
5. Change the beginnings and endings of words to make other words (*man–can, meat–meal, walk–talk,* etc.)
6. Substitute vowels to make other words (*cap-cup-cop, big-bag-beg-bug,* etc.)

Computers with speech-synthesizer components may be used with phonics software to provide additional practice for students who require special attention.

Reading Comprehension.
Students need to have good sight vocabularies and well-developed strategies for dealing with unknown words, but all this will be of little consequence if they only pronounce words and fail to comprehend much of what is read. Book and related experiences that begin in the early years and continue when they come to school should lead children to understand that meaning is to be expected and that they should constantly monitor their own comprehension to make sure that what is read to them and by them makes sense.

Comprehension should receive attention only following the reading of an entire text—an article, a story, or a book. Whether or not a sentence has been understood is not genuine *comprehension*.

Students need to see what the reading task is and then apply appropriate strategies, but even many adults can't manage this.

In this book we have taken the position that meanings are not given directly to readers. When the individual reads, he or she *constructs* a meaning, and this may or may not be the same for all who interact with that text. Several different kinds of meanings may result.

Individual Meanings. The reader comes to the reading situation with a background of knowledge, beliefs, and language understandings. What she or he constructs from a text will be individualistic, perhaps unique to that person. (One individual reads a pamphlet and finds it a logical analysis of a social problem; someone else sees it as nothing more than hate-filled propaganda.)

Young readers, almost by definition, know less and can do less than older readers, so their constructions are often viewed as peculiar. Certainly, when children in elementary classes are asked to set forth the meanings they have derived from something read the results are often viewed as "wrong" by teachers. (The same sort of thing occurs at the secondary-school and college levels when the instructor insists that students "didn't understand" the poem or novel; it's a matter of whose constructed meaning is preferred by those who decide that sort of thing.)

An elementary-school example might involve a child who reads a fable, *The Tortoise and the Hare,* and constructs a meaning: "The rabbit and the turtle had a race and the rabbit let the turtle win because he was tired." A well-informed teacher realizes that fables are likely to be only partially understood by younger children; they simply cannot think in terms of "lessons to be learned" or "underlying meanings." (Children's thinking has been discussed in several chapters of this book.) As adults we have to choose between accepting the child's construction of meaning as appropriate for her or him or "wrong" and in need of immediate correction.

Literal Meanings. When reading a text, the more mature reader may construct both a personal meaning ("That hare is like my brother when we clean our room") and a literal rendition of what the author intended to present. This direct type of comprehension is what most people mean by "reading for understanding" and is generally what is expected and valued in class and on achievement tests.

Literal meaning is often important. In reading material such as a business letter, instructions for assembling a bicycle, or directions for driving to a meeting, the reader is concerned with literal meaning—full and precise comprehension of what is on the page. Almost always in such circumstances the reader's questions are assumed to be self-evident (What do I have to do? Where do I turn?). Motivation is automatically present, then, and there is no reason to attempt to make inferences or otherwise look beyond the text for underlying meanings.

Literal reading can be too limited, of course. In the case of the tortoise's story, the reader may understand that this animal won the race but see nothing additional worthy of discussion.

Multiple or Competing Meanings. As educated adults, we commonly see several meanings in a text. (*Call of the Wild* may be seen as an adventure story, a book that follows the theme of "man over nature," or a message concerning the importance of protecting wilderness areas.) Again, the thinking abilities of the reader are important, especially the capacity for taking the point of view of others. The reader needs to ask questions such as: What was the author of this

Multiple possible meanings make for interesting discussions.

text intending to convey? What would someone who knew nothing about this understand it to mean? What are the messages intended by the author? What other meanings might someone get from it? What do I think of those interpretations?

Elementary students, then, do construct their own meanings as they read and can begin to understand that other meanings are possible, too. As they have further opportunities for discussions involving stories and other kinds of texts, their ability to think about what they read will expand rapidly.

Of course, questions about what a book, story, text, poem, or passage *means* abound and have occupied the attention of profound thinkers for many years. The meaning of *comprehension,* then, is relative to a reader and to a situation. As students reach the middle grades they are capable of such advanced thinking, as long as there is ample opportunity for discussion among themselves. Aspects of this matter of interpretation are discussed in Chapter 13, especially in the section Critical Reading and Thinking.

An Oral Reading Guide

1. Make sure there is a purpose.
2. Prepare in advance and practice.
3. Read carefully and clearly.
4. Speak loudly enough to be heard.
5. Read with appropriate expression.

Oral Reading. Reading aloud is an integral part of classroom functioning:

1. Reading aloud is done as an oral language activity, including choral reading, readers' theater, and interpretation of a poem or other piece of literature (see Chapter 5).
2. As a part of the writing process, the writer reads something she or he has written to a group of classmates for their suggestions and questions (see Chapter 10).

Reading orally into a tape recorder and then listening to the tape can be a useful activity.

3. In literature response groups, participants read selections aloud to make a discussion point or simply to enjoy the sound of the language the author has used.

4. When having a conference with a child, you will occasionally want him or her to read aloud to check particular skills or to do an informal reading assessment (see the section Reading Tests at the end of this chapter).

There are, then, legitimate reasons for children to practice the skills of reading aloud. Since competent silent reading is the behavior that ought to be emphasized in the school program, such practices as taking turns reading parts of a story aloud should not receive much attention.

Attitudes Toward Reading

A successful classroom reading program produces children who choose to read as an important life activity. Building children's interest in reading begins when they are quite young and being read to regularly and continues throughout the elementary-school years. All reading instruction should be meaningful and enjoyable; rigid and boring activities teach students to dislike reading, learning, and school itself. In addition to developing a student-oriented classroom program, there are other steps you can take.

1. Show delight yourself. Tell your students about something you have read or are reading.

2. Emphasize the utility of reading. When an interesting question comes up, seek out relevant reading material.

Reading in an informal setting is enjoyable.

3. Find out what your students need to do to obtain a card at the local library and help them do that.

4. Collaborate with school and public librarians on programs to encourage reading.

5. Bring in a rug, an easy chair, or some pillows for a classroom reading area (see also suggestions for a reading corner in Chapter 15).

6. Make a special effort to identify books in the school library that would likely be of interest to your pupils.

7. Dramatize episodes from popular books, do art activities depicting favorite characters or scenes, and select music to be played as background to oral reading.

READING AND THE CURRICULUM

Reading is involved in every school subject, not only literature but also music (words of songs), physical education (safety warnings), and art (directions for using materials). In most classrooms a substantial amount of reading is done in such areas as science and social studies, while reading and writing are becoming more significant in mathematics. (Chapter 13 focuses on informational reading, studying, and doing research.)

Literature and the Reading Program

A teacher needs extensive knowledge of children's books, both fiction and nonfiction.

In many classrooms there is ample opportunity for students to read literature in the form of stories, novels, plays, poems and other material. Basal reading series often contain a substantial amount of literature, and in some rooms nearly the entire reading program consists of literature.

Literature Response Groups. Response groups composed of five to eight students who have read the same book may meet during the reading period, or at other times during the day when possible. Such groups can make an important contribution to the reading program. In selecting books, children have something to say about which book they will read. If you have five or six groups in the room and make seven or eight titles available, it will usually be possible to accommodate nearly everyone with a first or second choice. Thus, motivation for reading a particular book will be high.

Procedures for Groups. Response groups meet on the basis of the members' choice of a particular book. Perhaps six students want to read *Where the Red Fern Grows* after you have told them a bit about it and the other titles available. There are no restrictions on reading ability, so some of the better readers and some of those who are not so accomplished are likely to be in the same group. This means that activities of the group will include helping a few members by reading portions to them and providing assistance with their reading.

Groups, sometimes called *reading circles,* make decisions about when to meet, how many pages to read by the next session, and how to organize their discussion. Younger students often meet as many as five times to discuss a book, whereas older ones often read the entire text before meeting to talk about it. The activities group members may engage in are many.

When several students are reading the same interesting book, there will be much to discuss.

Writing. All participants write about the book in their logs. At a minimum, they should record what pages they read on which day and make some notes about their reaction to the story, what new words they encountered, and what questions and comments they have. It is to be expected that some will want to write much more in the way of reaction, both before discussions take place and after. Since you will be talking with students about the content of their logs, the two of you will likely discuss the book at that time.

This is reading aloud for a *purpose.*

Reading Aloud. In discussing events and characters in the book being read, students will find it useful to refer to certain passages and read these to the other members of the group. They may even choose to tape-record content and play the tape for the others.

Partner Reading. In addition to meeting as a total group, students may wish to pair off and read to each other from the current book. (This may be very helpful to those who are finding the book a bit too difficult in spots.) Also, friendships may develop among children who enjoy reading very much.

Be sure that you have adequately demonstrated appropriate discussion behavior.

Group Discussion. If students are beginning to learn how to carry on a book discussion or if the book is one you are particularly interested in, you may wish to join them. Whether or not you participate directly, you should regularly provide guidance so that students will gain in their ability to participate in literature response groups.

Extension Activities. After a book has been read, members of the group may be interested in dramatizing parts of the story, producing related art work, talking about other writings by the same author, or considering books on the same or a related topic. Some may not wish to participate in these activities and should be permitted to go on to other reading.

Passages in some books (The Old Testament, for example) have been extensively discussed for hundreds of years.

Benefits of Group Book Discussions. There are many benefits to group book discussions, and these are preferable to the use of "study guides" for a book, exercises that resemble workbook pages on vocabulary, analysis of characters, and the other skills emphasized in some basal readers. Book discussions emphasize that

1. Reading is a transactional process between the reader and the text, as has been mentioned. Such transactions are more full and rich when each reader takes into account not only his or her own interpretations but also those of other members of the group.
2. Reading and discussing in a group builds the trust that is necessary if children are to feel comfortable in setting forth their own ideas.
3. Talking with classmates about the important life-related matters so often at the heart of good books benefits each child personally and usually leads to a deeper involvement with the book being read.
4. Positive experiences related to group reading will often encourage students to read more on their own and to discuss what they have read with others.

Benefits of Reading Literature. Whether or not literature response groups are used in a classroom there are many benefits to be gained by encouraging the reading of literature.

Current editions of basal reading series contain many literature selections but not many entire texts, of course.

1. Works of literature are more fully developed than conventional basal reading content and therefore more likely to capture children's interest.
2. Literature is written because authors are trying to communicate ideas important to them: reading is then a genuine writer-audience interaction.
3. The child's imagination is much more likely to be stimulated by a time-honored work of literature than by a basal selection.
4. The wider vocabulary and more expressive language of literature make a significant contribution to a child's cultural education.
5. Students are introduced to stories, characters, and authors that they will remember all their lives.
6. They are also learning about literature as a field of study, becoming familiar with forms of writing, story plots, character development, and dialogue.
7. Literature touches children's lives in significant ways—their hopes, fears, sense of humor, and personal experiences.

Relationships Between Reading and Writing

As was discussed in Chapters 10 and 11, there are advantages to capitalizing on relationships between writing and reading. As children write, they reread what they have written, and while doing this they assess the extent to which what they have written makes sense and accomplishes what they had hoped. If they have had many experiences in judging texts—noting what perspective the author takes, the logical order of presentation, and the choice of colorful and expressive language—they will be more likely to consider the use of such features in their own writing.

As students read, they learn more about writing, and writing experiences influence the development of reading strategies. Some examples are:

- When trying spelling approximations as they write first drafts and then checking these for accuracy later, students are learning more about phonics.
- Since maturing writers will think about finding just the right word to convey a particular meaning, they will be more likely to notice when an author has made a good choice.
- Young writers who are attempting to construct good sentences, paragraphs, and texts should be guided to examine those features in the materials they are reading. (This is better for elementary students than attempts to teach about formulas for "writing a paragraph.")

Reading in Other Subjects

Elementary students are usually expected to read in specific areas, most commonly mathematics, science, and social studies.

Mathematics. Appropriate teaching of mathematics in the elementary classroom begins with concrete experiences and real materials. As children use these counters, shapes, rulers, and other devices they learn to use the precise words of mathematics: "tens' place" as opposed to "tenths' place," "isosceles triangle" as opposed to "isosceles right triangle," and "common factor" as opposed to "common multiple."

After students demonstrate that they can discuss mathematical concepts and operations with competence, the next appropriate step is for them to write about mathematical situations: *Eighty-three means eight tens and three ones; If you have a blue shirt, a green shirt, white shorts, brown shorts, and black shorts, you will have six different outfits; The distance around a circle is a little more than three times the distance across the circle through the center.*

Only after ample experience in listening, speaking, and writing in relation to mathematics should students be asked to read about mathematical situations. This is because language is used very precisely in mathematics and this kind of control cannot be assumed in the absence of many high-quality learning experiences. (A student who appears to be thinking of the concept "half as much" says "twice as less," indicating that, although basic understanding is present, much more talk will be needed before exposure to related story problems.)

The primacy of oral language is evident in all aspects of a child's learning.

Some children may, however, be sufficiently interested in a topic that they can read about it and learn some mathematics at the same time. Youngsters who read the daily newspaper will call upon number concepts when reading the sports page (scores, batting averages), the weather report (average daily temperature, amount of precipitation), the stock market report (gains and losses), and advertisements (sale discounts, sizes). Such interests may lead students to read magazines and informational books on these mathematics-related topics.

Science. In science many technical words are used, so it is important to build a substantial amount of knowledge background through laboratory activities, discussion, and writing before expecting competent reading. In preparing students for reading science content, it is also very helpful to expose them to the common kinds of texts found in science—descriptions (solar system), discussions of processes (photosynthesis), classifications (species of fish), and cause-effect relationships (what causes rain). Some of this may be done in connection with discussions of types of thinking, too.

Because science is a topic that often appears in the daily news, children can read popular accounts of scientific issues such as the space program, changes in climate, conservation, disease, pollution, and animal life. When there is substantial interest, young students can often go on to read rather difficult articles and books about scientific matters. These sorts of books should be available in the classroom, along with equipment and supplies that can be used to carry out science activities. Also, there should be plants and animals in the room and books that tell about them.

Social Studies. Reading in social studies can be relatively easy for most children because the topics are likely to be close to their own experiences and events in the community. In addition to studying and doing reports (discussed in Chapter 13), there are many topics about which they can read:

> *Current Events:* Children can read about elections, the Olympics, the sales tax, our relations with other countries, and trade and commerce.
> *Holidays and Commemorations:* There are many books and other reading materials concerning Thanksgiving, presidents' birthdays, the birthdays of other famous people, Independence Day, and important dates and events in history.
> *Cultural Ties:* There will likely be interest in learning more about cultural events in the local community, histories of cultural groups, and the lives of people from particular cultural backgrounds.

Writing and reading often go together in the area of social studies.

Social Concerns: Areas such as health, drugs, pollution, conservation, family relationships, and one's own development are of concern to children, and appropriate reading materials should be made available to them.

Services and Occupations: Because of personal interest, perhaps career exploration, children may wish to read about law enforcement, medical care, computer science, business, or agriculture.

Books touching on many of these topics are discussed in Chapter 15.

ASSESSMENT OF READING

Because reading success is considered extremely important in our society, a great deal of attention is devoted to evaluating students' progress. In many states and districts, testing of reading performance is mandated at several points during the elementary years. Most assessment is intended to furnish information to interested groups: parents, school boards, administrators, state and national agencies, and, of course, teachers. (Students should also do self-evaluation regularly and receive some indication of how you view their progress.)

In this book we have suggested that assessment should be a continuous process, with you as the teacher collecting information that both contributes to planning and aids in understanding pupil performance. It has also been emphasized that samples of children's school work and information concerning the language processes they typically use ought to be collected in a comprehensive portfolio.

With regard to assessment of youngsters' reading performance, various approaches need attention, including observation and several kinds of testing.

Give attention to reading rates in the middle grades (combine this with teaching the use of the stopwatch and computing of averages).

Observation

As you meet with individual children and observe them in reading situations, numerous matters will come to your attention. If you do audio- and videotaping of students' oral reading it will be helpful to go over these tapes several times in order to consider the various aspects of their reading. At times of observation there are certain guidelines you ought to consider following:

1. Keep a page in a notebook (or a separate file card) for each child. Note what the student is reading, how fluently it is done, what sorts of reading materials are favored, and how well the reader comprehends different kinds of content.

2. Use observational aids such as checklists concerning, for example, which strategies are used to deal with unknown words, how fast sight vocabulary is accumulating, or what happens when the student encounters various forms of punctuation.

3. Make notes concerning a reader's apparent attitudes toward reading—the extent to which reading is selected as an activity when there are choices, how carefully books are examined in the library, the frequency with which references are made to books kept at home, and so forth.

Checklists, teachers' summaries of notes, and audio- and videotape recordings may all be added to each student's portfolio, either a comprehensive language arts portfolio or one limited to reading.

Reading Inventories

Informal Reading Inventories by Johnson, Kress, and Pikulski (International Reading Association, 1987) contains many useful suggestions.

Informal reading inventories, or "running records" of a child's reading performance may be used to assess levels of achievement and to identify specific difficulties. Such procedures involve taking careful note of how an individual student reads a particular selection orally. The notations are usually done directly on a copy of the passage, so you should have photocopies of texts at different difficulty levels available. Usually these selections are presented without the child having had any prior opportunity to read them.

Again, these may be videotaped (if you do this frequently students will become accustomed to it and it won't bother them) and preserved in a portfolio. They may well be shared with parents, too, as long as there has been some preparation for the experience and they have some knowledge of what it means.

Reading Tests

For a comprehensive discussion of reading tests, see *How to Increase Reading Ability* by Harris and Sipay (listed in the References).

There are a large number of reading tests available for use in the schools. Most are designed to obtain information concerning how the reading of an individual, class, or larger group compares with that done by other similar people. Tests are also commonly designed to be administered to groups. Other types of tests may be used, depending on the objectives of those doing the selection.

Standardized Reading Achievement Tests. By far the most significant reading achievement tests are classified as *standardized* and *norm-referenced.* A test, if it is to be thought of as standardized, must always be administered in the same way (the directions are provided) so that the results will be comparable in different situations. Achievement tests in reading are also usually *norm-referenced,* meaning that the test has been administered to a large number of selected individuals so that scores are relative to certain averages.

Results of norm-referenced tests are best reported as *percentiles,* numerical values that indicate where an individual's score is located on a scale from 1 to 99. When the score converts to a percentile value close to 50, for example, it is about average for her or his group, determined by age or grade level. Higher or lower scores and associated percentile ratings indicate how the scores compare with those of others. If the score is very high—yielding a percentile of 80, perhaps—indications are that the person tested reads better than about 80 percent of those who originally took the test. A low percentile rating of 25, however, would mean that about 75 percent of those taking the test scored higher than this person.

Other Reading Tests. Other tests are designed for individual administration, or test only a particular aspect of reading, are not standardized, or do not yield results that are readily compared from one person to another.

Uses of Reading Tests. The testing of reading poses numerous problems, most of which involve how the tests are used. No matter how much effort is made to develop an instrument, there is always potential for misinterpretation of results, so very important decisions (whether or not students should be placed in a particular group or program, to cite the most important example) should never be made on the basis of a single test score.

Another confusing aspect of reading tests arises when results are presented as *grade-level equivalents*. These equivalents are sometimes used to associate performance on reading tests with grade levels rather than the more meaningful percentiles described in a preceding section. Misunderstanding arises when, for instance, a student entering the fourth grade (grade level 4.0) does very well on a norm-referenced test and is reported as having a grade-level equivalent of 8.0. The problem is that this figure does not mean that the child should be given eighth-grade material to read. (Nor would a reported value of 2.0 indicate that second-grade books ought to be assigned.) All that such results can legitimately be interpreted as meaning is that the child is either a very good reader or a rather poor one, conclusions that could be reached by a teacher without administering any test. The reason given for continuing to report scores as grade-level equivalents, particularly for entire school districts or buildings, is that federal and state agencies and local school boards find them convenient.

See *Reading: What Can Be Measured?* by Farr and Carey (International Reading Association, 1986).

There are many reading achievement tests on the market and selecting one is a complex task. How the test was formulated, the nature of the group on which norms have been based, the ease with which it can be administered and scored, and the extent to which it is consistent with program objectives should all be considered important factors. A significant problem regarding the use of such tests is that teachers and others who receive the results must be very careful when interpreting what they mean and how they might be used responsibly.

One possible use of test results is to include them (or the tests themselves) in the child's portfolio along with the other types of assessment devices discussed in this section. You may wish to write commentaries on youngsters' performances on tests of all kinds and relate the outcomes to other materials in the portfolio.

A FINAL WORD

This chapter has emphasized two major concerns for the elementary-school reading program: children should read for enjoyment and what is read ought to mean something to them. Reading for meaning and enjoying reading are much more significant for children's lives than long lists of skills that simply are not as important as they have often been made out to be. It is the good story or well-written text on an interesting topic that is basic for children.

The next chapter will examine types of reading that involve learning content and doing library research. Again, active involvement is central, so you should be sure that, for each child, reading is for the purpose of accomplishing tasks that are intrinsically interesting, related to the classroom program, and intellectually challenging.

References

Alvermann, Donna E.; Dillon, Deborah R.; and O'Brien, David G. *Using Discussion to Promote Reading Comprehension.* International Reading Association, 1987.

Anderson, Richard C.; Hiebert, Elfrieda H.; Scott, Judith A.; and Wilkinson, Ian A. G. *Becoming a Nation of Readers.* U. S. Department of Education, 1984.

Choate, J. S., and Rakes, T. A. *Detecting and Correcting Special Needs in Reading.* Allyn and Bacon, 1988.

Cook, Doris M. *A Guide to Curriculum Planning in Reading.* Wisconsin Department of Public Instruction, 1986.

Cooper, J. David. *Improving Reading Comprehension.* Houghton Mifflin, 1986.

Cullinan, Bernice E., ed. *Children's Literature in the Reading Program.* International Reading Association, 1987.

Ekwall, Eldon E., and Shanker, James L. *Teaching Reading in the Elementary School.* Charles E. Merrill, 1985.

Hansen, Jane. *When Writers Read.* Heinemann, 1987.

Harris, Albert J., and Sipay, Edward R. *How to Increase Reading Ability: A Guide to Developmental and Remedial Methods,* 8th ed. Longman, 1985.

Jewell, Margaret Greer, and Zintz, Miles V. *Learning to Read Naturally.* Kendall/Hunt, 1986.

Karlin, Robert, and Karlin, Andrea. *Teaching Elementary Reading,* 4th ed. Harcourt Brace Jovanovich, 1987.

Laughlin, Mildred Knight, and Watt, Letty S. *Developing Learning Skills Through Children's Literature.* Oryx Press, 1986.

Moss, Joy F. *Focus Units in Literature: A Handbook for Elementary School Teachers.* National Council of Teachers of English, 1984.

Reinking, David, ed. *Reading and Computers.* Teachers College Press, 1987.

Routman, Regie. *Transitions from Literature to Literacy.* Heinemann Educational Books, 1988.

Short, Kathy G., and Pierce, Kathryn M. *Talking About Books.* Heinemann Educational Books, 1990.

Strickland, Dorothy S.; Feeley, Joan; and Wepner, Shelly. *Using Computers in the Teaching of Reading.* Teachers College Press, 1987.

Swift, Kathleen. "Try Reading Workshop in Your Classroom." *The Reading Teacher* 46 (February 1993), pp. 366–371.

Tway, Eileen, *Writing Is Reading: 26 Ways to Connect.* National Council of Teachers of English, 1985.

Vacca, J. L.; Vacca, R. T.; and Gove, M. K. *Reading and Learning to Read.* Little, Brown, 1987.

Weaver, Constance. *Reading Process and Practice.* Heinemann Educational Books, 1988.

Teaching Resources

KITS

Clues for Better Reading. Curriculum Associates (grades 1–5).

Developing Reading Power. Zaner-Bloser (grades 3–6).

Fantastic Reading. Dale Seymour (grades 5–6).

Reading Laboratory. Science Research Associates (several kits, with cassettes, teacher's handbook, and booklets; various grade levels).

Society for Visual Education produces kits for primary and upper grades that focus on comprehension (each has filmstrips, audiocassettes, skill sheets, and a guide).

LITERATURE SETS

Bridges. Scholastic (K–grade 6).

I Can Read Book and Cassette Library. Harper and Row (twenty-four storybooks and audiocassettes).

Language Works. Modern Curriculum Press (all grade levels).

MCP Literature. Modern Curriculum Press (grades 3–6).

Odyssey. Harcourt Brace Jovanovich (K–grade 6).

Quest Extenders. Scholastic (study guides; grades 4–6).

COMPUTER SOFTWARE

Cloze Plus. Milliken, 1983 (grades 1–6).

The Comprehension Connection. Milliken (grades 4–6).

Comprehension Power. Milliken (grades 4–6).

Context Clues. The Learning Well, 1984 (grades 1–4).

Customized Alphabet Drill. Random House (grades 1–6).

Explore-a-Story. D. C. Heath (K–grade 5).

Kittens, Kids, and a Frog. Hartley (primary grades).

Microcourse Reading. Houghton Mifflin (grades 3–6).

Mystery Mazes. Educational Activities (intermediate grades).

Reading to Learn. Society for Visual Education, 1986 (grades 3–6).

Return to Reading Series. Media Basics, 1984 (grades 4 and up).

Snoopy's Reading Machine. Random House (primary grades).

Sound Ideas. Houghton Mifflin, 1986 (grades 1–4).

Speed Reader 11. Davidson (intermediate grades).

Stickybear Reading Comprehension. Weekly Reader (grades 1–6).

Success with Reading. Scholastic, 1985 (grades 3–6).

Word Detective. Sunburst (grades 1–6).

Writing to Read. IBM, 1984 (intermediate grades).

FILMSTRIPS AND VIDEOTAPES

Encyclopedia Britannica has several collections of stories on sound filmstrips, including the following:

America's Legendary Heroes (intermediate grades), *Famous American Stories* (intermediate grades), and *Four for Fun!* (kindergarten and primary grades).

Fantastic Series. Thomas S. Klise (series of five filmstrips; intermediate grades).

Literature Study: One Classroom, One Session. Center for Establishing Dialogue in Teaching and Learning (video).

Mythology. Thomas S. Klise (series of four filmstrips; intermediate grades).

Teaching Reading Comprehension. WETN, 3319 West Beltline Highway, Madison, WI 53613-2899. (Fourteen 30-minute videos; grades 1–4).

The Writing Company distributes videotapes of such children's favorites as *Charlotte's Web, Heidi, The Hobbit, The Jungle Book, Old Yeller, The Red Pony, Where the Red Fern Grows,* and *The Yearling.*

BOOKS

McCracken, Robert A., and McCracken, Marlene J. *Stories, Songs, and Poetry for Teaching Reading and Writing.* American Library Association, 1986.

Moore, David W.; Readence, John E.; and Rickelman, Robert J. *Prereading Activities for Content Area Reading and Learning.* International Reading Association, 1982.

Rowell, Elizabeth, and Goodkind, Thomas B. *Teaching the Pleasures of Reading.* Prentice-Hall, 1982.

OTHER RESOURCES

Guinness Toucan Books for children eight and older include *Bullet Trains and Underwater Tricycles . . . and Other Amazing Mechanical Records* and *Bomber Bats and Flying Frogs . . . and Other Amazing Animal Records.* Sterling Publishing, 1986.

Little Books for children five to twelve include such titles as *The Great Wild Egg Hunt* and *The Bee That Could Never Be Killed.* Children's Art Foundation.

Spotlight on Vocabulary. Random House (books for grades 3 to 8).

TV and Movie Tie-Ins. Creative Education, 1983 (set of seven books that deal with movies and TV shows).

Activities for Preservice Teachers

1. Examine the teacher's manuals of several basal reading series for a particular grade level. How are word-attack skills taught? How much emphasis is there on phonics? What recommendations are made concerning the methods of teaching phonics? What do the manuals include on diagnosis and evaluation?

2. Select two standardized tests that have reading sections (*Stanford Achievement Test, Metropolitan Achievement Test,* or *Iowa Test of Basic Skills,* for example) for examination. What aspects of reading are covered by these tests? What kinds of tasks are pupils asked to do? How are the results compiled and reported?

3. Compare two or three basal reading series, focusing on how much literature is included. Are there fables, poems, legends, and so on? What authors are represented? Does it appear that the selections have been extensively rewritten for use in the basals?

4. Examine several computer programs designed to teach reading or to supplement reading instruction. Do you think that children would enjoy using them? How effective do you believe they would be for teaching reading skills, compared to other possible activities?

5. Interview teachers with twenty or more years of experience in teaching reading. Ask them to describe some of the changes they have seen in reading programs during this time. Also ask them what teaching problems still persist.

6. Find out if there is a chapter of Literacy Volunteers or other comparable agency in your community and explore the possibility of participating in helping adults learn to read.

7. Observe a reading session in a particular classroom for a week or more. What are the principal activities? What variations in lessons does the teacher use? Do the pupils appear to be paying attention and learning? How much actual reading do they do? What are their independent activities?

8. With some other college students, check your own reading rate, comprehension level, quality of oral reading, and other skills. Identify some areas you need to work on and see how much you can improve in a month or two.

9. Choose a grade level for which you can design exercises for finding the main idea, selecting important details, and understanding the organization of a selection. Compare what you have developed with commercial workbooks and worksheets.

Activities for Inservice Teachers

1. Examine your classroom program for opportunities to include realistic oral reading activities. For example, pupils might read directions to one another, a child could read selections from a favorite book in an attempt to get classmates interested in it, or two pupils might read actors' parts from a scene in a play.

2. Try having a SSR period in your class daily for two weeks. If it seems to be successful, invite the principal or reading teacher to participate occasionally.

3. Visit a curriculum materials center, district reading office, or library to find out what reading-related computer programs are available for examination. Select some to try out yourself for possible inclusion in your program.

4. Conduct a survey of reading interests in your class, and then work with a school or public librarian to see how many relevant titles can be made available to your pupils over the course of several months.

5. See what can be done in your school district to divert funds from the purchase of practice materials to library books. If changes in the law are necessary, find out how that might be accomplished.

6. Attend meetings of a local group of teachers affiliated with the International Reading Association. Find out what the benefits are of being a member at local, state, and national levels.

7. Consider having your two or three top readers and the same number of those with serious problems meet with you individually. Plan some activities for these students but mostly emphasize the reading of books they have selected. If this seems successful, add others to this program of individualized reading.

8. Organize a "book fair" if your school does not already have one. Pupils can be involved by making posters about their favorite books. An author of children's books might be available to make an appearance. Bookstores and public libraries may be willing to participate.

9. Develop a plan for keeping parents informed about your reading program and about how they can help.

10. Work with the school librarian to assemble a list of books related to topics you are planning for science, health, community studies, or geography. Send these lists home with the children with a note encouraging parents to extend the school's reading program using some of these books.

Activities for Children

1. Provide paragraphs in which a few words that may be unfamiliar to children are represented by blank spaces. (Make sure the content of each paragraph is of interest to the children.) A child reading such a paragraph attempts to understand what it says. Provide some way (perhaps by writing them on the back sides of the paragraph sheets or cards) for the child to find out what the omitted words are. The purpose is to show the significance of context in reading.

2. During sustained silent reading, children can identify particularly exciting, funny, or affecting parts of books that they can later read aloud to a partner or small group.

3. Children can work in pairs reading stories and rewriting them:
   a. From a different point of view
   b. In another setting
   c. With a different ending

4. Better readers can be introduced to genre reading in which they read nothing but Greek and Roman myths for a while, then science fiction, and then something else. This works best if children work as partners or in a small group.

5. Partners may read orally to one another. The listener should ask questions and attempt to predict what will come next in the story being read.

6. Activities such as the following can be done by individual children or small groups for practice in structural analysis:
   a. Match cards that have root words written on them with other cards containing prefixes or suffixes.
   b. Write the missing inflectional suffixes in sentences, for example:

      We are go to town.

      This is the small of the three balls.

      Put such sentences on cards and place them in a file.
   c. Prepare cards containing various words with common base forms. Have the child separate the cards into base-word categories. Words might be *green, greener, greenest; report, portal, portage, import;* and so on.
   d. Word cards can be sorted into those with particular endings (*-ed, -ing, -ness,* etc.), particular combina-

tions of letters (*ake, ime,* etc.), or particular beginnings (*b, gr, str,* etc.).

7. Supply children with maps, graphs, and charts suited to their level and ask them to interpret the information provided.

8. Activities can be constructed to provide practice in auditory discrimination and letter-sound association.
   a. Prepare sets of unlabeled pictures. A child can then group them according to the initial or final sound of their names.
   b. A child can sort words on cards according to the number of syllables in the words, words containing syllables that begin with a particular letter, those that rhyme, and so forth.

9. Prepare a bulletin board (one the children can reach) on which each section shows a letter or combination of letters. On each section thumbtack a box. Children can find pictures of objects whose names begin with the letters and place them in the correct boxes. This activity can be varied. For example, instead of showing letters, the bulletin board sections can contain pictures. Another variation is to find pictures of things whose names have ending sounds that match the letters on the board.

10. Children who like a particular character in a story may enjoy making a puppet of that character and dramatizing some scenes from the story.

11. To give individual children reading practice, prepare cards that children can read and then respond to by:
    a. Writing answers to questions about the selection
    b. Following directions
    c. Listing particular details given in the selection

12. Place small pictures from magazines or ones that you draw on three-by-five cards. Print the name of what is pictured on each card. With enough of these cards children can make up their own games, for example, matching pairs of homonyms, antonyms, or synonyms. After you get them started, children can make or find pictures to add to the set.

Chapter **13**

Reading
and Studying

Chapters 4 and 12 emphasized reading for its own sake—the enjoyment of stories, poems, magazines, and other similar materials. In this chapter we focus more attention on reading for information, through textbooks, reference sources, newspapers, and so forth.

Informational reading also involves studying assigned content and doing research for reports. In many classrooms elementary students do much reading of this kind. They write in learning logs, keep notebooks, and explore methods of organizing the knowledge they have gained. In addition, they do functional reading that includes such areas as completing forms, using telephone books and other directories, and following instructions—recipes, operation manuals, and directions of various kinds. Of course, learning to do all these types of reading is best done in meaningful settings and practiced in situations where they actually occur.

READING FOR INFORMATION

Study skills are an integral part of the instructional approach presented in Chapter 2, especially as they apply to information processing.

When reading for information—for personal reasons or in response to school requirements—children need to understand the nature of the task they confront, and you must explain this to them. In the middle grades of the elementary school, for example, students will begin to realize that reading an encyclopedia is different from reading a story. Certainly, many of the same abilities are used, from dealing with unfamiliar words to getting meaning from a lengthy text. The need to understand informational content to use it later, however, means that these aspects of reading have to receive systematic attention. In such circumstances students must be able to analyze the task involved, use the strategies that will likely work best, and make judgments about whether or not they are able to use what they have read effectively.

Undertaking Varied Tasks

Sometimes reading and studying experiences grow naturally from an interest the child has or that develops as a result of class activities in which she or he is involved. When a child is interested in horses, for instance, there will be little question about motivation for reading or the reader's background of related information needed to understand a text. Even if the material to be read is highly technical and apparently quite difficult, intense interest will enable the reader to make a good attempt.

Motivation is also often high when children are engaged in project work and need to study so they can carry out an activity that is intriguing to them. When students are to build a model of a seaport, for instance, they are likely to be strongly motivated to read extensively about docks, warehouses, tugs, and cranes.

For some school reading, though, you will need to concern yourself with building interest and background and checking on understanding (see Directed Reading Experiences in Chapter 12). To be maximally effective, such assigned reading tasks should not be isolated but, rather, ought to be one part of a total teaching-learning situation.

Study Assignments

Studying often grows out of assignments that, when properly made, lead to reading and other activities that have a good chance of being productive. The assignment should be something much more than a chalkboard notice that reads, "Social Studies—read pages 140–145," however. It should indicate that the reading is purposeful and closely integrated with other learning activities.

Any study-reading assignment should inform pupils concerning *what* they are to do, *why* it is to be done, and *how* to do it. All this requires more than simply assigning pages; it includes attention to study objectives, assessment of students' background knowledge, and establishment of motivation for task completion. (Also required are judgments concerning the reading ability of class members; if there are several who cannot read the required text, it will be necessary to see that they can hear it read aloud.)

Whether children are reading or listening, they will need some guidance. Suppose, for example, that pages 140–145 in the social studies book are devoted to a discussion of the colonial period in the Southeastern region of the United States. Assigning these pages could involve the following points.

I. *Motivation.* A means of motivating students could be class discussion centered around questions such as:
   A. When we talked about European colonization we discussed how the different colonies were begun. Do you remember how Virginia and the Carolinas started? What about Georgia?
   B. Do you suppose that life in the southern colonies was the same as that in New England or different? In what ways would it have been different?
   C. How is the southern winter different from that in the north? How would this affect the ways colonists earned their living?
   D. We know that there was slavery in the South rather than the North. Why was this so?

II. *Background.* Establishing student background for the assignment might include looking at a map, talking about use of rivers for transportation, and introduction of the concept of the *cash crop.*

III. *Reasons.* After introductory discussions it is usually beneficial to have readers establish reasons for studying the text. Some of these may come from the students and others will be supplied by you. Activities related to reasons and purposes could include the following:
   A. As you read, notice the titles and headings in dark print. Turn each of these into a question and see if you can answer it. For example, on page 141 there is the heading "Important Money Crops." Change this into a question: "What were the important money crops?" Read the section and see if you can answer that question in one sentence.
   B. While you are reading, try to identify a topic that you would like to find out more about and then prepare a report for a class presentation.

Using Appropriate Strategies

As students begin to read informational materials more extensively, they will require assistance in using the reading-study approaches that are likely to be helpful. They will learn these gradually as you provide help in seeing how they are used in raising questions about the content. Useful strategies include:

- Identifying the type of task:

  What is this—a narrative, description, explanation, argument, or what?

- Seeing how the material is structured:

  How is this organized? Are there headings? Are there places where questions are asked?

- Calling on existing knowledge:

  What do I already know about this? What does battery *mean in this sentence?*

- Raising questions about the content:

  What groups of people lived there? What kinds of houses did they build? Were they happy?

- Predicting what the content will be:

  Won't this tell about both wild and domestic dogs?
  And about different kinds of dogs?

- Identifying relationships between parts of the text:

  The first sections told where the iron ore and coal came from but will there be something on steel-making?

- Summarizing content:

  Does it say that using a credit card is like borrowing money?

- Checking understanding:

  Does it mean that all mountains come from volcanoes?

- Confirming or rejecting predictions:

  I thought dolphins were fish but according to this they aren't.

- Re-reading parts or the entire text:

  I understand the first part, but how did I get lost in here just before the end?

- Integrating content with prior knowledge:

  How does this fit in with what I already know about Rome?

Checking Outcomes. Readers are responsible for monitoring their understanding as they read a text, determining the degree to which it makes sense and relates to understanding they already possess. When understanding and meaning seem deficient, the reader should try strategies that may be more beneficial. At some point, however, it is useful to check on what is being understood. Several activities are likely to be productive:

Writing about a topic is an excellent way to study and learn about it.

Write a summary of what has been read. Just the act of writing will usually make gaps and inconsistencies in understanding apparent.

Discuss what has been read with someone who doesn't know much about the topic; trying to teach may improve understanding.

Discuss what was read with someone who has greater knowledge of the topic; they may be able to supply some useful cues.

Some learners are strongly visually oriented.

Draw a semantic map or topic web that shows how the major parts of the text are related to one another.

Using Specific Strategies. It is often helpful to students if a study plan is summarized as a series of steps. Studying a text is more complex than this, of course, but using a particular system may be a good beginning point for many youngsters. (Obviously, if someone is already proficient at informational reading, that person doesn't need to learn any such technique.) A number of approaches for aiding students in reading and retaining content have been developed, and most are known by acronyms or abbreviations, of which *SQ3R* (survey-question-read-recall-review) is the best known. The number of steps and their precise nature vary, but for most purposes study procedures emphasize four basic points:

1. *Preview:* Read the introduction if there is one. Look at section headings, pictures, diagrams, and other features of the text. This will help you get an idea of what the material is about.

2. *Purpose.* Consider any questions supplied by the text or the teacher or develop your own in preparation for reading. This will give you reasons for reading.

3. *Read.* Read the text carefully, probably more than once, keeping in mind the questions that have been identified.

4. *Review.* See if you can answer all the questions raised. Review the text, section by section, and identify materials that relate to the questions. Formulate answers in one or two sentences.

After students have learned how to use an outline for studying, they can add different strategies and learn to use the approach more flexibly. Also, students can work cooperatively in groups of four or five to raise questions, read the material, find answers to the questions, and read important sections aloud.

Teaching Study Strategies. Whatever reading-study approach you decide to use should be presented to the class and practiced by those who seem to need it the most. Individual variation in use is acceptable because the goal of teaching children to do informational reading and study of all kinds of content is to make them independent learners, able to pursue lines of inquiry on their own. (Chapter 12 discusses similar teaching principles in relation to the reading of literature.)

Discourage the kind of reading that is used only to find answers to specific questions listed in a textbook. Rather, stress thought-provoking questions.

Certainly, teaching study techniques will be done as an aspect of your developmental program as you make students aware of particular strategies and skills, then demonstrate these, and guide initial efforts to use them. By overseeing the actual use of recommended procedures when pupils are involved in information-processing activities (examining several sources to determine which is the world's largest dam) and providing appropriate embedded lessons (finding the scientific name of the water buffalo), you will be supporting their efforts to transfer what they know about reading and studying to new situations.

Awareness of Strategies. You should be sure that your students realize that such intellectual abilities and academic skills as seeing how a text is organized or understanding how to use an index will be extremely helpful in accomplishing significant learning tasks. It is your responsibility to identify these strategies for the class, describe them, discuss their use, and stress their importance. Many of the abilities are complex, so you should expect that you will need to call them to the attention of students numerous times, especially as they come up naturally in classroom activities.

Demonstrating Use of Strategies. Students, once they are aware of a strategy or skill, need to see it in use, either by you or someone else who is proficient. (As an enrichment activity, a gifted student could videotape the entire process as a classmate develops an outline or looks up a topic in encyclopedias.) Of course, you should regularly demonstrate what can be done with dictionaries, atlases, and other reference materials. Discussion of current news events will provide many opportunities to do that.

Teachers are important models for pupils. When planning and organizing study activities, you should explain what you are doing and demonstrate how to do it.

While reading stories and other texts aloud, capitalize on opportunities to demonstrate strategies such as making inferences, considering the author's purposes, defining a word by using the context, and so on. For instance, when the class is studying a science text you could do an embedded lesson in which you as the reader employ a particular strategy—looking for the relationship between a diagram and the text on the same page, for example.

Guiding Students' Use of Skills and Strategies. At the same time you are demonstrating the use of strategies and skills, you should provide students with opportunities to try them, too. For instance, everyone can look in the index for the entry on Washington, D.C., note the pages listed (47, 60, 72–79, 111), and decide which would be the best page to turn to first.

Encouraging Independent Use of Skills and Strategies. Students will need to be reminded regularly of what they have been taught and how to make use of the strategies practiced. When they are studying, or preparing to, you should review with them both the procedures discussed some time ago and those recently demonstrated. Of course, you should continue to make explicit your own use of targeted skills and strategies. (Even when you have on several occasions pointed out how to use indexes and tables of contents, you will find youngsters leafing through a book looking for specific content. Sometimes we adults do it ourselves!)

Using Learning Logs

By the time they reach the middle grades, students can use "learning logs" to aid them in their studies. In his or her log a pupil keeps a record of what is being done to study a particular topic, whether a project involving the entire class or a matter of personal interest. Several questions guide the use of learning logs.

Encourage pupils to use their logs to record questions that come to mind as they study. These may be points requiring clarification or topics for discussion or further reading.

What do I already know about this topic?
What do I want to know?
What are some sources I can use?
How is this new information I have found related to what I know and want to know?
Am I making the kind of progress I expected?
Should I revise my statement of what I want to know?
Should I look for new sources?
Am I ready to start organizing what I know?

When the strategy is complex the teacher should demonstrate and provide guidance.

Learning logs are different from journals and notebooks (see Chapter 11). Journals are more personal, touching, for example, on daily activities and experiences. Notebooks contain writings and other materials that mostly involve exploration of the writer's thoughts and feelings that might lead to some significant exploratory writing. Of course, studying a topic and writing about it in the learning log may lead the student to explore related ideas in a notebook or journal.

Just as with journals or notebooks, logs may become focal points for teacher–student conferences. The contents of the log will help you understand the study strategies being used by the child and which ones need to be worked on or introduced. Also, the log can be used to help students formulate the questions and concerns that they need to take up with you.

FINDING AND USING INFORMATION

In addition to learning how to study textbooks and similar sorts of materials, students need to know how to do research, that is, locating, organizing, and presenting information on a particular topic. The necessary materials to aid in such research ought to be available in school library media centers as discussed in Chapter 14.

Locating Information

A library user can become quite frustrated—as students at all levels know.

Library research is possible for elementary-school students if they have an adequate library and appropriate assistance. Too often the resources simply are not there. A child desiring to read in depth about endangered animal and plant species, for example, may find that the school library has only a few relevant pages in its entire collection. It is true, of course, that elementary-school library collections have usually been composed almost entirely of storybooks. Also, some libraries are not staffed full time with qualified librarians who have time to assist students properly.

Several developments have enhanced elementary-school students' access to varied sources of information:

- Elementary libraries are increasingly considered central to the school program. Those responsible for school planning now realize that the youngest children must have ready access to a good library media center.

- In school libraries and in many classroom libraries there are reference books of all kinds—encyclopedias, atlases, comprehensive dictionaries, guides to periodicals, biographical listings, and specialized yearbooks.

- The supply of informational books for elementary-age youngsters is growing rapidly in the diversity of topics and the numbers of copies. It is difficult to think of a topic for which children's informational books have not been printed, although these are not always selected for elementary libraries if the content is controversial.

- Electronic information-retrieval devices of several kinds are available in some elementary schools. Compact disk read-only-memory (CD-ROM) systems, for example, offer children the opportunity to sit at a computer and not only read text from the screen but also see still pictures and graphics of various kinds, watch films and animations, and even listen to speeches and music. (See Chapter 14.)

Using Resources

To make appropriate use of sources children must understand how to gain access to stored information. In Chapter 14 attention is given to how the school library is organized and what types of resources should be available there.

Preparation for Doing Research. In the classroom itself, though, there are ways in which you can help children increase their familiarity with reference works and how they may be used in research. If they have been using their dictionaries and the indexes in textbooks, encyclopedias, and other volumes, for example, that is a good start. From their acquaintance with fiction books students know about *authors* and *titles* and you can teach them how to think about the *subject* of an informational book. When they go to the library to learn how to use the card catalog system, then, they will already have some related understanding. There is much more to find out about, of course (using authors' last names when trying to find out what else they have written, for example).

Some reference books should be available in the classroom.

Using Alphabetical Order. Of course, students will have been using alphabetical order for some time before they begin to do independent research, but you should also see that they periodically review what they know and are able to do. (Basic understandings are presented in Chapter 4.) Some research skills related to alphabetical order are:

- Maintaining lists of new words and spelling words related to the topic being studied. (Using a word processor will enable them to insert new words in the existing alphabetical list without recopying.)
- Deciding which words related to a topic should be looked up first in an index or encyclopedia. For example, if the subject is the war that took place in the United States during the years 1861–1865, does the student search the index for *The War Between the States, The American Civil War, Civil War*, or what? Should *The* be included in the name and the search start with the letter *T*? (Such questions present

opportunities for you to teach valuable embedded lessons about history, research, and language—why there should be a disagreement about what name to give a war, for example.)

- Searching for names presents particular difficulties students should be aware of. When looking for *St. Augustine*, for example, will it be found nearer *saint* or *Stanford?* And what difference does it make if someone's name is Mac Donald MacDonald or McDonald? Sarah Louis-Phillips or Sarah Phillips?

- Use of different words or those that are spelled differently sometimes presents research problems. Even in English-speaking countries *kerosene* and *paraffin* may or may not be the same product. No matter what the language, the same city may be listed as either *Peking* or *Beijing, St. Petersburg* or *Leningrad.* Allowing students to confront these problems makes a valuable contribution to their educations, but you must intervene fairly quickly to avoid complete frustration.

Pronunciation Aids. As children study and do library research, they will increasingly come into contact with words (often in other languages) that are not in their listening and speaking vocabularies and it will be difficult for them to learn to pronounce these satisfactorily. Of course, diacritical marks for place names and people's names as well as unusual words are often supplied in various reference works.

It would be a good idea for you to review the pronunciation marks found in dictionaries from time to time and provide some practice for the students who seem to need it. Older students are probably better able to understand such matters as syllabication of words than they were when that was first introduced to them, and some don't fully grasp phonics understandings until they have read quite a bit.

Of course, there are electronic aids to pronunciation that can be kept in the classroom or added to the library resources. You can, for example, use word cards with strips of audiotape affixed to them, write the target word on the card (*Vienna,* perhaps), and then record the pronunciation (or have a student do it) on the tape. The student needs only to run the card through the machine. There are several types of devices that perform this function, and they can be used to give spelling words and to teach foreign language, too. Also, there are voice-synthesizer devices equipped with speakers and keyboards so that words typed in by students can be pronounced for them.

Combining Skills. When students have the ability to combine thorough knowledge of alphabetical order with other skills, they will be able to apply research strategies more smoothly. Only a substantial amount of practice with a variety of resources will make a person proficient, but more academically able and interested elementary students can make progress if they receive appropriate assistance. Some planned activities may help.

Learning to read a map is something some adults have not accomplished.

- Using a local map in conjunction with a telephone book, children may try to answer questions such as:
  1. What is the telephone number of a pizza restaurant within ten blocks of this school?
  2. What is the telephone number of the movie theater near the park?
  3. About how many miles is it from this school to the nearest hospital?

- Using a national map in conjunction with guides to national historic and scenic sites, children may try to answer questions such as:
  1. Which national park is closest to our school?
  2. How far is it from our school to where Abraham Lincoln is buried?
  3. If you were visiting the Carlsbad Caverns and wanted to drive to the Grand Canyon, what route would you use?

Activities related to your own class members' interests and backgrounds would be the best starting point for such experiences, of course. Sports cards or fan clubs might also serve well.

Note Taking

Once students have gone through the research steps of defining the questions that are important to them and finding sources that are related to those questions, their attention must turn to selecting the information that will be of most use. (Some may have already carried out similar activities in connection with making brief oral reports as described in Chapter 5.)

Various types of experiences could help to prepare your students to do their own notetaking:

1. Use an overhead projector to display a paragraph about some topic (a chicken's egg, perhaps). Emphasize a particular question: what are the parts of the egg? Take notes, writing on the chalkboard and discussing with the students what should be written. Stress that what is in the paragraph should not be copied entirely. (Do this sort of exercise several times, with two or three children leading the discussion.)
2. Have students take notes as a film or videotape is shown. Before the viewing, record a list of questions for which class members could seek answers. Following the viewing, during which the students take notes, ask them to use their notes to respond to questions.
3. Show a film or videotape two or three times. Have students take notes each time. Encourage them to check to see whether or not they changed their ideas about what the important content was.
4. Have students watch specific television programs or types of programs and take notes on advertising techniques, use of dialects, or new vocabulary items. Let children who have seen the same shows compare information gathered from their notes to check accuracy.
5. Prepare cassettes for children to use in the listening center. There should be questions to guide their listening, and they ought to be permitted to replay portions of the tape and take notes related to the questions.

After these preparatory experiences, students should undertake research activities that make use of sources they have identified as relevant for a research topic. With adult guidance they should follow these suggestions:

1. Look over the material. (See the section on skimming in this chapter. This is like the *survey* or *preview* aspect of studying.) Determine whether the text contains information relevant to the research question.

2. Record the name of the book or article, the author's name, and page numbers on which the information is found. For encyclopedias, write the name of the encyclopedia, volume number, subject heading, and page numbers.

3. Record only the information you are looking for. Use your own words; *don't copy content and include it as part of what you wrote yourself.*

4. If you decide to use an author's exact words, put quotation marks around what you copy and note the page numbers.

5. Check names, dates, and numerals for accuracy.

6. Skim once more to see if you have missed anything important.

The librarian may want to post a chart containing such suggestions at a time when much research is in progress.

Older students may work independently at times, taking notes on something they have decided to study. If they have had appropriate learning experiences in preceding years, they won't need more than a few reminders to function well.

When children first start making individual reports based on notes they have taken from several sources, guidance from you or the librarian is particularly important. They must learn to locate materials quickly, select the important information, and avoid the pitfalls of unintentional plagiarism by forgetting to write down sources. Use of simple note cards will aid them in following these guidelines.

Research Note Card

TOPIC	
SOURCE	**PAGES**
NOTES	

ORGANIZING AND REPORTING INFORMATION

The abilities needed to write the component sentences and paragraphs of a report are essentially those required for any writing; the steps of the writing process are described in Chapter 10. Of particular concern for report writing are organization of material before doing the first draft and acknowledgment of sources in the final editing.

Organizing for Writing

At the time of preparing to begin writing, reference should be made to notes kept in the learning log. Students should remind themselves of what their basic questions were when the project began. (Perhaps their research has taken them away from the original concern, and this is all right if they believe that the result will be a more useful report. But they should have a conference with you to explain what has happened and decide what to do.) If all is well, though, they can list their original major concerns and check their notes to see how the information they have found relates to these questions.

Probably the most difficult stage in the process of preparing a written report is that which occurs after a student has collected information and is ready to begin writing. Faced with what seems to be a jumble of disorganized notes and bits of information, the student must somehow put this material in a form that makes it accessible for writing. The solution is to use procedures specifically intended to assist with such organization.

Outlining and Diagrammatic Representations

The techniques that help a writer select the content and organize her or his report are *outlines,* which are essentially linear and verbal listings of content, and

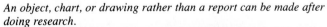

An object, chart, or drawing rather than a report can be made after doing research.

schematics, which are more like diagrams or maps of the materials to be reported.

These outlines and diagrams enable the research to go ahead with some direction but do not necessarily dictate exactly what content has to be covered. As the student proceeds in his or her research, changes can be made in outlines and other representations; that is, material can be added and deleted or entire sections moved or changed substantially. In other words, outlines and diagrams should be thought of as tools that the writer should use insofar as they help to produce a good report. Certainly, these aids should not become more important than the report itself.

Outlining. The outline form, which students will continually encounter as they progress in school, is useful in studying and in planning and carrying out a writing project. As with other sorts of writing and studying, you should first do whole-class and small-group outlining projects, then guide students as they begin to do their own outlining, and finally work with them as they achieve independence. The outline may be used as a guide for developing a report from the outset and then changed as necessary. Its forms increasing in complexity as children mature and gain practice, outlining is a developmental skill; therefore, activities are described here at three levels of sophistication.

A student doing research may work from a diagram, topic web, or outline.

Beginning Level. For younger children in the beginning primary grades a formal outline is usually not appropriate since they will not be able to keep it in mind as they do their reading. A more appropriate learning activity is for them to take some notes and then attempt to group these in some way that makes sense for a report (thus, "making an outline"). The notes taken should be few in number—four or five, perhaps. If the topic is "Spiders," for instance, they may have cards with these notes on them:

Spiders make webs.
Spiders eat insects.
Spiders have 8 eyes and 8 legs.
Insects get caught in the webs.

Younger students may use only one or two sources when writing.

Conferences with the child will give you the opportunity to teach embedded lessons on selecting and arranging the cards in order to stay with one idea that makes sense. Some children of this age will quickly see that the note on eyes and legs does not fit with the rest of the information very well. (Some pupils may be helped to find a reasonable sequence by starting with each card in turn as the first idea and seeing what other would follow. This is one advantage to having the notes on cards.)

If the child decides on the three sentences: *Spiders make webs, Insects get caught in the webs,* and *Spiders eat the insects,* she or he needs only to copy the sentences onto a piece of paper (or type them on a word processor) and add a drawing. The making of the note cards has been a "first draft," so it is possible to go directly to the finished report, which is much better for the age group involved than requiring two successive drafts.

When you want to introduce outlining more directly you can point out to the student that one main idea (how spiders get their food) has been reported and have her or him label it. Then the child might wish to continue to develop the report by identifying a second important idea (ask what the card on eyes and legs suggests).

Opportunities for using outlines in planning and reporting class activities are numerous. For instance, directions or plans for a class picnic or party can be outlined on the board. Or, when children have finished reading or listening to a story, ask them to provide a description of the sequence of events that occurred. Write these on the board or overhead projector; then reread the story to check the outline. This kind of activity will help demonstrate to children how their own stories can be improved if they jot down their ideas and organize them into a meaningful sequence.

Intermediate Level. Students in the middle grades (or especially able younger children) can profit from considering the details of outlining. A list of questions or a discussion can begin the outlining activity and lead to the identification of the most important ideas. If the topic is "Spiders," then the questions are likely to be about whether or not they are dangerous, what they look like, what they eat, and so forth. When a main idea is appearance, then the supporting points will involve information about the body parts, the head, legs, and eyes. An outline then evolves that can be used to begin the research for the report, with additions, deletions, and other changes made as needed.

At this level students can begin to understand main ideas and supporting ones, so what you do with outlining will strengthen their performance in such areas as listening, making oral reports, reading, and thinking, as well as writing. Outlines can be more than sequential at this time. This form includes three levels: main topics, subtopics, and details:

I. Use Roman numerals for main topics—the most important points.
   A. Indent and capitalize letters for subtopics.
      1. Use Arabic numerals for the details.
      2. Because you have one, you need at least one more detail about subtopic A.
   B. This is another subtopic of Roman numeral I.
      1. Give one detail about B.
      2. One B detail needs a second.
II. List another main topic.
   A. Subtopic. Details may or may not be needed here.
   B. Subtopic. Again, if there are two or more parts or details, there will need to be a division of the subtopic.

The discussion of content-area subjects in class also provides a good opportunity for teaching the value of outlining. As discussion takes place, write in outline form some of the information that you particularly want the class to remember. The children can copy it in their notebooks and use it as a basis for study.

Advanced Level. Once children have become fairly proficient at outlining with your assistance, encourage them to try to use this strategy independently. Only when they develop their own outlines will the activity have much effect on their thinking and study habits. Show that you rely on this skill by outlining important content on the board as it is discussed and by distributing study guides and other materials prepared in outline form.

At this level children may need help in correlating information from several sources for an oral or written report. When they do, the following procedure should prove helpful:

1. Using an overhead projector, present three brief articles about the same subject. All should contain some common information, but each should include facts not found in the others.
2. Have the children take notes on each selection. This may be a group effort, with notes being taken on the chalkboard.
3. With the children's help, outline the notes from each selection.
4. Make a composite outline, including important points from all three. You may wish to have the children place numbers (1, 2, 3) in parentheses after each point, both to illustrate how the material is correlated and to help them locate information quickly if they need to refer to the articles in writing their summaries (step 5).
5. Have small groups or individual students use the outline to write summaries of the information obtained from all three selections.

See the book on semantic mapping by Heimlich and Pittelman listed in the References section of this chapter.

Diagrammatic Representations. *Diagrams* or *graphic organizers* are like outlines in the sense that they show how aspects of a topic are related to one another. These organizational techniques are often called *semantic maps* or *topic webs*. (The use of simple webs in writing was described in Chapters 4 and 11.) These schematic guides are useful in the same way an outline is; they help in reading and studying and in organizing what is to be written.

The advantage of these modes of representation in the elementary school is that students are not required to think in linear fashion, something that is fundamental to outlining but difficult for youngsters to accomplish. When a child is thinking about spiders, she or he can consider the spider's *body* initially, then add *head* and *eyes* to the diagram (and then change *eyes* to *seeing* and make it a separate part of the web, if that seems to be a useful thing to do). Such changes are easily made during the research period and even when the first draft is being written.

Before doing a draft the student ought to examine the diagram and decide where to begin and in what order to take up the various subtopics (numbering them might help). At this time it may be apparent that some reorganization is necessary. In the sample provided, for instance, the writer might conclude that it would be an advantage to describe the spiders' mouth parts and manner of inserting poison when writing about *prey* rather than body parts.

Diagram of the Topic "Spiders"

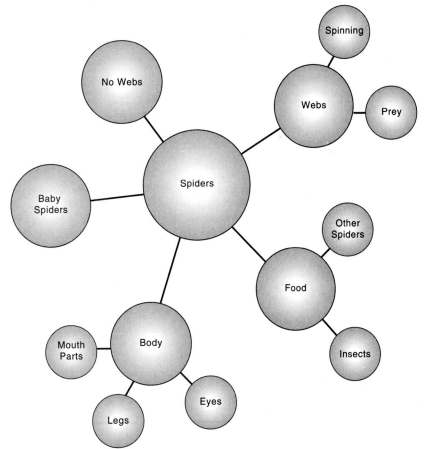

Bibliographies and Footnotes

Brief research reports are appropriate for most elementary students, but only the exceptional few should try a "term paper."

It is not often that an entire class of elementary students would be expected to use formal procedures such as providing footnotes and including a bibliography of sources used in a report. With the availability of much more resource material in school libraries, though, together with the possibilities presented by desktop publishing (see Chapter 11), it seems likely that some children will notice such writing features and want to include them in their own products.

As your more advanced students begin to use a variety of sources when carrying out research, help them to understand that appending a bibliography strengthens a report in two ways: first, if a writer has authorities to back up what is said, the reader will know that the subject has been studied and that the writer knows what he or she is talking about; and second, the bibliography gives readers the opportunity to go to the sources and find out more for themselves if they so choose.

Children love big words, and there is no reason why they should not use the term *bibliography* to label their list of sources. In the beginning, the form should be simple. A chart may be used to help with the punctuation and with the spelling of *bibliography.*

BIBLIOGRAPHY

Saywell, John T. *Government of Canada,* pages 106–113.
The World Book, Vol. 3.

When students use note cards, bibliographic information can be written on them and then transferred to a page of references at the end of the report. If a word processor is used, this can be done fairly easily. Students can examine punctuation forms used in several different sources to find out how bibliographic entries for books, magazines, encyclopedias, and newspapers are done.

Some students who are using quotations and facts may express interest in learning how to use *footnotes*. Footnotes ought to be in simple form, numbered for each page of the report and placed at the bottom of that page. Author, title, and page numbers are usually sufficient for any footnote at this level. The important understandings for children to gain are that they may not copy someone else's words without giving credit and that a footnote is the accepted way of acknowledging such use. Again, they may wish to examine how footnotes are punctuated in reading materials that they have examined (you should explain that they needn't include *ibid., op. cit.,* etc., however).

READING AND RESEARCH

Many skills and strategies are needed for effective reading. The foundational ones were discussed in Chapter 12 and those related to studying and doing research are examined in this chapter. This section discusses skimming and critical reading, which have particular relevance for research but are useful in other reading situations as well.

Skimming

Skimming is done for several reasons: as a preliminary to studying material, as a means of finding out whether or not a text is likely to have the content the reader needs for compiling a report, and as a way of locating a particular piece of information. All of these are legitimate purposes, so there is no doubt that skimming is a strategy that is appropriate for readers who are gaining maturity in the use of books and other texts. Most children in the middle grades of the elementary school are ready to learn something about skimming. Of course, whatever is taught will be best learned through embedded lessons related to authentic language experiences.

Even older students often cannot bring themselves to skim and not read every word.

Reading the First and Last Sentences of a Paragraph. Both you and the children should be aware that key sentences are not always first or last in a paragraph, but they do frequently appear in one of those positions, especially in materials prepared for elementary students. Even when such a sentence is not in one of those positions (or when there is no obvious topic sentence) reading first and last sentences should give clues to the general content. In longer selections, the first and last paragraphs might be read quickly as a means of skimming.

Looking for Cue Words. Cue words are of two types. First, if a child is looking for a specific piece of information, he or she should watch for words likely to be related to that kind of information. For example, if a pupil only wants to find out where a particular group of Indians lived, then place names—California, northern plains, or Mississippi River Valley, for instance—should be looked for. Second, there are general cue words. The way they are used is illustrated in this paragraph. The heading has given the main idea. The first sentence uses the words *two types;* the words *First* and *Second* lead immediately to these two types. Number words (or the numbers themselves) are perhaps the most helpful of all cue words. If these had been omitted, however, *For example* in sentence three should send the reader's eyes back to the preceding sentence to discover one of the two types. Other cue words that can help children to locate ideas are words like *causes, reason, however, principal,* and *furthermore* and phrases such as *in addition, on the other hand,* and *in conclusion.*

Using Format Clues. As was suggested in the section concerning study steps, one of the quickest ways to discover the general content of a long selection is to glance through it and read the various types of section headings, as well as the captions for pictures, graphs, maps, and other features. A child who is preparing a report can usually be led immediately to the information needed by using this technique, particularly if it is used in conjunction with the card catalog, table of contents, and/or index (see Chapter 14).

Materials used for teaching skimming should be selected carefully if appropriate habits are to be established. This does not mean that the materials should not be related to the subject matter or content area, only that you must select them with an eye to their suitability in developing a particular habit or skill. Specific teaching suggestions include the following:

1. Begin with short selections that clearly illustrate the strategies you are trying to encourage. The first few times you may wish to underline the parts that are important, that is, beginning and ending sentences, cue words, or topic headings. Give the children specific questions to answer and discuss what procedures might be used to find the answers. At first, simply ask them to decide what the selection

is about. Later, proceed to more detailed questions, such as "What kinds of homes did the Indians live in?" or "What are three ways trees help us?"

2. Use an overhead projector to present practice exercises; this makes it possible to control exposure time, demonstrating to students the advantage of skimming. Exposure time can be reduced as students become more proficient. (This activity is especially useful in encouraging line-by-line readers to try skimming.)

Divide a class into teams for "skimming contests." Award points for finding items in the least amount of time.

3. Regular, brief practice will improve speed. For example, say to the class "Turn to page 142 in your text and find the name of the Indian who guided the Smith family through the forest. As soon as you have found it, close your book and hold up your hand."

4. Providing some structure for scanning a page may help a child. Clear plastic overlays with a red line down the middle can be placed on the page to be read, for instance, and the youngster told to look only at the words that touch the line while trying to find a target phrase or word. (Students working together may enjoy cutting a "peephole" in the page so they can watch one another's eye movements to ensure that the eyes are moving only *down* the page and not *across.*)

Observe children as they study and work on reports based on supplementary reading. Guide individual children by reminding them of clues to look for, and provide reinforcement exercises when the need is indicated.

Critical Reading and Thinking

In Chapter 6 we discussed the importance of introducing thinking strategies along with listening and, of course, reading and thinking should also be taught

Some computer programs permit a reader to respond to a text in a variety of ways.

in conjunction with each other. While it often appears that young children are likely to believe everything they read, most older elementary students realize that not all that is in print will be true. Clearly, they are ready to approach reading critically if given the opportunity.

Teaching about Critical Reading. Certainly, providing children with opportunities to be critical about the validity of messages they receive (whether by means of radio, television, personal communication, or written texts) must be considered a significant part of their education. By the time they begin elementary school, some have seen so many misleading television commercials that they are vaguely aware that they should not take all communications at face value. They do need some specifics to watch out for, though, and you should have a plan for teaching about these.

To develop into critical readers children must learn to approach the printed word with inquiring minds, to evaluate what is read in the light of known facts or objective evidence, to examine the logic of a presentation, and to distinguish between fact and opinion. These thinking strategies should be stressed throughout the curriculum and in many different settings. Following are three examples.

1. *Evaluation in Terms of Evidence.*

   The reader has the opportunity to examine what is on the page and consider whether or not there is evidence to support what the author has written. In much the same way, a listener may hear a statement ("Our taxes are the highest in the state") unaccompanied by any evidence of its validity. The reader is in a much better position to note that the claim was not substantiated.

2. *Logic of a Presentation.*

   A speaker may be attractive and dynamic but deficient in logic. ("Since no one opposes us, we must be right.") The reader, on the other hand, can go over a passage several times and note deficiencies in reasoning.

3. *Differentiating Fact from Opinion.*

   Elementary students seem to have a great deal of difficulty in separating opinion and fact (as do many adults). Sample activities that may be of assistance to students are presented in the next section.

Teaching Activities: Fact and Opinion.

1. Have the children select famous personalities and write opinions about them: "I think Laura Ingalls Wilder lived in South Dakota" or "I believe that Jose Canseco hit more home runs last year than any other player in the American League." Then have them use their library skills to determine whether these are facts.

2. Obtain from magazines several full-page color advertisements, clipping off all printed material pertaining to the product. Show only the pictures to the children and ask them to write statements of fact and opinion about them. For example,

   Facts

   A woman is sitting on a patio with a collie.

   The woman is smiling.

   There are flowers and trees surrounding the patio.

Opinions

The woman is smiling because her new toothpaste got her teeth so white.

She is smiling because the flower seeds she bought made her yard beautiful.

She is smiling because a particular fertilizer made her garden grow especially well.

She is smiling because her dog likes that new dog food.

Check to make sure the facts are really facts, and lead the children into a discussion of whether such statements as "The woman is beautiful" and "The collie is a thoroughbred" are facts or opinions. Then show the printed material that was cut from the picture so children can find out which of their opinions were correct (at least according to the advertisement!).

3. Help children evaluate newspaper accounts by looking for key words that indicate opinion rather than fact. Here are some statements of the type to look for:

There is *probably* more snow here than any other place in the country.

The remains just discovered *may* be the missing link.

This *appears* to be the driest spot in North America.

The students *think* that this is the best school in the city.

4. A variation of the preceding activity is to have children separate fact from opinion within a single sentence:

Discuss use of the expression "true fact" with students and try to determine what it might mean to someone who uses it.

Yesterday's rain, which lasted for five hours, was probably the worst downpour in our history.

Facts: It rained yesterday. The rain lasted five hours.

Opinion: It was the worst downpour in our history.

Jim Simmons, who is exactly six feet tall, must be the tallest student in this school.

Fact: Jim Simmons is six feet tall.

Opinion: He is the tallest student in this school.

Mrs. Gotrocks, often said to be the wealthiest woman in the state, was shopping on Monday at Goodwill.

Fact: Mrs. Gotrocks was at Goodwill on Monday.

Opinion: Mrs. Gotrocks is the wealthiest woman in the state.

5. Have the children listen to television newscasts for several days and make a collection of phrases used to introduce statements that are not definitely known to be true: "It has been reported that," "Reliable sources inform us," "The alleged thief," and so on. Then have them look for these same qualifications in newspaper stories.

6. Children should also have opportunities to see how the choice of words can sway opinion. Let them try to find opposing descriptions of the same event:

Senator Wilkins smirked sardonically, then snapped, "I have nothing to say at this time."

The weary Senator attempted a smile, then said simply, "I have nothing to say at this time."

7. Have the class compare newspaper accounts of the same event written by different writers. (See the section Reading the Newspaper in this chapter.) A football game between teams from two cities, for example, would be written up quite differently by sports writers from each of those cities. Follow by having students attempt to separate facts and opinions.

Propaganda. In Chapter 6 we mentioned propaganda techniques in connection with listening activities. Of course, we are surrounded by propaganda, usually defined as the use of language to foster decision making based on emotions rather than critical thinking.

Although most propaganda involves advertising, getting consumers to buy one brand of cereal or make of automobile rather than another, the techniques can be used to foster other actions (support for a law that might be harmful in its effects) or beliefs (hate for certain groups). By the time children reach the middle grades they should be taught about the kinds of propaganda techniques commonly used:

- *Plain folks:* The president of the company started as a janitor. He still enjoys pitching horseshoes with the boys during the noon-hour break. (He understands ordinary people and wouldn't try to cheat them.)
- *Bandwagon:* More doctors recommend this pill than any other. (Notice that it doesn't say any other *what*.)
- *Repetition:* Sticky Goo holds your false teeth so you can munch, munch, munch for your lunch, lunch, lunch. (A more common type of repetition currently used involves frequently repeated slogans or jingles, which appear so often on television that even small children can repeat or sing them.)
- *Testimonial:* The star pitcher for the Rangers eats Ironies for breakfast. (If you eat Ironies, you can be a big leaguer too.)
- *Snob appeal:* Come out and see this executive house in an exclusive neighborhood. (Buy here and you can be part of an important group.)
- *Emotional words:* Concerned mothers buy Junkie sneakers for their children. (If you don't buy your child Junkie sneakers, you aren't a good mother.)
- *Rewards:* Buy at Smith Brothers' Store and get double coupon value. (Also common is the cash rebate.)

Teaching Activities: Propaganda. A bulletin-board display might be developed during a study of propaganda techniques. Ask children to bring in examples of various advertisements that appear to be using certain techniques, and have a panel decide which ones to post. Students may also enjoy collecting phrases commonly found in advertising. These might include the following:

huge savings	for better mileage
this week only	discount prices
buy with confidence	money-back guarantee
service with a smile	for preferred customers

An extension of this study that will appeal to children is to have them watch television commercials and decide which groups they are directed at (small children, women, teenagers, etc.) and which techniques are used for each group. They will be fascinated to discover that variations of the same technique are used for every age level: the four-year-old demands a certain cereal because there is a toy in the box, and the child's father buys a particular car because the company pays him a cash bonus.

As the children become expert in detecting the techniques, have them watch for overlapping ones. For example, "All responsible parents buy Dryer raincoats for their children. Your children deserve the best" includes the bandwagon, emotional, and snob-appeal approaches.

Coordinate the teaching of
listening strategies with
activities such as these.

As a concluding activity for the unit, divide the class into small groups and let each group select an item to "shop for." Each group should collect all the advertisements they can locate about their item. Then they may evaluate each one, write reactions to it, and report their findings to the class, including the reasons they decided to buy a particular brand or shop at a particular store. The items might include a swimming pool, a ping-pong table, a jar of peanut butter, a snowmobile, a video game, or a pair of jeans.

If it is valuable to recognize the advertising ploys used by those who are trying to sell their products, it is even more important to recognize that virtually the same techniques are used by those who want to sell *ideas*. During every political campaign, for example, we are bombarded by the same spot announcements on TV and radio to keep candidates' names before us; film stars and other entertainers endorse their favorites, and so on. In fact, we are surrounded daily by propaganda of many types.

Children should learn to recognize propaganda, but they should also learn that it is not necessarily bad. Rather, it is a part of our way of life. TV stations, for instance, commonly telecast what they often call "public service announcements," warning young people against the use of drugs, advertising public clinics that give immunizations against various diseases, and so on; prominent athletes plug not only shaving cream but also fundraising drives against multiple sclerosis or heart disease. No one is completely without bias; therefore, what a person writes or says is colored by his or her own beliefs. This "slanting" may be intentional, or the writer may make every effort to present an objective view. The important thing is that children should learn to search for bias or motive, to distinguish fact from opinion, to examine opposing views, and to draw their own conclusions. The following are some of the types of activities that can help your students to recognize and evaluate propaganda:

1. Use reading exercises that call for making inferences and for distinguishing fact from opinion as suggested earlier.

2. Begin even in the early grades to help children find themes in stories they read, for these are a type of propaganda—they represent the writers' beliefs. Begin with simple questions: "Do you think the person who wrote this story likes dogs? What makes you think so?" As children mature, they can grasp more subtle and complicated themes.

3. To help children think about the purposes and qualifications of writers when evaluating what they have to say, show a variety of articles from newspapers and magazines by means of an overhead projector. Then discuss questions such as the following:

   Did the writer simply want to sell more newspapers or magazines? (New Clues Uncovered!)

   Is the writer encouraging you to vote for a candidate or an issue. (Mr. Christopher is an all-around family man who lives in a neat, modest suburban home.)

   Is the writer qualified and competent to write on this subject? (Has the writer studied the subject sufficiently or had enough personal experience with it to know what he or she is talking about?)

   Does the writer present both sides of an issue or only one? (Those who oppose this issue base their objections on emotion alone; there can be no valid objection.)

4. Have children bring in two accounts of a political speech appearing in newspapers with opposing political views, or have them listen to reports of a speech on

different television channels, or both. Then compare these accounts and note the ways in which each supports its point of view.

5. An extension of the preceding activity is to videotape the speech itself and compare the various reports concerning it in terms of both accuracy and bias.

6. Have the children write papers either supporting or opposing a particular school or community issue on which opinions are strongly divided. Then have the class research the subject through whatever means are available—guest speakers, reading, and so on—and write new opinions based on what they have learned, telling why they have or have not changed their minds.

7. Bring in several articles concerning a current problem or issue. Display these on an overhead projector and have the children evaluate them in terms of propaganda techniques used, presentation of facts rather than opinions, use of "loaded" or highly emotional words, and use of reasoning.

Developing critical thinking takes time and effort. Broaden the children's horizons by providing many experiences and materials of various kinds. Make your classroom one in which a spirit of inquiry exists, where questions are freely asked and answers diligently sought. Help children to question what they read and hear and to acquire the desire and the skills to find answers.

NEWSPAPERS IN THE CLASSROOM

At several points in this book we have mentioned newspapers in connection with the elementary classroom. There are, of course, weekly national newspapers prepared especially for elementary students, and these make an important contribution to the program. In Chapter 11 we suggested that children produce their own school and classroom newspapers. Naturally, when preparing their own newspaper, children will be interested in learning about the papers read in their locality.

Despite the value in having students in the upper grades of the elementary school use daily newspapers as reading material on a regular basis, there are problems that must be confronted. Newspaper reports on crime, violence, and social problems often go into such explicit detail that some parents would not want their child's attention to be deliberately directed to it. If these objections can be dealt with, it will likely become apparent to everyone involved that the advantages of using the newspaper far outweigh any negative influences.

Newspaper Sections

In what sequence do you read the various sections of the newspaper? Which do you ignore?

Daily newspapers vary in size and scope but most present their readers with the same types of reading material. (Many departments are not represented every day.)

> *News Stories*
> International ("Threat to World Oil Supplies")
> National ("Presidential Campaign Begins")
> Regional ("Legislature May Increase Sales Tax")
> Local ("School Bus Accident Injures 5")
> *Other Sections and Departments*
> Sports (scores, teams, comment, etc.)
> Editorial (opinions, columnists, letters from readers)

Financial (business, agriculture, stock market, labor, comment, etc.)
Social Events (parties, weddings, etc.)
Home/Family (foods, child welfare, shopping, etc.)
Entertainment (TV, radio, movies, theater)
Arts (music, books, art galleries)
Science/Technology (computers, cars, inventions, etc.)
Religion (services, special days, activities)
Health (diseases, care, medical matters)
Human Interest Stories (people's relationships, pets, hobbies, people's problems)
Features (advice columns, crossword puzzles, horoscopes, comics)
Advertising (stores, services, classified ads, etc.)

Reading the Newspaper

Students can learn a great deal through regular reading of the newspaper, particularly if relevant materials are used in all curriculum areas, not only reading and the other language arts but also mathematics, science, social studies, and the special subjects. Opportunities for critical reading present themselves, too, as some of the examples in the preceding section indicate. Other examples include:

1. *Examining headlines and story titles.* Space is always a problem when titles are chosen, but which words are selected does often indicate what view the newspaper is taking of an event or person (see Critical Reading and Thinking for discussion of word choice).

   Reading for *the* main idea and using that for the title doesn't always work well. Students can discuss what alternative headlines they might use for the same story or even see that two newspapers have found quite different "main ideas." (Such a finding might lead to a discussion of the necessity to talk about "important ideas," recognizing that people will differ on which is more important.)

2. *Reading essays.* In Chapter 11 it was emphasized that essays—statements of opinion and arguments for and against particular positions and actions—are well represented in our daily newspapers by editorials, columns, and letters to the editor. Reading what various individuals have to say about a controversial matter (changing dog-control laws, for example) allows skills in identifying issues and analyzing a person's argument to be developed.

3. *Focusing on details.* Reading the newspaper presents many opportunities for considering significant details. When looking at want ads, for example, the reader needs to be sure to get the specifics (What year was that station wagon? Did the Ford have an automatic transmission?) Children whose families are considering the purchase of a car will probably be interested in such questions. Other possibilities are comparison shopping, keeping track of a favorite pitcher's earned run average, or finding out whether a stock went up 1/8 or 3/8 yesterday.

Obviously, many skills and strategies are useful in reading the newspaper. Reading newspapers in order to write better copy for the class newspaper is also important.

A FINAL WORD

This chapter has focused on informational reading—studying and doing research—and thus on the understandings, strategies, and skills students should have and use if they are to be genuinely successful in school. Basically, how effectively study skills are used depends on abilities in reading, abilities that go beyond mere word recognition and literal comprehension. But skills involve not only knowing how to use dictionaries and other reference sources, how to take notes and organize information for written and oral presentation, and how to read for various purposes, but how to do all this in the service of some worthwhile research effort. Such skills, then, are vital to success not only in the elementary school, but even more in later school years and in various activities of adult life after schooling is complete. Elementary-school children cannot learn all this but they can make a start. What is more, they can develop a positive view of what it means to learn important information and experience the satisfaction of organizing diverse materials in a way that makes sense to them and enables them to reach higher levels of understanding.

References

Askov, Eunice N., and Kamm, Karlyn. *Study Skills in the Content Areas*. Allyn and Bacon, 1985.

Beyer, Barry K. *Practical Strategies for the Teaching of Thinking*. Allyn and Bacon, 1987.

Bragstad, Bernice Jensen, and Stumpf, Sharyn Mueller. *A Guidebook for Teaching Study Skills and Motivation*, 2nd ed. Allyn and Bacon, 1987.

Cheyney, Arnold B. *Teaching Reading Skills through the Newspaper*. International Reading Association, 1992.

Cook, Doris M. *Strategic Learning in the Content Areas*. Wisconsin Department of Public Instruction, 1989.

Cross, Tracy L. "Have You Read? Content Area Literacy and Reading Comprehension." *The Reading Teacher* 46 (May 1993), pp. 708–710.

Cunningham, Patricia M., and Cunningham, James W. "Content Area Reading-Writing Lessons." *The Reading Teacher* 40 (February 1987), pp. 506–512.

Devine, Thomas G. *Teaching Study Skills*. Allyn and Bacon, 1987.

Duffy, Gerald G., and Roehler, Laura R. "Teaching Reading Skills as Strategies." *The Reading Teacher* 40 (January 1987), pp. 414–418.

Eggen, Paul D., and Kauchak, Donald P. *Strategies for Teachers: Teaching Content and Thinking Skills*. Prentice-Hall, 1988.

Fry, Edward B. *Skimming and Scanning*. Jamestown Publishers, 1982.

Heimlich, Joan E., and Pittelman, Susan D. *Semantic Mapping: Classroom Applications*. International Reading Association, 1986.

Norton, Donna E. "Webbing and Historical Fiction." *The Reading Teacher* 46 (February 1993), pp. 432–436.

Richards, Leah. "'Measuring Things in Words': Language for Learning Mathematics." *Language Arts* 67 (January 1990), pp. 14–25.

Rubin, Dorothy. *Teaching Reading and Study Skills in Content Areas*. Allyn and Bacon, 1992.

Tierney, Robert J.; Readence, John E.; and Dishner, Ernest K. *Reading Strategies and Practices: A Compendium*. Allyn and Bacon, 1990.

Winograd, Peter, and Smith, Lynne A. "Improving the Climate for Reading Comprehension Instruction." *The Reading Teacher* 41 (December 1987), pp. 304–310.

Wray, David. "Teaching Information Skills in the U.K. Elementary School." *The Reading Teacher* 41 (February 1988), pp. 520–524.

Teaching Resources

WORKBOOKS AND KITS

The Brigance Prescriptive Study Skills: Strategies and Practice. Curriculum Associates (kit of reproducible pages; grades 3–7).

Dictionary Skills. Curriculum Associates (workbook; grades 3–6).

Exploring Language with the Dictionary. Schoolhouse Press (workbooks; intermediate grades).

Flowcharting. Houghton Mifflin (workbook; upper grades).

HM Study Skills Program. NAESP Educational Products Center (guide, kit, and student text; grades 3–4).

Learning to Study. Jamestown Publishers (six workbooks and teacher editions; various grade levels).

More Lessons in Outlining. Curriculum Associates (skill-book; grades 5–8).

Reading and Thinking Strategies. D. C. Heath (kits; grades 3–6).

Sprint Reading Skills Program. Scholastic (kits; grades 1–5).

COMPUTER SOFTWARE

Alphabet, Sequences, and Alphabetizing. Random House, School Division (grades 2–4).

Building Comprehension. A. W. Peller and Associates (three sets; details, sequence, predicting outcome, etc.; K–grade 4).

The Cloze Technique for Developing Comprehension. A. W. Peller and Associates (two disks; grades 3–6).

How to Read in the Content Areas. Educational Activities (intermediate grades).

Let's Alphabetize. Unicorn Software (K–grade 3).

Library Adventure/Reference and Study Skills. Listening Library (grades 2–6).

Random House Dictionary. Sensible Software (intermediate grades).

Reading Comprehension: Main Ideas and Details. Milton Bradley (intermediate grades).

Report Writer. Society for Visual Education (teacher's guide; intermediate grades).

Storytree. Scholastic (intermediate grades).

Supermind: Advertising and Propaganda. Educational Activities (intermediate grades).

Tutorial Comprehension—Critical Reading. Random House (intermediate grades).

Who What When Where Why. Hartley (intermediate grades).

FILMSTRIPS AND VIDEOTAPES

Basic Thinking Skills. Society for Visual Education (videotape; intermediate grades).

Curious George Learns the Alphabet. Random House (filmstrips, cassettes, duplicating masters, and chart; primary grades).

Developing Effective Study Skills. Listening Library (six filmstrips with cassettes).

The Dictionary. Society for Visual Education (videotape, skill sheets, and guide; primary and intermediate grades).

The Dictionary. Thomas S. Klise (filmstrip and guide; upper grades).

Encyclopedia Brown Introduces Report-Writing Skills. Society for Visual Education (filmstrips, skill sheets, and teacher's guide; intermediate grades).

Go Find Out! Thomas S. Klise (intermediate grades).

How to Read the Newspaper Intelligently. Knowledge Unlimited (filmstrip; grades 5–6).

The Research Paper. Society for Visual Education (four filmstrips, four cassettes, worksheets, and guide; upper grades; also available in video).

Using the Encyclopedia. Thomas S. Klise (intermediate grades).

BOOKS

Don't Believe Everything You Read. PEM Press (intermediate grades).

Fact Finders. Dale Seymour (grades 4–6).

For the Love of Research. Dale Seymour (grades 4–6).

Independent Research Student Handbook. Dale Seymour (grades 4–6).

Margrabe, Mary. *Media Magic: Games and Activities for Total Curriculum Involvement.* Acropolis, 1979.

Meinbach, Anita Meyer, and Rothlein, Liz Christman. *Unlocking the Secrets of Research.* Scott, Foresman, 1985 (grades 5–8).

Pirie, Jennifer, and Pirie, Alex. *Thirty Lessons in Note Taking.* Curriculum Associates (worksheets; grades 5–8).

Reading a Newspaper. Janus (intermediate grades).

Research Skills. Coronado (grades 4–6).

Tassia, Margaret R. *Games for Information Skills.* Libraries Unlimited, 1983.

Activities for Preservice Teachers

1. Analyze your reading and study habits. Do you use any particular plan? Try some of the procedures described in this chapter, those you don't ordinarily use. Are any applicable to your situation?

2. Try skimming through magazine and newspaper articles about celebrities or political figures to find information concerning their childhood experiences or early education. What is your approach to skimming? Do you look at the first few words of each paragraph? Do you look for key sentences? Do you look for particular words?

3. Examine your local or campus newspaper and list all the types of reading experiences you find.

4. Talk with instructors who are subject-matter specialists in chemistry, economics, or other technical fields. Ask them to describe some of the reading and study problems in their fields.

5. Develop a lesson concerning one of the seasons, and plan some related encyclopedia activities for the children at a particular grade level.

6. Plan the assignment for a social-studies or science lesson at a particular grade level. Show exactly how you prepare the children for this assignment, assuming certain things about the children. Include motivation, background, and specific purposes.

7. Plan a lesson in drawing inferences for a specific grade level.

8. Collect materials for a bulletin-board display relating to a lesson on advertising techniques or propaganda.

9. Observe some classrooms where teachers are likely to ask children to study particular materials. Analyze the help given in terms of the points raised in this chapter. Note any attempts the teachers make to reinforce reading skills. Also note the extent to which they integrate the language arts with the teaching of content areas.

10. Examine some workbooks or worksheets that focus on specific reading skills, such as finding facts or following a sequence. Then find passages in science or social-studies textbooks for the same grade level that would be better vehicles for emphasizing the same skills.

Activities for Inservice Teachers

1. Evaluate the way you assign homework. Experiment with the techniques suggested in this chapter for helping children learn how to study. Note any improvements in children's attitudes about homework and the quality of learning that might be attributed to better assignments.

2. Coordinate dictionary activities with activities in various subject areas. For example, make a list of new words in a science lesson and after introducing these, have the children use a dictionary or thesaurus to find synonyms, related words, and variant meanings. This will not only help them to understand better the new words and to build vocabularies but will also give them practice in using these resources in their studying.

3. Collect a number of pictures from magazines. Have children write sentences, identifying facts and opinions. Have them look at headlines and captions for further instances of facts and opinions. This kind of activity can also be done using videotapes of television programs.

4. Show a film or videotape whose content lends itself to outlining and the use of a web or semantic map. Have children do a diagram first, showing what the main topic is and how the subtopics relate to it. Then help them convert the web into an outline.

5. Attend a meeting or conference where a variety of teaching materials are displayed. Examine these to see the ex-

tent to which they might make a worthwhile contribution to your program. Decide on the wisest way to spend any funds that might be available to support your reading program.

6. Choose a local public issue that is not too emotional (there aren't many) and have your class analyze pamphlets and news stories to see what advertising and other persuasive techniques are being used by the different sides.

7. With your class, select several topics for reports, perhaps from a social studies unit or a current event of local concern. Have each topic reported on by a group. Depending on the children's maturity and abilities, have the groups locate materials in the library, take notes, and collate information from several sources. Groups in the middle grades should be able to make outlines, write drafts, prepare bibliographies, and write (perhaps type) final reports.

8. After completing a story or a lesson in a subject area, ask the children to develop two or three good newspaper headlines based on the lesson or story. Then see if they can restate their headlines to alter the meaning. Discuss how the changes affected the meaning. An alternative to this is to give the children two slanted headlines for the same story; then have them listen to or read the story to select the headline that fits best.

Activities for Children

1. Have newspapers available so that children may use them to examine advertising copy, noting how words and sentences are used for certain purposes. Encourage the children to study how newspapers are organized into various sections (such study may lead to developing a class newspaper).

2. Children can prepare note cards to use when giving oral book reports by putting on each card a main idea followed by a list of important details they want to include.

3. Children can use a thesaurus to find synonyms and antonyms for words in spelling lessons and other words of interest to them.

4. A child can gain practice in finding the main idea by reading articles in the school newspaper, a local daily newspaper, or a children's newspaper such as *Weekly Reader* and then putting the main idea of each article into a single sentence.

5. Put lists of words on cards; on the front list the words in any order and on the back in alphabetical order. Vary the difficulty to allow for differences in the children's abilities. An individual child can select a card, put the words in alphabetical order on paper, and check the result by looking at the back of the card.

6. An individual child or a group of children might prepare a bulletin-board display showing the elements in a dictionary: guide words, entry words, pronunciation key, syllabication, and so on.

7. A child who needs more experience in putting events into sequence can draw a picture sequence of everything he or she did between getting up and arriving at school. The pictures might then be put into a strip like a comic, and dialogue added in "balloons" over the heads of the people.

8. Prepare a number of outlines by listing main topics in order on the left side of the page and subtopics in jumbled order on the right side. Children may select appropriate subtopics for each main idea and place them in appropriate sequences. On the back of each page, show how the subtopics should be placed.

9. Copies of current news articles related to children's interests (sports, local festivals, etc.) can be made available for study. Encourage the children to note how bias might be entering the articles, to determine fact and opinion, and to consider how certain expressions have been used. These aspects can be discussed in a group situation after enough children have read one or more of the articles.

10. Put out at least three issues of a class newspaper. Develop plans by having students read several different newspapers, inviting a reporter as a guest speaker, and visiting a newspaper's editorial offices.

11. Prepare specific questions related to the content being studied in social studies, science, or other subject area. Have children keep a log of the skills and strategies they used in finding answers.

12. Be sure that your listening center is well supplied with tapes designed to provide practice in finding main ideas, detecting the use of emotionally loaded words, putting information in sequence, and so on. Children need to learn how to do these things with content they both hear and read.

Chapter **14**

The Library
Media Center

*T*he term *information society,* often used to refer to today's world, has significant implications for education, including the elementary school. In the modern school, increasing attention must be given to methods of storing, processing, analyzing, and retrieving items of knowledge. This reality makes the school's library media center an integral part of all aspects of the curriculum and instructional program.

In this text we have emphasized matters related to dealing with information: learning to use computers and word processors, becoming familiar with all types of reading materials and electronic communication devices, and conducting research in order to reorganize knowledge and prepare oral and written reports. Of course, what can be done in the elementary school is limited but the beginnings are there. The extent to which a good start is made, however, depends on the availability of a well-equipped and competently staffed library media center.

THE SERVICES OF LIBRARY MEDIA CENTERS

One state recommends that library media centers have 6 square feet of floor space for each child enrolled—a total of 3,000 square feet for a school with 500 students.

The library media center has many roles to play in the elementary school. Not only is it a library and therefore a repository of books, but it is also a place where students go to learn about many other media, including sophisticated electronic devices. Teachers use the library in many ways—augmenting their classrooms with books from the building collection as well as other learning aids, and sending pupils for various kinds of assistance. In addition to these instructional services, however, the complete library media center fulfills other important responsibilities in the school community.

Roles in the School and the Community

In the school the library media center can play a significant role by taking responsibility for initiating and coordinating major activities and providing support for others.

Communitywide Projects. The library media center can be the school's representative when there are major local events such as festivals and celebrations. Exhibits can be organized by the center, for example, on special occasions, such as a state or local centennial, with displays of several kinds—murals, maps, books, and copies of historical documents. In communities with small populations, what is done in the local school often makes a very important contribution and certainly provides an excellent learning experience for the students directly involved in making the preparations.

School Events. Within the school community the library media center is often the focus of several activities. For example, a visit by an author of children's books would call for much preparation and fairly extensive follow-up activities. Book fairs where families have an opportunity to purchase children's books are often sponsored by parents' organizations in cooperation with librarians. Other events calling for book displays are science and craft fairs. In addition, "authors' teas," at which children read the books they have written to invited guests, are often held in library media centers.

Continuing Displays. Within the library media center itself and in building display cases or on bulletin boards throughout the school, the center specialists can exhibit book-related and other materials. These ongoing displays could include information on new magazines available, books focused on a particular topic (winter sports, Japan, or cooking, for example), reports done by students, computer art, and so forth. In certain cases exhibits might eventually be moved to public locations (town halls, local libraries, malls, super markets, etc.), serving to inform the community about what is being done at school.

A list of book clubs will be found at the end of this chapter.

Parents are usually pleased to support book clubs, and patronage of clubs often earns bonus books for the school.

"Clubs" for Purchasing Books. Commercially sponsored "book clubs" are popular in elementary schools and serve to provide students with regular opportunities to purchase books. Ordinarily teachers take the responsibility for promoting book sales. In some situations, however, the staff in the library media center may assume a leadership role so that children will have a more comprehensive view of what is available. Again, a display made up of possible purchases would probably be helpful.

Displays of Children's Products. When children come to the library media center they may be engaged in developing various sorts of products that can then be displayed. They may be working on a research report, a story for the classroom newspaper, a book produced on the word processor, a videotape on a science project, or some transparencies for an overhead projector. Any of these could result in something that would make an interesting display.

Retired teachers and other senior citizens make good library volunteers.

Center Volunteers. A program of adult volunteers and student aides can be very important in a library media center. When parents and other citizens are in the center on a regular basis, they not only help carry out the routine functions of the facility (thus freeing specialists to perform other more complex duties) but they also often bring specialized knowledge and skills to the school, helping students to do their research, type on the word processor, or put their books together, perhaps.

Older and especially interested students can also be library assistants. They can supervise book withdrawals and check in the returned books. Some will even be able to perform some of the same functions as the adult volunteers.

Cooperation with Teachers

New media must be planned for: innovations such as overhead transparencies, color copiers, and electronic mail don't just appear.

Staff members of library media centers need to understand each teacher and her or his classroom program so that optimal support services can be provided. This means that you must communicate your concerns and needs to staff members and be prepared to learn more about what services they are able to supply. Several areas are important.

Acquisition of Materials. As a teacher you should be prepared to suggest what ought to be acquired for the center collection. As far as books are concerned, it is not enough to request "more horse stories" or to remark that there should be "something better for the older girls." You need to confer with staff members regularly, examine lists of possible purchases, and read review copies or visit book stores in order to become informed about what might be acquired.

In addition to books you should become acquainted with what is available in other print media and also audio- and videocassettes, movies, filmstrips, and computer programs. This will require systematic searches and cooperation with the staff of the center.

Communicating about Program Directions. When you are planning to place emphasis on a particular aspect of your program, you should discuss such a venture with specialists in the library media center. They will then have ample time for planning and acquisition. If several teachers are expecting to make substantially more use of library books in their reading program, the implications of such a decision should be discussed with everyone concerned. Also, should you conclude that it would be helpful if some of your students doing research could come to the center in small groups, arrangements for such activity would have to be made in advance so that staff members would be available to assist them.

Sharing Instructional Responsibilities. Classroom teachers and center staff members are all responsible for teaching students how to use the library and media facilities. Certainly most teachers know a great deal about book collections and other print materials, but media centers often include electronic equipment and instructional-aid production facilities that teachers need to learn about. Time and commitment are required if teachers are to become competent to use these aids in their classrooms with students.

Sharing Center Facilities. A major problem with the management of centers is that it has been common to schedule entire classes to come to the library on a regular basis. When a school population is moderately large, this means that much space and time are taken up with these routine class sessions. Certainly children need to come to the library media center in order to find out about it, but if research is being given priority, some classroom periods must be reserved for intensive work with individuals and small groups undertaking fairly complex projects.

LIBRARY MEDIA CENTER COLLECTIONS

A library media center, when fully functioning, provides a wide range of services. Some of these are traditional (making books available) and some are not (providing students access to information stored in computer memories).

The Print-Materials Collection

Print materials can be acquired inexpensively through donations by parents and purchases made at auctions, charity shops, and neighborhood sales.

The books, magazines, and other printed items available in a center are basic to its functioning as a storehouse of items to be used there and borrowed by students and teachers. Several collections should be available.

Fiction Books. For most children, the library media center means stories, and this is certainly appropriate, since fiction books, hundreds or even thousands of them, ought to be available in the elementary school. (Of course, there should be a collection in each classroom, too.)

Classroom libraries are discussed in Chapter 15.

In the elementary library media center, there may be as many as three different collections of story books—picture or *easy books* for the youngest students, *juvenile books* for those in the later primary grades, and *young peoples'* or *young adult books* for older students, each with its own shelving organized according to the authors' last names.

Nonfiction Books. At the elementary level the library collection usually includes two kinds of nonfiction books: biographies and informational books about a variety of topics. As mentioned in several chapters, elementary students are making increasing use of informational books to supplement or replace textbooks and to do study and research on people and topics not sufficiently treated in the standard curriculum. Thus, the nonfiction collection must be given substantial consideration when additions to the library are made.

Reference Materials. Reference books are also increasingly important and must include several sets of encyclopedias (each classroom should also have one), comprehensive dictionaries (for teachers, mainly, but an occasional child with a particular need, too), and many other sorts of books (listed in another section of this chapter).

Children's magazines are listed at the end of this chapter.

Other Reading Materials. In addition to books, the library collection of reading materials should include newspapers, magazines, government documents, and pamphlets, as well as texts to be read on computer monitors. The many good children's magazines that are available deserve special attention.

The Media Collection

Increasingly, elementary schools use not only printed items but also pictorial representations of knowledge and electronic equipment. These approaches require systematic collection and procedures for making them accessible to teachers and children.

Audiovisual Materials. A library media center should have record collections related to music, oral language, stories, and books. These ought to include recordings of stories, book-cassette packages for reading along while listening to the story, and videotape versions of stories and books. (Other areas of language arts are also related to tapes—speech, dialect, listening and drama, for example.)

Students and teachers should have access to all kinds of audiovisual equipment in the center—slides and slide projectors, filmstrips and related projectors, overhead projectors, record players, cameras, and so forth. Students ought to be permitted to use this equipment and instructed in proper techniques.

Some elementary schools have access to electronic devices that provide much instructional assistance in making overhead transparencies, producing color copies, and storing electronic mail.

Electronic Equipment. Library media centers should make several types of electronic equipment available to teachers and their students. Important resources include audio recorders, videocassette recorders and playback equipment, and copy machines.

Computer-related possibilities ought to include computer-assisted instruction and tutoring, as well as simulation activities. In addition, some of the electronic devices required to assist special-needs students may be placed in the library media center. These are discussed in Chapter 16.

Stories, plays, and poetry are available on audiotapes.

The Instructional Materials Collection

Teaching aids of several different types may be found in the library media center, including pictures and graphics of many kinds, games, simulations, maps, kits, models, works of art, and practice materials. These may be used in the center by teachers and students or withdrawn for inclusion in a classroom program.

CHILDREN'S LEARNING AND THE CENTER

In several chapters we have described how children can make use of the library (for further discussion see Chapter 15). Besides learning how to do that, they must also learn how to use audiovisual materials. As in other areas of the classroom program, there needs to be a developmental program, a sequence of experiences that will gradually enable students to use the services and facilities of the library media center. These experiences are the joint responsibility of teachers and specialists in library and media areas.

Titles of books, videotapes, and computer programs about library use will be found at the end of the chapter.

In addition, use of the library media center involves many information-processing experiences, not only ordinary reading but also the sorts of study and research experiences described in Chapter 13. Experiences in the center also involve many embedded-lesson opportunities as children receive assistance from you and from staff members who are library specialists.

The Program for Younger Students

Children in the early grades should do most of their learning about books in conjunction with their own classroom library. There they learn to enjoy books and stories (as described in Chapters 4 and 12).

Caring for Books. Young children need guidance in how to take care of books, both at school and at home. A list of suggestions for them could include the following:

1. Handle all books carefully.
2. If you have been doing something messy, wash your hands before using a book.
3. Don't write in a book that isn't yours.
4. Protect books from getting wet.
5. Keep books away from young children who don't know how to treat them.
6. Watch pets when they are near books.
7. Return books as soon as you have finished with them.

When they make their first visits to the center, they can be reminded of these guidelines.

Learning Useful Terminology. As soon as they come to school, children can be exposed to the vocabulary of books, including terms such as *title, author,* and *illustrator.* The concept of title is relatively easy for young children to grasp—they have names, the school has a name, and the class gerbil has a name.

When a student knows the name of a book (*Curious George* or *The Very Hungry Caterpillar*), she or he can ask you to read it.

After they have heard "author" a few times as books are introduced and become authors themselves by helping to produce a class book or write their own, that concept will become well established in their minds. Then they can begin to recognize the names of a few popular writers, for instance, Dr. Seuss, Bill Martin, Jr., and Beverly Cleary. The same sort of progression will occur as children draw pictures for their books and notice how people called *illustrators* do art work for books including, in some cases, books for which the illustrator is also the author.

Children enjoy pasting in a "readers' comments" page at the end of their books and inviting classmates and others to respond.

Exposure to Books. Constant exposure to books will enable children to learn a great deal about how they are assembled—front cover and back cover, title page, dedication, and the name of the publisher. (If they are producing class or even individual books they can model theirs after the ones they have seen and supply this information, with you as the publisher). At the outset only a few students will show interest, but some will do so immediately while others will soon follow, very likely. Certainly the children should be exposed to all kinds of books: traditional stories, fairy tales, books about animals, humorous books, tall tales, fables, histories, and nonfiction informational books.

Becoming Acquainted with the Center. The first visits to the library media center may be for such purposes as hearing a book read or a story told,

Children should go to a school or public library frequently.

looking at a videotape of a story, or seeing a puppet show. Children can view or hear most of these in their own room, of course, but it is important that their initial center experience be an enjoyable one. Also, they need to become acquainted with the staff members, who are going to be important influences on their school experience.

Borrowing Books. After a few visits, children should be encouraged to take books back to their own room; usually they choose from a selection made available specifically for their group. Also, you should provide information to parents concerning how their child can go to the public library and become eligible to borrow from it.

The Program for Older Students

Children in the middle and upper grades will be familiar with the books and other collections in the library media center and will be going there as individuals, using the materials and, perhaps, serving as student assistants.

Books of All Kinds. Middle- and upper-grade students who have benefited from consistently good learning experiences with books and libraries will be not only reading their favorite kinds of materials but also branching off in many directions. They may become interested in a specific kind of fiction—science stories, for example, or historical novels—and want to try some adult-level reading not available in the school collection. Their readiness for these sorts of books would have to be discussed with the child's parents before you or a librarian could give the youngster any advice. Some realistic fiction, such as the books of Judy Blume, is appropriate for the age group, and interest in reading them should be anticipated.

Learning to use the local public library is crucial for students; it is a facility they will need all their lives.

Older children will likely begin reading nonfiction materials of all kinds, too. Again, some of this may be highly technical and involve materials not ordinarily included in the school collection, so you and members of the library media center staff may need to take steps to secure the sources that are needed.

Writing Activities. Whereas a limited number of young children may go to the library media center to do research, all older students should be involved in such reading-writing activity. As discussed in Chapter 13, those doing library research will require assistance in developing their outlines and topic webs, identifying relevant reading materials, using the word processor and printers, and so forth. It is important that teachers and center staff collaborate in ensuring that students are being taught about writing at the appropriate time and place.

Media and Electronic Equipment. Most children in the middle and upper grades can readily learn to operate electronic equipment of the conventional sort. Indeed, in some cases these students have access to camcorders and computers at home as well as record players and still cameras. They may need little more than opportunity to use the equipment and can be expected to be able to help one another learn about both hardware and software.

MAKING USE OF THE CENTER

To make maximum use of the library media center, students need to develop skills and understandings of several kinds. They need to know how the center is organized and what aids there are to finding what they need and making use of it.

Using the Book Collection

To assist students in making full use of the library collection, you and members of the library media staff must be sure that the children develop an understanding of the purposes and uses of the various parts of a book. This information is needed as they begin to use systematic organizational aids such as the card catalog and classification systems. Knowledge of book mechanics can be developed over a period of time, as children use various kinds of books and then refer to appropriate sections of them. They should gradually become familiar with the following terms:

Publisher	the company that printed the book and put it together
City	place where the book was published
Copyright date	when the book was published
Title page	a page giving the title, author, and publisher
Dedication	a special page in the book where the author thanks people, often special friends or members of his or her family
Introduction, Preface, or Foreword	any one of these names can be used for the section in the front of the book that briefly tells what the book is about or why it was written
List of illustrations	a list usually found in a book with many pictures, maps, or charts
Table of contents	a list of stories or chapters (Refer to this throughout the school year in all subject areas so that children become familiar with it.)
Glossary	a small dictionary that defines words used in this particular book (In elementary grades this is often found in the back of social studies or science books. Textbooks frequently provide experiences in using the glossary. Capitalize on these.)
Index	a list of subjects, found in the back of most books, that is the principal means for locating information (Several exposures will be needed for pupils to develop an understanding of the arrangement of indexes, their location, the format used, subtopic arrangements, and the relationship to the table of contents in the amount of detail.)

The Card Catalog. After children have visited the center a few times, the card catalog may be introduced and its use explained. Later, when the opportunity arises, this learning can be reinforced. A child may say, "This was a good book. I would like to read another one like it." That will be the time to suggest that he or she look in the card catalog to see if there is another book by the same author or on the same subject. Another child might report, "Someone told me the name of a good book, but I don't know how to find it in the library." Then the

Children should learn to use a card catalog by using one.

use of title cards can be introduced. Thus, when children are ready to prepare reports, the catalog will not be entirely unfamiliar to them. Before they can be truly independent in using it, however, they will need a lesson or series of lessons demonstrating the various kinds of cards and how they can be of help.

Begin with the physical setup of the card catalog or catalogs. In most libraries, author, title, and subject cards are all filed together, in alphabetical order. In some, however, each of these categories is filed separately; children should be aware of both possibilities. Similarly, cards for audiovisual materials may be filed in a separate catalog, or they may be included with those for books.

Libraries that middle-grade students use are likely to file all, or most, cards together. In such cases, they will probably use a color-coding system, which is especially useful because it helps both you and the children to discover quickly and easily whether the library has a filmstrip or cassette, for instance, that might be useful in presenting a report or teaching a particular unit. In this system, each type of material is assigned a particular color. That is, cards for filmstrips might have a strip of green tape across the top, sound cassettes a red one, videocassettes and films a blue one, and so on. These items will be filed alphabetically according to both subject and title.

A helpful teaching technique is to use a sketch of the external features of the card catalog, including guide letters. Then display this facsimile on a chart or bulletin board and use short oral drills to provide practice in deciding which drawer to look in for a particular entry. Stress the alphabetical arrangement, point out that even the books listed under an author's name are in alphabetical order, and call attention to the fact that articles *(a, an,* and *the)* are not considered in alphabetizing titles.

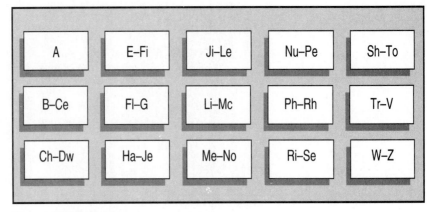

Chart or Bulletin Board

Ask questions, such as, "In which drawer would you find these entries":

- *How to Be a Perfect Person in Three Days?*
- information about space travel?
- skiing stories?
- a cassette recording of *And Now Miguel?*
- a Halloween poem?
- a biography of Michael Jordan?

Continue this type of activity only as long as seems necessary, making sure to include a variety of topic headings, as well as many entries that might be found under more than one. Help children learn to explore all possible headings; for example, a Halloween poem might be located under "Halloween," "holidays," or even "poetry" or "poems"; and the cassette of it could be listed in the general file or in a special one.

Children who are ready to explore the card catalog will have already had a great deal of experience in using other sources that are alphabetically arranged: dictionaries, indexes, and telephone directories, for instance. Therefore, they should have little difficulty in mastering the organizational features of the catalog. A significant aspect of this learning is understanding how to use the different kinds of cards in the catalog to find books and information. In conjunction with teaching about the physical setup of the catalog, then, describe and discuss the cards themselves.

A bulletin-board display with enlargements of actual cards (done on a copy machine, perhaps) will be needed. (See the examples of types of cards that on the next pages.) These reproductions can be placed below the chart showing the outside of the card catalog. Both interest and information can be added by putting explanatory notes on colored cards and attaching each to the item it refers to with colored yarn. Be sure to include all the types of cards and to keep the display up until after the children have had actual experience in using the catalog to find needed information.

author card

551.6
D
	Davis, Hubert
	      A January fog will freeze a hog, and
	other weather folklore. Compiled and
	edited by Hubert Davis. Illus. by John
	Wallner. Crown, 1977
	      unp. illus.
	      Thirty sayings used to predict the
	weather are accompanied by a factual
	explanation, the origin of the saying,
	and its general reliability.
	
	      1. Weather lore. I. Wallner, John
	II. Title

book is located in
nonfiction section

author
title

publisher

cards also under
these headings

title card

A January fog will freeze a hog, and
other weather folklore
 	
551.6   Davis, Hubert
D   A January fog will freeze a hog, and
other weather folklore. Compiled and
edited by Hubert Davis. Illus. by John
Wallner.   Crown, 1977
            unp.   illus.
 	
            1. Weather lore. I. Wallner, John
      II. Title

remember that this
card will be found
under J, not A

pages are not
numbered; book
is illustrated

subject card

WEATHER LORE
 	
551.6   Davis, Hubert
            A January fog will freeze a hog, and
other weather folklore. Compiled and
edited by Hubert Davis. Illus. by John
Wallner.   Crown, 1977
            unp.   illus.
            Thirty sayings used to predict the
weather are accompanied by a factual
explanation, the origin of the saying,
and its general reliability.
 	
            1. Weather lore. I. Wallner, John
      II. Title

note that cards are
alphabetized by first
letter at top of card,
regardless of
indentation

there will also be a card
for this book under the
illustrator's name

Catalog Cards: Dewey Decimal System

Continued

title card

	The great Gilly Hopkins
j Fiction	Paterson, Katherine
	The great Gilly Hopkins. New York: Crowell, 1978.
	I. Foster care homes—fiction
	I. Title

book may be found
in juvenile fiction

cards for fiction are
virtually the same in
Dewey Decimal and
Library of Congress
systems

author card

j Fiction	Paterson, Katherine
	The great Gilly Hopkins. New York: Crowell, 1978.
	I. Foster care homes—fiction
	I. Title

when illustrator
is important,
there may be a
third card

see and see also cards

WHITTLING   see

WOODCARVING

there is nothing catalogued
under this heading; look
under woodcarving for
information about whittling

AIRPLANES   see also

AERONAUTICS

some information can be
found under this heading;
you may find additional
information under the
second heading

Catalog Cards: Dewey Decimal System

author card

jPN	Bishop, Ann
6371.5	Noah riddle? Pictures by Jerry Warshaw.
B52	Chicago, J. Whitman, 1970.

call number—book is
in juvenile nonfiction

40 p.   col. illus.   22 cm.

book has 40 pages
and color illustrations

A collection of riddles about
Noah and the animals in his ark.

1. Riddles
I. Warshaw, Jerry
II. Title

title card

jPN
6371.5
B52   Noah riddle?

Bishop, Ann
    Noah riddle? Pictures by Jerry Warshaw.
Chicago, J. Whitman, 1970.

40 p.   col. illus.   22 cm.

A collection of riddles about
Noah and the animals in his ark.

1. Riddles
I. Bishop, Ann
II. Warshaw, Jerry

subject card

RIDDLES

jPN   Bishop, Ann
6371.5   Noah riddle? Pictures by Jerry Warshaw.
B52   Chicago, J. Whitman, 1970.

40 p.   col. illus.   22 cm.

A collection of riddles about
Noah and the animals in his ark.

1. Bishop, Ann   I. Warshaw, Jerry
II. Title

Catalog Cards: Library of Congress System

Continued

illustrator card

```
            Warshaw, Jerry

jPN         Bishop, Ann
6371.5          Noah riddle? Pictures by Jerry Warshaw.
B52         Chicago, J. Whitman, 1970.

            40 p.   col. illus.   22 cm.

            A collection of riddles about
            Noah and the animals in his ark.

            1. Riddles
            I. Bishop, Ann
            II. Title
```

cassette cards

Oversize probably
means that the
cassette is packaged
with the book by the
same name and kept
in a special place in
the library; ask the
librarian about
location

```
CASSETTE
j                 McDermott, Gerald
Oversize              Arrow to the sun.
PZ                [Sound recording.]—
8.1               Weston Woods, 1975
 .M159
Ar                    1 cassette [LTR 184C]

                      1. Pueblo Indians—Legends
                      I. title
```

publisher

order number of
cassette

```
CASSETTE          Arrow to the sun
j
Oversize          McDermott, Gerald
PZ                    Arrow to the sun.
8.1               [Sound recording.]—
 .M159            Weston Woods, 1975
Ar
                      1 cassette [LTR 184C]

                      1. Pueblo Indians—Legends
                      I. McDermott, Gerald
```

remember these cards
may be color-coded if
filed in the general file

cards for other media
will be similar to these

```
CASSETTE          PUEBLO INDIANS—Legends
j
Oversize          McDermott, Gerald
PZ                    Arrow to the sun.
8.1               [Sound recording.]—
 .M159            Weston Woods, 1975
Ar
                      1 cassette [LTR 184C]

                      1. McDermott, Gerald
                      I. Title
```

Catalog Cards: Library of Congress System

Children will probably have questions about the cards and the notes on them: "Is a book listed only once in the catalog? What does the call number mean?" Answer these questions as thoroughly as possible to help children feel competent and at ease in using library aids. Some questions may not have especially logical answers, and when this is true, simply say so. For example, why are an author's first *and* last names capitalized when only the first word of a book title is? Why does one card contain more complete information than another card on the same book?

If children have had a limited amount of library experience, they may need to do practice exercises to ensure they know how to use the card catalog. For example, they might report on how many books the library has by Lois Lenski, Judith Viorst, or some other author they like; they could begin with a list of book titles (both fiction and nonfiction) and find the names of the authors and where the books are located in the library; or each child could select a subject and find three books containing information about it, what subject headings they are listed under, and where they are located on the shelves. Again, provide this kind of practice only as much as seems necessary; if some children are already fairly adept at using the catalog, let them work on reports or serve as "assistant teachers" for those who need practice.

As soon as possible, each child should select a topic and go to the library to find information related to a class project; purposeful activities will provide greater reinforcement than any number of practice drills. Frequent opportunities to use the library in connection with units of study in all areas of the curriculum will both enrich the classroom program and help to establish important learnings. A special caution should be observed here, though: *know* your libraries and make sure that the children choose topics about which information is available. No amount of teaching about library procedures will be successful if a child's first efforts to find materials are *un*successful.

Activities related to using the card catalog should be designed to present essential information:

- Author, title, and subject cards are all arranged alphabetically.
- Cards for media items may be filed in the general catalog or in a separate one. These cards are also in alphabetical order, under both subject and title.
- Titles beginning with *A, An,* or *The* are alphabetized according to their second word. (Note that *And* is not included here.)
- A number in the title may or may not be spelled out but the title card is filed as though it were.
- Names beginning with *Mac* or *Mc* are filed together.
- Abbreviated words are listed as if they were spelled out. For example, for "U.S. Government," the alphabetical arrangement places this entry as if it were spelled out: "United States Government." The same applies to such abbreviations as *Dr., Mrs., Mr., St.,* and so on.
- Author cards for books by the same writer are filed according to the alphabetical order of the titles of the books: "Politi, Leo, *Butterflies Come, The*" comes before "Politi, Leo, *Song of the Swallows.*"

Call Numbers. Children may find out about call numbers while they are learning to use the card catalog. The following specifics are particularly important.

Organize an in-library "treasure hunt" to see who can find answers to such questions.

Communicate with the local public library when students are going to be in much need of services. Perhaps additional materials can be secured, special borrowing arrangements made, displays provided, and so forth.

1. It should be pointed out that fiction books will have the letter *j* (standing for *juvenile*) on their spine, possibly followed by a capital letter indicating the first letter of the author's last name. These letters constitute the call number of the book, enabling the reader to find the approximate place on the shelves where the book will be found in alphabetical order by the author's name. When the library has a separate collection for older children, books found there will be marked with a *y* or *ya* (meaning *young adult*). Cards for both of these categories, as well as picture books, will be found in the card catalog.

2. Biographies may be shelved in either of two ways. In most libraries children will use, biographies are likely to be together and have either the letter *B* or the call number *92* on their spines. Some libraries, however, are beginning to shelve biographies along with books about the subject's vocation or area of expertise; that is, a biography of Martina Navratilova will be found in the sports section, one about Duke Ellington in the music section, and so on. In either case, though, biographies are alphabetized according to the name of the person the book is about rather than the name of the author. Therefore, a biography will have the first letter of the subject's name beneath the call letter or number so that all books about the same person will be together. Thus, a child looking for a biography of a particular person will have only one place to look instead of several.

3. Other nonfiction books (biography is nonfiction) are arranged in numerical order according to numbers that indicate what each book is about. Thus, as with biographies, all the books about the same subject can be shelved together. Call numbers are assigned according to a classification system that has been worked out to include all subject areas. There are two of these systems; one or the other is used in almost every library of any size (see related sections in this chapter). General reference books such as encyclopedias and dictionaries, which contain information about many subjects, are another special category of nonfiction. These usually have the letter *R* on their spines, are kept in a special area, and can seldom be checked out of the library.

4. Media items have call numbers similar to those for books and are often grouped together for ease of care, use, and storage—that is, records are together, cassettes together, pictures in a special file, and so forth. In the juvenile sections of some libraries, however, a record might be found on the shelf next to the book that is recorded, a cassette could be packaged in a plastic bag with its book and kept in a special place, and so on. The librarian should be asked to help if these materials cannot be located.

Children who understand how to use the card catalog and what the call numbers mean are well on their way to being able to find what they are looking for, even in the large libraries they will encounter later. It is important to help them understand that this is not simply a complicated system set up by adults to try to confuse them. Rather, the card catalog is like a telephone directory; just as a child can look in the telephone directory to find out where a friend lives, so he or she can look in the card catalog to find out where a particular book, or information about a particular subject, can be located. The call number is the book's "address"; it shows where the book is shelved in the library, and it helps the librarian to put the book away quickly so that another person will be able to find it.

The important concept for children to learn is that the numbers will guide them in locating the books they want. If they are curious about what the numbers mean, a simple explanation can help them to understand why books about the same subject have the same or similar numbers and to recognize that there is order in the arrangement.

Although most university and other large libraries now use the Library of Congress system, many small libraries, including those in the schools, find the Dewey Decimal system better suited to their needs. Begin with whichever is used in libraries available to the children, although it would be a good idea to point out that this is not the only system. If neither system is used, teaching should be postponed until it can be meaningful.

Dewey Decimal System. In the Dewey Decimal System, books are arranged numerically on the shelves; therefore, anyone who knows the call number of the book he or she wants can find it easily; the call number, of course, is found by looking in the card catalog. The numbers represent ten general subject areas, as follows:

000–099	Reference books, such as encyclopedias and bibliographies (Many of these have the letter *R* on the spine and can seldom be checked out of a library; those that have call numbers usually can be checked out.)
100–199	Philosophy, psychology, ethics
200–299	Religion, including mythology and religions of all peoples
300–399	Social sciences: law, government, education, vocations, civics, economics
400–499	Language: dictionaries and books about the study of all languages
500–599	Science: mathematics, physics, chemistry, biology, zoology, botany
600–699	Useful arts: medicine, engineering, agriculture, aviation, manufacturing, etc.
700–799	Fine arts: painting, music, photography, recreation
800–899	Literature: poetry, plays, novels, and criticisms of these
900–999	History, geography, travel, biography

All of these general areas are divided into many subtopics, each of which has its own number. For example, the 630s are devoted to agriculture, so a book on forestry will be numbered 634, probably followed by a decimal point and another number to indicate a further subdivision of that subtopic.

The Library of Congress Classification. The Library of Congress classification may be explained if it is used in your library. By the time children reach the upper grades, they should at least be aware that there is more than one system of classification, since they may be using more than one library.

A	General works
B	Philosophy–religion
C	History–auxiliary science
D	History and topography (except America)
E & F	America
G	Geography–anthropology
H	Social science
J	Political sciences
K	Law
L	Education
M	Music
N	Fine arts
P	Language and literature
Q	Science
R	Medicine
S	Agriculture–plant and animal industry

T	Technology
U	Military service
V	Naval service
Z	Bibliography and library science

Additional letters and numerals are used to identify books within each sector of the Library of Congress system. *Education* is *L,* for example, so this textbook would have that designation. However, there are thousands of books related to education, so additional letters and numerals are needed.

Using Media

In some school library media centers, teaching aids, audiovisual equipment and electronic devices may be housed in a separate room or their own section of the center. They may be kept in an instructional materials center, for example. Also, the school's computer lab may be located near the library media center or organized as part of it. Wherever media materials are kept, learning to find and use them should be considered part of library instruction.

Children need practice both in locating the various audiovisual aids and in using them to supplement and add interest to reports and similar learning experiences. Therefore, as soon as they have become sufficiently familiar with the card catalog and the library itself to prepare simple reports using more than one source, plan for them to give reports in several subject areas, for which they may use various audiovisual aids. Make sure, however, that children understand that the aids chosen must fit the organizational plan for the report. Point out that if a particular videotape, for example, cannot be included in the outline for the report, it should not be a part of that report, however interesting it may be.

Such reports, when well prepared, not only enrich classroom activities but help to prepare children for the kinds of presentations that many will be expected to make during later school years and in adult life. This is an important beginning.

Caring for Media Materials. While many children have already had experiences with record players, audio- and videocassettes, electronic games, and other types of equipment and media when they come to school, all will need some guidance in learning how to use classroom and media center materials—overhead and other projectors, computers, video cameras, and so forth. They need to recognize that any such piece of equipment is not a toy and must be used and cared for properly. You and the media staff should work with them as they learn and assist them in establishing their own standards for media use, like the following:

When You Use Media

1. Work quietly and don't disturb others.
2. Don't get fingerprints on filmstrips, slides, tapes, or lenses.
3. Don't tear or bend filmstrips. Handle all materials carefully.
4. Be sure you know how to work machines before using them.
5. Put materials away when you are finished.

Selecting Media Materials. Selecting materials for the media center should receive as much attention as is given to selecting books for the library, since there is great variation in quality where each is concerned. Well-chosen materials can be used to enrich the curriculum as well as to guide children to books. For example, a beginning reader is likely to enjoy listening to a cassette recording as he or she "reads" Ezra Jack Keats's *Whistle for Willie,* and children will rush to find Pat Hutchins's *Rosie's Walk* after viewing the film.

The amount of computer software available is large and growing. Since the advent of the computer, the market has been flooded with software, much of it very poor in quality. (Review the software selection guidelines listed in Chapter 2.) This makes it necessary for teachers who want to use such materials to consult with the librarian, read current reviews in professional magazines, and check sources published by various organizations. And by all means, keep in mind that since the quality of these materials varies greatly, they should all be previewed before you use or recommend them for the library or media center.

Using Reference Materials

The use of an encyclopedia, atlas, almanac, biographical dictionary, fact book, or similar reference involves many of the same skills as those needed for effective use of a dictionary or a library card catalog. In addition, skillful use of most

Children will benefit from familiarity with many kinds of reference books.

reference books requires the ability to locate the particular passage, paragraph, or sentence within a section or a book that gives the specific information sought, and some familiarity with each of the reference sources—familiarity gained through practice in using them.

Encyclopedias. Even young children often have access to simplified encyclopedia-like sets of books that contain many illustrations and much information about animals and other topics likely to be of interest to them. Gradually they begin to use encyclopedias such as *Childcraft* and *World Book* that provide them with valuable experience in seeking and locating information as well as in general browsing.

You can introduce encyclopedia use by demonstrating that you use the index to find where to look for information and that you can then turn to the correct page and read the information you were looking for. Do this frequently as more information is needed on subjects being discussed. Tell and show the children what you are doing, and read what you find.

Intermediate-grade children should receive more direct instruction, which should include the following strategies and understandings:

- the form in which material in an encyclopedia is arranged, and differences in arrangement in the encyclopedias available for their use
- knowledge of the location of the index and the meanings of guide letters on the covers of volumes; particular attention should be given to boldface type, parentheses, italics, and so on
- the use of pronunciation keys, cross-reference listings, and bibliographies at the close of articles

Most school libraries have several different sets of encyclopedias. Children should have experience with all that are available to them. In connection with learning to take notes, each child can select a topic and look for information about it in all of the encyclopedias available. Comparing the information found will help children to discover the importance of looking in several sources for information. This should be done a number of times with several subjects; repeated experiences under guidance are essential for effective use of encyclopedias.

Children often enjoy using encyclopedias and other reference tools, and this type of experience provides opportunities for learning to locate information; to read critically; to take notes on, summarize, and outline what they have read; to prepare an oral or written report; to use handwriting, spelling, and punctuation skills; to compose with specific information and an audience in mind; and to do proofreading and editing. Thus, learning to use the encyclopedia not only is valuable in itself but also involves practice in a wealth of related language skills.

Other Reference Books. Much information is gathered in modern societies and among the public there is sufficient interest in almost any topic to warrant the publication of books devoted to it: baseball statistics, fishing atlases, film and television trivia, music yearbooks, and so on and on. Although an elementary-school collection cannot include all of these, some are certainly appropriate when it is likely that children would find a good use for them.

Atlases. Atlases are usually combinations of maps and tables of information, with some text included as well. At the elementary level, atlases are especially useful in social studies, although they can make a contribution to almost any area of the curriculum. If you emphasize current national and world events in your classroom program, you will want to have an atlas on the shelf so that it can be used regularly. This is the best way for children to learn geography—little by little and in connection with a meaningful discussion.

Almanacs. Students should have access to almanacs of several kinds in their classroom and the school library so that they can browse in them. They can find bits of information (What country produced the most rice last year?) and create their own trivia bulletin board. Then perhaps they can go on to start an almanac about the local community.

Famous First Facts. Intermediate-grade children have been known to get into the "yes, they did"—"no, they didn't" type of argument. Many times, such disputes can be settled by referring to *Famous First Facts,* a book that lists numerous items referring to events and people in the United States: the name of the first woman doctor, for example, or the date on which the accordion was patented.

Specific Sources. Just as readers can improve their performance by reading a great deal of material that is easy for them, they can improve their reference skills and strategies by spending time with less serious texts than encyclopedias. The following might be considered for inclusion in a school library media center.

- *The Guinness Book of World Records* lists accomplishments in a large number of categories, many of which are of interest to children. Students are likely to enjoy exploring the book's contents, maybe searching for an area in which they might compete for a record.

- *The Harper's Index Book* provides much numerical data about social matters. Students interested in making graphs will find many good possibilities.

- *Facts and Fallacies* contains 400 stories of unusual events—amazing feats of building, interesting customs, and so forth.

- A number of sources are mostly amusing: *It Is Illegal to Quack Like a Duck & Other Freaky Laws; The Dinosaur Is the Biggest Animal That Ever Lived and Other Wrong Ideas You Thought Were True;* and *Elephants Can't Jump and Other Freaky Facts about Animals.*

The Kid's World Almanac of Records and Facts, by Margo McLoone-Basta and Alice Siegel (World Almanac Publications, 1985), contains a special chapter of questions children ask, such as "How much does the earth weigh?" and "What makes popcorn pop?"

Children will be fascinated with the many kinds of one-volume references to be found in the library. A few are listed below; let them see how many others they can find.
Book of Lists
Dictionary of Art and Artists
Dictionary of Costume
The Ethnic Almanac
Geographical Dictionary

ELECTRONIC INFORMATION RETRIEVAL

Computerized information searches are available in most libraries used by adults and are beginning to appear in some elementary-school library media centers. When a computer-based book search system is in place, a child does not have to use the card catalog but may simply go to a computer terminal, type in the name of the author, and be able to see on the screen a list of all the books the library has by that author and the call number for each. (Of course, the title itself may be typed in, if known, and in some cases the child may be able to type in the subject and get a list of all the books related to it.) However, it is important for students also to know how to use the card catalog—computers are not always available.

In some library media centers students may use a computer to read, view pictures and graphs, and listen to sound presentations—all from a single disk.

In a well-equipped library media center students can combine sources and produce a computer presentation that includes text material, pictures, diagrams, videotapes, and sound recordings.

Encyclopedias and some other library reference materials are available in video disk formats in an increasing number of elementary schools. Some of these disks are *multimedia;* that is, they can produce not only texts on the monitor screen but also pictures and other graphic materials, speech, music, animations, and film clips—all in sound and color. Thus, students interested in volcanoes, by typing in the word, gain access not only to reading material on volcanoes but also to a map showing where most volcanoes occur, an animated depiction of what occurs in an eruption, a sound film of an actual eruption, a guided tour of a lava flow, and much else.

A FINAL WORD

In several important ways the library media center can be the focus of intellectual life in an elementary school. No matter what the curriculum area of interest—from art history to computer science—the center is the place to find relevant sources. And, of equal importance, in most situations all of the language arts are usually involved.

As electronic communications becomes more comprehensive, elementary library media centers will be connected with a vast network of information facilities, including research libraries, government agencies, satellite systems, and even elementary schools in other countries. Some day soon, instant, world-wide communication will be feasible for many children.

References

American Association of School Librarians, *Information Power: Guidelines for School Library Media Programs.* American Library Association, 1988.

Bell, Irene W., and Brown, Robert B. *Gaming in the Media Center Made Easy.* Libraries Unlimited, 1982.

Bell, Irene W., and Weikert, Jeanne. *Basic Media Skills Through Games,* 2nd ed. Libraries Unlimited, 1985.

Congress of the United States. *Power On! New Tools for Teaching and Learning.* Congress of the United States, 1988.

Hart, Thomas L. *Instruction in School Library Media Center Use,* 2nd ed. American Library Association, 1985.

Jay, M. Ellen, and Jay, Hilda L., *Building Reference Skills in the Elementary School.* Library Professional Publications, 1986.

Jones, Dorothy Blythe. *Children's Media Market Place.* Neal-Schuman, 1988.

Kulleseid, E. R., and Strickland, D. S. *Literature, Literacy, and Learning: Classroom Teachers, Library Media Specialists, and the Literature-based Curriculum.* American Library Association, 1989.

Language Arts 67:7 (November, 1990) (entire issue on "Libraries and Language Arts").

Lewis, Marguerite. *Hooked on Research.* Center for Applied Research in Education, 1984.

Margrabe, Mary. *Media Magic: Games and Activities for Total Curriculum Involvement.* Acropolis, 1979.

———. *New Library Media Center: A Stations Approach with Media Kit.* Acropolis, 1975.

Montgomery, Paula K., and Walker, H. Thomas. *Teaching Library Media Skills: An Instructional Program for Elementary and Middle School Students.* Libraries Unlimited, 1983.

Richardson, Selma K. *Magazines for Children: A Guide for Parents, Teachers, and Librarians.* American Library Association, 1983.

———. *Periodicals for School Media Programs.* American Library Association, 1972.

———, ed. *Children's Services of Public Libraries.* University of Illinois, Graduate School of Library and Information Science, 1978.

School Library Media Activities Monthly, published by LMS Associates.

Stoll, Donald R., ed. *Magazines for Children.* International Reading Association, 1990.

Urbanik, M. K. *Curriculum Planning and Teaching Using the Library Media Center.* The Scarecrow Press, 1989.

Teaching Resources

Adventures in Library Land. Random House (six sound filmstrips and teacher's guides; K–grade 6).

Brigance, Albert H. *Study Skills: Strategies and Practice.* Curriculum Associates (reproducible study sheets on reference skills, reading graphs, and maps; grades 3–8).

Curious George Visits the Library. CTB/Macmillan McGraw-Hill (software and related materials; ages 4–8)

Doing Research and Writing Reports. Scholastic (workbooks and teacher's editions; grades 4–6).

The Elementary School Library. Society for Visual Education (four filmstrips, four cassettes, worksheets, and teacher's guide; grades 3–6).

Knowlton, Jack. *Books and Libraries.* HarperCollins, 1991 (grades 2–6).

Lathrop, Ann. *How Can I Find It If I Don't Know What I'm Looking For: Library Skills.* Sunburst Communications, 1985 (computer program).

Library Skills. Scholastic (workbooks and teacher's editions; grades 2–6).

Library Skills Series. Random House (six filmstrips with cassettes and teacher's guide; grades 4–6).

Mallett, Jerry J. *Library Skills Activities.* Center for Applied Research in Education (workbook whose pages can be duplicated).

Meet the Card Catalog. Library Filmstrip Center (filmstrip, cassette, and teacher's guide; grades 4–7).

My Library. Spoken Arts (four filmstrips, four cassettes, and teacher's guide; upper grades).

Reference Skills. Random House (audiocassettes and worksheet masters; grades 4–9).

Ripley's Library Research Skills. Society for Visual Education, 1986 (four filmstrips, four cassettes, twenty-four skillsheets, two computer disks, and teacher's guide; intermediate grades).

Schwartz, Perry. *Make Your Own Video.* Lerner Books, 1991.

McInerney, Claire. *Tracking the Facts: How to Develop Research Skills.* Lerner Books (grades 4–8).

McInerney, Claire. *Find It! The Inside Story at Your Library.* Lerner Books (grades 4–8)

Using the Library. Society for Visual Education (four filmstrips, four cassettes, worksheets, and teacher's guide; upper grades).

CHILDREN'S BOOK CLUBS

Children's Book-of-the-Month Club
Time & Life Bldg.
1271 Avenue of the Americas
New York, NY 10020

Junior Library Guild
666 Fifth Avenue
New York, NY 10103

Scholastic Inc.
730 Broadway
New York, NY 10003

Trumpet Club
Bantam Doubleday Dell
666 Fifth Avenue
New York, NY 10103

Weekly Reader Book Clubs
245 Long Hill Road
Middletown, CT 06457

MAGAZINES FOR CHILDREN

Cobblestone: The History Magazine for Young People
Cobblestone Publishing
30 Grove Street
Peterborough, NH 03458

Cricket: The Magazine for Children
P.O. Box 51144
Boulder, CO 80321

Faces: The Magazine about People
30 Grove Street
Peterborough, NH 03458

Highlights for Children
P.O. Box 269
Columbus, OH 43272

Jack and Jill
P.O. Box 10003
Des Moines, IA 50340

Junior Scholastic
2931 E. McCarthy Street
P.O. Box 3710
Jefferson City, MO 65102

National Geographic World
P.O. Box 2330
Washington, D. C. 20077

Activities for Preservice Teachers

1. Investigate the possibility of involving parents as librarians or library helpers. Be prepared to report to the class.

2. Gather materials on book fairs. What has to be done to get a traveling exhibit to come to a school?

3. Survey several classrooms to determine how many pupils have public library cards. Inquire how often those with cards use them.

4. Plan a lesson for a particular primary grade that will necessitate looking up information in a beginning encyclopedia. Be sure to find out whether this information can be found in an encyclopedia that might be available to a class at this grade level.

5. Visit the library to obtain lists of Newbery and Caldecott award winners. Familiarize yourself with as many of these books as possible, and begin a card file of annotations for primary, middle, or upper grades.

6. Select a fifth-grade text for a specific subject area. Using the text as a base, make a unit lesson plan that would require children to go to the library for added information. Be sure to provide for differences in library experience and language skills.

7. Familiarize yourself with at least one set of encyclopedias, one atlas, and one of the other references listed in this chapter. Note particularly organization, teaching aids provided, types of information included, and grade levels for which each might be suitable.

8. Plan an activity designed to familiarize children with the use of a reference tool other than the encyclopedia. Demonstrate to the class exactly how you would present it.

9. Plan a unit for a particular subject area and grade level. Include at least three different types of audiovisual aids and tell how you would use them.

10. Examine a number of teaching aids such as those listed above and begin a file of ones you would like to use in teaching library skills at a particular grade level. Give reasons for your choices.

Activities for Inservice Teachers

1. Visit libraries in your area. Discuss with librarians the ages, interests, and reading abilities of your class. Find out what each library has to offer of a special nature for children. Find out what the librarian would like children of the ages of those in your class to know about the library.

2. Prepare a bulletin-board display designed to teach the use of the card catalog. Make large sample cards, similar to those in this chapter, with explanations (including pictures) of the various entries on the cards.

3. Plan a library skills unit for your class. Include visits to libraries in your plans.

4. Prepare activities that require children to use particular library skills—for example, finding several references about a topic, using an atlas, finding fiction books by a particular author, or locating a specific issue of a magazine.

5. Make a survey of the amount of library-use teaching done in your school. Report the results of your survey.

6. Plan a unit in a subject area for which children will prepare individual or group reports, using audiovisual aids. Report to the class on the number and types of aids used and how successful they were.

7. List the media aids or other resources you have used in teaching library skills to your class. Which would you use again and why?

Activities for Children

1. Individual children can go to the library and report back to the class about one or more kinds of reference books or sets. For example, one child might go to find out about the different kinds of atlases the library has. Each report should be complete enough for the children to appreciate the differences among the references in a category. Permission might be obtained to bring one or more of the reference works to the classroom at the time of the report for purposes of illustration.

2. Ability to read verbal and pictorial symbols related to air and auto travel is a true part of literacy. A child or group of children could prepare a chart or bulletin-board display showing the different types of signs that would be seen in an airport or on the highway, for example.

3. Ask a child to find the title and call letters for a book by each of these authors:

Tomie de Paolo	Virginia Hamilton
Maurice Sendak	Eve Bunting
Jane Yolen	Jack Prelutsky

Then reverse the process and give a few titles of books for which the child is to find the names of the authors.

4. Prepare sheets containing various informational statements, some true and some false. Individual children who need additional practice in library and study skills can find out whether or not the information is true. Sample statements might read as follows:

Julie of the Wolves was written by Roald Dahl.

Hailstones and Halibut Bones is a book of poems about holidays.

Chicago is approximately 850 miles from Boston by air.

The piranha is a flesh-eating fish that lives in the Amazon River.

5. During the football season (or that of baseball, hockey, etc.), a sports-minded pupil might prepare a bulletin-board display using pictures cut from magazines and newspapers and featuring information about the sport, gathered from almanacs and other sources.

6. Have a child prepare a report on the library to present to another class. This should include the use of visual aids—for example, reproductions of various types of cards from the card catalog, a floor plan of the library, books with different types of call numbers, and so forth.

7. A child can use an atlas to plan an imaginary trip, plotting the route to be taken, places of interest to visit, time necessary for traveling, method of travel, kinds of clothing needed, and so on.

8. An individual child can prepare a report for the class about the Caldecott or Newbery Medal. This might include information such as when the award was first given, what factors enter into the selection, and which books and authors have won it that the class is familiar with. Several books that have received the award might be used to illustrate the report.

9. When the class is working on a project for which supplementary material is needed (this will occur often in a program that is vital and broad), a child—or several children—can go to the library to locate and examine materials that might be useful. The child can either check out these materials for class use (arrangements will need to be made with the librarian for this) or prepare a list to be placed on the bulletin board, giving the title, the author, a few words about content, and the call number or location for each item.

Chapter **15**

Children and Books

*I*n the preceding chapter on library media centers the importance of making books available to children was emphasized. Certainly we all expect books to play a significant role in children's lives and for this reason consider that their full access to them is something so important as to require the attention of society's leaders.

In some families youngsters have many positive book-related experiences. They grow up in homes where there are dozens and even hundreds of volumes, where small children have books of their own, and where older girls and boys have bookcases that are completely full. Youngsters from this sort of background are also likely to visit public libraries regularly and attend elementary schools with good building and classroom libraries.

In other situations, sad to say, children have little access to the best kinds of books, in either homes, communities, or schools. Teachers who realize the inequity of such conditions are in the best position to educate the public concerning the importance of providing more and better books to libraries and schools. Also, as individuals they need to do whatever they can to bring books and students together.

BOOKS IN CHILDREN'S LIVES

In books children find much enjoyment, of course, but they also gain a better understanding of the world and their place in it as they read more and more widely. Many stories enable them to identify with characters involved in complex situations and events and to become acquainted with imaginary figures they often come to know well and even to identify with. Also, they can read informational nonfiction books that explore many significant topics, including aspects of daily life.

All children's books referred to are listed at the end of the chapter.

Areas of special importance are family and personal matters, the lives of others, and access to organized information that is relevant to all kinds of interests.

Family Relationships

Family matters are very important to children, including relationships with their parents and feelings about siblings and other relatives. There are numerous stories related to family situations, including many of the Ramona books (*Ramona and Her Father,* for instance); *Maudie in the Middle,* about the middle child in a family; and *It's Like This, Cat,* which tells about Dave who wants a cat, not the dog his father thinks would be better for him.

Relations between brothers and sisters receive much attention in storybooks. Judy Blume's *The Pain and the Great One* is a good example, as is *For Sale—One Sister—Cheap!* There are many others that relate to families, with titles indicating their story lines: *My Grandma's in a Nursing Home, Grandpa Loves Us* and *I Love My Grandma.* Some deal with specific situations: *Cracker Jackson* is about domestic violence and in *The Wednesday Surprise* one family member helps another learn to read. *The Relatives Came* provides some insights into the advantages and disadvantages of having a large family.

Reading a book about a sensitive topic is often helpful to a child.

Informational books on such topics as sibling rivalry, divorce, and other family matters are also available. These include *How It Feels When Parents Divorce, Coping with Step-families,* and *Coping with Sibling Rivalry.*

Experiences of Growing Up

Books for young children are listed in Chapters 3 and 4.

As they grow up, almost all children confront similar problems and many fiction and informational books have been written about these common situations. Relevant stories include *What's the Matter with A.J.?* about the arrival of a new baby, and *Will I Have a Friend?* about going off to school. Tomie de Paolo's *Nana Upstairs and Nana Downstairs* deals with the death of a family member, and Judith Viorst's *The Tenth Good Thing About Barney* is about a cat who died. Two stories concerning the death of a young person are *A Taste of Blackberries* and *Bridge to Terabithia.*

Older children may be ready for nonfiction materials about growing up. Titles you might recommend are *Self-Control, Responsibility, Everything You Need to Know about Growing Up Female* (or *Male*), *Coping with Death and*

Sharing a book leads to more sharing.

Grief, It's OK to be Shy, It's OK to be Angry, and *Celebrate You: Building Your Self-Esteem.* Eda LeShan has contributed *When Grownups Drive You Crazy.*

Learning About People's Lives

Books about how other people live and the experiences they have are of interest to children and can help them see events from various points of view. Series such as the *Little House* books enable children to understand what has happened to people at other times and in different places. Books also shed light on such matters as relations between older and younger people (*Wilfred Gardner McDonald Partridge*); the lives of those who reside in particular settings (*When I Was Young in the Mountains* and *Family Farm*); children with particular problems (*The Great Gilly Hopkins* is an unhappy foster child); or those from various cultural backgrounds, a topic discussed in another section of this chapter. *Through Grandpa's Eyes* is about visiting with a blind man. *Maniac McGee* tells of a boy who faces several difficulties, including being homeless.

Other titles related to special needs will be found in Chapter 16.

Informational books for children treat some of the same topics: different life circumstances (*Being Adopted*), challenging personal situations (*Why Am I Different?*), and biographies of people who have overcome obstacles (*Helen Keller*). Other books are about specific problems: *Finding a Common Language—Children Living with Deafness; Seeing in Special Ways—Children Living with Blindness; On Our Own Terms—Children Living with Physical Handicaps; We Laugh, We Love, We Cry—Children Living with Mental Retardation.* Jason Gaes, a boy with cancer, has written *My book for kids with cansur.*

CREATING AN APPROPRIATE CLIMATE

Children's Book Week in November can be a focus for many activities. Write to:
    The Children's Book
        Council
    67 Irving Place
    New York, NY 10003

In 1985 approximately twenty-five hundred new titles were published in the field of children's books. In 1990 the total was more than five thousand.

Just as you are the model for children's speaking and writing, you are also a model for their attitudes toward books, reading, and storytelling. As we said in Chapter 12, you should demonstrate to students that you enjoy stories and reading yourself and want to do everything you can to ensure that they love them, too.

First of all, it is vital that you become widely acquainted with books written expressly for children—all kinds of books. There are many resources you may use to find out about books for children. (Several guides to reviews and bibliographies are listed at the end of this chapter.) Such references can be helpful but you should also take a course or some workshops on children's books if you haven't, discuss books with librarians, and visit bookstores that have a good selection for children. Other considerations involve developing your room's library, reading aloud and telling stories, and using media appropriately.

The Room Library

The appeal of the area of the classroom devoted to the room library can be an important factor in creating an atmosphere that supports reading. If the library corner is nothing more than a place with a table and a few books, it will not do much to reinforce the idea that reading is a pleasant and rewarding experience.

An organized book area teaches about kinds of literature.

The room library should be warm and bright and occupy a prominent place in the room. Books ought to be attractively displayed and there should be comfortable seating.

In furnishing the library area appropriately, first arrange chairs invitingly around a low table near bookcases. There should likely be an area rug with, perhaps, an easy chair or a large bean-bag chair. Curtains, plants, and a lamp would be good additions. If there is space, a bathtub or small boat filled with cushions helps to create the informal atmosphere that is needed.

A bulletin board devoted exclusively to books is also an important feature of a reading corner. The children themselves can help put up displays and see that they are changed regularly. Here are a few ideas:

1. Display pictures of several authors and dust jackets of one of their books (with any photo of them removed). Fasten a length of yarn to each book cover and see if students can attach these to that writer's picture.

2. Use the same format and ask for matches between characters and the books they appear in or what they said in the story (*The Little Red Hen* and "Who will help me?"; *The Little Engine* and "I think I can," for example).

3. Children who have read a particular book (in their reading circle, perhaps) may wish to do a bulletin board on it, using the book cover, drawings they have done of scenes, and excerpts from the book and their written responses to it.

4. Encourage children to write captions for pictures taken from publishers' book advertisements or to make their own drawings and caption them. These can be used to make a bulletin board about a particular book, or about several books with a common theme or setting, or by the same author.

5. Have students write "advertisements" for favorite books and post them on the bulletin board. This could be combined with a study of advertising techniques.

6. Focus a display on a given event, group of people, or place (*Books About Immigrants,* for example, or *Stories from Mexico*)

7. Ask children to write letters to their favorite authors and make a display of any answers received. (Some are more likely to respond if several students from the same class write and their letters are sent as a packet.)

There are other uses to be made of a library corner:

- Students should browse in it when they first come into the room in the morning, if the schedule permits.
- Checking out books should be permitted once class members learn how to do that. Children may serve as librarians.
- The library corner may be used in conjunction with periods designated as Sustained Silent Reading (SSR) or Drop Everything and Read (DEAR).
- Students may use the corner when they are writing in their reading logs or literature response journals.
- Occasionally a literature response group or reading circle may meet in the room library corner.

SSR-type activities are described in Chapter 12.

Naturally, the most important furnishings in the room library are the books themselves. Beginning with the first day of the school year, the library should be well stocked with informational books and storybooks of many kinds. Audio- and videocassettes related to books should be in the library or in a media collection nearby. Of course, the books should have eye appeal, with many displayed so that the covers are visible to the students. A wide range of difficulty levels should be represented to enable children of all abilities to find something satisfying and challenging. A good proportion of the books should be changed regularly, but "old favorites" must be there, too.

As their teacher you know the children, their interests, and their abilities and are in the best position to select books for the classroom library, but the students can also participate. If it is at all possible, you might make arrangements to take a few children (not the same ones each time) to the local library. This will enable them to withdraw books and become familiar with library procedures. They could also help by "taking orders" from their classmates for particular types of books.

If you have a building library children can take turns going there in small groups and, with the aid of the librarian, selecting books to be brought back for the room library. In this way students can become increasingly aware of how the library in the classroom can be organized and operated.

Reading Aloud

As suggested in several chapters of this book, reading aloud to children ought to be considered very important, both at home and in school. Sometimes this will be spontaneous (it begins to shower and you quickly find a selection from *Rainy Day Rhymes* and read it to the class), but most of the time reading is planned.

There are reasons for this: it is not possible to have at hand every selection you might want to read, and reading aloud usually requires some preparation.

Of course, many poems and stories are available on cassettes, and children can listen to these. (Some books for young children and storytellers for all age groups are available on videocassettes, too.) However, just as family reading is personally satisfying for everyone involved, it is important that you and your class have shared experiences involving the reading of good literature. At these times you build rapport by sharing yourself, find out more about students and what they like, and have an opportunity to stretch their thinking through experiences they might well never have if it weren't for this opportunity.

Be selective—collect quality, not quantity.

In general, you should select for reading aloud stories or poems that you personally enjoy—your own enthusiasm will come through to the children. You must be constantly on the alert for selections that you like and that would be very good for reading aloud. Making a card file is one way to be sure that you will find the right piece for a specific situation. Cards might be organized according to the type of literature it is, the area of the curriculum involved, the special day or season to which the selection is related, or personal experiences and feelings likely to be attached to it. You may use categories of special meaning to you: "Holidays," "Personal Problems," or "Stories of Courage." Cards might include information regarding:

1. Genre (funny poem, Halloween story, essay, and so on)
2. Location (in a book, in a file, on the computer)
3. Title and author
4. Audiovisual possibilities (availability of illustrations, audio- and videotapes, related music)
5. Time required (estimate)
6. Summary (enough for an unfamiliar but interested potential user)

It may be that an entire faculty, perhaps with the leadership of the staff of the library media center, could build such a collection of cards for all to use. (Information could also be put on a computer and cross-referenced in several ways to make access easier; additions could then be made regularly, as well.)

Reading time is precious, so you should not choose material haphazardly but carefully, according to a plan of some kind, always including classics along with a few especially good contemporary titles. Some selections, for one reason or another, will be accessible to many children only when read aloud. The dialect spoken by certain characters in *The Secret Garden,* for example, will cause most readers a good deal of difficulty. The nonsense words in Roald Dahl's *The BFG* would likely be frustrating for some young readers (but delightful to others, of course).

In addition, children's classics often contain a number of words that children can understand in context but have difficulty reading for themselves (*quest,* for example, or *Transylvania*). Also, some items, once read aloud, are likely to get children started in a series of books; hearing *The Lion, the Witch and the Wardrobe* may introduce a child to the *Narnia Chronicles,* for example. Thus, reading aloud is an excellent way to widen children's latitude of choices. Other reasons for reading to children or for using audio- or videocassettes could include one or more of the following:

- The selection is high in interest level, but vocabulary and sentence structure are difficult for children (*Treasure Island,* perhaps).
- The work is of particular interest but copies are not available to children (someone's diary or other rare item).
- There is concern that the text has words in it that need to be explained as they are used or even avoided (*nigger* in *Huckleberry Finn,* for example).
- Some sections might be skipped entirely if they seem tediously descriptive (as is sometimes the case with older books) and likely to cause a class to lose interest.

The atmosphere for reading aloud or storytelling should be pleasant and informal. Some major guidelines are:

1. Select the material with regard to the group of children involved. Consider likely interest, length, and vocabulary.
2. Choose a book or story that is really worthwhile. Does it use interesting language, teach important values, or serve as an introduction to other significant works?
3. Read regularly so that children have the opportunity to develop appropriate habits of listening carefully and responding with their imaginations.
4. Establish a comfortable setting. Young children should sit on a rug and be close enough to see any illustrations. Older students needn't "sit up straight"; resting heads on desks while hearing a good story is perfectly acceptable.
5. Use visual aids where appropriate (flannel boards, puppets, related objects, maps) or use large-format books.

Controversies occur over children's books, so you should inquire about local practice before requiring a story that raises sensitive issues or reading it aloud. Remember, however, that almost all books will be objected to by someone.

Storytelling

Stories may be told as well as read, of course, and they were for thousands of years before reading and writing developed. Even today, a good storyteller is always appreciated. Telling a story works especially well with young children since the one telling can maintain good eye contact, develop a bond with the audience, and judge how well the presentation is going and, if need be, abbreviate the story before listeners' attention is lost.

The criteria for selecting a story to tell are much the same as those for choosing one to read, with one exception: it is important that the story not lose anything by being translated into your own words. Of course, it is possible to memorize a story, but that is not advisable except in very special cases. Memorization takes a great deal of time, and a story can be much less effective if something is forgotten at a crucial point. Therefore, if the original words are vital to full enjoyment, reserve the story for reading aloud.

A good storyteller commands an extensive vocabulary and can find exactly the right way to describe a character or an event. An effective storyteller loves words, enjoys telling stories, and communicates this enthusiasm to the listeners. There are few "born storytellers"; thorough preparation is the key to success.

Self-evaluation is also important. Using an audiotape recorder, you can experiment with sound effects, intonation, phrasing, and use of pauses. With a video recorder you can assess posture, effectiveness of visual aids, gestures, and facial expressions.

Like reading aloud, storytelling is an act of sharing, but it is even more intimate. Making choices carefully can help to produce the desired effect.

- Choose a physical setting that is comfortable and relaxing, perhaps on the rug and cushions in the library corner.
- Darken the room, play a record, or do whatever else will help to create the right mood.
- Select visual aids that might enhance the effectiveness of the story.
- Wear an article of clothing that would add something to the presentation.

Such matters may be discussed with students, too, as aspects of their listening and speaking experiences, since they, too, ought to have storytelling opportunities.

Using Media

In the preceding chapter we described a well-equipped library media center and urged you to consider using such aids. (We recognize that few schools have all the resources mentioned but hope that ways can be found to supply what children need.) You should take steps to familiarize yourself with what is available from school-system service centers, cooperative educational services agencies, state offices, public libraries, galleries, and museums. All could have materials related to books that you might borrow. Media-based activities ought to be of various kinds:

For recordings of stories and storytellers contact:
Catalog of Storytelling Resources
P.O. Box 12
Jonesboro, TN 37659

The Listening Library
Dept. MM
One Park Avenue
Old Greenwich, CT 06878

- Use audio- and videocassettes with professionals doing the reading or storytelling. This is particularly important when dialects are involved. (Then study the dialect as suggested in Chapters 5 and 7.)
- Use audio- or videocassettes of authors reading their own stories or poems. This will personalize the experience and help students to understand where these works come from.
- Use videotapes of parts of stories and plays as a way of encouraging students to read them.
- Showing the tape or movie after you have read the book (*Anne of Green Gables,* for instance) will provide much to talk about.

HELPING CHILDREN SELECT BOOKS

Take-offs on classics (*The True Story of the Three Little Pigs, by A. Wolf*) may stimulate similar writing attempts.

Developing an understanding of each child's interests, expanding those interests, and helping the child to find new ones is the responsibility of every teacher, and this includes selection of books. A librarian can be of assistance but cannot be expected to know as much about each of your students as you do. If your students keep their own reading logs, write in response to their reading, and regularly confer with you concerning their reading as well as their writing, you will have excellent opportunities for discussing many matters with them. These discussions, touching on such areas as school work, family experiences, hobbies, sports interests, pets, television, and travel, will allow you to suggest related books that children might find interesting.

Of course, knowledge of the youngsters is insufficient by itself. To make the best kinds of recommendations, you must have a comprehensive and detailed understanding of the books that are available.

Interests by Age

A list of books popular with children is published annually by the International Reading Association.

Certainly you should have a general view of which new books to examine as they become available. A principal consideration is the age group you teach. Fourth graders generally like particular kinds of books, as do first graders and other age groups.

Although gender differences in reading interests are becoming less marked—and certainly you should never reinforce them by influencing boys to select one kind of books and girls another—teachers and librarians do notice gender preferences in books.

Primary Grades. The youngest children select books principally on the basis of the illustrations. Bright colors are usually preferred over pastels, and illustrations should occupy a major portion of the space, with only a few words on a page. The pictures may be fanciful, but objects depicted should be readily recognizable. They love animal stories such as *Clifford* or *Koala Lou,* especially funny ones (*The Day Jimmy's Boa Ate the Wash*). There is often much interest in factual books on animals and prehistoric creatures (*Dinosaurs* by Gail Gibbons, *Dinosaur Time* by Peggy Parish, or Millicent Selsam's *Sea Monsters of Long Ago*).

Students in the early grades very much enjoy predictable and rhyming books such as *A House Is a House for Me* and *Drummer Hoff.* Stories about school and teachers are also popular (*Thomas' Snowsuit* and *Miss Nelson Is Missing* are entertaining.) Folk and fairy tales are perennial favorites and children love fantasy as long as the characters have human feelings and reactions. For example, Horton may sit on the egg without breaking it, but he must shiver when the winter winds blow and grow lonely sitting there on the nest alone. Gender differences may cause boys to resist reading about Ramona or other girls, for example, but this is not usually much of a problem.

Middle Grades. Middle-grade students continue to like fantasy and folk tales, but as their knowledge and experiences broaden so do their reading interests. They are interested in the world around them, both near and far, today and yesterday. Many types of books appeal to the middle-grader: histories (*Women of the West*), biographies (*Benjamin Franklin: A Man with Many Jobs*), adventure (*Pirates and Privateers*) and books that explain the wonders of the world around them (*Bats*). Mysteries begin to be popular, especially those with young detectives, such as Sobol's *Encyclopedia Brown.*

Gender differences begin to appear in the middle grades; boys in particular begin to restrict their reading to sports, athletic figures, and adventure. Girls are usually interested in a wider variety of topics but are beginning to evidence concern with books dealing with such matters as relationships—friendships mainly, but also books about families and, perhaps, boy-girl matters.

Upper Grades. Most of the interests pupils have in the middle grades continue into the upper grades. At this level, however, gender differences are often pronounced. Boys may be expected to emphasize sports, mysteries, adventure, and science fiction. Girls enjoy many of the same kinds of reading but also go on to biographies and books by authors such as Judy Blume, those that touch on serious matters of growing up, including romance. Boys of this age typically reject any book in which the central figure is female or in which there is a love interest, but they can be influenced to read *The Great Gilly Hopkins* and other books with much action.

At all ages children enjoy and should be exposed to humor as well as to stories about those who have problems to which they can relate. Humor is a safety valve to emotions, and it is important that children learn to laugh at themselves as well as others. What they think is funny at one age won't be laughed at when they are older, however. Very young children enjoy laughing at a baby bird who asks an elephant, "Are you my mother?" Somewhat older children are vastly amused at the troubles of Ramona Beasley, whereas ten-year-olds see the humor in such books as *How to Eat Fried Worms*.

Reading Ability

It is relatively easy to find books for good readers, but a major difficulty for most teachers is helping those children who have limited reading ability select books that will interest them and that they can read. This is a task requiring much patience and ingenuity. A few guidelines may prove helpful:

Some series of books published for children may be popular but of questionable value. You should resist using class time to read them aloud.

- Determine the level at which the student can read independently. Be sure the material is of interest to the child so that motivation is high. Consult a reading specialist if you require assistance.
- Make a special attempt to find out what else may interest the student.
- Using whatever information you have, ask a librarian or reading teacher for suggestions concerning reading selections.
- Branch out in selection of resources. Perhaps magazines and stories with a comic-book format would be good choices.
- Help the student maintain self-respect by finding easy-to-read materials not beneath his or her age level. Do whatever else you can to help the child make the most of other abilities and gain the approval of classmates.
- Make arrangements for readers with problems to read to younger children; this will give them a good reason to practice and a feeling of success. (Some may want to write books for kindergartners, too.)

Children have been known to extend themselves in reading if they are sufficiently motivated to read particular materials (a fourteen-year-old who "reads at the third-grade level" is somehow able to comprehend complex instructions for a video game). Such readers may be served rather well simply because there are many good fiction and informational books written at a low reading level (ask a remedial reading teacher for suggestions). Also there are materials on topics that are likely to be of interest to the youngster who seems to be two or more years behind in development. For example, Lerner Publications has its *Sports Illustrated for Kids* books and *Sports Achievers* packages. The Steck-

Vaughn Company offers several collections: *Superstars in Action* and *Spotlight* materials focus on sports and entertainment figures: *Great Heroes, Great Adventures,* and *Great Rescues.*

Students who read very well require attention, too. Certainly they should not be restricted in what they are allowed to read, although it is ethically required that you confer with parents with regard to any concerns they may have. Many schools have programs for gifted and talented children and you should be sure you know what book-related services are available to them. (See the related section in Chapter 16.)

THE TEACHING PROGRAM

In Chapter 12 it was stressed that a well-organized literature program should be central to learning to read in the elementary school. In that chapter and elsewhere in this text, we have stressed that literature makes important contributions not only to the reading and language arts programs but also to all phases of learning and to living itself. Certainly you should give careful thought to what you want your students to learn about literature and how you can best develop their understanding and appreciation.

Planning Considerations

Planning is important but should not be overdone. There should be no "assigning" of books to particular grade levels, either for your reading aloud to the class or for their self-selected reading. In some situations, regrettably, teachers have been told not to read a particular book to the class or even that they should discourage students from reading it because it is "taught" at a subsequent grade level. Of course, no one should be in the position of putting such restrictions on teachers. "Requiring" all children to read a particular piece of literature in the elementary school is also a mistaken practice—one that has caused many problems in secondary schools and colleges. Recall that in Chapter 12 we said that, even when there are literature response groups, children ought to get at least their second choice of a book to read.

Variety. Selections chosen to be read to the class should include a variety of kinds and styles of literature. Also, alternatives offered to response groups or reading circles should be varied: it should not always be a matter of choosing a sports book or a dog book or a funny book.

The variety ought to encompass *genres,* or different classifications of literature (short stories, novels, poems, plays); *themes* (family relationships, conflict between good and evil, facing equally desirable alternatives, etc.); *feeling tone* (cheerfulness, sadness, warmth, humor); and *type* of writing (fantasy, folklore, adventure, history, biography). In addition, there should be some classics; both older ones and newer ones are likely to become favorites. Not all of these are suitable at every grade level, of course, but every effort should be made to see that children at all levels become acquainted with many kinds of books and various styles of writing.

Experience Background. As with any other area of the program, you should take account of your students' backgrounds when making decisions about their literature experiences. When you read to them, you need to balance your selections between what will be light and easy for them to relate to and what will be rather more challenging. Also, you must judge whether or not content needs to be within their experience if they are to deal with it effectively. It is not true that children can relate only to that which is within their immediate experience. Part of the value of literature lies in the vicarious experiences it provides.

When you organize reading circles and several children in the circle do not have experiential background for the book involved, you may be tempted to intervene in the discussions. It is probably wise to hold off, though, since they may know more than you think, or other group members will help without much interruption in the flow of discussion. When conferring with an individual student, however, you should feel freer to explore her or his background for understanding a particular story.

Integration. When literature is to be an integral part of the curriculum, consideration must be given to how this integration is to be accomplished. Just as overall planning requires decisions about demonstrations, field trips, and use of electronic equipment, it is also necessary to select literary experiences that are relevant and that could possibly make an important contribution to learning.

The American Library Association Review provides lists of books considered especially appropriate for those reading below grade level.

Individual Growth. As we have pointed out, a comprehensive program will include reading aloud by you, small groups of children reading and responding to the same book, and individual children reading something of their own choice and discussing that with you.

Writing about what they have read is also an important aspect of the classroom program on books. In a classroom that provides opportunity and encour-

Many children enjoy reading several books by the same author.

agement for each child to explore in the areas of her or his own interests, to discover new ones, and to grow in understanding of the world, books of all kinds will assume an increasingly important role.

Responding to Books

In Chapter 13 children's responses to books were discussed in terms of having students read in small groups, write in their reading logs, and confer with you. Additionally, in other chapters there have been discussions of reading selections aloud, adapting passages for dramatization, writing dialogue based on a story, and other activities involving literature. In this section we will describe how those and other experiences may be expanded and reorganized and also applied to nonfiction materials. (Especially with younger children's books but with some of those for older students, too, the distinction between stories and informational books is occasionally not completely clear.)

Of course, there are numerous ways in which readers may respond. The typical "book report" usually involves writing a plot summary for a story that has been read. You may ask students to do that occasionally since the ability to summarize is a good indication of a reader's comprehension ability (and a way to learn how to study), but you wouldn't want to "spoil" the story by having these given orally or made available for others to read. Rather, responses should involve all kinds of attempts to give a reaction and, perhaps, to interest others in the book, whether fiction or informational.

One major alternative to conventional reports is to collect students' reactions in a systematic way. This information can even be put into a computer data bank, which would permit a child to type in the name of a book and call up a list of all classmates who have read it, together with their opinions. Ratings of books by students may also be kept in a card file that can be consulted by everyone.

Oral Activities.   Oral responses to books may take a variety of forms, and most suggestions can be adapted for either fiction or nonfiction works. Here are a few:

Make reporting on books—in science or any other subject—an integral part of the classroom oral language program.

1. A child could read a passage from the book aloud, perhaps a description of an incident or a place. This requires preparation so that it will be read well; also, the selection ought to be complete in itself or listeners will lose interest.

2. Several children who have read the same book could be involved in a presentation that is taken directly from it or summarizes a portion.

3. Children who have read several books involving the same historical period, science content, or genre (mystery stories, maybe) could organize a panel discussion on these topics.

Students can videotape book reviews and make these available to other class members.

4. A student could memorize a selection from a book and then combine this oral presentation with a well-practiced demonstration. Videotaping would reduce "stage fright."

5. A child could pretend to be a character from a story or an expert on the content of a nonfiction book and be interviewed by a classmate playing the role of newspaper or TV reporter. Both would need to have read the book, of course.

6. Someone might prepare a speech explaining why a particular character or a historical figure should have behaved differently or was misunderstood.

Written Activities. Writing as a reaction will vary according to the ages and abilities of the children. Some of the following will be appropriate to your situation:

1. an imaginary letter written by a character at a particular point in a story or by someone who disagrees with what the author has written in an informational book

2. a book advertisement written for the class or school newspaper or the reading-corner bulletin board

3. for a story, a first-person description of a particular event in the book, told as though the writer (a dog, maybe) had been an observer

4. for an informational book, a discussion of which parts were particularly interesting, difficult to understand, or helpful in some way

5. for a novel, a description of the setting in which the story took place and a discussion of the extent to which the setting was important to the story

6. for two informational books on the same topic, a description of the one that explains something better or that would be better to read first

7. a TV script based on part of the book (when actually videotaped, the activity includes thinking and good learning experiences in all the language areas)

Other Activities. Hands-on activities related to fiction and informational books are especially valuable for children who are not particularly verbal; some of them may be able to make something the others will admire. Also, art work and three-dimensional figures add color and interest to the book corner. (Art is communication, too!) Activities could include

1. making models, dioramas, or maps (reproducing the farm described in one of the *Little House* books or making a scale model of the *Kon Tiki*).

2. doing a collage from materials related to a particular book

3. drawing a cartoon strip (even inventing the characters) based on a book

4. making a mobile related to a book's content

5. constructing figures or masks to represent book characters

Becoming Acquainted with Authors

Some publishing companies distribute photos of and information sheets on authors. Obtain a pamphlet on Tomie dePaolo from:
  The Putnam & Grosset
    Group
  200 Madison Avenue
  New York, NY 10016.

When a reading program is effective in a school or classroom, the students may be expected to show a real interest in the people who write books—that is, the authors. (If children are doing a great deal of writing themselves, they also quite rightfully think of themselves as authors.) Students will want to know about favorite writers: where they live or lived, what their family is like, what kind of pets they have, and, especially, where they get their ideas. They are interested in the fact that Lee Bennett Hopkins was a teacher and want to know about Byrd Baylor's house in the desert.

Children usually know something about the work that authors and illustrators do. They may love Beverly Cleary's characters and Steven Kellogg's illustrations. Experience with poetry will lead them to be interested in Jack Prelutsky and Eloise Greenfield.

A book about authors and illustrators edited by Holtze is listed among the references for this chapter.

Chapters 6 and 11 also contain material on poetry.

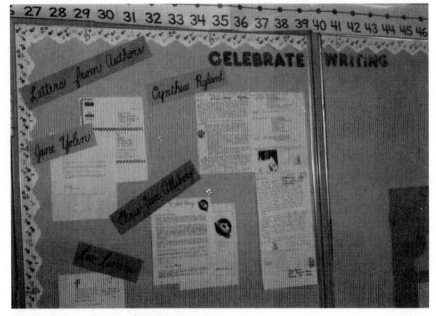

Writing to an author—and getting a response.

Several types of activities could revolve around authors and illustrators:

- Have a bulletin board on an author (Mem Fox, for instance) with dust jackets or illustrations from that person's books, lists of people in the class who have read particular books by that author, and notes on his or her life.
- Try to organize schoolwide efforts to bring a particular author to your school or locality.
- Organize a "Guess Who?" game in which clues are offered each day until the name of an author or illustrator is discovered and given to you individually by several students.
- Print excerpts from the books of authors and see who can identify most by the end of a two-week period.
- Print first lines from stories by the same author and see who can identify both the author and the stories.

POETRY IN THE LITERATURE PROGRAM

Since they enjoy rhythm, rhyme, and the sounds of words, children love poetry if given appropriate opportunities to experience it. Mother Goose has remained in good standing for centuries, and Dr. Seuss and Shel Silverstein are undisputed favorites of children today. Only unfortunate practices by adults—parents and teachers, and some textbook writers—cause large numbers of older students and grown-ups to be antagonistic to poetry. Selections not suitable to the age group (Wordsworth's *Daffodils* may not be right for your particular group of eight-year-olds), the listeners' experiences (paeans to rural life offered for the consumption of city residents), or their interests (the old masters wrote nothing about motorcycles) have made poetry a dull mystery in some instances.

Poetry is powerful because it offers important ways to express ideas and feelings; it stimulates the imagination and provides an outlet for the emotions. Poems often motivate children to express their own creativity, and they furnish a way of revealing to students the beauty and expressiveness of language.

Poetry Guidelines

When considering the use of poetry with children, you should keep in mind several general guidelines:

- With few exceptions poems are meant to be heard rather than seen. (There is no reason children should not follow along on a copy as a poem is read aloud, however.)
- You (or anyone else reading poetry to children) should prepare so that adequate attention can be given to speed, cadence, stress, tone, and pitch. As with other oral presentations, audio and video recording will be of benefit.
- Occasionally poems may be presented on recordings, especially when a particularly good effect has been achieved by a professional or if the voice is one that the children recognize with pleasure.
- As the teacher, your own voice is best, since your enjoyment of poetry will come through readily and be "caught" by the youngsters.

A list of collections of poetry is included at the end of this chapter.

As was mentioned in Chapter 5, poems, songs, and chants are all related. They should be done regularly, for their own sake and for their relevance to aspects of the curriculum. All bring high-quality learning experiences to the program—songs of boatmen pulling canal craft, magical chants of witches making their brews, and poems celebrating life.

Poems and Teaching

The valuable contributions to be made by poetry have been mentioned in several chapters of this text. Whether nursery rhymes, limericks, or whatever, poems are a significant part of our cultural heritage and merit a secure place in the curriculum. We hope, after having heard a great deal of poetry, that students in the elementary school will want to write some of their own. Several focal points for poetry are readily identified:

Everyday Experiences. It is important to include poems that children will understand and like immediately. A good example is one about mud:

MUD

Mud is very nice to feel
All squishy-squash between the toes!
I'd rather wade in wiggly mud
Than smell a yellow rose.
Nobody but the rosebush knows
How nice mud feels between the toes.*

*By Polly Chase Boyden. From *Child Life,* copyright © 1930. Used by permission.

We know that children prefer humorous poems to serious, meditative ones and that they like narrative poems and those about animals or about familiar and enjoyable experiences. Until they have had a substantial amount of exposure to poetry, they are not likely to react positively to poems that rely heavily on imagery and figurative language, finding these difficult to grasp.

You should, however, ask some questions that bring forth individual responses and also encourage appreciation for the special language of poetry. For example, if you read *Mud* you could ask "What are a rosebush's toes? Do you suppose that it can really feel the mud?"

A poem about a dog growling tells about a feeling that many children have experienced.

GROWL?

When a surly dog
Complete with scowl
Goes rumbly-grumbly
That's a growl.
Growl's sound is surly
Snarly-gray,
And when you hear it
Back away. . . . *

Word use in poems can be pointed out to children as something that is very important. They can see how the authors used *squishy-squash* and *rumbly-grumbly* to create appropriate sounds as well as to convey certain meanings. This helps students to appreciate that poetry is an art form that depends on finding just the right word.

As they discuss poems and poets they can also begin to appreciate how effects are created by the rhythm of the words (*galloping, galloping, over the hill*) and by the sound patterns of words arranged in particular ways (*beat, beat, beat of the tom-tom*). As they mature and gain experience, they can go on to look for images in poetry and to understand something of poetic forms (discussed in Chapter 11 in connection with writing of poetry).

Students can also be introduced to the idea that poetry often involves consideration of how the words are arranged on the page.

SOUND OF WATER

The sound of water is:
Rain,
Lap,
Fold,
Slap,
Gurgle,
Splash,
Churn,
Crash,
Murmur,
Pour,
Ripple,

*By Mary O'Neill from *What Is That Sound?* Copyright © 1966 by Mary O'Neill. Permission granted by Marian Reiner.

Roar,
Plunge,
Drip,
Spout,
Slip,
Sprinkle,
Flow,
Ice,
Snow.*

Of course they will first be impressed by the appearance of such a poem, but you can also interest them in looking for the rhyming and rhythmic elements in this one.

A Poetry File. Just as you keep a file of stories to read, you should have a systematic method of collecting poetry. There are several computer programs that will enable you to copy a poem only once but then be able to have access to it for various uses. *Mud,* for example, might be entered in a number of categories (Spring, Feelings, Weather, Rain, etc.) and filed according to its connection to such stories as *Mrs. Wishy Washy* as well. There are many good collections of children's poetry, several of which are listed at the end of this chapter.

BOOKS AND THE CURRICULUM

In Chapters 1 and 2, and in most of the others as well, we have suggested that you use units, topics, and themes to do the best type of teaching, including not only the language arts but all other areas of the curriculum, too. Stories, poetry, plays, and informational books related to such topics as The Civil War, Transportation, Electricity, and Oceans exist in plentiful numbers and can make an extremely important contribution to classroom activities.

A sampling of informational books for children appears at the end of this chapter.

Books are usually available on almost any subject, although you may sometimes need to look beyond the school collection. Such searching is worthwhile, however, because children will need resources that are much richer than ordinary textbooks. Some topics and examples include:

Pioneers

Sarah, Plain and Tall (fiction)
Little House series (fiction)
That Lonesome Prairie (fiction)
Old Yeller (fiction)
Log Cabin in the Woods—A True Story about a Pioneer Boy (nonfiction)
Children of the Wild West (nonfiction)

Space Travel

What If . . . I Were an Astronaut? (fiction)
Alistair in Outer Space (fiction)
Professor Noah's Spaceship (fiction)
Exploring the Night Sky (nonfiction)
Satellite (nonfiction)
My First Book of Space (nonfiction)

*By Mary O'Neill from *What Is That Sound?* Copyright © 1966 by Mary O'Neill. Permission granted by Marian Reiner.

Good informational books are usually more effective than textbooks.

BOOKS AND CULTURAL UNDERSTANDINGS

By the year 2020 the major-ity of children in our elementary schools will be people of color.

If people of the world, of a country, and of a society are to understand one another better, the reading of books will be one of the important aids to such understanding. By reading to children and guiding their choice of books, you can help them become acquainted with people who lived long ago or live today in places and ways remote from the experience of those in your class. Such acquaintance will help to relieve some of the difficulties we face in the modern world.

In our society there are many cultural groups, often with different languages, religions, ways of living, and outlooks on the world. Increasingly, children from many such groups attend school together and this makes it quite important that the classroom programs, including the books the children read, reflect this diversity of backgrounds. And, even in those situations where nearly all students are from the same cultural group, a wide variety of reading materials will help move the total society toward better understanding of the groups that compose it. There are many educational advantages to be realized by greater use of multicultural reading materials:

1. When children of racial and ethnic groups learn more about their own cultural heritage, their sense of self-worth and feeling of pride are enhanced and this has a positive effect on attitudes and academic progress.
2. When students are observed studying various racial and ethnic groups, the children from the groups read about are likely to develop improved self-concepts as a result.

3. Every student should have the opportunity to see that all cultures have made contributions to society, not only to writing but to many aspects of life.

4. Each culture has ways of looking at life that can expand every student's understanding of the world in which we all live.

5. Making superficial observations that other cultures are inferior deprives those who think that way of opportunities to broaden their basis for making choices regarding values and life experiences.

6. It is important to see that no one group is superior in creativity, expressiveness, and spiritual strength.

7. Readers are also able to see that all groups are made up of people with similar needs but how they meet these will differ.

World Understanding

Billions of people now live in the world and most are quite different from the Europeans who became dominant in the region in which most of us live. Except for the lucky few who can travel, the vast majority of people must watch television programs and movies to see people around the world. We can also listen to those who have traveled and met many different types of people (and view their slides and videotapes), and we can look at magazines from those places and sometimes read their newspapers. All of this helps anyone who is interested in learning about other people, but books are also very helpful in conveying such understanding and in sharing certain experiences. A number of cross-cultural books emphasize similarities among people from various countries: *Bread, Bread, Bread; Hats, Hats, Hats; Everybody Cooks Rice;* and *Favorite Folktales from around the World,* for example.

Of course, many of the stories we enjoy the most had their origins in other countries. Nursery rhymes have words like *pease porridge* or *sixpence,* identifying their origin as English. Most of our fairy tales come from European traditions, with the Grimm brothers being the most prominent source. Local names persist in the titles of stories—*The Brementown Musicians* or *The Pied Piper of Hamelin,* for instance.

Other tales are also from specific countries: *Hans Brinker and the Silver Skates* from the Netherlands, Hans Christian Andersons *The Ugly Duckling,* and many others from Denmark; *Pinnochio* and *Strega Nona* from Italy; and *Puss in Boots* from France. Others come from Africa (*Oh, Kojo! How Could You!*, *Why Mosquitoes Buzz in People's Ears,* and *Mufaro's Beautiful Daughters*), Asia (*Crow Boy* from Japan and *The Paper Crane, Tiki Tiki Tembo, Gung Hay Fat Choy,* and *Yeh-Shen* from China).

In reading these to children yourself and in discussing them, you can make the point that many peoples have produced similar stories as well as ones that are unique to their culture.

Cultural Groups In Our Society

Teach children to ask persons of various backgrounds how they wish references to their group membership to be made (for example, "Asian" is usually preferred over "Oriental").

The North American society is made up of people from different backgrounds and the population becomes more diverse every day with new arrivals. We need to understand one another better and, of course, books and stories help to promote such understanding. Children should be encouraged to read about groups that might very well live near them, with children attending the same school.

Books About the Early Inhabitants of the Western Hemisphere. Some groups have lived in North, Central, and South America for a long time, certainly thousands of years before the Europeans came. These include the people of the far north, the Inuit (or "Eskimos"), the Native Americans (or "Indians"), and the people of Mexico and countries south of Mexico.

Most children have several misconceptions about these groups. Mainly descended from the people who came from Asian areas, they crossed into the Western Hemisphere, settled in what we now call Alaska and Canada, and then moved south. It would no doubt be helpful if elementary children read more about these people and their histories and came to a fuller appreciation of what they had accomplished long before anyone else came to these regions.

There are books about the people of Central and South America:

Eye of the Heart
Brother Anansi and the Cattle Ranch
Magic Dogs of the Volcanoes
The Grandchildren of the Incas

and the people of the north:

Julie of the Wolves
The Enchanted Caribou
Dogsong
Happily May I Walk: American Indians and Alaska Natives Today
Arctic Memories

There are many books about Native Americans, a few of which are

Knots on a Counting Rope
Annie and the Old One
The Girl Who Loved Wild Horses
The Pueblo
The Great Sun Must Die
Hawk, I'm Your Brother
I Wear the Morning Star

(It must be kept in mind that Native Americans and the people of the north usually prefer to retain their cultural identities; they often request that they not be referred to as Eskimos or Indians. Such distinctions can be made clear for your students if you call their attention to literature such as Cree poems and Inuit stories.)

Books About Mexican Americans. Because of political and social changes over a long period of time "Mexican Americans" may be either long-time residents of the places in which they live or fairly recent arrivals. Many Mexican Americans speak both Spanish and English. Some books about Mexican Americans include

Hello, Amigos
Mother Goose on the Rio Grande
Famous Mexican Americans

Fiesta!
How We Came to the Fifth World
And Now Miguel

Books About African Americans. Most of the ancestors of African Americans came to North America during the period of slavery. More recently, people have immigrated voluntarily from countries in this hemisphere (some of whom are also descended from Africans who were enslaved) and from Africa itself. Children are interested in African stories (listed in another section of this chapter) and in books about the African-American experience:

Sounder
Roll of Thunder, Hear My Cry
Flossie and the Fox
The Stories Julian Tells
Amazing Grace
A Letter to Amy
The Hundred Penny Box
The Snowy Day
The People Could Fly

Books About Recent Arrivals. Many families arrived here during recent times, having come to live in a strange land for a variety of reasons. Their stories are important to them as they maintain contacts with the culture of their homeland. There are also stories about their experiences here. Such books will assist us and the children for whom we are responsible. Some examples were presented in another section of this chapter. Others are

The Beggar in the Blanket and other Vietnamese Tales
The Boy of the Three-year Nap
Dragonwings
Mail-order Kid
My Name Is San Ho

Puerto Ricans are American citizens, whether they reside in the United States or the island of Puerto Rico. Those making the decision to live on the mainland have increased in recent years. Many Puerto Ricans speak Spanish as their first language. Some books about Puerto Rico and Puerto Ricans are

Going Home
Felita, A Puerto Rican Child
Yagua Days
Stories from El Barrio
El Bronx Remembered
A Chair for My Mother

ASSESSING THE BOOKS PROGRAM

Since an important outcome of book reading is the pleasure and enrichment it brings to the individual and the role that books play in that person's life, the ultimate effect of your program cannot be determined until years after the

Students who enjoy books will care for them.

children leave you. During their time with you, however, you can observe the youngsters and try to respond to questions that will give you some basis for judging the success of your efforts:

1. Do the children choose to read on their own?
2. Do they have favorites and make requests?
3. Do they seek out titles that might be useful in particular situations?
4. Do they read across the spectrum of genres?
5. Do they share their reading with others?
6. Do they have their own library cards or are they planning to secure them?
7. Do they join book clubs to acquire their own books?

In Chapter 13 the point was made that a student's portfolio ought to list books read. Such a listing should include those read in connection with all aspects of the classroom program, perhaps with a note about how particular books contributed to the student's educational and personal background.

A FINAL WORD

We are fortunate to live at a time and in a place where thousands of trade books intended for children are published each year. Although only a few families can afford to purchase many of these, public and school libraries make them available to all. You can contribute much to society by informing yourself about books, introducing your students to the best of them, and giving storybooks and informational volumes a central place in your classroom program. Everyone agrees that the time and effort required to do this will pay rich dividends, but someone—you very likely—has to accept the responsibility for performing this crucially important service.

References

Bauer, Caroline Feller. *This Way to Books.* H. W. Wilson, 1983.

Bosma, Bette. *Fairy Tales, Fables, Legends, and Myths.* Teachers College Press, 1992.

Chambers, Aiden. *Introducing Books to Children,* 2nd ed. The Horn Book, 1983.

Cott, Jonathan. *Pipers at the Gates of Dawn: The Wisdom of Children's Literature.* McGraw-Hill, 1985.

Cullinan, Bernice. *Literature and the Child.* Harcourt Brace Jovanovich, 1981.

Fox, Mem. "Politics and Literature: Chasing the "isms" from Children's Books." *The Reading Teacher* 46 (May 1993), pp. 654–658.

Glazer, Joan I. *Literature for Young Children,* 2nd ed. Charles E. Merrill, 1986.

Harris, Violet J. "Multicultural Curriculum: African American Children's Literature." *Young Children* 46 (January 1991) pp. 37–44.

Huck, Charlotte S.; Hepler, Susan; and Hickman, Janet. *Children's Literature in the Elementary School.* Harcourt Brace Jovanovich, 1993.

Kruse, G. M., and Hornung, K. T. *Multicultural Literature for Children and Young Adults.* Cooperative Children's Book Center, 1991.

Lamme, Linda Leonard. *Raising Readers: A Guide to Sharing Literature with Young Children.* Walker, 1980.

Lukens, Rebecca. *A Critical Handbook of Children's Literature.* Scott, Foresman, 1990.

Pappas, Christine C. "Fostering Full Access to Literacy by Including Information Books." *Language Arts* 68 (October 1991) pp. 449–462.

Purves, Alan C., and Monson, Dianne L. *Experiencing Children's Literature.* Scott, Foresman, 1984.

Rosenblatt, Louise M. "Literature—S.O.S.!" *Language Arts* 68 (October 1991), pp. 444–448.

Shapiro, Jon E., ed. *Using Literature and Poetry Affectively.* International Reading Association, 1979.

Sloan, Glenna Davis. *The Child As Critic: Teaching Literature in Elementary and Middle Schools.* Teachers College Press, 1991.

Stewig, John Warren. *Children and Literature.* Houghton Mifflin, 1988.

Sutherland, Zena, et al. *Children and Books.* Scott, Foresman, 1986.

Trelease, Jim. *The New Read-Aloud Handbook,* Penguin, 1989.

Winkel, L., ed. *The Elementary School Library Collection: A Guide to Books and Other Media.* Brodart, 1990.

Teaching Resources

GUIDES FOR SELECTING BOOKS FOR CHILDREN

Arbuthnot, May Hill, et al. *Children's Books Too Good to Miss,* 7th ed. University Press Books, 1979.

Carroll, Frances Laverne, and Meacham, Mary. *Exciting, Funny, Scary, Short, Different, and Sad Books Kids Like about Animals, Science, Sports, Families, Songs, and Other Things.* American Library Association, 1984.

Doll, Carol A. *Nonfiction Books for Children: Activities for Thinking, Learning, and Doing.* Teacher Ideas Press, 1990.

Freeman, Judy. *Books Kids Will Sit Still For.* Alleyside Press, 1984.

Gillespie, John T., ed. *Elementary School Paperback Collection.* American Library Association, 1985.

Gillespie, John T., and Gilbert, Christin B., eds. *Best Books for Children: Preschool Through the Middle Grades.* R. R. Bowker, 1985.

Gillespie, J. T., and Naden, C. J. *Best Books for Children: Preschool Through Grade 6.* Bowker, 1990.

Griffin, Barbara. *Special Needs Bibliography.* The Griffin (P.O. Box 195, DeWitt, NY 13214), updated annually.

Haviland, Virginia, ed. *Children's Books of International Interest.* American Library Association, 1978.

Hopkins, Lee Bennett. *The Best of Book Bonanza.* Holt, Rinehart and Winston, 1980.

Kennedy, DayAnn; Spangler, Stella; and Vanderwurf, Mary Ann. *Science & Technology in Fact and Fiction: A Guide to Children's Books.* R. R. Bowker, 1990.

Kimmel, Margaret Mary, and Segel, Elizabeth. *For Reading Out Loud: A Guide to Sharing Books with Children.* R. R. Bowker, 1983.

Kobrin, Beverly. *Eyeopeners! How to Choose and Use Children's Books about Real People, Places and Things.* Penguin Viking, 1988.

LiBretto, Ellen V., ed. *High/Low Handbook,* 2nd ed. R. R. Bowker, 1985 (covers books, materials, and services for the problem reader).

Lima, Carolyn W. *A to Zoo: Subject Access to Children's Books.* R. R. Bowker, 1986.

O'Connell, S. M.; Montenegro, V. J.; and Wolff, K. *The Best Science Books and A-V Materials for Children.* American Association for the Advancement of Science, 1988.

Richter, B., and Wenzel, D. *The Museum of Science and Industry Basic List of Children's Science Books.* American Library Association, 1988.

Sinclair, Patricia Kennelly. *Children's Magazine Guide: Subject Index to Children's Magazines.* Pleasant T. Rowland, 1985.

Sunderlin, Sylvia, ed. *Bibliography of Books for Children.* Association for Childhood Education International, 1983.

Tway, Eileen, ed. *Reading Ladders for Human Relations.* National Council of Teachers of English, 1981.

Zarnowski, Myra. *Learning About Biographies: A Reading-Writing Approach for Children.* National Council of Teachers of English, 1990.

BOOKS OF POETRY

Greenfield, Eloise. *Honey, I Love.* Crowell, 1978.

Greenfield, Eloise. *Nathaniel Talking.* Writers and Readers, 1989.

Hopkins, Lee Bennett. *Side By Side: Poems to Read Together.* Simon and Schuster, 1988.

Hopkins, Lee Bennett, ed. *Still As A Star: A Book of Nighttime Poems.* Little, 1989.

Merriam, Eve. *A Sky Full of Poems.* Dell, 1986.

Merriam, Eve. *You Be Good & I'll Be Night: Jump on the Bed Poems.* Morrow, 1988.

O'Neill, Mary. *Hailstones and Halibut Bones.* Doubleday, 1973.

Prelutsky, Jack, ed. *The Random House Book of Poetry for Children.* Random House, 1983.

Prelutsky, Jack. *Read Aloud Rhymes for the Very Young.* Knopf, 1986.

Silverstein, Shel. *Where the Sidewalk Ends.* Harper, 1974.

Silverstein, Shel. *A Light in the Attic.* Harper, 1981.

CHILDREN'S BOOKS REFERRED TO IN THIS CHAPTER

Aardema, V. *Oh, Kojo! How Could You?* Dial, 1984.

Aardema, V. *Why Mosquitoes Buzz in People's Ears.* Dial, 1975.

Adler, K., and McBride, R. *For Sale—One Sister—Cheap!* Children's, 1986.

Alexander, F. *Mother Goose on the Rio Grande.* National Textbook, 1983.

Allard, H., and Marshall, J. *Miss Nelson is Missing.* Houghton Mifflin, 1982.

Anderson, H. *The Ugly Duckling.* Knopf, 1986.

Armstrong, W. *Sounder.* Harper and Row, 1969.

Bang, M. *The Paper Crane.* Greenwillow, 1985.

Balter, L. *What's the Matter with A. J.?* Barron, 1989.

Baylor, B. *Hawk, I'm Your Brother.* Macmillan, 1986.

Behrens, J. *Fiesta!* Children's, 1986.

Behrens, J. *Gung Hay Fat Choy.* Children's, 1982.

Bergman, J. *Finding a Common Language—Children Living with Deafness.* Gareth Stevens, 1989.

Bergman, T. *On Our Own Terms—Children Living with Physical Handicaps.* Gareth Stevens, 1989.

Bergman, T. *Seeing in Special Ways—Children Living with Blindness.* Gareth Stevens, 1989.

Bergman, T. *We Laugh, We Love, We Cry—Children Living with Mental Retardation.* Gareth Stevens, 1989.

Blum, J. *The Pain and the Great One.* Dell, 1985.

Bridwell, N. *Clifford.* Scholastic, 1985.

Brown, T. *Hello, Amigos.* Henry Holt, 1986.

Browning, R. *The Pied Piper of Hamelin.* Lothrop, Lee and Shepard, 1986.

Bunting, E. *The Wednesday Surprise.* Ticknor and Fields, 1989.

Burnett, F. *The Secret Garden.* Harper and Row, 1987.

Burt, D. *I Love My Grandma.* Gareth Stevens, 1985.

Byars, B. *Cracker Jackson.* Penguin, 1986.

Cameron, A. *The Stories Julian Tells.* Random House, 1981.

Cleary, B. *Ramona and Her Father.* Avon, 1990.

Cleaver, E. *The Enchanted Caribou.* Atheneum, 1985.

Cohen, M. *Will I Have a Friend?* Macmillan, 1967.

Cohen, S. *Coping with Sibling Rivalry.* Rosen Group, 1989.

Collins, A. *The Great Sun Must Die.* Science Research Associates, 1985.

Colodi, C. *Pinnochio.* Penguin, 1985.

Cruz, M. *Yagua Days.* Dial, 1987.

Dahl, R. *The BFG.* Penguin, 1989.

Davidson, M. *Helen Keller.* Scholastic, 1989.

de Paolo, T. *Nana Upstairs and Nana Downstairs.* Penguin, 1978.

de Paolo, T. *Strega Nona.* Harcourt Brace Jovanovich, 1982.

Delton, J., and Tucker, D. *My Grandma's in a Nursing Home.* A. Whitman, 1986.

Dickinson, T. *Exploring the Night Sky.* Camden House, 1987.

Dodge, M. *Hans Brinker and the Silver Skates.* Scholastic, 1988.

Dooley, N. *Everybody Cooks Rice.* Carolrhoda Books, 1991.

Ekoomiak, N. *Arctic Memories.* Holt, 1900.

Emberly, B. *Drummer Hoff.* Simon and Schuster, 1974.

Fox, M. *Koala Lou.* Harbrace, 1989.

Fox, M. *Wilfred Gardner McDonald Partridge.* Kane Miller Books, 1985.

Freedman, R. *Children of the Wild West.* Houghton Mifflin, 1983.

Gaes, J. *My book for kids with cansur.* Melius and Peterson, 1987.

George, J. *Julie of the Wolves.* Harper and Row, 1972.

Gibbons, G. *Dinosaurs.* Holiday, 1987.

Gipson, F. *Old Yeller.* Harper and Row, 1990.

Glassman, B. *Everything You Need to Know about Growing Up Female.* Rosen Group, 1991.

Glassman, B. *Everything You Need to Know about Growing Up Male.* Rosen Group, 1991.

Goble, P. *The Girl Who Loved Wild Horses.* Bradbury Press, 1978.

Golent, M., and Bahr, A. *It's OK to be Angry.* Macmillan, 1986.

Golent, M., and Bahr, A. *It's OK to be Shy.* Macmillan, 1986.

Graham, G. *The Beggar in the Blanket and Other Vietnamese Tales.* Dial, 1988.

Greene, C. *Benjamin Franklin: A Man with Many Jobs.* Children's Press, 1988.

Grimm, J. and W. *The Brementown Musicians.* Picture Book Studio, 1988.

Hamilton, V. *The People Could Fly.* Knopf, 1985.

Hansen, R., and Bell, R. *My First Book of Space.* Simon and Schuster, 1985.

Heegaard, M. *Coping with Death and Grief.* Lerner, 1990.

Henry, J., and Zarins, J. *Log Cabin in the Woods—A True Story about a Pioneer Boy.* Macmillan, 1988.

Highwater, J. *I Wear the Morning Star.* Harper and Row, 1986.

Hirschfelder, A. *Happily May I Walk: American Indians and Alaska Natives Today.* Macmillan, 1986.

Hoberman, M. *A House Is a House for Me.* Penguin, 1988.

Hoffman, M. *Amazing Grace.* Dial, 1991.

Jeffries, D. *Satellites.* Watts, 1987.

Johnson, J. *Celebrate You: Building Your Self-Esteem.* Lerner, 1990.

Johnson, L. *Responsibility.* Rosen Group, 1990.

Johnson, S. *Bats.* Lerner Publications, 1985.

Keats, E. *A Letter to Amy.* Harper and Row, 1968.

Keats, E. *The Snowy Day.* Penguin, 1962.

Kahaner, E. *Everything You Wanted to Know about Growing up Female.* Rosen Group, 1991.

Kaplan, L. *Coping with Step-families.* Rosen Group, 1991.

Knelp, M. *Self-control.* Rosen Group, 1991.

Krementz, J. *How It Feels When Parents Divorce.* Knopf, 1984.

Krumgold, J. *And Now Miguel.* Harper and Row, 1984.

Lake, A. *Women of the West.* Rourke Corp., 1990.

Lehtinen, R. *The Grandchildren of the Incas.* The World's Children Series, 1991.

Le Shan, E. *When Grownups Drive You Crazy.* Macmillan, 1988.

Lewis, C. *The Lion, the Witch, and the Wardrobe.* Macmillan, 1988.

Locker, T. *Family Farm.* Dial, 1988.

Louie, A. *Yeh-Shen.* Putnam, 1982.

McCall, E. *Pirates and Privateers.* Children's Press, 1980.

McDonald, J. *Mail-order Kid.* Putnam, 1988.

McKissack, P. *Flossie and the Fox.* Dial, 1986.

MacLachlan, P. *Sarah, Plain and Tall.* Harper and Row, 1985.

MacLachlan, P. *Through Grandpa's Eyes.* Harper and Row, 1980.

Martin, B. *Knots on a Counting Rope.* Henry Holt, 1987.

Mathis, S. *The Hundred Penny Box.* Penguin, 1975.

Miles, M. *Annie and the Old One.* Little, 1985.

Mohr, N. *El Bronx Remembered.* Harper and Row, 1975.

Mohr, N. *Felita, A Puerto Rican Child.* Dial, 1979.

Mohr, N. *Going Home.* Dial, 1986.

Morey, J., and Dunn, W. *Famous Mexican Americans.* Cobblehill Books, 1989.

Morris, A. *Bread, Bread, Bread.* Lothrop, Lee and Shepard, 1989.

Morris, A. *Hats, Hats, Hats.* Lothrop, Lee and Shepard, 1989.

Mosel, A. *Tiki Tiki Tembo.* Henry Holt, 1968.

Munsch, R. *Thomas' Snowsuit.* Firefly Books, 1983.

Naylor, P. *Maudie in the Middle.* Dell, 1990.

Neville, E. *It's Like This, Cat.* Harper and Row, 1985.

Noble, T. *The Day Jimmy's Boa Ate the Wash.* Penguin, 1980.

Parish, P. *Dinosaur Time.* Harper and Row, 1974.

Paterson, K. *Bridge to Terabithia.* Harper and Row, 1987.

Paterson, K. *The Great Gilly Hopkins*. Harper and Row, 1987.

Pettit, J. *My Name Is San Ho*. Scholastic, 1992.

Ridyard, D. *Grandpa Loves Us*. Gareth Stevens, 1985.

Rockwell, T. *How to Eat Fried Worms*. Dell, 1988.

Rohmer, N. *Brother Anansi and the Cattle Ranch*. Children's Book Press, 1989.

Rohmer, H., and Anchondo, M. *How We Came to the Fifth World*. Children's Press, 1988.

Rosenberg, M. *Being Adopted*. Lothrop, Lee and Shepard, 1984.

Round, G. *What If . . . I Were an Astronaut?* Barron's Educational, 1987.

Rylant, C. *The Relatives Came*. Bradbury Press, 1985.

Rylant, C. *When I Was Young in the Mountains*. Penguin, 1982.

Sadler, M. *Alistair in Outer Space*. Prentice-Hall, 1984.

Scieszka, J. *The True Story of the Three Little Pigs, by A. Wolf*. Viking, 1989.

Selsam, M. *Sea Monsters of Long Ago*. Macmillan, 1978.

Simon, N. *Why Am I Different?* A. Whitman, 1976.

Smith, D. *A Taste of Blackberries*. Crowell, 1973.

Snyder, D. *The Boy of the Three-Year Nap*. Houghton Mifflin, 1988.

Spinelli, J. *Maniac McGee*. Little, 1990.

Steptoe, J. *Mufaro's Beautiful Daughters*. Scholastic, 1987.

Stevenson, R. *Treasure Island*. Puffin, 1984.

Taylor, M. *Roll of Thunder, Hear My Cry*. Dell, 1976.

Twain, M. *Huckleberry Finn*. Raintree, 1988.

Twain, M. *Tom Sawyer*. Penguin, 1983.

Viorst, J. *The Tenth Good Thing About Barney*. Macmillan, 1988.

Wilder, L. *Little House in the Big Woods*. Harper and Row, 1932.

Wildsmith, B. *Professor Noah's Spaceship*. Oxford, 1980.

Williams, V. *A Chair for My Mother*. William Morrow, 1982.

Yashima, T. *Crow Boy*. Viking Penguin, 1955.

Yep, L. *Dragonwings*. Harper and Row, 1975.

Yolen, J. *Favorite Folktales from around the World*. Random House, 1986.

Yue, C. *The Pueblo*. Houghton Mifflin, 1986.

INFORMATIONAL BOOKS

Biracree, Tom. *Wilma Rudolph*. Chelsea House, 1988.

Birch, Beverly. *Marie Curie*. Gareth Stevens, 1988.

Bisel, Sara C. *The Secrets of Vesuvius: Exploring the Mysteries of an Ancient Buried City*. Scholastic, 1991.

Buchanan, Ken. *This House is Made of Mud*. Northland, 1991.

Butterfield, Moira. *People and Places*. Random House, 1991.

Brice, Raphaelle. *Rice: The Little Grain that Feeds the World*. Children's Press, 1991.

Carr, Terry. *Spill! The Story of the Exxon Valdez*. Franklin Watts, 1991.

Cross, Wilbur. *Solar Energy*. Children's Press, 1984.

di Franco, J. Philip. *The Italian-American*. Chelsea House, 1988.

Downer, Ann. *Don't Blink Now! Capturing the Hidden World of Sea Creatures*. Franklin Watts, 1991.

Embury, Barbara. *The Dream is Alive: A Flight of Discovery Aboard the Space Shuttle*. Harper and Row, 1990.

Farlow, James O. *On the Tracks of Dinosaurs: A Study of Dinosaur Footprints*. Franklin Watts, 1991.

Farre, Marie. *Long Ago in a Castle*. Children's Press, 1988.

Fritz, Jean. *Bully for You, Teddy Roosevelt*. Putnam, 1991.

Gallant, Roy A. *Earth's Vanishing Forests*. Macmillan, 1991.

Gentry, Tony. *Dizzy Gillespie*. Chelsea House, 1991.

Gibbons, Gail. *Whales*. Holiday House, 1991.

Humble, Richard. *Ships: Sailors and the Sea*. Franklin Watts, 1991.

Lambert, David. *Our World: Seas and Oceans*. Silver Burdette, 1988

Lambert, Mark. *The Brain and the Nervous System*. Silver Burdette, 1988.

Lavies, Bianca. *Wasps At Home*. Dutton, 1991.

Lazier, Christine. *Seashore Life*. Children's Press, 1991.

Lodge, Sally. *The Cheyenne*. Rourk, 1990.

Lohf, Sabine. *Building Your Own Toys*. Children's Press, 1989.

McCall. Edith. *Pirates & Privateers*. Children's Press, 1980.

McVey, Vicki. *The Sierra Club Book of Weatherwisdom*. Little, Brown, 1991.

Mell, Jan. *Grand Canyon*. Crestwood House, 1988.

Oliphant, Margaret. *The Egyptian World*. Warwick Press, 1989.

Reilly, Mary Jo. *Cultures of the World: Mexico*. Marshall Cavendish, 1991.

Sandelson, Robert. *Olympic Sports: Swimming and Diving*. Crestwood House, 1991.

Simon, Seymour. *Oceans*. Morrow, 1990.

Solomon, Chuck. *Major-League Batboy*. Crown, 1991.

Sullivan, George. *Sluggers! Twenty-Seven of Baseball's Greatest*. Atheneum, 1991.

Venezia, Mike. *Rembrandt*. Children's Press, 1988.

Williams, Lucy. *Beginning History: The American West*. Bookwright, 1991.

Activities for Preservice Teachers

1. Read several research studies about children's interests in literature and compare the results. Report your findings to the class.

2. Look in a media or instructional materials center for video- and audiocassettes, films, and filmstrips based on children's literature. View a variety of these and decide

which ones you would—or would not—use in a classroom. Give reasons for your decisions.

3. Begin a collection of biographies and pictures of authors of children's books.

4. Visit the children's section of a public library. Inquire about the most popular books, the frequency of children's visits, and the method used to select books for the collection.

5. Visit a library or bookstore and investigate collections of poetry for children. Select at least one that you would like to have as a part of your personal collection of children's literature.

6. Begin a collection of poems about holidays that occur during the normal school year. Confine your selections to those suitable for a particular age group (primary, middle, or upper grades), and try to include as many poems and as many holidays as possible.

7. Begin a file of stories for reading or telling to children. Concentrate on primary, middle, or upper grades.

8. Plan an activity designed to aid sixth-grade children in understanding and using figurative language. Use a story or poem as a motivating device. Outline carefully each step you would use in teaching the concept.

9. Visit a public library during the storytelling hour. Observe and report to the class on storytelling techniques used, choice of stories, and the children's reactions.

Activities for Inservice Teachers

1. Instead of, or in addition to, providing comfortable spots for readers in the library corner, some teachers like to set up "quiet areas" where children can sit on chairs or recline on mats while they enjoy books. Experiment with this, and, with the children, set up standards for behavior in these areas.

2. Investigate the availability of paperback books for children. Where can they be obtained? How durable are they? What do they cost?

3. Add to the independent activities for children suggested in this chapter.

4. Compile a file of poetry appropriate for particular days, such as the first day of spring, the first snow, a foggy day, Valentine's Day, and so on.

5. With your class, make a bulletin-board display about a favorite author.

6. With the children, organize a book fair and book swap. The children can bring favorite books, books they want to trade, and books obtained from neighbors (watch these for appropriateness). Assemble the books in an attractive and organized manner in an area of the room where children can easily go to browse and to make selections. Bulletin boards, book displays, mobiles, posters, and the children's own book-sharing devices (a card file of reactions to books that have been read, dioramas, art work, objects that have been constructed or collected, etc.) may be used to enhance the appeal of the area.

7. List the stories, poems, and books you have read to your class this year. Are you reading a variety of literature, presenting new authors, and introducing new literary forms?

8. List five media items you have used with your class this year. Describe your purposes and methods for using these and evaluate their effectiveness.

9. A walk to the local library with your class can be an enjoyable learning experience. Check with your library to make arrangements for a visit. A librarian may plan to read a special story to your class.

Activities for Children

1. Encourage children to make their own poetry anthologies and illustrate the poems with their own drawings or pictures cut from magazines. These should not be collected or graded (although they may be shared if the children wish). Poems might be written by the children themselves, might be ones they especially like, or both.

2. Have individual children select favorite poems and record them on tape. They can then use the tapes to judge their own reading for speed, expression, enunciation, and so forth. After a child feels that an effective reading level has been achieved, he or she may read the poem to the class.

3. Invite a child to go to the library and select books about a topic being studied by the class. This child may then be responsible for helping other children choose among them either for personal enjoyment or for reporting to the class.

4. Have a student interview classmates and other children in the school about their favorite books. Urge the child to

find out why each book is a favorite. He or she may report the results of the interviewing to the class and show copies of some of the books.

5. One child or several children might stage a puppet show based on an incident in a story or book.

6. Have a pupil look through magazines for pictures to illustrate a favorite story for telling to the class.

7. A child can prepare a bulletin-board display advertising a favorite book. A colorful jacket, sketches of characters, and a biography of the author might be included. Lists of "good" words, appealing passages, and chapter titles may also be part of the display.

8. Have children select characters from a story that they know well and find especially appealing. They can then list words, phrases, or sentences (either those used in the story or ones selected from their own impressions) that describe the character.

9. In the upper grades many children are beginning to play the guitar. Such a child may prepare for the class a program of ballads or folk songs from a particular era or locality in conjunction with a social studies or literature unit.

10. Mobiles illustrating a story or several stories may be made. These might show principal characters, location of action, or anything else the child wishes to express.

11. Audiovisual aids serve as a basis for many independent activities. Individual children or groups can listen to taped or recorded stories and poems, view videotapes or filmstrips, prepare flannelboard stories to tell, and so forth. Sometimes this individual activity can be followed up by class viewing or listening.

12. An upper-grade student might write a comparison of two versions of the same story, presented through different types of media, telling which he or she liked best and why.

13. A child may write a letter to an author or illustrator of a book that he or she has particularly enjoyed. Make sure that the letter includes particular reasons for liking the book (or the illustrations) or points out parts that were especially enjoyed. As an alternative, some piece of creative writing or art work that resulted from the reading might be sent to the author or illustrator.

Chapter 16

Serving Children
with Special Needs

For general information write to:

National Information
  Center for Children and
  Youth with Disabilities
P.O. Box 1492
Washington, DC 20013

Council for Exceptional
  Children
1920 Association Drive
Reston, VA 22091

National Easter Seal
  Society
70 East Lake Street
Chicago, IL 60601

*N*ot so many years ago it was common for large numbers of children with vision, hearing, speech, physical, mental, emotional, and learning problems to be assigned to special classes and even special schools and to find themselves isolated from other students. At the time, this provision of "extra" attention seemed a good idea, but the wisdom of such practice has been reconsidered in many school systems. Most decisions about the school placement of children with special needs are now governed by the principle of *inclusion,* the idea that, as much as possible, such youngsters ought to be included in the program of *regular education.* This means that teachers should increasingly expect that among the classroom group there will be one or more children who will require some additional services.

Other types of special-needs youngsters are likely to be enrolled in your class, too. In some situations large numbers of elementary-age children now come to school speaking a language other than English, so learning English is obviously an important need for them. And, of course, there are students whose abilities are exceptionally good, so much so that it is questionable that these *gifted and talented* students can make appropriate progress if not given a different kind of program.

In Chapter 2 we stressed that your planning should be comprehensive, encompassing consideration of students' individual characteristics and requirements—in all areas, of course, not just the language arts. We believe, however, that if your classroom program follows the guidelines we have presented in each succeeding chapter, the needs of nearly all of the children can be met.

SPECIAL-NEEDS CHILDREN

In the mid-1970s it was recognized in legislation at the national level that many students with impairments were not being adequately served through existing programs. It became public policy to consider the extent to which those with special needs could be served better if they were placed in a situation that could be designated as a *least restrictive environment,* somewhere that gave them maximum opportunity to function like everyone else while still providing the services needed.

Under these provisions, the most restrictive environment would be a hospital or residential center, and certain individuals can only be accommodated in such settings. A program considered less restrictive than total care would be a self-contained school or classroom devoted entirely to students requiring a high level of supervision and accommodation. Successively less restrictive environments would involve part-day or total placement in a regular classroom situation.

The Population to be Served

Approximately two million children of elementary-school age are classified as eligible for special educational services. The table below presents data concerning the number of students in each category and the percentage of the handicapped represented by that amount.

From these figures it is apparent that the largest single group of special-needs youngsters is composed of those who require speech assistance. It is known that most of these are children in the early grades, since data also indicate that about 60 percent of six-year-olds receive speech services, whereas only approximately 5 percent of eleven-year-old students do. Nevertheless, oral language is a major concern of teachers, so this area deserves much attention.

Examination of the table also indicates that, when the categories *learning disabled* and *mentally retarded* are combined, the proportion of special-needs children affected approaches 50 percent. (Controversies surround the degree of distinctiveness of these categories, but recommended teaching strategies are usually highly similar, so there is no need to separate them for a discussion of methods and instructional materials.) Thus, it is apparent that about 90 percent of younger students with special needs have substantial difficulties in the two areas of intellectual functioning and speech, clearly categories with substantial relevance for language learning. Language is also a prominent concern for those with deafness or significant hearing difficulties (an additional 1 percent of the special population) and blindness or serious vision limitations ($\frac{1}{2}$ of 1 per cent). Students in other categories seem unlikely to have problems specific to the language areas, except when a child with multiple challenges may have learning, speech, vision, or hearing difficulties (see the section Children with Physical Limitations). It is also true that some individuals with physical-movement limitations will require assistance in operating computers and other language-related devices.

In addition to students with limitations of various kinds, it is often mandated that schools give special attention to the education of gifted and talented children, those whose abilities are so far in advance of their classmates' that a teacher cannot be expected to provide appropriate learning experiences. It is generally accepted

Number and Percentage of Special-Needs Children in Categories

Information from the *Tenth Annual Report to Congress on the Implementation of the Education of the Handicapped Act* (1988).

CATEGORY	NUMBER	PERCENT OF HANDICAPPED
Speech Difficulties	820,000	41.0
Learning Disabled	780,000	39.0
Mentally Retarded	190,000	9.5
Emotionally Disturbed	120,000	6.0
Multiply Handicapped	30,000	1.5
Hard of Hearing or Deaf	20,000	1.0
Orthopedically Impaired	20,000	1.0
Health Impaired	20,000	1.0
Visually Handicapped	10,000	0.5

that 3 to 5 percent of school-age children are in this category. Certainly, among the students identified as having needs in the areas of physical handicap, hearing impairment, or whatever, some can also be identified as gifted or talented or both.

Although provisions for educating special-needs children do not include the entire population of students who are learning English as another language or who are participating in bilingual education programs, the needs of these students are covered by other national laws and regulations. Clearly, language arts teaching will be substantially affected when such youngsters are present in your classroom.

Labeling Children

Typically, various labels have been attached to special-needs children, often misleading ones. For example, students with relatively minor hearing losses may have in the past been sent to a rather restrictive school for the deaf. And mistakenly classifying individuals as emotionally disturbed or learning disabled has sometimes appeared to cause them to behave as if they actually did have the malady identified by the label—the so-called *self-fulfilling prophecy,* a phenomenon that may also affect those identified as *maladjusted* children or *slow learners.* Too often such labeling has been done for bureaucratic reasons: the child was difficult to teach and there was a class for the mentally retarded, so she or he was categorized and removed but did not receive the service actually needed. Even the *gifted* or *genius* label has caused difficulties for some so classified.

In some cases labeling is mandatory if a child is to receive certain services.

The Trend Toward Inclusion and Mainstreaming

At the very time when labeling the handicapped and placing them in segregated settings was at its height, some authorities, parents, and advocates for the disabled were beginning to recognize that less restrictive programming would probably be beneficial. The reasons for supporting this view were many.

Help parents accept their children's limitations and recognize their potential.

1. There was not much evidence that segregated special-needs students were succeeding well in school or society.
2. Parents of special-needs students were asking for fuller opportunities for their children.
3. The courts were considering arguments that conventional segregated environments violated the civil rights of the handicapped.
4. The fairness and the validity of much psychological testing used to identify and classify special-needs students were being questioned.
5. Children from minority backgrounds were overrepresented in several programs, especially those for the mentally retarded.
6. The capacity of the educational system to deliver special services to every classroom was being increased.
7. The view that the education of nonhandicapped children is incomplete without the opportunity to associate with the handicapped was becoming more widely accepted.
8. There was growing rejection of the labeling of children.

See the article by Schloss listed in the references at the end of the chapter.

Read about regular education for special needs students in Chapter 1 of *Exceptional Children* by Hallahan and Kauffman, listed in the References section at the end of the chapter.

These influences led to the adoption of laws and regulations that are usually summarized by the term *mainstreaming,* which means that special-needs children should spend at least some of their time in classes with the regular school-age population. In some cases mainstreaming involves attending both a special-education program and a regular classroom, with the balance between the two determined by all those involved—students, parents, teachers, and specialists. *Inclusion* means that significant efforts will be made to place special-needs children in regular classrooms. For many of those with special needs, then, the trend is to:

- provide each child with the most appropriate education in the least restrictive environment
- give most attention to the educational needs of children rather than to their clinical or diagnostic performance levels
- seek and create alternatives within the educational program of the regular classroom to better serve students with special needs
- unify special education programs with general education programs for the educational benefit of special-needs children

Placement of Special-Needs Children

The process of identifying childen with special needs and placing them in an appropriate setting is a complex one and often involves a lengthy and detailed set of procedures. Because labeling is a serious matter, the time and effort expended are considered worthwhile, however.

Of course, there are some youngsters who require full-time placement in a program for the handicapped (a day school or center, a residential facility, or a hospital). In this chapter the discussion will revolve around students who can be included in *regular education* and do not appear to need a segregated program on a full-time basis.

Among the individuals who can participate in a regular classroom program, several kinds of placements should be possible. In general, the challenge is to discover the extent to which a child needs assistance in order to succeed in a regular classroom situation. Although various governmental agencies and school systems use different terminology and criteria for placement (and don't all have the same number of options available), generally accepted procedures call for children not totally segregated to be placed in one of four types of situations.

1. *Regular Class Only.* A child placed in a regular class without additional services is, in general, treated the same as other students. The youngster is not labeled and does not leave the room for clinical attention. Ordinarily, the teacher will be aware of any existing situation and will be prepared to extend to the child the same sort of consideration any other pupil could expect. For example, a child in a wheelchair needs some room to maneuver; a child with poor vision or some hearing loss needs to be located differently; a mildly retarded or learning disabled or emotionally troubled student requires extra attention from time to time.

2. *Regular Class with Consultation.* A student's special needs may indicate that he or she can be placed in a regular classroom provided that the classroom

teacher has the opportunity to consult with a specialist on a regular basis. There may be no need to classify the student and no reason for him or her to leave the room for services.

Several conditions could produce a situation in which a classroom required a consultant. A child with low vision may need some materials enlarged; ones with serious hearing losses can be helped if the teacher wears a portable microphone and they a receiver; a slow learner or one with a learning problem can remember only one-step directions; or a tense youngster cannot do well in cooperative learning groups. In these circumstances the classroom teacher could probably do much for the affected youngster but would likely profit from having the advice of an expert.

3. *Regular Class with a Support Teacher.* When there is a support teacher who not only advises the regular teacher but is also scheduled to work with the special-needs student in the classroom each day or every few days, youngsters with fairly serious problems may be placed in that room. The classroom teacher continues to be responsible for that student's total educational program and provides almost all instruction. Very likely the child does not leave the room for services but may have to be identified as having a particular need.

Depending on academic ability and personal qualities, students who are blind or who have other serious limitations can succeed in regular classrooms when supported by a specialist. Also, it may be necessary to make room for a computer or other equipment required for a child.

4. *Regular Classroom Combined with Resource Room.* If it seems appropriate the special-needs child may spend a portion of the school day away from the regular classroom in a *resource room*. The resource-room teacher is a specialist who advises and confers with the regular teacher and also teaches and tutors the student on a regular basis. It is the classroom teacher that is responsible for the child's educational program, however.

In the resource room the special-needs child may be given clinical assistance (with a speech difficulty, perhaps), tutoring (mathematics, for instance), counseling (making friends and dealing with other concerns), access to services (a word processor that is a "talking computer"), or any of several other kinds of help. In general the resource room is intended to support students as they move toward full participation and inclusion in regular education.

SERVING SPECIAL-NEEDS CHILDREN IN THE CLASSROOM

A large proportion of children with special needs can be served while remaining in the regular classroom full time. Of course, each individual is different, so plans must be made for the specific youngster and her or his situation. Whether you wish to serve a child on your own, with some advice or services from a specialist in the room or in combination with services the student could receive in a resource room, would have to be decided in collaboration with all concerned. One advantage of the regular classroom placement is that you know the youngster well—something for which there is no substitute.

Hallahan and Kauffman present a sample IEP in their first chapter.

Regulations require that each student identified as requiring special assistance in such areas as those listed earlier, under The Population to be Served, should have an *individualized education program* (*IEP*) written for her or him. The IEP should be developed cooperatively by teachers and other members of the school district staff, parents or guardians of the student, and the child, if appropriate. It must include provisions to ensure that the special-needs student receives an education appropriate to her or his needs. Specifically, the IEP ought to consist of

1. a description of the child's current level of educational performance
2. a statement of goals for the year and short-term teaching objectives
3. a description of educational services to be provided and the extent to which the student will participate in the regular education program
4. a statement concerning how the child's program will be implemented and evaluated

Working relationships between teachers and parents are important in teaching all children, but are especially significant when special-needs students are involved.

It is also required that parents (or surrogates) agree to the provisions of the IEP and have access to information related to it. As a teacher you may have full responsibility for developing IEPs or opportunities to assist in developing them. Certainly you should be prepared to contribute to discussions concerning what might be best for the students you know well.

Children in Need of Speech Assistance

Although problems with their speech is the most common difficulty found among elementary-school students, the number of children in your classroom with serious speech disorders is likely to be rather small. However, it is important that you identify such youngsters and see that they receive the assistance they require, and you should be prepared to assist any pupil whose speech indicates the existence of less severe or transitory problems.

Write to:

American Speech-
Language-Hearing
Association
10861 Rockville Pike
Rockville, MD 20852

Minor Speech Difficulties. When a child first enters school, his or her speech may retain vestiges of "baby talk." Estimates indicate that over 40 percent of kindergarten children and 25 percent of first graders fall into this category. Such speech is characterized by one or more of several features: reversals (for example, "aminal" for "animal"), inability to articulate certain combinations ("st," "th," "str," etc.), and individual speech sounds, mispronunciations, and divergences in pitch and loudness. Children with any of these features may be referred to a speech therapist, who very likely will simply wish to observe their behavior, monitor their language development, and, perhaps, suggest activities similar to those described in this chapter.

The child of eight or nine (at the latest) certainly should be able to produce all of the speech sounds accurately unless he or she does have a serious speech problem. Any youngster, of course, may have certain habits (saying "tree" for "three," perhaps) that are attributable to the dialect spoken at home or in the community and are not, strictly speaking, speech problems.

Undesirable features of speech not associated with a psychological problem are discussed in the section that follows. Most of these difficulties call for the services of a speech therapist or other specialist, someone who works directly with the child or provides the classroom teacher with suggestions and assistance. When a specialist is not available, the teaching considerations and activities presented may be helpful.

Specific Types of Speech Difficulties. Speech problems may be manifested in a variety of forms. These can be grouped, though, in four major categories: *articulatory, voice, linguistic,* and *rhythmic* disorders.

Articulation problems. Very likely as many as 70 percent of all speech difficulties found in the elementary classroom involve the inability of a child to produce certain phonemes, either in isolation or in combination with other sounds. These articulatory difficulties consist mostly of sound substitutions, omissions, reversals, and additions in the speech of children eight years or older.

Persistence of young children's language characteristics in the speech of those who are older may be caused by such factors as problems with muscular coordination, illness, slow physical maturation, low intelligence, auditory memory limitations, restrictions on auditory perception, or various environmental influences (overprotection by a parent, desire for attention, sibling rivalry, etc.). There are other articulatory disorders identified by specialists, the most common of which is lisping, but they are also manifested in problems with particular speech sounds.

Never display impatience with a child who has speech difficulties. He or she must feel accepted and secure.

Voice Problems. Voice disorders are those in which speech sounds are articulated acceptably, but the voice has qualities that interfere with communication because they call too much attention to themselves. The most common voice problem is nasality, usually caused by a physical problem, the most serious of which is a cleft palate. Other voice features that interfere with communication include hoarseness, an unusually high or low pitch, and excessive loudness or softness.

A youngster with a speaking or hearing impairment may also be a "quiet one."

Language Problems. Optimal language development can be interfered with by various physical, environmental, or psychological problems. Major language disorders most often found in the elementary school are *delayed speech* and childhood *aphasia.* Delayed speech may mean that a child does not know some sounds or has a very limited vocabulary. Victims of delayed speech range from the child who suffers a mild delay in the appearance of a few sounds to the one who reaches the primary grades with the ability to say only three or four words. When seriously delayed language development is apparent the cause is usually brain damage and the condition is known as aphasia.

Rhythm Problems. The principal speech difficulty of a rhythmic nature is stuttering. Some stutterers block on producing sounds; some repeat sounds, syllables, or words; some speak very slowly or very rapidly; some prolongate sounds; and others have uncontrollable contractions of the speech mechanism. There may be combinations of the above in the speech of a stutterer, and there are cases in which there is no definite cause of stuttering, and no certain cure. However, many stutterers can learn procedures that enable them to control their speech.

Instructional Considerations. Children identified as possibly having a speech disorder should be referred for diagnosis. If the problem is considered to be serious the specialist doing the assessment should confer with parents and, if warranted, physicians and psychologists. If the child is of school age, the teacher should be included in discussions of remedial steps that ought to be taken.

Reduction of anxieties and tension is important in treating any speech problem. Interrupting a child's attempts to say what he or she wants to say often produces even more anxiety. Classmates must be helped to see that the affected individual deserves respect and should in no circumstances be mocked or ridiculed. Small-group discussions and cooperative learning experiences (see suggestions in Chapter 5) will often benefit a child with a speech problem.

Activities. Activities that have potential for modifying or remedying speech problems should be used to meet specific needs; they should not be used indiscriminately, however. It is much more important for children, including those who have speech handicaps, to engage in genuine communication situations than to practice speech exercises. Activities such as those suggested here are important and necessary at times, but they are only part of a total speech improvement program. Several types of interventions may be considered.

Relaxation. Relaxing exercises such as slumping in a chair, dropping the head and letting the arms dangle, shaking the hands and arms, and rotating the head on the chest and shoulders may help a child whose speech problem is related to tenseness. Of course you should strive to foster the kind of classroom atmosphere that is reasonably free of tension, since this will benefit all of the children.

Breathing. Breathing exercises, such as taking short quick breaths, inhaling deeply, taking in a quick breath and exhaling slowly (by counting), and doing specific acts (smelling a flower, saying "ah" for the doctor, showing surprise), may also be helpful. To deal with excessive nasality, try such exercises as yawning, forcing out air with vowel sounds (or blowing out a candle, blowing a pinwheel, etc.).

Hearing. Hearing exercises are often helpful, since good speech depends on aural acuity and the ability to discriminate between phonemes. These exercises include discriminating among sounds (the ringing of a small bell and the sound of a musical triangle being struck, for example), telling whether or not two words begin with the same sound (fine and vine), end with the same sound (star and start), or have the same middle sound (patted and padded).

Reducing "Baby Talk." The type of speech known as infantile perseveration is characterized by the use of such pronunciations as "muvver" for "mother" and "thithter" for "sister." Children still talking in this way may be helped if you make an audio- or videotape of you discussing this matter with them so that they can become more aware of what they are saying. Then a plan can be developed for substituting the more mature speech forms for the others.

See the article on electronic aids by Wisniewski and Sedlak listed at the end of the chapter.

Electronic Aids. In Chapter 5 it was suggested that children's oral language development could be advanced if audio- and videotape recorders were available to them in the classroom. Much the same can be said of special opportunities for those with fairly serious difficulties. Students who lack speech or whose speech is difficult for others to understand may be assisted in various ways:

1. With a computer and screen (especially a portable computer), they may type messages that others can read from the screen.
2. With a portable computer that prints out text on paper, affected individuals can type, print, and then give the sheet or strip to someone to read.

3. With a portable "talking computer," they can type-in messages that are then spoken to the listener by the machine.

4. Students who cannot speak and also have restrictions on their motor abilities can activate computers through switches controlled by even slight movements of almost any part of the body.

Children in Need of Assistance with Hearing

For information write to:
National Association for the Deaf
814 Thayer Ave.
Silver Spring, MD 20910
The association also serves the hearing impaired.

The total incidence of hearing losses among schoolchildren is not known, since these impairments range from very slight ones to absolute deafness. Hearing losses and learning difficulties are not necessarily related, but the fact that so much instruction depends on oral exchanges means that students who do not hear well will almost surely have some problems.

Screening for Hearing Losses. Most school systems have procedures providing that all students are periodically tested for hearing. Even though there has been screening, you may encounter children whose behavior and other symptoms indicate that they are not hearing properly. These include recurring earaches, a

The child attends a regular class because she hears through the receiver and the teacher wears a microphone.

tendency to favor one ear in listening, rubbing the ear, headaches, hearing buzzing or other noises, or dizziness. Excessive inattention, reflected in poor achievement and the failure to follow directions, may also signal a hearing problem. Sometimes, too, faulty pronunciation, heavy breathing through the mouth, and an unnatural pitch of voice are signs of impairment.

Children who appear to have hearing difficulties should be referred for professional attention. You should be prepared to cooperate with medical and clinical personnel in any way that you can to provide the assistance needed. Speaking face-to-face to a child who seems to have a hearing loss may give that student added help in focusing attention and learning to use clues.

Helping the Child. The child with a hearing impairment can be helped in various ways, and even a profoundly deaf student can be accommodated in the regular classroom. Possible adjustments are:

1. A plan for "total communication" should be undertaken, with a combination of strategies being used: lip reading, hearing aids, sign language, and so forth.

2. Face-to-face speech should be stressed with affected children; this may help them to focus attention and use clues.

3. Instruction in sign language should be offered for classmates (videotapes are available for practice).

4. The affected youngster should be seated to best advantage—with a child who has some proficiency in sign language, perhaps.

5. You may wear a lapel microphone in order to speak directly to any affected student who has a receiver.

6. Just as with students who need speech assistance, computers can be used by those with little or no hearing ability, since they can type in messages that can be read by someone else and read what others type for them.

7. A "talking computer" may also speak for the affected person who is able to type.

Children in Need of Assistance with Vision

Children who require vision assistance are common in schools, of course. Many devices are available for students whose vision is a problem for them: eye glasses, contact lenses, magnifying glasses (some large enough to cover a page in a book), and various electronic devices.

For information write to:
Council of Citizens with
Low Vision
1400 N. Drake Rd., No. 218
Kalamazoo, MI 20007

Identifying Children with Vision Problems. Symptoms of possible vision problems include

losing the place while reading
avoiding close work
peculiar posture when reading
holding the reading material closer or farther away than normal
holding the body rigid while looking at distant objects
rubbing the eyes
tilting the head to one side
frowning, blinking, or scowling while reading or writing
excessive head movement while reading
inflamed eyelids
frequent headaches

A few children in the elementary school, mostly boys, have problems with color perception and this may cause them difficulties with certain activities.

Instructional Considerations. When referred to a specialist, a child who has a vision problem usually receives attention: lenses, supervised muscle training, and so on. But even if a child does receive the kind of special assistance he or she needs, there are still some basic ways a teacher can help:

- Seat the child so that he or she can see the chalkboard, screen, and charts as well as possible.
- Place the desk so as to avoid glare on its surface.
- Prevent a situation in which the student would face sharp contrasts in the amount of direct light.
- Use reading materials that do not have a glossy surface.

Word processors can display large letters, which is very helpful with low-vision students.

There are also many ways in which children with little or no vision may be assisted in the area of the language arts through the availability of electronic aids:

1. Photocopy machines with enlargement capabilities located in the school, resource room, or even the regular classroom, make it possible for the low-vision student to be supplied with readable textbooks, practice materials, and library books.

2. Computers that produce a larger-than-ordinary display (letters several inches high) on their screens are also available.

3. Closed-circuit television cameras may be combined with color monitors so that ordinary pages and papers may be greatly enlarged for reading and other viewing.

4. Students with very little or no vision may type on a "talking computer" that reads back each letter and word typed and the entire text and also tells the typist where the cursor is located on the screen.

5. Children who type in braille may use machines that convert the braille to speech or conventional computer printing.

Children with Learning Problems

For information write to:

Association for Children with Learning Disabilities
4156 Library Road
Pittsburgh, PA 15234

Association for Retarded Citizens
500 East Border Street
Arlington, TX 76011

Council for Children with Behavioral Disorders
1900 Association Drive
Reston, VA 22091

This section presents a discussion of children who have substantial learning problems but who spend at least part of their day in the regular classroom. These students may be mentally retarded to some extent, may have learning disabilities, or may be unable to control their emotions and behavior at times.

Definitions and Characteristics. The actual learning problems of the students included in this category share certain similarities, but there are differences, of course. A youngster may not understand because of an inability to focus attention, a basically low intelligence, distractability, or one or another of several other difficulties.

Mental Retardation. Children classified as mentally retarded have many of the same needs as all other students. Those who are mildly retarded can also succeed at most developmental tasks; they simply perform these tasks (talk, ride a bicycle, read, divide) later than the average. (Those with substantial mental retardation will not be placed in regular education programs, of course.)

Learning Disabilities. Children said to be *learning disabled* are thought to be essentially normal but to have a condition that prevents them from succeeding at focusing attention, grasping knowledge, organizing experience, and expressing the synthesis of their thoughts at a level appropriate to their potential. Thus, the basic concern is that school achievement is highly unsatisfactory when compared to apparent ability. Most identifications of students as learning disabled occur because of the difficulties they have had with reading comprehension.

Possible Symptoms of Learning Disabilities

inattentiveness
aggressiveness
impulsiveness
incapacity to plan
perceptual difficulties
overexcitability
memory difficulties

Emotional and Behavior Problems. Nearly every child misbehaves occasionally or loses control and acts out feelings of anger, frustration, or sadness. Children who frequently behave in these ways and carry that behavior to extremes, perhaps causing harm to themselves or someone else, are kept away from others, just as adults with such problems are.

There are, however, children whose behavior appears to be neither within normal limits nor so problematical as to necessitate isolation. On the other hand, their feelings and conduct do prevent them from taking full advantage of the learning experiences made available in the classroom. Such students may be placed in a regular education situation as long as they are receiving some kind of assistance and the classroom teacher has an understanding of their status.

Instructional Considerations. Throughout this text we have discussed and recommended teaching procedures and materials that address the needs of a wide range of students. In dealing with youngsters who have been identified as having serious problems that interfere with their learning, you can only continue to use the varied approaches that you have found to be effective with all students. Also, the IEP and consultations with clinicians should provide you with specific suggestions that would be relevant for a particular student.

By continually reflecting on the needs of a pupil, you can, of course, identify strategies or activities that mesh well with his or her interests. For instance, a youngster who enjoys the classroom gerbils can have more time with the animals and do much reading and writing in connection with activities centering on them. The following general guidelines may help you think of specifics regarding a particular child.

Children from non-Western societies and those who are economically or socially disadvantaged may appear to have emotional and motivational problems in school settings. The likelihood is that the problem solution will require some adjustment by the school and some by the child.

1. *Be patient and understanding and sensitive to identified children's interests and needs.* All students need personal contact with you, but those with learning problems must receive constant assurance that you are there to help them and make their life better.

2. *Make sure the child attains a measure of success.* In the language arts area there are many opportunities for a child to succeed: improving handwriting and spelling, learning to type, participating in a televised play, and so on and on. Every student can make some kind of contribution.

3. *Make sure the child is aware of her or his accomplishments.* Not only can each youngster find success but there should be opportunities for you to point out that success. Most children can recognize that they are doing well and don't require much praise, but those with a history of learning difficulties need to have their accomplishments made public.

4. *Confer with identified children frequently and regularly.* In these pages reading and writing conferences have been discussed as important aspects of the program. These sessions will permit you and the child to talk about personal as well as instructional matters.

5. *Provide adequate time for the child to accomplish important goals.* Goals should be set in consultation with learning-problem students. You should gauge these carefully, seeing that they are significant but achievable within a time frame that is reasonable—reading a short book and responding to it in two weeks, for example.

6. *Provide appropriate materials and learning activities.* The kinds of activities we have recommended are in most cases open-ended. "Writing in journals" may mean a drawing with a few words for a youngster with a learning problem or a multi-page essay on the joys of skateboarding for an academically able child. This learning situation is quite different from one in which each student is given the same worksheet to complete.

Children with Physical Limitations

Many children with physical limitations can participate in a regular classroom. Youngsters with missing limbs or prosthetic devices, in wheelchairs, or using various means of assisted walking usually require no more than a bit of additional room and, perhaps, some furniture adjustments. Others, especially those with two or more kinds of problems, will need additional services.

Types of Limitations. For many youngsters their physical limitations are combined with other needs. A brain-injured child may be both partially paralyzed and unable to speak clearly, for example. Other multiply handicapped children could have special needs in both vision and hearing areas. Although it may at first seem likely that students with substantial needs cannot be accommodated in regular-education classrooms, much has already been accomplished and even more is being planned by experts in the fields of special education and technical adaptations for elementary-age children.

Instructional Considerations. Several of the procedures and devices mentioned in connection with the discussion of other special-needs children may be used with students who have physical limitations. To use a word processor, for example, some youngsters with movement restrictions will need large keyboards that permit them to activate a key by touching a knob with their entire hand rather than a finger. Others can successfully use a keyboard covered with a clear plastic screen with a hole over each key so that a tool strapped to the arm can be inserted and the key activated. As indicated in the discussions in other sections of this chapter, when students can use the word processor, the machine can speak for them if they do not have speech and can produce large-print type if they require that aid to vision.

Depending on what sorts of services may be available, then, even children with very serious difficulties can participate in regular classroom situations. Again the computer is central; if a way can be found to provide access to it, much else is possible. For instance, a person able to move the head only slightly can activate switches that move the cursor and select and type letters. With this, much else can be done and barriers to placement of the individual in a least restrictive environment are greatly diminished.

Gifted and Talented Children

Write to:

National Association for Gifted Children
1155 15th St. NW
No. 1002
Washington, DC 20005

The Association for the Gifted
c/o Council for Exceptional Children
1920 Association Drive
Reston, VA 22091

Government programs and school systems provide support services not only to students who have various difficulties that may interfere with learning but also to children with superior academic ability and other talents. As with any group considered unlikely to be educated adequately in the ordinary school situation, the question arises about whether or not gifted and talented children should be removed entirely and placed in programs exclusively for them, remain in the classroom with varying degrees of service, or receive only the conventional program with whatever extra attention the teacher can provide.

You may, then, have a student—hardly ever more than one in a class—whose academic ability or specific talents (music, art, drama, etc.) are so outstanding that you wonder if you can begin to provide what he or she requires. As with any other area of special need, each gifted child deserves individual attention—careful assessment of abilities, a cooperatively planned program of education, and much support.

Identifying the Students. In the area of language arts, gifted and talented students readily become visible to teachers because their outstanding characteristics are the very ones considered most important for classroom success.

1. *High Verbal Intelligence.* In nearly all programs for gifted children, intelligence is one of the most important selection criteria—and sometimes the only one. Certainly vocabulary is a significant factor involved in the assessment of intelligence, and knowledge of a large number of words and their meanings is important to success in reading, writing, and the other language areas.

2. *Sensitivity to Words.* In addition to knowing many words, gifted students are usually outstanding in their capacity to use them in just the right way: to select a word from among several synonyms and have it be precisely the one to convey the meaning intended, to relate words to one another in original ways, and express emotions and ideas through language much better than others of the same age can. In the language arts program such children often begin to write admirable poetry and to otherwise demonstrate their creativity.

3. *Grasp of Abstract Ideas.* Ideas are especially interesting to gifted students, and some need to express these in music, movement or art. In the language areas, however, in reading, listening, speaking, and writing, there are ample opportunities for children to call attention to their capacity to deal with such concepts as democracy, courage, friendship, and contrast.

4. *Rapid Progress in Reading and Writing.* Gifted children usually find it easy to read, and some do it a year or two before other youngsters. By first grade they may be reading a great deal, including materials at the fourth-grade level. Writing is often difficult because of handwriting limitations, but the availability of word processors in some households has made it more likely that even young students can get started. When invented spelling is encouraged, students in the early primary years sometimes write texts several dozen pages in length.

5. *Making Commitments to Activities and Projects.* Gifted youngsters are often highly motivated to undertake activities of special interest to them, even when such projects are very ambitious. In the language arts these may involve writing and producing a play, directing it, and taking the starring role (one first-grade girl came up with a production with parts for everyone—including her teacher). Publishing a collection of classmates' stories or a literary magazine for the school are other possibilities. Very often gifted students will invest many hours in such a venture—and learn much from it about planning and working with others.

6. *Concern with Issues and Problems.* High-ability children are usually more aware of adult concerns than are other students and often take an interest in becoming involved themselves. While most of these interests are related to health, government, and social problems, some are directly involved in language areas. A student may volunteer to read regularly to a blind person, for instance. And participating in the ecology movement will present opportunities for adult-level reading and writing experiences.

7. *Other Talents May Combine with Language Arts Experiences.* Children who are musically or artistically talented can make most welcome contributions to language arts activities. If someone writes a poem, a person with ability in music can devise a melody and thus produce a song, just as those with talent in drawing can be the illustrators of the class books. Students with dancing and dramatic ability can make contributions to learning activities and class or school productions.

The astrophysicist Stephen Hawking, who is almost entirely paralyzed, has written several important books about the universe.

Sometimes qualities of giftedness are evident when children are in the elementary school but not always. For this reason, you should not discourage a parent who seems to believe that a child has remarkable abilities. It is also important to remember that handicapped children may be gifted and talented.

Instructional Considerations. If the classroom experiences of gifted girls and boys are to meet their needs, adjustments in the program cannot mean only "more of the same." The gifted don't need longer lists of spelling words, more questions to answer, additional book reports, and the like. Rather, they should have opportunities that include contact with stimulating ideas, extensions of interests, and explorations of new areas of learning.

Even if a gifted child in your class works with a special teacher or you are advised by a consultant, the student's overall educational program remains your responsibility. You need to keep various factors and options in mind as you plan and supervise learning experiences.

- *Nature of Expectations.* The kinds of teaching recommended in this textbook stress self-evaluation and establishment of personal goals by the students themselves. This is particularly important for gifted children who too often lose interest because of an unchallenging regular program. They must be encouraged to strive for excellence in areas that are important to them, as long as the goals are their own.
- *Opportunities in the Language Arts.* The language arts area provides numerous opportunities for enrichment of a gifted child's experiences, whether the writing of poetry or the preparation of an exhibit of illustrations from selected stories. It is important for all children to have as many realistic and authentic experiences as possible, but this is particularly significant for those who may have mastered nearly all of what we think of as the developmental program of the elementary school.

*Both gifted children and those with learning problems can assist
younger students and profit from the experience.*

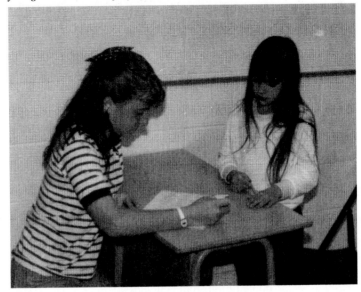

- *Independent Experiences and Leadership Opportunities.* Gifted and talented children often can profit from working independently or taking a leadership role in various projects. Independent activities could take place under the supervision of the school librarian or other member of the staff with expertise in the area of interest to the student. Leadership opportunities are important, too. For example, several students from different grade levels could cooperate to set up a postal system throughout the school, with one of the older high-ability youngsters as the organizer and manager serving under the supervision of the principal.

- *Research.* Chapters 13 and 14 emphasized study and research experiences. When such library work is combined with examination of real-life issues, realistic research situations are possible. Mostly they will consist of work in science or social studies, current events, community activities, or creative experiences. Students might do the research and then set up a display of local rocks or fossils, for example.

- *Technology.* When electronic technology is available to a gifted student, a large number of learning options open up to her or him. If the school has reference works on computer disks (as described in Chapter 14), research possibilities will be greatly enhanced. The collection of videotapes will be a very important resource, as will the capacity to tape-record telecasts of educational programs. Camcorders can make a substantial contribution to the range of study and creative experiences.

Although some people seem to believe that gifted and talented students should consider themselves fortunate and not expect to be eligible for additional services, others argue that such individuals will not fulfill their potential without assistance. Furthermore, according to this view, gifted students clearly have needs, too—need for exposure to more stimulating ideas, need for opportunities to extend their interests, and most of all need for a teacher who is neither threatened by their intellects and talents nor prone to be too demanding of them. You should support these students when they appear in your class, discussing many matters with them, particularly abstract ideas; introducing areas of potential interest; encouraging wide and deep exploration of topics; and posing questions that require critical thinking and problem solving.

Children Learning English as Another Language

For information write to:
Teaching English to
Speakers of Other
Languages
1600 Cameron St.
Suite 300
Alexandria, VA 22314

National Association for
Bilingual Education
Union Center Plaza
810 1st St. NE
Third Floor
Washington, DC 20002

Some children in our schools do not profit as much as they might from learning experiences because their language-cultural background is different from that of the majority of people in the society. Such youngsters have needs with special relevance to the language arts curriculum.

Depending on the location of a school, it may enroll a large number of children for whom English is not their first language. Some of these are from families that have lived in this country for a long time and whose home language is native (Navaho or Inuit, for instance) or a European language other than English (Spanish or French, most likely). Others who learn English as a second (or third, or fourth) language are recent arrivals who may speak Thai, Vietnamese, Russian, or one of several other languages. Such students are often classified as having *limited English proficiency.*

Understanding the Children. In planning ways to include students with limited English in your classroom program, you should keep in mind that family and cultural ties are significant and must receive prime consideration. Children's most important thoughts are of home and family, and their native language is an essential part of this background. To abuse or denigrate a family's heritage by condemning their language or other aspects of the culture degrades the student and shows a lack of sensitivity. In addition, there is the very practical matter that the desire a child has to learn a new language depends heavily on an attitude about his or her own worth as an individual.

A first step in helping students retain their identity while learning the language of the school is for you to understand something of their heritage. Learn as much as possible about the children's background. If it involves another country, study its history, current situation, traditions, and leaders. The culture—language, values, music, outlook on life, food, and pattern of family relationships—should also receive your attention. Although it will probably not be possible to learn the language, some expressions—greetings, common school and home words, and other frequently used vocabulary—can be taught and used with the whole class. (Language as a field of study can be a topic in the classroom, as mentioned in Chapter 1.)

Perhaps the children themselves can be encouraged to teach the other students words and customs that have been and still are important to them. An English-speaking person from the child's national or cultural group can be invited to school as a resource person. Since all children are interested in clothing, music, food, customs, and stories of other people, this is an excellent opportunity not only to enhance the self-images of children with limited English proficiency but also to help all students become knowledgeable about and appreciative of other cultures.

Motivating language learning with games.

Instructional Considerations. In developing a program for children learning English as another language, it is important to have sensible guidelines as well as specific teaching ideas:

- The focus should be on oral language; specific English expressions should receive the most attention.
- The form of English taught should be that used by children who are native speakers.
- Attention ought to be focused on the conversational fluency, intonation patterns and stress, and idiomatic speech of children who are native speakers of English.
- The child's first language should not be used during lesson periods when learning of English is being intensively pursued, as translation interferes with the necessary automatic responses.
- Making the sounds of English is difficult, so an accepting noncritical classroom climate is important; over-correction of students' pronunciation or speech patterns must be avoided.
- The program sets an example for quality of speech, so you must be an excellent model or provide someone who is or use audio and video recordings.

Specific teaching suggestions are also important:

1. Reduce the amount of teacher talk and place less emphasis on teacher-centered activities.
2. Emphasize peer-interaction and cooperative-learning activities.
3. Focus on content of communication, not extraneous matters.
4. Model good forms but do not correct structural mistakes.
5. Provide for frequent introduction of vocabulary items and idiomatic expressions.
6. Specific English expressions should receive the most attention.

For the most part, children who are learning English while maintaining their first language will profit from the kinds of activities described in this book, modified as necessary to take account of individual needs.

A FINAL WORD

We began this book with a discussion of how important it is for children to learn to use the English language well. Such learning ordinarily comes rather easily to most children and quite readily to gifted youngsters. While children who come to school speaking a language other than English usually become competent within a year or two, they often do require extra time and special instructional efforts. Also, there are students who have the specific sorts of limitations discussed in this chapter. They, too, can become effective communicators if provided with the appropriate kinds of teaching, whether in special education classes or in regular classrooms that they attend along with youngsters who have no apparent limitations.

References

Anderson, Betty, and Joels, Rosie Webb. *Teaching Reading to Students with Limited English Proficiencies.* Charles C Thomas, 1985.

Baum, Dale D. *The Human Side of Exceptionality.* PRO-ED, 1982.

Berdine, William H., and Blackhurst, A. Edward, eds. *An Introduction to Special Education.* Little, Brown, 1985.

Blatt, Burton. *The Conquest of Mental Retardation.* PRO-ED, 1987.

Breen, Michael J., and Altepeter, Thomas S. *Disruptive Behavior Disorders in Children.* Guilford, 1990.

Cohen, Sandra, and Plaskon, Stephen. *Language Arts for the Mildly Handicapped.* Charles E. Merrill, 1980.

Department of Education. *Tenth Annual Report to Congress on the Implementation of the Education of the Handiapped Act.* United States Government, 1988.

Edelsky, Carole. *Writing in a Bilingual Program: Habia Una Vez.* Ablex Publishing, 1986.

Ellis, Rod. *Understanding Second Language Acquisition.* Oxford, 1986.

Fitzgerald, Jill. "Literacy and Students Who are Learning English as a Second Language." *The Reading Teacher* 46 (May 1993), pp. 638–647.

Hallahan, Daniel P., and Kauffman, James M. *Exceptional Children.* Prentice-Hall, 1988.

Hewitt, Frank M. (with Steven R. Forness). *Education of Exceptional Learners,* 3rd ed. Allyn and Bacon, 1984.

Jeffree, Dorothy, and Skeffington, Margaret. *Reading Is for Everyone.* Prentice-Hall, 1984.

Lewis, Rena B., and Doorlag, Donald H. *Teaching Special Students in the Mainstream.* Charles E. Merrill, 1983.

Lim, Hwa-Ja Lee, and Watson, Dorothy J. "Whole Language Content Classes for Second-language Learners." *The Reading Teacher* 46 (February 1993), pp. 384–393.

Lucas, Linda, and Karrenbreck, Marilyn H. *The Disabled Child in the Library.* Libraries Unlimited, 1983.

Makohon, Linda, and Fredericks, H. D. Bud. *Teaching Expressive and Receptive Language to Students with Moderate and Severe Handicaps.* PRO-ED, 1985.

Morris, Richard J., and Blatt, Burton, eds. *Special Education: Research and Trends.* Pergamon, 1986.

Nevarez, Sandra; Mireles, Raquel C.; and Ramirez, Norma. *Experiences with Literature: A Thematic Whole Language Model for the K-3 Bilingual Classroom.* Addison-Wesley, 1990.

Norton, Donna. *Through the Eyes of a Child.* Charles E. Merrill, 1984.

Phelps-Terasaki, Diana; Phelps-Gunn, Trisha; and Stetson, Elton G. *Remediation and Instruction in Language.* Aspen Systems, 1983.

Pollette, Nancy, and Hamlin, Marjorie. *Exploring Books with Gifted Children.* Libraries Unlimited, 1980.

Rhodes, Lynn K., and Dudley-Marling, Curt. *Readers and Writers with a Difference: A Holistic Approach to Teaching Learning Disabled and Remedial Students.* Heinemann, 1988.

Rigg, Pat, and Allen, Virginia G., eds. *When They Don't All Speak English: Integrating the ESL Student into the Regular Classroom.* National Council of Teachers of English, 1989.

Schloss, Patrick J. "Mainstreaming Revisited." *Elementary School Journal* 92 (January 1992), pp. 233–244.

Schulz, Jane B., and Turnbull, Ann P. *Mainstreaming Handicapped Students,* 2nd ed. Allyn and Bacon, 1984.

Shore, Kenneth. *The Special Education Handbook.* Teachers College Press, 1986.

Spodek, Bernard; Saracho, Olivia N.; and Lee, Richard C. *Mainstreaming Young Children.* Wadsworth, 1984.

Wisniewski, Lech, and Sedlak, Robert. "Assistive Devices for Students with Disabilities." *Elementary School Journal* 92 (January 1992), pp. 297–314.

Zucker, Carol. "Using Whole Language with Students Who Have Language and Learning Disabilities." *The Reading Teacher* 46 (May 1993), pp. 660–670.

Teaching Resources

Ambert, Alba, and Melendez, Sarah E. *Bilingual Education: A Source Book.* Garland Publishing, 1985.

Azaknoff, Pat. *Health, Illness, and Disability: A Guide to Books for Children and Young Adults.* R. R. Bowker, 1983.

Baskin, Barbara H., and Harris, Karen H. *More Notes from a Different Drummer: A Guide to Juvenile Fiction Portraying the Handicapped.* R. R. Bowker, 1984.

Baskin, Barbara H. *Books for the Gifted Child.* R. R. Bowker, 1980.

Bos, Candace, and Vaughn, Sharon. *Strategies for Teaching Students with Learning and Behavior Problems.* Allyn and Bacon, 1991.

Friedberg, Joan B.; Mullins, June B.; and Sukiennik, Adelaide W. *Accept Me As I Am.* R. R. Bowker, 1985.

Griffin, Barbara. *Special Needs Bibliography*. The Griffin, 1984.

Leonard, Phyllis. *Choose, Use, Enjoy, Share: Library Skills for the Gifted Child*. Libraries Unlimited, 1985.

Lewis, Rena B., and Doorlag, Donald H. *Teaching Special Students in the Mainstream*. Charles E. Merrill, 1983.

Riekehof, Lottie L. *The Joy of Signing*. Gospel, 1987.

Renfro, Nancy. *Puppetry, Language, and the Special Child: Discovering Alternative Languages*. Watch Me Blossom Theatre Works.

Schon, Isabel. *A Hispanic Heritage, Series 11: A Guide to Juvenile Books about Hispanic People and Cultures*. Scarecrow Press, 1985.

Souweine, Judith, and Crimmins, Sheila. *Mainstreaming: Ideas for Teaching Young Children*. National Association for the Education of Young Children, 1981.

Webber, Margaret S. *Communication Skills for Exceptional Learners*. Aspen, 1981.

Suggested Children's Books

CHILDREN'S BOOKS ABOUT HANDICAPPING CONDITIONS

Bergman, Thomas. *On Our Own Terms—Children Living with Physical Handicaps*. Gareth Stevens, 1989.

Bradbury, Bianca. *The Girl Who Wanted Out*. Scholastic, 1981.

Brancato, Robin F. *Winning*. Knopf, 1987.

Killea, Marie. *Karen*. Dell, 1980.

Miner, Jane C. *New Beginning: An Athlete Is Paralyzed*. Crestwood House, 1982.

Powers, Mary Ellen. *Our Teacher's in a Wheelchair*. Whitman, 1986.

Seuling, Barbara. *I'm Not So Different: A Book about Handicaps*. Western Publishing, 1986.

Wepman, Dennis. *Helen Keller*. Chelsea House, 1989.

CHILDREN'S BOOKS ABOUT DEAFNESS AND HEARING LOSS

Arthur, Catherine. *My Sister's Silent World*. Children's Press, 1979.

Bergman, Thomas. *Finding a Common Language—Children Living with Deafness*. Gareth Stevens, 1989.

Bove, Linda. *Sesame Street Sign Language ABC*. Random House, 1986.

Peterson, Jeanne W. *I Have a Sister, My Sister Is Deaf*. Harper and Row, 1984.

Sullivan, Mary, and Bourke, Linda. *A Show of Hands: Say It in Sign Language*. Harper and Row, 1985.

Yeatman, Linda. *Buttons*. Children's Press, 1988.

CHILDREN'S BOOKS ABOUT BLINDNESS AND LOW VISION

Bergman, Thomas. *Seeing in Special Ways—Children Living with Blindness*. Gareth Stevens, 1989.

Brown, Marc. *Arthur's Eyes*. Avon, 1981.

Cohen, Miriam. *See You Tomorrow, Charles*. Greenwillow, 1983.

Marcus, Rebecca B. *Being Blind*. Hastings House, 1981.

Raskin, Ellen. *Spectacles*. Macmillan, 1988.

Reuter, Margaret. *My Mother Is Blind*. Children's Press, 1979.

Yeatman, Linda. *Perkins*. Children's Press, 1988.

CHILDREN'S BOOKS ABOUT SPEECH AND LANGUAGE DIFFICULTIES

Cunningham, Julia. *The Silent Voice*. Dutton, 1981.

Levine, Ellen. *I Hate English!* Scholastic, 1989.

Rounds, Glen. *Blind Outlaw*. Holiday, 1980.

CHILDREN'S BOOKS ABOUT PHYSICAL RESTRICTIONS

Kuklin, Susan. *Thinking Big: The Story of a Young Dwarf*. Lothrop, 1986.

Mendonca, Susan. *Broken Dreams*. Scholastic, 1984.

Rosenberg, Maxine. *My Friend Leslie*. Lothrop, 1983.

Yeatman, Linda. *Pickles*. Children's Press, 1988.

CHILDREN'S BOOKS ABOUT GIFTEDNESS

Fitzhugh, Louise. *Harriet the Spy*. Dell, 1986.

Hermes, Patricia. *I Hate Being Gifted*. Putnam, 1990.

Sadler, Marilyn. *Alistair's Time Machine*. Prentice-Hall, 1986.

Warren, Sandra, ed. *Being Gifted: Because You're Special from the Rest*. Trillium Press, 1987.

CHILDREN'S BOOKS ABOUT MENTAL AND LEARNING DIFFICULTIES

Bergman, Thomas. *We Laugh, We Love, We Cry—Children Living with Mental Retardation*. Gareth Stevens, 1989.

Garrigue, Sheila. *Between Friends*. Bradbury, 1978.

Giff, Patricia Reilly. *The Beast in Ms. Rooney's Room.* Dell, 1986.

Giff, Patricia Reilly. *The Candy Corn Contest*. Dell, 1984.

Prall, Jo. *My Sister's Special*. Children's Press, 1985.

Rabe, Bernice. *Where's Chimpy?* Whitman, 1988.

CHILDREN'S BOOKS ABOUT EMOTIONAL AND BEHAVIOR DIFFICULTIES

Clymer, Eleanor. *My Brother Stevie*. Dell Yearling, 1989

Hyde, Margaret O. *Is This Kid "Crazy"?* Westminster, 1983.

Paterson, Katherine. *The Great Gilly Hopkins*. Harper Junior, 1987.

Stolz, Mary. *The Bully of Barkham Street*. Harper and Row, 1985.

Activities for Preservice Teachers

1. Become familiar with procedures used to screen school children for various developmental, vision, hearing, and other problems. Participate in such activities if possible and report back to the class.

2. Do a case study on a child who has an identified difficulty and is being included in a *regular-education* classroom. Interview the teacher, the parents, and the consultant if there is one assigned. (Talk with the child, too, if possible.) Write a report on the situation of this youngster—protecting identities, of course.

3. Read about gifted and talented education and then visit some school programs for such children. Ask about such matters as identification of participants, general provisions for them, the role of the classroom teacher and any specialists, and what the evaluation of the program indicates.

4. Examine the educational literature published during the past five years for definitions of *learning disability.* What are your conclusions?

5. Organize a panel discussion on the appropriateness of placing special-needs children in regular classrooms. Include classroom teachers, parents, and staff members in special education on your panel.

6. Visit a classroom for mentally retarded students. Note the types of language arts instructional activities provided. Do these appear appropriate for the developmental levels of the children enrolled?

7. Visit a school where children from many different language backgrounds are in attendance. Make a list of the ways in which teachers are attempting to meet these students' needs.

8. Identify a child with very little vision or one who cannot hear and who is being assisted by a computer-based support system. Note in detail what the student does and how the system operates.

9. Examine some programs in teacher education and identify where college students are learning how to meet the needs of children with serious problems of movement, speech, hearing, vision, and so forth.

10. Develop a plan for learning the language, stories, songs, customs, and history of a particular group whose children you might someday have as students.

Activities for Inservice Teachers

1. Study the policies of your state and school district regarding the identification and placement of special-needs children. Ask administrators and supervisors how these are put into operation.

2. Survey teachers you know and ask them about any experiences they may have had in providing for special-needs children placed in their rooms. Try to find teachers who have had varying degrees of support from consultants and resource-room teachers.

3. In some situations class size is reduced in a regular-education room if a child with special needs is in attendance. Find out what is done in several school systems and report to the class.

4. If you have several childen who speak a language other than English at home, begin to make a list (or an audio recording) of some of their words that you and the other students should learn.

5. What categories of needs are used to identify or classify children considered handicapped in your school system? Find out what proportions there are of each in the general special-needs population and compare these figures with the ones presented in this chapter.

6. In many school situations a high proportion of children identified as mentally retarded live in poverty. Does this seem to be true in the districts you know about? What are possible explanations?

7. Many children have emotional problems that cause difficulties in their relationships at school—with adults and other students. What is the policy in your school with regard to disruptive students? Ask teachers and administrators how well such matters are being handled.

8. Do a case study of a child who a few years ago would have been placed in a special class and who can now participate reasonably well in regular education because of electronic aids that have been provided.

9. Examine an IEP for a student you do not know well. What are the recommendations related to what should be provided in the regular classroom? To what extent do you feel confident that you could successfully implement these recommendations?

10. Talk with parents of children who are gifted or talented. To what extent are they satisfied that their child's needs have been met in the school?

Children's Activities

1. Whenever there is a good reason (e.g., a child who uses a wheelchair may have moved into a student's neighborhood), direct the student to a book related to the special needs involved.

2. Have youngsters contribute to a list of words that can cause hurt to special-needs persons: *retard, weirdo, four-eyes, gimp,* and so forth.

3. Children can take turns using crutches or a wheelchair to better understand the problems users encounter.

4. If parents give permission, students who ordinarily see well can wear devices that distort their vision and allow them to experience that problem.

5. Provide books and videotapes so that interested children can begin to learn sign language.

6. Have a child who knows a language other than English begin to teach that to interested classmates.

7. Using only body and sign language, children can attempt to communicate without speaking or writing for an entire period or day.

8. After gaining parental permission, have students wear headsets that substantially reduce the ability to hear and then ask them to listen to records, watch TV, and converse with one another.

9. Encourage a special-needs child (including a gifted student) who operates a computer to teach others to use it.

Addresses of Publishers, Distributors, and Organizations

Ablex Publishing Corporation
355 Chestnut Street
Norwood, NJ 07648

Acropolis Books
2400 17th Street, NW
Washington, DC 20009

Addison-Wesley Publishing
   Company
1 Jacob Way
Reading, MA 01867

Allyn and Bacon, Inc.
160 Gould Street
Needham Heights, MA
   02194-2320

Amereon, Ltd.
P.O. Box 1200
Mattituck, NY 11952

American Library Association
50 E. Huron Street
Chicago, IL 60611

Aquarius People Materials, Inc.
Box 128
Indian Rocks Beach, FL 33535

Aspen Publishers, Inc.
1600 Research Boulevard
Rockville, MD 20850

The Association for Childhood
   Education International
11141 Georgia Avenue,
   Suite 200
Wheaton, MD 20902

Atheneum Publishers
866 Third Avenue
New York, NY 10022

Barr Films
P.O. Box 5667
3490 E. Foothill Boulevard
Pasadena, CA 91107

Basil Blackwell, Inc.
432 Park Avenue South, Suite 1530
New York, NY 10016

R. R. Bowker Company
245 W. 17th Street
New York, NY 10011

Boynton/Cook Publishers, Inc.
P.O. Box 860
52 Upper Montclair Plaza
Upper Montclair, NJ 07043

Bradbury Press
866 Third Avenue
New York, NY 10022

Broadman Press
127 Ninth Avenue North
Nashville, TN 37234

Broderbund Software
17 Paul Drive
San Rafael, CA 94903

William C. Brown Group
2460 Kerper Boulevard
Dubuque, IA 52001

C and C Software
5713 Kentford Circle
Wichita, KS 67220

Caedmon Records, Inc.
1995 Broadway
New York, NY 10023

Cambridge University Press
32 E. 57th Street
New York, NY 10022

Carolrhoda Books, Inc.
241 First Avenue North
Minneapolis, MN 55401

The Center for Applied
   Research in Education
P.O. Box 430
West Nyack, NJ 10995

Children's Art Foundation
Box 83
Santa Cruz, CA 95063

Children's Press
1224 W. Van Buren Street
Chicago, IL 60607

Clarion Books
52 Vanderbilt Avenue
New York, NY 10017

Computer Advanced Ideas, Inc.
1442A Walnut Street
Berkeley, CA 94709

Coronado Press
P.O. Box 3232
Lawrence, KS 66044

Coronet, The Multimedia Co.
108 Wilmot Road
Deerfield, IL 60015

Council For Indian Education
517 Rimrock Road
Billings, MT 59102

Coward-McCann (*See*
   Putnam's)

Creative Education, Inc.
P.O. Box 227
Mankato, MN 56001

Crestwood House, Inc.
P.O. Box 3427
Mankato, MN 56002

Crowell-Collier (*See*
Macmillan)

Curriculum Associates, Inc.
5 Esquire Road
North Billerica, MA
01862-2589

Davidson and Associates
3135 Kishawa Street
Torrance, CA 90505

Delacorte Press
1 Dag Hammarskjold Plaza
New York, NY 10017

Dell Publishing Company
245 E. 47th Street
New York, NY 10017

Delmar Publishers, Inc.
3 Columbia Circle
Albany, NY 12212-5105

Developmental Learning Materials
P.O. Box 4000
One DLM Park
Allen, TX 75002

Dial Press (*See* Doubleday)

Dillon Press, Inc.
242 Portland Avenue South
Minneapolis, MN 55415

DLM Teaching Resources
One DLM Park
Allen, TX 75002

Dodd, Mead and Company
71 Fifth Avenue
New York, NY 10003

Doubleday and Company, Inc.
501 Franklin Avenue
Garden City, NY 11530

E. P. Dutton, Inc.
2 Park Avenue
New York, NY 10016

EBSCO Curriculum Materials
Box 11542
Birmingham, AL 35202

Educational Activities
Box 392
Freeport, NY 11520

Educational Leadership
125 N. West Street
Alexandria, VA 22314-2798

Electronic Bookshelf, Inc.
Rt. 9, Box 64
Frankfort, IN 46041

Encyclopaedia Britannica, Inc.
310 S. Michigan Avenue
Chicago, IL 60604

Evans Publishing House
431 Post Road East, Suite 708
Westport, CT 06880

C. H. Fairfax Company, Inc.
P.O. Box 502
Columbia, MD 21045

Family Communications
4802 Fifth Avenue
Pittsburgh, PA 15213

Farrar, Straus and Giroux, Inc.
19 Union Square West
New York, NY 10003

Fearon Teaching Aids
19 Davis Drive
Belmont, CA 94002

First Byte
2845 Temple Avenue
Long Beach, CA 90806

Follett Publishing Company
1010 W. Washington Boulevard
Chicago, IL 60607

Four Winds Press
P.O. Box 824
Soquel, CA 95079

Freline, Inc.
P.O. Box 889
32 East Avenue
Hagerstown, MD 21740

Gale Research Company
Book Tower
Detroit, MI 48226

Garland Publishing Inc.
136 Madison Avenue
New York, NY 10016

Greenleaf Software
2101 Hickory Drive
Carrollton, TX 75006

Greenleaf Video, Inc.
3230 Nebraska Avenue
Santa Monica, CA 90404

Greenwillow Books (*See*
Morrow)

Grosset and Dunlap
51 Madison Avenue
New York, NY 10010

Harcourt Brace Jovanovich, Inc.
1250 Sixth Avenue
San Diego, CA 92101

Harper and Row Publishers,
Inc.
10 E. 53rd Street
New York, NY 10022

Hart Publications, Inc.
P.O. Box 1917
1900 Grant Street, Suite 400
Denver, CO 80201

Hartley's Courseware, Inc.
Dimondale, MI 48821

Harvest House Publishers
1075 Arrowsmith
Eugene, OR 97402

D. C. Heath and Company
125 Spring Street
Lexington, MA 02173

Heinemann Educational Books
70 Court Street
Portsmouth, NH 03801

Holt, Rinehart and Winston
383 Madison Avenue
New York, NY 10017

Holt, Rinehart and Winston of
Canada
55 Horner Avenue
Toronto, Ontario M8Z 4X6
Canada

The Horn Book
31 St. James Avenue
Park Square Building
Boston, MA 02116

Houghton Mifflin Company
One Beacon Street
Boston, MA 02108

Houghton Mifflin Educational
    Software
Box 683, Dept. 217
Hanover, NH 03755

Human Resources Development
    Press
22 Amherst Road
Amherst, MA 01002

Human Science Press, Inc.
72 Fifth Avenue
New York, NY 10011

Humanities Ltd.
P.O. Box 7447
Atlanta, GA 30309

Humanities Software
P.O. Box 590727
San Francisco, CA 94159

IBM
1133 Westchester Avenue
White Plains, NY 10604

InterLearn, Inc.
Box 342
Cardiff-by-the-Sea, CA 92007

International Reading
    Association
P.O. Box 8139
800 Barksdale Road
Newark, DE 19714-8139

Jamestown Publishers
P.O. Box 9168
Providence, RI 02940

JMH Software of Minnesota
7200 Hemlock Lane, Suite 103
Maple Grove, MN 55369

Kendall/Hunt Publishing
    Company
P.O. Box 539
2460 Kerper Boulevard
Dubuque, IA 52001

Thomas S. Klise Co.
P.O. Box 3418
Peoria, IL 61614

Alfred A. Knopf, Inc.
201 E. 50th Street
New York, NY 10022

Knowledge Unlimited
P.O. Box 52
Madison, WI 53701-0052

The Learning Company
545 Middlefield Road,
    Suite 170
Menlo Park, CA 94025

Learning Well
200 South Service Road
Roslyn Heights, NY 11577

Lerner Publications
241 First Avenue North
Minneapolis, MN 55401

Libraries Unlimited, Inc.
P.O. Box 263
Littleton, CO 80160-0263

J. B. Lippincott Company
227 E. Washington Square
Philadelphia, PA 19106-3780

Listening Library, Inc.
P.O. Box L
Old Greenwich, CT 06870

Little, Brown and Company
34 Beacon Street
Boston, MA 02106

Live Oak Media
P.O. Box 34
Ancramdale, NY 12503

Lodestar Books
2 Park Avenue
New York, NY 10016

Longman, Inc.
95 Church Street
White Plains, NY 10601

Lothrop, Lee and Shepard Books
105 Madison Avenue
New York, NY 10036

Macmillan Publishing Company
866 Third Avenue
New York, NY 10022

McDougal, Littell and Company
P.O. Box 1667
Evanston, IL 60204

McGraw-Hill Book Company
1221 Avenue of the Americas
New York, NY 10020

Media Basics
Larchmont Plaza
Larchmont, NY 10538

Charles E. Merrill Publishing
    Company
1300 Alum Drive
Columbus, OH 43216

Julian Messner
1230 Avenue of the Americas
New York, NY 10020

Methuen, Inc.
29 W. 35th Street
New York, NY 10001

Milliken Publishing Company
P.O. Box 21579
1100 Research Boulevard
St. Louis, MO 63132

Milton Bradley, Inc.
443 Shaker Road
East Longmeadow, MA 01028

Mindscape, Inc.
Dept. S
3444 Dundee Road
Northbrook, IL 60062

Modern Curriculum Press
13900 Prospect Road
Cleveland, OH 44136

William Morrow and Company,
    Inc.
105 Madison Avenue
New York, NY 10016

NAESP Educational Products
    Center
P.O. Box 1461
Alexandria, VA 22313

National Association for the
    Education of Young Children
1834 Connecticut Avenue, NW
Washington, DC 20009

National Council of Teachers of
    English
1111 Kenyon Road
Urbana, IL 61801

National Textbook Company
4255 W. Touhy Avenue
Lincolnwood, IL 60646

Navajo Curriculum Center Press
Rough Rock Demonstration School
Star Route 1
Rough Rock, AZ 86503

Thomas Nelson Australia
480 La Trobe Street
Melbourne 3000, Australia

New Plays Books
Box 273
Rowayton, CT 06853

Open University Press
242 Cherry Street
Philadelphia, PA 19106-1906

Oryx Press
2214 N. Central Avenue
Phoenix, AZ 85004-1483

Richard C. Owens Publishers, Inc.
Rockefeller Center, Box 819
New York, NY 10185

Oxford University Press
200 Madison Avenue
New York, NY 10016

Pantheon Books
201 E. 50th Street
New York, NY 10022

Paradigm Video
127 Greenbrae Boardwalk
Greenbrae, CA 94904

A. W. Peller and Associates
P.O. Box 106
249 Goffle Road
Hawthorne, NJ 07507

PEM Press
Box 3000
Communications Park
Mount Kisco, NY 10549

Penguin Books
40 W. 23rd Street
New York, NY 10010

Penguin Software
830 Fourth Avenue
Geneva, IL 60134

Philomel (*See* Putnam's)

Phoenix/BFA Films and Video
470 Park Avenue South
New York, NY 10016

Plays, Inc.
8 Arlington Street
Boston, MA 02116

Potomac MicroResources, Inc.
P.O. Box 277
Riverdale, MD 20737

Prentice Hall, Inc.
Route 9W
Englewood Cliffs, NJ 07632

PRO-ED
5341 Industrial Oak Boulevard
Austin, TX 78735

G. P. Putnam's Sons
200 Madison Avenue
New York, NY 10016

Raintree Publications, Inc.
310 W. Wisconsin Avenue,
   Mezzanine Level
Milwaukee, WI 53203

Rand McNally and Company
P.O. Box 7600
Chicago, IL 60680

Random House, Inc.
201 E. 50th Street
New York, NY 10022

Reading Is Fundamental, Inc.
Smithsonian Institution
600 Maryland Avenue, SW
Washington, DC 20560

Renfro Studios
1117 W. Ninth Street
Austin, TX 78703

St. Martin's Press, Inc.
175 Fifth Avenue
New York, NY 10010

Scarecrow Press, Inc.
Box 656
52 Liberty Street
Metuchen, NJ 08840

Scholastic, Inc.
P.O. Box 7501
2931 E. McCarty Street
Jefferson City, MO 63102

Scholastic Software
730 Broadway
New York, NY 10003

Schoolhouse Press (*See* Simon
   and Schuster)

Science Research Associates
155 N. Wacker Drive
Chicago, IL 60606

Scott, Foresman and Company
1900 East Lake Avenue
Glenview, IL 60025

Scribner-Laidlaw Educational
   Publishers
866 Third Avenue
New York, NY 10022

Seabury Press
Icehouse 1-401
151 Union Street
San Francisco, CA 94111

Sensible Software, Inc.
24011 Seneca
Oak Park, MI 48237

Dale Seymour Publications
P.O. Box 10888
Palo Alto, CA 94303

Shoe String Press, Inc.
P.O. Box 4327
Hamden, CT 06514

Simon and Schuster, Inc.
1230 Avenue of the Americas
New York, NY 10020

Society for Visual Education, Inc.
1345 Diversey Parkway
Chicago, IL 60614

Spinnaker Software
One Kendall Square
Cambridge, MA 02139

Spoken Arts
P.O. Box 289
New Rochelle, NY 10802

Springboard Software
7808 Creekridge Circle
Minneapolis, MN 53435

Standard Publishing Co.
8121 Hamilton Avenue
Cincinnati, OH 45231

Sterling Publishing Company
2 Park Avenue
New York, NY 10016

STL International, Inc.
P.O. Box 35918
Tulsa, OK 74153-0918

Stuart Finley
3428 Mansfield Road
Falls Church, VA 22041

Sunburst Communications
39 Washington Avenue
Pleasantville, NY 10570

Teachers College Press
Columbia University
1234 Amsterdam Avenue
New York, NY 10027

Charles C. Thomas, Publisher
2600 S. First Street
Springfield, IL 62794-9265

Thompson Book and Supply
    Company
P.O. Box 11600
Oklahoma City, OK 73136

Times Books
201 E. 50th Street
New York, NY 10022

Trillium Press
Box 209
Monroe, NY 10950

Unicorn Software Co.
1775 E. Tropicana Avenue, No. 8
Las Vegas, NV 89109

University of California Press
2120 Berkeley Way
Berkeley, CA 94720

University of Chicago Press
5801 Ellis Avenue
Chicago, IL 60628

University of Illinois
Graduate School of Library Service
249 Armory Building
505 E. Armory Street
Champaign, IL 61820

University of Wisconsin Press
114 N. Murray Street
Madison, WI 53715

University Park Press
P.O. Box 434
Grand Central Station
New York, NY 10163

University Press Books
Box 460
Middletown, NY 10940

Vanguard Press
424 Madison Ave.
New York, NY 10017

Viking Penguin Inc.
40 W. 23rd Street
New York, NY 10010

Wadsworth Publishing Co.
10 Davis Drive
Belmont, CA 94002

Walker and Company
720 Fifth Avenue
New York, NY 10019

Warner Books, Inc.
Juvenile Division
666 Fifth Avenue
New York, NY 10103

Western Publishing Company, Inc.
850 Third Avenue
New York, NY 10022

Westminster Press
925 Chestnut Street
Philadelphia, PA 19107

Weston Woods
389 Newtown Pike
Weston, CT 06883

Albert Whitman and Company
5747 W. Howard Street
Niles, IL 60648

The H. W. Wilson Company
950 University Avenue
Bronx, NY 10452

Windswept House, Publisher
P.O. Box 159
Mt. Desert, ME 04660

The Wright Group
10949 Technology Place
San Diego, CA 92127

Yale University Press
302 Temple Street
New Haven, CT 06520

Zaner-Bloser, Inc.
P.O. Box 16764
2300 W. Fifth Avenue
Columbus, OH 43216

Index

446